Fodor's

VIRGINIA & MARYLAND

10th Edition

Where to Stay and Eat for All Budgets

Must-See Sights and Local Secrets

Ratings You Can Trust

Fodor's Travel Publications   New York, Toronto, London, Sydney, Auckland
www.fodors.com

FODOR'S VIRGINIA & MARYLAND

Editor: Cate Starmer

Editorial Contributors: Mary Beth Bohman, Mike Lillis, Amy McKeever, Pete Nelson, Donna Owens, Alice Powers, Julie Scharper, Sam Sessa, Ginger Warder

Production Editor: Tom Holton

Maps & Illustrations: David Lindroth, Mark Stroud, *cartographers*; Bob Blake, Rebecca Baer, *map editors;* William Wu, *information graphics*

Design: Fabrizio La Rocca, *creative director*; Guido Caroti, Siobhan O'Hare, *art directors*; Tina Malaney, Chie Ushio, Ann McBride, Jessica Walsh, *designers*; Melanie Marin, *senior picture editor*

Cover Photo (Assateague Island): James L. Stanfield/National Geographic/Getty Images

Production Manager: Angela L. McLean

10th Edition

ISBN 978-1-4000-0816-2

ISSN 1075-0711

SPECIAL SALES

This book is available at special discounts for bulk purchases for sales promotions or premiums. Special editions, including personalized covers, excerpts of existing books, and corporate imprints, can be created in large quantities for special needs. For more information, write to Special Markets/Premium Sales, 1745 Broadway, MD 6-2, New York, New York 10019, or e-mail specialmarkets@randomhouse.com.

AN IMPORTANT TIP & AN INVITATION

Although all prices, opening times, and other details in this book are based on information supplied to us at press time, changes occur all the time in the travel world, and Fodor's cannot accept responsibility for facts that become outdated or for inadvertent errors or omissions. So **always confirm information when it matters,** especially if you're making a detour to visit a specific place. Your experiences—positive and negative—matter to us. If we have missed or misstated something, **please write to us.** We follow up on all suggestions. Contact the Virginia & Maryland editor at editors@fodors.com or c/o Fodor's at 1745 Broadway, New York, NY 10019.

PRINTED IN THE UNITED STATES OF AMERICA

10 9 8 7 6 5 4 3 2 1

Be a Fodor's Correspondent

Your opinion matters. It matters to us. It matters to your fellow Fodor's travelers, too. And we'd like to hear it. In fact, we need to hear it.

When you share your experiences and opinions, you become an active member of the Fodor's community. That means we'll not only use your feedback to make our books better, but we'll publish your names and comments whenever possible. Throughout our guides, look for "Word of Mouth," excerpts of your unvarnished feedback.

Here's how you can help improve Fodor's for all of us.

Tell us when we're right. We rely on local writers to give you an insider's perspective. But our writers and staff editors—who are the best in the business—depend on you. Your positive feedback is a vote to renew our recommendations for the next edition.

Tell us when we're wrong. We're proud that we update most of our guides every year. But we're not perfect. Things change. Hotels cut services. Museums change hours. Charming cafés lose charm. If our writer didn't quite capture the essence of a place, tell us how you'd do it differently. If any of our descriptions are inaccurate or inadequate, we'll incorporate your changes in the next edition and will correct factual errors at fodors.com immediately.

Tell us what to include. You probably have had fantastic travel experiences that aren't yet in Fodor's. Why not share them with a community of like-minded travelers? Maybe you chanced upon a beach or bistro or B&B that you don't want to keep to yourself. Tell us why we should include it. And share your discoveries and experiences with everyone directly at fodors.com. Your input may lead us to add a new listing or highlight a place we cover with a "Highly Recommended" star or with our highest rating, "Fodor's Choice."

Give us your opinion instantly at our feedback center at www.fodors.com/feedback. You may also e-mail editors@fodors.com with the subject line "Virginia & Maryland Editor." Or send your nominations, comments, and complaints by mail to Virginia & Maryland Editor, Fodor's, 1745 Broadway, New York, NY 10019.

You and travelers like you are the heart of the Fodor's community. Make our community richer by sharing your experiences. Be a Fodor's correspondent.

Happy traveling!

Tim Jarrell, Publisher

CONTENTS

ABOUT
THIS BOOK

Our Ratings

Sometimes you find terrific travel experiences and sometimes they just find you. But usually the burden is on you to select the right combination of experiences. That's where our ratings come in.

As travelers we've all discovered a place so wonderful that its worthiness is obvious. And sometimes that place is so experiential that superlatives don't do it justice: you just have to be there to know. These sights, properties, and experiences get our highest rating, **Fodor's Choice**, indicated by orange stars throughout this book.

Black stars highlight sights and properties we deem **Highly Recommended,** places that our writers, editors, and readers praise again and again for consistency and excellence.

By default, there's another category: any place we include in this book is by definition worth your time, unless we say otherwise. And we will.

Disagree with any of our choices? Care to nominate a place or suggest that we rate one more highly? Visit our feedback center at www.fodors.com/feedback.

Budget Well

Hotel and restaurant price categories from ¢ to $$$$ are defined in the opening pages of each chapter. For attractions, we always give standard adult admission fees; reductions are usually available for children, students, and senior citizens. Want to pay with plastic? **AE, D, DC, MC, V** following restaurant and hotel listings indicate if American Express, Discover, Diners Club, MasterCard, and Visa are accepted.

Restaurants

Unless we state otherwise, restaurants are open for lunch and dinner daily. We mention dress only when there's a specific requirement and reservations only when they're essential or not accepted—it's always best to book ahead.

Hotels

Hotels have private bath, phone, TV, and air-conditioning and operate on the European Plan (aka EP, meaning without meals), unless we specify that they use the Continental Plan (CP, with a continental breakfast), Breakfast Plan (BP, with a full breakfast), or Modified American Plan (MAP, with breakfast and dinner), or are all-inclusive (AI, including all meals and most activities). We always

list facilities but not whether you'll be charged an extra fee to use them, so when pricing accommodations, find out what's included.

Many Listings	
★	Fodor's Choice
★	Highly recommended
⊠	Physical address
✛	Directions
⌂	Mailing address
☎	Telephone
🖷	Fax
⊕	On the Web
✉	E-mail
🎫	Admission fee
⊙	Open/closed times
Ⓜ	Metro stations
▭	Credit cards

Hotels & Restaurants	
🏨	Hotel
⇗	Number of rooms
⌂	Facilities
❑	Meal plans
✕	Restaurant
⌂	Reservations
⬎	Smoking
ᗷᑫ	BYOB
✕🏨	Hotel with restaurant that warrants a visit

Outdoors	
🏌	Golf
⚠	Camping

Other	
☺	Family-friendly
⇨	See also
⊠	Branch address
☞	Take note

TOP EXPERIENCES

Explore an Island

Depart by ferry from Crisfield over the Chesapeake Bay to Smith Island, Maryland, a tiny, secluded community accessible only by boat, and home for generations to watermen and their families. The Smith Island Center tells the history of this traditional fishing enclave, a time-honored (though threatened) way of life for centuries. Enjoy a family-style meal featuring crabs or oysters, and for dessert, don't skip the island's nationally known cakes—stacked 8 to 10 layers high and frosted and recently designated Maryland's state cake by lawmakers. Tangiers Island in Virginia is similarly sleepy, while the northern Chesapeake Bay has more developed options like Kent Island.

Sample Heritage Music

Sample the musical soul of Virginia's country connections, by traveling "The Crooked Road," otherwise known as Virginia's Heritage Music Trail. Enjoy the beauty of the region's mountains and deep valleys, where the distinctive strains of mountain ballads and old-time toe-tapping music echo, especially in the heart of Appalachia and the southwest Blue Ridge Highlands regions. Plan ahead to attend two annual August events: the Carter Family Traditional Music Festival in Hiltons; and the Old Fiddlers Convention in Galax, held since 1935. Galax is the World's Capital of Old Time Mountain Music. Congress has designated one city here–Bristol—the "Birthplace of Country Music," and other towns are noteworthy for their music as well.

Discover New Communities

Discover two new waterfront communities with picturesque marinas. National Harbor, an enclave of lavish residences, retail stores, offices, and nightspots, is situated on 300 acres along the picturesque Potomac River in Oxon Hill, Maryland. It's home to Gaylord National, the largest nongaming combined hotel and convention center on the entire East Coast. Harbor East, one of Baltimore's newest neighborhoods, extends the city's scenic waterfront and world-renowned Inner Harbor. It boasts chic boutiques, an upscale movie theater, office high-rises with panoramic views, gourmet dining, and upscale accommodations.

Play Ball

Take yourself out to a ball game at Oriole Park at Camden Yards in downtown Baltimore. With its steel trusses and arched brick facade, the home of the Baltimore Orioles is considered one of America's most beautiful ballparks. The 48,000 seats provide fine views of the asymmetrical field; the natural grass turf is impeccably manicured; and, besides traditional ballpark fare, food offerings include pit beef and Maryland's famed crab cakes. If you have time, take the "Behind the Scenes" tour for all sorts of interesting factoids. Among them: Camden Station, now part of Oriole Park, was once a station along the Underground Railroad.

WHAT'S WHERE

The following numbers refer to chapters.

1 Washington, DC. The District is the urban pulse of the region, not to mention the political hub of the United States. The roughly 65-square-mi city has many of America's seminal museums, political buildings, monuments, and cultural institutions.

2 Northern Virginia & DC's Maryland Suburbs. Outside of DC is a mixture of old and new. There's a repository of Colonial and Civil War history; and also a bustling, sprawling clutch of corporate campuses, suburban neighborhoods, retail stores, and restaurants.

3 Central & Western Virginia. Mountains rule the horizons in dramatic interior Virginia, a favorite getaway for those seeking stunning scenery, old-fashioned mountain music, and outdoorsy activities. Dapper Charlottesville is the area's cultural center.

4 Richmond, Fredericksburg & the Northern Neck. Richmond, capital of the commonwealth, honors its history while embracing the "new" South. The rural Northern Neck peninsula, with its sylvan vistas and historic sites, extends east from Fredericksburg to the Chesapeake Bay.

5 Williamsburg & Hampton Roads. Colonial Williamsburg is just one of the area's many historic attractions. The Hampton Roads channel is surrounded by the port cities of Newport News and Norfolk, and the busy resort town of Virginia Beach.

6 Baltimore. Locals and tourists alike enjoy the lively Inner Harbor, Fort McHenry's hilltop vistas, and historic neighborhoods like Fells Point in this revitalized city.

7 Frederick & Western Maryland. Rugged, scenic mountains dominate the landscape around the small cities of Frederick and Cumberland. Each has its share of attractions, pastoral valleys, interesting parks, and swank restaurants and quaint inns.

8 Annapolis & Southern Maryland. Sailing enthusiasts and weekenders adore regal Annapolis, rich with Colonial architecture and history. Calvert and St. Mary's counties have inviting country inns, taverns, and gentle landscapes.

9 The Eastern Shore. Between the Chesapeake Bay and the Atlantic Ocean, this peninsula has classic resort towns like Ocean City, charming historic villages such as St. Michaels, and the wild ponies of Assateague and Chincoteague Islands.

Southwest Virginia

Blacksburg
Christiansburg
Cumberland Gap
Wytheville
Pulaski
81
Marion
Galax

PENNSYLVANIA

NEW JERSEY

Cumberland
Frostburg
Hagerstown
Martinsburg
Harpers Ferry
Winchester
Antietam
Westminster
Frederick
7
70
Brunswick
Columbia
Baltimore
Essex
Havre de Grace
Chesapeake City
Aberdeen
40
Dover
13
Delaware Bay
6
83
15
Strasburg
Woodstock
Leesburg
2
Arlington
66
Wheaton
Annapolis
8
WASHINGTON, D.C.
Greensboro
Easton
50
301
13
DELAWARE
Front Royal
Old Tavern
Annandale
Woodbridge
Alexandria
Brandywine
Cambridge
Federalsburg
Mt. Jackson
New Market
211
Culpeper
Stafford
Smithville
Salisbury
113
81
Harrisonburg
Orange
Fredericksburg
Potomac
Deal Island
Ocean City
Staunton
Waynesboro
Charlottesville
64
Cedon Ladysmith
Crisfield
9
3
29
Gum Spring
James River
Ruther Glen
17
Reedville
Chincoteague
BLUE RIDGE MTNS
Powhatan
360
Chesapeake Bay
13
Lynchburg
460
Burkeville
Colonial Heights
Richmond
64
Gloucester
Williamsburg
Cape Charles
ATLANTIC OCEAN
Keysville
360
Petersburg
James River
5
Hampton
Newport News
Chesapeake Bay Bridge-Tunnel
Alberta
85
Stony Creek
460
Windsor
Norfolk
Virginia Beach
South Hill
Emporia
95
Suffolk
Chesapeake
Clarksville
58
Franklin

NORTH CAROLINA

VIRGINIA & MARYLAND PLANNER

Climate

Maryland and Virginia each have four distinct seasons, different regions, and climates that vary accordingly. Summer in both states is generally hot and humid, with average temperatures in the 80s and 90s. Winters can be cold, with average temperatures in the 30s and 40s, and although snow is possible, frequent major snowstorms are not common in most parts of Maryland, nor in Virginia. In spring temperatures tend to be moderate and mild; in fall, cool and crisp. Neither state is especially rainy, although scattered showers and thunderstorms tend to occur seasonally. The mountainous regions can be as much as 10 to 15 degrees cooler.

When to Go

Spring brings horse racing to Baltimore, northern Virginia, and the Virginia Piedmont; the Preakness Stakes is highly festive, but many point-to-points and steeplechases are more interesting to watch and visit. Public gardens are in full bloom; garden clubs conduct tours of private properties throughout both states. In Shenandoah National Park, Skyline Drive overlooks a blooming panorama. If you happen to travel to Baltimore in early May, don't miss Sherwood Gardens, known for hundreds of thousands of tulips, azaleas, pansies, and blossoming trees.

Summer draws the largest numbers of visitors, particularly at Virginia Beach, Ocean City, and other resorts on the bay and the ocean. Baltimore's Inner Harbor can be thronged with tourists and yachters. On warm days the promenade is filled with visitors from around the world.

Autumn brings spectacular colors in the foliage of the rolling Piedmont region of Virginia and the Catoctin Mountains west of Baltimore; the temperatures become more comfortable for hiking and biking. Equestrian events resume, and in Maryland the sailboat and powerboat shows in Annapolis and the Waterfowl Festival in Easton attract thousands of people in October and November.

Winter temperatures may make it too cold to swim, yet the major resorts continue to draw vacationers with seasonal peace and quiet at much lower off-season rates. Other travelers come for romantic seclusion at a B&B. Virginia was the first Southern state to develop skiing commercially, and now both downhill and cross-country skiing are popular activities at resorts in the Shenandoah Valley and western Maryland.

Dining: The Basics

From haute cuisine to down-home diners, be it regional specialties or global ethnic fare, hailing from family farms or from Chesapeake Bay, the food of Maryland and Virginia is deliciously diverse. Favorites include the sweet, delectable meat of the famed blue crab, oysters, and local fish, as well as Virginia's famous ham.

In central Virginia, peanut soup and ham biscuits are among the traditional dishes, as is this region's version of barbecue: pork shoulder smoked tender and served in a savory sauce. In western Virginia home-style cooking rules. Small towns with generations-old restaurants serve good stick-to-your-ribs dishes. In larger cities like Richmond, Charlottesville, and Fredericksburg—as well as in Baltimore, Maryland—innovative chefs are emphasizing fresh, local ingredients in exquisite nouveau cuisine. In southern Maryland, stuffed ham with beaten biscuits is much beloved, while on Maryland's Eastern Shore crispy fried or baked chicken is a lunch or dinnertime staple. The Shore is also where the cakes of Smith Island have gained national acclaim: 8 to 10 layers, stacked high and frosted to perfection.

Restaurants aren't the only places to find good food here. Maryland's cornucopia of beautiful produce can be found at roadside stands crammed with white corn, tomatoes, and ripe melons. In Virginia the country markets in the mountains are sources for everything from freshly baked bread to homemade apple butter.

Lodging: The Basics

Maryland and Virginia have plenty of options for a good night's sleep, from sprawling luxury resorts and budget motels to cozy Colonial-era inns with a plethora of amenities: full-service spas and golf, cooking schools, sailing classes, and tours of wineries, to name a few.

Virginia has a wide assortment of elegant country inns. Throughout the Commonwealth, grand, historic hotels that conjure the golden age are enjoying a glorious renaissance and a new generation of guests.

For a relaxed setting, you may want to try a bed-and-breakfast; most are situated in small picturesque towns across Maryland, many with water views. In Baltimore, a new wave of upscale chain hotels with on-site restaurants and modern conveniences offers easy access to museums, sporting facilities, copious shopping, and dining options.

Getting Here & Around

Three major airports act as hubs for visitors to the region: **Baltimore/Washington International Airport** (BWI ⊕ www.bwiairport.com), **Dulles International Airport** (IAD) and **Ronald Reagan Washington National Airport** , (DCA ⊕ www.metwashairports.com).

Although it's not a hard-and-fast rule, it's true that the most convenient way to get around is by car. For example, in Maryland it only takes two hours to go from downtown Baltimore to the beaches of Ocean City; or three hours to get to Deep Creek Lake from the DC suburbs.

As for rush-hour warnings, both of the beltways (Baltimore or DC) get clogged during morning and evening rush hours, and arteries leading to same (I–95, I–83, I–270) can also get backed up under certain conditions. Also consider travel during off-peak hours on Maryland's busy Bay Bridge. On summer Friday nights and Saturday mornings, check current conditions (☎ 877/229–7726 ⊕ www.baybridge.com).

Outside of DC, with it's reliable **Metro** subway (⊕ www.wmata.com), public transportation options are limited but include: **Amtrak** (⊕ www.amtrak.com) and in Maryland, the **MARC** (⊕ www.commuterpage.com) commuter trains.

TOP VIRGINIA & MARYLAND ATTRACTIONS

Antietam National Battlefield

(A) As history buffs know, Antietam was the site of the deadliest one-day battle in American history, one that marked the first of two attempts by Confederate General Robert E. Lee to bring the Civil War north. Today the battlefield in Sharpsburg, Maryland, is maintained to look as it did on that fateful day of September 17, 1862.

Shenandoah National Park

(B) Imagine a postcard snapped by Mother Nature and you have Shenandoah. Perhaps the best-known element of this treasured historic park is the picturesque 105-mi long Skyline Drive. More than 500 mi of hiking trails run through the park. The park allows access to Virginia's Blue Ridge Mountains and the Appalachian Trail. Camping is allowed, but the park also offers modern lodging and sit-down restaurants.

Virginia Beach

(C) Of the myriad things to do in Virginia Beach—from kayaking to surfing—its well-maintained beaches and the lively 3-mi oceanfront boardwalk are what make folks come back year after year. Watch trained dolphins at the Virginia Aquarium & Marine Science Center or hike the trails through the wetlands at First Landing State Park.

Colonial Williamsburg

(D) Part of Virginia's "Historic Triangle," this restored 18th-century Colonial city features some 300 acres that include 88 original structures and hundreds of other homes, shops, and public buildings where patriots laid the groundwork for the nation's founding. Colonial Williamsburg operates several museums, and visitors can enjoy period dining at several dining taverns and even stay at historic Williamsburg Inn.

Baltimore's Inner Harbor

(E) The waterside promenade is home to a constellation of museums, specialty shops, restaurants, and new upscale hotels, with attractions geared to families and sophisticated adults. In warm weather, visitors can go paddleboating or take a water taxi to neighboring Fells Point for shopping and American history lessons. The National Aquarium, Maryland Science Center, American Visionary Art Museum, and the Reginald F. Lewis Museum of Maryland African-American History and Culture are all within walking distance.

City of Annapolis

(F) Maryland's state capital represents the many sides of this city: watch the noon formation of midshipmen at the U.S. Naval Academy; sail aboard a 74-foot schooner; or tour the quaint downtown to see numerous landmarks that illuminate American history. The Banneker-Douglass Museum is worth a stop for African-American culture, as is a chance to view lawmakers in action from the gallery of the Maryland State House, the oldest American state house in continuous legislative use.

Washington, DC

(G) There's a world to explore in DC—from cultural landmarks such as the Smithsonian Institution to monuments of the Mall. Indeed, America's full history—from Native American to African-American culture and beyond—come alive in this diverse and cosmopolitan world capital, where many attractions are free and open to the public. Locals and visitors from every corner of the globe enjoy the District's interesting and eclectic neighborhoods filled with shopping and dining options, and not the least a vibrant nightlife scene.

QUINTESSENTIAL VIRGINIA & MARYLAND

The Crab Craze

To Marylanders and Virginians alike, the humble crustacean known as the blue crab is king. Watermen in both states harvest the crabs from Chesapeake Bay (typically from April to November), but the region's most popular form of shellfish remains a menu staple year-round. First you have to decide how you want to eat this delectable edible. Choose from jumbo lump or back-fin crab cakes (fried or broiled); steamed in water or beer and liberally sprinkled with spicy Old Bay seasoning; soft-shell style (lightly floured or breaded then fried, and served on a sandwich with lettuce and tomato); deviled; or fluffed. Unless you're having some type of gourmet crab dish, it's practically heresy to ask for drawn butter or elaborate sauces. Concerns about overfishing have led to strict regulations by lawmakers, with the hope that the blue crab will survive for future generations.

Happy Trails

The sylvan scenery of Virginia and Maryland lends itself to all types of nature exploration. Along the eastern shores of both states, animal lovers can spy wild "ponies" (technically they're small horses) as you wander the terrain of Chincoteague and Assateague islands, in Virginia and Maryland respectively. The mountainous west delights ardent outdoors enthusiasts: you can hike through Shenandoah National Park in Virginia or Catoctin Mountain Park in Maryland, and nearly 600 mi of the famed Appalachian Trail passes through both states.

History Comes Alive

Virginia and Maryland, along with Washington, DC, have always played a seminal role in American history. While some very prominent attractions and sites reveal the ethic, spirit, and personality of the nation, even the smallest communities typically

If you want to get a sense of culture in Virginia and Maryland and indulge in some of the region's pleasures, start by familiarizing yourself with the rituals of daily life. These are a few highlights—things you can take part in with relative ease.

have historical societies, house-museums, and centuries-old inns and taverns brimming with character. In Virginia you can tour the homes of U.S. presidents ranging from George Washington and Thomas Jefferson to Harrison, Madison, Monroe, and Wilson. In Maryland, sites range from the venerable U.S. Naval Academy to the sweeping views of Fort McHenry, where a patriot was inspired to pen "The Star-Spangled Banner."

Other opportunities to step back in time abound: the legacy of America's earliest permanent settlement remains at Jamestown; one can experience living history at Colonial Williamsburg; and there are pivotal Civil War sites such as Antietam National Battlefield in Maryland and Appomattox Courthouse in Virginia. In Washington, DC, the National Mall is a celebration of monuments. Especially in recent decades, many of these key historic attractions have reinvented the way they interpret the past, with inclusionary histories that describe the contributions of enslaved African-Americans and others. You will also find more high-tech interactive exhibits, multimedia presentations, and dynamic reenactments.

Vintage Virginia

Virginia's vintners continue to win praise for the quality of their wines, not to mention sheer volume (more than 130 wineries produce hundreds of thousands of cases annually). But the real joy of Virginia wine comes from visiting the scenic vineyards and farms, sampling vintages in tasting rooms, and chatting with the winemakers themselves. You can also soak up the spirit of the viticulture at hundreds of annual wine events and festivals held annually across the state.

IF YOU LIKE

Great Battlefields

Some of the fiercest and most pivotal battles ever staged on American soil took place in Maryland and Virginia, including campaigns during the American Revolution, the War of 1812, and, of course, the Civil War. The National Park Service operates many of these battlefield sites as living-history museums, with carefully preserved or reconstructed fortifications; interpretive centers that show dramatic films and exhibits; and a wide range of narrated walking and driving tours. Battle reenactments are also held at many of these sites. You don't have to be a history buff to appreciate the significance of these seminal venues; in ways large and small, they helped determine the very course of U.S. history.

• At Maryland's Antietam National Battlefield, the single most bloody day of the Civil War occurred on September 17, 1862. When it was over, more than 23,000 Union and Confederate soldiers had been killed or wounded.

• During the War of 1812, Baltimore's star-shape Fort McHenry was where Francis Scott Key penned "The Star-Spangled Banner" while the British bombarded the beleaguered city.

• No tour of Civil War sites is complete without a stop at Manassas National Battlefield Park (aka "Bull Run") in Northern Virginia, where Union and Confederate troops met twice on the battlefield; the battles yielded two important victories for the Confederacy.

• When French and American troops led by General George Washington forced the British to surrender at Yorktown Battlefield, the Revolutionary War drew to a dramatic close.

Swank Country Inns

Small, tranquil, and increasingly sophisticated, the mountain towns and bay-side villages of Virginia and Maryland are home to some of the most sumptuous country inns in America. Many of these princely retreats boast talented chefs turning out innovative, regionally driven cuisine. And it's not uncommon to find great fly-fishing, hiking, golfing, and posh spas on-site or nearby. Here are a few places where you can experience luxury in a laid-back, bucolic setting.

• Antrim 1844 appeals to those who relish history and romance. The supremely elegant antebellum mansion—with 39 plush rooms and suites—has hosted weddings and celebrations. Located in Taneytown, Maryland, the inn is a short drive (about 15 mi south) to historic Gettysburg.

• Since 1766 the Homestead has been one of the most distinguished resorts in the Mid-Atlantic. This lavish resort in Hot Springs, Virginia has every amenity imaginable, including hiking, golfing, ice skating, spa treatments in the region's legendary healing waters, even falconry.

• The Inn at Little Washington in central Virginia is a favorite of top celebs and politicos and anyone who enjoys pampering. The legendary inn has become a must-do experience for those who appreciate its fabulous seven-course dinners, the beautiful English country-house decor, and its peaceful setting (no televisions in rooms; lovely gardens).

• Set on 220 sylvan acres on Maryland's Eastern Shore, amid a Chesapeake Bay tributary, the Kent Manor Inn earns praise for its 24 elegant rooms, panoramic water views, and the seafood served in the romantic restaurant.

Taking to the Water

Maryland and Virginia are not only traversed by countless rivers, they fringe the Atlantic Ocean and are both home to the Chesapeake Bay. So it's no wonder that there's great appreciation for maritime pursuits—boating, fishing, and kayaking. Companies around the region rent all types of boats and offer a wide range of tours and excursions. In the mountains of both states, you'll find exhilarating whitewater rafting. Even taking a ride on a tour boat in Baltimore's Inner Harbor or along the Potomac River in Washington, DC, offers plenty of interesting scenery. Here are a few great ways to take to the water in and around Virginia and Maryland.

• In Maryland you can spend a full day or take a sunset excursion by boat exploring the Chesapeake Bay. From Annapolis, Watermark Journeys schooner tours go as far as St. Michaels on the Eastern Shore.

• For an unusual view of Washington, DC's monuments and prominent buildings, take one of the kayaking tours on the Potomac offered by the Thompson Boat Center in Georgetown.

• Fans of deep-sea fishing need look no farther than Maryland's Ocean City Fishing Center, which has more than 30 vessels providing charter sportfishing trips to catch blue marlin, wahoo, and big-eye tuna.

National Parks & Forests

From the mountains to the seashore, a number of stunning—sometimes historic—national parks are in Virginia and Maryland. The parks provide wonderful opportunities for scenic country drives and bike rides, camping or stays in rustic park-service lodges, and up-close encounters with myriad wildlife, from bald eagles to wild horses. The famous Appalachian Trail cuts a rugged path through both states, and virtually every major park and forest has rigorous hikes and shorter nature walks. Here are some must-sees.

• A 37-mi-long barrier island that borders both Virginia and Maryland's shores, Assateague Island National Seashore is full of pristine beaches, wild horses, deer, and some 300 species of birds.

• Blackwater National Wildlife Refuge, southeast of Annapolis, is one of the East Coast's premier spots for viewing thousands of migratory geese and ducks in season, and birds ranging from bald eagles to ospreys. Visitors can explore the area by car, bike, or kayak.

• Catoctin Mountain Park in Western Maryland is home to the Camp David presidential retreat, but its other claim to fame is its beauty. The area boasts some 20 mi of scenic hikes, and the highest cascading waterfall in the state.

• The Potomac River, the waterway that divides Maryland and Virginia, is the route of the 185-mi linear park, the C&O Canal National Historical Park. It's a favorite with hikers and bicyclists.

• In Virginia's Shenandoah Mountains lies the breathtaking Skyline Drive, a celebrated 105-mi route through Shenandoah National Park.

GREAT ITINERARIES

THE BEST OF VIRGINIA, MARYLAND & WASHINGTON, DC

While Virginia, Maryland, and DC are too geographically and socially diverse to see everything during one visit, it is possible to glean a sense of the region with a little careful planning. This 10-day jaunt offers some of the best attractions in each area, from sea to city to mountains.

Days 1 & 2: Washington, DC

You could spend the entire 10 days of this itinerary exploring the nation's Capitol without running out of things to see and do. With two days, try the following strategy: spend the first day exploring the National Mall and checking out a handful of the Smithsonian museums and, another must in this neighborhood, the U.S. Holocaust Memorial Museum. Political buffs and those who simply want to see the seat of America's power might want to tour the White House (be sure to reserve at least three months in advance) or the Capitol. On your second day, venture into some of the city's diverse residential neighborhoods, such as Dupont Circle, U Street, Adams-Morgan, or Georgetown. Each abounds with chic shops, galleries, and handsome Victorian town houses. You'll also find many of the city's coolest hotels in these parts (the Hotel George, for example, an ultra-modern boutique hotel, has red themed eclectic decor) as well as restaurants serving everything from haute cuisine to authentic Ethiopian, Thai, and soul food. Culture-vultures shouldn't miss the Phillips Collection modern-art museum in Dupont Circle, and nature-lovers should spend a little time in sweeping Rock Creek Park, which divides Georgetown and Dupont Circle. The Newseum is another must for newshounds and the simply curious.

Day 3: Baltimore

On Day 3 drive up I–95 or Route 295 to Baltimore, the largest and best-known city in Maryland; it's a must-see for first-time visitors. Although quite different in look and feel from neighboring Washington, DC, Bmore, as locals call it, is historically and culturally interesting in its own right. Take in some of the major sights clustered around the colorful Inner Harbor, such as the National Aquarium of Baltimore, the American Visionary Art Museum, and, a few blocks away, the Reginald F. Lewis Museum of Maryland African-American History and Culture. The colorful museum (the exterior is red, gold, and black), is paces away from Little Italy, where there are many enjoyable Italian restaurants (and a place to get wonderful gelato) in different price ranges.

Be sure to save at least a little time to do some shopping and dining in four distinct neighborhoods—artsy Mount Vernon, historic Fells Point, upscale Canton, and the new and posh Harbor East. If you have time for a seasonal sporting event, do see Oriole Park at Camden Yards—one of the nation's most beautiful ballparks, or Ravens Stadium, home of the Baltimore Ravens.

Day 4: Annapolis & Solomons

On the morning of Day 4, head southeast from Baltimore via I–97 to experience Maryland's Colonial past in Annapolis, the state capital, which is also home to the impressive grounds of the vaunted U.S. Naval Academy. Harry Browne's, not far from the State House, is a great bet for one of Maryland's famous crab cakes or crab soup. Mid-afternoon, follow Route 2 into rural and scenic southern Maryland, eventually winding your way to the lovely town of Solomons, a cherished getaway for Chesapeake Bay boaters. The Back Creek Inn gets high marks as a lovely place to spend the night.

Day 5: Alexandria

The morning of Day 5 head south to the historic village of St. Mary's City, where archaeologists and other experts have been doing reconstruction work related to the area's early English settlement in the 1600s. Then head north up Route 5 and west on I–495 to reach Alexandria, an excellent base for exploring northern Virginia's top sites, such as Arlington Cemetery, Mount Vernon (George Washington's home), and Manassas National Battlefield Park. Alexandria has a little bit of everything: from a charming, historic Old Town district, complete with antiques shops, galleries, and boutiques, to the Torpedo Factory Art Center, where close to 200 artisans work and showcase their wares. History buffs may want to visit the Georgian-inspired Christ Church—where both George Washington and Robert E. Lee were pewholders, or the African-American museum, which touts Alexandria's leadership in early Civil Rights actions. Alexandria has fine restaurants and hotels—including the Morrison House, which offers some of the most stylish rooms in town.

Days 6 & 7: Charlottesville

From Alexandria head west on I–495 and then I–66, exiting at Front Royal and then driving along Skyline Drive through beautiful Shenandoah National Park. Keep in mind that it can take a while (about two to three hours) to drive along this meandering scenic road. At U.S. 33, travel east to U.S. 29, and then south to the lively and inviting university town of Charlottesville. Here you can find a number of hip restaurants as well as such appealing lodging options as the gorgeous hilltop expanse known as Keswick Hall, and the more-affordable Silver Thatch Inn. Use "C-ville" as a base for exploring Thomas Jefferson's life—be it his plantation home, Monticello, or the regal campus of the University of Virginia. If you have time, consider checking out one of the fine wineries in the general vicinity, such as Barboursville, which offers excellent tours and also has historic ties to Jefferson. Another presidential stop is James Madison's estate, Montpelier.

GREAT ITINERARIES

Day 8: Richmond

Drive east on I–64 from Charlottesville to reach Virginia's capital, Richmond, which is home to several fine museums, Civil War sites, and historic neighborhoods. An especially appealing section for a stroll is the Victorian Fan District, home to the excellent Virginia Museum of Fine Arts and close to the grand Jefferson Hotel. Richmond is a short drive from Petersburg and Pamplin Historical Park, where the historical interpretations are cutting-edge; they also incorporate the history of slavery. In the evening, venture into the revitalized Shockoe Bottom and Shockoe Slip areas downtown, whose cobblestone streets are lined with cool restaurants and lively bars and lounges.

Days 9 & 10: Williamsburg

Continue east from Richmond along I–64 to Williamsburg, your base for exploring such historic sites as the early English settlements of Jamestown and the Revolutionary battlefield at Yorktown. You'll want to spend at least a full day touring the museums and living history of Colonial Williamsburg, with its many house-museums staffed by costumed interpreters. Plan to spend the night in the Colonial Houses of Williamsburg, which offer the most authentically historic lodging experience. If you're traveling with kids, budget some time to enjoy the wild rides at nearby Busch Gardens. On your final day, if you still have energy and time, you might want to continue along I–64 east to the Hampton Roads area to spend a little time at the Mariners' Museum and the USS *Monitor* Center or the Chrysler Museum of Art in the maritime city of Norfolk. You could also continue directly to the resorts of Virginia Beach, or drive up U.S. 13, which affords you access to

both Virginia's and Maryland's Eastern Shore regions.

TIPS

This itinerary entails covering a lot of ground and spending nights at several different hotels. If you'd rather base your operations from two or three cities and visit the towns and attractions described above as day trips, consider spending the first three or four nights in Washington, DC (and visiting Baltimore, Annapolis, St. Mary's City, and Alexandria), and then the final five or six nights hunkered down in Richmond or Williamsburg, from where you can easily explore the rest of central Virginia.

For timing, consider that you'll battle significant crowds and possibly sultry weather in summer. The most delightful scenery and weather is in spring (when flowers bloom in radiant colors) and fall (when the foliage of Shenandoah Park is magnificent).

A CIVIL WAR TOUR

Civil War sites are among the most compelling reasons to visit Virginia and Maryland, and the Civil War itinerary below covers the standout attractions. When Virginia seceded from the Union in 1861, it would become a major battleground; thus, much of this tour is in Virginia, with a brief foray into Maryland.

Day 1: Hampton

Start your tour at Hampton, on the Virginia Peninsula, where the Union general George McClellan launched his drive toward Richmond. The Hampton History Museum contains excellent exhibits on Civil War ironclad ships. Nearby is

Fort Monroe—the Union stronghold in which the president of the Confederacy, Jefferson Davis, was imprisoned.

Day 2: Richmond

On Day 2 drive northwest on I–64 up the peninsula to Richmond's Museum and White House of the Confederacy and the National Battlefield Park Visitor Center. Also see the Virginia Historical Society Museum of Virginia History, which has some 800 pieces of Confederate weaponry, although only a few are on display. Proceed 20 mi south on I–95 to Petersburg, the city that was under an extended siege by Grant's army. Visit 1,500-acre Petersburg National Battlefield, the Siege Museum, and Pamplin Historical Park—which commemorates an important Union attack on Lee's supposedly impenetrable defense line—before returning to spend the night in Richmond.

Days 3 & 4: Fredericksburg

For Days 3 and 4, proceed north from Richmond up I–95 to Fredericksburg, which has blocks of historic Civil War–era homes and a Confederate Cemetery with the remains of more than 2,000 soldiers. Detour to see the four battlefields at Fredericksburg/Spotsylvania National Military Park, then venture an hour outside of town to see Stratford Hall plantation, where Robert E. Lee was born.

Days 5 & 6: Northern Virginia

For Days 5 and 6, base yourself around Arlington or Fairfax, which puts you close to the key attractions in this area—from Fredericksburg, you reach the area by heading north up I–95. Spend one day touring Manassas National Battlefield Park (aka "Bull Run"), site of two important Confederate victories—it's here that General Thomas Jonathan Jackson earned the nickname "Stonewall," when he and his brigade "stood like a stone wall." On your second day, head to Arlington National Cemetery and Arlington House (Lee's home for 30 years before the Union army confiscated it and turned the grounds into the cemetery).

GREAT ITINERARIES

Day 7: Frederick

From northern Virginia, head north on I–270 into Maryland. North of Frederick, catch Route 34 out of Boonsboro and follow it to the Antietam National Battlefield, site of the bloodiest single day of Civil War fighting (more than 23,000 troops were killed or wounded during the gruesome engagement). In Frederick, where you can spend the night, is the National Museum of Civil War Medicine with its 3,000 artifacts. Nearby is Monocacy National Battlefield, where Union troops thwarted a Confederate invasion of Washington, DC.

Days 8 & 9: Lexington

From western Maryland follow I–81 south back into Virginia and through the Shenandoah Valley to reach Lexington, a quaint and scenic college town (home to Washington and Lee University) where many buildings date back to the 1700s. Visit the Lee Chapel and Museum, where Lee is buried, and the Virginia Military Institute Museum, which has displays on Stonewall Jackson. Jackson is buried here as well; and you can see the only house he ever owned, which is now a museum.

TIPS

One of the most compelling times to visit a Civil War battlefield is when volunteers are staging a battle reenactment. Thousands of Civil War history enthusiasts participate in these events, which often last for several days. For more information, log on to ⊕ www.civilwarnews.com.

If you prefer to limit the number of times you change accommodations, consider basing your trip out of Alexandria or Arlington for the northern Virginia and western Maryland attractions, and out of Richmond for the central and eastern Virginia sites.

Day 10: Richmond

On your final day return to Richmond via Appomattox to spend some additional time exploring any of the city's Civil War–related attractions. Stop at Appomattox Court House, where Lee formally surrendered to Grant, thus officially ending the Civil War. The park here consists of some 27 original structures, and the self-guided tour is exceptionally good. From here it's a leisurely and scenic drive east on U.S. 460 and then northeast on U.S. 360 back to the state capital.

Washington, DC

WORD OF MOUTH

"All of the memorials are impressive, but the Korean War Memorial is especially impressive if you see it in the moonlight. It is eerily realistic. You can almost feel what it would be like to be with a group of soldiers on a patrol at night. For a vet like me, it was quite moving . . ."

—Travelermebe

"The obvious is that you will want to do the Smithsonian museums, but in addition to that, I highly recommend the Spy museum. I've taken guests to it and both my guests and I have really enjoyed it."

—npurpleh2

Updated by
Mary Beth
Bohman

THE BYZANTINE WORKINGS OF THE federal government, the sound bite–ready oratory of the well-groomed politicians, and the murky foreign policy pronouncements issued from Foggy Bottom cause many Americans to cast a skeptical eye on anything that happens "inside the Beltway." Washingtonians take it in stride—all in a day's work. Besides, such ribbing is a small price to pay for living in a city with charms that extend far beyond the bureaucratic. World-class museums and art galleries (nearly all of them free), tree-shaded and flower-filled parks and gardens, bars and restaurants that benefit from a large immigrant community and droves of young people, and nightlife that seems to get better with every passing year are as much a part of Washington as floor debates or filibusters.

The city that calls to mind politicking, back-scratching, and delicate diplomatic maneuvering is itself the result of a compromise. The deal was struck when Virginia's Thomas Jefferson agreed that the federal government would assume the war debts of the colonies if Alexander Hamilton and other Northern legislators would agree to locate the capital on the banks of the Potomac, near George Washington's estate at Mount Vernon. Soon after, in 1791, Pierre-Charles L'Enfant, a French engineer who had fought in the Revolution, designed a city with a "vast esplanade" now known as the "Mall," wide diagonal boulevards crossing a grid of streets, and a focal triangle formed by the Capitol, the president's house, and a statue where the Washington monument now sits. Although L'Enfant's plans seem grand now, for almost a century this city was little more than a sparsely populated swamp with empty dirt avenues. Cattle grazed on the Mall and America's famous early leaders worked in and inhabited dank, dilapidated buildings.

ORIENTATION & PLANNING

GETTING ORIENTED

The city is divided into the four quadrants of a compass (NW, NE, SE, SW), with the U.S. Capitol at the center. Because the Capitol doesn't sit in the exact center of the city (the Washington Monument does), Northwest is the largest quadrant.

If someone tells you to meet them at 6th and G, ask them to specify the quadrant, because there are actually four different 6th and G intersections (one per quadrant). Within each quadrant, numbered streets run north–south, and lettered streets run east–west (the letter J was omitted to avoid confusion with the letter I). The streets form a fairly simple grid—for instance, 900 G Street NW is the intersection of 9th and G streets in the NW quadrant of the city. Likewise, if you count the letters of the alphabet, skipping J, you can get a good approximation of an address for a numbered street. For instance, 1600 16th Street NW is close to Q Street, Q being the 16th letter of the alphabet if you skip J.

As if all this weren't confusing enough, Major Pierre L'Enfant, the Frenchman who originally designed the city, threw in diagonal avenues recalling those of Paris. Most of DC's avenues are named after U.S. states. You can find addresses on avenues the same way you find those on numbered streets, so 1200 Connecticut Avenue NW is close to M Street, because M is the 12th letter of the alphabet when you skip J.

PLANNING

WHEN TO GO

Washington has two delightful seasons: spring and autumn. In spring the city's ornamental fruit trees are budding, and its many gardens are in bloom. By autumn most of the summer crowds have left and you can enjoy the sights in peace. Summer can be uncomfortably hot and humid. Winter weather is mild by East Coast standards, but a handful of modest snowstorms each year bring this southern city to a standstill.

GETTING HERE & AROUND

BY AIR The major gateways to DC are Ronald Reagan Washington National Airport in Virginia, 4 mi south of downtown Washington; Dulles International Airport, 26 mi west of Washington, DC; and Baltimore/Washington International-Thurgood Marshall (BWI) Airport in Maryland, about 30 mi to the northeast. By Taxi, expect to pay $10–$15 to get from National to downtown, $50–$60 from Dulles, and $60–$70 from BWI, plus $1.50 airport surcharge for all. A $1 surcharge is added 7–9:30 AM and 4–6:30 PM.

The Metro subway ride downtown from Ronald Reagan Washington National Airport takes about 20 minutes and costs about $1.85, depending on the time of day and your final destination.

Washington Flyer links Dulles International Airport and the West Falls Church Metro station. The 25-minute ride is $9 for adults, free for children under six. Buses run every half hour from 5:45 AM to 10:15 PM. Fares may be paid with cash or credit card. The Washington Metropolitan Area Transit Authority (WMATA) operates express bus service between Dulles and several stops in downtown DC, including the L'Enfant Plaza Metro station. Bus 5A, which costs $3.10, runs every hour between 5:30 AM and 11:30 PM. Exact fare is required.

Free shuttle buses carry passengers between airline terminals and the train station at BWI. Amtrak and Maryland Rail Commuter Service (MARC) trains run between BWI and Washington, DC's Union Station from around 6 AM to 10 PM. The cost of the 30-minute ride is $17–$41 on Amtrak and $7 on MARC, which runs only on weekdays. WMATA also operates express bus service ($3.10) between BWI and the Greenbelt Metro station. Buses run between 6 AM and 10 PM. National, Dulles, and BWI airports are served by SuperShuttle. The approximately 20-minute ride from Reagan National to downtown averages $13; the roughly 45-minute ride from Dulles runs $32; the ride from BWI, which takes about 60 minutes, averages $35.

BY BUS Affectionately known as the Chinatown Bus, several bus lines run between Chinatown in New York City and Chinatown in Washington, DC. The most reliable is called Today's Bus. The buses are clean, the service is satisfactory, and the price—$20 one-way and $35 round-trip—can't be beat, except, perhaps by recent competitors BoltBus and Megabus. The buses offer more legroom, Wi-Fi hot spots, power outlets, and a loyalty ride-free program. Nonrefundable tickets can be purchased on the Web site or, if unreserved seats remain, before boarding.

The red, white, and blue WMATA buses ($1.35, $3.10 on express buses) crisscross the city and the nearby suburbs. Seven-day bus passes for $11 are available at the Metro Center sales office, open weekdays from 7:30 AM to 6:30 PM.

The DC Circulator offers $1 rides to cultural and entertainment destinations along three routes within the city's central core. The north–south route runs from the DC Convention Center at 6th Street and Massachusetts NW, to the Southwest Waterfront, at 6th Street and Maine Avenue. The east–west route runs from Union Station at Columbus Plaza NW, to Georgetown, at M Street and Wisconsin Avenue NW. A third loop, operating on weekends only from 10 AM to 6 PM, circles the National Mall and includes stops at the National Gallery of Art and the Smithsonian. Passengers can pay cash when boarding (exact change only) or use Metro Farecards, SmarTrip cards, all-day passes, and Metro bus transfers. Tickets also may be purchased at fare meters or multispace parking meters on the sidewalk near Circulator stops. Machines accept change or credit cards and make change. Buses run every 5–10 minutes from 7 AM to 9 PM, seven days a week.

BY CAR A car is often a drawback in Washington, DC. Traffic is horrendous, especially at rush hour, and driving is often confusing, with many lanes and some entire streets changing direction suddenly during rush hour. Interstate 95 skirts DC as part of the Beltway (also known as I–495 in parts), the six- to eight-lane highway that encircles the city.

Parking here is an adventure; the police are quick to tow away or immobilize with a boot any vehicle parked illegally. Private parking lots downtown often charge around $5 an hour and $25 a day. There's free three-hour parking around the Mall on Jefferson and Madison drives, though these spots are almost always filled. The closest free parking is in three lots in East Potomac Park, south of the 14th Street Bridge. Note that it's illegal to use a handheld phone while driving in Washington, DC, and that radar detectors are illegal in DC and Virginia.

BY METRO The Washington Metro is one of the country's cleanest and safest subway systems. It begins operation at 5 AM on weekdays and 7 AM on weekends and closes on weekdays at midnight and weekends at 3 AM. During the weekday peak periods (5–9:30 AM and 3–7 PM), trains come along every three to six minutes. At other times trains run about every 12–15 minutes.

The Metro's base fare is $1.65; the actual price you pay depends on the time of day and the distance traveled. Up to two children under age five ride free with a paying passenger. Buy your ticket at the Farecard machines, some of which accept credit cards. One-day passes are $7.80 and seven-day passes are $39. ■ TIP➜ **Make sure you hang on to your**

Farecard—you need it to exit at your destination. Locals use the SmarTrip card, a plastic card that can hold any fare amount and can be used throughout the subway system. Buy passes or SmarTrip cards at the Metro Center sales office.

BY TAXI You can hail a taxi on the street just about anywhere in the city, though they tend to congregate around major hotels. There are a number of different cab companies in the city, and as a result DC cabs do not have a uniform appearance (unlike New York's yellow cabs, for example). And you may find yourself in a taxi that's older and a bit run-down. Drivers are allowed to pick up more than one fare at a time.

After 70 years of a zone system, taxis in the District are now on time and distance meters. The base rate for the first ⅙ mile is $3. Each additional ⅙ mile and each minute stopped or traveling at less than 10 mph is 25¢. There is a $2 surcharge per piece of large luggage in the trunk and a 50¢ per bag handling charge. There is a $2 surcharge for radio dispatch.

BY TRAIN More than 80 trains a day arrive at Washington, DC's Union Station. Amtrak's regular service runs from DC to New York in 3¼–3¾ hours and from DC to Boston in 7¾–8 hours. Acela, Amtrak's high-speed service, travels from DC to New York in 2¾–3 hours and from DC to Boston in 6½ hours. Two commuter lines—Maryland Rail Commuter Service and Virginia Railway Express—run to the nearby suburbs. They're cheaper than Amtrak, but they don't run on weekends.

TOURS Old Town Trolley Tours ($32, $28.80 on the Web site), orange-and-green motorized trolleys, take in the main downtown sights and also head into Georgetown and the upper Northwest in a speedy two hours if you ride straight through. However, you can hop on and off as many times as you like. Tourmobile buses, authorized by the National Park Service, operate in a similar fashion, making 25 stops at historic sites between the Capitol and Arlington National Cemetery. Tickets, available at kiosks at Union Station and Arlington National Cemetery, are $25 for adults.

Special tours of government buildings with heavy security, including the White House and the Capitol, can be arranged through your representative's or senator's office. ■TIP→ **Plan up to six months in advance of your trip as limited numbers of these so-called VIP tickets are available.** Governmental buildings close to visitors when the Department of Homeland Security issues a high alert, so call ahead. The United States Capitol Vsitor Center leads free tours of the historic Capitol Monday through Saturday from 9 AM to 4:30 PM. Register in advance for tickets online or get them directly from the Center.

Guided walks around Washington, DC, and nearby communities are routinely offered by the Smithsonian Associates Program; advance tickets are required. Tour DC specializes in walking tours of Georgetown and Dupont Circle, covering topics such as the Civil War, the Underground Railroad, and Kennedy's Georgetown. Anecdotal History Tours leads tours in Georgetown, Adams-Morgan, and Capitol Hill, as well as tours of where Lincoln was shot and the homes of former presidents. Washington Walks has a wide range of tours, including "I've Got a Secret" featuring Washington, DC lore. The nonprofit group Cultural Tourism DC leads guided walking tours that cover the history and architecture of neighborhoods from the southwest waterfront to points much farther north.

ESSENTIALS

Air Contacts **Baltimore/Washington International-Thurgood Marshall Airport** (☎ *410/859-7100* ⊕ *www.bwiairport.com*). **Dulles International Airport** (☎ *703/572-2700* ⊕ *www.metwashairports.com/Dulles*). **Ronald Reagan Washington National Airport** (☎ *703/417-8000* ⊕ *www.metwashairports.com/National*).

Bus Contacts **BoltBus** (✉ *9th and G St. NW* ⊕ *www.boltbus.com*). **DC Circulator** (*District Department of Transportation* ☎ *202/962-1423* ⊕ *www.dccirculator.com*). **MegaBus** (✉ *9th and G St. NW* ⊕ *www.megabus.com*). **Today's Bus** (✉ *610 I St. NW* ☎ *202/408-8200* ⊕ *www.todaysbus.com*).

Metro Contacts **Metro Center sales office** (✉ *Metro Center Metro Station, 12th and F Sts. NW*). **Washington Metropolitan Area Transit Authority** (*WMATA* ☎ *202/637-7000, 202/638-3780 TTY, 202/962-1195 lost and found* ⊕ *www.wmata.com*).

Taxis & Shuttle Contacts **Amtrak** (☎ *800/872-7245* ⊕ *www.amtrak.com*). **DC Taxicab Commission** (☎ *202/645-6018* ⊕ *www.dctaxi.dc.gov*). **Diamond** (☎ *202/387-4011*). **Maryland Rail Commuter Service** (☎ *410/539-5000, 866/743-3682* ⊕ *www.mtamaryland.com*). **Mayflower** (☎ *202/783-1111*). **SuperShuttle** (☎ *800/258-3826 or 202/296-6662* ⊕ *www.supershuttle.com*). **Washington Flyer** (☎ *888/927-4359* ⊕ *www.washfly.com*). **Washington Metropolitan Area Transit Authority** (☎ *202/637-7000, 202/638-3780 TDD* ⊕ *www.wmata.com*). **Yellow** (☎ *202/544-1212*).

Tour Contacts **Anecdotal History Tours** (☎ *301/294-9514* ⊕ *www.dcsightseeing.com*). **Cultural Tourism DC** (☎ *202/661-7581* ⊕ *www.culturaltourismdc.org*). **Department of State** (☎ *202/647-3241, 202/736-4474 TDD* ⊕ *www.state.gov/m/drr*). **Old Town Trolley Tours** (☎ *202/832-9800* ⊕ *www.historictours.com*). **Smithsonian Associates Program** (☎ *202/357-3030* ⊕ *www.smithsonianassociates.org*). **Tour D.C** (☎ *301/588-8999* ⊕ *www.tourdc.com*). **Tourmobile** (☎ *202/554-5100 or 888/868-7707* ⊕ *www.tourmobile.com*). **United States Capitol Guide Service** (☎ *202/252-6827* ⊕ *www.visitthecapital.gov*). **Washington Walks** (☎ *202/484-1865* ⊕ *www.washingtonwalks.com*).

Train Contacts **Amtrak** (☎ *800/872-7245* ⊕ *www.amtrak.com*). **Maryland Rail Commuter Service** (*MARC* ☎ *800/325-7245* ⊕ *www.mtamaryland.com*). **Union Station** (✉ *50 Massachusetts Ave. NE* ☎ *202/371-9441* ⊕ *www.unionstationdc.com*). **Virginia Railway Express** (*VRE* ☎ *703/684-1001* ⊕ *www.vre.org*). **Washington Metropolitan Area Transit Authority** (☎ *202/637-7000, 202/638-3780 TDD* ⊕ *www.wmata.com*).

Visitor Information **DC Visitor Information Center** (✉ *1300 Pennsylvania Ave. NW, White House Area* ☎ *866/324-7386 or 202/289-8317* ⊕ *www.dcchamber.org*). **National Park Service** (☎ *202/619-7275 "Dial-a-Park" park information* ⊕ *www.nps.gov*). **Smithsonian** (☎ *202/633-1000 or 202/633-5285* ⊕ *www.si.edu*).

DISCOUNTS & DEALS

It's actually hard to spend money on activities in DC. All the Smithsonian museums and national memorials are free, as are many other museums and attractions. Summertime is heaven for budget travelers, when free outdoor concerts and festivals occur every week.

PLANNING YOUR TIME

Allow four or five hours to tour the monuments. This includes time to relax on a park bench and to grab a snack from a vendor or one of the snack bars east of the Washington Monument and near the Lincoln Memorial. If you're visiting during the first two weeks in April, take extra time around the Tidal Basin and the Washington Monument to marvel at the cherry blossoms.

EXPLORING WASHINGTON, DC

There's no denying that Washington, the world's first planned capital, is also one of its most beautiful. And although the federal government dominates many of the city's activities and buildings, there are always places where you can leave politics behind. Washington is a city of vistas—pleasant views that shift and change from block to block, a marriage of geometry and art. Unlike other large cities, Washington isn't dominated by skyscrapers, largely because, in 1899, Congress passed a height-restrictions act to prevent federal monuments from being overshadowed by commercial construction. Its buildings stretch out gracefully and are never far from expanses of green. Like its main industry, politics, Washington's design is a constantly changing kaleidoscope that invites inspection from all angles.

Washington's centerpiece is the National Mall, a mile-long stretch of grass that reaches from the Capitol past the bulk of the Smithsonian's grand museums to the Washington Monument. The White House, due north of the Washington Monument, and the other major monuments, to the southwest, are not far away. In recent years Downtown, north of Pennsylvania from the Capitol to the White House, has become the city's nerve center, quickly gentrifying with new bars, restaurants, world-class theaters, and a renovated Smithsonian Museum of American Art and National Portrait Gallery. The tree-shaded streets of Georgetown, up Pennsylvania Avenue from the White House, are lined with million-dollar row houses and the city's best upscale shopping. U Street, once Washington's Harlem, has regained its status as DC's hippest neighborhood. The neighborhoods along the Metro's red line—Dupont Circle, Woodley Park, and Cleveland Park—offer a pleasant respite from the federal bustle and some top-notch shops and art galleries.

THE MALL

The Mall is the heart of almost every visitor's trip to Washington. The front yard for nearly a dozen free museums, a picnicking park, a jogging path, and an outdoor stage for festivals, movies, musical performances, and fireworks, America's town green is the closest thing the capital has to a theme park.

TOP WASHINGTON, D.C. EXPERIENCES

■ **Shop in Georgetown:** Stroll the cobblestone streets and dip into shops offering cutting-edge fashion and priceless antiques.

■ **Explore the Smithsonian:** Spend days savoring a variety of brilliant exhibits in the Smithsonian's 13 museums, all free.

■ **Walk the Halls of Power:** At the White House, the Capitol, and the Supreme Court, take a peek behind the curtain.

■ **Taste the Emerging Theater Scene:** Feast your eyes on brilliantly staged productions at the Kennedy Center, Shakespeare Theatre, Arena Stage, and Woolly Mammoth.

■ **Get a Bird's-Eye View:** At the Old Post Office, Washington Monument, and Hotel Washington terrace, enjoy a full view of this marble- and monument-laden city.

MAIN ATTRACTIONS

⑩ **National Air and Space Museum.** The 23 galleries in this museum, thought ◔ to be the most-visited in the world, tell the story of aviation from the Fodor'sChoice earliest human attempts at flight. As you walk through, look up to ★ see the world's most famous aircraft, including the Wright 1903 Flyer, which Wilbur Wright piloted over the sands of Kitty Hawk, North Carolina; Charles Lindbergh's *Spirit of St. Louis;* the X-1 rocket plane in which Chuck Yeager broke the sound barrier; and an X-15, the first aircraft to exceed Mach 6. Other highlights include a 4-billion-year-old slice of moon rock and a backup model of the Skylab orbital workshop that you can walk through.

Films shown on the five-story-high IMAX screen—including the now classic *To Fly!*—employ swooping aerial scenes that make you feel as if you've left the ground. Upstairs, the Albert Einstein Planetarium's "all-dome" digital technology creates a feeling of movement through space. A shuttle bus runs from the museum entrance on the Mall to the **National Air and Space Museum Steven F. Udvar-Hazy Center** (*see Chapter 2*). ✉*Independence Ave. and 6th St. SW, The Mall* ☎*202/357–1729, 202/357–1686 movie information, 202/357–1729 TDD* ⊕*www.nasm.si.edu* ✉*Free, IMAX $10, planetarium $8.50* ⊘*Daily 10–5:30* Ⓜ*Smithsonian.*

❸ **National Gallery of Art, West Building.** The two buildings of the National ★ Gallery hold one of the world's foremost collections of paintings, sculptures, and graphics. ■ TIP→ **If you want to view the museum's holdings in (more or less) chronological order, start your exploration in the West Building, a gift to the nation from wealthy financier, industrialist, and Secretary of the Treasury Andrew Mellon.** The rotunda, with 24 marble columns surrounding a fountain topped with a statue of Mercury, sets the stage for the masterpieces on display in more than 100 galleries. But don't get overwhelmed; two serene gardens punctuate the center of each wing. The permanent collection includes *Ginevra de' Benci,* the only painting by Leonardo da Vinci on display in the Western Hemisphere; *The*

Adoration of the Magi by Fra Angelico and Filippo Lippi; *Daniel in the Lions' Den* by Peter Paul Rubens; a self-portrait by Rembrandt; Salvador Dalí's *Last Supper,* and works by impressionists such as Edgar Degas, Claude Monet, Auguste Renoir, and Mary Cassatt.

The **National Gallery of Art Sculpture Garden** is between 7th and 9th streets along the Mall. Granite walkways take you through the garden, which is planted with shade trees, flowering trees, and perennials. Sculptures on display include Roy Lichtenstein's playful *House I;* Alexander Archipenko's *Woman Combing Her Hair;* Miró's *Personnage Gothique, Oiseau-Eclair;* and Isamu Noguchi's *Great Rock of Inner Seeking.* The huge central fountain becomes a skating rink in winter. ⊠ *Constitution Ave. between 7th and 9th Sts. NW, The Mall* ☎ *202/737–4215, 202/842–6176 TDD* ⊕ *www.nga.gov* ✉ *Free* ⊗ *Mon.–Sat. 10–5, Sun. 11–6* Ⓜ *Archives/Navy Memorial.*

❹ National Gallery of Art, East Building. Architect I.M. Pei designed this dramatic structure, incorporating two interlocking spaces shaped like triangles. Despite its severe angularity, Pei's building is inviting. Inside, the sunlit atrium is dominated by a colorful 76-foot long Alexander Calder mobile. Masterpieces from every famous name in 20th-century art—Pablo Picasso, Jackson Pollock, Piet Mondrian, Roy Lichtenstein, Joan Miró, Georgia O'Keeffe, and dozens of others—fill the galleries. The collection of Henri Matisse's giant paper cutouts (on view only between 10 and 2 Monday through Saturday, and 11 to 3 on Sunday) is considered the world's greatest. The cheat sheet "What to See in An Hour" pinpoints 15 highlights of the East Building. An underground concourse lined with gift shops, a café, and a cafeteria links to the West Building. ⊠ *Constitution Ave. between 3rd and 4th Sts. NW, The Mall* ☎ *202/737–4215, 202/842–6176 TDD* ⊕ *www.nga.gov* ✉ *Free* ⊗ *Mon.–Sat. 10–5, Sun. 11–6* Ⓜ *Archives/Navy Memorial.*

❶ National Museum of American History. The 3 million artifacts in the country's largest history museum explore America's cultural, political, technical, and scientific past, with holdings as diverse and iconic as the desk on which Thomas Jefferson wrote the Declaration of Independence, the top hat Abraham Lincoln was wearing the night he was assassinated, and Judy Garland's ruby slippers from *The Wizard of Oz.* The museum reopened in November 2008 after a two-year, $85 million architectural renovation, aimed in part at reconfiguring the museum's infamously labyrinthine layout. Renovations are frequently subject to delay. Check the Web site to confirm that the museum has reopened. ⊠ *Constitution Ave. and 14th St. NW, The Mall* ☎ *202/633–1000, 202/633–5285 TDD* ⊕ *www.americanhistory.si.edu* ✉ *Free* ⊗ *Daily 10–5:30.*

❺ United States Holocaust Memorial Museum. A permanent exhibition tells the stories of the millions killed by the Nazis between 1933 and 1945, and it doesn't pull any punches. Upon arrival, you are issued an "identity card" that details the life of a holocaust victim. The museum recounts the Holocaust through documentary films, video- and audio-taped oral histories, and a collection that includes items such as a freight car like those used to transport Jews from Warsaw to the Treblinka death camp and the Star of David patches that Jews were made to wear. Like the history it covers, the museum can be profoundly disturbing; it's not recommended for children under 11, although Daniel's Story, a ground-floor exhibit not requiring tickets, is designed for children ages 8 and up. In addition to the permanent exhibition, the museum also has a multimedia learning center, a resource center for students and teachers, a registry of Holocaust survivors, and occasional special exhibitions. Timed-entry passes (distributed on a first-come, first-served basis at the 14th Street entrance starting at 10 AM or available in advance through tickets.com) are necessary for the permanent exhibition. ⊠ *100 Raoul Wallenberg Pl. SW, enter from Raoul Wallenberg Pl. or 14th St. SW, The Mall* ☎ *202/488–0400, 800/400–9373 tickets.com* ⊕ *www.ushmm.org* ☞ *Free* ☉ *Daily 10–5:30* Ⓜ *Smithsonian.*

ALSO WORTH SEEING

❽ Arthur M. Sackler Gallery. Arthur M. Sackler, who began collecting Asian art as a student in the 1940s, allowed Smithsonian curators to select 1,000 items from his ample collection and pledged $4 million toward the construction of this museum. The pan-Asian permanent collection includes Chinese ritual bronzes, Persian manuscripts, and Indian paintings in gold, silver, lapis lazuli, and malachite. ⊠ *1050 Independence Ave. SW, The Mall* ☎ *202/633–1000, 202/357–1729 TDD* ⊕ *www. asia.si.edu* ☞ *Free* ☉ *Daily 10–5:30* Ⓜ *Smithsonian.*

❻ Bureau of Engraving and Printing. The powerful presses here turn out more than $38 million a day, in addition to stamps, military certificates, and presidential invitations. You can only enter the bureau on the official tours, which last about 35 minutes. From March through August, same-day timed-entry tour passes are issued starting at 8 AM at the Raoul Wallenberg Place SW ticket booth. For the rest of the year, tickets aren't used. ⊠ *14th and C Sts. SW, The Mall* ☎ *202/874–8888, 877/874–4114 tour information* ⊕ *www.moneyfactory.com* ☞ *Free* ☉ *Sept.–Apr., weekdays 9–10:45 and 12:30–2; May–Aug., weekdays 9–10:45, 12:30–2, and 5–7* Ⓜ *Smithsonian.*

❼ Freer Gallery of Art. Home to one of the world's finest collections of Asian art, the Smithsonian's Freer Gallery of Art was made possible by an endowment from Detroit industrialist Charles L. Freer. Opened in 1923, the collection includes more than 27,000 works of art from the Far and Near East, including Asian porcelains, Japanese screens, Chinese paintings and bronzes, Korean stoneware, and Islamic manuscripts.

Freer's friend James McNeill Whistler is represented in the vast collection. The Peacock Room, a blue-and-gold dining room decorated with painted leather, wood, and canvas, was designed by Whistler for a British shipping magnate. Freer paid $30,000 for the entire room and moved it from London to the United States in 1904. The works of other American artists influenced by the Far East are also on display. ⊠ *12th St. and Jefferson Dr. SW, The Mall* ☎ *202/633–1000, 202/357–1729 TDD* ⊕ *www.asia.si.edu* ☞ *Free* ☉ *Daily 10–5:30* Ⓜ *Smithsonian.*

❾ Hirshhorn Museum and Sculpture Garden. Sculpture on the National Mall runs mostly to marble columns and dead presidents, but the Hirshhorn

The Mall

East Capitol St.

New Jersey Ave.

S. Capitol St.

US Capitol

Canal St.

1st St.

Bartholdi Park

U.S. Botanic Garden

3rd St.

Pennsylvania Ave.

4th St.

ARCHIVES/ NAVY MEMORIAL

THE MALL

Health and Human Services

Maryland Ave.

FEDERAL CTR. SW

7th St.

National Gallery Sculpture Garden

C St.

L'ENFANT PLAZA

9th St.

Jefferson Dr.

Constitution Ave.

Carousel

Independence Ave.

Forrestal Building

D St.

220 yards

200 meters

FEDERAL TRIANGLE

12th St.

SMITHSONIAN

Madison Dr.

KEY

M Metro station

14th St.

Auditors Building

Raoul Wallenberg Pl.

15th St.

presents a bold alternative: a 32-foot-tall yellow cartoon brush-stroke sculpture by pop-art iconographer Roy Lichtenstein. Conceived as the nation's museum of modern and contemporary art, the Hirshhorn holds more than 11,500 works by masters like Pablo Picasso, Joan Miró, Piet Mondrian, Willem de Kooning, and Andy Warhol. These are displayed in a round 1974 poured-concrete building designed by Gordon Bunshaft. Dubbed the "Doughnut on the Mall" when it was built, it's now seen as a fitting home for contemporary art. Outside, sculptures dot a grass-and-granite garden, an inspiring spot for a picnic. ✉ *Independence Ave. and 7th St. SW, The Mall* ☎ *202/633–1000, 202/633–8043 TDD* ⊕ *www.hirshhorn.si.edu* 🎫 *Free* ⊗ *Museum daily 10–5:30, sculpture garden 7:30–dusk* Ⓜ *Smithsonian or L'Enfant Plaza (Maryland Ave. exit).*

Ⓒ ⑪ **National Museum of the American Indian.** The Smithsonian's newest museum is the first national museum devoted to Native American artifacts, presented from a Native American perspective. The undulating exterior, clad in pinkish-gold limestone from Minnesota, evokes natural rock formations shaped by wind and water. Inside, four floors of galleries cover 10,000 years of history of the thousands of native tribes of the western hemisphere. The exhibits are arranged to showcase specific tribes and themes, rather than a chronological history. Live music, dance, theater, and storytelling are central to experiencing this museum. Free timed-entrance passes, required for entry, are distributed beginning at 10 AM from the museum's east entrance, but by midday, especially during winter months, you may find that you don't actually need one. You can also buy the passes in advance online. ✉ *4th St. and Independence Ave. SW, The Mall* ☎ *202/633–1000* ⊕ *www.americanindian. si.edu* 🎫 *Free* ⊗ *Daily 10–5:30* Ⓜ *L'Enfant Plaza.*

❷ Ⓒ **National Museum of Natural History.** This is one of the world's great natural history museums, filled with the largest African bull elephant ever found, dinosaur bones, fossils, and other natural delights—124 million specimens in all. The highlight of the second floor is the **Janet Annenberg Hooker Hall of Geology, Gems, and Minerals,** which includes a pair of Marie Antoinette's earrings, the Rosser Reeves Ruby, and, of course, the Hope Diamond. There are tarantula feedings Tuesday through Friday at 10:30, 11:30, and 1:30. The Samuel C. Johnson IMAX theater shows two- and three-dimensional natural-history films. ✉ *Constitution Ave. and 10th St. NW, The Mall* ☎ *202/633–1000, 202/357–1729 TDD* ⊕ *www.mnh.si.edu* 🎫 *Free, IMAX $8.50* ⊗ *Museum daily 10–5:30; Discovery Room Tues.–Fri. noon–2:30, weekends 10:30–3:30; free passes for Discovery Room near the room's entrance* Ⓜ *Smithsonian or Federal Triangle.*

THE MONUMENTS

Washington is a city of monuments. In the middle of traffic circles, on tiny slivers of park, and at street corners and intersections, statues, plaques, and simple blocks of marble honor the generals, politicians, poets, and statesmen who helped shape the nation. The monuments dedicated to the most famous Americans are west of the Mall on ground reclaimed from the marshy flats of the Potomac. This is also the location of Washington's greatest single display of cherry trees, gifts from Japan. And there will soon be a "King" among the presidents honored here. The Martin Luther King Jr. memorial is expected to be dedicated in 2010.

❼ **Franklin Delano Roosevelt Memorial.** This 7½-acre memorial to the 32nd president employs waterfalls and reflection pools, four outdoor gallery rooms—one for each of Roosevelt's terms as president—and 10 bronze sculptures. The granite megaliths that connect the galleries are engraved with some of Roosevelt's most famous quotes. Although today the memorial is one of the most popular in the District, it's had its share of controversy. When unveiled, the monument did not depict Roosevelt with a wheelchair, which he used for the last 24 years of his life, including those in which he led the nation through World War II. However, this was the first DC memorial purposely designed to be wheelchair accessible, and the first to honor a First Lady, Eleanor Roosevelt. ⊠ *West side of Tidal Basin, The Mall* ☎*202/426–6841* ⊕*www.nps.gov/fdrm* ⊠*Free* ☽*24 hrs; staffed daily 8* AM*–midnight* Ⓜ*Smithsonian.*

❽ **Jefferson Memorial.** The monument honoring the third president of the
Fodor'sChoice United States was modeled by John Russell Pope after a style that Jef-
★ ferson had used himself when he designed the University of Virginia. In the 1930s Congress decided that Jefferson deserved a monument positioned as prominently as those in honor of Washington and Lincoln, so workers scooped and moved tons of river bottom to create dry land on this spot directly south of the White House. Dedicated in 1943, it houses a statue of Jefferson, and its walls are lined with inscriptions based on the Declaration of Independence and his other writings. One of the best views of the White House can be seen from its top steps. ⊠*Tidal Basin, south bank, The Mall* ☎*202/426–6821* ⊕*www.nps. gov/thje* ⊠*Free* ☽*Daily 8* AM*–midnight* Ⓜ*Smithsonian.*

❺ **Korean War Veterans Memorial.** This memorial to the 1.5 million United States men and women who served in the Korean War (1950–53) highlights the high cost of freedom. Nearly 37,000 Americans were killed on the Korean peninsula, 8,000 were missing in action, and more than 103,000 were wounded. Nineteen oversize stainless-steel soldiers toil through a rugged triangular terrain toward an American flag; look beneath the helmets to see their weary faces. The reflection in the polished black granite wall to their right doubles their number to 38, symbolic of the 38th parallel, the latitude established as the border between North and South Korea in 1953, as well as the 38 months of the war. Etched with the faces of 2,400 unnamed servicemen and servicewomen, the wall says simply, "Freedom is not free." The circular Pool of Remembrance honors all who were killed, captured, wounded, or missing in action. ⊠ *West end of Mall at Daniel French Dr. and Independence Ave., The Mall* ☎*202/426–6841* ⊕*www.nps.gov/kwvm* ⊠*Free* ☽*24 hrs; staffed daily 8* AM*–midnight* Ⓜ*Foggy Bottom.*

L St.

FARRAGUT NORTH Ⓜ

McPHERSON SQUARE

Washington Circle

29

K St.

16th St.

21st St.

20th St.

19th St.

FOGGY BOTTOM

I St.

Ⓜ

FARRAGUT WEST

H St.

14th St.

Pennsylvania Ave.

G St.

23rd St.

22nd St.

18th St.

New York Ave.

The White House

F St.

Virginia Ave.

E St.

E St.

15th St.

D St.

The Ellipse

C St.

17th St.

50

Constitution Ave.

50

Henry Bacon Dr.

❷

❸

❹

Reflecting Pool

Daniel French Dr.

❶

West Potomac Park

John Paul Jones Statue

❺

D.C. War Veterans Memorial

Kutz Bridge

John Ericsson Memorial

Independence Ave.

Franklin Delano Roosevelt Memorial Park

❻

Boat House

Maine Ave.

W. Basin Dr.

Tidal Basin

Ohio Dr.

❼

Outlet Bridge

Potomac River

❽

Inlet Bridge

1

395

East Potomac Park

KEY

Ⓜ Metro station

Lady Bird Johnson Park

TO THE AWAKENING →

0   330 yards
0   300 meters

The Monuments

1 **Lincoln Memorial.** Henry Bacon chose a Greek Doric style for this white Colorado-marble temple to Lincoln because he felt that a great defender of democracy should be memorialized in the style found in the birthplace of democracy. Although detractors thought it inappropriate that the humble president be honored with what amounts to a modified but grandiose Greek temple, this memorial has become one of the nation's most recognizable

icons. Its powerful symbolism makes it a popular gathering place: In its shadow, Americans marched for integrated schools in 1958, rallied for an end to the Vietnam War in 1967, and laid wreaths in a ceremony honoring the Iranian hostages in 1979. It may be best known, though, as the site of Martin Luther King Jr.'s "I Have a Dream" speech. Daniel Chester French's 19-foot-high somber statue of the seated president, in the center of the memorial, is composed of 28 interlocking pieces of Georgia marble. ■TIP➜ **Although visiting the area around the Lincoln Memorial during the day allows you to take in an impressive view of the Mall to the east, the best time to see the memorial itself is at night, when spotlights illuminate the outside.** ✉ *West end of Mall, The Mall* ☎ *202/426–6895* ⊕ *www.nps.gov/linc* ✉ *Free* 🕑 *24 hrs; staffed daily 8 AM–midnight* Ⓜ *Foggy Bottom.*

6 **Martin Luther King Jr. National Memorial.** Located strategically between the Lincoln and Jefferson memorials and adjacent to the FDR Memorial, the crescent-shape King Memorial will sit on a 4-acre site on the curved bank of the Tidal Basin. Although the memorial is expected to be dedicated sometime in 2010, fourteen years after Congress approved it in 1996 and 80 years after the famed Civil Rights leader was born in 1929, don't be surprised if there are delays. Visitors will enter through a center walkway cut out of a huge boulder, the Mountain of Despair. From the Mountain, the Stone of Hope will be visible. The symbolism of the mountain and stone are explained by King's words: "With this faith, we will be able to hew out of the mountain of despair a stone of hope." The centerpiece Stone will be carved by Chinese sculptor Lei Yixin; his design was chosen from more than 900 entries in an international competition. Fittingly, Yixin first read about King's "I Have a Dream" speech at age 10 while visiting the Lincoln Memorial. The 28-foot tall granite boulder will include Lei's rendering of King, whose eyes will meet Jefferson's gaze. The themes of democracy, justice, hope, and love will be reflected through more than a dozen quotes on the south and north walls and on the Stone of Hope. The quotes reflect speeches, sermons, and writings penned by King from 1955 through 1968. Waterfalls in the memorial will reflect King's use of the biblical quote: "Let justice roll down like waters and righteousness like a mighty stream." ✉ *401 F. St. NW, The Mall* ☎ *202/737–5420 or 888/484–3373* ⊕ *www.buildthedream.org* ✉ *Free* Ⓜ *Foggy Bottom.*

CLOSE UP

A City of Statues

Washington, DC, has more equestrian statues than any other city in the nation; stone-and-metal men atop steeds are everywhere, watching the city from traffic circles, squares, and parks. The statues proliferated in the 19th century, when Civil War generals who went into politics seemed virtually assured of this legacy—regardless of their success in either endeavor.

Standing in Lafayette Square across from the White House, the statue of President Andrew Jackson is by sculptor Clark Mills, who had never seen an equestrian statue, much less created one. To get the proportions of the rearing horse correct, Mills had a horse trained to remain in an upright position so he could study the anatomy of its muscles.

Directly up 16th Street from Lafayette Square at Massachusetts and Rhode Island avenues is a statue of Lt. Gen. Winfield Scott, in the circle bearing his name. He was to be shown atop his favorite mount, a lightweight mare, but right before the statue was cast, some of Scott's descendants decided that a stallion would be a more-appropriate horse for him to ride into battle upon (regardless of historical accuracy). The sculptor, H. K. Brown, was forced to give the horse a last-minute sex change.

Farther up Massachusetts Avenue, at 23rd Street, is a statue of Civil War Gen. Philip Henry Sheridan, also in a circle bearing his name. The piece is by Gutzon Borglum, who completed more than 170 public statues, including the head of Abraham Lincoln in the Capitol Rotunda, and whose final work was Mount Rushmore's presidential faces. The statue of the leader riding Rienzi (who was later renamed Winchester for Sheridan's victory there) stands in the type of circle Pierre-Charles L'Enfant envisioned in his plan for Washington—a small, formal park where avenues come together surrounded by isolated houses and buildings.

The statue of Gen. William Tecumseh Sherman at 15th Street and Treasury Place is often overlooked—in summer, the general's head is obscured by trees, and all year long he presents his back and his mount's hindquarters to pedestrians. He's positioned where he is thought to have stood while reviewing the Union troops on their victorious return from Georgia. The bar at the Hotel Washington, which affords some of the best views of the city, is also the place for a good look at Sherman.

A long-held theory says that the number of raised legs on the mount of an equestrian statue reveals how the rider died: one leg raised means the rider died of wounds sustained in battle, two legs raised means the rider died in battle, and four feet on the ground means the rider died of natural causes. None of this is true, though, and of the more than 30 equestrian statues in Washington, only about a third (including Scott, Sheridan, and Sherman, but not Jackson) follow this "code."

—Lisa Greaves

③ National World War II Memorial. This monument honors the 16 million Americans who served in the armed forces, the more than 400,000 who died, and all who supported the war effort at home. An imposing circle of 56 granite pillars, each bearing a bronze wreath, represents the U.S. states and territories of 1941–45.

Four bronze eagles, a bronze garland, and two 43-foot-tall arches inscribed with "Atlantic" and "Pacific" surround the large circular plaza. The roar of the water comes from the Rainbow Pool, here since the 1920s but recently renovated as the centerpiece of the memorial. The Field of Stars, a wall of 4,000 gold stars, commemorates the more than 400,000 Americans who lost their lives in the war. Some people were critical when the site for the memorial was announced, because they felt it would interrupt the landscape between the Washington Monument and Lincoln Memorial and because it uses some of the open space that had been the site of demonstrations and protests. ⊠*17th St. east of Washington Monument, The Mall* ☎*202/426–6841* ⊕*www. wwiimemorial.com* ⊠*Free* ☉*24 hrs* Ⓜ*Smithsonian.*

② Vietnam Veterans Memorial. Opinions on this stark monument, now one of the most-visited sites in Washington, were once as divided as those on the conflict that it commemorates. The simple design by Maya Lin, a 21-year-old architecture student at Yale, was selected in a 1981 competition. Upon its completion in 1982, the memorial was decried by some veterans as a "black gash of shame." The names of more than 58,000 Americans are etched on the memorial's black granite panels, which reflect the sky, the trees, and the faces of those looking for the names of friends or relatives who died in the war. For help in finding a name, ask a ranger at the blue-and-white hut near the entrance. You can get paper and pencil from a park ranger if you'd like to make a rubbing. Thousands of offerings are left at the wall each year: letters, flowers, medals, uniforms, snapshots. The National Park Service stores these, and some are on display at the National Museum of American History. ⊠*Constitution Gardens, 23rd St. at Constitution Ave. NW, The Mall* ☎*202/426–6841* ⊕*www.nps.gov/vive* ⊠*Free* ☉*24 hrs; staffed daily 8 AM–midnight* Ⓜ*Foggy Bottom.*

④ Washington Monument. At the western end of the Mall, the 555-foot, 5-inch Washington Monument, the world's tallest masonry structure, punctuates the capital like a huge exclamation point. The cornerstone was laid in 1848, but building stopped in 1854 for 20 years, in part due to members of the anti-Catholic Know-Nothing party stealing and destroying a block donated by Pope Pius IX. During this period, herds of cattle grazed on the grounds of the half-finished monument. A clearly visible ring about a third of the way up the obelisk testifies to this unfortunate stage of the monument's history: the stone used for the second phase of construction came from a different stratum. The view from the top takes in most of the District and parts of Maryland and Virginia.

■TIP➔ The Washington Monument uses a free timed-ticket system. A limited number of tickets are available each day at the kiosk on 15th Street, beginning a half hour before the monument opens, though in spring and summer lines are likely to start well before then. ⊠ *Constitution Ave. at 15th St. NW, The Mall* ☏ *202/426–6841, 877/444–6777 for advance tickets* ⊕ *www.nps.gov/wamo; www.recreation.gov for advance tickets* 🎫 *Free, $2 service fee per advance ticket* ⊙ *Daily 9–5* Ⓜ *Smithsonian.*

> **CAPITAL FACTS**
>
> The White House wasn't ready for its first occupant, John Adams, the second U.S. president, until 1800: George Washington, who seems to have slept everywhere else, never stayed here.

THE WHITE HOUSE AREA

In a world full of recognizable images, few are better known than the whitewashed, 132-room mansion at 1600 Pennsylvania Avenue. The residence of perhaps the single most powerful person on the planet, the White House has an awesome majesty, having been the home of every U.S. president but George Washington. The president's neighborhood includes some of the city's oldest houses.

MAIN ATTRACTIONS

❷ **White House.** Irishman James Hoban's plan, based on the Georgian
Ⓒ design of Leinster Hall in Dublin and of other Irish country houses, was
★ selected in a 1792 contest. The building has undergone many structural changes since then. Major renovations occurred after the British burned the House in 1814 and a piano almost broke through the second-story floor during President Truman's Administration because of the House's deteriorating condition. Truman had the entire structure gutted and restored, adding a second-story porch to the south portico.

■TIP➔ Visitors wishing to tour the White House must make arrangements at least three months in advance through the office of their member of Congress. Non–U.S. citizens must make arrangements through their embassy. The self-guided tour includes several rooms on the ground floor and, on the State Floor, the large white-and-gold **East Room,** the site of presidential social events. In 1814 Dolley Madison saved the room's full-length portrait of George Washington from torch-carrying British soldiers by cutting it from its frame, rolling it up, and spiriting it out of the White House. The **State Dining Room,** second in size only to the East Room, is dominated by G. P. A. Healy's portrait of Abraham Lincoln, painted after the president's death.

❶ Since White House tours are self-guided, it's a good idea to come to the **White House Visitor Center** (⊠ *Entrance: Department of Commerce's Baldrige Hall, E St. between 14th and 15th Sts.* ☏ *202/208–1631, 202/456–7041 24-hr information line* ⊕ *www.nps.gov* ⊙ *Daily 7:30–4)* first to catch the photographs, artifacts, and videos that relate to the White House's construction, decor, and residents. ⊠ *1600 Pennsylvania Ave. NW, Downtown* ☏ *202/208–1631, 202/456–7041 24-hr information line* ⊕ *www.whitehouse.gov* Ⓜ *Federal Triangle.*

KEY

Ⓜ *Metro station*

The White
House Area

1

ALSO WORTH SEEING

6 Corcoran Gallery of Art. The Corcoran looks like a museum and acts like a gallery, blending classic elegance and experimental edge. Washington's first art museum, housed in a Beaux-Arts marble mansion, has an important collection of 18th-, 19th-, and 20th-century European and American art. Masterworks by the great earlier American artists, including John Copley, Gilbert Stuart, Rembrandt Peale, Mary Cassatt, and John Singer Sargent, are in constant rotation. As the parent of the Corcoran School of Art, the museum is also devoted to showcasing cutting-edge contemporary art, from established superstars to undiscovered talents. You're sure to see something contemporary and fun: mixed-media, sound, and video art transforming a room, or even live performance art. Purchase advance tickets for special exhibitions, as they tend to be popular. ⊠ *500 17th St. NW, White House area* ☎ *202/639–1700* ⊕ *www.corcoran.org* 🖾 *$6* ☉ *Sun., Mon., and Wed.* '*10–5; Thurs. 10–9; Fri. and Sat. 10–5* Ⓜ *Farragut West or Farragut North.*

4 Decatur House. This redbrick Federal-style building designed by Benjamin Latrobe for naval hero Stephen Decatur was the first private residence on Lafayette Square. Occupants of the house have included Henry Clay, Martin Van Buren, and the Beales, a prominent western family. The house, now operated by the National Trust for Historic Preservation, has a first floor furnished as it was in Decatur's time and a second floor done in the Victorian style favored by the Beales. Many of the row houses along Jackson Place date from the pre–Civil War or Victorian periods; even the more-modern additions, though—such as those at 718 and 726—are designed to blend in with their more historic neighbors. ⊠*748 Jackson Pl. NW, White House area* ☎*202/842–0920* ⊕*www. decaturhouse.org* ⊠*Free* ☉*Tues.–Sat. 10–5, Sun. noon–4; tours every hr at 15 mins past the hr* Ⓜ*Farragut West.*

❸ **Lafayette Square.** With such an important resident across the street, the National Capital Region's National Park Service gardeners lavish extra attention on this square's trees and flower beds. During the construction of the White House, workers' huts and a brick kiln were set up, and soon residences began popping up around the square, including the Blair House, which is now used by heads of state visiting Washington. Soldiers camped in the square during the War of 1812 and the Civil War, turning it both times into a muddy pit. Today protesters set their placards up in Lafayette Square.

In the center of the park is a large **statue of Andrew Jackson.** Erected in 1853 and cast from bronze cannons that Jackson captured during the War of 1812, this was the second equestrian statue made in America. The other statues in the park are of foreign-born soldiers who helped in America's fight for independence. In the southeast corner is the park's namesake, the **Marquis de Lafayette,** the young French nobleman who came to America to fight in the Revolution. ⊠*Bounded by Pennsylvania Ave., Madison Pl., H St., and Jackson Pl., White House area* Ⓜ*McPherson Sq.*

NEED A BREAK?

One block north of Pershing Park is the venerable **Hotel Washington** (⊠ 515 15th St. NW, White House area ☎ 202/638–5900 ⊕ www.hotelwashington. com Ⓜ Metro Center), where the view from the Rooftop Terrace is one of the best in the city. From May to October you can sit outside. (During cooler months, an extension shields you from the elements.) Drinks, coffee, and a light menu are available.

❺ **Renwick Gallery.** This luscious French Second Empire–style mansion is across the street from the White House. But even with such lofty neighbors, the fancy-gingerbread house is still the most appealing architecture on the block. It houses the Smithsonian American Art Museum's collection of decorative art and crafts. Check out Kim Schahman's 1955 *Bureau of Bureaucracy*: a beautifully crafted wooden cabinet full of cupboards to nowhere, bottomless drawers, drawers within drawers, and hidden compartments. This wonderful metaphor for the labyrinthine workings of government is appropriately set in a room with a view of the Executive Office Building. ⊠*Pennsylvania Ave. at 17th St. NW, White House area* ☎*202/633–2850, 202/633–5285 TDD* ⊕*www. americanart.si.edu* ⊠*Free* ☉*Daily 10–5:30* Ⓜ*Farragut West.*

CAPITOL HILL

The people who live and work on "the Hill" do so in the shadow of the edifice that lends the neighborhood its name: the gleaming white Capitol. More than just the center of government, however, the Hill also includes charming residential blocks lined with Victorian row houses and a fine assortment of restaurants, bars, and shops.

MAIN ATTRACTIONS

② **Capitol.** The Capitol's cornerstone was laid by George Washington in a Masonic ceremony on September 18, 1793. The "Congress House" grew slowly and suffered a grave setback on August 24, 1814, when British troops marched on Washington and set fire to the Capitol, the White House, and numerous other government buildings. In 1855, to keep the scale correct after the edifice was elongated to accommodate a growing government, work began on a taller, cast-iron dome. President Lincoln was criticized for continuing this expensive project while the country was in the throes of the Civil War, but he called the construction "a sign we intend the Union shall go on." This twin-shell dome, a marvel of 19th-century engineering, rises 285 feet above the ground and weighs 4,500 tons. It expands and contracts up to 4 inches a day, depending on the outside temperature.

Fodor'sChoice

★

Tours start under the center of the **Rotunda's** dome, at the center of which is Constantino Brumidi's 1865 fresco, *Apotheosis of Washington.* South of the Rotunda is **Statuary Hall,** once the legislative chamber of the House of Representatives. The room has an architectural quirk that maddened early legislators: a slight whisper uttered on one side of the hall can be heard on the other. To the north, on the Senate side, is the chamber once used by the Supreme Court, and, above it, the splendid Old Senate Chamber, both of which have been restored.

The **Capitol Visitor Center,** a $600-million subterranean education and information area beneath the east lawn of the Capitol, opened in December 2008. You can now register for tickets online or get them directly from the Center where tours will start. Free gallery passes to watch the House or Senate in session can be obtained only from your representative's or senator's office; both chambers are closed to the public when Congress is not in session. You can link to the e-mail of your representative at ⊕*www.house.gov* and ⊕*www.senate.gov.* Expect at least a 30-minute wait going through security when you enter the Capitol. Bags can be no larger than 14 inches wide, 13 inches tall, and 4 inches deep, and other possessions you can bring into the building are strictly limited. (The full list of prohibited items is posted on the Capitol Web site; click on "Visiting the Capitol.") There are no facilities for checking personal belongings. **If you're planning a visit, call ahead to check the status of tours and access; security measures may change.** ⊠*East end of Mall, Capitol Hill* ☎*202/224–3121 Capitol switchboard, 202/225–6827 guide service* ⊕*www.visitthecapital.gov* ⊠*Free* ☉*Tours weekdays 9–4:30* Ⓜ*Capitol S or Union Station.*

⑤ **Supreme Court Building.** It wasn't until 1935 that the Supreme Court got its own building: a white-marble temple with twin rows of Corinthian columns designed by Cass Gilbert. Before then, the justices had been moved around to various rooms in the Capitol; for a while they even met in a tavern. The Supreme Court convenes on the first Monday in October and remains in session until it has heard all of its cases and handed down all of its decisions (usually the end of June). On Monday through Wednesday of two weeks in each month, the justices hear oral arguments in the velvet-swathed court chamber. Visitors who want to listen can choose to wait in either of two lines. One, the "three- to five-minute" line, shuttles you through, giving you a quick impression of the court at work. If you choose the other, and you'd like to stay for the whole show, it's best to be in line by 8:30 AM. The *Washington Post* carries a daily listing of what cases the court will hear. ⊠ *1 1st St. NE, Capitol Hill* ☎ *202/479–3000* ⊕ *www.supremecourtus.gov* ⊠ *Free* ⊘ *Weekdays 9–4:30* Ⓜ *Union Station or Capitol S.*

ALSO WORTH SEEING

④ Library of Congress. Provisions for a library to serve members of Congress were originally made in 1800, when the government set aside $5,000 to purchase books that legislators might need to consult. This small collection was housed in the Capitol but was destroyed in 1814, when the British burned the city. Thomas Jefferson, then in retirement at Monticello, offered his personal library as a replacement, noting that "there is, in fact, no subject to which a Member of Congress may not have occasion to refer." Jefferson's collection of 6,487 books laid the foundation for the great national library. The largest library in the world now has almost 130 million items—2.7 million recordings, 12 million photographs, 4.8 million maps, and 58 million manuscripts—on approximately 530 mi of bookshelves.

Built in 1897, the copper-dome **Thomas Jefferson Building**, based on the Paris Opera House, is the oldest of the three that make up the library. The building's octagonal Main Reading Room contains a grand central desk surrounded by mahogany readers' tables under a 160-foot-high domed ceiling. Computer terminals have replaced card catalogs, but books are still retrieved and dispensed the same way: readers (18 years or older) hand request slips to librarians and wait patiently for their materials to be delivered. Items from the library's collection—which includes one of only three perfect Gutenberg Bibles in the world—are on display in the Jefferson Building's second-floor Southwest Gallery and Pavilion. Information about current and upcoming exhibitions, which can include oral history projects, presidential papers, photographs, and the like, is available by phone or on the library's Web site. To even begin to come to grips with the magnitude of scope and grandeur of the library, taking one of the free hourly tours is strongly recommended. Well-informed docents can decode the dozens of quirky allegorical sculptures and paintings throughout the building, and can bring you into spaces—such as the glassed-in observation deck over the Main Reading Room—that are closed to solo visitors. ⊠ *Jefferson Bldg., 1st St. and Independence Ave. SE, Capitol Hill* ☎ *202/707–4604, 202/707–5000, or 202/707–6400* ⊕ *www.loc.gov* ⊠ *Free* ⊘ *Mon.–Sat. 10–5:30; reading room hrs may extend later. Free tours Mon.–Sat. at 10:30, 11:30, 1:30, and 2:30; also 3:30 on weekdays* Ⓜ *Capitol S.*

Capitol Hill

TO
NATIONAL SHRINE,
JOHN PAUL II CULTURAL CENTER,
ROCK CREEK CEMETERY,
AND FRANCISCAN
MONASTERY

H St. NW

G St. NW

F St. NW

E St. NW

Massachusetts Ave. NW

G St. NW

New Jersey Ave. NW

North Capitol St.

H St. NW

2nd St. NE

3rd St. NE

G St.

TO
KENILWORTH
AQUATIC
GARDENS
AND UNITED
STATES
NATIONAL
ARBORETUM

1

**UNION
STATION**

**Columbus
Memorial
Fountain**

E St.NE

Massachusetts Ave. NE

D St. NE

**National
Japanese-
American
Memorial to
Patriotism**

Louisiana Ave. NE

1st St. NE

C St.

**Russell Senate
Office Building**

Delaware Ave. NE

1st St. NE

C St. NE

**Dirksen Senate
Office Building**

KENILWORTH →
AQUATIC
GARDENS &
UNITED STATES
NATIONAL
ARBORETUM

**Hart Senate
Office Building**

Constitution Ave. NW

Constitution Ave. NE

Maryland Ave.

**Frederick
Douglass
Townhouse**

A St. NE

**Capitol
Reflecting Pool**

Senate

2

**House of
Representatives**

Maryland Ave.

3

**Capitol
Visitor
Center**

1st St. SE

5

E. Capitol St.

**Folger
Shakespeare
Library**

4

A St.

**Adams
Building**

**Longworth
Building**

**Cannon House
Office Building**

Independence Ave. SW

**Rayburn
Bldg.**

Canal St.

C St. SW

South Capitol St.

New Jersey Ave. SE

TO MARINE CORPS BARRACKS,
WASHINGTON NAVY YARD AND
CONGRESSIONAL CEMETERY →

**Madison
Building**

2nd St. SE

3rd St. SE

D St. SW

D St. SE

*Folger
Square*

North Carolina Ave. SE

KEY

Ⓜ *Metro station*

E St.

0   220 yards
0   200 meters

L'Enfant, The City's Architect

The life of Pierre-Charles L'Enfant, architect of the city of Washington, has all the elements of a television miniseries: a handsome and idealistic 22-year-old Parisian volunteers in the American war for independence; he rises to the rank of major of engineers and is popular with fellow officers (and their wives); he becomes the toast-of-the-town architect in New York City and is selected by President George Washington to plan the new Federal City; he is fired amid controversy and dies bitter and broke; he is vindicated posthumously.

L'Enfant was educated as an architect and engineer in France, and at least one of his teachers profoundly influenced his career and, ultimately, his plan for Washington: he studied landscape architecture with André LeNotre, who designed the gardens at Versailles. Congress voted in 1785 to create a permanent Federal City, and in 1789 L'Enfant wrote to George Washington with an offer to create a capital "magnificent enough to grace a great nation." He got the job, and arrived in Washington in 1791 to survey the land.

L'Enfant's 1791 plan borrowed much from Versailles, including ceremonial circles and squares, a grid pattern of streets, and broad, diagonal avenues. He described Jenkins Hill, the gentle rise on which he intended to erect the "Congress House," as "a pedestal waiting for a monument." He envisioned the area west of the Congress House (what we now know as the Mall) as a "Grand Avenue, 400 feet in breadth, and about a mile in length, bordered with gardens, ending in a slope from the houses on each side."

Pennsylvania Avenue was to be a broad, uninterrupted line running from the Capitol to the site chosen for the Executive Mansion, but the construction of the Treasury Building in 1836 ruined this straight sight line. The area just north of the White House (basically the president's front yard) was to be part of "President's Park," but Thomas Jefferson, concerned that large, landscaped White House grounds weren't befitting a democratic country, ordered that the area be turned into a public park (now Lafayette Park).

Though skilled at city planning, headstrong L'Enfant had trouble with the game of politics. Things went slightly awry early on when L'Enfant had difficulty with the engravers of the city plan, they got worse when he expressed his resentment at dealing with Secretary of State Thomas Jefferson rather than the president, and they hit rock bottom when he enraged the city commissioners by tearing down a manor house being constructed where he had planned a street. The house belonged to Daniel Carroll—one of the commissioners. Only 11 months after his hire, L'Enfant was let go. He continued to work as an architect, but when he died in 1825 he was poor and bitter, feeling he hadn't been recognized for his genius. His contributions to the city were finally recognized, though, when in 1909, amid much ceremony, his body was moved from his original burial site in Maryland to Arlington Cemetery at the request of the Washington, DC, board of commissioners.

**NEED A
BREAK?**
True to its name, **The Hawk 'n' Dove** (⊠ *329 Pennsylvania Ave. SE, Capitol Hill* ☎ *202/543–3300* Ⓜ *Capitol South*) may well be the best place in town to overhear aides talk partisan politics over pints. The menu is long on the likes of pastrami sandwiches and old-fashioned chipped beef on toast.

❶ **Union Station.** Chicago architect and commission member Daniel H. Burnham patterned Washington's train depot after the Roman Baths of Diocletian (AD 305). In its heyday, during World War II, more than 200,000 people passed through the building daily. By the 1960s, however, the decline in train travel had turned the station into an expensive white-marble elephant, and by 1981 rain was pouring in through its neglected roof. The Union Station you see today is the result of a restoration, completed in 1988, intended to begin a revival of Washington's east end. Between train travelers and visitors to the shops, restaurants, and a nine-screen movie theater, 70,000 people a day pass through the Beaux-Arts building. The jewel of the structure is the main waiting room, with a 96-foot-high coffered ceiling inlaid with 8 pounds of gold leaf. Forty-six statues of Roman legionnaires, one for each state in the Union when the station was completed, ring the grand room. ⊠ *50 Massachusetts Ave. NE, Capitol Hill* ☎ *202/289–1908* ⊕ *www. unionstationdc.com* Ⓜ *Union Station.*

**NEED A
BREAK?**
On Union Station's lower level are more than 20 food stalls with everything from pizza to sushi.

❸ **United States Botanic Garden.** Established by Congress in 1820, this is the oldest botanic garden in North America. The recently renovated glass building, a Victorian design, sits at the foot of Capitol Hill, in the shadow of the Capitol building. It offers an escape from the stone and marble federal office buildings that surround it; inside are exotic rain-forest species, desert flora, and trees from all parts of the world. A special treat is the extensive collection of rare and unusual orchids. Walkways suspended 24 feet above the ground provide a fascinating view of the plants. A relatively new addition is the National Garden, which emphasizes educational exhibits. ⊠ *1st St. and Maryland Ave. SW, Capitol Hill* ☎ *202/225–8333* ⊕ *www.usbg.gov* ⊠ *Free* ☉ *Daily 10–5* Ⓜ *Federal Center SW.*

DOWNTOWN

In recent years developers have rediscovered the "East End," which had been a hole in the city since riots rocked the capital in 1968 after the assassination of Martin Luther King Jr. Buildings are now being torn down, built up, and remodeled at an amazing pace. **Penn Quarter,** the neighborhood immediately surrounding the once down-at-the-heels stretch of Pennsylvania Avenue, has blossomed into one of the hottest addresses in town for nightlife and culture. With its proximity to the venerable Ford's Theatre and the National Theater, a recently opened theater by the acclaimed progressive Woolly Mammoth company, and a major expansion and arts center from the prestigious Shakespeare Theatre, the neighborhood can rightfully claim to be Washington's own theater district. Meanwhile, new galleries, restaurants, and other cultural hot spots are constantly appearing.

MAIN ATTRACTIONS

International Spy Museum. Cryptologists, masters of disguise, and former officials of the CIA, FBI, and KGB are among the advisers of this museum, which displays the largest collection of spy artifacts anywhere in the world. There's a mix of flash and fun, with toys used by actual operatives as well as James Bond's Aston Martin and tales of celebrity spies like singer Josephine Baker, chef Julia Child, and actress Marlene Dietrich. "Operation Spy," a one-hour "immersive experience" works like a live-action game, dropping you in the middle of a high-stakes foreign intelligence mission. Advance tickets are recommended, particularly in spring and summer. ⊠800 F St. NW, East End ☎202/393–7798 ⊕www.spymuseum.org ⊠$18, children $15; Operation Spy only, $14; combination admission $25 ⊙Apr.–Oct., daily 9–8; Nov.–Mar., daily 10–6; hrs subject to change; check Web site before visiting Ⓜ Gallery Pl./Chinatown.

National Archives. The National Archives are at once monument, museum, and the nation's memory. Headquartered in a grand marble edifice on Constitution Avenue, the agency is charged with preserving and archiving the most historically important U.S. government records. Its 8 billion paper records and 4 billion electronic records date back to 1775. The star attractions are the Declaration of Independence, Constitution, and Bill of Rights. These are housed in the Archives' cathedral-like rotunda, each on a marble platform, encased in bulletproof glass, and floating in pressurized helium, which protects the irreplaceable documents. In the permanent exhibit you can find anything from the Emancipation Proclamation to the first issue of *Mad* magazine. Reservations are recommended. ⊠Constitution Ave. between 7th and 9th Sts. NW, The Mall ☎202/501–5000, 202/501–5205 tours ⊕www.nara.gov ⊠Free ⊙Mar. 15–Labor Day, daily 10 -7; Labor Day–Mar. 14, daily 10–5:30; tours weekdays at 10:15 and 1:15 Ⓜ Archives/Navy Memorial.

Newseum. Opened to great fanfare in 2008, this landmark $450 million glass-and-silver structure is on Pennsylvania Avenue, set smack between the White House and the Capitol: a fitting location for a museum devoted to the First Amendment and the essential role of a free press in maintaining democracy. The 90-foot-high media-saturated atrium is overlooked by a giant breaking-news screen and a news helicopter suspended overhead. From there, 14 galleries display 500 years of the history of news, including exhibits on the First Amendment, global news, and the way radio, television, and especially the Internet have transformed how we find out about the world. Live news programs—from presidential debates to town hall meetings—are regularly filmed in the museum's central live news studio, and audiences are often welcome to watch. Tickets for the Newseum are date specific and subject to availability; purchasing them in advance on the Web site is recommended. ⊠555 Pennsylvania Ave. NW, East End ☎888/639–7386 ⊕www. newseum.org ⊠$20 ⊙Daily 9 – 5 Ⓜ Archives/Navy Memorial.

ALSO WORTH SEEING

⑤ Ford's Theatre. On the night of April 14, 1865, during a performance of *Our American Cousin,* John Wilkes Booth entered the state box at this successful music hall and shot Abraham Lincoln in the back of the head. The stricken president was carried across the street to the house of tailor William Petersen and died the next morning. In 2007 the Ford's Theatre Society launched a two-year, $40-million campaign to transform the theater and its basement museum of Lincoln artifacts into a block-long, Lincoln-centered cultural campus commemorating the president. Opened in early 2009, it includes a renovated Ford's Theater, which will run a full schedule of plays; a new Lincoln museum; the historically restored home of William Peterson; and a new Center for Education and Leadership focused on Lincoln's life and presidency. ✉ *511 10th St. NW, East End* ☎ *202/426–6924* ⊕ *www.fords.org* ⌨ *Free* ◷ *Daily 9–5; theater closed to visitors during rehearsals and matinees, generally Thurs. and weekends; Lincoln museum in basement remains open at these times* Ⓜ *Metro Center or Gallery Pl.*

❶ National Building Museum. The open interior of this mammoth redbrick edifice is one of the city's great spaces, and has been the site of many inaugural balls. The eight central Corinthian columns, each made of brick covered with plaster, are among the largest in the world, rising to a height of 75 feet. The museum is devoted to architecture, design, landscaping, and urban planning. The permanent exhibit "Washington: Symbol and City" tells the story of the backwater that eventually became the nation's capital (beginning by debunking the myth that Washington was built on a swamp!). In the "Building Zone" kids ages two to six can get a hands-on introduction to building by constructing a tower or playing with bulldozers and construction trucks. Tours are offered at 12:30 Monday through Wednesday; 11:30, 12:30, and 1:30 Thursday through Saturday; and 12:30 and 1:30 Sunday. Family programs are available at 2:30 on weekends. ✉ *401 F St. NW, between 4th and 5th Sts., East End* ☎ *202/272–2448* ⊕ *www.nbm.org* ⌨ *Free* ◷ *Mon.–Sat. 10–5, Sun. 11–5* Ⓜ *Judiciary Sq.*

Dedicated to collecting images of those who have made "significant contributions" to America's "history, development and culture," the **National Portrait Gallery** is no longer bound by the stipulation that portraits must be of those dead 10 years or more. Along with the iconic "Lansdowne" portrait of George Washington by Gilbert Stuart, and Edgar Degas's portrait of Mary Cassatt, the gallery's 19,000 images now include visions of Tom Wolfe, Toni Morrison, and Shaquille O'Neal. ✉ *8th and F Sts. NW, East End* ☎ *202/633–1000* ⊕ *www.npg.si.edu* ⌨ *Free* ◷ *Daily 11:30–7* Ⓜ *Gallery Pl./Chinatown.*

❸ The **Smithsonian American Art Museum,** considered to be the world's biggest and most diverse collection of American art, has five times more of its collection on display post-renovation. Its more than 41,000 holdings span three centuries, from Colonial portraits to 20th-century abstractionists. Among the 7,000 American artists represented are John Singleton Copley, Winslow Homer, Mary Cassatt, Georgia O'Keeffe, Edward Hopper, David Hockney, and Robert Rauschenberg. ✉ *G St. between*

Downtown

F St.
E St.
New Jersey Ave.
1st St.
Old Adas Israel Synagogue
2nd St.
H St.
3rd St.
Massachusetts Ave.
JUDICIARY SQUARE
4th St.
General Accounting Office
MCI Center
5th St.
1 50
PENN QUARTER
6th St.
ARCHIVES-NAVY MEMORIAL
Constitution Ave.
Indiana Ave.
D St.
Louisiana Ave.
395

220 yards
200 meters
0
0

Washington Convention Center
Mt. Vernon Square
7th St.
GALLERY PLACE CHINATOWN
I St.
H St.
G Pl.
G St.
F St.
E St.
8th St.
9th St.
Old Patent Office Building
Tariff Commission Building
Justice Dept.
10th St.
Pennsylvania Ave.
11th St.
Internal Revenue

12th St.
METRO CENTER
13th St.
New York Ave.
Inter-American Development Bank Cultural Center
National Theatre
Pennsylvania Ave. N.
John A. Wilson Building
FEDERAL TRIANGLE
Constitution Ave.

McPHERSON SQUARE
14th St.
Willard Inter-Continental
15th St.
Pennsylvania Ave. S.
Department of Commerce Building
The Ellipse
50 1

FARRAGUT WEST
FARRAGUT NORTH
I St.
K St.
L St.
15th St.
16th St.
17th St.
Lafayette Park
The White House
Pennsylvania Ave.
D St.
C St.

KEY

M Metro station

Ford's Theatre **5**
International
Spy Museum **4**
National Archives **7**
National Building
Museum **1**
National
Portrait Gallery **2**

Newseum **6**
Smithsonian
American Art Museum **3**

7th and 9th Sts., East End ☎*202/633–1000* ⊕*www.americanart.si.edu*
✉*Free* ☉*Daily 11:30–7* Ⓜ*Gallery Pl./Chinatown.*

GEORGETOWN & FOGGY BOTTOM

Long before the District of Columbia was formed, Washington's oldest and wealthiest neighborhood was a separate city with a harbor full of ships and warehouses filled with tobacco. Washington has filled in around Georgetown over the years, but the former tobacco port retains an air of aloofness. Today

> **CAPITAL FACTS**
>
> The flat-front, redbrick Federal house at 3307 N Street was the home of then-Senator John F. Kennedy and his family before the White House beckoned.

some of Washington's most famous residents call Georgetown home, including former *Washington Post* executive editor Ben Bradlee, political pundit George Stephanopoulos, Senator (and 2004 presidential nominee) John Kerry, and *New York Times* op-ed doyenne Maureen Dowd. This is one of Washington's main areas for restaurants, bars, nightclubs, and boutiques.

Foggy Bottom, across the Potomac from Georgetown, has three main claims to fame: the State Department, the Kennedy Center, and George Washington University. Its name is derived from the wharves, breweries, lime kilns, and glassworks that were near the water. Smoke from these factories combined with the swampy air of the low-lying ground to produce a permanent fog along the waterfront.

☾ **C&O Canal.** When it opened in 1850, this waterway's 74 locks linked Georgetown with Cumberland, Maryland, 184 mi to the northwest, and kept Georgetown open to shipping after its harbor had filled with silt. Lumber, coal, iron, wheat, and flour moved up and down the canal, but it was never as successful as its planners had hoped. Today the canal is part of the National Park System; walkers follow the towpath once used by mules while canoeists paddle the canal's calm waters. You can glide into history aboard a mule-drawn canal boat ride. The National Park service provides the hour-long rides from about mid-April through late October; tickets cost $7 and are available across the canal, next to the Foundry Building. The schedule varies by season, with limited rides in spring and fall. In summer the boats run at least twice a day from Wednesday through Sunday. Call the visitor center for the exact schedule on the day of your visit. Canal-boat rides also depart from the Great Falls Tavern visitor center in Maryland. ⊠*Canal Visitor Center, 1057 Thomas Jefferson St. NW, Georgetown* ☎*202/653–5190* ⊕*www.nps.gov/choh*

Dumbarton Oaks. One of the loveliest places for a stroll in Washington is Dumbarton Oaks, the acres of enchanting gardens adjoining Dumbarton House in Georgetown. Planned by noted landscape architect Beatrix Farrand, the gardens incorporate elements of traditional English, Italian, and French styles such as a formal rose garden, an English country garden, and an orangery (circa 1810). You enter the gardens at 31st and R streets. In 1944 one of the most important events of the 20th century took place at **Dumbarton House**, when representatives of the United States, Great Britain, China, and the Soviet Union met in the music room to lay the groundwork for the United Nations. Career diplomat Robert Woods Bliss and his wife Mildred bought the property in 1920 and tamed the sprawling grounds, and removed later 19th-century additions that had obscured the Federal lines of the 1801 mansion. In 1940 the Blisses gave the estate to Harvard University, which maintains world-renowned collections of Byzantine and pre-Columbian art here. Both collections are small but choice. The Byzantine collection includes beautiful examples of both religious and secular items executed in mosaic, metal, enamel, and ivory. Pre-Columbian works—artifacts and textiles from Mexico and Central and South America by peoples such as the Aztec, Maya, and Olmec—are arranged in an enclosed glass pavilion designed by Philip Johnson. Normally on view to the public are the lavishly decorated music room and selections from Mrs. Bliss's collection of rare illustrated garden books. ⊠*1703 32nd St. NW, Georgetown* ☎*202/339–6401 or 202/339–6400* ⊕*www.doaks. org* ⊠*$7* ⊘*Gardens: Apr.–Oct. $8, Nov.–Mar. free.*

DUPONT CIRCLE & NORTHWEST DC

The main thoroughfares of Connecticut, New Hampshire, and Massachusetts avenues all intersect at Dupont Circle, with a small, handsome park and a splashing fountain in the center. Upscale restaurants, offbeat shops, coffeehouses, art galleries, and specialty bookstores give the neighborhood a distinctive, cosmopolitan air. Stores and clubs catering to the neighborhood's large gay community are abundant. Most of the sights in other sections of Northwest DC are immediately adjacent to Red Line Metro stops, but all can be easily reached by serious walkers, who will appreciate the leafy thoroughfares of these neighborhoods.

MAIN ATTRACTIONS

Ⓒ ★ **National Zoo.** For many years the zoo's most famous resident was Smokey the Bear, but the top attractions nowadays are the giant pandas. Tian Tian and Mei Xiang came from China in 2000, and will stay here until 2010. In 2005 their cub, Tai Shan, was born, the first giant panda cub to survive from birth at the National Zoo and only the third to survive in the United States. The pandas are stars, and their many fans cluster around their bamboo-filled compound.

Carved out of Rock Creek Park, the zoo is a series of rolling, wooded hills that complement the many innovative compounds showing animals in their native settings. Between 10 and 2 each day you can catch the orangutan population traveling on the "O Line," a series of cables and towers near the Great Ape House that allows the primates to swing hand over hand about 35 feet over your head. Part of the Smithsonian Institution, the National Zoo is one of the foremost zoos in the world. Created by an Act of Congress in 1889, the 163-acre park was designed by landscape architect Frederick Law Olmsted, who also designed the U.S. Capitol grounds. Before the zoo opened in 1890, live animals used as taxidermists' models were kept on the Mall. ✉ *3001 Connecticut Ave. NW, Woodley Park* ☎ *202/673–4800 or 202/673–4717* ⊕ *www.si.edu/natzoo* ✉ *Free, parking $16* ☉ *May–mid-Sept., daily 6 AM–8 PM; mid-Sept.–Apr., daily 6–6. Zoo buildings open at 10 and close before zoo closes* Ⓜ *Cleveland Park or Woodley Park/Zoo.*

President Lincoln's Cottage. In June of 1862, President Lincoln moved from the White House to this Gothic Revival cottage on the grounds of the Soldiers' Home to escape the oppressive heat of wartime Washington, and to grieve the loss of his son Willie. Lincoln and his wife lived in the cottage from June to November of 1862, 1863, and 1864—a quarter of his presidency—and it was here that he became consumed with the idea of emancipation and wrote the Emancipation Proclamation. Considered the most significant historic site of Lincoln's presidency outside the White House, Lincoln's Cottage opened for public tours in 2008. The tours attempt to re-create a visit to the cottage similar to what Lincoln's many visitors in the 1860s experienced, and to take visitors inside Lincoln's mind as he anguished over the Civil War and emancipation. Tours start and end at the visitor center, which has exhibitions and multimedia displays on Lincoln and the Civil War. **Advance reservations, available on the Web site, are highly recommended.** ✉ *Armed Forces Retirement Home at Rock Creek Church Rd. and Upshur St NW, Upper Northwest* ☎ *202/829–0436* ⊕ *www.lincolncottage.org* ✉ *$12* ☉ *Scheduled tours only. Nov. 1–Mar., Mon.–Sat. tours every hr 10–3, Sun. tours every hr noon–3; Apr.–Oct., Mon.–Sat. tours every hr 10–4, Sun. tours every hr noon–4* Ⓜ *Brookland or Georgia Ave. Metro, then take the H8 bus.*

ALSO WORTH SEEING

★ **Phillips Collection.** In 1918 Duncan Phillips started to collect art for a museum in his Georgian Revival house that would become America's first permanent museum of modern art. The museum was intended as a memorial to his father and brother, who had died within 13 months of each other. Having no interest in a painting's market value or its faddishness, Phillips searched for pieces that impressed him as outstanding products of a particular artist's unique vision. Holdings include works by Georges Braque, Georgia O'Keeffe, Paul Cézanne, Paul Klee, Henri Matisse, John Henry Twachtman, and Pierre Bonnard. Temporary exhibits frequently pay homage to Phillips's interest in illuminating aesthetic connections between artists. On Thursday the museum stays open late for live jazz and gallery talks. There is also a Sunday afternoon concert in the oak-paneled music room nearly every week. ✉ *1600 21st St. NW, Dupont Circle* ☎ *202/387–2151* ⊕ *www.phillipscollection. org* ✉ *Free for permanent collection on weekdays; admission varies on weekends and for special exhibitions* ☉ *Tues., Wed., Fri., and Sat. 10–5, Thurs. 10–8:30, Sun. 11–6* Ⓜ *Dupont Circle.*

🐾 **Rock Creek Park.** The 1,800 acres surrounding Rock Creek have provided a cool oasis for DC residents ever since Congress set them aside for recreational use in 1890. Bicycle routes and hiking and equestrian trails wind through the groves of dogwoods, beeches, oaks, and cedars, and 30 picnic areas are scattered about. Rangers at the **Nature Center and Planetarium** (✉ *South of Military Rd., 5200 Glover Rd. NW, Northwest* ☎ *202/426–6829*) introduce visitors to the park and keep track of daily events; guided nature walks leave from the center weekends at 2. The center and planetarium are open Wednesday through Sunday from 9 to 5. ☎ *202/282–1063 park information.* ⊕ *www.nps.gov/rocr.*

Washington National Cathedral. Construction of Washington National Cathedral—the sixth-largest cathedral in the world—started in 1907; it was finished and consecrated in 1990. Like its 14th-century Gothic counterparts, the stunning cathedral (officially the Cathedral Church of St. Peter and St. Paul) has a nave, flying buttresses, transepts, and vaults that were built stone by stone. The expansive view of the city from the Pilgrim Gallery is exceptional. The cathedral is Episcopalian, but has held services of many denominations, as well as state events such as the funerals of presidents. Its grounds have been shaped into the compact, English-style **Bishop's Garden.** Boxwoods, ivy, tea roses, yew trees, and an assortment of arches, bas-reliefs, and stonework from European ruins provide a restful counterpoint to the cathedral's towers. ✉ *Wisconsin and Massachusetts Aves. NW, Upper Northwest* ☎ *202/537–6200, 202/537–6207 tour information* ⊕ *www. cathedral.org/cathedral* ✉ *Suggested tour donation $3* ☉ *Weekdays 10–5, Sat. 10–4, Sun. 8–6:30 (8–2:45 for worship only). Tours Mon.– Sat. 10–4, every 30 mins. Gardens dawn–dusk* Ⓜ *Cleveland Park or Tenleytown.*

WHERE TO EAT

Wall-to-wall ethnic spots line 18th Street NW south from Columbia Road in Adams-Morgan. Parking can be impossible on weekends, but you can walk from the nearest Metro stop, Woodley Park/Zoo, in 10 to 15 minutes. In the East End, restaurants of all stripes (some casual and moderately priced, others upscale and trendy) have sprung up to serve the crowds that attend games at the MCI Center and that enjoy the increasingly chic bar scene. Chinatown, centered on G and H streets NW between 6th and 8th, hosts Chinese, Burmese, Thai, and other Asian restaurants. Capitol Hill has a number of bars that cater to congressional types who need to fortify themselves with food and drink after a day spent running the country, and Union Station houses a large food court offering quick bites that range from barbecue to sushi. Dupont Circle is dense with restaurants and cafés, many with outdoor seating. On Georgetown's main drags, Wisconsin Avenue and M Street, white-tablecloth establishments coexist easily with hole-in-the-wall joints. With some of the hippest bars in the District, quirky vintage stores, and small and lively nightclubs, the U Street neighborhood draws a young crowd day and night. Restaurants stay open late on weekend nights and serve everything from burgers to gourmet pizza and Ethiopian dishes at low prices.

One way to keep prices down at more-upscale places is to go for pretheater menus, where choices may be limited and the tab lower. Many high-end restaurants have separate bar menus that showcase the creativity of the chef at gentler prices. Going to a heavy hitter for lunch rather than dinner is another option. All restaurants are open daily for lunch and dinner unless stated otherwise.

WHAT IT COSTS					
	¢	$	$$	$$$	$$$$
AT DINNER	under $10	$10–$17	$18–$25	$26–$35	over $35

Prices are per person for a main course at dinner.

CAPITOL HILL

$-$$ ✕**Granville Moore's Brickyard.** This Belgian beer hall with a gourmet soul
BELGIAN is worth a visit despite its location in DC's Atlas District, an area that can be seedy after dark. Snag a seat at the bar or at one of the first-come, first-served tables, and linger over unfiltered artisanal brews that range from Chimay to the obscure, lip-smacking Brasserie des Rocs. The food is terrific, specifically the pots of steamed mussels served with crunchy, twice-fried frîtes paired with homemade dipping sauces. The bison burger and chicken with prosciutto are downright decadent. ✉*1238 H St. NE, Capitol Hill* ☎ *202/399–2546* ⊕*www.granvillemoores.com* ⌂*Reservations not accepted* ▤*AE, MC, V* ◷*No lunch.* ✛ *6G*

$-$$ ✕**Locanda.** Political combatants of all stripes lay down their arms at
ITALIAN day's end for an easygoing, welcoming meal at this new standby, minutes from the House of Representatives office buildings. The decor is minimalist, throwing the spotlight onto traditional Italian dishes that are rendered feather-light by Mediterranean accents. The grilled octopus starter is punched up by piquant fresh chorizo, braised pork coasts onto your fork with a coat of lentils, and the house-made pasta is simply revelatory. The frutti di mare is an emerald-green stunner that joins its shrimp and mussels with irresistible looped spaghetti, made from a squid-based dough. ✉ *633 Pennsylvania Ave. SE, Capitol Hill* ☎ *202/547–0002* ⊕*www.locandadc.com* ▤*AE, D, DC, MC, V* ◷*Closed Sun. and Mon.* Ⓜ*Eastern Market.* ✛ *6G*

¢-$ ✕**The Market Lunch.** A walk around the Capitol, a stroll through East-
AMERICAN ern Market, and then a hefty pile of blueberry pancakes from Market
◷ Lunch make for a perfect Saturday morning or afternoon on the Hill. The casual counter service and informal seating make it ideal for kids. Locals wait in long lines to dine on ham, eggs, grits, or pancakes in the morning or crab cakes, fried shrimp, or fish for lunch—and owner Tom Glasgow earned that loyalty by setting up a temporary location after historic Eastern Market was decimated by fire in 2007. But don't be mistaken: eating here has never been a leisurely experience. On Saturday you must be in line by noon. ■TIP➜**Follow convention and**

order quickly, eat, and give up your seat for the next customer. ✉ *Tent hall across the street from Eastern Market, 306 7th St. SE, Capitol Hill* ☎*202/547–8444* ▭*No credit cards* ⊘*Closed Mon. No dinner* Ⓜ*Eastern Market.* ✛*6G*

$$
AMERICAN

✕**Sonoma.** This chic multilevel wine bar has pours aplenty (in both tasting portions and full glasses) along with well-thought-out charcuterie boards piled with prosciutto, bresaola with house-made condiments like pickled ramps, and figs braised in wine. There's more conventional fare, too, like a juicy Wagyu burger with Taleggio cheese and grilled onions. By day the crowd skews to Senate staffers, by night the place becomes a hipster scene in the bar on the second level—think low tables and sofas—while a youngish crowd shares cheese plates in the crowded street-level dining room. ✉*223 Pennsylvania Ave. SE, Capitol Hill* ☎*202/544–8088* ⊕*www.sonomadc.com* ⌖*Reservations essential* ▭*AE, D, DC, MC, V* ⊘*No lunch weekends* Ⓜ*Capitol S.* ✛*6G*

DOWNTOWN

$–$$
LATIN AMERICAN

✕**Café Atlántico.** The menu is always exciting at this *nuevo Latino* restaurant with friendly service. Conch fritters come with tiny avocado ravioli, and scallops are served with coconut rice, ginger, squid, and squid-ink oil. On weekends Atlántico offers "Latino dim sum," tapas-size portions of dishes such as duck confit with passion-fruit oil, pineapple shavings, and plantain powder. À la carte, the plates are $3 to $9, but for $35 you can get a deluxe tasting menu ($25 for a vegetarian tasting menu). The bar makes mean cocktails with *cachaça*, a liquor distilled from sugarcane juice. You are unlikely to find a more-extensive selection of South American wines anywhere in the city. At Minibar, a six-stool bar on the second floor, you can explore a $95 tasting menu of about 30 creative morsels, such as a foie-gras "lollipop" coated with cotton candy, conjured up before your eyes. ■TIP→**Minibar is arguably the most adventurous dining experience in the city, which means you have to reserve at least a week in advance. The space generally closes from mid-August to mid-September.** ✉*405 8th St. NW, Downtown* ☎*202/393–0812* ⊕*www.cafeatlantico.com* ⌖*Reservations essential* ▭*AE, DC, MC, V* Ⓜ*Archives/Navy Memorial.* ✛*5E*

$$–$$$
FRENCH

✕**Central Michel Richard.** French powerhouse chef Michel Richard has set up camp downtown with this semicasual bistro offering up Franco-American spin-offs like fried chicken, leek-and-mussel chowder, and a ginger-flecked tuna burger. Rows of hams hang in a glass case. Light fixtures are subtly stamped with the word "Central." A jazzy portrait of Richard (think Andy Warhol) stares down from one wall. The mood is playful and low key; cocktails and champagne flow. And there are even a few carryovers from Richard's more-formal Citronelle in Georgetown like "Le Kit Kat," the chef's take on a Kit Kat bar. ✉*1001 Pennsylvania Ave. NW, Downtown* ☎*202/626–0015* ⊕*centralmichelrichard.com*

⚐ *Reservations essential* ▤ *AE, D, MC, V* ⊘ *Closed Sun. No lunch Sat.* Ⓜ *Metro Center.* ✛ *5E*

$
SPANISH

✕ **Jaleo.** You are encouraged to make a meal of the long list of tapas at this lively Spanish bistro, although entrées such as paella are just as tasty. Tapas highlights include the *gambas al ajillo* (sautéed garlic shrimp), fried potatoes with spicy tomato sauce, and grilled chorizo. Adventurers are encouraged to sample the octopus with paprika, and sweet tooths should save room for the crisp apple charlotte and the chocolate hazelnut torte. ⊠ *480 7th St. NW, Downtown* ☎ *202/628–7949* ⊕ *www.jaleo.com* ▤ *AE, D, DC, MC, V* Ⓜ *Gallery Pl./Chinatown.* ✛ *5E*

$–$$
AMERICAN
☾

✕ **Matchbox.** The miniburgers, served on toasted brioche buns with a huge mound of fried onion strings, get the most press, but the main clue to what to order at this convivial triple-decker bar-restaurant is the glowing wood-burning pizza oven. The personal pizzas are "New York–style," with a thin, crisp crust. You probably won't mistake them for the very best of New York, but the pizza margherita is good nevertheless. Homey plates such as grilled filet mignon with horseradish potatoes and spicy pecan-crusted chicken add substance to the menu. There's a great lineup of draft beers and oddball martinis. ⊠ *713 H St. NW, Downtown* ☎ *202/289–4441* ⊕ *www.matchboxdc.com* ▤ *AE, D, DC, MC, V* ⊘ *Closed Sun.* Ⓜ *Gallery Pl./Chinatown.* ✛ *4E*

¢–$
MEXICAN

✕ **Oyamel.** The specialty at this Mexican stunner is antojitos, literally translated as "little dishes from the street." But the high ceilings, gracious service, and gorgeous Frida Kahlo–inspired decor are anything but street, and even the smallest of dishes is bigger than life when doused with chocolatey mole poblano sauce or piquant lime-cilantro dressing. Standouts include house-made margaritas topped with a clever salt foam, the Veracruz red snapper in a hearty olive-tomato confit, and grasshopper tacos. Yes, those are bugs basted in tequila and pepper sauce—and they're delightful. ⊠ *401 7th St. NW, Downtown* ☎ *202/628–1005* ⊕ *www.oyamel.com* ▤ *AE, D, MC, V* Ⓜ *Archives/Navy Memorial.* ✛ *5F*

$$–$$$
INDIAN
Fodor'sChoice
★

✕ **Rasika.** This trendy Indian restaurant pairs an adventurous wine list with spicy fare in a supersleek setting. The chef, London export Vikram Sunderam (from Bombay Brasserie), comes from a town where curries never get short shrift. He has prepared a menu of traditional delights, like a fiery chicken green masala, alongside newer, more-inspired ones, like lamb miniburgers, tiny crab cakes with Indian spices, and fried spinach leaves with sweet yogurt sauce. Libations at the bar are concocted with as much creativity as the food. Muted shades of cream, applegreen, and cinnabar and dangling crystals evoke the subcontinent but in a stylish, modern way. ⊠ *633 D St. NW, Chinatown* ☎ *202/637–1222* ⊕ *www.rasikarestaurant.com* ▤ *AE, D, DC, MC, V* ⊘ *Closed Sun. No lunch weekends* Ⓜ *Archives/Navy Memorial.* ✛ *5F*

¢
JAPANESE
☾
Fodor'sChoice
★

✕ **Teaism.** This informal teahouse stocks more than 50 teas (black, white, and green) imported from India, Japan, and Africa, but it also serves healthful and delicious Japanese, Indian, and Thai food as well as teafriendly sweets like ginger scones, plum muffins, and salty oat cookies. You can mix small dishes—tandoori kebabs, tea-cured salmon, Indian flat breads—to create meals or snacks. There's also a juicy ostrich burger or *ochazuke*, green tea poured over seasoned rice. The smaller Connecticut Avenue branch (enter around the corner, on H Street; closed on weekends) is tucked neatly on a corner adjacent to Lafayette Park and the White House, a casual reprieve from neighboring high-priced restaurants. It's a perfect spot to grab lunch after touring the nation's power center. Breakfast is served daily. ⊠*400 8th St. NW, Downtown* ☎*202/638–7740* ⊕*www.teaism.com* ⊟*D, MC, V* Ⓜ*Archives/Navy Memorial* ⊠*800 Connecticut Ave. NW, Downtown* ☎*202/835–2233* Ⓜ*Farragut West* ⊠*2009 R St. NW, Dupont Circle* ☎*202/667–3827* ⊟*D, MC, V* Ⓜ*Dupont Circle.* ✛*2C, 4D, 5E*

$ ✕**Zaytinya.** This sophisticated urban dining room with soaring ceilings
MIDDLE EASTERN   is a local favorite for meeting friends or dining with a group. Zaytinya,
Fodor'sChoice   which means "olive oil" in Turkish, devotes practically its entire menu to
★   Turkish, Greek, and Lebanese small plates, known as mezes. To get the full experience, make a meal of three or four of these, such as the popular braised lamb with eggplant puree and cheese, or the locally made goat cheese wrapped in grape leaves with tomato marmalade. ■TIP➔**So many options make this a great choice for vegetarians and meat lovers alike.** Reservations for times after 6:30 are not accepted; come prepared to wait on Friday and Saturday nights. Belly dancers perform on Wednesday nights. ⊠*701 9th St. NW, Downtown* ☎*202/638–0800* ⊕*www.zaytinya.com* ⊟*AE, DC, MC, V* Ⓜ*Gallery Pl./Chinatown.* ✛*4E*

DUPONT CIRCLE

$–$$ ✕**Hank's Oyster Bar.** The watchword is simplicity at this popular and
SEAFOOD   chic take on the shellfish shacks of New England. A half-dozen oyster
Fodor'sChoice   varieties are available daily on the half shell, both from the West Coast
★   and local Virginia waters, alongside another half-dozen daily fish specials. An amuse-bouche of cheddar Goldfish crackers adds a touch of whimsy. Don't be shy about asking for seconds on the complimentary baking chocolate presented along with your check—the kitchen doesn't serve sweets, but it doesn't need to. ⊠*1624 Q St. NW, Dupont Circle* ☎*202/462–4265* ⊕*www.hanksdc.com* ⊟*AE, MC, V* ☉*Dupont Circle* ⊠*1026 King St., Alexandria, VA* ☎*703/739–4265* Ⓜ*King St.* ✛*3D*

$$$ ✕**Komi.** Johnny Monis, the young, energetic chef-owner of this small,
NEW AMERICAN   personal restaurant, offers one of the most adventurous dining experi-
Fodor'sChoice   ences in the city. The five-course prix-fixe is $74 and showcases contem-
★   porary fare with a distinct Mediterranean influence. ■TIP➔**Reservations open 30 days in advance—and the longer you wait, the smaller your chance at a coveted table.** Star plates include fresh sardines with pickled lemons, suckling pig over apples and bacon with polenta, and mascarpone-filled dates with sea salt. ⊠*1509 17th St., Dupont Circle* ☎*202/332–9200* ⊕*www.komirestaurant.com* ⚐*Reservations essential* ⊟*AE, D, MC, V* ☉*Closed Sun. and Mon. No lunch* Ⓜ*Dupont Circle.* ✛*3D*

$$–$$$ ✕**Nora.** Chef and founder Nora Pouillon helped pioneer the sustainable-
AMERICAN   food revolution with the first certified organic restaurant in the country, and her seasonal, sustainable ingredients are out of this world. Settle into the sophisticated and attractive quilt-decorated dining room and

start with the mushroom, leek, and Brie tart or a locally grown salad. Entrées such as pepper-crusted steak and roasted salmon with parsnips emphasize the well-balanced, earthy ingredients. ⊠*2132 Florida Ave. NW, Dupont Circle* ☎*202/462–5143* ⊕*www.noras. com* ✑*Reservations essential* ▤*AE, D, MC, V* ☾*Closed Sun. No lunch* Ⓜ*Dupont Circle.* ✛*2B*

$
ITALIAN
☾

✕**Pizzeria Paradiso.** A trompe-l'oeil ceiling adds space and light to a simple interior at the ever-popular Dupont Circle Pizzeria Paradiso. The restaurant sticks to crowd-pleasing basics: pizzas, panini, salads, and desserts. Although the standard pizza is satisfying, you can enliven it with fresh buffalo mozzarella or unusual toppings such as potatoes, capers, and mussels. Wines are well chosen and well priced. The intensely flavored gelato is a house specialty. At the larger location in Georgetown, the lower level has a Ratskeller-style beer pub. ⊠*2029 P St. NW, Dupont Circle* ☎*202/223–1245* ⊕*www.eatyourpizza.com* ▤*DC, MC, V* Ⓜ*Dupont Circle* ⊠*3282 M St. NW, Georgetown* ☎*202/337–1245* ▤*D, DC, MC, V* ✛*3C*

$$–$$$
NEW AMERICAN
Fodor'sChoice
★

✕**Blue Duck Tavern.** Many chefs are fond of artisanal and local ingredients. Chef Brian McBride is so committed to the cause that fixings are often strewn across marble counters in the restaurant's show kitchen. By now diners have gotten used to watching pastry chefs churn ice cream to be served minutes later in glass ice buckets, but sweets—and watching for the town's biggest political names to claim their favorite tables—aren't the only pleasures. The kitchen wows with Modern American riffs like a double-cut pork chop with bourbon-glazed peaches, a marrowbone with creamy insides, and a meaty hanger steak. The dining room is stylish, done up with Shaker furniture and quilts. ⊠*1201 24th St. NW, Foggy Bottom* ☎*202/419–6755* ⊕*www.blueducktavern.com* ✑*Reservations essential* ▤*AE, D, DC, MC, V* Ⓜ*Foggy Bottom/ GWU.* ✛*3B*

GEORGETOWN & FOGGY BOTTOM

$$$$
FRENCH
Fodor'sChoice
★

✕**Citronelle.** See all the action in the glass-front kitchen at chef Michel Richard's flagship California-French restaurant. Appetizers might include foie gras with lentils prepared three ways, and main courses run to lobster medallions with lemongrass, saddle of lamb crusted with herbs, and breast of squab. Desserts are luscious: a crunchy napoleon with filament-like pastry and the very special "chocolate bar," Richard's dense, rich take on a Snickers candy bar. A chef's table in the kitchen gives you a ringside seat (reserve at least a month ahead). The fixed-price menu costs $155, or $230 with wine pairings. The bar menu ($$–$$$) has morsels such as mushroom "cigars" and Serrano ham. ⊠*Latham Hotel, 3000 M St. NW, Georgetown* ☎*202/625–2150* ⊕*www.citro nelledc.com* ✑*Reservations essential. Jacket required* ▤*AE, D, DC, MC, V* ☾*No lunch* ✛*3A*

¢   ✕**Five Guys.** One of the quirky traditions of this homegrown fast-food
AMERICAN   burger house is to note on the menu board where the potatoes for that
⊙   day's fries come from, be it Maine, Idaho, or elsewhere. The place gets
just about everything right: from the grilled hot dogs and hand-patted
burger patties—most folks get a double—to the fresh hand-cut fries with
the skin on and the high-quality toppings such as sautéed onions and
mushrooms. Add an eclectic jukebox to all of the above and you've got
a great burger experience. There are also locations throughout the city.
⊠*1335 Wisconsin Ave. NW, Georgetown* ☎*202/337–0400* ⊕*www.
fiveguys.com* ⊟*MC, V.* ⊠*1645 Connecticut Ave. NW, Dupont Circle*
☎*202/328–3483* Ⓜ*Dupont Circle.* ✛*2A, 2C*

$$$–$$$$ ✕**Hook.** The old guard of Georgetown gourmands got a heavenly sur-
SEAFOOD   prise in 2006 when Barton Seaver, the young and charming chef at
Fodor'sChoice   Café Saint-Ex on U Street, opened this ode to the "sustainable-sea-
★   food" movement. From weakfish to yahoo, all of the uncommon fish
on the menu are caught using environmentally friendly methods that
preserve overfished seafood populations like swordfish and salmon.
Consciousness aside, your palate is in for a thrill for lunch, brunch,
or dinner. Seaver handed over his toque to longtime sous chef Joshua
Whigham, but the kitchen has not missed a beat. Pastry chef Heather
Chittum's fresh basil ice cream and homemade donuts stuffed with
Nutella are also not to be missed. ⊠*3241 M St. NW, Georgetown*
☎*202/625-4488* ⊕*www.hookdc.com* ⚱*Reservations essential* ⊟*AE,
MC, V* ⊙*No lunch Mon.* ✛*3A*

$–$$ ✕**Sushi-Ko.** At one of the city's best Japanese restaurants, daily specials
JAPANESE   are always innovative: sesame oil–seasoned trout layered with crisp
wonton crackers, and a sushi special might be salmon topped with a
touch of mango sauce and a sprig of dill. You won't find the restaurant's
delicious ginger, mango, or green-tea ice cream at the local Baskin-
Robbins. ⊠*2309 Wisconsin Ave. NW, Georgetown* ☎*202/333–4187*
⚱*Reservations essential* ⊟*AE, D, MC, V* ⊙*No lunch Sat.–Mon.*
✛*3A*

GLOVER PARK

¢–$ ✕**2 Amys.** Judging from the long lines here, the best pizza in DC is
PIZZA   uptown. Simple recipes allow the ingredients to shine through at this
⊙   Neapolitan pizzeria. You may be tempted to go for the D.O.C. pizza
Fodor'sChoice   (it has *Denominazione di Origine Controllata* approval for Neapoli-
★   tan authenticity), but don't hesitate to try the daily specials. Roasted
peppers with anchovies and deviled eggs with parsley-caper sauce
have by now become classics. At busy times the wait for a table can
exceed an hour, and the noisy din of a packed house may discourage
some diners. ⊠*3715 Macomb St. NW, Glover Park* ☎*202/885–5700*
⊕*www.2amyspizza.com* ⚱*Reservations not accepted* ⊟*MC, V* ⊙*No
lunch Mon.* ✛*1B*

U STREET

¢–$

AMERICAN

☺

✕**Ben's Chili Bowl.** Long before U Street became hip, Ben's was serving chili. Chili on hot dogs, chili on Polish-style sausages, chili on burgers, and just plain chili. Add cheese fries if you dare. The faux-marble bar and shiny red-vinyl stools give the impression that little has changed since the 1950s, but turkey and vegetarian burgers and meatless chili are a nod to modern times. Ben's closes at 2 AM Monday through Thursday, at 4 AM on Friday and Saturday, and at 8 PM Sunday. Southern-style breakfast is served from 6 AM weekdays and from 7 AM on Saturday. ⊠*1213 U St. NW, U Street corridor* ☎*202/667–0909* ⊕*www.bens chilibowl.com* ⊟*No credit cards* Ⓜ*U Street/Cardozo.* ✛*2E*

¢–$

AFRICAN

✕**Etete.** The best of the city's Ethiopian restaurants, Etete doesn't hold back on the spices. Savory pastries known as *sambusas* are filled with fiery lentils, and ginger brightens a stew of vegetables. The sharing of dishes and the mode of eating—rather than using utensils diners tear off pieces of *injera*, a spongy pancake-like bread to scoop up stews and sautées—make for exotic and adventurous dining at this style-conscious eatery. ⊠*1942 9th St. NW, U Street* ☎*202/232–7600* ⊕*www.eteterestaurant. com* ⊟*AE, D, DC, MC, V* Ⓜ*U St./African-American Civil War Memorial/Cardozo.* ✛*2E*

¢–$

THAI

✕**Sala Thai.** Who says Thai food has to be sweat-inducing? Sala Thai makes the food as spicy as you wish, because this chef is interested in flavor, not fire. Among the subtly seasoned dishes are *panang goong* (shrimp in curry-peanut sauce), chicken sautéed with ginger and pineapple, and flounder with a choice of four sauces. Mirrored walls and warm lights soften this small dining room, as do the friendly service and largely local clientele. The Dupont and U Street locations are most popular, but Arlington, Bethesda, and the Upper Northwest neighborhood all host winning Sala locations. ⊠*1301 U St. NW, U Street corridor* ☎*202/462–1333* ⊕*www.salathaidc.com* Ⓜ*U St./Cardozo* ⊠*2016 P St. NW, Dupont Circle* ☎*202/872–1144* ⊟*AE, D, DC, MC, V* Ⓜ*Dupont Circle.* ✛*2D*

WHERE TO STAY

Forced to cater to all stripes, from lobbyists with expense accounts to those in town for the free museums, from bigwigs seeking attention to those flying under the radar, Washington's rooms suit everyone. The high-end and business-class hotels are located mainly near the halls of power, whether in Georgetown row houses, near the White House, or on Capitol Hill. Downtown, quickly becoming the city's nerve center, also has its fair share. There's a good chance that if you stay in one of the pricier digs in these areas you can sign a guest register touched by diplomats and then sleep in beds where royalty rested. The District's boutique hotels and cool guesthouses tend to congregate in the shadier areas of northwest DC.

DC HOTEL TIPS

If you can stand semitropical weather, come in August, during the congressional recess, when Washington is calm and less expensive. Rates also drop in late December and January, except around an inauguration.

Reservations: With more than 63,000 guest rooms, Washington can almost always provide a place to stay—though it's always prudent to reserve. Hotels often fill up with conventioneers, politicians in transit, families, and, in spring, school groups. Hotel rooms in DC can be hard to come by during the Cherry Blossom Festival in late March or early April, and also in May, when so many graduate from college. Late October's Marine Corps Marathon also increases demand for rooms. The **Washington, DC Convention and Tourism Corporation** (☎ *800/422–8644* ⊕ *www.washington.org*) runs a reservation service.

Parking: Hotel parking fees range from free (often in the suburbs) to $30 (plus tax) per night. This sometimes involves valet parking, with its implied additional gratuities. Street parking is free, but sparse, on Sunday and usually after 6:30 PM weekdays.

WHAT IT COSTS					
	¢	$	$$	$$$	$$$$
FOR TWO PEOPLE	under $125	$126–$210	$211–$295	$296–$399	over $400

Prices are for a standard double room in high season, excluding 14.5% room tax.

CAPITOL HILL

$$$$
Fodor'sChoice
★

⊞ **Hotel George.** Rooms at this cool boutique hotel offer duvet-covered beds with the softest Egyptian cotton sheets, granite-topped desks, silk-screen prints, CD players, and seating areas with a lounge chair and ottoman. Most have marble bathrooms and terry robes, and each room comes with a complimentary in-room television "yoga program" (mat, block, and strap provided). Portraits of America's first president, by Andy Warhol protégé Steve Kaufman, adorn public areas. Bistro Bis serves updated versions of classic French dishes. **Pros:** stylish hotel; popular restaurant; men's and women's steam rooms. **Cons:** expensive; some reports of street noise; ultramodern feel not everyone's cup of tea. ⊠ *15 E St. NW, Capitol Hill* ☎ *202/347–4200 or 800/576–8331* ⊕ *www.hotelgeorge.com* ➾ *138 rooms, 1 suite* ⬩ *In-room: safe, DVD, Ethernet. In-hotel: restaurant, room service, bar, gym, concierge, laundry service, parking (fee), some pets allowed, no-smoking rooms* ⊟ *AE, D, DC, MC, V* Ⓜ *Union Station.* ✛ *5G*

DOWNTOWN

$$$ 🏨**Renaissance Mayflower Hotel.** The magnificent block-long lobby with its series of antique crystal chandeliers and gilded columns is a destination in itself. Guest rooms at this grande dame hotel, which opened its doors in 1925 for Calvin Coolidge's inauguration, are done in soothing yellows, green, tans, and blues. Town and Country, the hotel's inside-the-Beltway power bar, has been a place for political wheeling and dealing for nearly as long as the hotel. Sam the bartender mixes up 101 martinis to keep guests happily in the drink. Work off the booze and the crab cakes, a favorite on the menu at the hotel's elegant Café Promenade, in yjr spa-like fitness center. **Pros:** gorgeous lobby; fitness center with natural light and well-maintained equipment; a few steps from the Metro. **Cons:** rooms vary in size; no pool. ⊠*1127 Connecticut Ave. NW, Downtown* ☎*202/347–3000 or 800/228–9290* ⊕*www.marriott. com* ⇔*580 rooms, 74 suites* ⚙*In-room: Ethernet. In-hotel: public Wi-Fi, restaurant, room service, bar, gym, concierge, laundry service, executive floor, parking (fee), no-smoking rooms* ▤*AE, D, DC, MC, V* Ⓜ*Farragut North.* ✛*4C*

$$$$ 🏨**St. Regis Washington, DC.** Don't forget to look up and admire the

Fodor'sChoice ⋆ ornate, hand-painted ceiling in the newly restored lobby of the St. Regis, a 1926 landmark hotel that reopened in January 2008 after an extensive 16-month restoration. Pratesi linens dress the beds, a 15-inch LCD TV is recessed behind the bathroom mirror in every guest room, and personal butlers now carry BlackBerrys, so while you're out you can e-mail requests like "Please pack my bags." Just two blocks from the White House, this Italian Renaissance–style hotel attracts a formal business crowd. If you check in with kids, hotel staff will give them F.A.O. Schwarz teddy bears and bring minirobes to your room. The concierge also keeps a selection of toys and games on hand and can arrange babysitting. A new health club and restaurant were added in late 2008. **Pros:** two blocks from White House; renovated historic property; exceptional service. **Cons:** no pool; most rooms don't have great views; pricey. ⊠*923 16th and K Sts., NW, Downtown* ☎*202/638–2626 or 877/787–3447* ⊕*www.stregis.com/washington* ⇔*175 rooms, 25 suites* ⚙*In-room: safe, refrigerator (some), DVD (some), Ethernet, Wi-Fi. In hotel: restaurant, room service, bar, gym, spa, laundry service, concierge, public Wi-Fi, parking (fee), some pets allowed, no-smoking rooms* ▤*AE, D, DC, MC,V* Ⓜ*Farragut North.* ✛*4D*

$ 🏨**Washington Doubletree Hotel.** Just off Scott Circle, the Doubletree ☾ offers spacious guest rooms that have recently been renovated, with comfortable beds, well-equipped workstations, CD players, coffeemakers, and robes. An American bistro, 15 Ria, brings a New York sensibility to the hotel, which is only six blocks from the White House. **Pros:** child-friendly; good location; updated rooms and fitness center. **Cons:** no pool; limited street parking at times. ⊠*1515 Rhode Island Ave. NW, Downtown* ☎*202/232–7000 or 800/222–8733* ⊕*www.washington. doubletree.com* ⇔*181 rooms, 39 suites* ⚙*In-room: safe, Ethernet, refrigerator. In-hotel: public Wi-Fi, restaurant, gym, concierge, parking (fee)* ▤*AE, D, DC, MC, V* Ⓜ*Dupont Circle.* ✛*3D*

Where to Stay & Eat in Washington

KEY
☐ Hotels
◼ Restaurants
▨ Restaurant in Hotel

U STREET-CARDOZO

Ben's Chili Bowl

Etete

SHAW-HOWARD UNIVERSITY

Rhode Island Ave.

U St.

T St.

S St.

R St.

Q St.

Logan Circle

P St.

O St.

N St.

New York Ave.

M St.

Morrison-Clark Inn

Massachusetts Ave.

Mt. Vernon Square

MT. VERNON SQUARE-UDC

Marrakesh

L St.

Massachusetts Ave.

METRO CENTER

Match Box

GALLERY PLACE-CHINATOWN

Zaytinya

Central Michel Richard

Hotel Monaco

Poste

Jaleo

Café Atlántico

Teaism

Rasika

Oyamel

ARCHIVES-NAVY MEMORIAL

FEDERAL TRIANGLE

JUDICIARY SQUARE

Hotel George

Holiday Inn on the Hill

UNION STATION

Union Station

Pennsylvania Ave.

National Museum of Natural History

National Gallery of Art

US Capitol

Smithsonian Institution

THE MALL

Jefferson Dr.

Independence Ave.

SMITHSONIAN

National Air and Space Museum

◼ Sonoma
◼ Market Lunch
◼ Locanda
◼ Granville Moore's Brickyard

DUPONT CIRCLE

$–$$

Fodor's Choice
★

The Inn at Dupont Circle South. This is the inn where everybody knows your name. Innkeeper Carolyn jokes that her guests are "her babies," and the personal attention shows: there are many repeat customers here, and some keep in touch even when they are not in town. Most rooms have private baths; all have TVs, featherbeds, and typical inn decor complete with doilies, bric-a-brac, and impressionist posters. Carolyn serves a hot breakfast in the parlor or on the sun porch. ■ TIP→ **The Nook Room is aptly named and budget friendly at $95 per night.** Pros: personable innkeeper; personalized service; great Dupont location across from Metro; children welcome. Cons: older home complete with creaking floors; no elevator; not all rooms have private baths. ⊠ *1312 19th St. NW, Dupont Circle* ☎ *202/467–6777 or 866/467–2100* ⊕ *thedupontcollection.com* ⤳ *8 rooms* ⚭ *In room: safe, refrigerator, Wi-Fi. In-hotel: no elevator, laundry facilities, public Wi-Fi, airport shuttle, parking (fee), no-smoking rooms* ☰ *AE, MC, V* ⦿⊢*BP* Ⓜ *Dupont Circle.* ✢*3C*

$$–$$$

Jurys Washington Hotel. The Irish-run Jurys chain has breathed new life into this older building on Dupont Circle. Half the guest rooms here were updated several years ago with a more modern flair in the spirit of the hotel's shining white marble lobby. At check-in it's a good idea to request one of the newer rooms, but whichever room you wind up with you'll be right in the heart of hip and urban Dupont Circle. Rooms have writing desks, coffeemakers, hair dryers, and complimentary newspaper delivery. Biddy Mulligan's, the hotel bar, draws a Guinness-guzzling crowd. Pros: free Wi-Fi; great location; fun neighborhood bar. Cons: busy area; no pool. ⊠ *1500 New Hampshire Ave. NW, Dupont Circle* ☎ *202/483–6000 or 866/534–6835* ⊕ *www.jurysdoyle.com* ⤳ *314 rooms, 6 suites* ⚭ *In-room: safe, Wi-Fi. In-hotel: public Wi-Fi, restaurant, room service, bar, gym, concierge, laundry service, parking (fee), no-smoking rooms* ☰ *AE, D, DC, MC, V* Ⓜ *Dupont Circle.* ✢*3C*

$$$–$$$$

Mansion on O Street. Rock and roll palace meets urban thrift shop in this utterly oddball supper club–cum–guesthouse, a scramble of five side-by-side town houses crammed with art, junk, and everything in between. Nothing here suggests a hotel: from a two-story log-cabin suite with fish tanks and pony-skin chairs to the John Lennon–theme room with a signed guitar case and hologrammed bathroom floor, this is the most unusual sleep in town. Squander your evenings shooting pool in the billiards room, or pick up one of the ubiquitous guitars and write a song about the place—you won't be the first. Breakfast (included) is self-service in the giant, funky turquoise kitchen, and 24-hour room service is now available—just tell the chef what you are in the mood for and wait for the knock on your door. Watch for secret doorways, some left from when the Mansion was a dorm for Hoover's G-Men. Pros: one-of-a-kind; serious about privacy; glamorous common areas. Cons: layout makes for many dark rooms; eccentric staff and service; expensive. ⊠ *2020 O St. NW, Dupont Circle* ☎ *202/496–2020* ⊕ *www.omansion.com* ⤳ *18 rooms, 11 suites* ⚭ *In-room: DVD (some), VCR (some), Ethernet, Wi-Fi. In-hotel: room service, bar, laundry service, parking (fee), no-smoking rooms* ☰ *AE, D, DC, MC, V* ⦿⊢*BP* Ⓜ *Dupont Circle.* ✢*3C*

GEORGETOWN

$$$$ ⊞ **Four Seasons Hotel.** Having completed a whopping $40 million reno-
⟳ vation in 2005, the Four Seasons has reasserted its role as Washington's
Fodor's Choice leading hotel. Impeccable service and a wealth of amenities have long
★ made this a favorite with celebrities, hotel connoisseurs, and families.
Luxurious, ultramodern rooms offer heavenly beds, flat-screen digital
TVs with DVD players, and French limestone or marble baths with
separate showers and sunken tubs. A 2,000-piece original art collection
graces the walls, and a walk through the corridors seems like a visit
to a wing of the MoMA or the Met. The formal Seasons restaurant
offers traditional dishes with an elegant twist, as well as a popular
Sunday brunch. The sophisticated spa here is one of the best in town.
Pros: edge of Georgetown makes for a fabulous location; lap of luxury
feel; Four Seasons service. **Cons:** expensive; challenging street parking;
expensive ($42 a night) valet service. ⊠*2800 Pennsylvania Ave. NW,
Georgetown* ☎*202/342–0444 or 800/332–3442* ⊕*www.fourseasons.
com/washington* ⇆*160 rooms, 51 suites* ⌂*In-room: safe, Ethernet.
In-hotel: restaurant, room service, bar, pool, gym, concierge, children's
programs (ages 5–16), parking (fee), some pets allowed, no-smoking
rooms* ▤*AE, D, DC, MC, V* Ⓜ*Foggy Bottom.* ✛*4A*

$$–$$$ ⊞ **Washington Suites Georgetown.** Just outside the center of Georgetown,
this older all-suites accommodation offers families and long-term-stay
travelers an alternative to standard hotel rooms. Each suite has a fully
equipped kitchen, a small living and dining area, and a separate bedroom and bath. ■**TIP**➡ **Stock your fridge at the Trader Joe's across the
street.** Fresh pastries, juices, and cereal are served each morning in the
breakfast room. Many of the staff members have worked at the hotel
for years and know regular guests by name. **Pros:** friendly staff; good
for long-term stays; good value. **Cons:** no-frills; breakfast room can be
crowded when hotel is full. ⊠*2500 Pennsylvania Ave. NW, Georgetown* ☎*202/333–8060 or 877/736–2500* ⊕*www.washingtonsuites
georgetown.com* ⇆*124 suites* ⌂*In-room: kitchen, Ethernet. In-hotel:
gym, laundry facilities, parking (fee), no-smoking rooms* ▤*AE, D, DC,
MC, V* ❘◯❘*CP* Ⓜ*Foggy Bottom.* ✛*4B*

WEST END & FOGGY BOTTOM

$$–$$$ ⊞ **Embassy Suites.** Plants cascade over balconies beneath a skylight in
⟳ this modern hotel's atrium, which is filled with classical columns, plaster
lions, wrought-iron lanterns, waterfalls, and tall palms. Within walking
distance of Georgetown, the Kennedy Center, and Dupont Circle, the
suites here are suitable for both business travelers and families. Beverages are complimentary at the nightly manager's reception, and the rate
includes cooked-to-order breakfast. There's a kids' corner with movies
and games, and the Italian restaurant, Trattoria Nicola's, serves lunch
and dinner. **Pros:** family-friendly; all suites; pool to keep the little ones—
and sweaty tourists—happy. **Cons:** not a lot of character; museums not
in walking distance. ⊠*1250 22nd St. NW, West End* ☎*202/857–3388
or 800/362–2779* ⊕*www.embassysuites.com* ⇆*318 suites* ⌂*In-room:
refrigerator, Wi-Fi. In-hotel: restaurant, room service, bar, pool, gym,*

laundry service, parking (fee), no-smoking rooms ⊟*AE, D, DC, MC,*
V ⏐○⏐*BP* Ⓜ*Foggy Bottom/GWU or Dupont Circle.* ✛*3B*

$$$$ 🏨**Fairmont Washington.** The large glassed-in lobby and about a third of
☾ the bright, spacious rooms overlook the Fairmont's central courtyard
and gardens. Rooms are comfortable, if not the city's most modern. The
informal Juniper restaurant serves mid-Atlantic fare and has courtyard
dining; there's a champagne brunch on Sunday in the Colonnade Room.
■TIP➡**The health club is one of the best in the city.** Families have access
to the pool, kids' menus and crayons in the restaurant, and a babysitting
referral service. The Fairmont also offers family packages, such as the
"Panda Package," a trip to visit the pandas at the National Zoo. **Pros:**
fitness-focused guests will love the health club; lots of kid-friendly features. **Cons:** pricey; not many attractions in walking distance. ⊠*2401
M St. NW, Foggy Bottom* ☎*202/429–2400 or 877/222–2266* ⊕*www.*
fairmont.com ⤴*406 rooms, 9 suites* ♿*In-room: safe, Ethernet. In-*
hotel: restaurant, room service, bar, pool, gym, concierge, executive
floor, parking (fee), some pets allowed, no-smoking rooms ⊟*AE, D,*
DC, MC, V Ⓜ*Foggy Bottom/GWU.* ✛*3B*

$ 🏨**George Washington University Inn.** This boutique hotel is in a quiet
neighborhood a few blocks from the Kennedy Center, the State Department, and George Washington University. Wrought-iron gates lead
through a courtyard to the hotel's front entrance, where beveled-glass
doors open onto a small lobby with a gray marble floor. Rooms, which
vary in size and configuration, have Colonial-style furniture and complimentary high-speed Internet access. Guests also receive free entry to
the nearby Bally Total Fitness club. **Pros:** good price; close to Metro.
Cons: not many amenities; far from museums. ⊠*824 New Hampshire
Ave. NW, Foggy Bottom* ☎*202/337–6620 or 800/426–4455* ⊕*www.*
gwuinn.com ⤴*64 rooms, 31 suites* ♿*In-room: safe, kitchen (some),*
refrigerator, Wi-Fi. In-hotel: restaurant, bar, laundry facilities, laundry
service, parking (fee), no-smoking rooms ⊟*AE, DC, MC, V* Ⓜ*Foggy*
Bottom/GWU. ✛*4B*

WOODLEY PARK & UPPER NORTHWEST

$$$–$$$$ 🏨**Omni Shoreham Hotel.** A $15 million dollar facelift has enhanced this
☾ already elegant hotel overlooking Rock Creek Park, and the historic
Fodor's Choice property is aging gracefully. The light-filled guest rooms have a sooth-
★ ing garden palette and feature flat-screen TVs and marble bathrooms.
The vast art deco–and–Renaissance–style lobby welcomes visitors, who
in the past have ranged from the Beatles to heads of state (the hotel
has played host to inaugural balls since its 1930 opening). There is
even a resident ghost said to haunt Suite 870. Families will love the
larger-than-typical guest rooms, kiddie pool, bird-watching, bike rent-
als, and movie nights. ■TIP➡**Parents: Ask the concierge about story time
and cuddles with the guide dog for the blind who trains at the hotel. Pros:**
renovated historic property; great outdoor pool and sundeck; good
views from many rooms. **Cons:** not downtown; big. ⊠*2500 Calvert
St., NW, Woodley Park* ☎*202/234–0700 or 800/545–8700* ⊕*www.*
omnihotels.com ⤴*818 rooms, 16 suites* ♿*In-room: safe, refrigerator*

(some), DVD (some), VCR (some), Wi-Fi. In-hotel: restaurant, room service, bar, pool, gym, spa, bicycles, children's programs (ages 3–13), concierge, laundry service, parking (fee), some pets allowed, no-smoking rooms ▤*AE, D, DC, MC, V* Ⓜ*Woodley Park/Zoo.* ✛*1A*

NIGHTLIFE & THE ARTS

From buttoned-down political appointees to laid-back folks who were born here, Washingtonians have plenty of options when they head out for the night. Most bars are clustered in several key areas. Penn Quarter, near the Verizon Center and U Street NW between 12th and 15th streets, is quickly becoming one of the hottest spots in town. Georgetown has dozens of bars, nightclubs, and restaurants at the intersection of Wisconsin and M streets. A host of small live-music venues and popular bars line the 18th Street strip in Adams-Morgan between Columbia Road and Kalorama Avenue. The stretch of Pennsylvania Avenue between 2nd and 4th streets SE has a half-dozen Capitol Hill bars. Hill staffers also hang out on Barrack's Row, 8th Street SE south of D Street. For a high-powered happy hour, head to the intersection of 19th and M streets NW, near lawyer- and lobbyist-filled downtown.

DC has also gone from being a cultural desert to a thriving arts center in the past 40 years. To satiate the educated young professionals who flock here for opportunities in government, the arts scene has exploded. To sift through the flurry of events, check out the daily "Guide to the Lively Arts," in the *Washington Post,* and the "Weekend" section on Friday. On Thursday, look for the free weekly *Washington CityPaper* (⊕*www.washington citypaper.com*). The *Washington Post* (⊕*www.washingtonpost.com/city guide*) also publishes an Internet-based entertainment guide.

TICKETplace sells half-price, day-of-performance tickets for select shows. ▨*Old Post Office Pavilion, 406 7th St. NW, Downtown* ☏*202/842–5387* ⊕*www.ticketplace.org* Ⓜ*Archives/Navy Memorial.*

LIVE MUSIC

The Birchmere. A legend in the DC area, the Birchmere is one of the best places outside of the Blue Ridge Mountains to hear acoustic folk, country, and bluegrass. Enthusiastic crowds have enjoyed performances by artists such as Mary Chapin Carpenter, Lyle Lovett, Leon Redbone, and Emmylou Harris. Recently, the club has expanded its offerings to include jazz and blues. ▨*3701 Mt. Vernon Ave., AlexandriaVA* ☏*703/549–7500* ⊕*www.birchmere.com.*

★ **Black Cat.** Come here to see the latest local bands as well as indie stars such as Neko Case, Modest Mouse, and Clinic. Dave Grohl, lead singer of the Foo Fighters and formerly of Nirvana, owns a stake in the club. The post-punk crowd whiles away the time in the Red Room, a side bar with pool tables, an eclectic jukebox, and no cover charge. The club also is home to Food for Thought, a vegetarian café. ▨*1811 14th St. NW, U Street corridor* ☏*202/*

667–7960 ⊕ *www.blackcatdc.com*
Ⓜ *U Street/Cardozo.*

Blues Alley. Head here for a classy evening in an intimate setting, complete with great music and outstanding New Orleans–style grub. The cover charge is typically $25 for well-known performers such as Moses Allison, and more for top acts like Wynton Marsalis. There is also a $10 food or drink minimum. ■TIP➔ You can come for just the show, but those who enjoy a meal get better seats. ✉ *1073 Wisconsin Ave. NW, near M St., Georgetown* ☎ *202/337–4141* Ⓜ *Foggy Bottom.*

PERFORMANCE VENUES

FodorśChoice **John F. Kennedy Center for the Performing Arts.** On the bank of the Potomac
★ River, the gem of the DC arts scene is home to the National Symphony Orchestra, the Washington Ballet, and the Washington National Opera. The best out-of-town acts perform at one of three performance spaces— the Concert Hall, the Opera House, or the Eisenhower Theater. Eclectic performers can be found at the Center's smaller venues, including the Terrace Theater, showcasing chamber groups and experimental works; the Theater Lab, home to cabaret-style performances like the audience-participation hit Sheer Madness; the KC Jazz Club; and a 320-seat family theater. But that's not all. On the Millennium Stage in the center's Grand Foyer you can catch free performances almost any day at 6 PM. ■TIP➔ On performance days, a free shuttle bus runs between the Center and the Foggy Bottom/GWU Metro stop. ✉ *New Hampshire Ave. at Rock Creek Pkwy. NW, Foggy Bottom* ☎ *202/467–4600 or 800/444–1324* ⊕ *www.kennedy-center.org* Ⓜ *Foggy Bottom/GWU.*

THEATER

Arena Stage. The first regional theater company to win a Tony Award, Arena Stage performs mainly American theater, reviving some classic plays and showcasing the country's best new writers. While its waterfront location undergoes renovation, Arena Stage will hold its performances in Crystal City at the Crystal Forum. ✉ *1800 S. Bell St., Crystal City* ☎ *202/488–3300* Ⓜ *Crystal City.*

★ **Shakespeare Theatre.** This acclaimed troupe crafts fantastically staged and acted performances of works by Shakespeare and his contemporaries. For two weeks in late spring they perform Shakespeare for free at Carter Barron Amphitheatre. ✉ *450 7th St. NW, Downtown* ☎ *202/547–1122* Ⓜ *Gallery Pl./Chinatown or Archives/Navy Memorial.*

★ **Woolly Mammoth.** Unusual avant-garde shows with edgy staging and solid acting have earned Woolly Mammoth top reviews and favorable comparisons to Chicago's Steppenwolf. The troupe's talent is accentuated by its modern, 265-seat theater in Penn Quarter near the MCI Center. ⊠ *641 D St. NW, Downtown* ☎*202/393–3939* Ⓜ *Gallery Pl./ Chinatown or Archives/Navy Memorial.*

SPORTS & THE OUTDOORS

Washington's 69 square miles are in part a fantastic recreational backyard, with dozens of beautiful open spaces. Rock Creek Park has miles of wooded trails and paths for bikers, runners, and walkers that extend to almost every part of the city. The National Mall connects the Lincoln Memorial and the Capitol building. With the monuments as a backdrop, you can spike a volleyball, ride a bike, or take a jog. Into watching more than doing? Washington's myriad professional sports teams will sate your hunger for top-level competition no matter what your favorite game.

BOATING & SAILING

Surrounded by the beloved cherry trees and overlooked by the Jefferson Memorial, the **Tidal Basin** is a scenic spot for paddleboating.Canoeing, sailing, and powerboating are all popular on the **Potomac River** north and south of the city. You can dip your oars just about anywhere along the river—go canoeing in the C&O Canal, sailing in the widening river south of Alexandria, or even kayaking in the raging rapids at Great Falls, a 30-minute drive from the capital.

RENTALS

A few miles east of Glen Echo Park in Georgetown, **Fletcher's Cove** (⊠ *4940 Canal Rd., at Reservoir Rd., Foxhall* ☎*202/244–0461*) rents rowboats, canoes, and bicycles and sells tackle, snack foods, and DC fishing licenses. Here you can catch shad, perch, catfish, striped bass, and other freshwater species. Canoeing is allowed in the canal and, weather permitting, in the Potomac. Bicycles are for rent here; the C&O Canal path connects to Virginia bike paths via Key Bridge. There's a large picnic area along the riverbank.

Thompson's Boat Center (⊠ *2900 Virginia Ave. NW, Foggy Bottom* ☎*202/333–4861* Ⓜ *Foggy Bottom*) is near Georgetown and Theodore Roosevelt Island. The center rents canoes for $8 per hour and $22 per day. Single kayaks are $8 per hour and $24 per day, and double kayaks are $10 per hour and $30 per day.

Tidal Basin (⊠ *Bordered by Independence Ave. and Maine Ave., The Mall* ☎*202/479–2426* Ⓜ *Farragut West*) rents paddleboats beginning in April and usually ending in September, depending on how cold the water gets. The entrance is at 1501 Maine Avenue SW, on the east side of the Tidal Basin. You can rent two-passenger boats at $8 per hour and four-passenger boats at $16 per hour.

ICE-SKATING

Fodor'sChoice   The **National Gallery of Art Ice Rink** (⊠ *Constitution Ave. NW, between*
★   *7th and 9th Sts., Downtown* ☎ *202/289–3361* Ⓜ *Navy Memorial/
Archives*) is surrounded by the gallery's Sculpture Garden. The art deco
design of the rink makes it one of the most popular outdoor winter sites
in Washington. In spring the rink becomes a fountain.

PROFESSIONAL SPORTS

DC United (⊠ *Robert F. Kennedy Stadium, 2400 E. Capitol St. SE, Capi-
tol Hill* ☎ *202/547–3134* Ⓜ *Stadium*) is one of the best Major League
Soccer (U.S. pro soccer) teams. International matches, including some
World Cup preliminaries, are often played on RFK Stadium's grass field.
Games are April through September.

One of pro hockey's better teams, the **Washington Capitals** (⊠ *Verizon
Center, 6th and F Sts., Downtown* ☎ *202/432–7328* Ⓜ *Gallery Pl./
Chinatown*), playz home games October through April.

The WNBA's **Washington Mystics** (⊠ *Verizon Center, 6th and F Sts.,
Downtown* ☎ *202/432–7328* Ⓜ *Gallery Pl./Chinatown*) perennially
lead the WNBA in attendance, despite a losing record. The games,
which run from late May to August, are loud, boisterous events.

Major League Baseball has returned to DC, where the **Washington
Nationals** (⊠ *Potomac and 1st Sts. SW* ☎ *202/675–6287* Ⓜ *Navy Yard*)
of the National League play in their spectacular home, Nationals Park.
■ TIP➜ The Metro is a hassle-free and inexpensive way to get to the ball
park. The closest and most convenient stop is the Navy Yard on the Green
Line.

The **Washington Redskins** (☎ *301/276–6000 FedEx Field stadium*) have
the largest football stadium in the NFL, but all 80,000 seats are held
by season-ticket holders. Occasionally you can find tickets advertised
in the classifieds of the *Washington Post* or buy them from online ticket
vendors and auction sites—at top dollar, of course. ■ TIP➜ Fans can see
the players up close and for free at training camp, held in August.

The NBA's **Washington Wizards** (⊠ *Verizon Center, 6th and F Sts., Downtown* ☎ *202/432–7328* Ⓜ *Gallery Pl./Chinatown*) play from October
to April.

RUNNING & BIKING

The numerous cycling trails in the District and its surrounding areas
are well maintained and clearly marked. Running is one of the best
ways to see the city. It can be dangerous to run at night on the trails,
although the streets are fairly well lighted. Even in daylight, it's best to
run in pairs when venturing beyond public areas or heavily used sections of trails.

The 89-mi-long **C&O Canal Towpath** is mostly gravel and dirt, making it
easy on knees and feet.

★ The most popular running and cycling route in Washington is the 4.5-mi loop on the **Mall** around the Capitol and past the Smithsonian museums and the major monuments.

Rock Creek Park has 15 mi of trails, a bicycle path, a bridle path, picnic groves, playgrounds, and the boulder-strewn rolling stream that gives it its name. Starting one block south of the corner of P and 22nd streets on the edge of Georgetown, Rock Creek Park runs all the way to Montgomery County, Maryland. The roadway is closed to traffic on weekends.

RENTALS & TOURS

Thompson's Boat Center (⊠ *2900 Virginia Ave. NW, Foggy Bottom* ☎ *202/333–4861* Ⓜ *Foggy Bottom*) allows easy access to the Rock Creek Trail and the C&O Towpath and is close to the monuments. All-terrain bikes are $8 per hour and $25 per day. Fixed-gear and children's bikes are $8 per hour and $15 per day. Children's trailers (attachments to adult bikes) rent for $4 per hour or $15 per day.

SHOPPING

African masks; kitchenware as objets d'art; bargains on Christian Dior, Hugo Boss, and Burberry; paisley scarves from India; American and European antiques; books of every description; handicrafts from almost two dozen Native American tribes; busts of U.S. presidents; textiles by the armful; fine leather goods—all this and more can be found in the nation's capital. **Georgetown** is not on a subway line and parking is difficult at best, but people still flock here for tony antiques, elegant crafts, and high-style shoe and clothing boutiques, along with national chains. **Dupont Circle,** a younger, less staid version of Georgetown, has many art galleries, offbeat shops, and specialty book and record stores that give it a cosmopolitan air. Northeast of Dupont, **U Street,** once known for its classy theaters and jazz clubs and then its decline, has been revitalized with a string of chic clothing stores and home-wares shops. As the **Capitol Hill** area has become gentrified, unique shops and boutiques have sprung up, many clustered around the redbrick **Eastern Market,** where a weekend flea market presents nostalgia and local crafts by the crateful. And don't forget the **museum shops**—especially at the National Gallery of Art, the National Museum of the American Indian, the National Building Museum, and the National Museum of Natural History—where you can pick up unique items like prints of masterpiece paintings, models of dinosaur skeletons, and period jewelry.

CAPITOL HILL/EASTERN MARKET

MARKET

★ **Eastern Market.** Vibrantly colored produce and flowers; quality meat, poultry, and fish; and fragrant cheeses are sold by independent vendors at this 134-year-old landmark. On weekends a flea market and an arts-and-crafts market add to the fun. The redbrick building was gutted by fire in April 2007, but the restoration is scheduled for completion by the end of 2009. In the interim, a temporary structure across the street houses vendors. ✉ *306 7th St. SE, Capitol Hill* ⊕ *www.easternmarketdc. com* ⊙ *Closed Mon.* Ⓜ *Eastern Market.*

DUPONT CIRCLE

ART GALLERIES

Hemphill Fine Arts. This spacious gem of a gallery shows established artists such as Jacob Kainen and William Christenberry as well as emerging artists, including Colby Caldwell. ✉ *1515 14th St. NW, 3rd fl., Logan Circle* ☎ *202/234–5601* ⊙ *Closed Sun. and Mon.* Ⓜ *Dupont Circle.*

BOOKS

★ **Kramerbooks & Afterwords.** One of Washington's best-loved independents, this cozy shop has a small but choice selection of fiction and nonfiction. Open 24 hours on weekends, Kramerbooks shares space with a café that has late-night dining and weekend entertainment. ✉ *1517 Connecticut Ave. NW, Dupont Circle* ☎ *202/387–1400* Ⓜ *Dupont Circle.*

HOME FURNISHINGS

Dragonfly. Dragonfly's expert owner hand-selects antiques on her trips to Asia. Finds from eight provinces in China, Vietnam, and Mongolia fill this inviting shop. ✉ *1457 Church St. NW<* ☎ *202/265–3359* ⊕ *www. dragonflydd.com* ⊙ *Closed Mon. and Tues.* Ⓜ *Dupont.*

WOMEN'S CLOTHING

Betsy Fisher. Catering to women of all ages and sizes in search of contemporary and trendy styles, this store stocks one-of-a-kind accessories, clothes, shoes, and jewelry by well-known designers like Diane Von Furstenberg. A small selection of up-and-coming local designs is also available. ✉ *1224 Connecticut Ave. NW, Dupont Circle* ☎ *202/785–1975* ⊕ *www.betsyfisher.com* Ⓜ *Dupont Circle.*

GEORGETOWN

ANTIQUES & COLLECTIBLES

Jean Pierre Antiques. Very Georgetown, this gorgeous shop sells antique furniture from France, Germany, and Italy. ✉ *2601 P St. NW, Georgetown* ☎ *202/337–1731* Ⓜ *Dupont Circle.*

Old Print Gallery. Here you'll find the capital's largest collection of old prints, with a focus on maps and 19th-century decorative prints (including Washingtoniana). ✉ *1220 31st St. NW, Georgetown* ☎ *202/965–1818* ⊙ *Closed Sun.* Ⓜ *Foggy Bottom/GWU.*

HOME FURNISHINGS

A Mano. The store's name is Italian for "by hand," and it lives up to its name, stocking colorful hand-painted ceramics, hand-dyed tablecloths, blown glass stemware, and other home and garden accessories by Italian and French artisans. ✉ *1677 Wisconsin Ave. NW, Georgetown* ☎ *202/298–7200.*

SHOES

★ **Sassanova.** There are high-end shoes in this girly shop for every occasion—be it a walk on the beach or through a boardroom. Brands carried include Lulu Guinness, Emma Hope, and Sigerson Morrison. Jewelry, bags, and shoes for kids round out the selection. ✉ *1641 Wisconsin Ave. NW, Georgetown* ☎ *202/471–4400* ⊕ *www.sassanova.com.*

SPAS & BEAUTY SALONS

Blue Mercury. Hard-to-find skin-care lines—Laura Mercier, Eve Lom, and Paula Dorf are just a few—are what set this small national chain apart. At the "skin gym" you can treat yourself to facials, waxing, massage, and oxygen treatments. ✉ *3059 M St. NW, Georgetown* ☎ *202/965–1300* Ⓜ *Foggy Bottom/GWU.*

WOMEN'S CLOTHING

Urban Chic. Gorgeous suits, jeans, cocktail dresses, and accessories from designers like Catherine Malandrino, Paul & Joe, Ella Moss, Rebecca Taylor, and Susana Monaco can be had for a price at this fashionista hangout. The handbags are a highlight. ✉ *1626 Wisconsin Ave. NW, Georgetown* ☎ *202/338–5398* .

U STREET

ANTIQUES & COLLECTIBLES

Good Wood. This friendly shop sells vintage and antique wood furniture, including wonderful 19th-century American pieces, along with stained glass and other decorative items. ✉ *1428 U St. NW, U Street corridor* ☎ *202/986–3640* ⊘ *Closed Mon.–Wed.* Ⓜ *U Street/Cardozo.*

HOME FURNISHINGS

Muléh. You'll find exquisite contemporary Balinese and Filipino home furnishings and trendy clothes from LA and New York at this expansive showroom. ✉ *1831 14th St. NW, U Street corridor* ☎ *202/667–3440* ⊘ *Closed Mon.* Ⓜ *U Street/Cardozo.*

WOMEN'S CLOTHING

Nana. The hip, friendly staff here is one of the reasons DC women love this store, which stocks both new and vintage women's clothes at affordable prices. You'll also find handmade jewelry and cool handbags. ✉ *1528 U St. NW, Upstairs, U Street corridor* ☎ *202/667–6955* Ⓜ *U Street/Cardozo.*

Northern Virginia & D.C.'s Maryland Suburbs

WORD OF MOUTH

"There are lots of nice shops and restaurants in Old Town Alexandria and it makes for pleasant strolling in the evening."

—longhorn55

"Don't forget Arlington National Cemetery . . . the changing of the guard is not to be missed."

—Lmaev

Updated
by Amy
McKeever

ALTHOUGH DC GETS ALL THE recognition for its place in the nation's history, visitors to the region might be surprised by the richness of Northern Virginia and the Maryland suburbs. These border regions—which each originally contributed the land to create DC—are chockablock with historical references and diverse cultural experiences. Some of the greatest presidents used DC's neighbors both for their own plantation homes or to build experimental cooperative communities under the New Deal. An influx of immigration has also brought an exciting variety of cuisines to both regions to satisfy anyone's palate.

Traffic between the District and Northern Virginia and the Maryland suburbs goes both ways (each way slowly). Nearby areas have grown significantly in the recent past and have modern housing, government, and office buildings. Tysons Corner in Fairfax County has major retail outlets clustered close to the I–495 Beltway and has office buildings sprawling across 25.8 million square feet. The area employs about 128,000 people, many of them commuters. Expansion toward Dulles International Airport has been particularly massive, especially along the toll road to the airport. Federal agencies that maintain offices in Maryland include the National Institutes of Health, the Internal Revenue Service, and the National Aeronautics and Space Administration. Because of their proximity to DC, many residents consider themselves Washingtonians, though some Washingtonians think otherwise.

ORIENTATION & PLANNING

GETTING ORIENTED

Enveloping the nation's capital are two regions equally steeped in early American history. Although Northern Virginia and DC's Maryland suburbs are now home to mainly federal employees, past residents have included George Washington and Robert E. Lee. These are ideal regions in which to learn about Colonial and Civil War–era America and enjoy the diversity of a region that continues to attract immigrants from around the world.

Alexandria. Among the northernmost cities in Virginia, Alexandria was once part of the District of Columbia and now shares its border. Buildings in Alexandria's old downtown, referred to often as "Old Town," are reminiscent of the Federal period (1780–1830). Alexandria was a thriving Colonial port, and these days Old Town is also a bustling nightspot with a variety of ethnic restaurants and dozens of pubs.

Arlington. Slightly to the west of Alexandria and also along the DC border lies Arlington. Home to Arlington National Cemetery, the Pentagon, and the Marine and Air Force memorials, Arlington is to military history what Alexandria is to Colonial history.

Mount Vernon, Woodlawn & Gunston Hall. These three estates on the shores of the Potomac were home to some of the most important figures in Colonial America. George Washington resided at Mount Vernon

TOP REASONS TO GO

■ **Take a moment to reflect at Arlington National Cemetery:** See Arlington House and its Washington view; learn about prominent early Virginia families: Washington, Custis, Randolph, and Lee. Visit the Tomb of the Unknowns, the Kennedy graves, and those of other famous Americans, all within these sacred grounds.

■ **Get to know the first president at Mount Vernon:** Visit the historic plantation and learn about George Washington's many contributions as a farmer, patriot, general, and president. See his threshing barn, gristmill, distillery, and personal artifacts, and experience the new interactive displays.

■ **Return to the first shot of the Civil War:** Explore the site of the first Civil War battle at Manassas National Battlefield Park in the peaceful Virginia countryside. A second Battle of Manassas lasted three days and resulted in 3,300 killed. (The Confederacy won both battles.)

■ **Wonder at the views in Great Falls and C&O Canal parks:** Visit the scenic fall line of the Potomac River, a barrier to upriver navigation that necessitated settlements at Georgetown and Alexandria and the Patowmack Canal, remnants of which are in the park, and later the C&O Canal. Or cross over to the Maryland side of the Potomac and climb the Billy Goat Trail in the C&O Canal National Historical Park.

plantation. He gave his step-granddaughter a portion of the land, upon which she and her husband constructed Woodlawn. Another Revolutionary figure, George Mason, lived at Gunston Hall, where he developed a strong philosophy that heavily influenced the Bill of Rights.

Fairfax County. Moving even farther south and into the heart of Northern Virginia, Fairfax County is one of the most rapidly developing counties in the region, with office buildings and upscale shopping overtaking the Tysons Corner area. However, Northern Virginia's rural roots have been preserved in Manassas, where the Manassas National Battlefield Park honors the soldiers of two major Civil War battles, and at Great Falls Park, an ideal site for hiking and boating.

Loudoun County. Farthest away and to the west of DC, visitors can find the capital of Virginia's horse country. Loudoun County plays host to various fox hunts and steeplechases each year. It is also the home of a burgeoning Virginia wine industry.

Montgomery County. The large swath of land across the northwest border with DC is Maryland's Montgomery County. Bethesda and Silver Spring, two of DC's most popular suburban cities, are in Montgomery County. There's also plenty for those who love the outdoors, including Glen Echo Park and the C&O Canal National Historical Park.

Prince George's County. East of Montgomery County, also bordering the District, is Prince George's County, best known for being home to the University of Maryland Terrapins. But it also had an important role in America's aviation history, as it boasts the oldest continuously operating airfield. Fort Washington Park and the Merkle Wildlife Sanctuary provide a shady relief from the urban sprawl.

PLANNING

WHEN TO GO

Washington, DC, was built on a swamp, so expect muggy weather if visiting in the summer months. Winter usually doesn't get extremely cold, but spring and fall are the best bets for a trip. Expect large crowds at Arlington Cemetery around holidays such as Veterans Day and Memorial Day. Major events in DC such as the Cherry Blossom Festival in March and April do affect hotel prices and crowds in these areas.

In December the **Historic Alexandria Candlelight Tour** (☎ *703/838–4242* ⊕ *www.oha.alexandriava.gov*) is a one-night visit to historic houses for light refreshment and performances of period music of the holiday season. Over Presidents Weekend in February, **George Washington's Birthday** (☎ *703/549–7662* ⊕ *www.washingtonbirthday.net*) is celebrated in Alexandria, Virginia, with a parade—175 floats and marching units— and a reenactment of a Revolutionary War skirmish at Fort Ward nearby. **Virginia Gold Cup** (☎ *540/347–2612* ⊕ *www.vagoldcup.com*) steeplechase horse races, held in May near Middleburg in Northern Virginia, have been among the most prominent social and sporting events of the state since the 1920s. Every May, Andrews Air Force Base plays host to the **Joint Services Open House & Air Show** (☎ *301/981–4424* ⊕ *www.jsoh.org*). It's the largest military open house in the United States, complete with demonstrations and an impressive air show. The first Saturday of October, Bethesda restaurants sell samples of their fare at the food festival, **Taste of Bethesda** (☎ *301/215–6660* ⊕ *www.bethesda.org*).

GETTING HERE & AROUND

BY AIR   Three major airports serve both suburban Maryland and the Washington, DC, area. Baltimore-Washington International (BWI) Airport, 10 mi south of Baltimore off I–95 and Route 295, is closer to Montgomery and Prince George's counties than Ronald Reagan National Airport or Washington Dulles International Airport. Alexandria is only a few miles from Ronald Reagan Washington National Airport.

BY CAR   An automobile is a must to travel throughout the counties, but avoid the Capital Beltway (I–495) during morning and afternoon rush hours. At those times the congestion is second only to that of Los Angeles.

The Capital Beltway, I–495, circles the District of Columbia through Virginia and Maryland (and enters the District very briefly, as it crosses the Wilson Bridge), providing a circular bypass for I–95 around Washington. During commute hours it becomes congested—toward Tysons Corner in the morning, and away in the evening—so if you plan to spend most of your time in downtown Washington or within the Beltway, it would be prudent to select lodging north of the I–95/I–495 interchange. Note that HOV restrictions prohibit single-person vehicles on I–66 inside the Beltway eastbound during morning rush hour and westbound during evening rush hour.

2

Roads that run through the region and into downtown Washington include Wisconsin, Connecticut, Georgia, New Hampshire, and Pennsylvania avenues; Routes 1 and 50 (the latter turns into New York Avenue upon entering the District); Baltimore Washington Parkway; and I–295, all of which get busy 7:30–9 AM and 5–6:30 PM. Giving parking tickets is one of the things capital-area jurisdictions do best, so if you park at meters, be careful and keep the meter fed. Also read parking signs carefully. There are many variations, and they are often quite confusing.

The outer loop in Maryland around the intersection with I–270 is congested in the morning rush, as is the inner loop in the evening rush. Interstate 270, which intersects with I–495 in Montgomery County, reaches destinations north of Rockville in Montgomery County. The Custis Memorial Parkway, I–66, runs east–west between Washington, DC, and I–81 near Front Royal, which takes you south through the Shenandoah or north to West Virginia.

BY METRO   Washington Metropolitan Area Transit Authority (WMATA) provides subway service (Metrorail) in the District and in the Maryland and Virginia suburbs. The Orange, Blue, and Yellow lines serve Northern Virginia. Maryland's Montgomery County is served by the system's busiest route, the Red Line, and Prince George's County is served by the Blue, Orange, and Green lines. It begins operation at 5 AM on weekdays and 7 AM on weekends and closes on weekdays at midnight and weekends at 3 AM. During the weekday peak periods (5–9:30 AM and 3–7 PM), trains come along every three to six minutes. At other times trains run about every 12–15 minutes.

The Metro's base fare is $1.65; the actual price you pay depends on the time of day and the distance traveled. Up to two children under age five ride free with a paying passenger. Buy your ticket at the Farecard machines, some of which accept credit cards. One-day passes are $7.80 and seven-day passes are $39. ■TIP➡ **Make sure you hang on to your Farecard—you need it to exit at your destination.** Locals use the SmarTrip card, a plastic card that can hold any fare amount and can be used throughout the subway system. Buy passes or SmarTrip cards at the Metro Center sales office.

BY TAXI   Taxicabs are free to operate in adjoining jurisdictions and this is vital, considering that there are two states plus the District and several counties and cities in a small area. Virginia and Maryland taxis are metered with rates set by the jurisdiction (about $4 to board and plus 40¢ for each quarter mile in Maryland and a $2.75 flag fare with 30¢ for every sixth of a mile in Virginia). Taxis are usually waiting near the busier Metrorail stations like Ballston, King Street, and Rosslyn, and the bigger hotels.

Taxis at the Virginia airports are very tightly regulated. Washington Flyer cabs serve Dulles International Airport exclusively from the airport but any taxi can deliver there. A starter outside the arrivals area at Reagan National loads taxicabs from a regulated line of incoming taxis and will provide a fare sheet if desired. An airport fee of $1.75

Northern Virginia & DC's Maryland Suburbs

is added to your fare to pay for this service. Some taxi drivers accept credit cards, but ask first.

BY TRAIN Amtrak serves the region with six trains to Alexandria and one to Manassas in each direction daily. Amtrak's Autotrain terminal is in Lorton, between Springfield and Woodbridge and just off I-95. The Alexandria station is colocated with a major bus hub and a Metrorail station. Virginia Railway Express (VRE) provides cheap workday service between Union Station in Washington, DC, and Fredericksburg and Manassas, with 17 stops, including all Amtrak stations along the route. VRE offers discounted multiride, five-day, monthly, and senior ticket fares. Free parking is available at most suburban VRE stations.

Amtrak has scheduled stops in New Carrollton and at BWI Airport as part of its East Coast service. The MARC commuter train has two lines that go through Montgomery and Prince George's counties, and it also goes into Washington's Union Station.

ESSENTIALS

Air Contacts SuperShuttle (☎ 800/258-3826 or 202/296-6662 ⊕ www.super shuttle.com). **Washington Flyer** (☎ 888/927-4359 ⊕ www.washfly.com).

Metro Information Metrorail (☎ 202/637-7000 ⊕ www.wmata.com).

Train Contacts Maryland Rail Commuter Service (☎ *410/539-5000, 410/539-3497 TTY, 866/743-3682* ⊕ *www.mtamaryland.com*). **Maryland Transportation Authority (for Penn Line)** (☎ *410/539-5000 or 866/743-3682* ⊕ *www.mtamaryland.com*). **Virginia Railway Express** (*VRE* ☎ *800/743-3873* ⊕ *www.vre.org*).

DISCOUNTS & DEALS

Purchase either the Market Square or Tricorn pass from the Alexandria Visitors Center for discounted admission to three museums in the historic Old Town ($9). Both passes include admission to Carlyle House Historic Park and Gadsby's Tavern Museum, but the Market Square pass also includes the Stabler-Leadbeater Apothecary Museum, while the Tricorn pass includes the Lee-Fendall House Museum & Garden instead. Note that these passes are only a deal if used for all three museums.

ABOUT THE RESTAURANTS

There is no need to go into the District to find a decent restaurant. Alexandria and Arlington have a wide variety of ethnic and American restaurants at reasonable prices. Alexandria has several good restaurants near the river on and around King Street, but parking is tough and the Metrorail station is far away. In Arlington there is a good variety of dining between the neighborhoods of Ballston and Rosslyn around five closely spaced Metrorail stations. The Shirlington area, just off Shirley Highway south of the Pentagon and with loads of free parking, has become a convenient and reasonable dining destination for both Arlington and Alexandria. Many Washington restaurants have opened Bethesda branches, and alfresco dining is available during good weather at most places. Bethesda's largest concentration of restaurants (about 75) is within the Woodmont Triangle, bounded by Old Georgetown Road, Wisconsin Avenue, and Rugby Avenue.

ABOUT THE HOTELS

It's best to book your hotel room in advance. Occupancy rates are high, and you're likely to pay only a little less than you would in Washington. Tourists coming to see Washington's cherry blossoms make spring the busiest season. December and January tend to be the slowest and least expensive months, except around a presidential inauguration.

Lodging choices range from familiar hotel chains to homes with 18th-century architecture blended with modern amenities. **Alexandria & Arlington Bed and Breakfast Network** (✉ *4938 Hampden La., Suite 164, Bethesda* ☎ *703/549–3415 or 888/549–3415* ⊕ *www.aabbn.com*) can arrange accommodations in Northern Virginia.

WHAT IT COSTS					
	¢	$	$$	$$$	$$$$
Restaurants	under $10	$10–$16	$17–$23	$24–$30	over $30
Hotels	under $100	$100–$160	$161–$230	$231–$300	over $300

Restaurant prices are per person for a main course at dinner. Hotel prices are for a standard double room, excluding state and local taxes.

PLANNING YOUR TIME

You'll want to devote most of your time to the areas closest to Washington, DC, such as Arlington, Alexandria, Bethesda, and Silver Spring. These are easily connected to one another via Metrorail and Metrobus. It wouldn't be unusual to spend the day visiting Arlington's monuments to the military, yet end the day with a seafood dinner in Silver Spring. Allow about an hour for travel across the District of Columbia via Metrorail, however, especially on weekends or during non–rush hours. Another quick trip from Virginia to Maryland is to ride the ferry across the Potomac River from either Mount Vernon or Alexandria to stroll the National Harbor in Maryland. These trips take 50 and 20 minutes, respectively. On the other side of the District, there is also an automobile ferry—White's Ferry—that connects Loudoun and Montgomery counties. For all other vehicular crossings, the Capital Beltway traverses the Potomac as well, via the American Legion and Woodrow Wilson bridges. The former connects Virginia's Fairfax County to Maryland's Montgomery County, while the Woodrow Wilson Bridge connects Alexandria to Prince George's County, Maryland.

If you have more time, drive away from the capital towards Manassas, Middleburg, Occoquan, Kensington, or Glen Echo. Plan to spend at least half a day or more in each outlying town. Enjoy the slower pace of life and go wine tasting, antique shopping, or picnicking in the many parks.

EXPLORING NORTHERN VIRGINIA & SUBURBAN MARYLAND

Northern Virginia is generally defined as the area close to and south and west of the Potomac River, including Arlington and Alexandria, Fairfax County, Loudoun County, and Prince William County, to the south. Most attractions, restaurants, and shops in Montgomery County are clustered "down-county" in areas closest to DC. In Prince George's County, places to explore are sprinkled throughout the area.

ALEXANDRIA

A lively mix of historic homes, taverns, restaurants, and shops, Alexandria seems to exist in two or three centuries at once. Founded in 1749 by Scottish merchants eager to capitalize on the booming tobacco trade, Alexandria first emerged as one of the most important ports in Colonial America. The city dwarfed Georgetown—Washington's oldest neighborhood—in the days before the Revolution, and through the Civil War had one of the country's largest slave markets. Alexandria is linked to many significant events and personages of the Colonial, Revolutionary, and Civil War periods. Members of the Lee family of Revolutionary and Civil War fame lived here, and George Washington had a town house and attended church here, though he lived a few miles south in Mount Vernon.

For many African-Americans fleeing slavery, part of their journey on the Underground Railroad included a stop in Alexandria. This was true of one of the largest and most celebrated slave escapes, in which 77 individuals, many of whom labored in homes in Alexandria, took refuge on the *Pearl,* a ship bound for New Jersey, which left from Washington's 7th Street Wharf in April 1848. Unfortunately the ship was captured in Maryland and most of its passengers were returned to Bruin's Slave Jail. Harriett Beecher Stowe modeled her account of the slave trade in *Uncle Tom's Cabin* on this establishment.

This vibrant past remains alive in the historic district of **Old Town Alexandria**—an area of cobbled streets, restored 18th- and 19th-century homes, churches, and taverns close to the water. The main arteries of this district are Washington Street (the G.W. Parkway as it passes through town) and King Street. Most points of interest are on the east (Potomac) side of Washington Street.

GETTING HERE & AROUND
Alexandria is only a few miles from Ronald Reagan Washington National Airport. It's easy to get there by Metrorail, taxi, water taxi, or Metrobus. Visit the Old Town sights on foot if you're prepared to walk 20 blocks or so; parking is usually scarce, especially close to the river, and the parking police seem to catch every violation (especially in alleys). ■ TIP→ **The visitor center at Ramsay House will give you a 24-hour permit for free parking at any two-hour metered spot.**

TOURS Old Town Experience runs walking tours that leave from the Ramsay House Visitors Center 10:30 AM Monday through Saturday and 2 PM Sunday; tickets are $15. Another tour operator, Footsteps to the Past, also leads tours from the visitor center at 11:30 AM and 1:30 PM Monday through Saturday and 10:30 AM on Sunday; tickets are $10. Alexandria Colonial Tours leads guided walking tours of historic Alexandria by reservation. Ghost-and-graveyard tours (reservations not required) are conducted Friday, Saturday, and Sunday nights, although in summer you can also take a tour on Wednesday and Thursday nights.

TIMING & PRECAUTIONS
As with anywhere in the DC area, beware main roads at rush hour, from 7:30 AM to 9 AM and 5 PM to 6:30 PM. King and Duke streets in Alexandria will be tough to navigate in those hours, and the Metro will be crowded. The Woodrow Wilson Bridge is also notorious for delays at this hour.

ESSENTIALS
Taxi **Alexandria Yellow Cab** (☎ *703/548–7505*).

Tours **Alexandria Colonial Tours** (☎ *703/519–1749*).**The Old Town Experience** (☎ *703/836–0694*). **Footsteps to the Past** (☎ *703/683–3451*).

Train Contacts **Alexandria Amtrak station** (✉ *110 Callahan Dr.* ☎ *703/836–4339*).

Visitor Information **Alexandria Convention and Visitors Association** (✉ *Ramsay House, 221 King St. Alexandria* ☎ *703/838–4200 or 800/388–9119* ⊕ *www.visitalexandria.com*).

Numbers in the text correspond to numbers in the margin and on the Alexandria map.

MAIN ATTRACTIONS

Appomattox Confederate Statue. In 1861, when Alexandria was occupied by Union forces, the 800 soldiers of the city's garrison marched out of town to join the Confederate Army. In the middle of Washington and Prince streets stands a statue marking the point where they assembled. In 1885 Confederate veterans proposed a memorial to honor their fallen comrades. This statue, based on John A. Elder's painting *Appomattox*, is of a lone soldier glumly surveying the battlefields after General Robert E. Lee's surrender. The names of 99 Alexandria Confederate dead are carved on the base. ⊠ *Washington and Prince Sts., Old Town.*

⑩ Boyhood Home of Robert E. Lee. The childhood home in Alexandria of the commander of the Confederate forces of Virginia is a fine example of a 19th-century Federal town house. The house is privately owned and not open to visitors. ⊠ *607 Oronoco St., Old Town.*

❼ Carlyle House. Alexandria forefather and Scottish merchant John Carlyle built a grand house here, completed in 1753 and modeled on a country manor house in the old country. Students of the French and Indian War will want to know that the dwelling served as General Braddock's headquarters. The house retains its original 18th-century woodwork and is furnished with Chippendale furniture and Chinese porcelain. An architectural exhibit on the second floor explains how the house was built; outside there's an attractive garden of Colonial-era plants. ⊠ *121 N. Fairfax St., Old Town* ☎ *703/549–2997* ⊕ *www.carlylehouse.org* ☞ *$4* ⊙ *Tues.–Sat. 10–4, Sun. noon–4, guided tour every ½ hr.*

⑬ Christ Church. Both Washington and Robert E. Lee were pewholders in this Episcopal church, which remains in nearly original condition. (Washington paid quite a lot of money for Pews 59 and 60.) Built in 1773, this fine example of an English Georgian country-style church has a Palladian window, an interior balcony, and an English wrought-brass-and-crystal chandelier. Docents give tours during visiting hours. ⊠ *118 N. Washington St., Old Town* ☎ *703/549–1450* ⊕ *www.historicchristchurch.org* ☞ *$5 donation suggested* ⊙ *Mon.–Sat. 9–4, Sun. 2–4.*

❽ Gadsby's Tavern Museum. The two buildings that now comprise this
☾ museum—a circa-1785 tavern and the 1792 City Hotel—were centers
★ of political and social life. George Washington celebrated his birthdays in the ballroom. Other noted patrons included Thomas Jefferson, John Adams, and the Marquis de Lafayette. The taproom, dining room, assembly room, ballroom, and communal bedrooms have been restored to their original appearance. The tours on Friday evenings are led by a costumed guide carrying a lantern. ⊠ *134 N. Royal St., Old Town* ☎ *703/838–4242* ⊕ *www.gadsbystavern.org* ☞ *$4, lantern tour $5* ⊙ *Nov.–Mar., Wed.–Sat. 11–4, Sun. 1–4, last tour at 3:45; Apr.–Oct., Tues.–Sat. 10–5, Sun. and Mon. 1–5, last tour at 4:45; tours 15 mins before and after the hour. Half-hour lantern tours Mar.–Nov., Fri. 7–9:30.*

2

⑯ **George Washington Masonic National Memorial.** Because Alexandria, like
★ Washington, DC, has no really tall buildings, the spire of this memorial dominates the surroundings and is visible for miles. The building overlooks King and Duke streets, Alexandria's major east–west arteries. It's a respectable uphill climb from the King St. Metrorail and bus stations. From the ninth-floor observation deck (reached by elevator) you get a spectacular view of Alexandria and Washington, DC, but access above the first and mezzanine floors is by guided tour only. The building contains furnishings from the first Masonic lodge in Alexandria. George Washington became a Mason in 1752 in Fredericksburg, and became Charter Master of the Alexandria lodge when it was chartered in 1788, remaining active in Masonic affairs during his tenure as president, 1789–97. ☒ *101 Callahan Dr., Old Town* ☎ *703/683–2007* ⊕ *www.gwmemorial.org* ▧ *Free* ☉ *Daily 9–4; 1-hr guided tour of building and observation deck daily at 10, 11:30, 1:30, and 3.*

❾ **Lee-Fendall House.** At historic Lee Corner at North Washington and Oronoco streets, the Lee-Fendall House was built in 1785; over the course of the next 118 years it was home to 37 members of the Lee family and served as a Union hospital. The house and its furnishings, of the 1850–70 period, present an intimate study of 19th-century family life. Highlights include a splendid collection of Lee heirlooms, period pieces produced by Alexandria manufacturers, and the beautifully restored, award-winning garden. ☒ *614 Oronoco St., Old Town* ☎ *703/548–1789* ▧ *$4* ☉ *Feb.–mid-Dec., Tues., Thurs., Fri., and Sat. 10–4; Wed. and Sun. 1–4; sometimes closed weekends, closed Dec. 15–Feb. 1.*

⑭ **Lyceum.** Built in 1839 and one of Alexandria's best examples of Greek Revival design, the Lyceum is also the city's official history museum. Over the years the building has served as the Alexandria Library, a Civil War hospital, a residence, and offices. Restored in the 1970s for the Bicentennial, it has an impressive collection including examples of 18th- and 19th-century silver, tools, stoneware, and Civil War photographs taken by Mathew Brady. ☒ *201 S. Washington St., Old Town* ☎ *703/838–4994* ⊕ *www.alexandriahistory.org* ▧ *$2 donation suggested* ☉ *Mon.–Sat. 10–5, Sun. 1–5.*

❶ **Ramsay House.** The best place to start a tour of Alexandria's Old Town is at the **Alexandria Convention and Visitors Association,** in Ramsay House, the home of the town's first postmaster and lord mayor, William Ramsay. The structure is the site of the first house in Alexandria. The unusually helpful staff hands out brochures, maps for self-guided walking tours, and 24-hour permits for free parking at any two-hour metered spot. ☒ *221 King St., Old Town* ☎ *703/838–4200, 800/388–9119, 703/838–6494 TDD* ⊕ *www.funside.com* ▧ *Guided tours $10–$15* ☉ *Daily 9–5; tours Mon.–Sat. 10:30 and 11:30, Sun. 10:30 and 2.*

❻ **Torpedo Factory Art Center.** Torpedoes were manufactured here by the
☾ U.S. Navy during World War II. Now the building, housing the studios
★ and workshops of about 160 artists and artisans, has become one of Alexandria's most popular attractions. You can observe printmakers,

jewelry makers, sculptors, painters, and potters as they create original work in their studios. The Torpedo Factory also houses the Alexandria Archaeology Museum, which displays artifacts such as plates, cups, pipes, and coins from an early tavern, and Civil War soldiers' equipment. If digging interests you, call to sign up for the well-attended public digs (offered once a month from June to October; ☎703/838–4399; 🖼$5 ♟*Reservations are required*). ✉*105 N. Union St., Old Town* ☎*703/838–4565* ⊕*www.torpedofactory.org* 🖼*Free* ☉*Daily 10–5.*

ALSO WORTH SEEING

⓫ Alexandria Black History Museum. This museum, devoted to the history of African-Americans in Alexandria and Virginia, is at the site of the Robert H. Robinson Library, a building constructed in the wake of a landmark 1939 sit-in protesting the segregation of Alexandria libraries. The federal census of 1790 recorded 52 free African-Americans living in the city, and the port town was one of the largest slave exporting points in the South, with at least two bustling slave markets. ✉*902 Wythe St., Old Town* ☎*703/838–4356* ⊕*oha.ci.alexandria.va.us/bhrc* 🖼*Free* ☉*Tues.–Sat. 10–4.*

❹ Athenaeum. One of the most noteworthy structures in Alexandria, this striking, reddish-brown Greek Revival edifice at the corner of Prince and Lee streets stands out from its many redbrick Federal neighbors. Built in 1851 as a bank (Robert E. Lee had an account here) and later used as a Union Army hospital, then as a talcum powder factory for the Stabler-Leadbeater Apothecary, the Athenaeum now houses the gallery of the Northern Virginia Fine Arts Association. They also offer ballet classes through the Washington School of Ballet. This block of Prince Street between Fairfax and Lee streets is known as **Gentry Row,** after the 18th- and 19th-century inhabitants of its imposing three-story houses. ✉*201 Prince St., Old Town* ☎*703/548–0035* ⊕*www.nvfaa.org* 🖼*Free* ☉*Thurs.–Sun. noon–4. Times subject to change so call to confirm.*

❺ Captain's Row. Many of Alexandria's sea captains once lived on this block. The ships sailing to America during the Revolution weren't fully loaded with cargo, and they used stones to balance the ship during the passage. These stones were then used to pave the streets, as can be witnessed best on Prince and Princess streets. ✉*Prince St. between Lee and Union Sts., Old Town.*

⓯ Friendship Fire House. Alexandria's showcase firehouse dates from 1855 and has the appearance and implements of a typical 19th-century firehouse. The Friendship Fire Company, however, was established in 1774 and bought its first engine in 1775. Among early fire engines on display is a hand pumper built in Baltimore in 1851. Most everything can be seen through the windows even when the firehouse is closed. ✉*107 S. Alfred St., Old Town* ☎*703/838–3891* ⊕*oha.ci.alexandria.va.us* 🖼*Free* ☉*Fri. and Sat. 10–4, Sun. 1–4.*

❸ Old Presbyterian Meeting House. Except from 1899 through 1949, the Old Presbyterian Meeting House has been the site of an active Presbyterian congregation since 1775. Scottish pioneers founded the church, and Scottish patriots used it as a gathering place during the Revolution.

Old Town
Alexandria,
Virginia

Four memorial services were held for George Washington here. The tomb of an unknown soldier of the American Revolution lies in a corner of the small churchyard, where many prominent Alexandrians—including Dr. James Craik, physician and best friend to Washington and John Carlyle—are interred. The original sanctuary was rebuilt after a lightning strike and fire in 1835. The interior is appropriately plain; if you'd like to visit the sanctuary you can borrow a key in the church office, or just peek through the many wide windows along both sides. ⊠*321 S. Fairfax St., Old Town* ☎*703/549–6670* ⊕*www.opmh.org* ☞*Free* ⊗ *Weekdays 9–4:30.*

② **Stabler-Leadbeater Apothecary.** Once patronized by George Washington and the Lee family, the Stabler-Leadbeater Apothecary is among the oldest apothecaries in the country (the reputed oldest is in Bethlehem, Pennsylvania). Some believe that it was here, on October 17, 1859, that Lt. Col. Robert E. Lee received orders to lead Marines sent from the Washington Barracks to help suppress John Brown's insurrection at Harpers Ferry (then part of Virginia). The shop now houses a museum of 18th- and 19th-century apothecary memorabilia, including one of the finest collections of apothecary bottles in the country. In fact, they have so many that curators are still processing them all. ■ TIP→ **Tours include discussions of Alexandria life, as well as the history of the family that owned**

and ran the shop for 141 years. Tours designed especially for children are available. ✉*105–107 S. Fairfax St., Old Town* ☎*703/838–3852* ⊕*www.apothecarymuseum.org* ✉$4 ⊘*Tues.–Sat. 10–5, Sun. and Mon. 1–5.*

NEED A BREAK?   Grab a seat on the deck beside the Potomac River at the **Afterdeck Cafe at Washington Sailing Marina** (✉*1 Marina Dr.* ☎*703/548–0001*), beside the Potomac, where you can watch sailboats and airport operations and enjoy salads, sandwiches, flatbread pizzas, several reasonable draft beers, soft drinks, and coffee. It's ½- mi south of Ronald Reagan National Airport just off the George Washington Memorial Parkway.

WHERE TO EAT

$ ✕**Bugsy's Pizza Restaurant and Sports Bar.** With a huge salad bar and a
PIZZA   large, ever-changing assortment of good, hot pizzas, this is a great place to stop for a late dinner Friday or Saturday. Every day, this pizza place also offers an all-you-can-eat pizza and salad buffet for $6.95. Upstairs, the authentic sports bar is loaded with interesting memorabilia, heavy on hockey—the personable owner used to play in the NHL. Catch every game you can imagine on their 16 TVs, including 8 HDTVs. ✉*111 King St.* ☎*703/683–0313* ⊕*www.bugsyspizza.com* ⚒*Reservations not accepted* ▤*AE, MC, V* ⊘*No lunch Sun.*

$$$ ✕**Gadsby's Tavern.** In the heart of the historic district, this circa-1792
AMERICAN   tavern provides a taste of the interior decoration, cuisine, and entertainment of the early Republic. A strolling balladeer usually makes the rounds on Friday and Saturday nights. The tavern was a favorite of Thomas Jefferson and George Washington, who is commemorated on the menu: George Washington's Favorite Duck is half a duck roasted with peach-apricot dressing and served with Madeira sauce. Other period offerings are Gentlemen's Pye (made with game), Sally Lunn bread, and a rich English trifle. Brunch is served on Sunday. ✉*138 N. Royal St.* ☎*703/548–1288* ⊕*www.gadsbystavernrestaurant.com* ▤*AE, D, DC, MC, V.*

$$$–$$$$ ✕**The Grille at the Morrison House.** On a quiet street in central Alexandria,
AMERICAN   this hotel dining room serves breakfast and dinner only. The cuisine is French and American with Southern influences and an emphasis on local ingredients. Entrées include three seafood dishes such as Oysters Rockefeller, all accompanied by vegetables. Or try the burger with prosciutto and manchego on toasted brioche. A pianist entertains in the intimate dining room on Thursday. The Grille hosts an afternoon tea every third Saturday of the month for $38. ✉*Morrison House, 116 S. Alfred St.* ☎*703/838–8000 or 866/834–6628* ⊕*www.morrisonhouse. com* ▤*AE, DC, MC, V* ⊘*No lunch.*

$ ✕**Il Porto.** Inside an old building just one block from the Potomac, Il Por-
ITALIAN   to's interior is reminiscent of Italy, with plaster walls, exposed wooden beams, and checkered tablecloths. The menu includes traditional Italian versions of veal, seafood, pasta, and chicken, and creative interpretations such as *Paradiso Terra e Mare* (chicken, shrimp, scallops, and chopped clams in white-wine-and-lemon sauce). For healthy foodies,

Il Porto uses whole-wheat pasta and organic wines. ⊠*121 King St.* ☎*703/836–8833* ⊕*www.ilportoristorante.com* ▭*AE, D, MC, V.*

$$-$$$ ✕**La Porta's.** At the west end of Old Town and about two blocks from
AMERICAN the King St. Metrorail station, La Porta's combines great food with
★ a variety of gentle, good music nightly in an intimate setting. Fresh
seafood is the strong suit here, especially the crab cakes. Monday and
Tuesday you can choose two entrée specials plus a bottle of wine for
$28 per couple—a great deal. Park free in their enclosed lot beside
the restaurant. Brunch is served Sunday 11–3:30. ⊠*1600 Duke St.*
☎*703/837–9117* ⊕*www.laportas.net* ▭*AE, D, DC, MC, V* ⊗*No
lunch Sat.* Ⓜ*King St.*

$$ ✕**Las Tapas.** A big, bright, authentic Spanish restaurant, Las Tapas spe-
SPANISH cializes in, what else? There are 59 tapas on the menu, such as tortilla
espanola, plus substantial entrées, including six kinds of paella. Indeed,
Paella Valenciana is the signature dish in this friendly restaurant. Order
a jug of the red, white, or specialty sangrias to accompany your meal.
Then sit back and watch the flamenco dancers, who perform Tuesday
through Thursday nights; Friday and Saturday nights bring Spanish
guitar music. ⊠*710 King St.* ☎*703/836–4000* ⊕*www.lastapas.us*
▭*AE, D, DC, MC, V.*

$$$ ✕**Le Refuge.** This petite French restaurant one block from Alexandria's
FRENCH busiest intersection has been a local favorite for 25 years. It is Alex-
andria's oldest French restaurant with its original owners, Jean Fran-
cois and his wife Francoise. Enjoy lovingly prepared, authentic French
country fare with beaucoup flavor; popular selections include trout,
bouillabaisse, garlicky leg of lamb, frogs' legs, and beef Wellington.
Polish it all off with an order of profiteroles or crème brûlée. Personal
service (they don't like to keep you waiting between courses) makes this
cozy restaurant popular. ⊠*127 N. Washington St.* ☎*703/548–4661*
⊕*www.lerefugealexandria.com* ▭*AE, DC, MC, V* ⊗*Closed Sun.*

¢–$ ✕**Rocklands.** This homegrown barbecue stop is known for its flavorful
BARBECUE pork ribs smoked over hickory and red oak. Sides like silky corn pud-
♺ ding, rich mac 'n' cheese, and crunchy slaw are as good as the meats,
which cover everything from beef brisket and chopped pork barbecue to
chicken and fish. The family crowd comes for dinner, but they also do
popular take-out. There is another branch in Arlington at 3471 Washington Blvd. ⊠*25 S. Quaker La., Alexandria, VA* ☎*703/778–9663*
⊕*www.rocklands.com* ▭*AE, MC, V*

$$ ✕**Taverna Cretekou.** Whitewashed stucco walls and colorful macramé
GREEK tapestries bring a bit of the Mediterranean to the center of Old Town.
On the menu are *exohikon* (lamb baked in a pastry shell) and sword-
fish *xiphoias* (kebab), and the extensive wine list includes only Greek
choices, such as the special Taverna Cretekou wine made in the south
of Kalamata. In warm weather you can dine in the canopied garden.
◼**TIP**➔ **Thursday evenings bring live music, and if you are so moved, plates
for breaking are $2 each—opa!** A buffet brunch is served on Sunday.
⊠*818 King St.* ☎*703/548–8688* ⊕*www.tavernacretekou.com* ▭*AE,
MC, V* ⊗*Closed Mon.*

WHERE TO STAY

$–$$ ⊞**Best Western Old Colony Inn.** Just north of Old Town in a peaceful location within walking distance of most local attractions, this red-brick two-story hotel offers free shuttle service to the Braddock Road Metrorail stop, Old Town, and Washington Reagan National Airport. Rooms have Federal-style cherry furnishings with a work desk, upholstered lounge chair, hair dryer, iron, ironing board, and coffeemaker. **Pros:** rates include a full continental breakfast, free local calls, and a newspaper; good location. **Cons:** rooms are a bit drab, with quilted floral bedspreads; rollaway beds cost $10 a day. ⊠*1101 N. Washington St.* ☎*703/739–2222 or 800/937–8376* ⊕*www.bestwestern.com* ➪*49 rooms* ⌂*In-room: refrigerator, DVD, Ethernet. In-hotel: restaurant, gym, laundry facilities, laundry service, airport shuttle, parking (no fee), no-smoking rooms* ⊟*AE, D, DC, MC, V* ❡*BP.*

$$–$$$ ⊞**Embassy Suites Old Town Alexandria.** The relaxing sound of rushing
    ☾   water from the atrium fountain adjacent to the restaurant greets you inside this modern all-suites hotel three blocks from Alexandria's landmark George Washington Masonic Temple. Train buffs should request a suite facing the Amtrak and Metrorail stations across the street. Each suite has a living room with overstuffed sofa and chairs and a work desk; beds have an abundance of fluffy pillows. A free shuttle is available to transport you to the scenic Alexandria riverfront, which has shops and restaurants. **Pros:** the cooked-to-order breakfast is complimentary; kids can romp in the playroom. **Cons:** train station across the street can be noisy; Wi-Fi use costs $9.95 a day. ⊠*1900 Diagonal Rd.* ☎*703/684–5900 or 800/362–2779* ⊕*www.embassysuites.com* ➪*268 suites* ⌂*In-room: kitchen, refrigerator, Ethernet. In-hotel: restaurant, pool, gym, laundry facilities, laundry service, public Wi-Fi (fee), parking (fee)* ⊟*AE, D, DC, MC, V* ❡*BP* Ⓜ*King St.*

$$–$$$ ⊞**Morrison House.** The architecture, parquet floors, crystal chandeliers,
    ★   decorative fireplaces, and furnishings here are so faithful to the Federal period (1790–1820) that it's often mistaken for a renovation rather than what it is: a structure built from scratch in 1985. The hotel blends Early American charm with modern conveniences. Some rooms have fireplaces, and all have four-poster beds, hair dryers, and bathrobes. The highly regarded Grille restaurant serves American contemporary cuisine. **Pros:** in the heart of Old Town, about a 15-minute walk from the train and Metrorail stations; modern building with historic charm. **Cons:** can be a little pricey; fireplaces are decorative only. ⊠*116 S. Alfred St.* ☎*703/838–8000 or 800/367–0800* ⊕*www.morrisonhouse.com* ➪*42 rooms, 3 suites* ⌂*In-room: DVD. In-hotel: 2 restaurants, room service, bars, public Wi-Fi, parking (fee)* ⊟*AE, DC, MC, V* Ⓜ*King St.*

NIGHTLIFE & THE ARTS

BARS & PUBS

Murphy's Irish Pub (⊠*713 King St., Old Town* ☎*703/548–1717*) has authentic Irish entertainment nightly and a blazing fire when winter comes. Aficionados praise Alexandria's **Shenandoah Brewing Company** (⊠*652 S. Pickett St.* ☎*703/823–9508*) for its stouts and ales, especially the Bourbon Stoney Stout, aged in oak casks previously used to make premium bourbon. Inside, the atmosphere is slightly industrial and the menu is limited to foods grown or made in Virginia: peanuts, potato chips, chili, and a delicious beer-queso dip. **Union Street Public House** (⊠*121 S. Union St., Old Town* ☎ *703/548–1785* ⊕*www.usphalexandria.com*) has three dining rooms and two bars that twist through this 200-year-old building. Although it's also a restaurant, come late for a beer in the busy main bar or chat with friends in the cozy OysterBar area.

LIVE MUSIC

The **Birchmere** (⊠*3701 Mt. Vernon Ave.* ☎*703/549–7500* ⊕*www. birchmere.com*)is one of the best places outside the Blue Ridge Mountains to hear acoustic folk and bluegrass. It also gets more than its share of headliners, including frequent visitors Mary Chapin Carpenter, Lyle Lovett, and Dave Matthews. Tickets are on the expensive side, with big names fetching up to $95. **La Porta's** (⊠*1600 Duke St.* ☎*703/683–6313* Ⓜ*King St.*) has jazz combos nightly. **Las Tapas** (⊠*710 King St., Old Town* ☎*703/836–4000*) has flamenco dancing Tuesday through Thursday nights and Spanish guitar music Friday and Saturday nights, without cover charge.

SPORTS & THE OUTDOORS

BOATING

If you can't snag one of the boats at the Washington Sailing Marina, try **Belle Haven Marina** (⊠*George Washington Pkwy.* ☎*703/768–0018*), south of Wilson Bridge just off George Washington Memorial Parkway. This rustic outfit rents Sunfish ($30 for two hours weekdays, $35 weekends), Flying Scots ($46 for two hours weekdays, $54 weekends), and canoes and kayaks ($20 for two hours), from April to October. All-day rates are available. The **Washington Sailing Marina** (⊠*1 Marina Dr.* ☎*703/548–9027* ⊕*www.washingtonsailingmarina.com*), on the George Washington Memorial Parkway just south of the airport, rents sailboats from around mid-May to mid-October. Aqua Fins are $10 per hour, the larger Flying Scots are $19 per hour. There's a two-hour minimum, and reservations are required (along with certification from a sailing school or passing a written test). Phone early; boats are limited.

HIKING

Huntley Meadows Park (⊠*3701 Lockheed Blvd.* ☎*703/768–2525* ⊡*Free* ☉*Park daily dawn–dusk; visitor center Mon. and Wed–Fri. 9-5; call for weekend hrs*), a 1,460-acre refuge, is made for birders. You can spot more than 200 species—from ospreys to owls, egrets, and ibis. Much of the park is wetlands, home to a variety of aquatic species. A boardwalk circles through a marsh, enabling you to spot beaver lodges, and 4 mi of trails wind through the park, making it possible that you'll see deer, muskrats, and river otters as well.

The **Mount Vernon Trail** is a favorite with Washington runners and bikers. You can access it from the north just short of Key Bridge in Rosslyn, beside the I–66 off-ramp. The path crosses the George Washington Parkway, going to Theodore Roosevelt Island (directly across the river from the Kennedy Center), past Ronald Reagan Washington National Airport, and on to the Alexandria waterfront. This stretch is approximately 9½ mi one-way. South of National Airport, the trail runs beside the Washington Sailing Marina. The southern section of the trail (approximately 9 mi) takes you along the banks of the Potomac from Alexandria all the way to Mount Vernon. It passes Jones Point (under the Wilson Bridge), the southern apex of the original District of Columbia, just before entering protected wetlands for about 2 mi beginning at Hunting Creek.

> **RENT A BIKE**
>
> Rent a bike at the idyllic **Washington Sailing Marina**, on the Mount Vernon Bike Trail. A 12-mi ride south will take you to the front doors of Mount Vernon, and a 6-mi ride north across the Memorial Bridge will put you at the foot of the Washington Monument. All-terrain bikes rent for $6 per hour or $22 per day; cruisers cost $4 per hour or $16.50 per day. The marina is open 9–5 daily.

SHOPPING

Old Town Alexandria is dense with antiques shops—many of them quite expensive—that are particularly strong in the Federal and Victorian periods. The Alexandria Convention and Visitors Association has maps and lists of the dozens of stores (available at Ramsay House).

The **Antique Guild** (✉ *113 N. Fairfax St., Old Town* ☎ *703/836–1048 or 800/518–7322* ⊕ *www.theantiqueguild.net*) is where silver flatware and estate jewelry goes when it's ready for a new home. Dating to 1753, the **Saturday Morning Market at Market Square** (✉ *City Hall, 301 King St.*) may be the country's oldest operating farmers' market. Vendors sell baked goods, fresh produce, plants, flowers, and high-quality crafts. Come early; the market opens at 6 AM, and by 10 AM it's all over. **Sumpter Priddy III, Inc.** (✉ *323 S. Washington St., Old Town* ☎ *703/299–0800* ⊕ *www.sumpterpriddy.com*) specializes in American furniture from the early 19th century and folk art in different mediums.

ARLINGTON

★ Arlington has evolved since the end of World War I from a farming community into one of sprawling homes, large-scale retailing, and office buildings small to colossal. Connected to Washington by four bridges and three subway lines, the county is vital to the capital, providing office space to the federal government and housing to its employees. First the War Department, then Department of Defense and all military service headquarters were moved to the Pentagon, then numerous other government offices and bureaus moved to Arlington and nearby Virginia communities like Langley (home of the C.I.A.) as they required larger quarters than were available in Washington. This trend continues. For the visitor, Arlington offers somber reflection at the nation's cemetery, a plethora of dining and lodging options, and easy access to the attractions of Washington.

Carved out of Fairfax County when the District of Columbia was created, Arlington was returned to Virginia along with the rest of the state's contribution in 1846, and until 1920 was the County of Alexandria. In the 19th century, members of the Custis family, including Martha Washington's first husband, had extensive land holdings in the area. Arlington was the name of the Custis family home that became the home of Robert E. Lee, now the Custis-Lee Mansion in Arlington Cemetery.

GETTING HERE & AROUND

If you arrive at Reagan National Airport, Arlington is an easy drive west along the George Washington Parkway. Many parts of Arlington are easily accessible via Metrorail, as both the Orange and Blue lines run through parts of the county. The Orange Line heads through Clarendon and Ballson, while the Blue Line takes riders through Rosslyn and Pentagon City. The Yellow Line also meets up with the Blue Line for a portion of its trip through Arlington. Taxis are also readily available throughout the area.

TIMING & PRECAUTIONS

Rush hour, which lasts from 7:30 AM to 9 AM and 5 PM to 6:30 PM on weekdays, slows down traffic through Arlington, especially on the heavily trafficked I–66, Route 50, and George Washington Parkway. Also be careful driving at these times through urban centers such as Rosslyn.

ESSENTIALS

Bus Contacts **Arlington Depot** (⊠ *Pentagon*). **Arlington Transit** (☎ *703/ 228-7433* ⊕ *www.commuterpage.com/art*).

Taxi **Arlington Blue Top Cab** (☎ *703/243-8294*).

Visitor Information **Arlington County Visitor Center** (⊠ *1301 S. Joyce St., Arlington* ☎ *703/228-5720 or 800/677-6267* ⊕ *www.stayarlington.com*).

Numbers in the text correspond to numbers in the margin and on the Arlington National Cemetery map.

MAIN ATTRACTIONS

❸ **Arlington House.** It was in Arlington that the two most famous names in Virginia history—Washington and Lee—became intertwined. George Washington Parke Custis, raised by Martha and George Washington, his grandmother and step-grandfather, built Arlington House (also known as the Custis-Lee Mansion) between 1802 and 1818 on his 1,100-acre estate overlooking the Potomac. After Custis's death, the property went to his daughter, Mary Anna Randolph Custis. In 1831 Mary married Robert E. Lee, a graduate of West Point. For the next 30 years she lived at Arlington House while Lee went wherever the Army sent him, including the superintendency of West Point.

In 1861 Lee was offered command of the Union forces in Washington. It was understood that the first order of business would be a troop movement into nearby Virginia. He declined and resigned from the U.S. Army, deciding that he could never take up arms against his native Virginia. The

Lees left Arlington House that spring, never to return. Federal troops crossed the Potomac not long after that, fortified the estate's ridges, and turned the home into the Army of the Potomac's headquarters. Arlington House and the estate were confiscated in May 1864 when the Lees failed to pay $92 and change in property taxes in person. (General Lee's eldest son sued the U.S. government, and after a 5–4 decision by the U.S. Supreme Court, was eventually compensated for the land.) Two hundred nearby acres were set aside as a national cemetery in 1864. One thousand soldiers were buried there by the end of that year. Soldiers from the Revolutionary War and the War of 1812 were reinterred at Arlington as their bodies were discovered in other resting places.

The building's heavy Doric columns and severe pediment make Arlington House one of the area's best examples of Greek Revival architecture. The plantation home was designed by George Hadfield, a young English architect who, for a while, supervised construction of the Capitol. The view of Washington from the front of the house is superb. In 1933 the National Park Service acquired Arlington House and continued the restoration that the War Department had begun, and in 1972 Congress designated the Custis-Lee Mansion as Arlington House, the Robert E. Lee Memorial. It looks much as it did in the 19th century, and a quick tour takes you past objects once owned by the Custises and the Lees.

In front of Arlington House, next to a flag that flies at half staff whenever there's a funeral in the cemetery, is the flat-top **grave of Pierre Charles L'Enfant,** designer of Washington, DC ⌧*Between Lee and Sherman Drs.* ☎*703/235–1530* ⌷*Free* ⊙*Daily 9:30–4:30.*

Fodor'sChoice   **Arlington National Cemetery.** More than 250,000 American war dead,
★   as well as many notable Americans (among them Presidents William Howard Taft and John F. Kennedy, General John Pershing, and Admiral Robert E. Peary), are interred in these 624 acres across the Potomac River from Washington, established as the nation's cemetery in 1864. While you're at Arlington there's a good chance you'll hear a bugler playing taps, or the sharp reports of a gun salute. Approximately 28 funerals are held daily (it's projected that the cemetery will be filled in 2060).To get here, you can take the Metrorail to either the Rosslyn or Arlington Cemetery station and then walk about 0.5 mi, arrive by Tourmobile tour bus, walk across Arlington Memorial Bridge (southwest of the Lincoln Memorial), or drive to the large paid parking lot at the skylighted visitor center on Memorial Drive ($1.75 per hour for
❶   the first three hours, then $2 per hour). Stop at the **Visitor Center** for a free brochure with a detailed map of the cemetery. If you're looking for a specific grave, the staff can consult microfilm records and give you directions to it. You should know the deceased's full name and, if possible, his or her branch of service and year of death.

Tourmobiles leave daily 8:30–6:30 (in fall and winter, daily 8:30–4:30) from just outside the visitor center, where you can buy tickets ($7.50) good all day for unlimited reboarding in the cemetery. The Tourmobile stops at the Kennedy grave sites, the Tomb of the Unknowns, and Arlington House. Arlington Cemetery is included in the Washington

Arlington National Cemetery, Virginia

KEY

Ⓜ Metro station

ROSSLYN Ⓜ

Theodore Roosevelt Island

Theodore Roosevelt Br.

Theodore Roosevelt Island

Lincoln Memorial

George Washington Memorial Pkwy.

12th Ave.

Marshall Dr.

Ord and Weitzel Dr.

Custis Walk

Columbia Island

Arlington Memorial Bridge

Ohio Dr.

50

110

ARLINGTON CEMETERY Ⓜ

Lady Bird Johnson Park

Potomac River

Schley Dr.

Memorial Dr.

Sherman Dr.

Sheridan Dr.

Weeks Dr.

Roosevelt Dr.

❶ Women in Military Service for America Memorial

27

George Washington Memorial Pkwy.

King Dr.

❷

❸

ARLINGTON NATIONAL CEMETERY

Crook Walk

Grant Dr.

Eisenhower Dr.

McClellan Dr.

Marshall Dr.

❺

❹

Roosevelt Drive

York Dr.

Porter Dr.

Grant Dr.

Bradley Dr.

Jesup Dr.

Arnold Dr.

Patton Dr.

27

110

Pentagon

0 — 440 yards

0 — 400 meters

Patton Dr.

Columbia Pike

❻

244

TO DRUG ENFORCEMENT MUSEUM

Ⓜ PENTAGON

Tourmobile ticket ($20), which includes transportation across the Potomac from the Lincoln Memorial to the visitor center. ■TIP→ **Touring the cemetery on foot means a fair bit of hiking, but it can give you a closer look at some of the thousands of graves spread over these rolling Virginia hills.** If you decide to walk, from the visitor center head to the ornate Memorial Gate, then west on Roosevelt Drive, and turn right on Weeks Drive. ⊠*West end of Memorial Bridge* ☎*703/607–8000 to locate a grave* ⊕*www.arlingtoncemetery.org* ✒*Free* ⊙*Apr.–Sept., daily 8–7; Oct.–Mar., daily 8–5.*

❷ **Kennedy graves.** A moving part of any visit to Arlington National Cem-
★ etery is a visit to the graves of John F. Kennedy and other members of his family. President Kennedy is buried under an eternal flame near two of his children, who died in infancy, and his wife, Jacqueline Bouvier Kennedy Onassis; his is the most-visited grave site in the country. The graves are a moderate walk west of the visitor center. Across from them is a low wall engraved with quotations from Kennedy's inaugural address. Nearby, marked by a simple white cross, is the grave of his brother Robert Kennedy. ⊠*Sheridan and Weeks Drs.*

❺ **Section 7A.** Many distinguished veterans are buried in this area of Arlington National Cemetery near the Tomb of the Unknowns, including boxing champ Joe Louis, ABC newsman Frank Reynolds, actor Lee Marvin, and World War II fighter pilot Colonel "Pappy" Boyington. ⊠*Crook Walk near Roosevelt Dr.*

❹ **Tomb of the Unknowns.** Many countries established a memorial to their war dead after World War I. In the United States, the first burial at the Tomb of the Unknowns took place at Arlington National Cemetery on November 11, 1921, when the unknown soldier from the "Great War" was interred under the large white-marble sarcophagus. Unknown servicemen killed in World War II and Korea were buried in 1958. The unknown serviceman killed in Vietnam was laid to rest on the plaza on Memorial Day 1984, but was disinterred and identified in 1998. Officials then decided to leave the Vietnam War unknown crypt vacant. Soldiers from the Army's 3rd Infantry ("The Old Guard") keep watch over the tomb 24 hours a day, regardless of weather conditions. Each sentinel marches exactly 21 steps, then faces the tomb for 21 seconds, symbolizing the 21-gun salute, America's highest military honor. The guard is changed with a precise ceremony during the day—every half hour from April through September and every hour the rest of the year. At night the guard is changed every hour.

The Memorial Amphitheater west of the tomb is the scene of special ceremonies on Veterans Day, Memorial Day, and Easter. Mementos from foreign governments are displayed in an indoor trophy room. Across from the amphitheater are memorials to the astronauts killed in the 1986 *Challenger* space shuttle explosion and to the servicemen killed in 1980 trying to rescue American hostages in Iran. Rising beyond that is the main mast of the USS *Maine,* the American ship sunk in Havana Harbor in 1898, killing 299 men and sparking the Spanish-American War. ⊠*End of Crook Walk.*

ALSO WORTH SEEING

⑥ Air Force Memorial. Dedicated in 2006, this memorial honors the service and sacrifices of the men and women of the U.S. Air Force and its predecessor organizations of the U.S. Army. Three curved spires—up to 270 feet tall—represent the bomb burst maneuver famously performed by the USAF Thunderbird Demonstration Team. The memorial is just uphill from the Pentagon, beside the Navy Annex on Columbia Pike, and easy to see from a distance. ⊠ *Columbia Pike at Joyce St.*

OFF THE BEATEN PATH

Drug Enforcement Administration Museum. The very compact DEA Museum, inside one entrance to DEA headquarters, is across the street from the Fashion Centre at Pentagon City. It displays the methods and effects of dangerous drugs on America, starting with quaint 19th-century ads for opium-laced patent medicines and cocaine tooth drops (opiates, cannabis, and cocaine were unregulated then). Displays show current methods of illegal drug production, international drug smuggling, and the means of intercepting illegal drug shipments. Some displays are too stark for children. ⊠ *700 Army Navy Dr., at Hayes St.* ☎ *202/307–3463* ⊕ *www.deamuseum.org* ⊠ *Free* ☉ *Tues.–Fri. 10–4* Ⓜ *Pentagon City.*

⑧ Netherlands Carillon. Outside the Arlington National Cemetery is the lovely and unusual 49-bell musical carillon presented to the United States by the Dutch people in 1960 in gratitude for aid received during World War II. For a good view of Washington, look to the east across the Potomac. From this vantage point the Lincoln Memorial, the Washington Monument, and the Capitol appear side by side. ⊠ *Meade and Marshall Drs.*

Pentagon. This office building, the headquarters of the U.S. Department of Defense, is one of the largest in the world. The Capitol could fit into any one of its five wedge-shape sections. Approximately 23,000 military and civilian people work here. Astonishingly, this mammoth office building, completed in 1943, took less than two years to construct. Construction was overseen by General Leslie Grove, then a colonel, who later led the Manhattan Project to develop the atom bomb.

Parts of the structure were rebuilt following the September 2001 crash of hijacked American Airlines Flight 77 into the northwest side of the building. The damaged area was removed in just more than a month, and rebuilding proceeded rapidly (in keeping with the speed of the original construction). Renovations on all areas damaged by the terrorist attack were completed by spring 2003.

Tours of the building are given on a limited basis to educational groups by advance reservation. ■ TIP➔ **Tours for the general public can be arranged through your congressional office with two weeks advance notice.** You can also drive right by, fairly close, with unobstructed views of all sides. ⊠ *I–395 at Columbia Pike and Rte. 27* ☎ *703/695–1776* ⊕ *pentagon.afis.osd.mil.*

⑦ Section 27. Nearly 3,800 former slaves are buried in this part of Arlington National Cemetery. They're all former residents of Freedman's Village, which operated at the Custis-Lee estate for more than 30 years beginning in 1863 to provide housing, education, and employment training for ex-slaves who had traveled to the capital. In the cemetery the headstones are marked with their names and the word "Civilian" or "Citizen." Buried at Grave 19 in the first row of Section 27 is William Christman, a Union private who died of peritonitis in Washington on May 12, 1864. He was the first soldier (but not the first person) interred at Arlington. ⊠ *Ord and Weitzel Dr. near Custis Walk.*

OFF THE BEATEN PATH

Theodore Roosevelt Island. The island wilderness preserve in the Potomac River has 2½ mi of nature trails through marsh, swampland, and upland forest. It's an 88-acre tribute to the conservation-minded 26th president. Cattails, arrowarum, pickerelweed, willow, ash, maple, and oak grow on the island, which is also a habitat for frogs, raccoons, birds, lizards, and the occasional red or gray fox. The 17-foot bronze statue of Roosevelt, toward the center of the woods, was done by Paul Manship. A pedestrian bridge connects the island to a parking lot on the Virginia shore, which is accessible by car only from the northbound lanes of the George Washington Memorial Parkway. ✢ *From downtown DC, take Constitution Ave. west across Theodore Roosevelt Bridge to George Washington Memorial Pkwy. north; follow signs or walk or bike across bridge beginning at Kennedy Center* ☎ *703/289–2500 for park information* ☜ *Free* ☉ *Island daily dawn–dusk* Ⓜ *Rosslyn.*

❾ **United States Marine Corps War Memorial.** Better known simply as "the Iwo Jima," this memorial, despite its familiarity, has lost none of its power to stir the emotions. Honoring Marines who gave their lives since the Corps was formed in 1775, the statue, sculpted by Felix W. de Weldon, is based on Joe Rosenthal's Pulitzer Prize–winning photograph of five Marines and a Navy corpsman raising a flag atop Mt. Suribachi on the Japanese island of Iwo Jima on February 19, 1945. By executive order the U.S. flag flies day and night from the 78-foot-high memorial. On Tuesday evenings from early June to mid-August there's a Marine Corps sunset parade on the grounds of the memorial. Call ☎ 202/433–6060 for start times. On parade nights a free shuttle bus runs from the Arlington Cemetery visitors parking lot.

Women in Military Service for America Memorial. What is now this memorial next to the visitor center was once the Hemicycle, a huge carved retaining wall faced with granite at the entrance to Arlington National Cemetery. Built in 1932, the wall was restored, with stairways added leading to a rooftop terrace. Inside are 16 exhibit alcoves showing the contributions that women have made to the military—from the Revolutionary War to the present—as well as the history of the memorial itself. A 196-seat theater shows films and is used for lectures and conferences. A computer database has pictures, military histories, and stories of thousands of women veterans. A fountain and reflecting pool front the classical-style Hemicycle and entry gates.

WHERE TO EAT

$–$$ ✕**Carlyle.** Whether you eat at the bustling bar or in the dining room
AMERICAN upstairs, you'll find an imaginative, generous interpretation of modern
American cooking. Start with the blue crab fritters, then move on to
entrées such as pecan-crusted trout. The warm, flourless, chocolate-mac-
adamia nut waffle with vanilla ice cream is classic. Carlyle is especially
known for its fantastic weekend brunch, where you can pair brioche
French toast with a glass of Virginia sparkling cider. You can even buy
a loaf of bread at the restaurant's own bakery, the Best Buns Bread
Company, next door. ⊠*4000 S. 28th St., Shirlington* ☎*703/931–0777*
▤*AE, MC, V.*

¢–$ ✕**Nam Viet.** Arlington has several Vietnamese restaurants, most on Wil-
VIETNAMESE son Boulevard, and this one a block off Wilson probably has the best
food. Autographed photos of U.S. military and political leaders gaze
down from the walls. The sweet-and-spicy salmon soup has many fans,
as do the *cha gio* (spring rolls) and the green-papaya salad (with shrimp
or beef jerky). Dine outside in good weather. Try to arrive early in the
evening to find a parking space, as residents tend to fill up the street
parking later on. ⊠*1127 Hudson St., Clarendon* ☎*703/522–7110*
⊕*www.namviet1.com* ▤*AE, D, DC, MC, V* Ⓜ*Clarendon.*

$$–$$$ ✕**Willow Restaurant.** This handsome restaurant and bar in mahogany
CONTINENTAL and jewel tones with 1930s-style photographs has a jazz-era feel. Its
elegance can be felt in the polished wooden floors and the spacious dining rooms outfitted with white tablecloths. The cuisine combines the
freshest ingredients with classic French and Italian influences. Featured
are grilled flat breads with innovative toppings, vegetarian French green
lentil ragu with goat cheese, a minirack of pork wrapped in house-made
sausage, and crispy potato-wrapped rockfish. Park free in the building's
garage to avoid the conscientious parking enforcement. ⊠*4301 N.
Fairfax Dr., Ballston* ☎*703/465–8800* ⊕*www.willowva.com* ▤*AE,
D, DC, MC, V* Ⓜ*Ballston.*

WHERE TO STAY

$$ 🏨 **Hilton Arlington and Towers.** Traveling to Arlington Cemetery, Wash-
ington, and Alexandria sights is easy from this hotel, just above the
Ballston Metrorail stop. Rooms make use of neutral colors and tradi-
tional mahogany furniture. The hotel has direct access via a skywalk to
an adjacent shopping mall. **Pros:** renovated fitness center; all suites have
hot tubs; you can't get any closer to the Metro and shopping. **Cons:** fee
for Internet use in rooms; parking fee of $17 a day; the busy neighbor-
hood can get noisy. ⊠*950 N. Stafford St., Ballston* ☎*703/528–6000
or 800/445–8667* ⇱*204 rooms, 5 suites* ⚑*In-room: Ethernet (fee).
In-hotel: restaurant, room service, bar, laundry service, parking (fee),
no-smoking rooms* ▤*AE, D, DC, MC, V* Ⓜ*Ballston.*

¢–$ 🏨 **Holiday Inn Arlington at Ballston.** You can get to the major sights of
☾ Northern Virginia and DC quickly from this hotel, two blocks (or a
free shuttle ride) from the Ballston Metrorail station. It is also across
the street from the Custis jogging trail. Guest rooms have a navy and
burgundy color scheme with duvet comforters, an overstuffed chair

with ottoman, and a mahogany dresser and work desk. Kids love the suspended model railroad at Lacey Station Dining Car Restaurant (named for the railroad station that was once 200 feet away); hotel guests 12 and under eat free from the kids' menu. Parking is free Friday and Saturday nights. **Pros:** perks for kids; free shuttle to the Metro; free parking on weekends. **Cons:** service sometimes suffers with a busy staff; fee for parking during the week. ⊠ *4610 N. Fairfax Dr., Ballston* ☎ *703/243–9800* ⊕ *www.hiarlington.com* ⤴ *221 rooms, 2 suites* ⚬ *In-room: Ethernet. In-hotel: restaurant, room service, bar, pool, gym, laundry facilities, parking (fee)* ⊟ *AE, D, DC, MC, V* Ⓜ *Ballston.*

$$$$ 🖼 **Hotel Palomar Arlington.** Ideally situated on the banks of the Potomac, with the Rosslyn Metrorail station across the street and walkable across the Key Bridge from Georgetown, the Hotel Palomar Arlington is a trendy boutique hotel. Rooms are decorated in neutral hues with splashes of teal and orange. The headboards of the soft beds are upholstered in a chocolate and cream houndstooth pattern. Rooms facing the river have telescopes for stargazing. The hotel's Mind.Body. Spa program allows guests to order in-room spa services, or they can ask for a complimentary yoga bag of accessories to use with television fitness programming. **Pros:** nice extra touches like the telescopes and yoga accessories; small feel for a larger hotel; close to Georgetown's restaurants, shopping, and nightlife. **Cons:** parking is tough to find in downtown Rosslyn; hotel provides only valet parking. ⊠ *1121 N. 19th St., Rosslyn* ☎ *703/351–9170* ⊕ *www.hotelpalomar-arlington. com* ⤴ *154 rooms, 24 suites* ⚬ *In room: Ethernet, safe, DVD. In-hotel: restaurant, room service, bar, gym, spa, laundry service, parking (fee), some pets allowed, no-smoking rooms* ⊟ *AE, D, DC, MC, V.*

$$$$ 🖼 **Marriott Crystal Gateway.** This elegant, modern Marriott caters to the business traveler and those who want to be pampered. Its two towers rise 17 stories above the highway; inside is mahogany, marble, and lots of greenery. Rooms have contemporary styling with fabrics in hues of gold and red blended with mahogany furniture. Amenities include hair dryers, irons, ironing boards, and coffeemakers. Concierge Lounge serves a Continental breakfast, evening hors d'oeuvres, and all-day beverages to concierge-floor guests. Although the hotel does offer unlimited in-room high-speed Internet access and long-distance phone calls in the 48 contiguous states as part of its "Wired for Business" package, there is a cost of $9.95 per day. **Pros:** rooms come with flat-screen HD TVs that allow you to connect your iPod, laptop, video camera, or camcorder; great for business travelers. **Cons:** fee for Internet access; area has a corporate feel. ⊠ *1700 Jefferson Davis Hwy., Crystal City* ☎ *703/920–3230 or 800/228–9290* ⊕ *www.marriott.com/wasgw* ⤴ *615 rooms, 82 suites* ⚬ *In-room: Ethernet, Wi-Fi. In-hotel: 3 restaurants, bars, pool, gym, concierge, laundry facilities, laundry service, airport shuttle, parking (fee)* ⊟ *AE, DC, MC, V* Ⓜ *Crystal City.*

NIGHTLIFE & THE ARTS

The Colorado-based **Rock Bottom Brewery** (✉ *4238 Wilson Blvd., No. 1256, Ballston* ☎ *703/516–7688* Ⓜ *Ballston-MU*) pours ales, lagers, and porters alongside fixings such as fried chicken, barbecued ribs, pizza, and cheesecake made with the house stout.

MUSIC

IOTA. The bands at IOTA play alt-country or rock to unpretentious, attentive crowds. Expect to fight your way to the bar—it gets crowded quickly. There's music for a cover charge of $10 to $15 almost every night, except in the café, which serves food and charges no cover. ✉ *2832 Wilson Blvd., Clarendon* ☎ *703/522–8340* ⊕ *www.iotaclubandcafe.com* Ⓜ *Clarendon.*

SHOPPING

Crystal City Shops (☎ *703/922–4636* ⊕ *www.thecrystalcityshops.com*) is comprised of more than 200 street-level and underground stores and restaurants connected to the Crystal City Metrorail station and near a Virginia Railway Express (VRE) station. **Fashion Centre at Pentagon City** (✉ *1100 S. Hayes St., Pentagon City* ☎ *703/415–2400* ⊕ *www.fashioncentrepentagon.com* Ⓜ *Pentagon City*) is anchored by Macy's and Nordstrom. This four-story mall includes such shops as the Coach Store, Swatch, babyGap, Sephora, Williams-Sonoma, and an Armani Exchange. In addition to a skylighted food court, there are two full-service restaurants to choose from, including the popular Arlington chain Harry's Tap Room.

MOUNT VERNON, WOODLAWN & GUNSTON HALL

Long before Washington was planned, the shores of the Potomac had been divided into plantations by wealthy traders and gentlemen farmers. Most traces of the Colonial era were obliterated as the capital grew in the 19th century, but several splendid examples of plantation architecture remain on the Virginia side of the Potomac, 15 mi or so south of DC. In one day you can easily visit three such mansions: Mount Vernon, the home of George Washington and one of the most popular sites in the area; Woodlawn, the estate of Washington's step-granddaughter; and Gunston Hall, the home of George Mason, author of the document on which the Bill of Rights was based. (Expect the longest wait times at Mount Vernon, particularly in spring and summer.) Set on hillsides overlooking the river, these estates offer magnificent vistas and bring back to vivid life the more palatable aspects of the 18th century. They are all accessible from I–95, south of Alexandria.

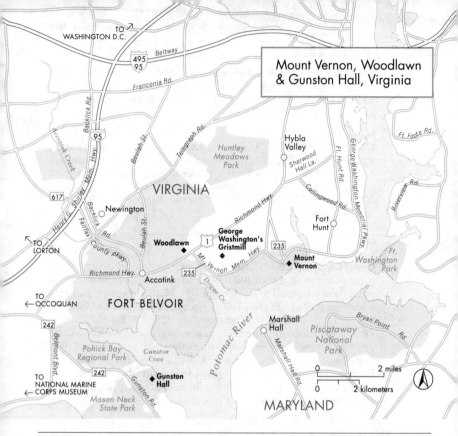

Mount Vernon, Woodlawn & Gunston Hall, Virginia

MOUNT VERNON

16 mi south of Washington, DC, 8 mi south of Alexandria, VA.

Mount Vernon and the surrounding lands had been in the Washington family for nearly 70 years by the time George inherited it all in 1743. Before taking over command of the Continental Army, Washington was an accomplished farmer managing the 8,000-acre plantation, operating five farms on the land. He oversaw the transformation of the main house from an ordinary farm dwelling into what was, for the time, a grand mansion. The inheritance of his widowed bride, Martha, is partly what made that transformation possible.

The red-roof main house is elegant though understated, with a yellow pine exterior that's been painted and coated with layers of sand to resemble white-stone blocks. The first-floor rooms are quite ornate, especially the formal large dining room, with a molded ceiling decorated with agricultural motifs. The bright colors of the walls, which match the original paint, may surprise those who associate the period with pastels. Throughout the house are smaller symbols of the owner's eminence, such as a key to the main portal of the Bastille—presented to Washington by the Marquis de Lafayette—and Washington's presidential chair.

As you tour the mansion, guides are stationed throughout the house to describe the furnishings and answer questions.

The real treasure of Mount Vernon is the view from around back: beneath a 1,400-foot piazza, the home's dramatic riverside porch overlooks an expanse of lawn that slopes down to the Potomac. In springtime the view of the river (a mile wide where it passes the plantation) is framed by dogwood blossoms. In the 19th century, steamboats rendered honors when passing the house during daylight hours.

You can stroll around the estate's 500 acres and three gardens, visiting the workshops, kitchen, carriage house, greenhouse, slave quarters, and—down the hill toward the boat landing—the tomb of George and Martha Washington. There's also a pioneer farmer site: a 4-acre hands-on exhibit with a reconstruction of George Washington's 16-side treading barn as its centerpiece. Among the souvenirs sold at the plantation are stripling boxwoods that began life as clippings from bushes planted in 1798, the year before Washington died. A tour of house and grounds takes about 4½ hours. A limited number of wheelchairs are available at the main gate. Evening candlelight tours are offered Friday–Sunday evenings in late November and early December.

Just inside the main entrance, the orientation and education centers on either side illustrate George Washington's life and contributions with interactive displays, movies, life-size models, and objects such as furnishings, Revolutionary War artifacts, books, and personal effects.

George Washington's Gristmill—a reproduction—operates on the site of his original mill and distillery. Records kept by Washington helped archaeologists excavate the distillery in the late 1990s, and it was reconstructed and reopened to the public in 2007. During the guided tours, led by costumed interpreters, you meet an 18th-century miller and watch the water-powered wheel grind grain into cornmeal just as it did 200 years ago. The mill is 3 mi from Mount Vernon on Route 235 between Mount Vernon and U.S. Route 1, almost to Woodlawn. Tickets can be purchased either at the gristmill itself or at Mount Vernon's Ford Orientation Center. ⊠ *Southern end of George Washington Pkwy., Mount Vernon* 🕾 *703/780–2000* ⊕ *www.mountvernon.org* 🎫 *$13, gristmill $4, combination ticket $15* ⊙ *Mar., Sept., and Oct., daily 9–5; Apr.–Aug., daily 8–5; Nov.–Feb., daily 9–4.*

WOODLAWN

3 mi west of Mount Vernon, 15 mi south of Washington, DC.

Ↄ Woodlawn was once part of the Mount Vernon estate. From here you can still see the five trees of the bowling green that fronted Washington's home. The house was built for Washington's step-granddaughter, Nelly Custis, who married his favorite nephew, Lawrence Lewis. (Lewis had come to Mount Vernon from Fredericksburg to be his Uncle George's social secretary so that the statesman could have more time to manage his five farms.)

The Lewises' home, completed in 1805, was designed by William Thornton, a physician and amateur architect from the West Indies who drew up the original plans for the U.S. Capitol. Like Mount Vernon, the Woodlawn house is constructed wholly of native materials, including the clay for its bricks and the yellow pine used throughout its interior. Built on a site selected by George Washington, the house has commanding views of the surrounding countryside and the Potomac River beyond. In the tradition of Southern riverfront mansions, Woodlawn has a central hallway that provides a cool refuge in summer. Inside the house is a bust of George Washington set on a pedestal so the crown of the head is at 6 feet, 4 inches. Washington's actual height is believed to have been 6 feet, 2 inches, however, the pedestal was built two inches taller to accommodate for the inches lost when it was placed outside and sunk into the garden.

Woodlawn was once a plantation where more than 100 people, most of them slaves, lived and worked. As plantation owners, the Lewises lived in luxury. Docents talk about how the family entertained and how the slaves grew produce and prepared these lavish meals as well as their own. As intimates of the Washingtons' household, the Lewises displayed a collection of objects in honor of their illustrious benefactor. Many Washington family items are on display today. Woodlawn opened its doors to the public as a National Trust for Historic Preservation site in 1952.

Also on the grounds of Woodlawn is the **Pope-Leighey House.** One of Frank Lloyd Wright's "Usonian" homes, the structure was built in 1941 as part of the architect's mission to create affordable housing. It was moved here from Falls Church, Virginia, in 1964, to save it from destruction during the building of Route 66. By design a very small, sparsely furnished home, it features many of Wright's trademark elements, including the use of local materials. Visitors are mostly students of architecture or of Wright. An in-depth tour is given on the first Sunday of the month. ⊠*9000 Richmond Hwy., Alexandria* ☎*703/780–4000* ⊕*www.woodlawn1805.org* ▣*$7.50 each for Woodlawn and Pope-Leighey House, combination ticket $13* ⊙*Mar.–Dec., daily 10–5; limited guided tours in Mar.; tours leave every hr; last tour at 4.*

GUNSTON HALL

9 mi south of Woodlawn, 24 mi south of Washington, DC.

☾ Gunston Hall Plantation, down the Potomac from Mount Vernon,
Fodor's Choice was the home of another important George. Gentleman farmer George
★ Mason was a colonel of the Virginia militia and author of the Virginia Declaration of Rights, the model for the U.S. Bill of Rights, which called for freedom of the press, tolerance of religion, and other fundamental democratic principles. Mason was a framer of the Constitution but refused to sign the final document because it didn't stop the importation of slaves, adequately restrain the powers of the federal government, or include a bill of rights. Mason's objections spurred the movement for the inclusion of the Bill of Rights into the Constitution.

Mason's home was begun about 1755. The Georgian-style mansion has some of the finest hand-carved ornamented interiors in the country. It's the handiwork of the 18th century's foremost architect, William Buckland, who also designed the Hammond-Harwood and Chase-Lloyd houses in Annapolis, but was at the time an indentured servant carpenter/joiner. Gunston Hall is built of native brick, black walnut, and yellow pine. The style of the time demanded absolute symmetry in all structures, which explains the false door set into one side of the center hallway and the "robber" window on a second-floor storage room. The house's interior, with carved woodwork in styles from Chinese to Greek, has been meticulously restored, with paints made from the original formulas and carefully carved replacements for the intricate mahogany medallions in the moldings. Restored outbuildings include a kitchen, dairy, laundry, and smokehouse, and a schoolhouse has also been reconstructed.

The formal gardens, recently under excavation by a team of archaeologists, are famous for their boxwoods—some were planted during George Mason's time, making them among the oldest in the country. The Potomac is visible past the expansive deer park, and Mason's landing road to the river was recently found and cleared. Also on the grounds is an active farmyard with livestock like those of Mason's era. Special programs, such as archaeology tutelege and hearth-cooking demonstrations, are available throughout the year. A tour of Gunston Hall takes at least 45 minutes; tours begin on the front porch of the house. Buy tickets at the visitor center, which includes a museum and gift shop. ⊠*10709 Gunston Rd., Mason Neck* ☏*703/550–9220* ⊕*www.gunstonhall.org* ⌸*$8* ☉*Daily 9:30–5; 1st tour at 10, last tour at 4:30, tours every ½ hr on the hr.*

OFF THE BEATEN PATH

Ⓒ

Fodor's Choice

★

National Museum of the Marine Corps. Eighteen miles south on I–95, next to the Marine Corps Base Quantico, the glassy atrium of the National Museum of the Marine Corps soars into the sky. The design for this 118,000-square-foot homage to the military's finest was inspired by the iconic photograph of Marines lifting the American flag on Iwo Jima. Inside the museum, visitors are able to see the flag itself, as well as experience the life of a Marine. The museum is completely interactive, from the entrance where drill instructors yell at new "recruits" in surround-sound, to the Korean War exhibit, where visitors walk through a snowy mountain pass and shiver from the cold while listening to the 2nd Platoon fight on the other side of the mountain. The museum also has a staggering collection of tanks, aircraft, rocket launchers, and other weapons. There is even a rifle range simulator ($5) where guests of all ages can learn how to hold a rifle and practice hitting targets. Ooh-rah! ⊠*18900 Jefferson Davis Hwy., Triangle* ☏*877/635–1775* ⊕*www. usmcmuseum.org* ⌸*Free* ☉*Daily 9–5.*

HISTORIC OCCO-QUAN

In between visits to others sites off I–95 like Gunston Hall and Woodlawn, pop over to Occoquan for a relaxing afternoon. This tiny village on the shores of the Occoquan River was founded in 1734 as a trading post. It was the main delivery point for mail between the North and South during the Civil War.

Occoquan today is an ideal getaway for antiques and art shopping, or fishing and boating along the river.

Family-run **Occoquan Antiques** (✉ *405 Mill St.* ☎ *703/499–9312* ⊕ *www. occoquanantiques.com* ⊗ *Open Tues.–Sun.*) specializes in mahogany furniture from the 1920s and 1930s. The**Artists' Undertaking Gallery** (✉ *309 Mill St.* ☎ *703/494–0584* ⊕ *www.theartistsundertaking.com* ⊗ *Daily 11–5.*) displays the work of local artisans, including basket weavers, painters, and potters. **The Story Tellers** (✉ *308-D Poplar Alley* ☎ *703/494–1994* ⊕ *www.3storytellers.com* ⊗ *Closed Mon.–Wed.*) is dedicated entirely to children and specializes in multicultural and award-winning books.

After working up an appetite browsing, be sure to stop by **Mom's Apple Pie Company** (✉ *126A Commerce St.* ☎ *703/497–7437* ⊕ *www.MomsApple-PieCo.com*.) to indulge in a forkful of the mind-blowing black raspberry pie (or whatever is seasonal). **The Garden Kitchen** (✉ *404 Mill St.* ☎ *703/494–2848*) has a homey atmosphere that perfectly matches its low-key lunch menu, which includes peanut-butter-and-jelly sandwiches and quiche lorraine.

FAIRFAX COUNTY

In 1649 King Charles II of England gave the land that would become Fairfax County to seven English noblemen. It became a county in 1742 and was named after Thomas, sixth Lord Fairfax. Widespread tobacco farming, the dominant industry in the 18th century, eventually depleted the land. After tobacco, dairy farming became the major agricultural activity, and by 1925 Fairfax was first among all Virginia counties in dairy production. Today the economy depends upon business and government, and Fairfax County has one of the highest per capita incomes in the country. Wolf Trap, the only national park dedicated to the performing arts, is here, and throughout the year it draws concertgoers from miles around.

Fairfax County Visitors Center (✉ *8180A Silverbrook Rd., Lorton* ☎ *800/732–4732* ⊕ *www.visitfairfax.org*).

CHANTILLY

8 mi northwest of Fairfax.

Located in western Fairfax County, Chantilly is home to Dulles International Airport as well as the Smithsonian's National Air and Space Museum Steven F. Udvar-Hazy Center. During the Civil War, Union and Confederate troops clashed here in the Battle of Chantilly.

EXPLORING

★ Opened in 2003 to commemorate the 100th anniversary of the Wright brothers' flight, the **National Air and Space Museum Steven F. Udvar-Hazy Center** is beside Washington Dulles International Airport. The gargantuan facility displays 123 aircraft and 141 large space artifacts, including rockets, satellites, experimental flying machines, a Concorde, the Space Shuttle *Enterprise,* the *Enola Gay,* and a Lockheed SR-71 Blackbird, which in 1990 flew from Los Angeles to Washington, DC, in just over an hour. An IMAX theater here shows films about flight. Parking is free after 4 PM. ✉ *14390 Air and Space Museum Pkwy.* ☎ *202/633–1000* ⊕ *www.nasm.si.edu/udvarhazy* ☜ *Free, IMAX $8.50, parking $12* ⊙ *Daily 10–5:30.*

The main attraction for those who come to Chantilly is a Federal-period home called **Sully.** The house has changed hands many times since it was built in 1794 by Richard Bland Lee, Northern Virginia's first representative to Congress. Citizen action in the 20th century saved it from destruction during construction of nearby Dulles Airport. In the 1970s the house and its outbuildings were restored to their original appearance, with a representative kitchen and flower gardens. A 45-minute tour is offered every hour on the hour, and tours of the outbuildings and slave quarters are available daily at 2 PM. Educational programs, special events, and living-history programs are held here throughout the year. ✉ *Rte. 28, 3601 Sully Rd.* ☎ *703/437–1794* ⊕ *www.fairfaxcounty.gov/parks/sully* ☜ *$6* ⊙ *Wed.–Mon. 11–4.*

MANASSAS

16 mi southwest of Fairfax.

EXPLORING

☾ The Confederacy won two important victories—in July 1861 and Fodor'sChoice August 1862—at **Manassas National Battlefield Park,** or Bull Run. General ★ Thomas Jonathan Jackson earned his nickname Stonewall here, when he and his brigade "stood like a stone wall." When the second battle ended, the Confederacy was at the zenith of its power. Originally farmland, the battlefield bore witness to casualties of nearly 30,000 troops. The Stone House, used as an aid station during the war, still stands. President Taft led a peaceful reunion of thousands of veterans here in 1911—50 years after the first battle. The "Peace Jubilee" continues to be celebrated at the Manassas courthouse every summer. A self-guided walking or driving tour of the park begins at the visitor center, whose exhibits and audiovisual presentations greatly enhance a visit. Bull Run is a 26-mi drive from Washington; from Arlington and Fairfax take I–66 west (use I–495 to get to I–66 from Alexandria) to Exit 47B (Sudley Road/Route 234 North). Don't be fooled by the earlier Manassas exit for Route 28. The visitor center is ½-mi north on the right. ✉ *6511 Sudley Rd.* ☎ *703/361–1339* ⊕ *www.nps.gov/mana* ☜ *$3 for 3 days* ⊙ *Park daily dawn–dusk, visitor center daily 8:30–5.*

WHERE TO STAY

$$ ▥ **Courtyard Manassas Battlefield Park.** You can't get any closer to the Manassas Battlefield than this—it's down the block from the main entrance. Business travelers appreciate the hostelry's location near the Dulles High Tech Corridor, with plenty of dining and shopping nearby. This beautifully landscaped, three-story hotel has comfy guest rooms that feature luxurious linens, down comforters, thick mattresses, and

fluffy pillows. Included are a coffee-maker, hair dryer, iron, and ironing board. **Pros:** close to the Manassas Battlefield; complimentary newspaper delivered to each room. **Cons:** restaurant serves breakfast only; no shuttle bus offered; area is light on public transportation. ⊠ *10701 Battleview Pkwy.* ☎ *703/335–1300*

WORD OF MOUTH

"Bloody but unavoidable history, told with an unflinching eye for detail. There were two battles of Manassas; the site allows you to trace both." —Neal Sanders

🖨 *703/335–9442* ⇆ *137 rooms, 12 suites* ⌂ *In-room: refrigerator, dial-up. In-hotel: restaurant, pool, gym, laundry facilities, parking (no fee), no-smoking rooms* ▤ *AE, D, DC MC, V.*

TYSONS CORNER

11 mi northwest of Alexandria.

A highly developed commercial area of office buildings, hotels, restaurants, and two major shopping centers, Tysons Corner is a fashionable address in the Washington, DC, area.

TIMING & PRECAUTIONS
Beware of the grating traffic jam on every road, side street, and parking lot at rush hour. Routes 123 and 7 and International Drive are the worst; I–495, the Beltway, is less affected. Weekends can also bring bumper-to-bumper traffic on these roads, as residents from throughout Fairfax County and beyond like to shop at the malls in Tysons.

ESSENTIALS
Tyson's Westpark Transit Station (⊠ *Tyco Rd. and International Dr., off the Dulles Toll Rd.*).

WHERE TO EAT

$$$–$$$$　✕**Capital Grille.** A small group of urban restaurants are tucked in a
AMERICAN　pocket of high-end stores in the suburb of Tysons Corner. Among them is the Capital Grille, where meat and potatoes means fine dry-aged porterhouse cuts and delicious cream-based traditional mashed potatoes. Pair it with a selection off the list of more than 30 premium wines. Another don't-miss is the panfried calamari with hot cherry peppers. Dine in elegance, as Oriental carpets meet dark mahogany wood and plush leather seating, and gold-framed portraits hang on the walls. ⊠ *1861 International Dr., at Rte. 7, McLean* ☎ *703/448–3900* ⊕ *www. thecapitalgrille.com* ▤ *AE, D, DC, MC, V* ⊗ *No lunch weekends.*

$–$$　✕**Clyde's of Tysons Corner.** A branch of a popular Georgetown pub,
ECLECTIC　Clyde's has four art deco dining rooms, one or more of which may be devoted to private parties. The Palm Terrace has high ceilings and lots of faux greenery; less formal dining rooms adjoin each other and a couple of bars. Clyde's mostly attracts workers from the nearby corporate buildings, who appreciate the attentive service and high-quality fare. The lengthy, eclectic menu always includes fresh fish dishes, such as trout Parmesan. The wine list is equally long. ⊠ *8332 Leesburg Pike, Tysons Corner* ☎ *703/734–1900* ⊕ *www.clydes.com* ▤ *AE, D, DC, MC, V.*

WHERE TO STAY

$$–$$$ Hilton McLean/Tysons Corner. The staff has a reputation for friendliness at this upscale hotel, where rooms are decorated in an autumn color scheme with restful green carpeting and upholstered furniture. The large guest rooms have two overstuffed lounge chairs and a desk; many also have a matching sofa, work desk, hair dryer, iron, ironing board, and coffeemaker. The Cafe Restaurant serves American cuisine from 6:30 AM to 11 PM daily. **Pros:** free shuttle service to the two vast shopping malls at Tysons Corner and elsewhere in a 3-mi radius; free copy of *USA Today* available. **Cons:** traffic can be difficult in this area of Northern Virginia near I–495 and Route 123; fee for Wi-Fi use. ✉ *7920 Jones Branch Dr., McLean* ☎ *703/847–5000* ⊕ *www.mclean.hilton.com* ⤴ *458 rooms, 18 suites △ In-room: dial-up. In-hotel: 2 restaurants, room service, bar, pool, gym, spa, executive floor, public Wi-Fi* ▭ *AE, D, DC, MC, V.*

$$$$ Ritz-Carlton, Tysons Corner. One of the most elegant hotels in the DC area has large guest rooms with modern furniture and flat-screen TVs. Booking a concierge room gives you access to an exclusive club with five complimentary mini-meals and appetizer services throughout the day and sweeping views of the Virginia countryside. On the third floor is the expansive European Day Spa. The lobby lounge's dark-panel walls and safari animal bronzes make it feel like a 19th-century club room. The hotel adjoins the exclusive Tysons Galleria mall. **Pros:** true luxury experience; the location adjoining the Tysons Galleria mall is ideal for browsing Saks Fifth Avenue or Neiman Marcus; there's also a multitude of dining options, from Legal Sea Foods to P.F. Chang's China Bistro. **Cons:** like any hotel in the Tysons Corner area, it's burdened with heavy shopper and commuter traffic; a stay here is a hit to the wallet. ✉ *1700 Tysons Blvd., McLean* ☎ *703/506–4300* ⊕ *www.ritzcarlton. com* ⤴ *348 rooms, 50 suites △ In-room: Ethernet. In-hotel: restaurant, bar, pool, gym, spa, concierge, laundry service, executive floor, parking (fee), no-smoking rooms* ▭ *AE, D, MC, V.*

SHOPPING

The **Galleria at Tysons II.** Across a busy highway from Tysons Corner Center, the Galleria has about 100 generally upscale retailers, including Saks Fifth Avenue, Versace, and Neiman Marcus, and a variety of average to good restaurants (like Maggiano's) and fast-food outlets. ✉ *2001 International Dr., McLean* ☎ *703/827–7700.*

Tysons Corner Center. Anchored by Bloomingdale's and Nordstrom, Tysons Corner Center houses more than 300 stores and restaurants and a 16-screen AMC Theatre. Traffic is extremely heavy around the evening rush. ✉ *1961 Chain Bridge Rd., McLean* ☎ *703/893–9400* ⊕ *www.shoptysons.com.*

WOLF TRAP

13 mi west of Alexandria.

★   A major venue in the greater DC area, **Wolf Trap National Park for the Performing Arts** hosts a wide variety of performances throughout the year. In warmer months popular and classical music, opera, dance, and comedy performances are given in a partially covered pavilion, the Filene Center, and in the Barns at Wolf Trap—two 18th-century barns transported from upstate New York—the rest of the year. Many food concessions are available; picnicking is permitted on the lawn, but not in the fixed seating under the pavilion.

Children's programs are emphasized at the outdoor Theatre in the Woods, including mime, puppetry, animal shows, music, drama, and storytelling. (No food or drink other than water is allowed in the theater.) A major event in September is the International Children's Festival. At any event, allow extra time for parking, and expect a traffic jam after the performance. The 100-plus acres of hills, meadows, and forests here are closed to general use from two hours before to one hour after performances. Parking is free, and on performance nights Metrorail operates a $3 round-trip shuttle bus between the West Falls Church Metrorail station and the Filene Center. The fare is exact change only, and the bus leaves 20 minutes after the show, or no later than 11 PM— but it's almost unheard-of for any show to last longer than that. ⊠ *1551 Trap Rd., Vienna* ☎ *703/255–1900, 703/938–2404 Barns at Wolf Trap* ⊕ *www.wolf-trap.org* ☉ *Daily dawn–dusk* Ⓜ *West Falls Church, then bus to Filene Center only.*

ⓒ **Colvin Run Mill Historic Site,** about 3 mi southeast of Wolf Trap, dates from the first decade of the 19th century, although the country store was added in the early 20th century. In addition to the restored gristmill, there are two exhibit rooms inside the miller's home. It offers tours every hour on the hour, with the last tour leaving at 4; educational programs; special events; and occasional outdoor concerts. You can picnic on the grounds, feed the ducks, and learn about America's technological roots. The Colvin Run Mill General Store originally served the local community and today offers penny candy, freshly ground cornmeal and wheat flour, and various old-fashioned goods. The mill itself usually operates Sunday afternoons from April to October. Call ahead to see if conditions permit grinding. ⊠ *Rte. 7 at 10017 Colvin Run Rd., Great Falls* ☎ *703/759–2771* ⊕ *www.co.fairfax.va.us/parks/crm* ⊠ *$6* ☉ *Mar.–Dec., Wed.–Mon. 11–5; Jan. and Feb., Wed.–Mon. 11–4.*

GREAT FALLS PARK

20 mi northwest of Alexandria.

★ Facing the C&O Canal National Historical Park across the Potomac River on the Maryland side is **Great Falls Park,** where the steep, jagged falls of the Potomac roar into the narrow Mather Gorge, the rocky narrows that make the Potomac churn.

The 800-acre park is a favorite for outings; here you can follow trails past the old Patowmack Canal and among the boulders and forests lining the edge of the falls. There are three overlooks in the park, two of which are handicap accessible. Horseback riding is permitted—maps are available at the visitor center—but you can't rent horses in the park. Swimming, wading, overnight camping, and alcoholic beverages are not allowed, but you can fish (a Virginia or Maryland license is required for anglers 16 and older), climb rocks (climbers must register at the visitor center or lower parking lot beforehand), or—if you're an experienced boater with your own equipment—go white-water kayaking (*below* the falls only). As is true all along this stretch of the river, the currents are deadly. Despite frequent signs and warnings, there are those who occasionally dare the water and drown.

A tour of the visitor center and museum takes 45 minutes. Staff members conduct special tours and walks year-round. ⊠*Rte. 193/Old Georgetown Pike; Exit 44 off Rte. 495, the Capitol Beltway to Rte. 738, follow signs* ☎*703/285–2966* ⊕*www.nps.gov/grfa* ⊠*$5 per vehicle; $3 for entry on foot, horse, or bicycle; admission good for 3 days* ☉ *Year-round, daily 7–dusk. Visitor center Apr.–Oct., daily 10–5; Nov.–Mar., daily 10–4.*

Downriver about 8 mi from Great Falls Park, the **Chain Bridge** links the District of Columbia with Virginia. It is named for the chains that held up the original structure. The Virginia side of the river in the area around Chain Bridge is known for its good fishing and narrow, treacherous channel.

WHERE TO EAT

$$$$ ✕**L'Auberge Chez François.** Set in the Virginia countryside, this sprawling
FRENCH restaurant serves the German-influenced cuisine of Alsace. The decor is
★ romantic—a fireplace dominates the main dining room, and red-jacketed waiters courteously guide you through the all-inclusive six-course meal. *Choucroute* (sausage, duck, smoked pork, and foie gras served atop sauerkraut), and *Le sauté gourmandise Papa Ernest*—medallions of fillet of beef and veal, a grilled lamb chop, and half a roasted Maine lobster tail—are a few of the generously portioned entrées. You are asked in advance whether you'd like a soufflé. Say yes, unless the Alsatian plum tart is calling you instead. Make reservations up to a month in advance. ⊠*332 Springvale Rd., Great Falls* ☎*703/759–3800* ⊕*www.lauberge chezfrancois.com* ⚐*Reservations essential. Jacket and tie required* ⊟*AE, D, DC, MC, V* ☉*Closed Mon. No lunch.*

LOUDOUN COUNTY

Loudoun County, capital of Virginia's horse country and an hour away from DC, abounds with historic villages and towns, antiques shops, wineries, farms, and heritage sites; the countryside is littered with stables, barns, and stacked-stone fences. The Potomac River borders the county on the north. In the major towns in Loudoun, such as Leesburg, Middleburg, and Waterford, residents keep alive traditional rural Virginia pursuits like fox hunts, steeplechases, and high-profile entertaining.

Loudoun Tourism Council (⊠ *222 Catoctin Circle SE, Suite 100, Leesburg* ☎ *703/771–2617 or 800/752–6118* ⊕ *www.visitloudoun.org*).

MIDDLEBURG

40 mi west of Alexandria.

The area around here was surveyed by George Washington in 1763, when it was known as Chinn's Crossroads. It was considered strategic because of its location midway on the Winchester–Alexandria route (roughly what is now U.S. 50). Loudoun County also had the largest militia in the state of Virginia during the Revolutionary War. Many of Middleburg's homes include horse farms, and the town is known for its steeplechases and fox hunts in spring and fall. Attractive boutiques and stores line U.S. 50 (the main street). Roads out to the vineyards are often unpaved and narrow.

EXPLORING

Two miles east of town is the **Chrysalis Vineyard,** a 412-acre-and-growing vineyard dedicated to producing both old- and new-world varieties of wine and hoping to revive interest in the fabled Norton, a grape native to Virginia. The owner says she'd rather grow the world's best Norton than the 400th best cabernet. Wine tastings here emphasize the educational experience, as volunteers present each wine in detail to tasters. The entire experience takes about 45 minutes. Afterward, buy a bottle of wine and snag a picnic table near the tasting tents. Grills are available on a first come, first served basis. Chrysalis is also host to a number of music (mostly bluegrass and jazz) festivals throughout the year, including a jazz festival in May and the Norton festival the first weekend in October. ⊠ *23876 Champe Ford Rd.* ☎ *540/687–8222 or 800/235–8804* ⊕ *www.chrysaliswine.com* ⊙ *Daily 10–5.*

The vineyards in the Middleburg area often have tastings and tours. Three miles south of Middleburg, **Piedmont Vineyards and Winery** has 10 acres of vines, as well as an early-18th-century manor house. Piedmont specializes in white wines such as chardonnay and semillon, but also makes some reds. ⊠ *Rte. 626* ☎ *540/687–5528* ⊕ *www.piedmont wines.com* ⊙ *Tours Sat. 11:30; tasting room Sat.–Mon. 11–5.*

One mile east of Middleburg is the **Swedenburg Estate Vineyard.** The winery's modern building sits on a working farm, which raises Angus beef cattle. The Bull Run mountains form a backdrop for the vineyards. Swedenburg vineyard grows chardonnay, cabernet sauvignon, pinot noir, and Riesling. ⊠ *Valley View Farm, Rte. 50/23959 Winery La.* ☎ *540/687–5219* ⊕ *www.swedenburgwines.com* ⊙ *Weekends 11–5, weekdays by appointment.*

WHERE TO STAY

$$ 📷 **Middleburg Country Inn.** This three-story structure, built in 1820 and enlarged thereafter, was the rectory of St. John's Parish Emmanuel Episcopal Church until 1907. Its medium-size rooms are furnished with antiques and period reproductions. Unusual for a small inn, each guest room has its own phone and free wireless Internet. A full country breakfast includes your choice of three entrées, and, when weather permits, you can eat your meal alfresco. The inn is within walking distance of the historic downtown. **Pros:** historic inn with free Internet; rooms include film library and complimentary ice cream. **Cons:** there's a $70 surcharge if you book a room for Saturday night only; cancellations must be made 10 days in advance of stay to avoid one-night's lodging charge. ☒*209 E. Washington St., Box 2065* ☎*540/687–6082 or 800/262–6082* ⊕*www.middleburgcountryinn.com* ⇨*5 rooms, 3 suites* ♿*In-room: Ethernet, Wi-Fi. In-hotel: restaurant, no elevator, public Wi-Fi* ☐*AE, D, MC, V* ⑩*BP.*

$$ ☷ **The Red Fox Inn and Tavern.** Built in 1728 of local fieldstone, Mr. Chinn's Ordinary (tavern) was sited on the vast estate of Thomas, sixth Lord Fairfax. George Washington visited the popular tavern in 1748. During the Civil War the inn served as a headquarters and hospital for Confederates. Today it is on the National Register of Historic Places. Fresh flowers, bathrobes, and the *Washington Post* delivered to your four-poster bedroom are extras that make for a special stay. **Pros:** romantic inn; in the center of town. **Cons:** the limited number of rooms can make this a difficult reservation to secure; pricey lodging option. ☒*2 E. Washington St., Box 385* ☎*540/687–6301 or 800/223–1728* ⊕*www.redfox.com* ⇨*13 rooms* ♿*In-room: dial-up. In-hotel: restaurant, public Wi-Fi* ☐*AE, D, MC, V* ⑩*BP.*

EN ROUTE

Fodor's Choice
★

Five miles south of Leesburg on Route 15, **Oatlands** is a former 3,408-acre plantation built by a great-grandson of Robert "King" Carter, one of the wealthiest pre-Revolution planters in Virginia. The Greek Revival manor house was begun in 1804 in the Federal style; a stately portico and half-octagonal stair wings were added in the 1820s. The house, a National Trust Historic Site, has been meticulously restored, and the manicured fields remain host to equestrian events from spring to fall. Among these is the Loudoun Hunt Point-to-Point in April, a race that brings out the entire community for tailgates and picnics on blankets. The terraced walls here border a restored English garden of 4.5 acres. ☒*20850 Oatlands Plantation La. (Rte. 15)* ☎*703/777–3174* ⊕*www. oatlands.org* ☷*$10; additional fee for special events* ☉*Mar. 30–Dec. 30, Mon.–Sat. 10–5, Sun. 1–5; tours on the hr.*

LEESBURG

36 mi northwest of Alexandria.

Leesburg is one of the oldest towns in Northern Virginia. Its numerous fine Georgian and Federal buildings now house offices, shops, restaurants, and homes. In an early sign of changing allegiances, "George Town" changed its name to Leesburg in 1758 to honor Virginia's illustrious Lee family. When the British burned Washington during the War of 1812, many government records, including originals of the Declaration of Independence and the U.S. Constitution, went to Leesburg for safekeeping at the homes of Sheriff John Littlejohn and Clerk of Court Charles Binns.

EXPLORING

Within the 1,200 acres that make up **Morven Park** are the Morven Park International Equestrian Institute (a private riding school) and two museums: Winmill Carriage Museum and the Museum of Hounds and

Hunting. The elegant mansion was originally a fieldstone farm house built in 1781. It evolved into a Greek Revival building that bears a striking resemblance to the White House (completed in 1800). Scenes from the Civil War film *Gods and Generals* and other movies were filmed here. In fact, the land was once a Confederate camp, remnants of which they are still finding today. Two governors have also lived here. The mansion and the Museum of Hounds and Hunting have been closed for an extensive renovation since 2003, although some rooms in the mansion have reopened; call to check. The Winmill Carriage Museum, housing more than 50 historic vehicles including one belonging to Grace Kelly and another belonging to Tom Thumb, is open to those taking the tours. ■TIP→ **Morven Park hosts Civil War reenactments the third Saturday of each month from April to mid-November.** Call for the latest info. ⊠*Old Waterford Rd., 1 mi north of Leesburg* ☎*703/777–2414* ⊕*www.morvenpark.org* ✑*$5* ⊙*Tours Apr.–Nov., Fri.–Mon. 1–4; tours on the hr.*

WHERE TO STAY & EAT

$$ ╳**Lightfoot Restaurant.** Housed in a Romanesque-Revival building
AMERICAN   (1888), this restaurant was the Peoples National Bank for more than half a century. Restored to its original grandeur, the restaurant was named in honor of Francis Lightfoot Lee, a signer of the Declaration of Independence. One of the wine "cellars" is actually the bank's vault. The seasonal American cuisine, based on local ingredients, includes Blue Ridge spinach salad, a variation on oysters Rockefeller, seared salmon topped with artichoke gratin and crab over apricot couscous, balsamic vinegar-and-sage-glazed pork chop with Asiago-potato soufflé, and many kinds of seafood. ⊠*11 N. King St.* ☎*703/771–2233* ⊕*www.lightfootrestaurant.com* ⊟*AE, MC, V.*

$$$$ ⌂**Lansdowne Resort.** With 312 acres of hills and tall trees bordered by the Potomac River, Lansdowne specializes in outdoor activities and has miles of hiking and jogging trails. Polished wood furniture, handsome wall decorations, and marble-accented bathrooms help make the property elegant. On the Potomac restaurant serves a seasonal menu with fresh fish options. The Riverside Hearth, an upscale café overlooking an 18-hole golf course and driving range, is best known for its decadent Sunday brunch buffet. **Pros:** there's always something to do here between its tennis courts, pools, and 45 holes of championship golf courses; some areas of the hotel have beautiful views. **Cons:** the resort gets mixed reviews when it comes to service and friendliness of front desk staff; prices are high. ⊠*44050 Woodridge Pkwy., off Rte. 7* ☎*703/729–8400 or 800/541–4801* ⊕*www.lansdowneresort.com* ⤶*305 rooms, 14 suites* ⌂*In-room: WiFi. In-hotel: 2 restaurants, bars, golf courses, tennis courts, pools, gym, spa, bicycles, concierge, laundry service, parking (no fee), no-smoking rooms* ⊟*AE, D, DC, MC, V.*

CLOSE UP

Virginia's Winemaking Roots

In 1609 English settlers in Jamestown, Virginia, produced the first wine—however humble—in America. In the nearly 400 years since, it has been sink or swim for the state's wine industry—mostly sink. But after numerous tries, Virginia can claim some 135 wineries.

In 1611 the Virginia Company, eager to establish wine making in the Colonies, brought over French wine-growers along with slips and seeds of European vine stocks. For the next two centuries, French viticulturists attempted but failed to transplant European rootstock to the New World. In 1769 the Virginia Assembly appointed the Frenchman Andrew Estave as winemaker and viticulturist. He couldn't get the European stock to take either, but realized that the problem lay with Virginia's harsher climate of cold winters and hot, humid summers. Estave believed that growers should therefore use native American grapes, which were more likely to flourish.

Thomas Jefferson was anxious to promote grape growing, to encourage wine drinking for itself, and to create a cash-crop alternative to tobacco. Although he appreciated European wines, Jefferson believed that successful wine making in America would depend on native varietals. By 1800 he and other Virginians had begun developing hybrids of American and European varieties, resulting in grapes that combined American hardiness with European finesse and complexity. The most popular are still grown today.

A strong wine-making industry developed in Virginia between 1800 and the Civil War. The war's fierce battles destroyed many vineyards but as recently as 1950 only 15 acres of grapes were being grown. In the 1960s the Virginia grape industry began a revival that has made it the sixth-largest wine-producing state. The revival began with American hybrids but has shifted to French hybrids.

Today Virginia's wines are winning national and international acclaim. The state sells more than 357,000 cases of wine yearly from 2,800 acres of wine grapes. The most popular variety, chardonnay, comes as a medium- to full-bodied dry white. It may be fruity, with a hint of apples or citrus. Other whites include vidal blanc, viognier, Riesling, Gewürztraminer, sauvignon blanc, and a Seyval blanc. Virginia's reds include cabernet franc, petit verdot, cabernet sauvignon, merlot, pinot noir, and Chambourcin.

Virginia's wineries are spread around the state in six American Viticultural Areas. The wine industry begun by Jefferson is in the Monticello region in central Virginia. Other areas are the Shenandoah, Northern Neck George Washington Birthplace, North Fork of Roanoke, Rocky Knob, and Virginia's Eastern Shore. Each area has been designated for its unique wine-growing conditions.

The "Virginia Winery Guide" lists each of the state's wineries (many offer tours and tastings). It's free and can be picked up at visitor information centers throughout the state or by contacting the **Virginia Wine Board**(☎*800/828–4637* ⊕*www. virginiawine.org*). From there you can also find descriptions of more than 500 wine events and festivals that take place each year, attracting half a million visitors.

WATERFORD

5 mi northwest of Leesburg, 45 mi northwest of Alexandria.

The historic community of Waterford was founded by a Quaker miller and for many decades has been synonymous with fine crafts; its annual Homes Tour and Crafts Exhibit, held the first weekend of October, includes visits to 18th- and19th-century buildings. Waterford and more than 1,400 acres around it were declared a National Historic Landmark in 1970 in recognition of its authenticity as an almost-original, ordinary 19th-century village. Visit the **Waterford Foundation** (✉ *40183 Main St.* ☎ *540/882–3018* ⊕ *www.waterfordva.org* ۞ *Weekdays 9–5)* to pick up booklets for your self-guided walking tour of the town.

MONTGOMERY COUNTY, MARYLAND

In 1776 Montgomery County, named after Revolutionary War hero General Richard Montgomery, became the first Maryland county to drop the custom of naming jurisdictions after royalty. In between housing developments, strip malls, and office parks, the northern portion of the county retains traces of the area's agrarian beginnings.

ESSENTIALS

Montgomery County Conference & Visitors Bureau (✉ *111 Rockville Pike, Suite 800, Rockville* ☎ *240/777–2060 or 877/789–6904* ⊕ *www.cvbmontco.com).*

BETHESDA

2 mi north of Washington, DC.

Bethesda was named in 1871 after the Bethesda Meeting House, which was built by the Presbyterians. The name alludes to a biblical pool that had great healing power. Today people seek healing in Bethesda at the National Institutes of Health and the soothing aqua vitae available in the suburb's relatively tame restaurants and bars. Bethesda has changed from a small community into an urban destination, but in certain ways time has stood still east of Bethesda in Chevy Chase, a tony town of country clubs, stately houses, and huge trees.

GETTING HERE & AROUND

You can hail a taxi on the street just about anywhere in Bethesda or Silver Spring. Bright blue signs identify parking; on weekends you can park free in public garages.

ESSENTIALS

Taxi Contact **Montgomery Taxi Cab** (☎ *301/926–9300).*

EXPLORING

A self-guided nature trail winds through a verdant 40-acre estate and around the **Audubon Naturalist Society.** The estate is known as Woodend, as is the mansion, which was designed in 1927 by Jefferson Memorial architect John Russell Pope. The society leads wildlife identification walks, environmental education programs, and—September through

Montgomery
County,
Maryland

June—a weekly Saturday bird walk at its headquarters. The bookstore stocks titles on conservation, ecology, and birding, as well as nature-related gifts such as jewelry and toys. ✉ *8940 Jones Mill Rd., Chevy Chase* ☎ *301/652–9188, 301/652–1088 for naturalist tape* ⊕ *www.audubonnaturalist.org* ✉ *Free* ⊙ *Grounds daily dawn–dusk; bookstore weekdays 10–5, Sat. 9–5, Sun. noon–5.*

National Institutes of Health (NIH). One of the world's foremost biomedical research centers, with a sprawling 322-acre campus, the NIH offers tours for the public, including an orientation tour at the NIH Visitor Information Center and one at the National Library of Medicine, that will likely be quite interesting to those interested in medicine and a little dry to everyone else. The visitor center tour discusses how health and medicine has been transformed through discovery—discoveries that have kept the blood supply safe from disease and begun mapping the human genome. There are about 1,500 ongoing clinical trials at this facility at any given time, and tours will take you through the pediatric day unit, which offers a playroom for children and a program for them to connect with pediatric patients across the country via Internet. Then the tour continues to the pediatric oncology lab, where researchers are working to improve methods to help these very children. Although best known for its books and journals—there are about 35 mi worth of them—the National Library of Medicine also houses historical medical references dating from the 11th century. A library tour includes a look at historical documents, the library's databases, and "visible human" anatomical simulator. The library was built during the Cold War, and as guides will explain, the building's roof was designed to collapse in the event of an attack from the Soviet Union, protecting the books kept below ground. ⊠ *Visitor Information Center, 9000 Rockville Pike, Bldg. 10* 🕾*301/496–1776* ⊠*National Library of Medicine, 8600 Rockville Pike, Bldg. 38A* 🕾*301/496–6308* ⊕*www.nih.gov* 🖃*Free* ⊙*Call for tour times, library hrs, and information on forms of ID to bring, plus other security measures* Ⓜ*Medical Center.*

WHERE TO EAT

$$
MEDITERRANEAN
✕**Andalucia.** Don't be put off by the spartan location, hidden in an office-and-shopping strip mall. Inside its doors, Andalucia's dim lighting and candles set the scene for a romantic evening out. Sample specialties from Portugal, Spain, and Italy, including a succulent Paella Valenciana. But the real treat here isn't on the menu—if you ask nicely, waiters will bring you a 1-pound steak on a scalding hot rock that you cook at your table. It comes with three sauces on the side: spicy, sweet and creamy. Andalucia hosts a five-course wine dinner the last Sunday of every month ($69). ⊠*12300 Wilkins Ave., Rockville* 🕾*301/770–1880* 🖃*AE, D, DC, MC, V* ⊙*Closed Mon.*

$$
MIDDLE
EASTERN
✕**Bacchus of Lebanon.** The lamb dishes and appetizers ("mezze") are excellent at this Lebanese restaurant. The lamb dishes are cooked so tender that the meat comes apart at the slightest touch of your fork. Try the Fatte Bel Lahm, lamb cooked in sizzling butter on a bed of pita chips and smothered in yogurt sauce, garlic, and pine nuts. Outdoor seating is available in a pretty courtyard with a stone fountain in the corner. Both vegetarians and meat eaters will find good options on the creative menu. ⊠*7945 Norfolk Ave.* 🕾*301/657–1722* ⊕*www.bacchus oflebanon.com* 🖃*AE, D, MC, V.*

¢
SOUTHWESTERN
✕**California Tortilla.** Friendly, quick service helps make this counter-service restaurant—which describes itself as "darned spunky"—a local favorite. The blackened chicken Caesar burrito is one of the top three sellers in the joint. Add spice to your meal with a dash or two from 75 hot sauces lined up on the wall, and grab a seat inside or out. On Monday nights, spin the Mystery Prize Burrito Wheel for discounts and freebies. Patrons can also subscribe to the restaurant's "Taco Talk" newsletter, which is read worldwide. ⊠*4862 Cordell Ave.* 🕾*301/654–8226* ⊕*www.californiatortilla.com* ⊠*7727 Tuckerman La., Potomac* 🕾*301/765–3600* 🖃*MC, V.*

$
INDIAN
✕**Passage to India.** Although the delivery is sometimes stiff, the regional Indian dishes in this stately, quiet dining room are delicious and made with local ingredients. Anything tandoori is not to be missed, as are the goat curry and the *kamal-kakri masala,* a lotus-stem-and-pea stew. Pictures of rajas adorn the walls in this authentic Indian restaurant, while the windows are fitted with wooden lattice screens that create a more dramatic and romantic ambience. Sitar music plays softly in the background, rounding out your experience. ⊠*4931 Cordell Ave.* 🕾*301/656–3373* 🖃*AE, D, MC, V.*

2

$-$$ ✕**Tara Thai.** Blue walls and paintings of sea life reflect the owner's child-
THAI hood home in Thailand; so does the extensive menu at this branch of
a busy chain, whose many seafood dishes include fresh flounder and
rockfish. Favorites include the mild and traditional pad thai; the spicy
Goong Phuket, grilled black tiger shrimp topped with crabmeat and
chicken sauce; and the chicken satay. Service is quick and friendly,
making Tara Thai an excellent place to stop and rest while shopping
in nearby stores. ✉*4828 Bethesda Ave.* ☎*301/657–0488* ✉*12071
Rockville Pike, Rockville* ☎*301/231–9899* ▤*AE, D, DC, MC, V.*

¢–$ ✕**Tastee Diner.** The Tastees are part of the culinary past in the Washing-
AMERICAN ton area, with a handful still left in Silver Spring, Laurel, and Bethesda,
the flagship location. These 24-hour diners are sentimental favorites
among many area residents, who value them for their hand-formed
hamburgers, the tastiness of which is subjective. Students and others on
low budgets (or little sleep) ignore the dust and relish the coffee, which
flows endlessly. Breakfast is served around the clock. ✉*7731 Woodmont Ave.* ☎*301/652–3970* ⊕*www.tasteediner.com* ⚃*Reservations
not accepted* ▤*MC, V.*

WHERE TO STAY

$–$$ ▦**American Inn of Bethesda.** At the north end of downtown Bethesda,
the American Inn breaks no new fashion frontiers for motel decor,
but the rooms are clean, generally bright, and affordable. The hotel
houses Guapo's restaurant, serving moderately priced Tex-Mex fare.
Use of the business center—including Internet access—is free. The hotel
also provides a free shuttle to the National Institutes of Health and
the Naval Hospital. **Pros:** many other restaurants and nightclubs are
within walking distance; the Bethesda Metro is a 10-minute walk away.
Cons: service is sometimes slow and unhelpful; not a tranquil setting.
✉*8130 Wisconsin Ave.* ☎*301/656–9300 or 800/323–7081* ⊕*www.
american-inn.com* ⇨*75 rooms, 1 suite* ⚃*In-room: refrigerator. In-
hotel: restaurant, bar, pool, laundry facilities, laundry service, public
Internet, public Wi-Fi, parking (no fee), no-smoking rooms* ▤*AE, D,
DC, MC, V* ⑩*CP* Ⓜ*Bethesda.*

$$$–$$$$ ▦**Embassy Suites.** Shopping and sightseeing couldn't be more convenient
★ at this all-suites hotel, which adjoins the upscale Chevy Chase Pavilion
and is an elevator ride up from the Friendship Heights Metro station.
Each suite includes a bedroom and separate living room with a sleeper
sofa, kitchen space, and a table suitable for dining and working. The fit-
ness center has more than 20 exercise stations and a personal trainer for
a fee. A dozen restaurants and no fewer than three large shopping malls
are within walking distance. **Pros:** complimentary breakfast and evening
cocktails in the sun-filled atrium; great location adjacent to shopping
and Metro. **Cons:** although rooms come outfitted with noise-strip seal-
ers and triple-pane windows, that won't always be enough to keep out
streets sounds from busy Wisconsin below; street parking is scarce, and
the garage is available only for a fee. ✉*4300 Military Rd., Washington,
DC* ☎*202/362–9300 or 800/362–2779* ⊕*www.embassysuites.com*
⇨*198 suites* ⚃*In-room: dial-up. In-hotel: restaurant, room service,
pool, gym, laundry service, public Wi-Fi, parking (fee), no-smoking
rooms* ▤*AE, D, DC, MC, V* ⑩*BP* Ⓜ*Friendship Heights.*

$$$–$$$$ ▦ **Hyatt Regency Bethesda.** Part of a busy nexus of restaurants, world-class shops, and movie theaters, this hotel, next to the Metro entrance, is a convenient refuge for weary travelers. Rooms are classically understated, with spacious mahogany desks and iPod docks. The rooftop covered pool shares space with a large gym that even has a hot towel bar. If you're staying over on a Saturday night, shell out the $10 to watch local comics perform at the Laugh Riot at the Hyatt—you can get on stage after the show and tell your own joke for a cash prize. **Pros:** entertaining amenities; great for business travelers; discounts for weekend stays. **Cons:** rooms are on the average size compared to the price you pay for them; parking available only for a fee. ⊠*1 Bethesda Metro Center, on 7400 block of Wisconsin Ave.* ☎*301/657–1234 or 800/233–1234* ⊕*www.hyatt.com* ⬠*390 rooms, 5 suites* △*In-room: Ethernet. In-hotel: 2 restaurants, room service, bar, pool, gym, laundry service, public Wi-Fi, parking (fee)* ▤*AE, D, DC, MC, V* Ⓜ*Bethesda.*

NIGHTLIFE & THE ARTS

Free concerts are held on Wednesday afternoons in summer at Bethesda Place Plaza, and Thursday evenings at Veterans Park. Catch anything from rock, reggae, and Hawaiian swing to jazz, funk, and blues.

THE ARTS

★ A sharp, state-of-the-art facility, the 400-seat **Round House Theatre** (⊠*4545 East-West Hwy.* ☎*240/644–1100* ⊕*www.round-house.org* Ⓜ*Bethesda*) primarily produces local premieres of quirky, contemporary, off-Broadway plays. The season usually also includes at least one world premiere, a traditional favorite, and a holiday musical.

Strathmore Hall Arts Center. Local and national artists exhibit in the galleries and jazz, chamber, folk, and popular musicians perform year-round at this mansion built around 1900. Whimsical pieces, part of the permanent collection, are on display in the sculpture garden. A Wednesday evening concert series features local musicians for $10. The 1,976-seat Music Centre, home to the Baltimore Symphony Orchestra in Montgomery County, opened in 2005. Strathmore's Tea is served in a well-lighted wood-panel salon Tuesday and Wednesday at 1 (reservations essential). On Tuesday and Thursday in summer, concertgoers spread out on the expansive lawn to listen to free concerts—everything from classical to Cajun and Brit pop. ⊠*10701 Rockville Pike* ☎*301/530–0540* ⊕*www.strathmore.org* ⬡*Free, Backyard Theater $6, tea $21* ⊙*Mon., Tues., Thurs., and Fri. 10–4; Wed. 10–9; Sat. 10–3* Ⓜ*Grosvenor/Strathmore.*

NIGHTLIFE

With a space large enough to accommodate loungers and dancers, karaoke (on Thursday), DJs spinning hip-hop and reggae, live music, and dance lessons, swanky **Juste Lounge** (⊠*6821 Reed St.* ☎*202/393–0939* ⊕*www.justelounge.com*) draws an eclectic crowd. Smoke a hookah on the patio on weekends.

SPORTS & THE OUTDOORS

One of the best playgrounds in the Washington area, **Cabin John Regional Park** (⊠*7400 Tuckerman La.20852* ☎*301/299–0024*) has plastic slides, bouncing wooden bridges, swings, and mazes to delight both toddlers and preteens. On the park grounds there's also an ice rink, indoor and outdoor tennis courts, a nature center, hiking trails, and a train that operates seasonally. An outdoor amphitheater brings the occasional concert or theater production.

The paved **Capital Crescent Trail** runs along the old Georgetown Branch, a B&O Railroad line completed in 1910 that saw its last train in 1985. Bicyclists, walkers, in-line skaters, and strollers take the 7½-mi route from near Key Bridge in Washington's Georgetown to Bethesda and Woodmont avenues in central Bethesda. The trail picks up again at a well-lighted tunnel at the Elm Street Park (4600 Elm Street) and continues into Silver Spring. From Bethesda to the outskirts of Silver Spring, the 3½-mi trail is gravel. The Georgetown Branch Trail, as this section is officially named, connects with the Rock Creek Trail, which goes to Rockville in the north and Memorial Bridge past the Washington Monument in the south. For more information, contact the **Coalition for the Capital Crescent Trail** (☎*202/234–4874* ⊕*www.cctrail.org*). You can rent bikes at **Big Wheel Bikes** (⊠*6917 Arlington Rd., Bethesda* ☎*301/652–0192*).

SHOPPING

Bethesda isn't known for bargains, although one of its best-known malls contains a Filene's Basement. Shoppers who love discounts should head north on Wisconsin Avenue to Rockville Pike (Route 355). Four of the area's seven regional malls are in Bethesda and the Chevy Chase section of Washington, DC. Downtown Bethesda has no fewer than eight bookstores, including a huge Barnes & Noble.

CLOTHING

Lemon Twist. Inside this boutique are classic women's wear and children's clothes, gifts, and more from designers such as Lilly, Vera Bradley, and Vineyard Vines. But most of all Lemon Twist has been known for its customer service since 1977. ⊠*8534 Connecticut Ave., Chevy Chase* ☎*301/986–0271.*

Wear It Well. From funky jackets and slacks to tailored business suits, this local shop specializes in items that wear and travel well. ⊠*4816 Bethesda Ave., Bethesda* ☎*301/652–3713.*

DEPARTMENT STORES

Filene's Basement. The Boston-based upscale fashion discounter attracts bargain hunters looking for steep discounts on designer clothing—if you find something that suits you, it'll be the best deal in town by far. Off-price shoes, children's clothing, household goods, perfume, and accessories are sold as well. ⊠*5300 Wisconsin Ave. NW, Washington, DC* ☎*202/966–0208* Ⓜ*Friendship Heights.*

Saks Fifth Avenue. Despite its New York origin and name, Saks is a Washington institution. It has a wide selection of European and American couture clothing; other attractions include the shoe, jewelry, fur, and lingerie departments. ⊠*5555 Wisconsin Ave., Chevy Chase* 🖀*301/657–9000* Ⓜ*Friendship Heights.*

MALLS

Chevy Chase Pavilion. Across from Mazza Gallerie is the newer, similarly upmarket Chevy Chase Pavilion. Its women's clothing stores range from Alpaca International to Ann Taylor Loft and Talbots. ⊠*5335 Wisconsin Ave. NW, Washington, DC* 🖀*202/686–5335* ⊕*www.ccpavilion. com* Ⓜ*Friendship Heights.*

The Collection at Chevy Chase. This mall is the latest addition to the luxurification of Friendship Heights, which now can claim Bulgari, Dior, Ralph Lauren, Louis Vuitton, Jimmy Choo, and Barney's Co-op. ⊠*5471–5481 Wisconsin Ave. NW, Washington, DC* ⊕*www.the collectionatchevychase.com* Ⓜ*Friendship Heights.*

Mazza Gallerie. This four-level mall is anchored by the ritzy Neiman Marcus department store and the discounter Filene's Basement. Other draws include Williams-Sonoma's kitchenware and a seven-screen movie theater. ⊠*5300 Wisconsin Ave. NW, Washington, DC* 🖀*202/966–6114* ⊕*www.mazzagallerie.com* Ⓜ*Friendship Heights.*

White Flint Mall. Bloomingdale's, Lord & Taylor, and Borders Books & Music, plus 125 other stores, pull in the serious shoppers. ⊠*11301 Rockville Pike, North Bethesda* 🖀*301/231–7467* ⊕*www.shopwhite flint.com* Ⓜ*White Flint.*

GLEN ECHO

4 mi west of downtown Bethesda, 2.5 mi from the Capital Beltway.

Glen Echo, now a charming village of Victorian houses, was founded in 1891 by Edwin and Edward Baltzley, inventors of a type of mechanical eggbeater. The brothers fell under the spell of the Chautauqua movement, an organization that ran what can best be described as an educational summer camp with prominent lecturers and performers. To further their dream, the brothers sold land and houses, but the Glen Echo Chautauqua lasted only one season.

EXPLORING

The **Clara Barton National Historic Site** is a monument to the founder of the American Red Cross. Known as the "angel of the battlefield" for nursing wounded soldiers during the Civil War, Barton used the striking Victorian structure at first to store Red Cross supplies (it was built for her by the town's founders). It later became both her home and the organization's headquarters. Today the building is furnished with many of her possessions and period artifacts. Access is by guided tours, which last approximately 35 minutes. ⊠*5801 Oxford Rd., next to Glen Echo Park parking lot, Glen Echo* 🖀*301/492–6245* ⊕*www.nps.gov/clba* 🎫*Free* ⊙*Daily 10–5; tours on the hr 10–4, last tour leaves at 4.*

The Baltzley brothers' 10-acre compound, **Glen Echo Park**, was once known for its whimsical architecture, including a stone tower, from the Chautauqua period. The area was later the site of an amusement park,

FodorsChoice
★

and you can still see the skeletons of the once-thriving rides. Only the splendid 1921 Dentzel **carousel** still runs (May–June, Wednesday and Thursday 10–2, weekends 1–6; July and August, Wednesday–Friday 10–2, weekends noon–6; September; weekends noon–6), with musical accompaniment from a rare Wurlitzer military band organ. The National Park Service now administers the property, which is the site of a puppet company and a children's theater that operate nights and Sunday afternoons. Social dances and classes from jazz to swing to salsa are held in the 1933 Spanish Ballroom. Art galleries have ongoing exhibits and demonstrations. ✉ *7300 MacArthur Blvd.* ☎ *301/492–6229* ⊕ *www.glenechopark.org* 🎟 *Carousel rides $1, puppet shows $8, plays $12, cost of dances vary* ⊗ *Daily dawn–dusk.*

WHERE TO EAT

$$$
IRISH
★

✕ **Irish Inn at Glen Echo.** This turn-of-the-20th-century inn used to be a biker bar and a brothel. Now it's a cozy, popular destination with a pub and a restaurant, each serving excellent Irish comfort food. Try the boiled ham and cabbage, shepherd's pie, or the salt-crusted salmon or braised lamb shank with roasted root vegetables. The pub, which has an attractive selection of Irish whiskey and a relatively affordable menu, stays open until 2 AM, with live music on Sunday and Monday evenings. ✉ *6119 Tulane Ave.* ☎ *301/229–6600* ⊕ *www.irishinnglenecho.com* ▭ *AE, D, DC, MC, V.*

POTOMAC

8 mi north of Glen Echo, 7 mi northwest of Bethesda.

The popular translation of the Native American name "Patawomeck" is "they are coming by water." Although today's visitors are likely to drive, it is still possible to view the mighty Potomac River by hiking along the towpath of the C&O Canal and climbing the rocks at Great Falls, which Maryland and Virginia share a view of from opposite banks. Potomac is also known for its elegant estates and houses, as it is one of the wealthiest communities in the United States.

EXPLORING

The C&O Canal National Historical Park extends along the Potomac River 184½ mi from Washington, DC, to Cumberland, Maryland. Three miles south of the town of Potomac, the **Great Falls Tavern,** a museum and visitor center, serves as the park's local anchor. Barge trips and a vista on the powerful Great Falls are the draws here. A ½-mi, wheelchair-accessible walkway to the platform on Olmsted Island provides a spectacular view of the churning waters. Swimming and wading are prohibited, but you can fish (a Maryland license is required for anglers 16 and older) or climb the rocky Billy Goat Trail; only experienced boaters can go white-water kayaking below the falls—all along this stretch of the river, the currents are deadly. ■ TIP→ **The tavern ceased food service long ago, so if you're hungry, head for the seasonal snack bar a few paces north or bring your own picnic.** ✉ *11710 MacArthur Blvd.* ☎ *301/767–3714* ⊕ *www.nps.gov/choh* 🎟 *$5 per vehicle, $3 per person without vehicle, good for 3 days on MD and VA sides of park*

⊘*Park, daily sunrise–sunset; tavern and museum, daily 9–4:45; barge trips, Apr.–Oct., Tues.–Sun. 11, 1:30, and 3.*

WHERE TO EAT

$$–$$$ ✕**Normandie Farm.** Built on top of a half-finished country club that was
FRENCH   foreclosed on during the Great Depression, Normandie Farm maintains the French-American provincial cuisine and romantic, rustic surroundings that the original 1930s owners (sisters) grew to love during their time at cooking school in Normandy, France. The classic menu has likewise remained nearly unchanged; the most popular dishes are beef Wellington, poached salmon, and lamb chops accompanied by fabulous popovers. Although French flavor imbues the farm, famous locals—like Maryland crab—also have a starring role. ✉*10710 Falls Rd.* ☎*301/983–8838* ▤*AE, D, MC, V* ⊘*Closed Mon.*

$$$$ ✕**Old Angler's Inn.** The inn, where Civil War soldiers from the North
AMERICAN   and South found respite and Teddy Roosevelt stopped after hunting and
★   fishing, was restored in 1957 and began its foray into fine dining. Diners like the cozy fireplace and menu favorites like the Maryland crab-cake appetizer with sesame seaweed salad and chateaubriand of veal. Everything is made fresh—the inn even makes its own ice cream and sorbet. Sit outside on the patio and garden to hear live music Thursday–Sunday in good weather. ✉*10801 MacArthur Blvd.* ☎*301/299–9097* ⊕*www. oldanglersinn.com*▤*AE, MC, V* ⊘*Closed Mon.*

KENSINGTON

4 mi northeast of Bethesda.

Established in 1890 as Knowles Station, Kensington was one of Montgomery County's first villages. Borrowing both its name and architecture from the tony London neighborhood, Kensington was a planned Victorian community from the start. Its neighbor Garrett Park even has a few "Chevy houses." Built in the 1920s, these smallish houses came with a mortgage that financed a Chevrolet in the driveway and an RCA radio inside. Start on Armory Avenue and wander through the historic district to see the entire spectrum of domestic architecture here.

The **Temple of the Church of Jesus Christ of Latter-day Saints** is impossible to miss from the Beltway near Silver Spring. One of its white towers is topped with a golden statue of the Mormon angel Moroni. It's closed to non-Mormons, but a visitor center provides a lovely view of the mammoth white-marble temple and runs a film about prophet Joseph Smith and an interactive exhibit hall. Tulips, dogwoods, and azaleas bloom in the 56-acre grounds each spring. In December locals of all faiths enjoy the Festival of Lights—650,000 of them—and Nativity scenes. ✉*9900 Stoneybrook Dr.* ☎*301/587–0144* ⊘*Grounds and visitor center daily 10–9.*

WHERE TO EAT

¢   ✕**Café 1894.** This little counter-service café, named in honor of Kensing-
CAFÉ   ton's christening, is also a full-service 70-seat restaurant with a charming courtyard linking the two. The egg soufflés, quiches, and Belgian

2

waffles are popular for breakfast, while a variety of wraps and salads are on the lunch menu. Café 1894's signature dish is turkey meat loaf with homemade mashed potatoes and fresh steamed vegetables. An ice-cream counter offers fresh berry toppings, homemade whipped topping, and specialty cones. The chef's emphasis is on organic and fair-trade products. ⊠*10417 Armory Ave.* ☎*301/946–9404* ▤*AE, D, MC, V* ☾*Closed Mon. No dinner Tues.*

SHOPPING

Fodor's Choice ★ At Kensington's **Antique Row** (⊠*Howard Ave.* ☎*301/949–5333* ⊕*www.kensingtonantiquerow.com*), east of bustling Connecticut Avenue, more than 80 shops sell jewelry, china, art, toys, silver, and furniture in buildings as old as some of the items. On the west side of Connecticut Avenue, Howard Avenue alternates auto-body repair shops with 100,000 square feet of antiques warehouses that specialize in furniture from Belgium, England, Italy, France, and the United States. For a full listing of the **Antique Dealers of West Howard Avenue,** visit ⊕*www.westhowardantiques.com*. **Antique Market** (⊠*3776 Howard Ave.* ☎*301/949–2318*) stocks vintage magazine covers, sports memorabilia, West German pottery, and vintage linens. At **Antiques & Uniques** (⊠*3762 Howard Ave.* ☎*301/942–3324*) you can find porcelain dolls, Tiffany lamps, and china. **Maria's Place** (⊠*3758 Howard Ave.* ☎*301/949–2378*) sells Victorian furniture, porcelain, and fine jewelry. The **Prevention of Blindness Antiques Shop** (⊠*3716 Howard Ave.* ☎*301/942–4707*) sells furniture, linens, and vintage clothing.

SILVER SPRING

5 mi southeast of Kensington via Rte. 97.

With a population of more than 220,000, the greater Silver Spring area is one of Washington, DC's largest suburbs and is currently undergoing something of a rebirth, with businesses and entertainment venues staking their claims in the original downtown area. Silver Spring was named when Francis Preston Blair, editor of the *Washington Globe,* friend to President Andrew Jackson, and owner of the Blair House (now the nation's official guest quarters for foreign dignitaries), was riding his horse through the countryside, looking for a pastoral retreat from Washington. His horse threw him, and, as he looked for his mount, he noticed a spring in which sand and mica shone like silver. Wheaton, a more-suburban locale 4 mi to the north, is home to the popular National Capitol Trolley Museum.

EXPLORING

Fodor's Choice ★ **American Film Institute Silver Theatre & Cultural Center.** This three-screen, state-of-the-art center for film is a restoration of architect John Eberson's art deco Silver Theatre, built in 1938. The AFI hosts film retrospectives, new releases, on-stage appearances, and tributes to stars that have included Jeanne Moreau and Russell Crowe. Each June, in partnership with the Discovery Channel, the AFI hosts the glitzy SILVERDOCS documentary film festival, one of the world's best. ⊠*8633 Colesville Rd.* ☎*301/495–6700* ⊕*www.afi.com/silver* Ⓜ*Silver Spring.*

At the rolling 50-acre **Brookside Gardens,** the series of theme areas highlight roses, azaleas, flowers with particularly potent fragrance, and plants that attract butterflies, among many others. Inside, two conservatories house seasonal displays and exotic tropicals throughout the year. The visitor center has an auditorium, classrooms for adults and children, a 5,000-volume horticulture library, a gift shop, and an information booth. ⊠*1800 Glenallan Ave., Wheaton, MD* ☎*301/962–1400* ⊕*www.brooksidegardens.org* ⊠*Free, class fees $11–$50* ⊙*Conservatories daily 10–5, visitor center daily 9–5, gift shop Mon.–Sat. 10–4 and Sun. noon–4, horticulture library weekdays 10–3.*

A selection of historic trolleys has been rescued and restored at the **National Capital Trolley Museum,** along with streetcars from Europe, Canada, the District of Columbia, and elsewhere in America. The museum is run by volunteers whose childhood fascination with trains never left them at the station. For a nominal fare you can go on a 2-mi ride through the countryside. ⊠*1313 Bonifant Rd., Wheaton, MD* ☎*301/384–6088* ⊕*www.dctrolley.org* ⊠*Museum free, trolley ride $4* ⊙*Hrs. vary seasonally. Please call to check latest information. Last train leaves station ½ hr before closing time.*

ᘓ **National Museum of Health and Medicine.** Opened in 1862 to train doctors during the Civil War, this medical museum now features displays on the Lincoln assassination and one of the world's largest collections of microscopes. Because some exhibits are fairly graphic (the wax surgical models and the preserved organs in particular), the museum may not be suitable for young children or the squeamish. Adult visitors must present a photo ID to enter. ⊠*6900 Georgia Ave. NW* ☎*202/782–2200* ⊕*nmhm.washingtondc.museum* ⊠*Free* ⊙*Daily 10–5:30; tours 2nd and 4th Sat. at 1* Ⓜ*Silver Spring.*

WHERE TO EAT

$–$$
LATIN
AMERICAN
★
✕**Ceviche.** This hip Latin restaurant offers a selection of creative comfort food in its modern red-and-white dining room, which buzzes with the chatter of lounging twentysomethings. Try the popular *lomo saltado,* tender beef medallions in a soy reduction, and, of course, the various takes on Ceviche's citrus-and-raw-seafood namesake for an appetizer. Flaky empanadas, filled with beef, cheesy spinach, and other flavors, come three for $9. Aside from the dish it is named for, Ceviche's best entrées are its meat options. However, vegetarian meals are becoming more prominent on the Andean-inspired menu, and there are a few salmon and mahimahi options and more on the way. ⊠*921–J Ellsworth Dr.* ☎*301/608–0081* ⊕*latinconcepts.com/ceviche* ⊟*AE, D, DC, MC, V.*

$$$$
AMERICAN
✕**Mrs. K's Toll House.** In one of the last tollhouses in Montgomery County, Mrs. K's has welcomed diners since 1930 and continues to please both those in search of comfort food and those with adventurous palates. Designed to resemble a country inn, the restaurant is filled with antique furniture, "Historic Old Blue" Staffordshire plates, and Nicholas Lutz glass. Try the New Zealand lamb chops, perhaps marinated in juniper berries, garlic, and rosemary. Both the menu and the decorations change seasonally. The restaurant serves a popular brunch on Sunday. ⊠*9201*

Colesville Rd. ☎301/589–3500 ⊕www.mrsks.com ☰AE, D, DC, MC, V. C Closed Mon.

$$ ╳**The Original Crisfield Seafood Restaurant.** With not much more elegance
SEAFOOD than a neighborhood barbershop, the prices here might seem absurd. But you get your money's worth: no-nonsense seafood and an eyeful of Old Maryland arrested in time. Crab cakes don't get any more authentic than these, presented with just enough structural imperfection to guarantee they're made by hand; the clam chowder—creamy, chunky, and served with a bottomless bowl of oyster crackers—is rendered with similar, down-home care. ✉8012 Georgia Ave. ☎301/589–1306 ☰AE, MC, V ⊙Closed Mon.

WHERE TO STAY

$–$$ ⬚**Comfort Inn.** This unpretentious hotel is close to Silver Spring's growing entertainment and dining hub on Colesville Road, as well as to the Silver Spring Metro. Rooms are decorated in green and burgundy, with flat-screen TVs, ergonomic desk chairs, and mahogany headboards. There isn't any room service, but many local restaurants will deliver. Silver Spring also offers a free Metro station shuttle that stops one block away from the hotel. **Pros:** a free continental breakfast in the lobby breakfast area offers cereals and even waffles; hotel was completely renovated in 2008. **Cons:** although it is only a few blocks from downtown Silver Spring, the location is in a more run-down and developing section of the neighborhood; fairly basic amenities. ✉7990 Georgia Ave. ☎301/565–3444 ⊕www.ramada.com ⬚130 rooms ⬚In-room: Ethernet. In-hotel: gym, laundry facilities, public Wi-Fi, parking (no fee), no-smoking rooms ☰AE, D, MC, V ⊙CP ⓂSilver Spring.

$–$$ ⬚**Crowne Plaza Hotel.** Three blocks from the Silver Spring Metro, this chain hotel doesn't offer many luxuries, but is a dependable, pleasant place to stay. Some rooms have refrigerators, couches, or recliners. The bedding is so comfortable here that due to popular demand guests can order it online for their own homes. A shuttle bus runs within a 3-mi radius daily. **Pros:** the Crowne Plaza's Sleep Advantage program provides guests with complimentary ambient-sound CDs to help them sleep; if the hotel forgets your wake-up call, you get a free night's stay; on a main thoroughfare with much to do. **Cons:** on a main thoroughfare with plenty of noise; rooms fill up quickly during the week, so book early. ✉8777 Georgia Ave. ☎301/589–0800 ⊕www.crowneplaza. com ⬚221 rooms, 11 suites ⬚In-room: Wi-Fi In-hotel: restaurant, room service, bar, pool, gym, parking (no fee) ☰AE, D, DC, MC, V ⓂSilver Spring.

PRINCE GEORGE'S COUNTY, MARYLAND

Named in 1696 for Denmark and Norway's prince (the husband of the heir to the throne of England, Princess Anne), the county was once famous for its tobacco auctions, which are still held in its southern end. Tobacco created a wealthy leisure class that enjoyed cricket, fox hunting, and horse racing, a sport still popular in the area. Much of the county today remains affluent.

Nature lovers should try to make a visit to the National Wildlife Visitor Center and the Merkle Wildlife Sanctuary. Flight fans can check out the world's oldest continuously operating airport in College Park. For those who prefer 60-second thrills, Six Flags is full of roller coasters, waterslides, and kiddie rides. Sports fans may not be able to see the Redskins, but they can get a fix at a Maryland Terrapins game or at a Bowie Baysox minor-league baseball game. Historic sites, including the Surratt House Museum, are scattered throughout the county.

To tour the county, start in College Park and work your way up to Laurel. Then head south to the heart of the county before visiting sites along the Patuxent and Potomac rivers.

Prince George's County Conference & Visitors Bureau (⊠ *9200 Basil Ct., Suite 101, Largo* ☎ *301/925–8300 or 888/925–8300* ⊕ *www.co.pg.md.us/subSites/ Visitors/index).*

COLLEGE PARK

6 mi east of Silver Spring via I–495, 9 mi north of Washington, DC.

As its name implies, College Park is primarily a university town on gently rolling terrain.

EXPLORING

One of the largest campuses in the country, the **University of Maryland at College Park** has an enrollment of about 35,000. The College Park campus began as an agricultural college in 1856, and became part of the University of Maryland in 1920. The university's athletic teams (the Terrapins) participate in the highly competitive Atlantic Coast Conference and draw large crowds to Byrd Stadium and the 17,950-seat Comcast Center. In Turner Hall, visitor-center staff provide information about the university and maps for getting around the sprawling campus of 1,200 acres and 270 buildings. At the dairy, ice cream made from campus cows' milk is available by the cone or carton. ⊠ *Turner Hall, U.S. Rte. 1 at Rossborough La.* ☎ *301/314–7777* ⊕ *www.umd. edu* ☉ *Turner Hall weekdays 8–5, Sat. 9–3. Dairy Oct.–Apr., weekdays 8–5; May–Sept., weekdays 10–4, Sat. noon–3.*

The Wright Brothers once trained military officers to fly at College Park Airport, the world's oldest continuously operating airport, which is now affiliated with the Smithsonian Institution. The **College Park Aviation Museum** is a tribute to the Wright Brothers and early aviation. Children can spin propellers and dress up like aviators. In fall, the museum hosts the Hollywood Flyers film series, showing blockbusters and documentaries about flight. Screenings take place at 2 PM on Sunday, and are free with museum admission. At the Peter Pan program, preschoolers make airplanes and hear stories on the second and fourth Thursday of the month (10:30 to noon). On their Web site, the museum offers podcast audio tours in English, Spanish, and French. ⊠ *College Park Airport, 1985 Corporal Frank Scott Dr.* ☎ *301/864–6029, 301/861–4765 TDD* ⊕ *www.collegeparkaviationmuseum.com* ⊠ *$4* ☉ *Daily 10–5.*

WHERE TO STAY & EAT

$–$$
PIZZA
✕**Ledo's.** Students, alumni, and locals have made Ledo's pizza popular throughout the state. There are dozens of Ledo's franchises in Maryland, but many insist that the best pizza—with smoked provolone so gooey you need a knife and fork—comes from the original restaurant, which opened here in 1955 and is still family run. (The other franchises are under separate management.) This original location also serves up homemade lasagna and other dishes made with fresh ingredients. Adelphi is just outside College Park city limits. ✉*2420 University Blvd., Adelphi* ☎*301/422–8622* ⊕*www.ledopizza.com* ▭*MC, V.*

$–$$
▦**The Inn and Conference Center/University of Maryland and University College.** Renovated in 2004, the center is a certified green building, with an air-conditioning system that is chlorofluorocarbon free. Guests can use the campus recreation center and indoor pool for free. The university offers a complimentary shuttle that links the hotel with both the College Park and Prince George's Plaza Metro stops. **Pros:** guests in need of their daily coffee fix can visit the Starbucks in the hotel lobby; two restaurants provide plenty of food options. **Cons:** it's tough to get a reservation in late May and early June; parents start booking rooms months before graduation. ✉*3501 University Blvd. E, at Adelphi Rd.* ☎*301/985–7300 or 800/727–8622* ⊕*marriott.com* ⬦*237 rooms, 7 suites* ♿*In-room: Ethernet, refrigerator. In-hotel: 2 restaurants, bar, pool, gym, parking (fee)* ▭*AE, D, MC, V.*

NIGHTLIFE

While the food is decent, **R.J. Bentley's** is better known as the favorite watering hole of University of Maryland Terrapins fans. The walls are covered with license plates and gas-pump memorabilia, except the "wall of fame," hung with jerseys from the university's past athletes. Signed floorboards from the 2002 NCAA Men's basketball Final Four hang in the terrace area, where diners and drinkers can watch games on mounted television sets. Students and alumni head to this hangout for beer, chili, wings, and sandwiches; the bar packs in fans after home games. ✉*7323 Baltimore Ave.* ☎*301/277–8898* ▭*AE, MC, V.*

| OFF THE BEATEN PATH |

Planned as part of a New Deal program during the Great Depression, **Greenbelt** was one of three cooperative communities built for low- and middle-income families (the others are outside Milwaukee and in Ohio). These quasi-utopian "greenbelt" communities, constructed and planned by the U.S. Department of Agriculture, were meant to be self-sufficient areas, with the side benefit that they would relieve some of the housing pressure in nearby metropolitan areas. The town is now a National Historic Landmark. Walk down Crescent Road to the Greenbelt Museum (15 Crescent Road) for a glimpse at some representative houses, including one International Style house (10b Crescent Road) filled with artifacts from the 1930s such as Fiestaware and children's toys. Three miles northeast of Greenbelt, the Agricultural Research Service's (ARS) **Beltsville Agricultural Research Center** has developed everyday innovations such at backyard fly traps, orange juice from concentrate, and seedless grapes. Today the emphasis is on charting environmental stress, such as the depletion of the ozone layer, but you can also catch up on the latest in food technology. The visitor center is inside a log lodge built in 1937 by the Civilian Conservation Corps, and tours take at least two hours. Because of their length and technical nature, tours are not recommended for children below middle-school age. There are neither free food samples nor cafeterias on-site. Reservations are essential; call at least two weeks in advance. (⊠ *Bldg. 302, 10300 Baltimore Ave. Beltsville* ☎*301/504–9403* ⊕*www.ars.usda.gov* 🖃*Free* ⊗ *Weekdays 8:30–4.*)

LAUREL

11 mi north of College Park.

Three other Maryland counties claim a section of this town (Anne Arundel, Howard, and Montgomery) but most of the suburb is in Prince George's.

EXPLORING

On 70 acres of parkland, **Montpelier Mansion** is a masterpiece of Georgian architecture that George Washington used as a guesthouse on the way to and from the Constitutional Convention. It was built and owned by the Snowdens, who earned their wealth through tobacco and an iron foundry. Interesting features include a 35- by 16-foot reproduction of a hand-painted floor cloth and an offset central hall staircase. Also on the property is an 18th-century summerhouse where ladies took their tea, boxwood gardens, an herb-and-flower garden with plants grown in the 1800s, and a cultural arts center with three galleries and artists' studios. ⊠ *Rte. 197 and Muirkirk Rd.* ☎*301/953–1376, 301/953–1993 arts center* 🖃*$3* ⊗ *Dec.–Feb., Sun. tours at 1 and 2; Mar.–Nov., Mon.–Thurs. 11–3, Sun. noon–3, guided tours on the hr. Art center daily 10–5.*

One of the Department of the Interior's largest science and environmental education centers, the **Patuxent National Wildlife Visitor Center,** between Laurel and Bowie, showcases interactive exhibits on global environmental issues, migratory bird routes, wildlife habitats, and endangered species. A viewing station overlooks a lake area that beavers, bald eagles, and Canada geese use as a habitat. Weather permitting, you can take a 30-minute tram tour through meadows, forests, and wetlands and then explore the trails on your own. The paved Loop Trail runs 1/3-mi; another 3½ mi of trails crisscross the property. ⊠ *10901 Scarlet Tanager Loop, off Powder Mill Rd.* ☎*301/497–5763* ⊕*patuxent.fws. gov* 🖃*Free, tram ride $3* ⊗ *Daily 9–4:30; tram mid-Mar.–mid-Nov., weekends 11:30, 1, 2, and 3, summer weekdays 11:30; late June–Aug., weekdays 11:30; trails daily sunrise–4:30.*

SPORTS & THE OUTDOORS
FISHING & HUNTING
The mission of **Patuxent Research Refuge** is to conserve and protect wildlife through research and habitat management, and to educate the public. The North Tract of the refuge is available for fishing. Educational programs are also available here. To enter, every visitor must check in and receive an access pass. A Maryland nontidal fishing license is also required for anglers. ⊠ *230 Bald Eagle Dr.* ☎*410/674–3304, 410/674–4625 TDD* ⊕*patuxent.fws.gov* 🖃*Free* ⊗ *Daily 8–4.*

HORSE RACING

Maryland has a long-standing love for the ponies. You can watch and wager on Thoroughbreds at **Laurel Park** (⊠ *Rte. 198 and Race Track Rd.* ☎ *301/725–0400*) from January to April, a 10-day period in August, and September to December. Call to see when horses will be running, but races are simulcast seven days a week.

BOWIE

13 mi southeast of Laurel, 15 mi east of College Park.

Bowie started as a few buildings around a railroad junction in 1870, but has grown into the largest municipality in Prince George's County and the home of Bowie State University, a historically black college within the University of Maryland system.

EXPLORING

Built in the mid-1700s as a country retreat for provincial Maryland governor Samuel Ogle, the Georgian-style **Belair Mansion** was subsequently owned in the early 1900s by William Woodward. Ogle was instrumental during Colonial times in importing horses that improved the American Thoroughbred. The house displays British and Early American paintings, silver, and furniture. In 1908 Woodward built additions to the house, including the **Belair Stable,** which began the modern legacy of the Belair Stud, the line responsible for Omaha and his sire Gallant Fox, each of whom won the Triple Crown in the mid 1900s. One-hour tours of the mansion and stable emphasize the contributions of the families and their horses to racing history. ⊠ *12207 Tulip Grove Dr.* ☎ *301/809–3089* ⊡ *Free, donations accepted* ☉ *Tues.–Sun. noon–4.*

SPORTS & THE OUTDOORS

Ⓒ **Bowie Baysox** (⊠ *4101 N.E. Crain Hwy.* ☎ *301/805–6000* ⊕ *www. baysox.com*), the AA affiliate of the Baltimore Orioles, play at the 10,500-seat Prince George's Stadium. Children have major-league fun off the field at a carousel, moonbounce, child-oriented concession stands, and a playground. Fireworks light up the sky at every home game held on Friday and Saturday evenings between April and Labor Day. Tickets cost $9.

LARGO

9 mi south of Bowie

Largo is an entertainment hub of suburban Maryland, boasting both Six Flags America as well as FedEx Field, where DC's popular Redskins play.

EXPLORING

Ⓒ Maryland's only amusement park, **Six Flags America** combines a theme park with Hurricane Harbor, a water park. On the "dry" side, high-speed revelers enjoy eight old-fashioned wood or modern steel coasters. "Batwing" puts riders headfirst, face and belly down, with nothing between them and the ground but a safety strap. Children under 48 inches can coast on a minimodel, "drive" an 18-wheeler, and earn their wings flying minijets. On the "wet" side, children of all ages beat the heat whizzing down waterslides and swimming in pools. The five-story Crocodile Cal's (named for Cal Ripkin, legendary star of the Baltimore Orioles) Caribbean Beach House dumps 1,000 gallons of water on unsuspecting passersby every few minutes. When your body has been through enough, sit back for the stage and musical entertainments. ⊠*13710 Central Ave., Largo* ☎*301/249–1500* ⊕*www.sixflags.com/ America* ☞*$50, kids under 48" $25, kids 2 and under free; parking $15* ☉*Late Apr.–Labor Day, call ahead or check Web site calendar for hrs; Fright Fest, Oct., Fri. 5–10, weekends 1–10.*

WHERE TO STAY & EAT

$–$$ ✕**Jasper's.** Locals come here as much to be seen as to eat. The Largo
AMERICAN location is one of four in the state. On the American menu, lobster bisque, rainbow trout stuffed with crabmeat, and the grilled-chicken Caesar salad are among the favorites; all desserts, including the peanut butter pie are made in-house. Food is served well into the night, as late as 1 AM on Friday and Saturday nights. A giant full-wall television screen plays Redskins games throughout the football season. ⊠*9640 Lottsford Ct., near FedEx Field, Largo* ☎*301/883–2199* ⊕*www.jaspers restaurants.com* ⊟*AE, D, DC, MC, V.*

$$ ⊞**New Carrollton Landover Courtyard by Marriott.** This business-district hotel caters to a corporate crowd, but it's also a convenient roosting spot for visitors to Six Flags and other sights in suburban Maryland.Guests can indulge in a hot breakfast every morning or take a daily dip in the on-site pool. Prices for the basic rooms drop below $100 on weekends. **Pros:** free shuttle service runs in a 3-mi radius to the DC Metro and to Amtrak's New Carrollton station; no fee for parking. **Cons:** Wi-Fi available only in lobby; room service is limited to dinner between 5 and 10 PM. ⊠*8330 Corporate Dr., Landover* ☎*301/577–3373* ⊕*marriott. com* ⊅*136 rooms, 14 suites* ⚹*In-room: Ethernet. In-hotel: restaurant, room service, pool, gym, public Wi-Fi, parking (no fee), no-smoking rooms* ⊟*AE, D, DC, MC, V.*

CLINTON

10 mi southwest of Upper Marlboro.

The origin of the name Clinton is unclear—the town used to be called Surrattsville for Mary Surratt's husband, the postmaster John Surratt.

EXPLORING

☉ **Oxon Cove Park** preserves 19th-century farm life on a site where the Piscataway Native Americans once lived. Children can feed chickens, milk cows, and take a wagon ride. There's a fine view of Washington over the Potomac River. Throughout the year, the National Park Service offers programs such as sheep shearing in May, cider making in September, and "Talking Turkey," when kids can learn about and feed domestic and wild turkeys in November. ⊠*6411 Oxon Hill Rd., 5 mi northwest of Clinton* ☎*301/763–1062* ⊕*www.nps.gov/oxhi* ☞*Free* ☉*Daily 8–4:30.*

★ The **Surratt House Museum,** once a house and tavern, is where John Wilkes
Booth sought refuge after assassinating President Lincoln. For her role
in the conspiracy, Mary Surratt became the first woman to be executed
by the federal government. She was said to have told one of her ten-
ants to get the "shooting irons ready" for Booth as he was fleeing after
the assassination. You can trace Booth's escape route on an electronic
map at the visitor center. Costumed docents give tours of the house,
talk about 19th-century life in Prince George's County, and discuss the
Civil War, but they won't get into debates about Surratt's innocence or
guilt. The Surratt Society sponsors a 12-hour John Wilkes Booth escape
route tour in April and September that covers the 12 days Booth spent
on the run in Maryland, Virginia, and Washington, DC. ✉ *9118 Brandywine Rd.* ☎ *301/868–1121* ⊕ *www.surratt.org* ▤ *$3* ☉ *Wed.–Fri.
11–3, weekends noon–4; tours every ½ hr.*

FORT WASHINGTON PARK

5 mi southwest of Clinton, 7 mi south of Oxon Hill.

George Washington chose this site on a narrow portion of the Potomac
River for the first fort to protect the nation's capital. It was destroyed
during the War of 1812, only five years after its completion; the current
fort was completed in 1824. Half-hour tours of the fort are given on
request. On the first Sunday of each month, costumed volunteers fire
the fort's cannons. If you cross the drawbridge over the moat, you can
see the 7-foot-thick stone and masonry walls, gun positions, and other
defenses. Although the fort is impressive, most people visit the park to
picnic along the river. ✉ *13551 Fort Washington Rd.* ☎ *301/763–4600*
▤ *$5 per car; $3 pedestrian, bike, or bus* ☉ *Early Apr.–Oct., daily 9–5;
Nov.–early Apr., daily 9–4:30.*

ACCOKEEK

10 mi south of Fort Washington.

By fighting off developers in the 1950s, the Accokeek Foundation helped
keep the view from Mount Vernon as George Washington would have
seen it. Today the once-rural area is being developed into a suburban
community. Locals call Piscataway Park, tucked away at the end of the
road by the river, a hidden treasure.

☾ On 4,000 acres of land bought to protect the view from Mount Vernon across the river, **Piscataway Park** attracts history buffs, horticul-
turists, naturalists, hikers, and families. At **National Colonial Farm**
you can walk through a middle-class 18th-century farm dwelling and
tobacco barn and reproductions of a meat house and out-kitchen used
by farmers not quite as prosperous as the Washingtons on the other
side of the Potomac. Guides point out the farmhouse's most valuable
materials: the glass in the windows and its nails. Whenever a house
burned down in the 18th century, the owners would rummage through
the remains for the nails. Old-time animal breeds and heirloom crop
varieties are both raised here. Also on hand is an herb garden as well

as bluebirds, great blue herons, and bald eagles. ✉ *3400 Bryan Point Rd., 5 mi south of Fort Washington Park* ☎ *301/283–2113 Accokeek Foundation, 301/283–0112 National Park Service* ⊕ *www.nps.gov/pisc* 🎟 *$2, families $5* ⊘ *Park daily dawn–dusk; National Colonial Farm mid-Mar.–mid-Dec., Tues.–Sun. 10–4; tours weekends at 1; mid-Dec.– mid.-Mar., weekends 10–4.*

NATIONAL HARBOR

12 mi south of downtown Washington, DC, 2 mi west of Oxon Hill.

The National Harbor sprawls across 300 acres of the previously abandoned banks of the Potomac River across from Old Town Alexandria. Although it is still in development and construction is to be expected, the location already offers world-class accommodations, dining, and water taxi tours to other hot spots on the Potomac.

GETTING HERE & AROUND

The easiest way to reach National Harbor is by car via I–295, I–95, or I–495. Water taxis from Old Town Alexandria or Georgetown are also convenient. Once in National Harbor, all you need to get around is a good pair of shoes.

ESSENTIALS

Visitor Information National Harbor Marina Office (✉ *163 Waterfront St.National Harbor* ☎ *301/749–1582* ⊕ *www.nationalharbor.com*).

EXPLORING

American Market. Shop for local produce at this upscale outdoor market, which also features crafts such as hand-sewn dolls, hot glass jewelry, and folk-art prints. Pick up pecan butter tarts or applesauce sweetbreads to appease your sweet tooth. ✉ *137 National Plaza, across from the Gaylord National Resort* ⊕ *www.americanmarketnh.com* ⊘ *Memorial Day–mid.–Oct., Sat. 9–2.*

Art Whino. This exhibition showcases a collection of 133 artists specializing in pop-surrealism, low-brow, and urban contemporary art. ✉ *173 Waterfront St.,* ☎ *301/567–8210* ⊕ *www.artwhino.com* ⊘ *Sun and Mon. noon–6, Tues.–Sat. 10 AM–10 PM.*

Fodor'sChoice ★ **The Awakening.** This sculpture depicts a 100-foot giant struggling to free himself from the earth. The display is actually five separate pieces buried in the ground, and was created by J. Seward Johnson. Its original location was at Hains Point in Alexandria, but it moved to National Harbor in 2008. ✉ *National Plaza* 🎟 *Free.*

Potomac Riverboat Company. Jump aboard a cruise ship from National Harbor's dock for a water tour of Mount Vernon, Alexandria, Georgetown, or the monuments of Washington. The ferry to Mount Vernon includes admission to the grounds. The company also operates hourly water taxis across the Potomac to the dock in Alexandria, where National Harbor's visitors can find even more shopping and dining options. On Thursday evenings, dogs can join their owners for a tour of Alexandria's seaport. ✉ *Commercial Pier* ☎ *703/548–9000 or*

877/511–2628 ⊕*www.potomacriverboatco.com* ✉*Taxis and tours* *$9–$38* ☉*Call ahead for hrs.*

WHERE TO STAY & EAT

$$–$$$
SEAFOOD

✗**Moon Bay Coastal Cuisine.** Meander through the Gaylord National's 18-story atrium, across a small wooden bridge, and straight into an historic Chesapeake fish market with bare wooden walls and a high ceiling exposing vents. Although it may look drab at first sight, Moon Bay Coastal Cuisine serves upscale seafood dishes and boasts a top-flight wine cave. Start off with the chopped salad or a selection of unique sushi and sashimi creations. Entrée options include pan-seared scallops served on a truffled potato plank and smothered in creamed corn with bacon. If you're up for a culinary challenge, order the crispy striped bass which comes whole with stone-ground cheddar grits. Moon Bay also offers a few non-seafood options, such as the cherry maple glazed pork loin. ✉*201 Waterfront St.* ☎*301/965–2000* ▤*AE, D, DC, MC, V.*

$$$$
AMERICAN
Fodor'sChoice
★

✗**Old Hickory Steakhouse.** The signature restaurant of the Gaylord National Resort, Old Hickory serves prime cuts of meat in an elegant setting. It's perfect for a romantic evening with the sun setting over the harbor or for an expense-account evening of cocktails and fine cigars out on the terrace. Order filet mignon or a 24-ounce porterhouse with four sauce choices, including béarnaise, bordelaise, green peppercorn, and bleu cheese; try the slightly crispy truffle fries on the side and you won't be disappointed. Old Hickory also has its own full-time Maître d'Fromage who presents guests with artisanal cheese from around the world. Fish and chicken options are available, but the real draw is the expensive steak. ✉*201 Waterfront St.* ☎*301/965–4000* ⚑*Jacket required* ▤*AE, D, DC, MC, V.*

$$$$

▦ **Gaylord National Resort & Convention Center.** The $800 million Gaylord National Resort & Convention Center is larger than life (and everything else around it). Guests at the 2,000-room resort can dine, shop, get pampered, and even go clubbing without ever leaving the property, which anchors the newly developed National Harbor waterfront in Prince George's County, Maryland. About a 25-minute ride to the National Mall, the Gaylord is shaping up to be a fun alternative for the DC-bound who don't mind commuting to museums and monuments. Room balconies opening on to the 230-foot-high glass atrium are a good place to watch the nightly dancing fountain show in the massive lobby below. **Pros:** 30-foot-wide media wall in the National Pastime Sports Bar and Grill; waterfront location. **Cons:** cab, car, or public bus necessary to get downtown; might be a bit too big for some; area still in development. ✉*201 Waterfront Street, National Harbor* ☎*301/965–2000 301/965–2001* ⊕*www.gaylordnational.com* ⇋*2,000 rooms* ⚐*In-room: safe, kitchen (some), refrigerator, DVD (some), Wi-Fi. In-hotel: 4 restaurants, 7 bars, pool, gym, spa, laundry service, concierge, public Wi-Fi, parking (fee), no smoking rooms.* ▤*AE, D, DC, MC, V.*

Central & Western Virginia

WORD OF MOUTH

"Go to Shenandoah National Park, it is very scenic and I love it . . . consider going in fall, in October or so, but even when the leaves are not changing it is still pretty."

—asdaven

"If you are looking for cool little towns, Floyd, Va. is nice, also Château Morrisette Winery near Meadows of Dan."

—Chewy1

Updated
by Ginger
Warder

REFINED ELEGANCE. RUGGED COUNTRY. Much like the contrast between two of the region's Revolutionary War–era giants—Thomas Jefferson, the renowned statesman who steered the early United States into existence, and Patrick Henry, a rough-and-tumble rebel who demanded liberty or death—central and western Virginia presents both of these experiences to the traveler, often simultaneously.

Eastern Virginia's coastal plains start rolling into the gently undulating Piedmont west of I–95. Charlottesville, 71 mi northwest of Richmond, epitomizes the refined elegance of this region, a center of culture amid vineyards and the homes of early-American presidents. Jefferson, our nation's third president and a principal writer of the Declaration of Independence, left an indelible imprint on the region through his neoclassical Monticello homesite, the University of Virginia, and his summer retreat, Poplar Forest, farther south near Lynchburg. In fact, Jefferson's design aesthetic is evident in public buildings, monuments, and private homes throughout Virginia.

ORIENTATION & PLANNING

GETTING ORIENTED

West of Richmond, Virginia stretches toward West Virginia and Kentucky, with its most southwestern point more than a 400-mi drive from the state's capital city. Rolling countryside is broken up by the dramatic Blue Ridge and Appalachian mountains. The fourth-largest of the South Atlantic states, Virginia stretches 470 mi from the Eastern Shore to its western extremities.

Charlottesville & the Blue Ridge. Charlottesville, just east of the Blue Ridge, centers around Thomas Jefferson's architectural genius—Monticello and the University of Virginia. To the south, the restored Civil War–era village of Appomattox Court House is a peek back in time. Farther west the Blue Ridge juts suddenly out of the landscape. Skyline Drive in Shenandoah National Park and the Blue Ridge Parkway ride the spine of the Blue Ridge.

Shenandoah Valley. Beyond the Blue Ridge is the famed Shenandoah Valley, a 150-mi stretch of picturesque meadows and farms framed by mountains on either side. Along the western rim of Virginia is Winchester, which changed hands no fewer than 72 times during the Civil War. Farther south is Lexington, known for its ties to Confederate generals Robert E. Lee and Stonewall Jackson.

Southwest Virginia. In Roanoke, Virginia's largest city west of Richmond, the new 81,000-square-foot Taubman Museum of Art adds to the city's growing reputation as a cultural center. In this area you can hike and camp in the George Washington and Jefferson national forests, float along on the New River, and photograph wild ponies near the state's highest mountain. West of these valleys, the country becomes its most rugged, in the Allegheny Mountains along the Virginia–West Virginia

TOP REASONS TO GO

■ **Thomas Jefferson:** Explore the contours of his mind at Monticello, the University of Virginia, and Poplar Forest.

■ **Presidential history:** Get up close and personal not only with Jefferson, but also James Madison, James Monroe, and Woodrow Wilson at their restored homes.

■ **Proud in defeat:** Relive the final days of the Civil War at Appomattox and honor the revered Southern general who surrendered there at Lee Chapel in Lexington.

■ **Mountain sights:** Ride the Appalachian crests along the Blue Ridge Parkway and Skyline Drive. See a city beneath your feet from Roanoke's Mill Mountain, and soak in history at the Homestead Resort's Jefferson Pools, originally designed by that great statesman.

■ **Mountain sounds:** Dance to the twang of fiddles and banjoes outside the Floyd Country Store and all along the Crooked Road.

border, and the deeply gorged Appalachian Plateau coal country in the state's far southwest tip. Known as the Allegheny Highlands, this region is undergoing a renaissance after years of neglect.

PLANNING

WHEN TO GO

The climate is temperate in this region from April through October, although summers tend to be very humid. Spring and fall are beautiful, filled with flowers and colorful foliage, but winter driving through this mountainous part of the state can be hazardous. Crowds are largest at major attractions during the summer months, and peak vacation weeks like Easter and Christmas.

Summer festivals include the two-week-long **Virginia Highlands Festival** (☎800/435–3440 or 276/676–2282 ⊕www.vahighlandsfestival.org) in Abingdon, during late July–early August, which celebrates Appalachia with juried displays and demonstrations of arts and crafts, exhibitions of animals, sales of antiques, and performances of country music. During the first three weekends of August, "Shakespeare at the Ruins" at **Barboursville Vineyards** (☎540/832–3824 ⊕www.barboursvillewine.com) brings outdoor performances of the Bard's classics to these beautiful vineyards, between Charlottesville and Orange. The **October Homes Tour and Crafts Exhibit** (☎540/882–3018 ⊕www.waterfordva.org) in Waterford draws tens of thousands to this historic community. Also in October, the **Virginia Film Festival** (☎800/882–3378 ⊕www.vafilm.com), in Charlottesville, is becoming a major event in the motion-picture industry, with screenings of important new movies and appearances by their stars.

GETTING HERE & AROUND

BY AIR Many travelers to western Virginia prefer to fly into international airports in the Washington-Baltimore area (Dulles, Reagan National,

Baltimore-Washington International), Richmond, or Greensboro, North Carolina, then commute by rental car; all three areas are within two hours' drive of western Virginia destinations.

The region's three largest airports—Charlottesville-Albermarle, Lynchburg, and Roanoke—are small and relatively hassle-free. Regional carriers using small jets and turboprops are the norm, though larger jets sometimes serve Roanoke. Tri-Cities Regional Airport is just across the state line in Blountville, Tennessee, for easy access to the Abingdon area.

BY CAR   The many pleasant highways and routes that snake through western Virginia's rolling countryside make driving a particularly good way to travel. The region's interstates (I–64, I–81, and I–77) are remarkably scenic, but the same mountainous terrain that contributes to their beauty can also make them treacherous. Dense valley fog banks, mountain-shrouding clouds, and gusty ridge-top winds are concerns at any time of the year, and winter brings ice and snow conditions that can change dramatically in a few miles when the elevation changes.

Interstate 81 and U.S. 11 run north–south the length of the Shenandoah Valley and continue south into Tennessee. Interstate 66 west from Washington, DC, which is 90 mi to the east, passes through Front Royal to meet I–81 and U.S. 11 at the northern end of the valley. Interstate 64 connects the same highways with Charlottesville, 30 mi to the east. Route 39 into Bath County connects with I–81 just north of Lexington. Interstate 77 cuts off the southwest tip of the state, running north–south and crossing I–81 at Wytheville. Interstate 77 crosses two major ridges and passes through two mountain tunnels in Virginia.

Travelers will rarely find bumper-to-bumper traffic jams in Charlottesville or any other city in the region. The major exception: autumn Saturdays when the University of Virginia has a home football game. Virginia Tech games can similarly snarl traffic in the Roanoke–New River valley area, including on I–81.

BY TAXI   Taxis are generally ordered instead of hailed. If travel in the region takes you outside the city, a rental car is a better way to go.

BY TRAIN   Amtrak has service to Charlottesville and Staunton, en route from New York and Chicago. The same train stops at Clifton Forge for the Homestead Resort in Bath County. A complimentary shuttle bus on Sunday, Wednesday, and Friday connects Roanoke (Campbell Court and Roanoke Airport Sheraton) and Clifton Forge Rail Station. Amtrak's *Crescent* runs between New York City and New Orleans and stops daily in Lynchburg and Charlottesville.

ESSENTIALS

Air Contacts Charlottesville-Albemarle Airport (✈ *8 mi north of Charlottesville at intersection of Rtes. 606 and 649 off Rte. 29* ☎ *434/973–8342* ⊕ *www.gocho.com*). **Lynchburg Regional Airport** (✉ *Rte. 29 S* ☎ *434/455–6090*). **Roanoke Regional Airport** (✉ *Off I–581* ☎ *540/362–1999* ⊕ *www.roanokeairport.com*). **Tri-Cities Regional Airport** (✉ *Blountville, TN* ☎ *423/325–6000* ⊕ *www.triflight.com*).

DISCOUNTS & DEALS

A Presidential Pass, purchased for $29 at Monticello, Ash Lawn-Highland, or Michie Tavern, grants access to these three sites with a $5 combined savings.

ABOUT THE RESTAURANTS

Since Charlottesville is a college town, most restaurants are very casual. You will need reservations for popular fine-dining options like the C&O, and business casual is more appropriate for these upscale venues.

ABOUT THE HOTELS

Both locally owned and major chain motels and hotels are plentiful along the interstate highways (I–81, I–64, I–77, I–66), with a particularly heavy concentration in the Charlottesville and Roanoke areas. Accommodations in private homes and converted inns are available through the Bed and Breakfast Association of Virginia (✉*Box 1077, Standardsville* ☎*888/660-2228 or 800/296-1246* ⊕*www.innvirginia. org*) and various accommodations in and near Charlottesville can be found through Guesthouses (✉*Box 5737, Charlottesville 22905* ☎*434/979-7264* ⊕*www.va-guesthouses.com*).

WHAT IT COSTS					
	¢	$	$$	$$$	$$$$
Restaurants	Under $10	$10–16	$17–$23	$24–$30	over $30
Hotels	under $100	$100–$169	$161–$230	$231–$300	over $300

Restaurant prices are per person for a main course at dinner. Hotel prices are for a standard double room, excluding state and local taxes.

PLANNING YOUR TIME

You'll need at least half a day for each of the president's homes, and you should allow a day for a scenic drive to some of the region's well-known wineries: there are 130 in or near Charlottesville. Plan to spend two to three days exploring Jefferson's hometown and the surrounding areas.

CHARLOTTESVILLE & THE BLUE RIDGE

Surrounded by a lush countryside, Charlottesville is the most prominent city in the foothills of the Blue Ridge Mountains. Thomas Jefferson's hilltop home and the University of Virginia, the enterprise of his last years, draw appreciators of architecture. Twenty-five miles northeast, Orange County is where you find the estate of Jefferson's friend and compatriot James Madison. The tiny town of Washington, 30 mi beyond Orange, bears the stamp of another president: George Washington surveyed and plotted out this slice of wilderness in 1749. Lynchburg, to Charlottesville's south, is near the site of Jefferson's retreat home, the octagonal Poplar Forest, and the ending battle of the Civil War, Appomattox. On the Blue Ridge itself are popular Shenandoah National Park, the park's spectacular but often-crowded Skyline Drive, and Wintergreen Resort, a haven for outdoor sports.

CHARLOTTESVILLE

Charlottesville is 71 mi northwest of Richmond via I–64.

Charlottesville is still Jefferson's city, focused on Monticello and the University of Virginia. The downtown pedestrian mall, a brick-paved street of restored buildings that stretches along six blocks of Main Street, is frequented by humans and canines. Outdoor restaurants and cafés, concerts, street vendors, and impromptu theatrical events keep things lively.

GETTING HERE & AROUND

Charlottesville is off of I–64, just an hour from Richmond or two hours from Washington, DC. Although the pedestrian mall in downtown Charlottesville is walkable, you'll need a car to see the historic presidential homes, wineries, and attractions in the region. CTS offers a free trolley service daily between downtown and the university. The University Transit Service at the University of Virginia has service to and from university buildings and parking lots, the hospital, on- and off-campus student housing, and the Barracks Road shopping center.

Van on the Go shuttles is a car service that shuttles guests from the Charlottesville airport to hotels, downtown, and area tourist attractions, but it's more expensive ($59–$99) than a local taxi. Average taxi fare is around $32.

TIMING & PRECAUTIONS

Charlottesville is full of energy during the school year and can be very crowded on fall football weekends. If you want to avoid crowds in town or long waits at restaurants and attractions, visit on a weekday.

ESSENTIALS

Taxi Companies AC Airport Cab & Wahoo Cab (☎ 434/981–0585). **Quicksilver Taxi** (☎ 434/825–3499). **Taxinet** (☎ 434/245–8294). **Van on the Go** (✉ *Charlottesville-Albermarle Airport* ☎ 434/975–8267 *or* 866/725–0200 ⊕ *www.vanonthego.com*).

Train Station Union Station (✉ *810 W. Main St.,* ☎ 434/296–4559).

Transportation Information Charlottesville Transit Service (CTS ✉ *315 4th St. NW* ☎ 434/296–7433). **University Transit Service at the University of Virginia** (✉ *1101 Millmont St.* ☎ 434/924–7231).

Visitor Information Charlottesville/Albemarle Convention and Visitors Bureau (✉ *Rte. 20 S, Box 178, Charlottesville* ☎ 434/293–6789 *or* 877/386–1102 ⊕ *www.charlottesvilletourism.org*).

EXPLORING

Standing in contrast to the grandiose Monticello is the modest **Ash Lawn–Highland.** James Monroe, who held more major political offices than any other U.S. president, intentionally kept it a simple farmhouse, building the home in 1799, 2 mi from his friend Jefferson's estate. A later owner added on a more prominent two-story section where two original Monroe rooms burned down. Though it definitely has a more common feel than Monticello, the small rooms in Ash Lawn–Highland are similarly crowded with gifts from notables and souvenirs from Monroe's time as envoy to France. Allow a couple of hours to visit Monroe's estate, a perfect way to complete a day that begins at Monticello. The outdoor Ash Lawn Opera Festival draws music aficionados in July and August. ⊠*1000 James Monroe Pkwy., Rte. 795 southwest of Monticello* ☎*434/293–9539* ⊕*www.ashlawnhighland.org* ☎*$9* ⊙*Apr.–Oct., daily 9–6; Nov.–Mar., daily 11–5.*

Housed in a converted 1916 school building, **McGuffey Art Center** contains the 2nd Street Gallery and the studios of painters, printmakers, metalworkers, and sculptors, all of which are open to the public. ⊠*201 2nd St. NW, Downtown* ☎*434/295–7973* ⊕*www.mcguffeyartcenter. com* ☎*Free* ⊙*Tues.–Sat. 10–6, Sun. 1–5.*

Fodor'sChoice **Monticello,** long featured on the back of the U.S. nickel, is well worth the
★ admission and the almost inevitable wait. Arrive early, ideally on a weekday, and allow at least three hours to explore the nuances of Jefferson's life as exemplified by the architecture, inventions, and layout throughout his grand, hilltop estate. Monticello (which means "little mountain") is the most famous of Jefferson's homes, constructed from 1769 to 1809. Note the narrow staircases—hidden because he considered them unsightly and a waste of space—and his inventions, such as a seven-day clock and a two-pen contraption that allowed him to make a copy of his correspondence as he wrote it without having to show it to a copyist. Onsite are re-created gardens, the plantation street where his slaves lived, and a gift shop. ⊠*Rte. 53* ☎*434/984–9822* ⊕*www.monticello.org* ☎*$15* ⊙*Mar.–Oct., daily 8–5; Nov.–Feb., daily 9–4:30.*

★ The **University of Virginia** is simply called "The University" by many associated with it, annoying its rivals. Unquestionably, though, it is one of the nation's most notable public universities, founded and designed by 76-year-old Thomas Jefferson, who called himself its "father" in his own epitaph. Even if you're not an architecture or history buff, the green terraced expanse called the Lawn, surrounded by redbrick, columned buildings, is inviting. The Rotunda is a half-scale replica of Rome's Pantheon, suggesting Jefferson's Monticello and the U.S. Capitol. Behind the Pavilions, where senior faculty live, serpentine walls surround small, flowering gardens. Edgar Allan Poe's room—where he spent one year as a student until debt forced him to leave—is preserved on the West Range at No. 13. Campus tours (daily at 10, 11, 2, 3, and 4) begin indoors in the Rotunda, whose entrance is on the Lawn side, lower level. The **University of Virginia Art Museum** (⊠*Bayly Bldg., 155 Rugby Rd.* ☎*434/924–7458* ☎*Free* ⊙*Tues.–Sun. noon–5*), one block north of the Rotunda, exhibits art from around the world from ancient times to the present day. ⊠*University* ☎*434/924–3239* ⊕*www.virginia. edu* ☎*Free* ⊙*Rotunda daily 9–4:45. University closed during winter break in Dec. and Jan. and spring exams 1st 3 wks of May.*

☾ At the **Virginia Discovery Museum** children can step inside a giant kaleidoscope, explore a reconstructed log cabin, or watch bees in action in a working hive. The hands-on exhibits are meant to interest children (and their parents) in science, the arts, history, and the humanities. The

Thomas Jefferson

One of the nation's foremost states-men, Jefferson is best known for his first contribution to the country: draft-ing the Declaration of Independence in 1776. The sum of the 33-year political career that followed is bet-ter remembered than its milestones, which do, however, bear repeating.

His first office of weight was that of governor of his beloved Virginia, beginning in 1779. In 1790 he served as secretary of state under his friend George Washington, and resigned in 1793. A Republican presidential can-didate in 1796, he lost by just three electoral votes to Federalist John Adams, and as rules then dictated, Jefferson became vice president. By the 1800 race, tensions between the Federalist and Republican parties were high and debilitating to a nation still finding its way. Jefferson won the nation's third presidency at this critical juncture and served two terms, after which he retired to Monticello.

The breadth of Jefferson's skills is astounding. He was a statesman, farmer and zealous gardener, writer, scientist, musician, and philosopher. One admiring contemporary described Jefferson as a man who could "calcu-late an eclipse, survey an estate, tie an artery, plan an edifice, try a cause, break a horse, dance a minuet, and play a violin." And as a lover of great wine, Jefferson introduced European vinifera grapes to Virginia. He has even been hailed as the father of the American gastronomic revolution, importing from France olive oil, Par-mesan cheese, raisins, and pistachios. The *Garden Book*, which he kept for upward of half a century, contains a wealth of minutiae, from planting times to the preferred method of grafting peach trees.

It's often noted that this architect of democracy was also a slave owner. He owned about 200 slaves at any given time, and freed only 7 after his death, and one of the most enduring myster-ies surrounding Jefferson has been his relationship with Sally Hemings, one of his slaves. Jefferson went through an inquiry into his conduct during his last year as governor of Virginia, and while president, Federalists accused him of improper relations with a white woman and with Hemings.

Virginians love Jefferson because he loved Virginia. Monticello, his experi-ment in architecture that had him making changes until the day before he died, attracts 500,000 people every year. The University of Virginia, which Jefferson called "the hobby of my old age," is now one of the nation's elite public universities. Charlottesville honors its most famous resident in a number of ways. On April 13—Jeffer-son's birthday—the Thomas Jefferson Center for the Protection of Free Expression presents the Muzzle Award to those guilty of trying to quash free speech. On the anniversary of his death, Independence Day, Monticello is the site of a naturalization cer-emony for new Americans.

museum is at the east end of the downtown mall. ⊠ *524 E. Main St., Downtown* ☎ *434/977–1025* ⊕ *www.vadm.org* 💲 *$4* ⊙ *Tues.– Sat. 10–5, Sun. 1–5.*

WHERE TO EAT

¢ AMERICAN ★ ✕ **Bodo's Bagels.** You may have to wait in line at one the three locally owned locations, especially at breakfast, but locals swear these are the best bagels south of the Big Apple. In true New York style, bagels are boiled before being baked, and all 10 varieties are true water bagels made with no fats or preservatives. Lunchtime is also popular, and the low prices appeal to both students and visitors. There are also locations at 505 Preston Avenue and 1609 University Avenue. ⊠ *1418 Emmet St., Downtown* ☎ *434/293–6021* ⊕ *www.bodosbagels.com* 🍴 *Reservations not accepted* 🚭 *MC, V* ⊙ *No dinner Sunday.*

$$–$$$ ECLECTIC ★ ✕ **C&O Restaurant.** Don't let the exterior fool you: behind the boarded-up storefront hung with an illuminated Pepsi sign is an exemplary restaurant. The formal dining room upstairs, the lively bistro downstairs, and the cozy mezzanine in between share a French-influenced menu that has Pacific Rim and American Southwest touches. The heated patio and urban terrace are also lovely dining spaces in fall and spring. For a starter try the panfried sweetbread medallions; the entrées include steak *chinoise* with fresh ginger, tamari, and scallion cream sauce. The chefs source their products from local markets and farms, so the menu changes seasonally. The wine list is 300 strong. ⊠ *515 E. Water St., Downtown* ☎ *434/971–7044* ⊕ *www.candorestaurant.com* 🚭 *AE, MC, V.*

MEALS ON WHEELS While you're strolling the downtown pedestrian mall, pick up a gourmet nosh from Hamdinger's Food Cart (⊕ www.hamdingerscart.com). This one-man show makes global cuisine from local ingredients. Try the Moroccan chicken or masala curry. He's open weekdays from 11:30 until 2.

¢–$ SOUTHWESTERN ✕ **Continental Divide.** A neon sign in the window of this locals' favorite says "Get in here"—you might miss the small storefront restaurant otherwise. The food is Southwestern cuisine, with quesadillas, burritos, spicy pork tacos, and enchiladas. The margaritas are potent. Cactus plants decorate the front window, and the booths have funky lights. It can get crowded and convivial, but customers like it that way. ⊠ *811 W. Main St., Downtown* ☎ *434/984–0143* 🍴 *Reservations not accepted* 🚭 *D, DC, MC, V* ⊙ *No lunch.*

$–$$ PIZZA ★ ✕ **Crozet Pizza.** It may look like a shack, but this red clapboard restaurant 12 mi west of Charlottesville has been serving up what is renowned as some of Virginia's best pizza since 1977. You have about three dozen toppings to choose from, including seasonal items such as snow peas and asparagus spears. Like its outside, the interior is rustic, with portraits of the owners' forebears and one wall covered with business cards from around the world. On weekends, takeout must be ordered hours in advance. ✉*5794 3 Notched Rd. at Rte. 240, Crozet* ☎*434/823–2132* ▭*No credit cards.*

$$$ ✕**Duner's.** This former motel diner 5 mi west of Charlottesville fills up
AMERICAN early, and since they don't accept reservations, be prepared to wait up to 30 minutes. The fanciful menu, which changes daily, emphasizes fresh, seasonal fare in its seafood and pasta dishes. Appetizers may include lamb and green peppercorn pâté with grilled bread. Several fish selections appear daily on the menu, along with specialties like veal sweetbreads or duck breast, continental style. While there isn't a kids' menu, the chef will make a burger or kid-friendly meal, as well as special vegetarian or dietary requests. ✉*Rte. 250 W, Ivy* ☎*434/293–8352* ⊕*www.dunersrestaurant.com* ⚠*Reservations not accepted* ▭*AE, MC, V* ◷*No lunch.*

WHERE TO STAY

$$$–$$$$ ⛳**Boar's Head Inn.** Set on 55 acres in west Charlottesville, this local landmark resembles an English country inn, with flower gardens, ponds, and a gristmill from 1834. The rooms have king-size four-poster beds and Italian Anichini linens; many have balconies. Some suites have fireplaces. There are lots of activities here, from cooking classes and wine tastings to hot-air ballooning. The Old Mill Room restaurant is open for a lunch buffet and dinner and there are two other restaurants on-site. **Pros:** true luxury; tons of amenities; sumptuous lunch buffet. **Cons:** add-on activities can make this a pricey stay; compared to other inns, this larger property can feel impersonal. ✉*U.S. 250 W, Ednam Dr.* ☎*434/296–2181* ⊕*www.boarsheadinn.com* ⚓*160 rooms, 11 suites* ⚐*In-room: Ethernet. In-hotel: 3 restaurants, golf course, tennis courts, pools, gym, spa* ▭*AE, D, DC, MC, V.*

$$$$ ⛳**Clifton Country Inn.** This small inn is a member of the Relais & Cha-
★ teaux group, the ultimate in luxury. Top-shelf amenities include Mascioni linens and robes and Molton Brown toiletries in the 18 uniquely appointed rooms and suites, situated on 100 acres with spectacular views of the Blue Ridge Mountains. Many of the rooms are named to reflect the property's ties to the Jefferson family. About 350 acres passed to Thomas Jefferson's daughter and her husband, Thomas Mann Randolph, who established their home Edgehill on the property. The foundations of the main building are thought to be the original foundations of one of Mann's warehouses. **Pros:** great food; luxury in a small setting; massive private lake. **Cons:** far from downtown Charlottesville; expensive. ✉*1296 Clifton Inn Dr.* ☎*434/971/1800* ⊕*www.cliftoninn. net* ⚓*18 rooms* ⚐*In-room: Ethernet. In-hotel: 2 restaurants, pool, tennis court* ▭*AE, D, MC, V*

$$–$$$ ⛳**High Meadows Vineyard Inn.** Federalist and Italianate architecture are joined by a hall in this bed-and-breakfast (and working vineyard), combining houses from 1832 and 1882, respectively. This 13-acre property is 15 mi south of Monticello and close to several top wineries. Their own vineyard is known for its pinot noir. All of the rooms have been recently renovated, with the addition of luxury linens and Arbonne toiletries. Dinner is served in the dining room by reservation Wednesday through Saturday, and a substantial breakfast is included in the room

rate. The inn even keeps its own hens for true farm-to-table organic eggs. **Pros:** luxury amenities; winery on-site; historic property. **Cons:** farther from town; small size books up quickly. ✉ *55 High Meadows La., Scottsville* ☎ *434/286–2218 or 800/232–1832* ⊕ *www.highmeadows. com* ➡ *9 rooms, 2 cottages* ⌂ *In-room: Wi-Fi, no TV. In-hotel: restaurant* ⊟ *MC, V* ⦿ *BP.*

$$$$ ▣ **Keswick Hall at Monticello.** If you've got the money for it, this 1912
Fodor's Choice Tuscan villa on 600 lush acres 5 mi east of Charlottesville is a luxuri-
★ ous, cosmopolitan retreat. Since it is now owned by the Orient-Express, you can expect the ultimate in luxury amenities and service. The 48 guest rooms and suites contain all the modern amenities like high-speed Internet and flat screens, which exist in harmony with English and American antiques and claw-foot tubs. Some rooms have whirl-pool baths and balconies. The 18-hole golf course, designed by Arnold Palmer, spreads across the rear of the estate. There's no check-in desk here; you are welcomed inside as if you are entering someone's home. The facilities of the private Keswick Club are open to those staying overnight. **Pros:** two restaurants and pub on-site; top-shelf toiletries. **Cons:** expensive for the area; lacking Colonial history of many inns. ✉ *701 Club Dr., Keswick* ☎ *434/979–3440 or 888/778/2565* ⊕ *www. keswick.com* ➡ *40 rooms, 8 suites* ⌂ *In-room: Ethernet, safe. In-hotel: 2 restaurants, golf course, tennis courts, pools, gym, spa, bicycles, some pets allowed* ⊟ *AE, D, DC, MC, V.*

$$$ ▣ **Omni Charlottesville.** This attractive member of the luxury chain looms over one end of the Downtown Mall. The triangular rooms at the point of the wedge-shape building get light from two sides. Cherry-color furnishings and sage fabrics decorate the guest quarters, and potted plants soften the bright seven-story atrium lobby. **Pros:** steps from pedestrian mall; nice market and gift shop; modern hotel. **Cons:** some rooms are small; no historical connection. ✉ *235 W. Main St., Downtown* ☎ *434/971–5500 or 800/843–6664* ⊕ *www.omnihotels.com* ➡ *204 rooms, 7 suites* ⌂ *In-room: Wi-Fi. In-hotel: restaurant, bar, pools, gym* ⊟ *AE, D, DC, MC, V.*

$$ ▣ **Silver Thatch Inn.** Four-poster beds and period antiques are just part of
★ the charm of this 1780 white-clapboard Colonial farmhouse 8 mi north of town. The friendly hosts help their guests arrange outdoor activities at nearby locations. The original structure was built to house Hessian soldiers captured during the Revolutionary War and still remains as the Hessian Room. **Pros:** fascinating Colonial history; romantic fireplaces; canopy beds; pub and restaurant on-site. **Cons:** small size means few amenities, particularly in the rooms. ✉ *3001 Hollymead Dr.* ☎ *434/978–4686 or 800/261–0720* ⊕ *www.silverthatch.com* ➡ *7 rooms* ⌂ *In-room: Wi-Fi, no phone, no TV. In-hotel: restaurant, pool, no kids under 14, no-smoking rooms* ⊟ *AE, DC, MC, V* ⦿ *BP.*

$$$ ▣ **200 South Street Inn.** Two Georgian houses, one of them a former brothel, have been combined and restored to create this old-fashioned inn in the historic district, two blocks from the Downtown Mall. Furnishings throughout are English and Belgian antiques. Several rooms come with a canopy bed, sitting room, fireplace, and whirl-pool. **Pros:** central location; charming decor; historic inn. **Cons:** limited availability; two-night minimum on weekends. ⊠*200 South St., Downtown* ☎*434/979–0200 or 800/964–7008* ⊕*www.southstreetinn.com* ⤴*16 rooms, 3 suites* ⚹*In-hotel: no-smoking rooms* ▭*AE, DC, MC, V* ⎮◎⎮*CP.*

$ ⊡**Wintergreen Resort.** This is a great place to get away any time of year and still have access to cultural attractions, 25 mi southwest of Charlottesville (via I–64, U.S. 250, and Route 151). With 6,700 acres of forest, six restaurants, and three golf courses, Wintergreen is more like a community in itself than just a resort. Skiing and snowboarding are the central attractions, with 20 downhill slopes and five chairlifts. One of the golf courses, Devils Knob at over 3,800 feet, is the highest in Virginia. Accommodations at the resort include everything from studio apartments to seven-bedroom houses. Most rooms have fireplaces and full kitchens; the housing units' wood exteriors blend into the surrounding forest. **Pros:** good skiing and summer outdoor activities; cozy rooms complete with fireplaces; many restaurants and other resort options. **Cons:** crowded in season; half-hour drive from Charlottesville. ⊠*Rte. 664, Wintergreen* ☎*434/325–2200 or 800/266–2444* ⊕*www.wintergreenresort.com* ⤴*305 units* ⚹*In-room: kitchen (some), Wi-Fi. In-hotel: 6 restaurants, bar, golf courses, tennis courts, pools, gym, spa, bicycles, laundry facilities, laundry service* ▭*AE, D, MC, V.*

A SIP OF A SIDE-TRIP

The Starr Hill Brewery (⊠ *5391 Three Notched Rd., Crozet* ☎ *434/823–5671*) is one of the most well-respected breweries on the East Coast, featuring four house brews including Amber Ale, Pale Ale, Jomo Lager, and Dark Starr Stout and open for tastings on Saturdays from noon to 5. If apple cider is more to your taste, visit **Carter's Mountain Orchard** (⊠ *1435 Carters Mountain Trail, Charlottesville* ☎ *434/977–1833*) for stunning views of Charlottesville and some of the best apples in the state.

NIGHTLIFE & THE ARTS

For listings of cultural events, music, and movies, and a guide to restaurants, pick up a free copy of the *C-Ville Weekly* (⊕*www.c-ville.com*), an arts-and-entertainment newspaper available in restaurants and hotels throughout the city. If you're near the University of Virginia campus, grab a free copy of the student newspaper, the *Cavalier Daily* (⊕*www.cavalierdaily.com*), for the latest on college sports and events.

FESTIVALS

In March, **Virginia Festival of the Book** (☎*434/924–6890* ⊕*www.vabook.org*) draws authors that have included Garrison Keillor and Michael Ondaatje. Thousands attend the festival, which is open to the public and promotes literacy while celebrating the book. Every autumn, Charlottesville hosts the **Virginia Film Festival** (☎*800/882–3378* ⊕*www.vafilm.com*), with screenings of important new movies, panel discussions, and appearances by stars of the cinema. The movies are shown at four sites around the university and downtown.

SPORTS & THE OUTDOORS
CANOEING & KAYAKING

James River Runners Inc (✉10082 Hatton Ferry Rd., Scottsville ☎434/286–2338), about 35 minutes south of Charlottesville, offers canoe, kayak, tubing, and rafting trips down the James.

SHOPPING

Charlottesville, at heart an academic community, supports a large number of independent bookstores, especially specialists in used and antiquarian books. Whether it's a rare first edition you are seeking or just some unique bargains, try **Blue Whale Books** (✉115 W. Main St., Downtown ☎434/296–4646). Run by an antiquarian book dealer, the shop has thousands of books in all categories and price ranges, from one dollar to several hundred. **Daedalus Bookshop** (✉123 4th St. NE, Downtown ☎434/293–7595) has three floors of books crammed into every nook and cranny. **Heartwood Books** (✉5 Elliewood Ave., University ☎434/295–7083), close to the university campus, stocks scholarly works, including a good collection of theology and philosophy. Legal-thriller master John Grisham kicks off book tours at **New Dominion Bookshop** (✉404 E. Main St.,Downtown ☎434/295–2552).

★ The **Downtown Mall** (✉Main St., Downtown ⊕www.downtowncharlottesville.net) is a six-block brick pedestrian mall with specialty stores, cinemas, art galleries, restaurants, and coffeehouses in restored 19th- and early-20th-century buildings.

> **WORD OF MOUTH**
>
> "Orange is a little less than 2 hours from DC in the direction of Charlottesville. Within a short drive you have historic homes—Monticello (Jefferson), Montpelier (Madison), and Ash Lawn (Monroe). You have lots of vineyards, including Barboursville, which lots of wine buffs have identified as an up-and-comer. You have fantastic B&Bs and antiques shops all over the place. Nice dinners are not hard to come by, either." —flo77

ORANGE

25 mi northeast of Charlottesville via Rte. 20, 60 mi northwest of Richmond.

Orange is a fertile agricultural area bearing reminders of the Civil War. Among the many estates dotting the countryside is the home of our nation's fourth president.

EXPLORING

During the Civil War, a handsome Greek revival hotel, now the **Exchange Hotel Civil War Museum,** was transformed into a Confederate receiving hospital for wounded and dying soldiers. In addition to weapons, uniforms, and the personal effects of Union and Confederate soldiers, the museum displays the often crude medical equipment used for amputations, tooth extractions, and bloodletting. One room re-creates a hospital ward; an estimated 70,000 soldiers were treated here between 1862 and 1865. The museum hosts an annual ghost walk every October. ✉400

S. Main St., Gordonsville ☎*540/832–2944* ⊕*www.hgiexchange.org* ✉*$6* ⊘*Mar.–mid Nov., Mon.–Sat. 10–4, Sun. 1–4.*

Just outside Orange is **Montpelier,** the former residence of James Madison (1751–1836), the fourth president of the United States. A massive renovation was completed in 2008, removing parts of the mansion added by its 20th-century owners, the duPont family. In her will, Marion duPont Scott left the estate to the National Trust for Historic Preservation with the stipulation that it be returned to its original state. The mansion is now restored to its early-19th-century Madisonian state, a project that totaled $24 million. Some of the Madisons' possessions, as well as a tribute to the "Father of the Constitution," have been set up in an Education Center on the grounds. The walking tour includes a stop at the cemetery where James and his wife, Dolley, are buried. Exotic conifers planted by the duPonts dot the meadowlike grounds, and a walking path wanders amid an old-growth forest. The annual Montpelier Hunt Races, a steeplechase, have been held since 1934. When they run, on the first Saturday in November, the house tour is canceled. Admission to the races is $15. ✉*Rte. 20, 4 mi southwest of Orange, 11395 Constitution Way, Montpelier Station* ☎*540/672–2728* ⊕*www.montpelier.org* ✉*$11* ⊘*Apr.–Oct., daily 9:30–5; Nov.–Mar., daily 9:30–4:30.*

St. Thomas's Episcopal Church (1833), the one surviving example of Jeffersonian church architecture, is a replica of Charlottesville's demolished Christ Church, which Jefferson designed. It's here that Robert E. Lee worshipped during the winter of 1863–64. The church's biggest decorative asset is its Tiffany window. ✉*119 Caroline St.22960* ☎*540/672–3761* ⊕*www.ndearing.com/stthomas.html* ✉*Donations accepted* ⊘*Tours by appointment.*

WHERE TO STAY

$$–$$$ 🏨**Mayhurst Inn.** An architectural rarity in the South, this Italianate Victorian mansion was built in 1859 by a grandnephew of James Madison, and generals Stonewall Jackson and Robert E. Lee were early guests. Now Mayhurst is a cozy and comfortable B&B surrounded by 37 acres of woods with hiking trails. Its rooms have floor-to-ceiling windows, marble fireplaces, and antique furnishings; some have whirlpool baths. Included with the room rate is a sumptuous three-course breakfast, evening wine and cheese, and soft drinks and snacks. **Pros:** antiques; historic; complimentary snacks. **Cons:** limited availability. ✉*12460 Mayhurst La.* ☎*540/672–5597 or 888/672–5597* ⊕*www. mayhurstinn.com* ⇆*8 rooms, 2 suites* ⌂*In-room: no TV (some). In-hotel: no-smoking rooms.* ▭*AE, MC, V* ⊙❙*BP.*

WASHINGTON

63 mi north of Charlottesville.

Known as Little Washington to differentiate it from its big sister about 60 mi away, this tiny town packs in antiques shops, galleries, custom jewelry shops, and two theaters in roughly five blocks—perfect for an afternoon stroll. In 1749 young surveyor George Washington laid out

Virginia's Wineries

Jamestown's Colonial settlers are believed to have made the first wine in Virginia, but only in the past 30 years has the Commonwealth's wine industry truly come into its own. The number of wineries here has grown from fewer than 10 in the 1970s to more than 130 wineries in the Charlottesville area alone. As you drive through the state, keep an eye out for grape-cluster signs on the highway, which identify nearby wineries. Virginia Tourism offers a free wine trail map. The Monticello Wine Trail connects 22 area vineyards, including the Jefferson Vineyards (⊕ *www. jeffersonvineyards.com*), located on land where Thomas Jefferson himself grew grapes. Virginia is becoming well known on the national oenophile radar for its viogniers, and for vintages from vintners like Kluge.

For more information on Virginia vineyards and wineries, contact the Virginia Wineries Association (☎ *800/828–4637* ⊕ *www.virginia wine.org*) or the Jeffersonian Wine Grape Growers Society (☎ *434/ 296–4188* ⊕ *www.monticellowine trail.org*), sponsor of the Monticello Wine Trail.

Among central and western Virginia's more popular wineries are Barboursville Vineyards, near Charlottesville, and Château Morrisette Winery, on the Blue Ridge Parkway in the southern part of the state.

Barboursville Vineyards. This vineyard between Charlottesville and Orange was the first in the state to grow only vinifera (old-world) grapes. The grapes were planted in 1976 on the former plantation of James Barbour, governor from 1812 to 1814. His house, designed by Thomas Jefferson, was gutted by fire in 1884; the ruins remain. ⊠ *17655 Winery Rd., near intersection of Rtes. 20 and 23, Barboursville* ☎ *540/832–3824* ⊕ *www. barboursvillewine.com* ⊡ *Tours free; tastings $4* ⊙ *Tastings Mon.–Sat. 10–5, Sun. 11–5.*

Château Morrisette Winery. With the Rock Castle Gorge nearby, this winery has spectacular surroundings. Tastings allow you to sample the dozen different wines produced here. ⊠ *Winery Rd. off Rte. 726, west of Blue Ridge Pkwy. at milepost 171.5, Meadows of Dan* ☎ *540/593–2865* ⊕ *www.thedogs.com* ⊡ *Tour and tasting $5* ⊙ *Mon.–Thurs. 10–5, Fri. and Sat. 10–6, Sun. 11–5.*

Kluge Estate. Established in 1999 just 9 mi from the birthplace of Virginia viticulture at Monticello, Kluge is making world-class whites, reds, and rosé in its 2,000-acre vineyard on Carter's Mountain. Grapes are harvested by hand and most of the wines are made in *methode traditionelle*. Taste one of the chardonnays, a blanc de blanc, or a Bordeaux blend at the estate's Farm Shop, which also offers food and wine pairings. ⊠ *100 Grand Cru Dr., Charlottesville* ☎ *434/977–3895 or 434/984–4855* ⊕ *www.klugeestateonline.com* ⊙ *11 AM–5:30 PM.*

the five-block-by-two-block grid; the town claims to be the very first Washington of all.

WHERE TO STAY

$$$$

Fodors Choice

★

🍽 **The Inn at Little Washington.** What began as a small-town eatery in 1978 has grown into a legend. The rich interior of the three-story white-frame inn is the work of Joyce Conway-Evans, who has designed theatrical sets and rooms in English royal houses. Plush canopy beds, marble bathrooms, and fresh flowers make the rooms sumptuous. Recent additions include two luxurious cottages: the 3,200-square-foot Claiborne House and the smaller but equally charming Gamekeeper's Cottage, both steps from the main inn. Chef Patrick O'Connell's much-loved New American food is served in a slate-floor dining room with William Morris wallpaper, and his restaurant consistently wins respect from international critics. The seven-course dinner costs $178 per person on Saturday, $158 on Friday, and $148 Sunday through Thursday, not including wine and drinks; rooms are equally pricey. **Pros:** ultimate luxury; amazing in-house restaurant. **Cons:** must reserve months in advance; limited number of rooms. ⊠*309 Middle St., at Main. St.* ☎*540/675–3800* ⊕*www.theinnatlittlewashington.com* ⇱*18 rooms, 3 suites, 2 cottages* ♨*In-room: safe. In-hotel: restaurant, bicycles* ▤*MC, V* ⊗*Hotel and restaurant closed Tues. except in May and Oct.* ¶◎*CP.*

LYNCHBURG

66 mi southeast of Charlottesville via Rte. 29, 110 mi west of Richmond.

Lynchburg was founded by John Lynch, a Quaker pacifist, but its most prominent landmark is Monument Terrace, a war memorial: at the foot and head of the 139 limestone and granite steps that ascend to the Old City Courthouse are statues honoring a World War I doughboy and a Confederate soldier. Lynchburg is also known as the home of evangelist Rev. Jerry Falwell, his Thomas Road Baptist Church, and Christian college, Liberty University.

ESSENTIALS

Train Station Kemper Street Station (⊠*825 Kemper St.* ☎*434/847–8247*).

Visitor Information Lynchburg Regional Convention and Visitors Bureau (⊠*216 12th St.* ☎*434/847–1811 or 800/732–5821*).

EXPLORING

At the **Anne Spencer House and Gardens** you can step into "Edankraal," the studio of this late poet of the Harlem Renaissance. Hers is the only work of a Virginian to appear in the *Norton Anthology of Modern American and English Poetry*. A librarian at one of Lynchburg's segregated black schools, Spencer (1882–1975) penned most of her work in this back-garden sanctuary, which has been left completely intact with her writing desk, bookcases, mementos, and walls tacked with photos and news clippings. ⊠*1313 Pierce St.* ☎*434/845–1313* ⊕*www.anne spencermsueum.com* ⊒*$5* ⊗*Tours by appointment.*

At the **Legacy Museum of African-American History,** the rotating exhibits focus on such themes as health and medicine, education, business, the civil rights struggle, and the contributions African-Americans have made to society, the arts, and politics. ✉ *403 Monroe St.* ☎ *434/845–3455* ⊕ *www.legacymuseum.org* 🎫 *$5* ⊗ *Wed.–Sat. noon–4, Sun. 2–4, and by appointment.*

The mansion on Daniel's Hill, **Point of Honor,** was built in 1815 on the site of a duel. Once part of a 900-acre estate, this redbrick house surrounded by lawns retains a commanding view of the James River. The facade is elegantly symmetrical, with two octagonal bays joined by a balustrade on each of the building's two stories. The interiors have been restored and furnished with pieces authentic to the early-19th-century Federal period. ✉ *112 Cabell St.* ☎ *434/847–1459* ⊕ *www.pointof honor.org* 🎫 *$6* ⊗ *Mon.–Sat. 10–4, Sun. noon–4.*

A must-see on the Thomas Jefferson tour of Virginia is his "occasional retreat," **Poplar Forest.** The octagonal architecture, now standing in a residential neighborhood and surrounded by only a few remaining poplars, was conceived and built by Jefferson, and he sometimes stayed here between 1806 and 1813. This Palladian hermitage exemplifies the architect's sublime sense of order that is so evident at Monticello. Erected on a slope, the house has a front that's one story high, with a two-story rear elevation. The octagon's center is a square, skylighted dining room flanked by two smaller octagons. The restoration to its Jefferson-era state is ongoing, and likely to continue for years to come. Every July 4 there's a free celebration that includes a reading of the Declaration of Independence and living-history exhibits. ✉ *1548 Bateman Bridge Rd., Rte. 661, Forest* ☎ *434/525–1806* ⊕ *www.poplarforest.org* 🎫 *$9 full tour, $4 grounds only* ⊗ *Apr.–Nov., Wed.–Mon. 10–4.*

OFF THE BEATEN PATH

FodorsChoice
★

Appomattox Court House. To many in Virginia, the Civil War has never ended, but the history books say it ended here, 25 mi east of Lynchburg, on April 9, 1865, when Confederate General Lee surrendered the Army of Northern Virginia to General Grant, leader of pursuing Union forces. There are 27 structures in the national historical park, restored to its 1865 appearance; most can be entered. A highlight is the reconstructed McLean House, in whose parlor the articles of surrender were signed. ✉ *3 mi north of Appomattox, on Rte. 24* ☎ *434/352–8987* ⊕ *www. nps.gov/apco/* 🎫 *June–Aug. $4; Sept.–May $3* ⊗ *Daily 8:30–5.*

Red Hill–Patrick Henry National Memorial. In the town of Brookneal is the final home of Revolutionary War patriot Patrick Henry, whose "Give me liberty or give me death" speech inspired a generation. The 1770s house has been reconstructed on its original site and contains numerous furnishings owned by the Henry family. Henry's grave is on the property. ✉ *1250 Red Hill Rd.,35 mi southeast of Lynchburg, off Rte. 619,*

Brookneal ☎*434/376–2044* ✆*$6*
⊙*Apr.–Oct., daily 9–5; Nov.–Mar.,*
daily 9–4.

WHERE TO EAT

$–$$ ✕**Meriwether's Market Restaurant.**
AMERICAN Dubbing itself a "casual gourmet
restaurant," Meriwether's offers
American dishes generally made
with local and regional ingredients, from game to seafood. For an
entrée, try the spicy shrimp and grits or a specialty pizza. This restaurant
offers portions to suit any size appetite, with plates in small, medium,
and large categories from Plantation tenderloin to pan-roasted quail to
a small plate of cornmeal-crusted fried oysters. It's in the Boonsboro
Shopping Center. ⊠*4925 Boonsboro Rd.* ☎*434/384-3311* ⊕*www.
meriwethers.com* ▤*AE, D, MC, V* ⊙*Closed Sun.*

$$ ✕**Shoemakers.** This elegant steak-and-seafood house is in the converted
AMERICAN tobacco warehouse district known as the Bluffwalk. With warm exposed
brick walls and an urban sensibility, the restaurant offers a wide variety
of steaks, chops, and classic seafood dishes. Think traditional, with a
variety of cuts and preparations, in addition to seafood standards from
surf 'n turf to shrimp cocktail and lobster bisque. ⊠ *1312 Commerce
St.* ☎*434/455–1510* ⊕*www.shoemakersdining.com* ▤*AE, MC, V.*

SHENANDOAH NATIONAL PARK

*Southern entrance is 18 mi west of Charlottesville via I–81; northern
entrance is at Front Royal.*

Though Shenandoah National Park is only a narrow ribbon on the
map, stretching 80 mi along the Blue Ridge but rarely more than 5 mi
wide, it is easy to imagine being much deeper in the wilderness as you
travel through it or spend a night camping here. Steep, wooded ridges
with rocky slopes stand out in the foreground of vistas taking in the
Shenandoah Valley to the west and the Piedmont to the east. Skyline
Drive traverses the park end to end, from Waynesboro to Front Royal,
and is the most common way to see the park. But hikers can find beau-
tiful terrain just yards from the drive on some of the park's 500 mi of
trails, trout fishers may wade into more than 25 streams, and riders can
rent horses for wilderness trail rides. Those who want to know more
about the area's flora and fauna may want to take a guided hike, which
naturalists lead daily throughout the summer. The seasonal activities of
the park are outlined in the *Shenandoah Overlook,* a free newspaper
you can pick up on entering the park.

TIMING & PRECAUTIONS

Skyline Drive and the rest of Shenandoah Park can get crowded on
weekends and holidays, so avoid these times if possible. Winter is a
wonderful time to experience the park's rugged beauty with few crowds,
but many facilities are closed and bouts of ice and snow bring out bar-
ricades on parts of the drive.

ESSENTIALS

Visitor Information ⌂ *Park Superintendent, Box 348, Rte. 4, Luray 22835* ☎ *540/999–3500* ⊕ *www.nps.gov/shen* ✉ *Park and Skyline Dr. $15 car ($10 car Dec.–Feb.), $10 motorcycle, $8 bicycle or pedestrian; tickets are valid 7 days.*

EXPLORING

Fodor'sChoice ★ **Skyline Drive** runs 105 mi, alternating between open vistas and forest-hemmed stretches and offering easily accessible wilderness. Designated as a National Historic Landmark, the two-lane highway runs from Rockfish Gap at Afton, Virginia, to Front Royal. During weekends and holidays it can seem a little too much like city driving—a 35-mph speed limit, rubber-necking leaf-lookers, narrow overlook turnouts, and the occasional black bear sighting can back traffic up uncomfortably. It's best to choose a weekday and allow the entire day; you may want to spend an hour or two resting on one roadside boulder.

■ TIP➡ **Continue south on Skyline Drive past the park gates and over Interstate 64, and the road becomes the Blue Ridge Parkway, which continues 471 mi south to Cherokee, North Carolina. Unlike Skyline Drive, the parkway is free, and the speed limit is 45 mph.**

Luray Caverns, 9 mi west of Skyline Drive on U.S. 211, are the largest caverns in the state. The world's only "stalacpipe organ" is composed of stalactites (calcite formations hanging from the ceilings of the caverns) that have been tuned to concert pitch and are tapped by rubber-tip plungers. The organ is played electronically for every tour and may be played manually on special occasions. A one-hour tour begins every 20 minutes. ✉ *U.S. 211, 101 Cave Hill Rd.,Luray* ☎ *540/743–6551* ⊕ *www.luraycaverns.com* ✉ *$19* ⊙ *Mid-Mar.–mid-June, daily 9–6; mid-June–Labor Day, daily 9–7; Labor Day–Oct., daily 9–6; Nov.–mid-Mar., weekdays 9–4, weekends 9–5.*

WHERE TO STAY

$–$$ ▦ **Jordan Hollow Farm.** The oldest of the four buildings here is a 1790 farmhouse, now a restaurant serving American regional cuisine. The youngest structure, built of hand-hewn logs almost 200 years later, contains four of the inn's most luxurious rooms, which include a fireplace, whirlpool, and TV. The 150-acre horse farm is near the tiny town of Stanley, 6 mi from Luray and 15 mi from Shenandoah National Park. From here you can gaze out over pastures full of horses and playful llamas toward a backdrop of the Blue Ridge Mountains. The only "pets" allowed are horses, which can be boarded here. Nearby trails are good for hiking and mountain biking. **Pros:** equestrian friendly; rustic luxury. **Cons:** a 20-minute drive from the park; limited availability. ✉ *326 Hawksbill Park Rd., Stanley* ☎ *540/778–2285 or 888/418–7000* ⊕ *www.jordanhollow.com* ➽ *8 rooms, 7 suites* ♿ *In-room: refrigerator, DVD. In-hotel: restaurant, bar, bicycles, no-smoking rooms, no kids under 18* ☰ *AE, D, DC, MC, V* ⚑*BP.*

¢–$ ▦ **Skyland Resort.** At the highest point on Skyline Drive (3,680 feet), with views across the Shenandoah Valley, this facility has lodging that ranges from rustic cabins and motel-style rooms to suites. This resort is one of three different properties within the park: **Big Meadows Lodge,** originally built by the Civilian Conservation Corps, is in a spectacular setting surrounding by grassy meadows full of deer and wildlife. **Lewis Cabins** are the real and very rustic thing for an authentic outdoor adventure. Since these three properties in the park are in sought-after locations, you'll need to book up to a year in advance. There's no air-conditioning, but days above 80°F are rare at this altitude. Pros: stunning scenery; alternative to in-park camping. Cons: must plan far in advance; no phones or TVs in many rooms; closed in winter. ⊠*Milepost 41.7 on Skyline Dr.* ☎*800/778–2851* ⊕*www.visitshenandoah.com* ➦*177 rooms* ♿*In-room: no a/c, no phone, no TV (some). In-hotel: restaurant, bar* ▭*AE, D, DC, MC, V* ⊗*Closed Dec.–mid-Mar.*

SPORTS & THE OUTDOORS

CANOEING

At **Downriver Canoe** (⊠ *884 Indian Hollow Rd. Rte. 613 near Front Royal, Bentonville* ☎*540/635–5526* ⊕*www.downriver.com*), day and overnight trips start at $49 per canoe (or $32 per kayak, $16 per tube, and $79 per raft). **Front Royal Canoe** (⊠ *8567 Stonewall Jackson Hwy.,U.S. 340, near Front Royal* ☎*540/635–5440 or 800/270–8808* ⊕*www.frontroyalcanoe.com*) offers a $16 tube trip as well as canoe, kayak, and raft trips of from one hour up to three days for $40–$130. The company also rents boats and sells fishing accessories. **Shenandoah River Outfitters** (⊠*6502 S. Page Valley Rd., Rte. 684, Luray* ☎*540/743–4159* ⊕*www.Shenandoah-river.com*) rents canoes and kayaks for $20 to $84, and tubes from $18.

HIKING

The **Appalachian Trail** is more than 2,000 mi long, but you don't have to go that far, or even 2,000 feet, along it to see glorious foliage, rock formations, and wildlife. The trail zigzags across Skyline Drive through the park, offering easy access by car, variable hike lengths from a few feet to many miles, and connections with the more than 500 mi of the park's own trail network.

SHENANDOAH VALLEY

The fertile hills of the Shenandoah Valley reminded Colonial settlers from Germany, Ireland, and Britain of the homelands they left behind. They brought an agrarian lifestyle and Protestant beliefs that eventually spread across much of the Midwest. Today the valley is full of historic, cultural, and geological places of interest, including Civil War sites; Woodrow Wilson's birthplace and a reproduction of Shakespeare's Globe Theatre, both at Staunton; many beautifully adorned caverns; and the famous hot mineral springs in aptly named Bath County.

ESSENTIALS

Shenandoah Valley Travel Association (⊠*I–81, Exit 264* ✉*Box 1040, New Market 22844* ☎*540/740–3132 or 800/847–4878* ⊕*www.shenandoah.org*).

WINCHESTER

129 mi north of Charlottesville, 136 mi northwest of Richmond.

The historic town of Winchester is widely known as the birthplace of one of country music's most beloved stars, Patsy Cline. Cline hit it big when she won the Arthur Godfrey talent show, but died tragically in a plane crash at the peak of her career in 1963. She is buried in Winchester's Shenandoah Memorial Park, where a bell tower was erected in her honor.

Winchester served as a headquarters for Colonel George Washington during the French and Indian War. During the Civil War it was an important crossroads near the front line. It changed hands 72 times during the war, and was General Stonewall Jackson's headquarters for nearly two years.

Today the Old Town features a multiblock pedestrian mall filled with boutiques and restaurants, as well as must-see museums including George Washington's Office Museum and the Civil War Museum in the Old Courthouse.

The **Museum of the Shenandoah Valley** brings together fine and decorative art collections and multimedia presentations that reflect the region's cultural history. Designed by renowned architect Michael Graves, the museum's modern exterior belies the four centuries of historical artifacts, fine arts, and decorative arts on display inside its mammoth 50,000-square-foot space. In contrast, the Glen Burnie House and gardens, adjacent to the museum, are a gracious walk through the 18th and 19th centuries. The 1736 Georgian country estate that was the home of Winchester's founder, Colonel James Wood is surrounded by 25 acres of formal gardens. The collections within it include a gallery with furniture, fine arts, and decorative objects gathered by the last family member to live in the house, Julian Wood Glass Jr., who died in 1992. Another gallery assembles shadow-box rooms and miniature furnished houses. ⊠ *901 Amherst St.* ☎ *540/662–1473 or 888/556–5799* ⊕ *www.shenandoahmuseum.org* 🎟 *$12 for museum, house, and gardens; $6–$10 for other combinations* ⊘ *Museum Tues.–Sun. 10–4, house and gardens Mar.–Nov., daily 10–4.*

OFF THE BEATEN PATH

State Arboretum of Virginia. This arboretum, 9 mi east of Winchester, has the most extensive boxwood collection in North America. Hands-on workshops and tours are available throughout spring, summer, and fall. You can stroll through the perennial and herb gardens and have a look at more than 8,000 trees. The arboretum is a wonderful place to bird-watch or to have a picnic. ⊠ *Rte. 50 E* ☎ *540/837–1758* 🎟 *Free* ⊘ *Daily dawn–dusk.*

Stonewall Jackson's Headquarters Museum is a restored 1854 home. Jackson used this as his base of operations during the Valley Campaign in 1861–62. Among the artifacts on display are his prayer book and camp table. The reproduction wallpaper was a gift from the actress Mary Tyler Moore; it was her great-grandfather Lieutenant Colonel Lewis T. Moore who lent Jackson the use of the house. A $10 block ticket purchased at the museum also includes entry to two nearby historic attractions: **George Washington's Office Museum,** a preserved log cabin where Washington briefly lived during the French and Indian War, and **Abram's Delight Museum,** the oldest residence in Winchester. The stone house was owned by Isaac Hollingsworth, a prominent Quaker. ⊠*415 N. Braddock St.* ☎*540/667–3242* ⊕*www.winchesterhistory.org* ☞*$5 each or $10 block ticket* ⊙*Apr.–Oct., Mon.–Sat. 10–4, Sun. noon–4; Nov.–Mar., Fri. and Sat. 10–4, Sun. noon–4.*

WHERE TO EAT

$$$$
FRENCH
Fodor'sChoice
★

✕**L'Auberge Provencale.** Tucked away in the small town of White Post is a slice of Provence in a historic inn. L'Auberge Provencale is the epicurean getaway of choice for Washingtonians, and it's true that Chef Alain Borel has been on the gourmand radar for years. Borel and his wife Celeste grow their own herbs, vegetables, and fruit, and source their other sustainable foods locally from the bounty of the Valley. L'Auberge features not only an excellent list of French vintages, but many of Virginia's top wines as well. Reserve way ahead of time for the authentic Provencale prix-fixe dinner ($90 per person). ⊠ *Rte. 340, White Post* ☎*540/837–1375 or 800/638–1702* ⌖*Reservations essential* ☐*AE, D, MC, V* ⊙*Closed Jan.*

$$$
ITALIAN

✕**Violino Ristorante Italiano.** Homemade pasta—about 20 different kinds—fills the menu in this cheery, yellow-stucco restaurant in the city's Old Town. Owners Franco and Marcella Stocco and their son Riccardo (the men are chefs; Marcella manages the dining room) serve up their native northern Italian cuisine, including lobster *pansotti* (lobster-filled ravioli in a sauce of white wine and lemon). Try the Trio Violino, an antipasto platter with duck breast prosciutto, homemade venison bresaola, and duck salami with a raspberry vinaigrette. A strolling violinist entertains diners on weekends. The outdoor patio, enclosed by potted plants, is a quiet spot in the midst of street bustle. ⊠*181 N. Loudoun St.* ☎*540/667–8006* ☐*AE, D, DC, MC, V* ⊙*Closed Sun.*

WHERE TO STAY

$

▣**The George Washington Hotel.** The recently renovated George Washington Hotel, which reopened in the spring of 2008, is perfectly situated within walking distance of all of the charming town's attractions. Built in 1924, the historic hotel once hosted the many celebrities, such as Ed Sullivan, who served as Grand Marshall at the Shenandoah Valley Apple Blossom Parade. The stunning lobby with its original Tennessee marble floors features a pictorial history of the grand hotel, along with a hip new lounge and upscale restaurant called the Dancing Goat. As it's now part of the Wyndham group, guests can expect rooms furnished with period reproductions, luxury bedding, and modern amenities from flat screens to high-speed Internet. **Pros:** great location in historic downtown; luxury setting; **Cons:** smallish rooms. ⊠*103 E. Picadilly St., Winchester* ☎*540/678–4700* ⊕*www.wyndham.com* ⇖*90 rooms* ⌖*In-room: Ethernet. In-hotel: restaurant, bar* ☐*AE, D, MC, V.*

$$–$$$
Fodor'sChoice
★

▣**L'Auberge Provencale.** Chef-owner Alain Borel and his wife Celeste, of Avignon, France, bring the warm elegance of the south of France to this 1750s country inn, originally a sheep farm owned by Lord Fairfax.

3

Rooms are eclectically decorated with French art and fabrics, and Victorian wicker and antiques; some have fireplaces. Breakfast includes fresh homemade croissants and apple crepes with maple syrup. This is considered one of the most romantic inns in Virginia. The L'Auberge Provencale restaurant itself is also in high demand *(see full review above).* **Pros:** European luxury; stellar cuisine at in-house restaurant. **Cons:** limited number of rooms; must reserve well in advance. ✉ *Rte. 340, White Post* ☎ *540/837–1375 or 800/638–1702* ⊕ *www.laubergeprovencale. com* ⤶ *10 rooms, 4 suites* ♿ *In-room: no phone, no TV. In-hotel: restaurant, pool, no kids under 10, no-smoking rooms* ⊟ *AE, D, MC, V* ⊘ *Closed Jan.* ⭘ *BP.*

MIDDLETOWN

6 mi south of Winchester.

Middletown has one of the area's loveliest historic homes. **Belle Grove,** an elegant farmhouse and 100-acre working farm, is a monument to the rural and the refined, two qualities that exist in harmony in the architecture here and throughout the region. Constructed in 1797 out of limestone quarried on the property, the building reflects the influence of Thomas Jefferson, said to have been a consultant. Originally built for Major Isaac Hite and his wife Nelly (President James Madison's sister), this was the headquarters of the Union general Philip Sheridan during the Battle of Cedar Creek (1864), a crucial defeat for the Confederacy. Part of the battle was fought on the farm. ✉ *Rte. 11* ☎ *540/869–2028* ⊕ *www.bellegrove.org* ⌖ *$7* ⊘ *Apr.–Oct., Mon.–Sat. 10–3:15, Sun. 1–4:15; Nov., Sat. 10–4, Sun. noon–5.*

WHERE TO STAY

$–$$ ⊡ **The Inn at Vaucluse Springs.** Midway between Winchester and Belle
★   Grove Plantation, the Inn at Vaucluse Springs sits on 100 acres of rolling orchards. The 200-year-old Manor House serves as the gathering spot for an elegant three-course breakfast and end-of-the-day socializing. Six private guest houses include the Old Mill House, once an artist's studio, on the spring's edge, and the Gallery Guest House with panoramic meadow views. Innkeepers Neil and Barry Myers offer genial Southern hospitality and elegant accommodations have earned them top accolades for almost two decades. **Pros:** small retreat in gorgeous apple-orchard setting; first-class organic breakfast. **Cons:** hard to find; a bit removed from local sites. ✉ *231 Vaucluse Spring La., Stephens City* ☎ *540/862–0200 or 800/869–0525* ⊕ *www.vauclusespring.com* ⤶ *6 guest houses* ♿ *In-room: no phone.* ⊟ *AE, MC, V.*

**EN
ROUTE**
The **Strasburg Antique Emporium** (✉ *150 N. Massanutten St., Strasburg* ☎ *540/465–3711* ⊘ *Fri. and Sat. 10–7, Sun.–Thurs. 10–5*), 5 mi south of Middletown, covers 1.4 acres. It's in the quirky and historic downtown of Strasburg, which was settled by Germans. Inside the emporium, more than 100 dealers and artisans sell everything from furniture to jewelry to vintage clothing.

NEW MARKET

35 mi southwest of Middletown via I–81.

At New Market the Confederates had a victory at the late date of 1864. Inside the Hall of Valor, in the 260-acre **New Market Battlefield Historical Park,** a stained-glass window mosaic commemorates the battle, in which 257 Virginia Military Institute cadets, some as young as 15, were mobilized to improve the odds against superior Union numbers; 10 were killed. This circular building contains a chronology of the war, and a short film deals with Stonewall Jackson's legendary campaign in the Shenandoah Valley. A farmhouse that figured in the fighting still stands on the premises. The battle is reenacted at the park each May. ⊠ *I–81, Exit 264* ☎ *540/740–3101* ✆ *$8* ⊘ *Daily 9–5.*

The **Shenandoah Valley Apple Blossom Festival** (☎ *540/662-3864* ⊕ *www. thebloom.com* ✆ *Free*) has been, for more than 80 years, the biggest event of the year. Held in April, the 10-day festival includes more than 30 events including a huge parade led by a celebrity grand marshall. The apple industry, once the largest employer in the valley, is celebrated with food from apple candy to apple butter.

NIGHTLIFE & THE ARTS

The **Shenandoah Valley Music Festival** brings classical, jazz, and folk music to the Allegheny Mountains on weekends from May to September. The events are held at the Orkney Springs Hotel, an early-19th-century spa that's now an Episcopal retreat. Arts and crafts displays and an ice-cream social precede each concert. Concertgoers can sit on the lawn for $14 or in one of two pavilions for around $21; call ahead to reserve tickets. A bus to the festival from Woodstock (I–81, Exit 283) costs $5. ⊠ *Rte. 263, 2 mi south of Bryce Resort* ☎ *540/459–3396* ⊕ *www. musicfest.org.*

The **Wayside Theatre** (⊠ *7853 Main St., Middletown* ☎ *540/869-1776* ⊕ *www.waysidetheatre.org*) is the second-oldest regional theater company in Virginia and has just completed a total renovation of the theater and the adjoining Curtain Call Café. Check the Web site for the seasons schedule.

HARRISONBURG

18 mi southwest of New Market via Exit 251 from I–81.

Harrisonburg is a workaday market town surrounded by rich farmlands. Settled in 1739, it's a stronghold of Mennonites, who wear plain clothes and drive horse-drawn buggies. The city is also a center of higher education, with James Madison University and Eastern Mennonite College in town and Bridgewater College nearby. The **Hardesty-Higgins House,** an 1848 Georgian Greek revival, is now the center of the district and home to the visitor center. Harrisonburg is also the home of James Madison University, where you can stroll through a world of natural beauty at the **Edith J. Carrier Arboretum and Botanical Gardens** (⊕ *www.jmu.edu/arboretum*).

EXPLORING

At the **Virginia Quilt Museum** you can see examples of quilts made throughout the mid-Atlantic region and learn about the international heritage of quilting. ⊠ *301 S. Main St.* ☎ *540/433–3818* ⊕ *www. vaquiltmuseum.org* ⊠ *$5* ⊘ *Mon. and Thurs.–Sat. 10–4, Sun. 1–4.*

WHERE TO STAY & EAT

¢–$ ✕ **Dave's Taverna.** Get a bird's-eye
GREEK   view of Harrisonburg from the rooftop dining area at Dave's. Like many casual Greek eateries, the menu runs from American classics like burgers and pizzas to Greek and Italian fare from souvlaki and Greek chicken to caprese salad and linguine. But vegetarians need not worry, as veggie pitas and burgers round out the menu. ⊠ *121 S. Main St.* ☎ *540/564–1487* ⊟ *MC, V.*

$$–$$$ ▦ **By the Side of the Road Bed and Breakfast.** This 1789 home features four luxurious suites and three intimate cottages overlooking the rolling hills of Harrisonburg. The inn combines 21st-century amenities with the Old World elegance of featherbeds and fireplaces. The three cottages feature whirlpool spa tubs set in front of the fireplace and four-inch-thick featherbeds. All rooms and suites are furnished with period antiques and reproductions from Colonial in the 1790s main house to Victorian in the 1840s addition. **Pros:** no two-night minimum; close to skiing, Skyline Drive, and the Blue Ridge. **Cons:** expensive option for the area; limited availability. ⊠ *491 Garbers Church Rd.* ☎ *540/801–0430* ⊕ *www. bythesideoftheroad.com* ↩ *4 suites, 3 cottages* ⑂ *In-room: Wi-Fi. In-hotel: no-smoking rooms* ⊟ *MC, V* ⑩ *BP.*

¢–$ ▦ **Joshua Wilton House.** A row of trees guards the privacy of this circa
★   1888 B&B decorated in the Victorian style and set on a large yard at the edge of the "Old Town" district. The sunroom and back patio are built for relaxation. Ask for Room 4; it has a lace-draped canopy bed and a turret sitting area with a view of the Blue Ridge Mountains looming over Main Street. Room 2 has a fireplace. The restaurant's menu changes daily, its components supplied by many small, local organic farmers. **Pros:** restaurant on-site; charming decor; nice downtown location. **Cons:** few amenities; limited number of rooms. ⊠ *412 S. Main St.* ☎ *888/294–5866 or 540/434–4464* ⊕ *www.joshuawilton.com* ↩ *5 rooms* ⑂ *In-room: no TV, Wi-Fi. In-hotel: restaurant, no kids under 8, no-smoking rooms* ⊟ *AE, MC, V* ⑩ *BP.*

DAYTON

2 mi west of Harrisonburg via Rte. 33 off I–81.

Dayton is best known for its large Mennonite population, whose black horse-drawn buggies share the road with latter-day SUVs, and for its extensive farmer's market with handcrafted goods and foods from the region.

At the **Harrisonburg–Rockingham Historical Society,** multimedia folk art reflects the largely German and Scotch-Irish culture of the valley. One Civil War exhibit includes an electric map that traces Stonewall Jackson's famous 1862 Valley Campaign. ✉*382 High St.* ☎*540/879–2616 or 540/879–2681* ⊕*www.heritagecenter.com* ✇*$5* ⊙*Mon.–Sat. 10–4.*

Also known as the Daniel Harrison House, **Fort Harrison** (from circa 1749) is of fortified stone and decorated in prosperous frontier style. Harrison was Dayton's first settler, and this is the oldest house in the town. Costumed interpreters discuss how the furnishings—beds with ropes as slats and hand-quilted comforters—were made. Artifacts on display come from recent excavations undertaken adjacent to the house. ✉*Rte. 4* ☎*540/879–2280* ✇*Donation welcome* ⊙*Mid-May–Oct., weekends 1–5.*

SHOPPING

The **Dayton Farmers Market** (✉ *3105 John Wayland Hwy.,Rte. 42, south of Dayton* ☎*540/8793801*), an 18,000-square-foot area, has homemade baked goods and fresh fruits and vegetables as well as butter churns and ceramic speckle ware, made by the Mennonites who live in the area. It's one place to mingle with the craftspeople, as well as with students from James Madison University in nearby Harrisonburg. It's open Thursday through Saturday from 9 to 6.

STAUNTON

27 mi south of Dayton via I–81, 11 mi west of southern end of Skyline Dr. at Waynesboro off I–64.

Staunton (pronounced *stan*-ton) was once the seat of government of the vast Augusta County, which formed in 1738 and encompassed present-day West Virginia, Kentucky, Ohio, Illinois, Indiana, and the Pittsburgh area. After the state's General Assembly fled here from the British in 1781, Staunton was briefly the state's capital. Woodrow Wilson (1856–1924), the nation's 27th president and the eighth president from Virginia, was a native son.

TOURS The Historic Staunton Foundation offers free one-hour walking tours Saturday morning at 10, Memorial Day through October, departing from the Woodrow Wilson Birthplace (24 North Coalter Street). A brochure for a self-guided tour is available from the Staunton/Augusta County Travel Information Center.

ESSENTIALS

Train Station (✉*1 Middlebrook Ave.*).

Visitor Information Historic Staunton Foundation (✉*1205 Augusta St.* ☎ *540/885–7676*). **Staunton-Augusta County Travel Information Center** (✉*1290 Richmond Rd.* ☎*540/332–3972*).

EXPLORING

⟳ The **Frontier Culture Museum,** an outdoor living-history museum, re-cre-
★ ates agrarian life in America. The four illustrative farmsteads, American, Scotch-Irish, German, and English, were painstakingly moved from

their original sites and reassembled on the museum grounds. A West African village and an American Indian village are also among the exhibits. The livestock and plants here resemble the historic breeds and varieties as closely as possible. Special programs and activities, held throughout the year, include soap and broom making, cornhusking bees, and supper and barn dances. ⊠*1250 Richmond Rd., off I–81, Exit 222 to Rte. 250 W* ☎*540/332–7850* ⊕*www.frontiermuseum.org* ☞*$10* ⊙*Dec.–mid-Mar., daily 10–4; mid-Mar.–Nov., daily 9–5.*

Seven miles east of Staunton, the **P. Buckley Moss Museum** is a free full-scale gallery of paintings and drawings by one of the Valley's most recognized artists. Moss, who moved to Waynesboro in 1964, was inspired by the quiet dignity and simplicity of the "plain people"—those in the Mennonite communities of the Shenandoah Valley—and has made these neighbors her subject matter. Don't miss the large-scale dollhouse built into a staircase. Her studio, a converted barn about 2 mi from the museum, opens a few times a year to the public. ⊠*150 P Buckley Moss Dr., I–64, Exit 94, Waynesboro* ☎*800/343-8643* ⊕*www.pbuckley moss.com* ☞*Free* ⊙*Mon.–Sat. 10–6, Sun. 12:30–5:30.*

The **Woodrow Wilson Presidential Library** has period antiques, items from Wilson's political career, and some original pieces from when this museum was the residence of Wilson's father, a Presbyterian minister. Wilson's presidential limousine, a 1919 Pierce-Arrow sedan, is on display in the garage. The site is being expanded to become a full presidential library, with space for scholarly research. ⊠*24 N. Coalter St.* ☎*540/885–0897 or 888/496–6376* ⊕*www.woodrowwilson.org* ☞*$12* ⊙*Mar.–Oct., Mon.–Sat. 9–5, Sun. noon–5; Nov.–Feb., Mon.–Sat. 10–4, Sun. noon–4.*

WHERE TO EAT

¢–$

SOUTHERN

★

✕**Mrs. Rowe's Restaurant.** A homey restaurant with plenty of booths, Rowe's has been operated by the same family since 1947 and enjoys a rock-solid reputation for inexpensive and delicious Southern meals. The fried chicken—skillet-cooked to order—is a standout. A local breakfast favorite is oven-hot biscuits topped with gravy (your choice of sausage, tenderloin, or creamy chipped beef). For dessert, try the mince pie in fall or the rhubarb cobbler in summer. ⊠*74 Rowe Rd., I–81, Exit 222* ☎*540/886–1833* ▭*D, MC, V.*

$$$

SOUTHERN

Fodor'sChoice

★

✕**Staunton Grocery.** Featuring contemporary interpretations of Southern classics, the chef here focuses on local produce from the valley, and the menu changes seasonally. The Grocery is in the center of historic downtown Staunton. Look for pork belly with plums in a red-wine reduction or Southern fried quail on braised greens. Tasting menus of four or six courses are also offered, with wine pairings suggested by the house sommelier. ⊠*105 W. Beverly St.* ☎*540/886-6880* ▭*AE, D, MC, V* ⊙*Closed Mon.*

WHERE TO STAY

$–$$

▥**Belle Grae Inn.** The sitting room and music room of this restored 1870 Victorian house have been converted into formal dining rooms, with brass wall sconces, Oriental rugs, and candles at the tables. In the heart of historic Staunton just seven blocks from the birthplace of Woodrow Wilson, the inn consists of a main house, circa 1873, and three nearby 19th-century houses, one of which has a full kitchen and laundry facilities. A meal plan is available, in addition to the standard complimentary breakfast included in the room rate. Accommodations are furnished with antique rocking chairs and canopied or brass beds, and many have fireplaces. **Pros:** historic ambience; Wi-Fi; eco-friendly certified as a Virginia Green Lodging. **Cons:** limited availability. ⊠*515 W. Frederick St.* ☎*540/886–5151 or 888/541–5151* ⊕*www.bellegrae. com* ➵*8 rooms, 7 suites, 2 cottages* ⌂*In-hotel: restaurant, public Wi-Fi, no-smoking rooms* ⊟*AE, D, MC, V* ⧖*EP.*

$-$$ ⚏**Stonewall Jackson Hotel.** Built in 1928, this elegantly restored hotel in historic downtown is known for its richly appointed rooms and suites and top-of-the-line amenities. With more than 100 rooms, the hotel also has an indoor pool, fitness center, business center, lounge, restaurant, and conference facilities. The historic past is reflected in the period decor. **Pros:** extras like free Internet and daily paper; great location. **Cons:** busy conference hotel. ⊠*24 S. Market St.* ☎*540/885–4840 or 866/880–0024* ⊕*www.stonewalljacksonhotel.com* ➵*124 rooms* ⌂ *In-room: Wi-Fi. In-hotel: pool, gym, executive floor* ⊟*AE, D, MC, V.*

NIGHTLIFE & THE ARTS
THEATER

★ Experience Shakespeare's plays the way the Elizabethans did at **Blackfriars Playhouse** (⊠*10 S. Market St.* ☎*540/885–5588* ⊕*www.shenandoah shakespeare.com*), the world's only re-creation of Shakespeare's indoor playhouse, which has gained acclaim for its attention to detail. Unlike the open-air Globe Theatre styled around a courtyard, Blackfriar's was, in its time, an innovative indoor winter venue. As in 17th-century London, most seating consists of benches (modern seat backs and cushions are available), and some stools are right on stage.

LEXINGTON

30 mi south of Staunton via I–81.

Two deeply traditional Virginia colleges sit side by side in this town, each with a memorial to a soldier who was also a man of peace.

TOURS For $16 the Lexington Carriage Company will take visitors around town in a horse-drawn carriage for 45–50 minutes, from April through October. Tours begin and end at the Lexington Visitor Center, where a self-guided walking-tour brochure of the town is also available.

ESSENTIALS

Visitor Information Lexington Carriage Company (☎ *540/463–5647* ⊕ *www.lexcarriage.com*). **Lexington Visitor Center** (⊠*106 E. Washington St.* ☎*540/463–3777*).

EXPLORING

The **George C. Marshall Museum** preserves the memory of the World War II army chief of staff. Exhibits trace his brilliant career, which began when he was aide-de-camp to John "Black Jack" Pershing in World War

I and culminated when, as secretary of state, he devised the Marshall Plan, a strategy for reviving postwar Western Europe. Marshall's Nobel Peace Prize is on display; so is the Oscar won by his aide Frank McCarthy, who produced the Academy Award–winning Best Picture of 1970, *Patton*. An electronically narrated map tells the story of World War II. ⊠ *VMI campus, Letcher Ave.* ☎*540/463–7103* ⊕*www.marshall foundation.org* ✒*$5* ⊙*Mon.–Sat 9–5, Sun. 1–5.*

Confederate general Jackson's private life is on display at the **Stonewall Jackson House,** where he is revealed as a dedicated Presbyterian who was devoted to physical fitness, careful with money, musically inclined, and fond of gardening. The general lived here only two years, while teaching physics and military tactics to the cadets, before leaving for his command in the Civil War. This is the only house he ever owned; it's furnished now with period pieces and some of his belongings. ⊠*8 E. Washington St.* ☎*540/463–2552* ⊕*www.stonewalljackson.org* ✒*$6* ⊙*Mon.–Sat. 9–5, Sun. 1–5.*

Adjacent to Washington and Lee University are the imposing Gothic buildings of the **Virginia Military Institute** *(VMI)* , founded in 1839 and the nation's oldest state-supported military college. With an enrollment of about 1,300 cadets, the institute has admitted women since 1997. After a two-year expansion and renovation effort, the **Virginia Military Institute Museum,** now includes a 3,000-square-foot main exhibit hall in Jackson Memorial Hall, dedicated to the VMI Heritage. Displays include 15,000 artifacts, including Stonewall Jackson's stuffed and mounted horse, Little Sorrel, and the general's coat, pierced by the bullet that killed him at Chancellorsville, and on the lower level, the Henry Stewart antique firearms collection. ⊠*Letcher Ave.* ☎*540/464–7232* ⊕*www.vmi.edu* ✒*$3* ⊙*Daily 9–5.*

Washington and Lee University, the ninth-oldest college in the United States, was founded in 1749 as Augusta Academy and later renamed Washington College in gratitude for a donation from George Washington. After Robert E. Lee's term as its president (1865–70), it received its current name. Today, with 2,000 students, the university occupies a campus of white-column, redbrick buildings around a central colonnade. Twentieth-century alumni include the late Supreme Court Justice Lewis Powell, newsman Roger Mudd, and novelist Tom Wolfe. The campus's **Lee Chapel and Museum** contains many relics of the Lee family. Edward Valentine's statue of the recumbent general, behind the altar, is especially moving: the pose is natural and the expression gentle, a striking contrast to most other monumental art. Here you can sense the affection and reverence that Lee inspired. ⊠*Jefferson St., Rte. 11* ☎*540/458–8400* ⊕*www.wlu.edu* ✒*Free* ⊙*Chapel Apr.–Oct., Mon.–Sat. 9–5, Sun. 1–5; Nov.–Mar., Mon.–Sat. 9–4, Sun. 1–4. Campus tours Apr.–Oct., weekdays 10–4, Sat. 9:45–noon; Jan.–Mar., weekdays 10 and noon, Sat. 11.*

OFF THE BEATEN PATH

Natural Bridge of Virginia. About 20 mi south of Lexington, this impressive limestone arch (which supports Route 11) has been gradually carved out by Cedar Creek, which rushes through 215 feet below. The Monacan Native American tribe called it the Bridge of God. Surveying

3

the structure for Lord Halifax, George Washington carved his own initials in the stone; Thomas Jefferson bought it (and more than 150 surrounding acres) from King George III. The after-dark sound-and-light show may be overkill, but viewing and walking under the bridge itself and along the wooded pathway beyond are worth the price of admission. On the property are dizzying caverns that descend 34 stories, a wax museum, a toy museum, and an 18th-century village constructed by the Monacan Indian Nation. ⊠*I–81 S, Exit 180; I–81 N, Exit 175* ☎*540/291–2121 or 800/533–1410* ⊕*www.naturalbridgeva.com* ⊠*Bridge $13, all attractions $28* ☉*Mar.–Nov., daily 8 AM–dark.*

WHERE TO STAY & EAT

$-$$ ✕**The Palms.** Once a Victorian ice-cream parlor, this full-service restaurant in an 1890 building has indoor and outdoor dining. Wood booths line the walls of the plant-filled room; the pressed-metal ceiling is original. Specialties on the American menu include broccoli-cheese soup, charbroiled meats, and teriyaki chicken. The menu features traditional soups and salads, burgers and sandwiches, and steaks and pasta. The Palms is open for lunch as well. ⊠*101 W. Nelson St.* ☎*540/463–7911* ⊕*www.thepalmslexington.com* ♟*Reservations not accepted* ☰*AE, D, MC, V.*

AMERICAN

¢–$ ⌂**Maple Hall.** For a taste of Southern history, spend a night at this country inn of 1850. Once a plantation house, it's on 56 acres 6 mi north of Lexington. Individually decorated rooms have period antiques and modern amenities; most have gas log fireplaces as well. On the property are a fishing pond and miles of scenic walking trails. Many celebrities have slept here, from Elizabeth Taylor and Richard Gere to Bill Clinton and Lady Bird Johnson. **Pros:** historic setting; outdoor activities. **Cons:** a bit far from downtown. ⊠*Rte. 11* ☎*540/463–6693 or 877/283–9680* ⊕*www.lexingtonhistoricinns.com/maplehall.htm* ⊠*17 rooms, 4 suites* ♟*In-hotel: restaurant, tennis court, pool* ☰*D, MC, V* ☉*BP.*

¢–$ ⌂**Natural Bridge Hotel.** The first hotel on this site was built in 1828, but visitors have been attracted to the Natural Bridge since Colonial times. Within walking distance of the spectacular rock arch of the same name (there's also a shuttle bus), the Colonial-style brick hotel has a beautiful location as well as numerous recreational facilities. Long porches with rocking chairs allow leisurely appreciation of the Blue Ridge Mountains. Rooms are done in a Colonial Virginia style. The hotel is similar in style to the Homestead Resort but at a fraction of the price. **Pros:** walk to the Natural Bridge; budget-friendly; stunning scenery. **Cons:** far from local towns; larger hotel may lack Southern hospitality feel. *Rte. 11, Box 57, Natural Bridge* ☎*540/291–2121 or 800/533–1410* ⊕*www.naturalbridgeva.com* ⊠*180 rooms* ♟*In-hotel: restaurant, bar, tennis courts, pool* ☰*AE, D, DC, MC, V.*

¢–$ ⌂**Sheridan Livery Inn.** This historic property is in the heart of downtown, within walking distance of shops, restaurants, and attractions. Built in 1887 as the stable and carriage service of prominent Lexington businessman John Sheridan, the historic structure was carefully renovated and opened as an inn in 1997. The rooms are spacious, with high ceilings, and include the charm of 19th-century furnishings along with modern amenities like Wi-Fi. A continental breakfast is included in the room rate. **Pros:** great location; good breakfast. **Cons:** only 15 rooms. ⊠ *35 N. Main St., Lexington* ☎ *540/464–1887* ⊕ *www.sheridan liveryinn.com* ⊅ *12 rooms, 3 suites* ♿ *In-room: Wi-Fi. In-hotel: restaurant, bar, no-smoking rooms* ⊟ *AE, MC, V* �|◎| *BP.*

> **DID YOU KNOW?**
>
> In Virginia, Allegheny is spelled with an "e", but across the border in West Virginia, the mountain range's name is spelled Alleghany with an "a."

BATH COUNTY

20 mi northwest of Lexington via Rte. 39.

Bath County, known as the Allegheny Highlands, is where Virginia's rugged outdoors and refined elegance intermingle most delightfully. Amid its steep ridges and dense forests is the Homestead, a historic and elegant resort. Forgotten when the C&O Railroad moved its headquarters from Clifton Forge, this region is going through a renaissance. The county's name is fitting: healing thermal springs were what originally brought visitors to town in the 1700s. The sulfurous waters still flow at Warm Springs, Hot Springs, and Bolar Springs, their temperatures ranging from 77°F to 104°F. Thomas Jefferson designed the octagonal buildings that house the Jefferson Pools, now operated by the Homestead.

GETTING HERE & AROUND

Bath County is about a three-hour drive from Richmond on I–64, but Amtrak also services Clifton Forge. Trains only run a few times a week from Richmond, but daily from Charlottesville and Washington, DC, and they're a wonderful way to soak up the stunning mountain vistas.

TIMING & PRECAUTIONS

In winter the mountain roads can be treacherous, and throughout the year, keep an eye out for wildlife from deer to badgers.

WHERE TO EAT

$$–$$$
AMERICAN

✕ **The Company Store.** The 19th-century mining company commissary in Low Moor is now a local gathering spot, with the ambience of an earlier era supplied by its jukebox and a broad selection of merchandise from country ham, vintage postcards, and penny candy to household products, local art, and Virginia wines. Chef Michel Neutelings, whose background includes over two decades of experience at resorts including the Homestead, has turned the restaurant into a dining destination worth the drive, featuring a seasonal menu sourced locally. In fall you might get grilled pork chops in an apple-cider reduction or butternut squash with chestnuts, while in other seasons updated classics like rack of lamb or fire-grilled prime sirloin with a red-wine-and-shallot sauce. There's also a lounge with live music for weekend entertainment. ⊠ *100 Old Church St., Low Moor* ☎ *540/862–0098* ⊟ *AE, MC, V.*

$$–$$$
AMERICAN
★

✕ **Waterwheel Restaurant.** Part of a complex of five historic buildings, this restaurant is in a gristmill that dates from 1700. A walk-in wine cellar, set among the gears of the original waterwheel, has 100 wine selections; diners may step in and choose for themselves. The dining area is decorated with Currier & Ives and Audubon prints. Some menu favorites are fresh smoked trout and chicken Fantasio (breast of chicken stuffed with wild rice, sausage, apple, and pecans). Desserts include such Old Virginny recipes as a deep-dish apple pie baked with bourbon. On Sunday look for the hearty but affordable brunch. ⊠ *128 Old Mill Rd. Grist Mill Sq., Warm Springs* ☎ *540/839–2231* ⊟ *D, MC, V* ☯ *Closed Tues. Nov.–May.*

> **JEFFERSON POOLS**
>
> Don't miss the pools, about 5 mi from the Homestead resort: designed by Thomas Jefferson himself. A host of American notables have soaked in the restorative mineral springs. The resort operates the pools and runs a free shuttle service to and from them several times a day. Day visitors can soak in history for $17.

WHERE TO STAY

$$–$$$ **The Homestead.** An evening at the Homestead is like taking a cruise
Fodor'sChoice ship through the mountains. Soothing orchestra music plays as guests
★   stroll the column-adorned hallways, sauntering into the ornately decorated dining room for a luxurious six-course meal of regional and continental cuisine. Daytime activities include far more than shuffleboard: there are three championship-grade 18-hole golf courses, 4 mi of streams stocked with rainbow trout, 100 mi of riding trails, skeet and trap shooting, and nine ski slopes (the Homestead was the site of the South's first downhill skiing in 1959). Host to a prestigious clientele since 1766, the Homestead has evolved from a country spa to a 15,000-acre resort-and-conference facility. Rooms in the sprawling redbrick building, built in 1891, have Georgian-style furnishings; some have fireplaces. European-style meal plans are a better value than paying just the room rate. **Pros:** Southern luxury; outdoor activities; even the spa has history. **Cons:** everything costs extra, even coffee; size can be overwhelming. ⊠ *Rte. 220, Hot Springs* ☎ *540/839–1766 or 800/838–1766* ⊕ *www.thehomestead.com* ⮒ *429 rooms, 77 suites* ⌂ *In-room: Wi-Fi. In-hotel: 6 restaurants, golf courses, tennis courts, pools, spa, bicycles, airport shuttle* ⊟ *AE, D, DC, MC, V* ⦿ *EP.*

$–$$ **Inn at Gristmill Square.** Occupying five restored buildings at the same
★   site as the Waterwheel Restaurant, the rooms of this state historical landmark inn are in a Colonial Virginia style. Four units are in the original miller's house; others occupy the former blacksmith's shop, hardware store, gristmill, and cottage. Some of the rooms have fireplaces and patios. **Pros:** historic; good location for shoppers; nice inhouse restaurant. **Cons:** limited availabilty. ⊠ *Rte. 645, Box 359, Warm Springs* ☎ *540/839–2231* ⊕ *www.gristmillsquare.com* ⮒ *12 rooms, 5 suites, 1 apartment* ⌂ *In-room: Wi-Fi. In-hotel: restaurant, bar, tennis courts, pool* ⊟ *D, MC, V* ⦿ *BP.*

NIGHTLIFE & THE ARTS

Garth Newel Music Center (⊠ *Rte. 220, Warm Springs* ☎ *540/839–5018 or 877/558–1689*) has weekend chamber-music performances in summer, and hosts more than 50 concerts a year. You can make reservations and plan to picnic on the grounds, or consider staying over at the Homestead just down the road.

SPORTS & THE OUTDOORS

GOLF

The Homestead has three excellent 18-hole golf courses. The par-70, 6,679-yard Cascades course, the site of USGA and Senior PGA events, has gently sloped fairways amid rugged terrain. The par-72, 6,752-yard Lower Cascades course, designed by Robert Trent Jones, has more wide-open fairways with many bunkers and breaks. The par-72, 6,211-yard Old Course is most famous for its first tee, established in 1892. It's the oldest tee still in continuous use in the United States.

HIKING & MOUNTAIN BIKING

At **Douthat State Park** (⊠*Exit 27, 7 mi north of I–64 near Clifton Forge* ☎*540/862–8100*) there are more than 40 mi of well-signed, smoothly groomed, and sometimes steep trails for hiking and biking. The trails pass by waterfalls and majestic overlooks. The Warm Springs Ranger District of the **George Washington and Jefferson National Forests** (☎*540/839–2521*) has information on hundreds of miles of local trails.

EN ROUTE

The small town of **Clifton Forge** was once the heartbeat of the Chesapeake and Ohio Railway, and generations of travelers sped through the countryside on its trains. In its boom days, the Smith Creek Station saw as many as 100 trains a day passing through on their way west over the Alleghany mountain, east over the Blue Ridge, or down the James River. Clifton Forge is now home to the **C&O Heritage Center,** a railroad museum full of model trains and memorabilia, including an excellent gift shop featuring many items dedicated to the C&O Railway's cuddly kitten mascot, Chessie. Kids love the replica signal tower and the 7½-inch gauge ride-on train that circles the museum. ⊕*www. cohs.org.*

SOUTHWEST VIRGINIA

Southwest Virginia is a rugged region of alternating mountain ridges and deep valleys. Modern urban life is juxtaposed with spectacular scenery in the Roanoke and New River valleys. Other areas retain the quiet charm of yesteryear: they have many pleasant meadows, old country churches, and towns with just one stop sign. The gorge-incised Appalachian Plateau in far southwest Virginia is abundant in coal. Interstate 81 and Interstate 77 form a kind of "X" across the region, and the Blue Ridge Parkway roughly defines southwest Virginia's eastern edge.

ROANOKE

49 mi south of Lexington (via I–81).

They once called this city "Big Lick." But today Roanoke, with a population of 95,000, is Virginia's largest city west of Richmond, the largest city on the Blue Ridge Parkway, and in many ways, the capital of southwest Virginia. The metropolitan area of 230,000 has enough city flavor to provide a degree of culture and elegance, but its location between the Blue Ridge Parkway and Appalachian Trail means that the wilds aren't too far away either; mountains dominate its horizons in all directions.

DISCOUNTS & DEALS

The Roanoke Valley RED Card offers discounts to regional attractions. It's free at the visitor center.

ESSENTIALS

Taxi Companies Liberty Cab (☎ 540/344–1776). Yellow Cab Services of Roanoke (☎ 540/345–7711).

Visitor Information Roanoke Valley Convention and Visitors Bureau (✉ 101 Shenandoah Ave. NE ☎ 540/342–6025 or 800/635–5535 ⊕ www.visitroanokeva. com).

EXPLORING

Market Square is the heart of Roanoke, with Virginia's oldest continuous farmers' market, a multiethnic food court inside the restored City Market Building, and several restaurants, shops, and bars. In a restored warehouse, **Center in the Square** (✉ 1 Market Sq. SE ☎ 540/342–5700 ⊕ www.centerinthesquare.org) contains the Mill Mountain Theatre and regional museums covering science, history, and art. A combined ticket grants access to the science museum, which has many interactive exhibits, as well as the MegaDome theater and Hopkins Planetarium,

Even in daylight, the Roanoke skyline is dominated by a star. The 100-foot-tall **Mill Mountain Star,** constructed in 1949, stands in a city park 1,000 feet above the Roanoke Valley. It is lighted in red, white, and blue each evening. From either of the park's two overlooks, Roanoke, the "Star City of the South," looks like a scale model of a city, framed by wave after wave of Appalachian ridgelines. Hike or bike the mountain's greenway trail. ✉ Mill Mountain Park; follow Walnut St. south 2 mi from downtown Roanoke; or take Pkwy. Spur Rd. 3 mi north from Blue Ridge Pkwy. at milepost 120.3.

☾ Sharing the mountaintop with the star is the **Mill Mountain Zoo.** Asian animals are center stage here, including a rare Siberian tiger, snow leopards, and red pandas. Ride the Zoo Choo train for $2. ✉ Mill Mountain Park; follow Walnut St. south 2 mi from downtown Roanoke; or take Pkwy. Spur Rd. 3 mi north from Blue Ridge Pkwy. at milepost 120.3 ☎ 540/343–3241 ⊕ www.mmzoo.org ⌨ $7.12 ☾ Daily 10–5; gate closes at 4:30.

★ You can relive the final days of steam trains at the **O. Winston Link Museum,** inside a renovated passenger train station. Link spent several years in the late 1950s and early 1960s photographing Norfolk & Western's last steam engines in the railroads of southwest Virginia. The hundreds of stunning black-and-white photographs on display do much more than evoke nostalgia—they also capture day-to-day life: a horse-drawn carriage awaiting an oncoming train, a locomotive rocketing past lovers watching a drive-in movie. ☒ *101 Shenandoah Ave.* ☎ *540/982–5465* ⊕ *www.linkmuseum.org* ☜ *$5* ⊗ *Mon.–Sun. 10–5.*

★ **Taubman Museum of Art.** Opened in the fall of 2008, this Randall Stout–designed faceted-glass structure soars amid the surrounding mountains, the contemporary architecture striking a balance with its natural location. Formerly known as the Art Museum of Western Virginia, the Taubman's new 81,000-square-foot home quadruples the previous exhibit space, housing 19th- and 20the-century American art, modern art, and small special collections of European and ancient Mediterranean art. The museum honors the American Ambassador to Romania and his wife, Nicholas and Eugenia Taubman. ☒ *110 Salem Ave. SE* ☎ *540/342–5760* ⊕ *www.taubmanmuseum.org* ☜ *$8.50* ⊗ *Tues.–Sat. 10–5.*

☾ Near Market Square, the **Virginia Museum of Transportation** has the largest collection of diesel and steam locomotives in the country—not surprising, considering that Roanoke got its start as a railroad town and was once the headquarters of the Norfolk & Western railroad. The dozens of original train cars and engines, some of which can be boarded and many built here in town, include a massive nickel-plate locomotive—just one of the many holdings that constitute an unabashed display of civic pride. The sprawling model-train and miniature-circus setups please young and old alike. ☒ *303 Norfolk Ave. SW* ☎ *540/342–5670* ⊕ *www.vmt.org* ☜ *$8* ⊗ *Weekdays 11–4, Sat. 10–5, Sun. 1–5.*

OFF THE BEATEN PATH

National D-Day Memorial. This site stirs the soul, bringing the sacrifice of D-Day home. When Allied forces landed at Normandy on June 6, 1944, in what would be the decisive military move of World War II, the small town of Bedford lost 19 of its young men, and 4 more in days to come. The memorial's focal point is a huge granite arch and flag plaza on a hill overlooking the town. There are also granite statues of soldiers in combat and a reflecting pool that periodically shoots up spurts of water, as if struck by bullets. Don't be surprised if you see some D-Day veterans sitting near the memorial. ☒ *3 Overlord Circle, U.S. 460, 27 mi east of Roanoke, at junction of 122, Bedford* ☎ *540/587–3619* ⊕ *www.dday.org* ☜ *$5* ⊗ *Daily 10–5.*

Booker T. Washington National Monument. It would have been hard for Booker T. Washington to imagine the farm on which he was born into slavery hosting a national monument. But this restored tobacco farm 25 mi southeast of Roanoke and 21 mi south of Bedford is a fitting tribute to the humble origins of Washington (1856–1915), who broke through the yoke of oppression to become a remarkable educator and author, advising presidents McKinley, Roosevelt, and Taft and taking tea with Queen Victoria. More important, he started Tuskegee Institute in Alabama and inspired generations of African-Americans. Covering 224 acres, the farm's restored buildings; tools; crops; animals; and, in summer, interpreters in period costume all help show what life during slavery was like. ☒ *Rte. 122, 21 mi south of Bedford* ☎ *540/721–2094* ⊕ *www.nps.gov/bowa* ☜ *Free* ⊗ *Daily 9–5.*

NEED A BREAK?

At the **Homestead Creamery** (✉ *Rte. 122, just east of intersection with Rte. 116, Burnt Chimney* ☎ *540/721–5808*), you can sample farm-fresh milk and ice cream. No plastic or paper cartons here—the milk is stored and sold in glass bottles, the way milkmen used to bring it. Gulping the chocolate milk is like drinking a chocolate cake. Unusual milk flavors such as mocha and orange cream are often available.

WHERE TO EAT

$$–$$$
BRAZILIAN
★

✕**Carlos Brazilian International Cuisine.** High on a hill with a spectacular sunset view, this lively restaurant has French, Italian, Spanish, and Brazilian dishes. Sit in the Olinda Room with its wall of windows. Try the *porco reacheado* (pork tenderloin stuffed with spinach and feta cheese) or the *moqueca mineira* (shrimp, clams, and whitefish in a Brazilian sauce). Brazilian radio often accompanies the meal. If you love chicken, try the sautéed version with pineapple and papaya. ✉*4167 Electric Rd.* ☎*540/342-6455* ⊕*www.carlosbrazilian.com* ⊟*AE, MC, V* ✣*Closed Sun.*

$
SOUTHERN
Fodor'sChoice
★

✕**The Homeplace.** Bring a big appetite with you on the drive up and over Catawba Mountain to get to the Homeplace. Famished Appalachian Trail hikers in grimy shorts and suave diners in their Sunday best eat side by side family-style in this farm home in a tiny country hamlet— come as you are. Old-fashioned cooking is dished up grandma style, with all-you-can-eat fried chicken, mashed potatoes and gravy, green beans, pinto beans, baked apples, and hot biscuits. ✉*4968 Catawba Valley Dr., 7 mi west of Salem on Rte. 311 N, I–81, Exit 141, Catawba* ☎*540/384-7252* ⚖*Reservations not accepted* ⊟*MC, V* ✣*No lunch Thurs.–Sat., no dinner Sun.*

¢–$
AMERICAN

✕**Mac 'N' Bob's.** The enormous growth in seating since 1980, from 10 to 250, testifies to the popularity of this establishment in downtown Salem. Sports memorabilia line the walls of the attractive redbrick building near Roanoke College, and sporting events are likely to be on the many TVs near the bar. The menu runs from hamburgers to steak to seafood to pizza. If you have a big appetite, try a fully loaded calzone, which flops off the sides of your plate. ✉*316 E. Main St., Salem* ☎*540/389–5999* ⊕*www.macandbobs.com* ⊟*AE, D, MC, V.*

WHERE TO STAY

$–$$

⌂**Hotel Roanoke and Conference Center.** This elegant Tudor Revival building, listed on the National Register of Historic Places, was built in 1882 by the Norfolk & Western Railroad. The richly paneled lobby has Florentine marble floors and ceiling frescos. The formal restaurant serves regional Southern cuisine. A $6.5 million renovation of guest rooms and suites includes new furnishings, flat screens, and Sweet Dreams beds. The Market Square Bridge, a glassed-in walkway, goes from the hotel to downtown attractions. **Pros:** historic building but newly decorated; great Market Square location. **Cons:** busy conference hotel. ✉*110 Shenandoah Ave.* ☎*540/985–5900* ⊕*www.hotelroanoke.com* ↪*313 rooms, 19 suites* ⋔*In-room: Wi-Fi. In-hotel: 2 restaurants, bar, pool, gym, airport shuttle* ⊟*AE, D, DC, MC, V.*

SPORTS & THE OUTDOORS
HIKING

The **Appalachian Trail** is north and west of Roanoke, crossing the valley at Troutville, 5 mi to the north. Two of the most-photographed formations on the entire 2,000-mi route from Georgia to Maine, McAfee Knob and Dragon's Tooth, are accessible from trailheads on the Virginia 311 highway, west of the valley. The **Star Trail** (⊠ *Trailhead on Riverland Rd., 2 mi southeast of downtown Roanoke*) winds through a forest oasis amid the metropolitan area as it works its way up 1½ mi to the Mill Mountain Star. Other trails can be found along the Blue Ridge Parkway to the east and south and in the George Washington and Jefferson national forests to the north and west. For more information, contact the national forests' **Supervisor's Office** (⊠ *5162 Valleypointe Pkwy., Roanoke* ☎ *540/265–5100 or 888/265–0019*).

BLUE RIDGE PARKWAY

5 mi east of Roanoke.

The Blue Ridge Parkway takes up where Skyline Drive leaves off at Waynesboro, weaving south for 471 mi to the Great Smoky Mountains National Park in North Carolina. The parkway goes up to higher elevations than the drive, up to 4,200 feet at Apple Orchard Mountain, and even higher in North Carolina. In Virginia the parkway is especially scenic between Waynesboro and Roanoke, winding through the George Washington National Forest, visiting numerous ridge-top overlooks that provide views of crumpled-looking mountains and patchwork valleys.

Milepost 0 is at Rockfish Gap. There are no gas stations on the parkway, so you'll have to exit if you need to refuel, and be prepared for a leisurely drive as the speed limit is 45 mph. Visit the **Blue Ridge Parkway Visitors Center,** open 9–5 daily year-round, 1.5 mi north of milepost 115 near Roanoke, or call the National Park Service's office in Vinton (☎ 540/857–2490) for information on Virginia's section of the parkway.

EXPLORING

Mabry Mill, north of Meadows of Dan and the Blue Ridge Parkway's junction with U.S. 58 at milepost 176, 55 mi south of Roanoke, is one of the parkway's most popular stops for photographers. The restored water-powered, weatherworn gristmill grinds cornmeal and buckwheat flour, which are for sale. ⊠ *Blue Ridge Pkwy., milepost 176* ☎ *276/952–2947* ⊠ *Free* ⊙ *May–Oct., daily 8–6.*

Peaks of Otter Recreation Area, 25 mi northeast of Roanoke, offers a close-up view of cone-shape Sharp Top Mountain, which no less an authority than Thomas Jefferson once called America's tallest peak. At 3,875 feet it's not even the tallest in the park—nearby Flat Top is 4,004 feet. You can hike to both peaks and to little brother Harkening Hill, as well as to Fallingwater Cascades, a thrilling multitier waterfall. For those not up to the climb, a bus heads most of the way up Sharp Top hourly throughout the day. The peaks rise about the shores of Abbott Lake, a bucolic picnic spot. A pleasant lakeside lodge and campground along the placid lake below are an ideal base for local trekking. ☒*Blue Ridge Pkwy., milepost 86* ☎*540/586–4357* ⊕*www.peaksofotter.com* ☜*Free*

OFF THE
BEATEN
PATH

Crabtree Falls. A series of cascades fall a distance of 1,200 feet. Taken together, Virginia claims these cascades as the highest waterfall east of the Rockies, though no single waterfall within the series would qualify as such. Whatever the superlatives or qualifications, the falls are a wondrous sight. A trail winds up a steep mountainside all the way to the top, but the first overlook is an easy stroll 700 feet from the lower parking lot. The best time to see the waterfalls is winter through spring, when the water is high. ☒*Rte. 56, 6 mi east of Blue Ridge Pkwy., or 19 mi from Wintergreen by following Rte. 151 south and then Rte. 56 west at Roseland.*

WHERE TO STAY

¢–$ ▦**Peaks of Otter Lodge.** This unpretentious, peaceful lodge is so popular that reservations are accepted beginning October 1 for the following year. Every room looks out on Abbott Lake from a private terrace or balcony, and their interiors have a folksy quality. Nestled between two of the three peaks of its namesake, the lodge was built in 1964 and is the flagship of a chain of visitor concessions along the Blue Ridge Parkway. In non-winter months a complimentary bus takes you to Sharp Top Mountain if you prefer not to hike, and you can see the same mountaintop from the lodge's Lake View Restaurant. **Pros:** restaurant and lounge on-site; ADA-accessible rooms; nice views. **Cons:** may be too rustic for some; must reserve far in advance. ☒*85554 Blue Ridge Pkwy., milepost 86, Rte. 664, Box 489, Bedford* ☎*540/586–1081 or 800/542–5927* ⊕*www.peaksofotter.com* ⇄*63 rooms* ⚒*In-room: no a/c, no phone, no TV. In-hotel: restaurant, bar* ☰*MC, V.*

BLACKSBURG & THE NEW RIVER VALLEY

41 mi southwest of Roanoke via I–81.

Despite its name, derived from being "new" to explorers when it was first discovered, the New River is actually one of the oldest rivers in the world: legend says only the Nile is older. The only river that flows from south to north completely through the Appalachian Mountains, the New River cuts a bluff-graced valley through its Virginia section for 60 mi from Galax near the North Carolina line to Pearisburg, just over the West Virginia line. Visitors will find cozy downtown areas in towns like Blacksburg, Christiansburg, Radford, and Pulaski, and many opportunities for outdoor recreation just outside the towns' limits.

EXPLORING

Almost a century before Virginia Tech's founding in 1872, the **Historic Smithfield** plantation was built in what was then the frontier wilds. Aristocratic colonist and Revolutionary War patriot William Preston moved his family to the estate in 1774, a year before the war began. Among his descendants were three Virginia governors and four U.S. senators. Today costumed interpreters, authentic period furniture, and Native American artifacts reveal how different life in the New River valley was more than two centuries ago. ✉ *1000 Smithfield Plantation Rd., Blacksburg* ☎ *540/231–3947* ⊕ *www.civic.bev.net/smithfield* ☜ *$6* ☾ *Mon., Tues., and Thurs.–Sat. 10–5; Sun. 1–5.*

With 26,000 students, **Virginia Tech** is Virginia's largest university. A small college just a few decades ago, Tech is now known for top-notch research programs and its Hokies football team, regularly ranked in the top 10. The focal point of the sprawling campus is the Drillfield, a vast green space surrounded by hefty neo-Gothic buildings built of what is known locally as "Hokie Stone" masonry. The **Virginia Museum of Natural History** at Virginia Tech (✉ *428 N. Main St.* ☎ *540/231–3001*) presents rotating exhibits on local and national wildlife; a separate geology museum in Derring Hall displays gems and minerals. ✉ *Blacksburg* ☎ *540/231–6000* ⊕ *www.vt.edu.*

What is now the **Wilderness Road Regional Museum** was once lodging for settlers making their way west on a Native American route that went from Pennsylvania through the Cumberland Gap. The man who founded the town of Newbern built this house in the same year, and the structure has since served as a private home, a tavern, a post office, and a store. Today the house contains antique dolls, swords and rifles, an old loom, and other artifacts of everyday life. A self-tour map of Newbern, the only Virginia town entirely within a National Register of Historic Places district, is available at the museum. ✉ *5240 Wilderness Rd.I–81, Exit 98, Newbern* ☎ *540/674–4835* ☜ *$2* ☾ *Mon.–Sat. 10:30–4:30, Sun. 1:30–4:30.*

WHERE TO EAT

$–$$
SOUTHERN

✕ **Boudreaux's Restaurant.** Ever eaten gator bites or buffalo crawfish? Be sure and try them at Boudreaux's. What started as a project in business marketing for a pair of Virginia Tech students is now an established part of Blacksburg's downtown. The canopied rooftop is a particularly relaxing place to enjoy jambalaya or Cajun catfish, and they serve brunch on both Saturday and Sunday. Live bands often perform in the evening. ✉ *205 N. Main St., Blacksburg* ☎ *540/961–2330* ⊕ *www.boudreauxs. com* ⊟ *AE, D, MC, V.*

¢–$
MEDITERRANEAN

✕ **The Cellar.** A gathering place and watering hole near the Virginia Tech campus, this storefront restaurant serves eclectic, inexpensive dishes. Try the Greek spaghetti with sautéed feta, garlic, and olives, or the "Mac Daddy": a single large meatball in marinara sauce and Parmesan. Local bands perform here often. ✉ *302 N. Main St., Blacksburg* ☎ *540/953–0651* ⊕ *www.the-cellar.com* ⊟ *MC, V.*

WHERE TO STAY

¢–$

🏨 **Holiday Inn University.** This hotel is across the street from Virginia Tech, with a golf course, movie theater, numerous restaurants and shopping areas, and even a beach volleyball court nearby. The imposing entrance made from native stone doesn't look anything like a chain hotel. The rooms are modern and comfortable, with two phone lines in each one. **Pros:** close to Virginia Tech. **Cons:** no historical connection. ✉*900 Prices Fork Rd., Blacksburg* ☎*540/552–7001* 🖨*540/552–0827* ☛*148 rooms, 1 suite* ♿*In-room: Wi-Fi. In-hotel: restaurant, bar, tennis court, pools, airport shuttle* ▭*AE, D, DC, MC, V.*

\$\$\$ 🏨**Mountain Lake.** Centered around the highest natural lake east of the Mississippi, this resort is a great place to cool off during a hot summer. Accommodations range from spartan cottages to plush suites in a majestic sandstone hotel from 1930 (the resort itself predates the Civil War). Atop 4,000-foot Salt Pond Mountain, outdoor activities abound: you can hike, mountain bike, ride horses, swim, and boat within the 2,500-acre Mountain Lake Wilderness, which surrounds the hotel. The adjacent Jefferson National Forest offers even more recreation, including a segment of the Appalachian Trail. **Pros:** gorgeous scenery; outdoor activities. **Cons:** crowded in summer; far from Blacksburg. ✉*115 Hotel Circle, 7 mi north of U.S. 460 on Rte. 700, Pembroke* ☎*540/626–7121* ⊕*www.mountainlakehotel.com* ☛*28 cottages, 16 lodge rooms, 43 hotel rooms* ♿*In-room: no a/c, refrigerator (some), no TV, Wi-Fi. In-hotel: restaurant, pool, bicycles* ▭*AE, D, MC, V* ⫟*MAP* ⊘*Closed Dec.–Apr.*

SPORTS & THE OUTDOORS
BIKING
Mountain Lake (✉*115 Hotel Circle, 7 mi north of U.S. 460 on Rte. 700, Pembroke* ☎*540/626–7121*) has more than 20 mi of mountain-bike trails, with bicycles available at the hotel. The 52-mi **New River Trail,** Virginia's narrowest state park, runs from Pulaski to Galax following what was once a railroad bed. It parallels the river for 39 of those miles, passing through two tunnels. The trail is also open to hikers and horseback riders. The Jefferson National Forest's **Pandapas Pond Recreation Area,** on the edge of Blacksburg, is a popular place for mountain biking.

HIKING
The **Appalachian Trail** crosses the New River valley, visiting overlook sites such as Angel's Rest and Wind Rock. For more information on area hikes in the Jefferson National Forest, contact the **Blacksburg Ranger Station** (✉*110 Southpark Dr., Blacksburg* ☎*540/552–4641*). The 4-mi loop at **Cascades Recreation Area** (✉*Jefferson National Forest, off U.S. 460, 4 mi north of Pembroke on Rte. 623*) passes a rushing stream and a 60-foot waterfall. This hike is popular locally and becomes crowded on weekends when the weather's good.

ABINGDON

135 mi southwest of Roanoke (via I–81).

Abingdon, near the Tennessee border, is a cultural crossroads in the wilderness: the town of nearly 7,000 draws tens of thousands of people each year because of a fine theater company and exuberant local celebrations.

By far the most popular event here is the **Virginia Highlands Festival** during the first two weeks of August: 200,000 people come to hear live music performances ranging from bluegrass to opera, to visit the exhibitions of mountain crafts, and to browse among the wares of more than 100 antiques dealers (⊕*www.vahighlandsfestival.org*).This is followed by the **Burley Tobacco Festival,** held in September, during which country-music stars perform and prize farm animals are proudly displayed.

ESSENTIALS

Visitor Information **Abingdon Convention & Visitors Bureau** (✉ *335 Cummings St.* ☎ *276/676–2282* ⊕ *www.abingdon.com/tourism*).

WHERE TO STAY & EAT

$$$ ☷**Camberley's Martha Washington Inn.** Constructed as a private house in
★   1832, turned into a college dormitory in 1860, and then used as a field hospital during the Civil War, the Martha Washington finally became an inn in 1935. Across from the Barter Theatre, the inn has rooms furnished with Victorian antiques; some have fireplaces. A natatorium, pool, and full-service spa add to the old world luxury. **Pros:** historic luxury; spa and pool facilities. **Cons:** pricey compared to nearby options. ✉*150 W. Main St.* ☎*276/628–3161 or 800/555–8000* ⊕*www.martha washingtoninn.com* ⤶*51 rooms, 11 suites* ⟐*In-room: refrigerator, Wi-Fi. In-hotel: restaurant, bar, pool, gym, spa, laundry service, public Internet, airport shuttle* ▤*AE, D, DC, MC, V* ⏋*BP.*

NIGHTLIFE & THE ARTS

From February through the Christmas season, audiences flock to the prestigious **Barter Theatre** (✉*133 W. Main St.* ☎*276/628–3991*), America's longest-running professional repertory theater. Founded during the Depression by local actor Robert Porterfield, the theater got its name in the obvious way: early patrons who could not afford the 40¢ tickets could pay in produce. Patricia Neal, Ned Beatty, and Gregory Peck are among the many stars who began their careers at the Barter, which today presents classics, dramas, comedies, musicals, and new and Appalachian works. Although times have changed since Noël Coward was given a Virginia ham for his contributions, patrons can still barter for their seat a few times a year. But don't just show up at the box office with a bag of arugula—all trades must be approved by advance notice.

THE OUTDOORS

HIKING

Wild ponies on open grasslands studded with rocky knobs give the area around **Mt. Rogers** an appearance distinct from any other in Virginia. At 5,729 feet, Mt. Rogers is Virginia's highest point, but you don't need to hike all the way to its summit to experience the grandeur of Western-like terrain—a short walk of about a mile from **Grayson Highlands State Park** (✉*U.S. 58, 20 mi east of Damascus* ☎*276/579–7092* ⤳*$2*) into the adjacent **Mount Rogers Recreation Area** is all that's required. Through the 5,000-acre state park and 120,000-acre recreation area run an extensive network of riding and hiking trails; the Appalachian Trail passes through on its way to North Carolina and Tennessee, just to the south. ✉*Mount Rogers National Recreation Area, 3714 Hwy. 16, Marion* ☎*276/783–5196* ⤳*Free.*

Mountain Music

Southwest Virginia's hills and valleys have long reverberated with the sounds of fiddles, banjoes, mandolins, and acoustic guitars. Scotch-Irish settlers brought these sounds with them, and for the generations before radio and television, front-porch gatherings and community dances entertained local families isolated, geographically and culturally, from the rest of civilization.

Virginia has designated a 250-mi route snaking through the hills as **The Crooked Road: Virginia's Music Heritage Trail.** What connects the communities and sites along this route is a passion for traditional mountain music—bluegrass, gospel, roots, and old-time country. Many people point to this region as the birthplace of the country-music industry. In 1927 talent scout Ralph Peer set up a makeshift recording studio in the Virginia-Tennessee border town of Bristol. From these sessions came such seminal acts as the Carter Family and Jimmie Rodgers. For more information, go to ⊕ *www.thecrookedroad.org.* Sites are listed here from west to east.

Ralph Stanley Museum and Traditional Mountain Music Center (✉ *Clintwood* ☎ *276/926–5591* ⊕ *www.ralphstanleymuseum.com*). The Ralph Stanley Museum opened in 2004 to preserve traditional mountain music. Focusing on the life and career of local legend Ralph Stanley, the exhibits allow visitors to hear the music of Stanley and other artists.

Carter Family Fold (✉ *U.S. 58/421, 19 mi west of Bristol, Hiltons* ☎ *276/386–6054 or 276/386–9480* ⊕ *www.carterfamilyfold.org*). At this 1,000-seat auditorium, live music is performed on Saturday night; a two-day festival is held each August. A museum in an adjacent building displays memorabilia from the Carter Family; descendants often perform in the shows.

Old Fiddlers Convention (✉ *Galax* ☎ *276/236–8541* ⊕ *www.oldfiddlers convention.com*). Hundreds of musicians and thousands of fans gather the second week of August for performances, contests, and jam sessions.

Rex Theatre (✉ *113 E. Grayson St., Galax* ☎ *276/236–0329 or 276/236–0668* ⊕ *www.rextheatere galax.com*). Bluegrass, country, and gospel music is broadcast from here each Friday night on WBRF, FM–98.1.

Blue Ridge Music Center (✉ *Blue Ridge Pkwy. milepost 213, near NC line* ☎ *276/236–5309* ⊕ *www. blueridgemusiccenter.net*). The center's outdoor amphitheater is the site of an ambitious concert series of regional and national musicians that has included the likes of Ricky Skaggs and Doc Watson. Impromptu jam sessions often break out in the center's plaza area.

Floyd Country Store (✉ *206 S. Locust St.Floyd* ☎ *540/745–4563* ⊕ *www.floydcountrystore.com* ✉ *$3*). What were once just sessions have evolved into a Friday Night Jamboree attended by local folks and visitors from far off. In summer, music often breaks out all around the store as well. "Granny Rules" are in effect— "no smokin,' no cussin,' and no drinkin." But clogging on the dance floor is fine.

3

At the end of Abingdon's Main Street is the beginning of the 34-mi **Virginia Creeper Trail**, a former rail bed of the Virginia-Carolina Railroad. You can hike it, bike it, or take to it on horseback. The trail has sharp curves, steep grades, and 100 trestles and bridges. It joins the Appalachian Trail at Damascus, a town known for its friendly attitude and the many businesses targeted toward hikers and cyclists. In May the town celebrates Trail Days, a festival celebrating hikers. ⊠ *Trailhead at end of Main St.* ☎ *540/676–2282 or 800/435–3440.*

Richmond, Fredericksburg & the Northern Neck

WORD OF MOUTH

"We decided to take a day trip from the DC area and drove down to Fredricksburg. It is a wonderful town . . . We went on the trolley ride. It gives you a good overview of the history of the area and shows you the location of the sites . . . We felt it was very worthwhile. We brought a picnic lunch but there were a lot of cute places to eat on the main strip of town."

—suzanne97

"I know you have great art museums in NYC, but you should visit the Virginia Museum of Fine Arts. I especially love the Fabergé eggs and other Fabergé objects."

—longhorn55

Updated
by Ginger
Warder

A HOST OF PATRIOTS AND presidents have lived and worked in the heart of the Old Dominion, an area that takes in Richmond, Fredericksburg, Petersburg, and the Northern Neck. Virginia is often called "The Mother of Presidents," since eight of America's leaders, including George Washington, were born here. The birthplaces, boyhood homes, or graves of notable figures such as George Washington, James Monroe, John Tyler, and Robert E. Lee can be found here, and the area has many associations with other leaders, including Patrick Henry and Thomas Jefferson. William Byrd II named the city Richmond in 1737 because the bend in the James River reminded him of the Thames in Richmond, England. George Washington designed the nation's first canal system here, the Kanawha, and Richmond has been home to many other "firsts," including the first African-American governor in the country, the first hospital, and the South's first television station.

Richmond's renovated State Capitol was originally designed by Jefferson, and its rotunda features portraits and statues of Virginia's presidents, including the famous Houdoun marble sculpture of George Washington. At St. John's Church, in one of the city's oldest neighborhoods, Patrick Henry gave his incendiary "Give me liberty or give me death" speech that helped ignite the American Revolution.

ORIENTATION & PLANNING

GETTING ORIENTED

South of Washington, DC, I–95 easily connects this region of Virginia, bordered by the Chesapeake Bay to the East.

Richmond. It's within a day's drive of half of the U.S. population, easily reached from Interstates 95 and 64. Serving as Virginia's capital since 1780, Richmond is also the former capital of the Confederacy. Besides numerous Revolutionary War and Civil War sites, the city also contains the Fan District, full of 19th-century homes; the Museum District, which contains several world-class Virginia institutions; historic Monument Avenue; the vibrant shopping district known as Carytown; and a wealth of restaurants and nightclubs in Shockoe Slip and Shockoe Bottom. In nearby Ashland (about 20 mi north of Richmond), Patrick Henry honed his oratory skills at the historic Hanover Courthouse. This quaint railroad town is also home to charming shops, the Henry Clay Inn, Randolph Macon College, and Henry's former residence, Scotchtown.

Petersburg. Thirty minutes south of Richmond, Petersburg is a delightful antebellum city with many historic attractions. Besieged by the Union Army in 1864, the townspeople bravely did their best to protect the Confederacy. The Petersburg National Battlefield, Pamplin Park, and the historic Blandford Church and Cemetery are must-sees for Civil War buffs. Blandford Church has an incredible collection of 15 stained-glass windows designed by Louis Comfort Tiffany as a tribute to the Confederate states and their brave soldiers.

TOP REASONS TO GO

■ **Soak up art from around the world:** Richmond's Virginia Museum of Fine Arts, the most outstanding museum in the region, has among its treasures the Mellon collections of British sporting art and French impressionist and postimpressionist art—and those precious five Fabergé eggs.

■ **Reflect at the somber Petersburg National Battlefield:** On the site where more than 60,000 Union and Confederate soldiers died during the siege of the city, today a 1,500-acre park is laced with several miles of earthworks and includes two forts.

■ **Combine Revolutionary history with architecture appreciation:** Stratford Hall Plantation is the birthplace of the legendary Robert E. Lee, the only person to be a general in both the Confederate and Union armies. Built in the 1730s and the center of a 1,600-acre working plantation, it's one of the country's finest examples of Colonial architecture, and offers wonderful views of the Potomac River to boot.

■ **Return to Colonial days at Fredericksburg's Kenmore:** The mansion was built in 1775 on a 1,300-acre plantation owned by Colonel Fielding Lewis, a patriot, merchant, and brother-in-law of George Washington. Among the gems here are the outstanding plaster moldings in the ceilings and over the fireplace in the dining room—even more ornate than those at Mount Vernon.

Fredericksburg. Less than an hour north of Richmond sits the appealing city of Fredericksburg, a quaint historic city full of both Colonial and Civil War history, with hundreds of impressive 18th- and 19th-century homes and a treasure trove of art and antiques stores. The nearby Fredericksburg/Spotsylvania National Military Park presents the story of the area's role in the Civil War.

The Northern Neck. East of Fredericksburg, away from the blood-soaked and fought-over grounds, peace and quiet reign in a 90-mi-long peninsula Virginians call "The Northern Neck." This outdoorsman's escape was the birthplace of three presidents, including the Father of Our Country. Don't miss George Washington's birthplace and the quintessential seaside town of Irvington. Here wide rivers and the briny Chesapeake Bay entice water lovers and sports anglers.

PLANNING

WHEN TO GO
Richmond's mild climate welcomes visitors year-round. Since Virginia Commonwealth University is spread throughout the downtown area, traffic is more congested from September through May when school is in session.

Spring is spectacular, especially during **Virginia's Annual Garden Week** in April (⊕ *www.vagardenweek.org*). In July the **Hanover Tomato Festival** (⊕ *www.hanovertomatofestival.com*), and in August, the **Carytown Watermelon Festival** (⊕ *www.carytown.org/wmfestival.htm)* celebrate

Richmond, Petersburg, and the Northern Neck

KEY
⊢——— Rail Lines

that county's bounty. In May and September the Richmond International Raceway hosts NASCAR. In September the **Virginia State Fair** (☎804/228–3200 ⊕*www.statefair.com*), in Richmond, is a classic conglomeration of carnival rides, livestock shows, displays of farm equipment, and lots of food for sale. The **Richmond Folk Festival** (⊕*www.richmondfolkfestival.org*) takes place in October downtown, and Lewis Ginter Botanical Garden is ablaze with 450,000 lights during December's **Garden Festival of Lights** (⊕*www.lewisginter.org*).

GETTING HERE & AROUND

BY AIR Richmond International Airport, 10 mi east of the city, Exit 197 off I–64, has scheduled flights by eight major carriers. Undergoing a massive renovation, Richmond Airport's traffic patterns change frequently due to construction.

Other nearby airports include Dulles International and Reagan National in Washington, DC, as well as Patrick Henry in Newport News and the Charlottesville-Albemarle Airport. A taxi ride to downtown Richmond from the airport costs $25, and the Groom Transportation shuttle is $21.50.

BY CAR Having a car is advisable in Richmond and Fredericksburg. It's essential for touring outlying attractions, including historic homes and battlefields, and the Northern Neck. Avoid the major interstates such as 64 and 95 during morning and evening rush hours if possible.

BY TRAIN   Richmond has two Amtrak stations: Main Street Station downtown and Staples Mill, about 10 mi to the west. Only the trains on the Northeast corridor stop at Main Street; more routes are offered from Staples Mill. Amtrak trains operate between Washington's Union Station, Alexandria, Fredericksburg, Richmond, and a number of commuter stops several times daily. A one-way ticket costs $25 between Fredericksburg and Washington and $41 between Washington and Richmond. Amtrak service between New York City and Newport News or Florida passes through Richmond daily. The Virginia Rail Express, which uses the same tracks and station as Amtrak, provides workday commuter service between Fredericksburg and Washington's Union Station, with additional stops near hotels in Crystal City, L'Enfant Plaza, and elsewhere. A round-trip ticket from Washington's Union Station to Fredericksburg costs $18.20. There's no mass transit to the Northern Neck, but you can take the train to Fredericksburg and rent a car.

4

ESSENTIALS
Air Contacts Richmond International Airport (✉ *Airport Dr.* ☎ *804/226–3000* ⊕ *www.flyrichmond.com).*

Train Information Virginia Rail Express (☎ *703/684–1001 or 800/743–3873* ⊕ *www.vre.org).*

Visitor Information Potomac Gateway Visitor Center (✉ *3540 James Madison Pkwy., King George* ☎ *540/663–3205* ⊕ *www.northernneck.org).*

ABOUT THE HOTELS & RESTAURANTS
Keep in the mind that hotel rooms can be hard to come by during Richmond's NASCAR Nextel Cup races, held over two weekends in May and September.

WHAT IT COSTS				
¢	$	$$	$$$	$$$$
Restaurants	under $10	$10–$16	$17–$23	$24–$30	over $30
Hotels	under $100	$101–$160	$161–$230	$231–$300	over $300

Restaurant prices are per person for a main course at dinner. Hotel prices are for a standard double room, excluding state tax.

EXPLORING THE AREA

Richmond, 100 mi south of Washington, DC, on the James River, is the state's historic capital. It's easy to get here on I–95. Midway between Washington and Richmond on I–95, Fredericksburg is a lovely place to relax and retrace 18th- and 19th-century history in homes and museums and on nearby battlefields. About 20 mi east of Fredericksburg, the Northern Neck begins. There's no public transportation to this rural area, but a car lets you wander at will among its many historic sites and water views. Ashland, in Hanover County about 20 mi north of

Richmond, is the birthplace of Patrick Henry. Petersburg, with its Civil War history, is a mere half hour south of Richmond.

RICHMOND

Centered on the fall line of the James River, about 75 mi upriver from the Chesapeake Bay, Richmond completes the transition from Tidewater Virginia into the Piedmont, the central section of rolling plains that reaches toward the mountain barrier in the west. Not only is Richmond the capital of the Commonwealth, but it was also the capital of the Confederacy. As a result, the city is studded with historic sites. At the start of the Civil War, Richmond was the most industrialized city in the South, and it remains an important city for national industries. After years of urban decay, Richmond transformed itself into a lively and sophisticated modern town, adding high technology to traditional economic bases that include shipping and banking.

GETTING HERE & AROUND

By car, Interstates 95 and 64 come directly to Richmond, and state routes 1, 5, and 301 are scenic alternatives. Richmond has two Amtrak stations: one downtown and one on the west side at Staples Mill Road. Cabs are metered in Richmond; they charge $2.50 for the first mile and $1.50 for each additional mile. Greater Richmond Transit operates bus service in Richmond. Buses run daily, 5 AM–1 AM; fares are $1.25 (exact change required). ■TIP➔ **A free lunch express shuttles throughout the downtown area weekdays from 11:30 to 2:30. Three 22-passenger vans loop around downtown, stopping at nine restaurants every 10 minutes. This is a great way to get around the downtown area during midday. See ⊕www. ridegrtc.com for the lunch express route map.**

TOURS   Historic Richmond Tours, a service of the Valentine Richmond History Center, offers guided tours that cover such topics as the historic Hollywood Cemetery and the River District and Jackson Ward. You can take either a walking tour or one of the thematic bus tours with topics that change monthly. Richmond Discoveries' excursions include tours that highlight Civil War history and customized trips for large groups or small families. Segway tours offers a 2½-hour tour by Segway of the historic sites of the city and includes a training lesson before departing. Tours meet at the Richmond Visitors Center on 3rd Street.

TIMING & PRECAUTIONS

Both Interstates 95 and 64 will be affected by rush-hour traffic. With many major businesses on the West End of Richmond, 64 West will be heavy in the mornings, and 64 East returning to the city will be busy from 4 PM to 6 PM. Similarly, 95 North in the morning and 95 South in the evening will also see increased traffic, and in summer, with many Richmond residents heading to the beaches, both 64 East and 95 South can experience mile-long backups. The Downtown Expressway and the Powhite Parkway are toll roads (25¢–$1.50) that service the suburban areas, especially on the south side of the city, and these will also be busy during rush hours.

Also, be aware that since this is a large, urban city, there are some downtown areas that you should visit with caution, especially after dark.

ESSENTIALS

Taxi Companies Groome Transportation (✉ *Richmond Airport* ☎ *804/222–6464*). **Metro Taxicab Service** (✉ *2405 Westwood Ave.* ☎ *804/353–5000*). **Yellow Cab Service Inc** (✉ *3203 Williamsburg Rd.* ☎ *804/222–7300*).

Train Stations Richmond train station (✉ *7519 Staples Mill Rd., at Main Street Station* ☎ *804/553–2903*).

Tour information Historic Richmond Tours (☎ *804/649–0711* ⊕ *www.rich mondhistorycenter.com*). **Richmond Discoveries** (☎ *804/222–8595* ⊕ *www. richmonddiscoveries.com*). **Segway Tours** (✉ *405 N. 3rd St.* ☎ *800/979–3370* ⊕ *www.segwayofrichmond.com* ⊠ *$65* ⊙ *Daily tours at 10 AM and 2 PM*).

Visitor Information Richmond Regional Visitor Center (✉ *401 N. 3rd St.* ☎ *800/370–9004* ⊕ *www.visit.richmond.com*). **Virginia Tourism Corporation** (✉ *901 E. Byrd St.* ☎ *800/847–4882* ⊕ *www.virginia.org* ✉ *Bell Tower at Capitol Sq., 9th and Franklin Sts.* ☎ *800/545–5586 Information by mail:* ✉ *403 N. 3rd St.*). **Visitor Center at Richmond International Airport** (✉ *1 Richard E. Byrd Terminal Dr.* ☎ *804/236–3260* ⊕ *www.richmond.com/visitors*).

Numbers in the text correspond to numbers in the margin and on the Richmond map.

DOWNTOWN

Richmond's historic attractions lie north of the James River, which bisects the city with a sweeping curve. The heart of Old Richmond is the Court End district downtown. This area, close to the Capitol, contains seven National Historic Landmarks, three museums, and 11 additional buildings on the National Register of Historic Places—all within eight blocks. Just a mile east of Court End is historic Church Hill, a neighborhood of 19th-century homes and historic St. John's Church, which offers a free reenactment of Patrick Henry's "Give me liberty" speech on Sunday at 2 PM.

Running west from the Court End district is Main Street, lined with banks; Cary Street, an east–west thoroughfare, becomes, between 12th and 15th streets, the cobblestone center of Shockoe Slip, and the west end of Cary Street, known as Carytown, is Richmond's most popular shopping district. Shockoe Slip (once the city's largest commercial trading district and the heart of the slave trade) and Shockoe Bottom (on land formerly occupied by a Native American trading post) are unique restored areas filled with trendy shops, restaurants, and nightlife. Shockoe Bottom landmarks include the 17th Street Farmers' Market, operating since 1775, and Main Street Station, an elaborate Victorian structure capped by red tiles that was Richmond's first train station. Drive west beyond the historic downtown to see a fascinating group of close-in, charming, and distinctive neighborhoods. Not far from the Capitol is Jackson Ward, called the "Home of Black Capitalism," a cultural and entrepreneurial center after the Civil War.

MAIN ATTRACTIONS

⓫ **American Civil War Center.** This museum weaves the stories of the Union, Confederate, and African-American experiences during the Civil War into a national context. The permanent exhibit *In the Cause of Liberty* is housed in the old Gun Foundry, where more than 1,100 Confederate cannons were made. ⊠ *500 Tredegar St.* ☎ *804/780–1865* ⊕ *www. tredegar.org* ⌐ *$8* ☉ *Daily 9–5*

⓮ **Black History Museum & Cultural Center of Virginia.** The goal of this museum in the Jackson Ward is to gather visual, oral, and written records and artifacts that commemorate the lives and accomplishments of blacks in Virginia. On display are 5,000 documents, fine art objects, traditional African artifacts, textiles from ethnic groups throughout Africa, and artwork by Sam Gilllam, John Biggers, and P.H. Polk. ⊠ *3 Clay St., at Foushee St.* ☎ *804/780–9093* ⊕ *www.blackhistorymuseum.org* ⌐ *$5* ☉ *Tues.–Sat. 10–5.*

OFF THE BEATEN PATH

Citie of Henricus. Visit the home of Pocahontas and the second successful English settlement in the New World. Costumed interpreters reenact the lives of Virginia's Native Americans and English settlers who helped create the nation we know today. ⊠ *251 Henricus Park Rd., Chester* ☎ *804/706–1340* ⊕ *www.henricus.org* ⌐ *$7* ☉ *Tues.–Sun. 10–5.*

❸ **Edgar Allan Poe Museum.** Richmond's oldest residence, the Old Stone House in Shockoe Bottom, just west of Church Hill Historic District, now holds a museum honoring the famous writer. Poe grew up in Richmond, and although he never lived in this early- to mid-18th-century structure, his disciples have made it a monument with some of the writer's possessions on display. ⊠ *1914 E. Main St.* ☎ *804/648–5523 or 888/213–2703* ⊕ *www.poemuseum.org* ⌐ *$6* ☉ *Tues.–Sat. 10–5, Sun. 11–5. Guided tours on the hr; last tour departs at 4.*

❼ **John Marshall House.** John Marshall (1755–1835) was chief justice of the U.S. Supreme Court for 34 years—longer than any other. He built his redbrick Federal-style house with neoclassical motifs in 1790. Appointed to the court by President John Adams, Marshall also served as secretary of state and ambassador to France. The house, fully restored and furnished, has wood paneling and wainscoting, narrow arched passageways, and a mix of period pieces and heirlooms. The house has been a beautifully maintained museum since 1913. ⊠ *818 E. Marshall St.* ☎ *804/648–7998* ⊕ *www.apva.org/marshall* ⌐ *$6* ☉ *Tues.–Sat. 10–4:30, Sun. noon–5.*

❺ **Museum and White House of the Confederacy.** These two buildings provide a look at a crucial period in the nation's history. The museum (a good place to start) has elaborate permanent exhibitions on the Civil War era. The "world's largest collection of Confederate memorabilia" includes such artifacts as the sword Robert E. Lee wore to the surrender at Appomattox. Next door, the "White House" has in fact always been painted gray. Made of brick in 1818, the building was stuccoed to give the appearance of large stone blocks. Preservationists have painstakingly re-created the interior as it was during the Civil War, when Jefferson Davis lived in the house. During the 45-minute guided tour,

Fodor'sChoice
★

Richmond, Virginia

440 yards
400 meters

you see the entry hall's period 9-foot-tall French rococo mirrors and its floor cloth, painted to resemble ceramic tiles. You can park free in the adjacent hospital parking garage; the museum will validate tickets. ✉ *1201 E. Clay St.* ☎ *804/649–1861* ⊕ *www.moc.org* ✉ *Combination ticket $11; museum only, $8; White House only, $8* ⊙ *Mon.–Sat. 10–5, Sun. noon–5.*

⑫ **Richmond National Battlefield Park Visitor Center.** Inside what was once the
☾ Tredegar Iron Works, this is the best place to get maps and other materials on the Civil War battlefields and attractions in the Richmond area. A self-guided tour and optional tape tour for purchase covers the two major military threats to Richmond—the Peninsula Campaign of 1862 and the Overland Campaign of 1864—as well as the impact on Richmond's home front. Three floors of exhibits in the main building include unique artifacts on loan from other Civil War history institutions. Other original buildings on-site are a carpentry shop, gun foundry, office, and company store.

Kids can participate in the Junior Ranger program. They're given a workbook which leads them through the exhibits in search of "clues." Once they've completed their book, they receive their choice of an embroidered Ranger patch or a Ranger pin.

Built in 1837, the ironworks, along with smaller area iron foundries, made Richmond the center of iron manufacturing in the South. When the Civil War began in 1861, the ironworks geared up to make the artillery, ammunition, and other material that sustained the Confederate war machine. Its rolling mills provided the armor plating for warships, including the ironclad CSS *Virginia.* The works—saved from burning in 1865—went on to play an important role in rebuilding the devastated South; it also produced munitions in both world wars. The center has a pay parking lot ($3), but free parking is available next door at the Belle Isle lot. Also, be aware that the American Civil War Center is also on this site, but is a private museum that charges admission. ✉ *5th and Tredegar Sts.* ☎ *804/771–2145* ⊕ *www.nps.gov/rich* ✉ *Free* ⊙ *Daily 9–5.*

Richmond Slave Trail. Walk in the footsteps of Richmond's slaves from the Manchester Docks, down the Slave Trade path along the James River, past former slave auction houses in cobblestoned Shockoe Bottom and Lumpkin's Jail. Free booklets for a 1.3-mi self-guided walk are available from the city park system, or join in the big Freedom Celebration annually on June 19. (✉ *Manchester Docks* ☎ *804/646–8911* ⊕ *www. ci.richmond.va.us/departments/parks/james.aspx* ✉ *Free*).

❷ **St. John's Episcopal Church.** For security reasons, the rebellious Second
Fodor'sChoice Virginia Convention met in Richmond instead of Williamsburg; it was
★ in this 1741 church on March 23, 1775, that Patrick Henry delivered the speech in which he declared, "Give me liberty or give me death!" His argument persuaded the Second Virginia Convention to arm a Virginia militia. The speech is reenacted Memorial Day to Labor Day on Sunday at 2 PM. The cemetery includes the graves of Edgar Allan Poe's mother, Elizabeth Arnold Poe, and many famous early

Virginians, notably George Wythe, a signer of the Declaration of Independence. The visitor center, in a restored redbrick schoolhouse, has Colonial crafts and other items for sale. Guided tours are led on the half-hour. ⊠ *2401 E. Broad St. , at 24th St.* ☏ *804/648–5015* ⊕ *www. historicstjohnschurch.org* ≣ *$6* ⊙ *Mon.–Sat. 10–3:30, Sun. 1–4.*

⑥ Valentine Richmond History Center. For more than 100 years the Valentine Richmond History Center, established in 1898, has celebrated one of America's most historic cities. It has collected more than a million objects—one of the nation's largest

collections focusing on a single city—including preserved photographs, textiles, and artifacts, and interprets 400 years of Richmond's history through items of everyday life. The large collection is kept in the History Center Archives, and is available for study and research by appointment. **Wickham House** (1812), a part of the Valentine, is more rightly a mansion; it was designed by architect Alexander Parris, the creator of Boston's Faneuil Hall. John Wickham was Richmond's wealthiest citizen of the time, and Daniel Webster and Zachary Taylor were frequent guests. The last owner of the house, Mann Valentine Jr., left a bequest in his will to turn the home into a museum. Mann's brother, sculptor Edward Valentine, worked from his carriage house studio to create the Robert E. Lee memorial at Washington & Lee University, and the famous statue of Thomas Jefferson in Richmond's grand Jefferson Hotel. His studio is one of only four surviving 19th-century sculptors' studios in the United States open to the public. ⊠ *1015 E. Clay St.* ☏ *804/649–0711* ⊕ *www.richmondhistorycenter.com* ≣ *$10, includes John Marshall House and Wickham House* ⊙ *Tues.–Sat. 10–5, Sun. noon–5; guided Wickham House tours Tues.–Sat. 11–4 and Sun. 1–4.*

㉛ Virginia Museum of Fine Arts. The panorama of world art here, spanning
Fodor'sChoice the ages from ancient times to the present, features such important
★ works as the Mellon collections of British Sporting Art and French impressionist and postimpressionist art—including nine original wax sculptures and seven bronzes by Edgar Degas; works by Goya, Renoir, and Monet; classical and Egyptian art; Roman marble statues; and one of the world's leading collections of Indian, Nepalese, and Tibetan art. The museum's most beloved pieces are its five Fabergé eggs. At this writing, the museum is undergoing a major expansion until early 2010, which will double existing gallery space, create a sculpture garden, and enlarge parking. During this time some galleries and collections will be off view: call ahead for specific information. ⊠ *200 North Blvd.* ☏ *804/340–1400* ⊕ *www.vmfa.state.va.us* ≣ *Free, $5 suggested donation* ⊙ *Wed.–Sun. 11–5.*

9 ★ **Virginia State Capitol.** Thomas Jefferson designed this grand edifice in 1785, modeling it on a Roman temple—the Maison Carrée—in Nîmes, France. After an extensive renovation, the Capitol has a new handicapped-accessible entrance on Bank Street. A visitor's center is in the adjacent Bell Tower, and the expanded Capitol features an exhibit gallery, gift shop, and Meriwether's Capitol Café. Indoor guided tours last one hour and include the Old House and Senate chambers, the Rotunda, and two rooms restored in 2007. A map for self-guided tours is also available. ✉*1000 Bank St.* ☎*804/698–1788* ⊕*www.virginiacapitol. gov* ✆*Free* ⊗*Mon.–Sat. 8:30–5, Sun. 1–4*

ALSO WORTH SEEING

10 **Canal Walk.** The 1.25-mi Canal Walk meanders through downtown Richmond along the Haxall Canal, the James River, and the Kanawha Canal, and can be enjoyed on foot or in boats. Along the way, look for history exhibits such as the Flood Wall Gallery, bronze medallions, and other exhibits placed on Brown's Island and Canal Walk by the Richmond Historical Riverfront Foundation. Many sights intersect with Canal Walk, including the Richmond National Battlefield Park Civil War Visitor Center, and 5th, 7th, Virginia, 14th, 15th, and 17th streets meet the water along it.

The James River–Kanawha Canal was proposed by George Washington to bring ships around the falls of the James River, and to connect Richmond to major trade routes. Brown's Island, once the location of an ammunition factory during the Civil War, hosts festivals and concerts in warmer months. **River District Canal Cruises** (✉*139 Virginia St.* ☎*804/649–2800*) operates a 40-minute ride on the canal in a 38-seat open boat. Tours, which cost $5, depart from the Turning Basin near 14th and Virginia streets. Tours run from April through mid-November and depart on the hour. If you're in a car, try to find the site before parking. Lack of prominent signage makes it challenging to find, and parking lots are a few blocks away. ⊕*www.richmondriverfront.com/ canalwalk.shtml.*

7 **Chimborazo Medical Museum.** This was once the Confederacy's largest and best-equipped hospital. Chimborazo opened in 1861 and treated more than 76,000 Confederate soldiers between 1862 and 1865. It could house more than 3,000 patients in its 100 wards. This site—once more than 40 acres—now contains a National Park Service visitor center and a small medical museum that tells the story of the patients, hospital, caregivers, and physicians through uniforms, documents, and other artifacts. ✉*3215 E. Broad St.* ☎*804/226–1981* ⊕*www.nps.gov/rich* ✆*Free* ⊗*Daily 9–5.*

8 **Library of Virginia.** As the official state archive, this library preserves and provides access to more than 99.5 million manuscript items documenting four centuries of Virginia history—fascinating to researchers and less so to everyone else. Its collections include 240,000 photographs, prints, engravings, posters, and paintings. The building has free underground parking. ✉*800 E. Broad St.* ☎*804/692–3500* ⊕*www.lva.lib. va.us* ✆*Free* ⊗*Mon.–Sat. 9–5.*

⑬ Maggie L. Walker National Historic Site. From 1904 to 1934, this restored 28-room brick building was the home of a pioneering African-American businesswoman and educator whose endeavors included banking, insurance, and a newspapers. You can take a 45-minute tour of the house and see a movie about her accomplishments. ⊠ *Visitor center, 600 N. 2nd St.* 🕾 *804/771–2017* ⊕ *www.nps.gov/malw* 🎫 *Free* ⊙ *Mon.–Sat. 9–5.*

Virginia Aviation Museum. The legendary SR-71 Blackbird spy plane, once able to travel faster than three times the speed of sound and at an elevation of more than 85,000 feet (near the edge of Earth's atmosphere) sits proudly outside this museum. The U.S. Air Force's 32 Blackbirds were used on reconnaissance missions from 1964 to 1990. The museum also has Captain Dick Merrill's 1930s open-cockpit mail plane; airworthy replicas of the Wright brothers' 1900, 1901, and 1902 gliders; a replica 1903 Flyer; and a World War I SPAD VII in mint condition. Virginia's Aviation Hall of Fame is also housed at this branch of the Science Museum of Virginia. To get here, take Exit 197 off I-64 East and follow signs to the museum. ⊠ *Richmond International Airport, 5701 Huntsman Rd.* 🕾 *804/236–3622* ⊕ *www.vam.smv.org* 🎫 *$6* ⊙ *Mon.–Sat. 9:30–5, Sun. noon–5.*

⑱ Virginia Center for Architecture. Richmond's museum is housed in a Tudor Revival mansion on Monument Avenue designed by John Russell Pope. See the rotating exhibitions and learning center on a self-guided tour. One of the permanent exhibits is "The House that Pope Built," a tribute to the architect of the Thomas Jefferson Memorial, the National Gallery of Art West Building, and Richmond's Union Station which now houses the Science Museum. Touring exhibitions range from American classicism to iconic furniture design. ⊠ *2501 Monument Ave.* 🕾 *804/644–3041* ⊕ *www.virginiaarchitecture.org* 🎫 *Free* ⊙ *Tues.– Fri. 10–5, weekends 1–5.*

❹ Virginia Holocaust Museum. The city's most poignant museum is housed in the former Climax Warehouse, which stored tobacco in Richmond's Shockoe Bottom. In keeping with the museum's aim to further "tolerance through education," the museum details the experiences of Holocaust survivors from across Virginia who have recorded their stories and shared their memories. One permanent exhibit, the Ipson Saga, follows the life of a family who went from prewar Lithuania to the Kovno ghetto concentration camp, as well as their escape and eventual resettlement in Virginia. After an introductory film in which six Richmond-based survivors tell their stories, visitors receive a book for a self-guided tour; a free audio tour (in English, Spanish, German, French, or Polish) is also available. The museum's auditorium, the Chore Shul, is a replica of the beautiful 18th-century interior of the only surviving synagogue in Lithuania. Because of the nature of the exhibits, the museum is not recommended for young children. ⊠ *2000 E. Cary St.* 🕾 *804/257–5400* ⊕ *www.va-holocaust.com* 🎫 *Donations accepted* ⊙ *Weekdays 9–5, weekends 11–5.*

RICHMOND'S NEIGHBORHOODS

Richmond is divided into four quadrants: Northside (north of the James River), Southside (south of the James River), West End, and East Richmond. The main attractions, sites, hotels, restaurants, and shopping are spread out between several popular neighborhoods. Starting with Church Hill at the east end of downtown, heading west you'll come to Shockoe Bottom and Shockoe Slip, downtown, the Fan District which is home to Virginia Commonwealth University, the Museum District, the popular shopping area Carytown, and finally to the West End, a major residential and business area.

To the west of downtown, Monument Avenue, 140 feet wide and divided by a verdant median, is lined with statues of Civil War heroes, as well as a newer one commemorating Arthur Ashe, and the stately homes of some of the first families of Virginia. A block south, a series of streets fanning out southwesterly from Park Avenue near Virginia Commonwealth University creates the Fan District, a treasury of restored turn-of-the-20th-century town houses that has become a popular neighborhood. Adjacent to it is Carytown, a restored area of shops and eateries along Cary Street.

MAIN ATTRACTIONS

15 **Beth Ahabah Museum and Archives.** This repository contains articles and documents related to the Richmond and Southern Jewish experience, including the records of two congregations. ⊠ *1109 W. Franklin St.* ☎ *804/353–2668* ⊕ *www.bethahabah.org* ✉ *Free, $3 donation suggested* ⊘ *Sun.–Thurs. 10–3.*

17 **Children's Museum of Richmond.** A welcoming, hands-on complex for children and families, the museum is a place to climb, explore, experiment, ⚅ and play until every surface area is smudged with fingerprints. Bright, ★ colorful, and crowded, the museum's different sections focus on educational fun. How It Works lets children experiment with tools, materials, and their own endless energy. Our Great Outdoors houses the museum's most popular attraction, the Cave, where children explore a 40-foot replica of a limestone cave and are introduced to earth science, oceanography, and rock collecting. ⊠ *2626 W. Broad St.* ☎ *804/474–2667* ⊕ *www.c-mor.org* ✉ *$7* ⊘ *Tues.–Sat. 9:30–5, Sun. noon–5.*

OFF THE BEATEN PATH

Lewis Ginter Botanical Garden. You'll find year-round beauty on this historic property with more than 40 acres of spectacular gardens, dining, and shopping. The classical domed conservatory is the only one of its kind in the Mid-Atlantic, and houses ever-changing displays, tropical plants, and more than 200 orchids in bloom. The rose garden features 80 varieties, with more than 1,800 roses, and a pavilion for special events including wine tastings and evening jazz concerts. A Children's Garden offers a wheelchair-accessible tree house—fun for kids and adults—an Adventure Pathway, sand- and water-play areas, as well as an international village. More than a dozen theme gardens include a Healing Garden, Sunken Garden, Asian Valley, and Victorian Garden. The marvelous display of Christmas lights has become a Richmond tradition. Dining options include the Garden Café and the Tea House, and the shop offers an interesting selection of attractive gifts. ⊠*1800 Lakeside Ave.* ☎*804/262–9887* ⊕*www.lewisginter.org* ⊠*$9* ⊙*Daily 9–5.*

🔆 **Meadow Farm** This living-history complex has programs, exhibits, and interpretive demonstrations of the life and culture on a working farm in 1860. On weekends, costumed interpreters work in the fields, the barns, the doctor's office, the blacksmith forge, and the farmhouse, offering a glimpse into the daily activities of original owner Dr. John Mosby Sheppard and his family. The grounds are open year-round from dawn to dusk, and there are special activities for children. Other scheduled events include storytelling days, Civil War lantern tours, and harvest-picking parties, and best of all, these programs are free. ⊠*3400 Mountain Rd., Glen Allen* ☎*804/501–5520* ⊕*www.co.Henrico.va.us/ rec* ⊠*Free* ⊙*Tues.–Sun. noon–4; closed 1st 2 wks Jan.*

16 **Science Museum of Virginia.** Aerospace, astronomy, electricity, physical sci-
🔆 ences, computers, crystals, telecommunications, and the Foucault pen-
★ dulum are among the subjects covered in exhibits here, many of which strongly appeal to children. The biggest spectacle is the Ethyl IMAX Dome and Planetarium, which draws the audience into the movie or astronomy show. The Virginia Tech Solar Decathlon House is a working model of a green home of the future. The museum is in a former train station with a massive dome. ⊠*2500 W. Broad St.* ☎*804/864–1400* ⊕*www.smv.org* ⊠*Museum $10; IMAX $8.50; IMAX and planetarium $17.50* ⊙*Mon.–Sat. 9:30–5, Sun. 11:30–5.*

19 **Virginia Historical Society Museum of Virginia History.** With 7 million manuscripts and 200,000 books, the library here is a key stop for researchers and genealogists. The visitor-friendly museum mounts regularly changing exhibits and has permanent exhibitions that include an 800-piece collection of Confederate weapons and equipment and "The Story of Virginia, an American Experience," which covers 16,000 years of history and has galleries on topics such as Becoming Confederates and Becoming Equal Virginians. The Society also operates the Virginia House (⇨ *see below*) and sells combination admission tickets for just one dollar more. ⊠*428 North Blvd., at Kensington Ave.* ☎*804/358–4901* ⊕*www.vahistorical.org* ⊠*$5, free on Sun.* ⊙*Mon.–Sat. 10–5, Sun., galleries only, 1–5. Research library closed Sun.*

RICHMOND'S PARKS AND ESTATES

Not far from downtown are mansions and country estates, two with buildings transported from England. Presidents and Confederate leaders are buried in Hollywood Cemetery.

EXPLORING

22 **Agecroft Hall.** Built in Lancashire, England, in the 15th century during the reign of King Henry VIII, Agecroft Hall was transported here in 1926. It's one of the finest Tudor manor houses in the United States. Set amid gardens planted with specimens typical of 1580–1640, the house contains an extensive assortment of Tudor and early Stuart art and furniture (1485–1660) as well as collector's items from England and elsewhere in Europe. A Tudor kitchen lets visitors learn about the culinary tools of that age. ✉*4305 Sulgrave Rd.* ☎*804/353–4241* ⊕*www. agecrofthall.com* ✉*$8* ⊘*Tues.–Sat. 10–4, Sun. 12:30–5.*

㉕ Hollywood Cemetery. Designed in a garden style along the banks of the James River, the cemetery requires at least an hour to stroll through the grounds. Many noted Virginians are buried here, including Presidents John Tyler and James Monroe; Confederate President Jefferson Davis; Generals Fitzhugh Lee, J. E. B. Stuart, and George E. Pickett; the statesman John Randolph; and Matthew Fontaine Maury, a naval scientist. See the pyramid memorial to Confederate soldiers. ✉*412 S. Cherry St. Albemarle* ☎*804/648–8501* ✉*Free* ⊘*Mon.–Sat. 7–5, Sun. 8–5.*

㉔ Maymont. On this 100-acre Victorian estate are the lavish Maymont
ⓒ House museum, a carriage collection, and elaborate Italian and Japa-
★ nese gardens. A true family attraction, Maymont's complex includes the Nature Visitor Center, native wildlife exhibits, and a children's farm. Kids love the pair of playful otters in the aquarium and the waterfall above the Japanese garden. A Bald Eagle Habitat and Raptor Valley are popular additions to the wildlife areas of the park. Take the hop-on, hop-off tram for $3 to see this huge park and its exhibits. Guided mansion tours are on the hour and half hour until 4:30 PM. A café is open for lunch. Carriage rides are also available for $3. ✉*2201 Shields Lake Dr.* ☎*804/358–7166* ⊕*www.maymont.org* ✉*Donation welcome* ⊘*Grounds Apr.–Oct., daily 10–7; Nov.–Mar., daily 10–5. Mansion, nature center, and barn Tues.–Sun. noon–5.*

㉑ Virginia House. Alexander and Virginia Weddell had this 16th-century manor house, originally built on the site of a 12th-century English monastery, shipped across the Atlantic and up the James River in the 1920s. After three years of reconstruction and the planting of lush year-round gardens, the couple realized their dream of a re-created European estate. Alexander Weddell spent a lifetime in the diplomatic service in Mexico, Argentina, and Spain, and the house contains an extensive collection of Spanish and Latin American antiques. The estate (named after Mrs. Weddell, and not the state) passed to the Virginia Historical Society when the Weddells died in a New Year's Day train accident in 1948. Combination tickets including the Virginia Historical Society are only one dollar more. ✉*4301 Sulgrave Rd.* ☎*804/353–4251* ⊕*www. vahistorical.org* ✉*$5* ⊘*Fri. and Sat. 10–4, Sun. 12:30–5; last tour begins 1 hr before closing.*

㉓ Wilton. William Randolph III built this elegant Georgian house in 1753 on what is now the only James River plantation in Richmond. Once 14 mi downriver, the home was moved brick by brick to its current site when industry encroached upon its former location. Wilton is the only house in Virginia with complete floor-to-ceiling panels in every room, and the pastel-painted panels and sunlit alcoves are a large part of its beauty. The home's 1815 period furnishings include the family's original desk bookcase and an original map of Virginia drawn by Thomas Jefferson's father. The Garden Club of Virginia landscaped the terraced lawns that overlook the James River. ✉*215 S. Wilton Rd.*

☎*804/282–5936* ⊕*www.wiltonhousemuseum.org* ⊜*$10* ⊙*Mar.–Jan., Tues.–Fri. 1–4:30, Sat. 10–4:30, Sun. 1:30–4:30.*

ASH-LAND & AROUND

The historic town of Ashland, where Patrick Henry honed his oratory skills, is about 20 mi north of Richmond. An easy day trip or stop on the way north to Fredericksburg, Ashland was home to both Henry and fellow orator Henry Clay. Visit the historic courthouse andPatrick Henry's plantation, **Scotchtown** (⊠*16120 Chiswell La., Beaverdam* ☎*804/227-3500* ⊕*www.apva.org/scotchtown*). If you plan to stay over, the **Henry Clay Inn**, a charming Georgina Revival home, is in the heart of the historic town (⊠*114 N. Railroad Ave., Ashland* ☎*804/798-3100* ⊕*www.henryclayinn.com*). The **Iron Horse** restaurant is a local favorite for lunch and dinner (⊠*100 S. Railroad Ave., Ashland* ☎*804/752-6410*). Catch a show at the **Barksdale Theatre** (⊠*1601 Willow Lawn Dr.* ☎*804/282-2620* ⊕*www.barksdalerichmond.org*). Kids love the nearby 400-acre amusement park, **Paramount Kings Dominion** (⊠*I-95, Doswell Exit 98* ☎*804/876-5000* ⊕*www.kingsdominion.com*).

WHERE TO EAT

¢–$
AMERICAN

✕**Café Gutenberg.** If you're craving a cup of Illy Coffee and a decadent pastry, head for Shockoe Bottom. Directly across the street from the Farmers' Market, this café has a Viennese coffeehouse vibe, complete with loaner books and free Wi-Fi. Richmond residents have been drawn here for years, but now the food is the star. Extensive offerings for vegetarians and vegans include vegan biscuits and gravy and mock duck skewers, but there's plenty of choice for carnivores. Chefs Jen Mindel and Garrett Berry use local and seasonal ingredients to create soul-satisfying meals from breakfast to dinner, like miso-crusted rainbow trout and mixed grill of spring lamb and curried chicken satay. On the pastry side, try the mixed-berry turnover, bursting with ripe blueberries and other luscious fruits. ⊠ *1700 E. Main St* ☎*804/497-5000* ⊕*www.cafegutenberg.com* ≜*Reservations not accepted* ▤*AE, MC, V.*

$–$$
EUROPEAN
★

✕**Café Rustica.** Chef/owner Andy Howell is a star on the Richmond culinary scene. Opened in 2008, his latest success is a European bistro in the heart of downtown. Howell sources his ingredients regionally and whips up European comfort food for breakfast, lunch, and dinner. The roast chicken with vegetables will transport you to the south of France, while the schnitzel is pure Heidelberg. A wine bar and daily cheese plate specials make Café Rustica a great pre-and-post event stop as well. Seating is limited, but they don't take reservations. ⊠ *14 E. Main St.* ☎*804/225-8811* ≜*Reservations not accepted* ▤*AE, D, MC, V* ⊙*Closed Mon.*

$–$$
MEDITERRANEAN

✕**Chez Foushee.** This hip bistro just off Broad Street near Virginia Commonwealth University is a popular lunch and brunch spot, and also has a take-out operation. It's a regular stop on the free GRTC lunch express, with a wide variety of seasonal soups, salads, wraps, and hot entrées. The wine list features French vintages to complement the simple continental fare. ■TIP➔ **The restaurant opens for special dinners once a month for** the First Friday Art Walk; reservations for these nights are a must. ☒ *203 N. Foushee St.* ☎*804/648–3225* ⊕*www.chezfoushee.com* ▭*AE, D, MC, V* ☉*Closed weekends. No dinner except for Art Walk nights.*

$$–$$$ ✕**Comfort.** This local favorite is
SOUTHERN always packed, partly because of its proximity to the National Theater, a popular concert venue. Specializing in Southern comfort food from fried catfish to macaroni and cheese, each entrée is marked with two prices so you can choose either two or three of the seasonal sides like squash casserole and fried okra. If you're looking for small-batch bourbon, Comfort's whiskey bar stocks more than 40 of the best. ☒ *200 W. Broad St.* ☎*804/780–0004* ⊕*www. comfortrestaurant.com* ⚑*Reservations not accepted* ▭*AE, D, MC, V* ☉*Closed Sun. No lunch Sat.*

¢–$ ✕**Halligan Bar & Grill.** This hole-in-the-wall barbecue joint has taken
BARBEQUE off like a house on fire . . . literally. Owned by a 17-year fire service
☺ veteran, and staffed by Henrico County's finest, Halligan is a tribute to firefighters with a 1973 Seagrave fire truck that serves as a backdrop to the bar, authentic helmets doubling as pendant lights, and walls covered with memorabilia. Meat is smoked in-house for hearty Southern favorites like the Carolina-style pulled-pork sandwich, classic chicken, and Texas-style beef brisket. Don't be surprised to hear sirens and see lights set off periodically to salute the customers. ☒ *3 N. 17th St.* ☎*804/447–7981* ▭*AE, D, MC, V.*

$$–$$$ ✕**The Hard Shell.** This fun and unpretentious restaurant has many fresh
SEAFOOD and local seafood dishes, and those with other tastes can choose from such options as filet mignon and prime rib; even vegetarians are well cared for. Raw bar enthusiasts will be enticed, too, with the option of getting a half pound of steamed shrimp, Dungeness crab legs, snow crab legs, or littleneck clams. From live Maine lobsters to blue-point oysters, this is the place for any kind of seafood you crave. Although the interior is romantic, with exposed brick and dark wood, if the weather's nice, dine alfresco on one of the city's favorite patios. The Sunday brunch is especially attractive, as are the specialty drinks, particularly the martinis. ☒*1411 E. Cary St.* ☎*804/643–2333* ⊕*www.thehardshell.com* ▭*AE, D, DC, MC, V* ☉*No lunch weekends.*

$$–$$$ ✕**Julep's.** In the River District, and in the city's oldest commercial build-
AMERICAN ing (1817), Julep's has a spiral staircase joining the upper and lower dining areas. The specialty here is New Southern cuisine, with seasonal lunch and dinner menus that include tempting dishes such as roasted game hen stuffed with a risotto of country ham, green peas, and mushrooms. The wine list is one to linger over. Try not to leave without sampling one of the restaurant's namesakes. ☒*1719–21 E. Franklin St.* ☎*804/377–3968* ⊕*www.juleps.net* ▭*AE, MC, V* ☉*Closed Sun. No lunch Sat., no dinner Mon.*

$$$$ ✕**Lemaire.** Named after Etienne Lemaire, Maître d'Hôtel to Thomas
AMERICAN Jefferson from 1794 until the end of his presidency, this is the grandest restaurant in Richmond. Jefferson's tastes included adding light sauces and fresh herbs to dishes prepared with the region's more than abundant

supply of ingredients. Today the menu follows the same theme with updated regional Southern cuisine that includes dashes of European classical and American contemporary influences. Typical dishes might include rack of venison, or crispy-skin Chesapeake Bay rockfish, and a tasting menu with wine pairings is available in addition to the regular offerings. ⊠*Jefferson Hotel, 101 W. Franklin St.* ☎*804/788–8000* ⊕*www.jeffersonhotel.com* ⊟*AE, D, DC, MC, V.*

¢–$ ✕**Millie's Diner.** Be prepared to wait in line to check out Richmond's
AMERICAN favorite diner. Locals often bring lawn chairs and games to pass the time while waiting for their chance to try the upscale, contemporary selections at this quirky eatery. This is the place for brunch for everything from huevos rancheros to the signature Devil's Mess kitchen-sink omelet. Although the vibe is straight out of the '50s, with personal jukeboxes in every booth, the food is strictly 21st century, with contemporary takes on Southern classics, as well as global offerings like Thai spicy shrimp. Try the mac 'n cheese with oyster mushrooms, asparagus, and foie gras butter or the pan-seared venison with black grapes and Yorkshire pudding. The dinner menu changes every three weeks, although the most popular lunch and breakfast offerings are always available. ⊠*2603 E. Main St.* ☎*804/643–5512.* ⌁*Reservations not accepted* ⊟*AE, D, MC, V* ☾*Closed Mon.*

$$$$ ✕**Old Original Bookbinder's.** Opened in 1865, the original branch of this
AMERICAN restaurant has been a Philadelphia institution and has played host to the likes of astronauts, princesses, movie stars, and many other celebrities. Now the tradition continues in a beautifully renovated old tobacco warehouse near the James River. Surrounded by exposed brick walls, a live lobster tank, and an open kitchen, you can enjoy meat and seafood dishes such as a grilled bone-in pork chop, sweet crusted mahimahi, Bookbinder's Signature Crab Cakes, and Bookbinder's Steak. On nicer days eat on the open-air patio with a modern, cooling, nearby fountain. ⊠*2306 E. Cary St.* ☎*804/643–6900* ⊕*www.bookbindersrichmond. com* ⊟*AE, MC, V* ☾*No lunch.*

WHERE TO STAY

$$–$$$ ▦**Berkeley Hotel.** Although built in the style of the century-old ware-
★ houses and buildings that surround it, this boutique hotel dates from 1988. Those seeking extra space and luxury should opt for the Governor's Suite, which has a luxurious king bed, a private terrace, and a living room with panoramic views over the historic Shockoe Slip area. Norman guest rooms have four-poster beds and traditional furnishings. Guests staying here get free entry to the YMCA health and fitness facilities. **Pros:** complimentary car service; steps from several restaurants and shops. **Cons:** extremely busy street; limited parking. ⊠*1200 E. Cary St.* ☎*804/780–1300 or 888/780–4422* ⊕*www.berkeleyhotel.com* ⌁*54 rooms, 1 suite* ⌂*In-room: Wi-Fi. In-hotel: restaurant, bar, gym, concierge, laundry service, parking (fee), no-smoking rooms* ⊟*AE, D, DC, MC, V.*

$–$$ ▦**Commonwealth Park Suites Hotel.** When it was the Rueger back in
★ 1846, this hotel was a bootlegging saloon with rooms for its clientele.

After a fire during the Civil War it fell into disrepair for 50 years. It was rebuilt in 1912, and after several renovations it now has 59 luxurious rooms and suites. Because the Commonwealth is across from the Capitol, some senators and representatives make this their home when the state legislature is in session. Maxine's Café is open for breakfast, lunch, and dinner. **Pros:** across the street from Capitol and visitor center; large suites for extended stays. **Cons:** limited food service on-site. ⊠*901 Bank St.* ☎*804/343–7300 or 888/343–7301* ☐*804/343–1025* ⇘*10 rooms, 49 suites* ⌂*In-room: Ethernet. In-hotel: restaurant, laundry service, no-smoking rooms* ⊟*AE, D, DC, MC, V.*

$–$$ ▧ **Crowne Plaza Hotel.** Shaped like a piece of cheese, this is Richmond's most easily identifiable hotel. In the city's River District, the Crowne Plaza is close to the new Canal Walk and the James River. Club level floors include high-end amenities like fluffy bathrobes and access to the private Concierge Lounge with complimentary continental breakfast Tuesday to Friday and hors d'oeuvres and beverages weekday evenings. The rooms of choice are the two Bi-Level Point Suites with the floors connected by a spiral staircase, and classy extras like Oriental carpets and a wet bar. **Pros:** close to river and Tredegar Visitor Center. **Cons:** must drive to restaurants and downtown historic sites; borders busy highway. ⊠*555 E. Canal St.* ☎*804/788–0900 or 800/227–6963* ⊕*www.crowneplaza.com/ric-eastcanal* ⇘*270 rooms, 29 suites* ⌂*In-room: Ethernet. In-hotel: restaurant, bar, pool, gym, executive floor* ⊟*AE, D, DC, MC, V.*

$$$ ▧ **Jefferson Hotel.** A 70-foot-high ceiling with a stained-glass skylight
Fodor'sChoice   and 10 of the original Louis Comfort Tiffany stained-glass windows,
★   rich tapestries, and replicas of traditional Victorian furniture make this the most elegant hotel in Richmond.The Palm Court Lobby is home to Edward Valentine's full-size statue of the president and to a magnificent sweeping staircase reminiscent of the one in *Gone With the Wind*. The rooms are done in a total of 57 different styles, and the 1,550-square-foot Presidential Suite has its own private balcony. Since the hotel is older, the rooms are somewhat small, but exquisitely appointed with period furnishings and top-of-the-line amenities including Frette linens and robes. **Pros:** luxury lodging; pet-friendly; excellent concierge service. **Cons:** standard rooms are small; some older amenities. ⊠*101 W. Franklin St., at Adams St.* ☎*804/788–8000 or 800/424–8014* ⊕*www.jeffersonhotel.com* ⇘*228 rooms, 36 suites* ⌂*In-hotel: 2 restaurants, room service, bar, pool, gym* ⊟*AE, D, DC, MC, V.*

$–$$ ▧ **Omni Richmond.** Part of the historic Shockoe Slip area, this hotel looks classically Southern. The rooms on the club level come with private concierge service and access to a club lounge; Get Fit rooms come with a portable treadmill. Many restaurants and stores are in the James Center itself, and just outside is Shockoe Slip. If you stay here, you have access to the nearby Capital Club health and fitness facilities. **Pros:** close to restaurants and shopping. **Cons:** limited parking. ⊠*James Center, 100 S. 12th St.* ☎*804/344–7000* ⊕*www.omnihotels.com* ⇘*353 rooms, 8 suites* ⌂*In-room: Wi-Fi. In-hotel: 2 restaurants, room service, bar, pool, gym, parking (fee), no-smoking rooms* ⊟*AE, D, DC, MC, V.*

NIGHTLIFE & THE ARTS

The National Theater (✉ *708 E. Broad St.* ☎ *804/612–1900* ⊕ *www. nationalva.com*) This locally owned venue hosts everything from the Richmond Symphony to the Black Crowes, with a full schedule throughout the year.

The **Richmond Coliseum** (✉ *601 E. Leigh St.* ☎ *804/780–4956* ⊕ *www. richmondcoliseum.net*) has been a Richmond institution since the early 1970s. With 11,330 permanent seats, and nearly 2,000 more for concerts, it hosts top entertainers and artists, the Ringling Brothers circus, Richmond Riverdogs hockey team, wrestling, and other large events.

BARS

From the college bars in the Fan District to upscale martini and wine bars, Richmond has a vibrant nightlife. One local favorite is **Havana 59** (✉ *16 N. 7th St.* ☎ *804/780–2822* ⊕ *www.havana59.net*) in Shockoe Bottom. Styled after the Cuban clubs that gave Havana the nickname "the Paris of the '50s," this multilevel club is decked out in palm trees and twinkling white lights, with both outdoor terraces and an open-fronted cavernous ground floor, where slow-moving ceiling fans circulate. Latin music, traditional mojitos, and a cigar-friendly atmosphere keep Havana hopping into the wee hours.

THEATER

Carpenter Center (✉ *600 E. Grace St.* ☎ *804/225–9000* ⊕ *www.carpenter center.org*), a restored 1928 motion-picture palace, is now a performing-arts center that mounts opera, traveling shows, symphonic music, and ballet. **Landmark Theatre** (✉ *6 N. Laurel St.* ☎ *804/646–4213*) was built in an extremely elaborate style with towering minarets and desert murals: when it was built by the Shriners in 1926, it was called "the Mosque," and still is by locals. Just west of downtown, the Landmark is known for its excellent acoustics and has the largest permanent proscenium stage on the East Coast. Many of America's most famous entertainers have performed here, and it continues to be used for the road versions of Broadway shows, symphony performances, ballet, children's theater, concerts, and fashion shows.

SPORTS & THE OUTDOORS

GOLF

In Richmond aficionados tee off most of the year. The area has 24 golf courses open to the public—the **Virginia State Golf Association** (⊕ *www. vsga.org*) has a good handle on them all; its Web site even allows you to book tee times online.

RAFTING

Richmond is the only city within the United States that has rafting within its city limits. **Richmond Raft** (☎ *804/222–7238 or 800/222–7238* ⊕ *www.richmondraft.com*) conducts white-water rafting trips through the city on the James River (Class III and IV rapids), as well as float trips from March through November.

SHOPPING

Carytown is a nine-block shopping-and-entertainment district (⊠ *West end of Cary St. from the Powhite Pkwy. to Boulevard* ⊕*www.carytown. org*). More than 300 shops and more than 25 restaurants are packed into this district. Parking is scarce on weekends. The 17th Street **Farmers' Market** (⊠*100 N. 17th St., at Main St.* ⊕*www.17thstreetfarmersmarket. com*), beside the old Main Street Station, has been a public gathering place since 1737, and is within walking distance to art galleries, boutiques, and antiques shops, many in converted warehouses and factories. Market days are Thursday, Saturday, and Sunday. **Shockoe Slip** (⊠*E. Cary St. between 12th and 15th Sts.*), a neighborhood of tobacco warehouses during the 18th and 19th centuries, has boutiques, antiques stores, and international furniture stores like the multilevel, supermodern La Difference.

PETERSBURG

Historic **Petersburg,** 20 mi south of Richmond on I–95, lies along the Appomattox River. During the Civil War the city was under siege for 292 days by Union forces from June 1864 to April 1865—the so-called last stand of the Confederacy. A major railroad hub, the city was a crucial link in the supply chain for Lee's army, and its surrender brought about the evacuation of Richmond and the surrender at Appomattox. Lee's Retreat is a 26-stop self-guided driving tour from Petersburg to Appomattox. For a route map and other information, contact the Petersburg Visitor Center.

These days, like many other small Southern towns, it is struggling to overcome decades of depression, and this is readily apparent on the drive from l–95 to the downtown area. However, a great effort has been made in the area around the Petersburg Visitor Center, and there are many beautifully maintained houses in the historic residential area just to the west.

TIMING & PRECAUTIONS

Although the parks and historic downtown area have been restored and revitalized, be careful in the transitional neighborhoods on the edges of the city.

EXPLORING

Centre Hill Mansion. This, the third home of the Bolling family, was originally built in 1823. Having been remodeled twice since then, it illustrates changing architectural styles; it was and is the grandest home in Petersburg. Inside are ornate woodwork, plaster motifs, period furnishings, and an 1840s service tunnel in the basement that once connected the work area of the house to the street below. For many years on January 24, the residents of Centre Hill heard the ghosts of Civil War soldiers marching up and down the staircase. You can listen for those boots at the annual Ghost Watch. ⊠*1 Centre Hill Circle* ☎*804/733–2401* ⊠*$5* ☉*Daily 10:30–4:30.*

A parish church from the 18th century, **Old Blandford Church** is a memorial to the Southern soldiers who died during the Civil War. Some 30,000 Confederate soldiers are buried in the churchyard, which is surrounded by ornamental ironwork. The church's 15 spectacular stained-glass windows by Louis Comfort Tiffany are memorials donated by the Confederate states. The Memorial Day tradition is said to have begun in this cemetery in June 1866, inspired by the women's group of the church who not only raised the funds for the memorial, but also decorated the graves every year. ⊠ *319 S. Crater Rd., 2 mi south of town* ☎ *804/733–2396* 🖃 *$5* ⊙ *Daily 10–5.*

★ On April 2, 1865, in what is now **Pamplin Historical Park,** Union troops successfully attacked General Robert E. Lee's formerly impenetrable defense line, forcing Lee to abandon Petersburg. Today you are greeted by the 300-foot-long facade of the Battlefield Center, a concrete representation of the Confederate battle lines. Besides the center, which focuses on the April 2 battle, there's a 2-mi battle trail with 2,100 feet of 8-foot-high earthen fortifications, reconstructed soldier huts, and original picket posts. Also on the grounds is Tudor Hall, an 1812 plantation home that served as the 1864 headquarters for Confederate general Samuel McGowan. Costumed interpreters bring the era to life, and reconstructed outbuildings have exhibits and displays. The **National Museum of the Civil War Soldier** on the grounds has interactive displays and nearly 1,000 artifacts. You can select an audio guide that includes the actual letters and diaries of a soldier. The park also has a café and a large store. Allow at least two hours to visit the park and museum. ⊠ *6125 Boydton Plank Rd., off U.S. 1, I–85S to Exit 63A* ☎ *804/861–2408 or 877/726–7546* ⊕ *www.pamplinpark.org* 🖃 *$15* ⊙ *Mid-Aug.–mid-June, daily 9–5; mid-June–mid-Aug, daily 9–6.*

Fodor's Choice ★ To walk **Petersburg National Battlefield** is to be where more than 60,000 Union and Confederate soldiers died during the siege of the city. A pronounced depression in the ground is the eroded remnant of the Crater, the result of a 4-ton gunpowder explosion set off by Union forces in one failed attack. The 1,500-acre park is laced with several miles of earthworks and includes two forts. In the visitor center, maps and models convey background information vital to the self-guided driving tour, during which you park at specified spots on the tour road and proceed on foot to nearby points of interest. ⊠ *Rte. 36, 2.5 mi east of downtown* ☎ *804/732–3531* ⊕ *www.nps.gov/pete* 🖃 *$5 per car, $3 per cyclist or pedestrian* ⊙ *Daily 9–5.*

The **Petersburg Visitor Center** sells the Fort Henry Pass, which allows admission to the Siege Museum, Centre Hill Mansion, and Blandford Church for $11. The center also has information about Lee's Retreat Trail, a 26-stop driving tour around the area. Free parking is plentiful near the center. ⊠ *McIlwaine*

> **WORD OF MOUTH**
>
> "There are also very good battlefield interpretations at Fredericksburg, 45 mi south of Washington, and Richmond-Petersburg, 100 mi south. The latter was a siege, ineptly carried out by the Union army which had the effect of prolonging the war by nearly a year."
> —Neal Sanders

House, 425 Cockade Alley ☎*804/733–2400 or 800/368–3595* ⊕*www.*
petersburg-va.org.

★ The **Siege Museum,** inside a former commodities market from 1839, tells
the story of how the city's lavish lifestyle gave way to a bitter struggle
for survival during the Civil War: a single chicken could cost as much
as $50 in Confederate currency. A 16-minute movie narrated by Peters-
burg-born actor Joseph Cotten dramatizes the upheaval. ⊠*Exchange*
Bldg., 15 W. Bank St. ☎*804/733–2404* 🎫*$5* ⊗*Daily 10–5.*

WHERE TO EAT

$$–$$$ ✕**Alexander's Fine Food.** White tablecloths flare from beneath glass tops
GREEK   at the tables of this Greek-American restaurant, which also has a bar.
A souvlaki platter, leg of lamb, and Athenian-style chicken are specialties. Lunch favorites include the "grill and chill" and the variety of
hearty salads, while the stuffed chicken breast and the crab cakes are
best-sellers at dinner. ⊠*101 W. Bank St.* ☎*804/733–7134* ▤*No credit*
cards ⊗*Closed Sun. and Wed.–Sat. No dinner Mon. and Tues.*

$ ✕**Andrades.** Although the faux pergola and grapes might make you
MEXICAN   think Italian, Andrades is a locally owned Mexican eatery in the heart
of the historic downtown area. Popular for both lunch and dinner, the
cuisine has a Southwestern and Mexican flair and includes such tempting dishes as *Zarzuela de Mariscos,* a seafood casserole, and *Masitas*
de Puerco, Cuban-style pieces of pork marinated in criollo sauce and
roasted in Sevilla's bitter oranges. The menu is rounded out with traditional selections including tacos and enchiladas. Complimentary tortilla chips and salsa are made fresh daily, and the large outdoor terrace
is popular in spring and fall. ⊠*7 Bollingbrook St.* ☎*804/733–1515*
▤*MC, V.*

$–$$ ✕**The Brickhouse Run.** Tucked away in a small alley in the historic dis-
BRITISH   trict, this British pub occupies one of the oldest buildings in the city.
Traditional and authentic pub grub includes fish-and-chips and shep-
herd's pie, and of course, a good selection of imported ales. The well-
rounded menu includes American favorites like burgers and pasta.
Salads are always a good bet, since the chef sources his produce
locally, and desserts including crème brûlée are outstanding. Both the
chummy bar area and the dining room are filled with British-theme
accessories and memorabilia. Reservations are not required and dress
is casual. ⊠ *407-409 Cockade Alley* ☎*804/862–1815* ▤*AE, MC, V*
⊗*Closed Sun. and Mon.*

WHERE TO STAY

¢–$ 🖼️**High Street Inn.** In the heart of the historic district, this beautiful
Queen Anne mansion dating from 1891 was built by J. A. Gill, a
wealthy local merchant, of natural fired brick. Opened in late 2004,
the public areas and rooms—all named after people or places that influenced Petersburg's history—are charmingly classical, and the intricacy
of the woodwork on the king-size bed in the BollingBrook Room has
to be seen to be believed. **Pros:** in historic district; vegetarian friendly.

Cons: no Wi-Fi. ⊠*405 High St.* ☎*804/722–0800 or 888/474–1898* ⊕*www.thehighstreetinn.com* ⟿*5 rooms* ⟳*In-room: Wi-Fi. In-hotel: parking (no fee)* ⊟*AE, D, DC, MC, V* ⎊*CP.*

¢ ⊞**Howard Johnson Steven Kent.** Formerly a Best Western, but although the name has changed, this budget-friendly hotel hasn't. The pristine two-story motel has a home-style family restaurant, an Olympic-size swimming pool, and nearly 20 acres of recreational facilities. Local calls and newspapers are free, and rooms have a coffeemaker, hair dryer, iron, and ironing board. Room rates include a complimentary continental breakfast. **Pros:** full on-site amenities; least-expensive option in area. **Cons:** older property; not near historic downtown. ⊠*12205 S. Crater Rd.* ☎*804/733–0600 or 800/284–9393* ⊜*804/862–4549* ⟿*133 rooms* ⟳*In-room: Ethernet. In-hotel: restaurant, bar, tennis courts, pool, laundry facilities* ⊟*AE, D, DC, MC, V* ⎊*CP.*

¢ ⊞**Ragland Mansion.** This stunningly attractive Italianate villa dates from the 1850s; it was the residence of General "Black Jack" Pershing during World War I. Inside are large formal rooms with crown moldings, French windows, 14-foot ceilings, mosaic parquet floors, and European and American artworks. The rooms and suite are furnished with antique furniture, claw-foot tubs, brass and iron beds, and paintings and engravings. It's a short walk from downtown and the historic district. **Pros:** historic home; period furnishings; good value. **Cons:** no food service on-site other than breakfast. ⊠*205 S. Sycamore St.* ☎*804/861–1932 or 800/861–8898* ⊜*804/861–5943* ⊕*www.raglandmansion.com* ⟿*6 rooms, 3 suites* ⟳*In-hotel: parking (no fee)* ⊟*AE, MC, V.*

FREDERICKSBURG

Halfway between Richmond and Washington, near the falls of the Rappahannock River, Fredericksburg is a popular destination for history buffs. The town's 40-block National Historic District contains more than 350 original 18th- and 19th-century buildings, including the house George Washington bought for his mother; the Rising Sun Tavern; and Kenmore, the magnificent 1752 plantation owned by George Washington's sister.

Although its site was visited by explorer Captain John Smith as early as 1608, Fredericksburg wasn't founded until 1728. It was named after England's crown prince at the time, Frederick Louis, the eldest son of King George II. The streets still bear names of his family members: George, Caroline, Sophia, Princess Anne, William, and Amelia. Established as a frontier port to serve nearby tobacco farmers and iron miners, Fredericksburg was at one point the 10th largest port in the colonies.

George Washington knew Fredericksburg well, having grown up just across the Rappahannock on Ferry Farm, his residence from age 6 to 19. The myths about chopping down a cherry tree and throwing a coin (actually a rock) across the Rappahannock (later confused with the Potomac) refer to this period of his life. In later years Washington often visited his mother here on Charles Street.

Fredericksburg prospered in the decades after independence, benefiting from its location midway along the route between Washington and Richmond—an important intersection of railroad lines and waterways. When the Civil War broke out, it became the linchpin of the Confederate defense of Richmond and therefore the target of Union assaults. In December 1862, Union forces attacked the town in what was to be the first of four major battles fought in and around Fredericksburg. In the battle of Sunken Road, Confederate defenders sheltered by a stone wall at the base of Marye's Heights mowed down thousands of Union soldiers who charged across the fields.

At Chancellorsville in April 1863, General Robert E. Lee led 60,000 troops to a brilliant victory over a much larger Union force of 134,000, and this resulted in Lee's invasion of Pennsylvania. The following year, Grant's troops battled Lee's Confederates through the Wilderness, a region of dense thickets and overgrowth south of the Rapidan River, then fought them again at Spotsylvania. Although neither side was victorious, Grant continued heading his troops toward the Confederate capital of Richmond.

By the war's end, fighting in Fredericksburg and at the nearby Chancellorsville, Wilderness, and Spotsylvania Court House battlefields resulted in more than 100,000 dead or wounded. Fredericksburg's cemeteries hold the remains of 17,000 soldiers from both sides. Miraculously, despite heavy bombardment and house-to-house fighting, much of the city remained intact.

A few decades ago Fredericksburg was one of the numerous small Southern cities facing another battle for survival, but today the city is being overrun for a different reason. The charming, historic town appeals to commuters fleeing the Washington, DC, area for kinder, less-expensive environs. The railroad lines that were so crucial to transporting Civil War supplies now bring workers to and from the nation's capital an hour away, and the sacred Civil War battlegrounds share the area with legions of shopping centers. Tourists aren't scarce either, and not just to visit the historical sights. These days Fredericksburg has reinvented itself as a cute small town chock-a-block with boutiques and antiques and specialty stores, as well as a lively selection of small cafés and restaurants.

GETTING HERE & AROUND
By car, Fredericksburg is easily accessible from Interstate 95 or Route 1, about an hour north of Richmond or south of Washington, DC. The unmanned Fredericksburg train station is two blocks from the historic district.

TOURS   Trolley Tours of Fredericksburg runs a 75-minute narrated tour of Fredericksburg's most important sights. Tours cost $17 and leave from the visitor center.

The tour coordinator at the Fredericksburg Visitor Center can arrange a group walking tour of the city as well as of battlefields and other historic sites to which you can drive. Reservations are required. The

Fredericksburg Department of Tourism (in the visitor center) publishes a booklet that includes a short history of Fredericksburg and a self-guided tour covering 29 sights.

ESSENTIALS

Taxi Companies Bumbreys Independent Cab Service (⊠ *209 Lafayette Blvd.* ☎ *540/373–6111).* **City Cab** (☎ *540/372–4484).* **Yellow Cab of Fredericksburg** (⊠ *2217 Princess Anne St.* ☎ *540/368–8120).*

Tours Trolley Tours of Fredericksburg (☎ *540/898–0737* ⊕ *www.fredericksburg trolley.com).*

Numbers in the text correspond to numbers in the margin and on the Fredericksburg map.

4

DOWNTOWN FREDERICKSBURG

Fredericksburg, a modern commercial town, includes a 40-block National Historic District with more than 350 original 18th- and 19th-century buildings. No play-acting here—residents live in the historic homes and work in the stores, many of which sell antiques. A walking tour through the town proper takes three to four hours; battlefield tours will take at least that long.

MAIN ATTRACTIONS

❶ Fredericksburg Visitor Center. Beyond the usual booklets, pamphlets, and maps, this visitor center offers a money-saving pass to city attractions ($32 for entry to nine sights including Washington's boyhood home, a better than 40% discount over individual admission prices). Before your tour, you may want to see the center's 10-minute orientation slide show. The center building itself was constructed in 1824 as a residence and confectionery; during the Civil War it was used as a prison. ⊠ *706 Caroline St., Historic District* ☎ *540/373–1776 or 800/678–4748* ⊕ *www. visitfred.com* ☉ *Daily 9–5; hrs extended in summer.*

NEED A BREAK? For freshly made soups, sandwiches, and desserts, drop by **Olde Towne Wine and Cheese Deli** (⊠ *707 Caroline St., Historic District* ☎ *540/373-7877* ☉ *Daily 11–4),* in operation for more than a quarter century and directly opposite the Fredericksburg Tourism Center.

⑬ Gari Melchers Home and Studio. The last owner of this 1790s Georgian-style house was American artist Gari Melchers, who chaired the Smithsonian Commission to establish the National Gallery of Art in Washington. His wife, Corinne, deeded the 27-acre estate and its collections to Virginia. The home is now a public museum and a Virginia National Historic Landmark administered by the University of Mary Washington. You can take a one-hour tour of the spacious house, which is furnished with a rich collection of the owners' antiques. Galleries in the stone studio, built by the Melchers in 1924, house the largest repository of the artist's work. An orientation movie is shown in the reception area, which was once the carriage house. ⊠ *224 Washington St.* ☎ *540/654–1015* ⊕ *www.garimelchers.org* ☜ *$10* ☉ *Mon.–Sun. 10–5.*

Fredericksburg, Virginia

NEED A BREAK?

Goolrick's Pharmacy (⊠ *901 Caroline St., Historic District* ☎ *540/373–9878*) opened in 1869 and has been in its present location since the late 1890s. In 1912 the soda fountain was installed, and it is now the oldest operating in the United States. In addition to malts and egg creams (made of seltzer, milk, and syrup, but not egg or cream), Goolrick's serves light meals weekdays 8:30–7 and Saturday 8:30–6.

Hugh Mercer Apothecary Shop. Offering a close-up view of 18th- and 19th-century medical instruments and procedures, the apothecary was established in 1761, and demonstrates the work of Dr. Mercer, a Scotsman who served as a brigadier general of the Continental Army (he was killed at the Battle of Princeton). Dr. Mercer may have been more careful than other Colonial physicians, but his methods might still make you cringe. A costumed hostess explicitly describes amputations and cataract operations before the discovery of anesthetics. You can also hear about therapeutic bleeding, see the gruesome devices used in Colonial dentistry, and watch a demonstration of leeching. ⊠ *1020 Caroline St., at Amelia St., Historic District* ☎ *540/373-3362* ⊒ *$5* ⊙ *Mar.–Nov., Mon.–Sat. 9–5, Sun. 11–5; Dec.–Feb., Mon.–Sat. 10–4, Sun. noon–4.*

⑤ **Kenmore.** Named Kenmore by a later owner, this house was built in 1775

Fodor's Choice   on a 1,300-acre plantation owned by Colonel Fielding Lewis, a patriot,

★   merchant, and brother-in-law of George Washington. Lewis sacrificed his fortune to operate a gun factory and otherwise supply General Washington's forces during the Revolutionary War. As a result, his debts forced his widow to sell the home following his death. The outstanding plaster moldings in the ceilings and over the fireplace in the dining room are even more ornate than those at Mount Vernon. It's believed that the artisan responsible for them worked frequently in both homes, though his name is unknown, possibly because he was an indentured servant. A recent multiyear renovation has returned the grand house to its original state. It is interesting to note that the walls vary in thickness: 36 inches in the basement, 24 inches on the ground floor, and 18 inches upstairs. Guided 45-minute architectural tours of the home are conducted by docents; the subterranean Crowningshield Museum on the grounds displays Kenmore's collection of fine Virginia-made furniture and family portraits as well as changing exhibits on Fredericksburg life. ⊠ *1201 Washington Ave., Historic District* ☎ *540/373–3381* ⊕ *www. kenmore.org* ⊠ *$8* ☉ *Jan.–July, daily 10–5; Aug.–Dec, daily 10–4; last tour begins at 4:15.*

④ **Mary Washington House.** George purchased a three-room cottage for his

★   mother in 1772 for £225, renovated it, and more than doubled its size with additions. She spent the last 17 years of her life here, tending the garden where her original boxwoods still flourish today, and where many a bride and groom now exchange their vows. The home has been a museum since 1930. Inside, displays include Mrs. Washington's "best dressing glass," a silver-over-tin mirror in a Chippendale frame; her teapot; Washington family dinnerware; and period furniture. The kitchen, in a rather lopsided wooden house in the pretty gardens, and its spit are original. Tours begin on the back porch with a history of the house. ⊠ *1200 Charles St., Historic District* ☎ *540/373–1569* ⊕ *www. apva.org/marywashingtonhouse* ⊠ *$5* ☉ *Mar.–Nov., Mon.–Sat. 9–5, Sun. 11–5; Dec.–Feb., Mon.–Sat. 10–4, Sun. noon–4.*

OFF THE
BEATEN
PATH
Potomac Point Winery. Just 15 mi north of town off Route 1, this winery has a gorgeous tasting room and beautiful restaurant in its French Mediterranean–style building. One of Potomac Point's most notable wines is the viognier. For romantics, it's also got a private "proposal tower" and a dedicated engagement and wedding coordinator. ⊠ *275 Decatur Rd., Stafford* ☎ *540/446–2266* ⊕ *www.potomacpointwinery. com* ⊠ *Free* ☉ *Sun.–Thurs. 11–6, Fri. and Sat. 11–9.*

③ **Rising Sun Tavern.** In 1760 George Washington's brother Charles built as his home what later became the Rising Sun Tavern, a watering hole for such patriots as the Lee brothers (the only siblings to sign the Declaration of Independence); Patrick Henry, the five-term governor of Virginia who said, "Give me liberty or give me death"; and future presidents Washington and Jefferson. Two male indentured servants and a "wench" in period costume lead a tour without stepping out of character. From them, you hear how travelers slept and what they ate and drank at this busy institution. ⊠ *1304 Caroline St., Historic*

4

District ☎*540/371–1494* ⊕*www.apva.org/risingsuntavern* ⌨*$5*
🕐*Mar.–Nov., Mon.–Sat. 9–5, Sun. 11–5; Dec.–Feb., Mon.–Sat. 10–4,
Sun. noon–4.*

ALSO WORTH SEEING

❼ Confederate Cemetery. This cemetery contains the remains of more than
2,000 soldiers (most of them unknown) as well as the graves of generals
Dabney Maury, Seth Barton, Carter Stevenson, Daniel Ruggles, Henry
Sibley, and Abner Perrin. ✉*1100 Washington Ave., near Amelia St.,
Historic District* 🕐*Daily dawn–dusk.*

❾ Fredericksburg Area Museum and Cultural Center. In an 1816 building once
used as a market and town hall, this museum's six permanent exhibits
tell the story of the area from prehistoric times through the Revolutionary and Civil wars to the present. Recently, the museum acquired the
historic bank building and has added seven permanent exhibitions in the
new space, as well as a learning center. Opened in 2008, the bank annex
is home to an exhibit titled "Fredericksburg at War," which details the
area's history from the Revolutionary War to World War II. The Civil
War exhibits emphasize the civilian experience, although attention is
also paid to the soldier. Military items on display include a Henry rifle,
a sword with "CSA" carved into the basket, and a Confederate officer's
coat. Most weapons and accessories were found on local battlefields.
Other displays include dinosaur footprints from a nearby quarry, Native
American artifacts, and an 18th-century plantation account book with
an inventory of slaves. The first and third floors have changing exhibits.
✉*907 Princess Anne St., Historic District* ☎*540/371–3037* ⊕*www.
famcc.org* ⌨*$7* 🕐*Mar.–Nov., Mon.–Sat. 10–5, Sun. 1–5; Dec.–Feb.,
Mon.–Sat. 10–4, Sun. 1–4.*

❽ James Monroe Museum and Memorial Library. This tiny one-story building—
on the site where Monroe, who became the fifth president of the United
States, practiced law from 1787 to 1789—contains many of Monroe's
possessions, collected and preserved by his family until the present day.
They include a mahogany dispatch box used during the negotiation of
the Louisiana Purchase and the desk on which the Monroe Doctrine was
signed. ✉*908 Charles St., Historic District* ☎*540/654–1043* ⊕*www.
umw.edu/jmmu* ⌨*$5* 🕐*Mar.–Nov., Mon.–Sat. 9–5, Sun. 1–5; Dec.–
Feb., Mon.–Sat. 10–4, Sun. 1–4.*

❻ Mary Washington Grave and Monument. A 40-foot granite obelisk, dedicated by President Grover Cleveland in 1894, marks the final resting
place of George's mother. It was laid at "Meditation Rock," a place on
her daughter's property where Mrs. Washington liked to read. ✉*Washington Ave. at Pitt St.*

❿ University of Mary Washington Galleries. On campus are two art galleries.
The Ridderhof Martin Gallery hosts art exhibitions from various cultures and historical periods. The duPont Gallery, in Melchers Hall, displays paintings, drawing, sculpture, photography, ceramics, and textiles
by art faculty, students, and contemporary artists. Free gallery-visitor
parking is available in the lot at the corner of College Avenue at Thornton Street. ✉*1301 College Ave., Historic District* ☎*540/654–1013*

⊕*www.edu/umw_galleries* ⊡*Free* ⊙ *When college is in session, Mon., Wed., and Fri. 10–4, weekends 1–4.*

AROUND FREDERICKSBURG

Surrounding the town of Fredericksburg are historic sites and gorgeous vistas where, in 1862, Union forces once stood. Today you see only the lively Rappahannock and beautiful homes on a lovely drive across the river.

EXPLORING

⑫ Chatham. Now part of the Fredericksburg/Spotsylvania National Military Park, Chatham was built between 1768 and 1771 by William Fitzhugh, a plantation owner, on a site overlooking the Rappahannock River and the town of Fredericksburg. Among Fitzhugh's guests were the likes of George Washington and Thomas Jefferson. During the Civil War, Union forces commandeered the house and converted it into a headquarters and hospital. President Abraham Lincoln conferred with his generals here, Clara Barton (founder of the American Red Cross) tended the wounded, and poet Walt Whitman visited for a few hours looking for his brother, who had been wounded in a battle. After the war, the Georgian house and gardens were restored by private owners and eventually donated to the National Park Service. The home itself is now a museum. Five of the 10 rooms in the 12,000-square-foot mansion house exhibits spanning several centuries and are open to the public. ⊠*120 Chatham La., Falmouth, VA* ☎*540/370–0802* ⊕*www.nps.gov/ frsp* ⊡*Free* ⊙ *Daily 9–4:30.*

⑭ Fredericksburg/Spotsylvania National Military Park. The 9,000-acre park

Fodor'sChoice actually includes four battlefields and four historic buildings. At the

★ Fredericksburg and Chancellorsville visitor centers you can learn about the area's role in the Civil War by watching a 22-minute film ($2) and viewing displays of soldiers' art and battlefield relics. In season, park rangers lead walking tours. The centers offer recorded tours ($4.95 rental, $7.50 purchase) and maps that show how to reach the battlefields, Chancellorsville (where General Stonewall Jackson was mistakenly shot by his own troops), and Spotsylvania Court House battlefields—all within 15 mi of Fredericksburg.

Just outside the Fredericksburg Battlefield Visitor Center is Sunken Road, where on December 13, 1862, the Confederates achieved a resounding victory over Union forces attacking across the Rappahannock (there were 18,000 casualties on both sides). Much of the stone wall that protected Lee's infantrymen is now a re-creation, but 100 yards from the visitor center part of the original wall overlooks the statue *The Angel of Marye's Heights,* by Felix de Weldon (sculptor of the famous *Marine Corps War Memorial* statue in Arlington). This memorial honors Sergeant Richard Kirkland, a South Carolinian who risked his life to bring water to wounded foes; he later died at the Battle of Chickamauga. ⊠*Fredericksburg Battlefield Visitor Center, 1013 Lafayette Blvd. at Sunken Rd., Historic District* ☎*540/373–6122* ⊠*Chancellorsville Battlefield Visitor Center, Rte. 3 W, Plank Rd.,*

Chancellorsville ☎*540/786–2880* ⊕*www.nps.gov/frsp* ✉*Free* ☉*Visitor centers daily 9–5 with extended hrs in summer; walking tours on a seasonal basis dawn–dusk.*

⓫ **George Washington's Ferry Farm.** If it hadn't been for the outcries of his-
☾ torians and citizens, a Wal-Mart would have been built on this site, the
★ boyhood home of our first president. The land was saved by the George
Washington's Fredericksburg Foundation, and the discount store found
a location farther out on the same road. Recently, archaeologists have
uncovered the original fireplaces and four cellars from the house where
Washington was raised, as well as thousands of new artifacts. Ferry
Farm, which once consisted of 600 acres, is across the Rappahannock
River from downtown Fredericksburg and was the site of a ferry crossing. Living here from ages 6 to 19, Washington received his formal
education and taught himself surveying while *not* chopping a cherry
tree or throwing a coin across the Rappahannock—legends concocted
by Parson Weems. The mainly archaeological site also has an exhibit
on "George Washington: Boy Before Legend." The ongoing excavations
include a summer program for children and adults, "Digging for Young
George." Ferry Farm became a major artillery base and river-crossing
site for Union forces during the Battle of Fredericksburg. ⊠*Rte. 3
E, 268 Kings Hwy., at Ferry Rd., Fredericksburg* ☎*540/370–0732*
⊕*www.kenmore.org* ✉*$5* ☉*Daily 10–5; last tour begins at 4:15.*

⓯ **National Cemetery.** The National Cemetery is the final resting place of
15,000 Union dead, most of whom have not been identified. ⊠*Lafayette Blvd. at Sunken Rd., Historic District* ☎*540/373–6122* ☉*Daily
dawn–dusk.*

WHERE TO EAT

$$$–$$$$ ✕**Augustine's at Fredericksburg Square.** Named after Augustine Washing-
AMERICAN ton, George's father, who owned most of the property along Caroline
Street, the 1837 mansion is the place to go in Fredericksburg for formal
dining. The well-spaced tables are set in the traditional European style,
including the use of gold charger plates and service by white-gloved
waiters. The creative and attractively presented dishes, prepared in a
New American style, might include saffron-braised angler fish and Vir-
ginia pheasant. A five-course prix-fixe dinner is offered for $87. The
wine list is not only extensive in its selections but also creatively pre-
sented. ⊠*525 Caroline St.* ☎*540/310–0063* ⊕*www.augustinesrest.
com* ⊟*AE, D, MC, V* ☉*Closed Sun. and Mon. No lunch.*

$$–$$$ ✕**Bistro Bethem.** In an 1833 storefront that served as a general store,
AMERICAN buttermilk-color walls display local art. Copper chandeliers and original
heart-of-pine floors lend a warm glow; when the weather's fine, tables
are brought out onto the sidewalk for alfresco dining. The menu changes
with the seasons and features modern American cuisine with a Southern
accent, including fresh fish and wild game. The award-winning wine list
features the most diverse, multicultural varietal selections in the Fred-
ericksburg region. ⊠*309 William St.* ☎*540/371–9999* ⊕*www.bistro
bethem.com* ⊟*AE, D, MC, V* ☉*Closed Mon. No dinner Sun.*

$$$–$$$$ ✕**Chords.** Opened in 2005 in a historic building, this mulitifaceted
AMERICAN restaurant has jazz- and blues-theme decor and a frequently changing
menu that might include such delicacies as baby cod Wellington, gnocchi
with sun-dried tomatoes and oyster mushrooms, and fruits de mer, and
can also cater to those with food allergies. Steaks, chops, and chicken
round out the classic offerings. Expect expensive and traditional food,
although the early-bird specials offer a substantial discount from 5 to 7.
The Cellar Nightclub is open Tuesday through Saturday and is known
for its great lineup of jazz artists. ✉*917 Caroline St., Historic District*
☎*540/372–3434* ⊕*www.chordsinc.com* ▭*AE, D, DC, MC, V.*

$$–$$$ ✕**Claiborne's.** On the walls of this swank eatery in the 1910-era Fred-
SOUTHERN ericksburg train station are historic train photographs. The restaurant,
decorated in dark green and navy with mahogany-and-brass bars,
specializes in Low Country Southern dishes, including crawfish, grits,
and collard greens. Accompanying the steaks, chops, and seafood are
ample vegetable side dishes served family style. ✉*200 Lafayette Blvd.,
Historic District* ☎*540/371–7080* ⊕*www.claibornesrestaurant.com*
▭*AE, MC, V.*

$–$$ ✕**La Petite Auberge.** Housed in a pre–Civil War brick general store, this
FRENCH white-tablecloth restaurant actually has three dining rooms decorated
like a French garden, with numerous paintings by local artists for sale.
For over two decades, this has been a Fredericksburg favorite for its
consistently good food and service. The interesting menu changes with
the seasons, and the chef sources his products locally. Specialties like
house-cut beef, French onion soup, and seafood are all served with
a continental accent. A fixed-price ($17) four-course dinner is served
from 5:30 to 7 Monday through Thursday. ✉*311 William St.,Historic
District* ☎*540/371–2727* ▭*AE, D, MC, V* ⊗*Closed Sun.*

$–$$ ✕**Poppy Hill Tuscan Kitchen.** In the heart of the downtown shopping dis-
ITALIAN trict, you'll have to look down to find this cozy basement eatery, but it's
worth the search. A "farm-to-table restaurant," Poppy Hill's regionally
sourced produce changes seasonally. Warm earth tones infuse the space
and rustic Tuscan favorites include hearty soups and salads, seafood
stew, prosciutto-wrapped tilapia, and balsamic glazed chicken. The
antipasto platter is a mountain of artisanal cheeses, crostini, olives,
and charcuterie, and is big enough to share with four. Lunch is a great
value with sandwiches and pasta dishes under $9. A nice list of chianti,
sangiovese and other Italian wine favorites, both white and red, comple-
ments the menu. It is open for brunch on Sunday. ✉*1000 Charles St.,
Historic District* ☎*540/373–2035* ⊕*www.ciaopoppyhill.com* ▭*AE,
MC, V* ⊗*Closed Mon.*

$$–$$$ ✕**Ristorante Renato.** This family-owned restaurant, decorated with lace
ITALIAN curtains, red carpeting, and walls covered with paintings, specializes
in traditional northern and southern Italian cuisine, including veal,
chicken, pasta, and seafood. Standouts include veal Florentine, fettuccine Alfredo, eggplant parmigiana, steamed mussels, and lasagna. The
260-seat restaurant is also open for lunch on weekdays. Save room for
the Italian desserts such as cannoli, spumoni, and tiramisu. ✉*422 William St., Historic District* ☎*540/371–8228* ⊕*www.ristoranterenato.
com* ▭*AE, MC, V* ⊗*No lunch weekends.*

4

¢–$ ✕ **Sammy T's.** Vegetarian dishes, healthful foods, and homemade soups
AMERICAN and breads share the menu with hamburgers, oyster and crab-cake sandwiches, and dinner platters at this unpretentious place. Eclectic vegetarian and vegan offerings from tzatziki and tabbouleh to black-bean cakes
and veggie chili make this the go-to place for noncarnivores, but it's the
list of more than 20 sandwiches and wraps that make Sammy T's a hot
spot for the in-town lunch crowd. The bar is stocked with nearly 50
brands of beer. There's a separate no-smoking section around the corner,
but a tin ceiling, high wooden booths, and wooden ceiling fans make
the main dining room much chummier. ✉ *801 Caroline St., Historic
District* ☏ *540/371–2008* ⊕ *www.sammyts.com* ⊟ *AE, D, MC, V.*

$–$$ ✕ **Smythe's Cottage & Tavern.** Entering this cozy dining room in a black-
AMERICAN smith's house built in the early 1800s is like taking a step back in time,
and may remind you of the Colonial taverns in Williamsburg. The lunch
and dinner menus are classic Virginia: seafood pie, quail, stuffed flounder, peanut soup, and Smithfield ham biscuits. The wine list features
Virginia vintages as well. Smythe's is in the heart of the historic district,
making it a convenient stop for lunch. ✉ *303 Fauquier St., Historic
District* ☏ *540/373–1645* ⊟ *MC, V* ☉ *Closed Tues.*

WHERE TO STAY

$$ ▦ **Homewood Suites.** In a newly developed area locals call the "cam-
pus," this new all-suites hotel is a sister property to the Hampton Inn,
and in addition to one-bedroom suites, features the only two-bedroom
suites in Fredericksburg. A sumptuous complimentary breakfast in the
lobby lounge is included in the rate, as is an afternoon happy hour.
The spacious suites are like having your own well-appointed apart-
ment making them perfect for families or extended stays since they have
full kitchens that include dishes and dishwashers. **Pros:** largest suites
in town; free breakfast and happy hour included. **Cons:** not close to
historic attractions; 10-minute drive to town. ✉ *1040 Hospitality La.*
☏ *540/786–9700* ⊕ *www.homewoodsuites.com* ↬ *124 suites* ⚏ *In-
hotel: pool, gym, public Wi-Fi* ⊟ *AE, D, DC, MC, V.*

¢ ▦ **Inn at the Olde Silk Mill.** This 1920s motel with moss-green siding
and forest-green awnings has a beautifully decorated central staircase
in the lobby. Each of the 30 rooms is furnished with antiques and
appointments from the Civil War period, and the lobby has an old-time
upright piano, as well as many historic photographs of Fredericksburg.
Efficiency suites for extended stays feature more modern decor and all
rooms have high-speed wireless Internet. Breakfast includes beverages,
cereal, and coffee cake. The inn is situated just at the edge of the historic
district and has private, off-street parking. **Pros:** period rooms; nice
breakfast; good value. **Cons:** on the outer edge of the historic district.
✉ *1707 Princess Anne St., Historic District* ☏ *540/371–5666* ⊕ *www.
fci1.com* ↬ *27 rooms* ⚏ *In-room: refrigerator. In-hotel: parking (no
fee), no-smoking rooms* ⊟ *AE, MC, V* ❑ *BP.*

$–$$ ▦ **Kenmore Inn.** This 18th-century historic home is easily recognizable
by its magnificent and inviting front porch. There are two types of
rooms. The deluxe ones, in the original part of the house, have working

fireplaces and canopy beds; the slightly smaller standard rooms have Colonial furnishings. The English pub, with its Mahogany Horseshoe Bar, serves lighter dishes and imported draft beer; it's open Tuesday to Sunday evenings. **Pros:** charming decor; restaurant on-site; high-speed Internet. **Cons:** limited availability; some rooms are small. ⊠ *1200 Princess Anne St., Historic District* ☎ *540/371–7622* ⊕ *www.kenmoreinn. com* ⤳ *9 rooms* ⚭ *In-room: no TV (some), Wi-Fi. In-hotel: restaurant, bar* ⊟ *AE, D, DC, MC, V* ❙❉❙ *CP.*

$$ ⚏ **Richard Johnston Inn.** This elegant B&B was constructed in 1793 and
★ served as the home of Richard Johnston, mayor of Fredericksburg from March 1809 to March 1810. Guest rooms are decorated with period antiques and reproductions, and have working fireplaces, along with high-speed wireless and the purely Southern amenity of complimentary cream sherry. The aroma of freshly baked breads and muffins entices you to breakfast in the large Federal-style dining room, where the table is set with fine china, silver, and linens. The inn is just across from the visitor center and two blocks from the train station. Ample private parking is behind the inn. **Pros:** Wi-Fi in a historic setting; massage therapy; true Southern experience. **Cons:** advance deposit required; expensive. ⊠ *711 Caroline St., Historic District* ☎ *540/899–7606 or 877/557–0770* ⊕ *www.therichardjohnstoninn.com* ⤳ *7 rooms, 2 suites* ⚭ *In-room: VCR, Wi-Fi. In-hotel: parking (no fee), no-smoking rooms* ⊟ *AE, MC, V* ❙❉❙ *CP.*

THE NORTHERN NECK

Between Fredericksburg and the Chesapeake Bay is the "Northern Neck," an area attractive to nature lovers, anglers, and boaters. This 90-mi-long peninsula has a 1,200 mi total shoreline and is bathed on three sides by the Potomac and Rappahannock rivers, and the mighty Chesapeake Bay. Settled by Europeans more than 300 years ago, the Northern Neck is the birthplace of presidents George Washington, James Monroe, and James Madison, as well as General Robert E. Lee and Washington's mother, Mary Ball.

The Northern Neck peninsula is as unspoiled today as when Captain John Smith first visited in 1608. Even at the peninsula's start, the area is forested and tranquil. You can find charming B&Bs; fresh-off-the-boat seafood; excursion boats to islands in the Chesapeake Bay; historic homes and museums; and places to commune with nature.

The sites below are listed in geographical order beginning at the intersection of Routes 3 and 301. Though it's unusual that three presidents' birthplaces are in such proximity, those of James Madison and James Monroe are just markers off the highway, whereas Washington's is a national monument. A marker on Highway 301 in Port Conway, King George County, memorializes the onetime plantation where James Madison was born in 1751; an outline of the house and a marker in neighboring Westmoreland County identifies the birthplace of James Monroe, born in 1758, on Highway 205 between Oak Grove and Colonial Beach.

Numbers in the text correspond to numbers in the margin and on the Northern Neck map.

GEORGE WASHINGTON BIRTHPLACE NATIONAL MONUMENT

32 mi east of Fredericksburg on Rte. 3.

After you pass the town of Oak Grove on Route 3, all signs point to the national park on the Potomac River. At Pope's Creek, **George Washington Birthplace National Monument** is a 550-acre park mirroring the peaceful rural life our first president preferred. The house in which Mary Ball Washington gave birth to George in 1732 burned in 1779, but native clay was used to make bricks for a representative 18th-century plantation home. Costumed interpreters lead tours through the house, which has items dating from the time of Washington's childhood. The grounds include a kitchen, garden, cemetery with 32 Washington family graves, and the Colonial Living Farm, worked by methods employed in Colonial days. Picnic facilities are available year-round, and children under 15 are admitted free. ⊠ *Rte. 3* ☎ *804/224–1732* ⊕ *www.nps.gov/gewa* ✉ *$4* ☉ *Daily 9–5.*

WHERE TO STAY

¢ ⊡ **Westmoreland State Park.** This 1,300-acre, full-service park is one of Virginia's most beautiful campgrounds, with hiking trails winding through marshlands, woods, and meadows and along the Potomac River. There are also places to fish, rent boats or kayaks, or simply picnic. The comfortable, climate-controlled cabins have complete kitchens with microwave oven and toaster, dishes, silverware, and cooking utensils. Living rooms have a sofa, dining table, and working fireplace. The basic furnishings include linens for four beds. From Memorial Weekend to Labor Day Weekend there is a one-week minimum; at all other times the minimum is two nights. Westmoreland also has 133 campsites available and six camping cabins that provide a shelter but few other amenities. **Pros:** extensive outdoor activities; beautiful setting off the beaten path. **Cons:** no restaurants nearby; limited amenities; minimum stay required. ⊠ *1650 State Park Rd., Rte. 1, Box 600, Montross* ☎ *804/493–8821 or 800/933–7275* ⊕ *www.dcr.state.va.us/parks/westmore.htm* ⇆ *27 cabins, 133 campsites* ♿ *In-room: no phone, kitchen, no TV. In-hotel: pool, laundry facilities* ▭ *AE, MC, V.*

STRATFORD HALL PLANTATION

8 mi east of George Washington Birthplace National Monument via Rte. 3.

Robert E. Lee, who became the commander of the Confederate Army, was born in the Great House of **Stratford Hall Plantation,** one of the country's finest examples of Colonial architecture. Eight chimneys in two squares top the H-shape brick home, built in the 1730s by one of Lee's grandfathers, Colonial governor Thomas Lee. The house contains Robert E. Lee's crib, original family pieces, and period furnishings. The working Colonial plantation covers 1,600 acres and has gardens, a kitchen, smokehouse, laundry, orangery, springhouses, coach house, stables, slave quarters, and a gristmill that grinds from 11 AM to 2 PM on the first whole weekend of each month from April through September. The Plantation Dining Room, a log cabin restaurant, serves meals and sandwiches daily from 11 to 3. Its outdoor screened deck overlooks the woodlands. ⊠ *Rte. 3, Stratford* ☎ *804/493–8038 or 804/493–8371* ⊕ *www.stratfordhall.org* ☞ *$10* ☉ *Visitor center daily 9:30–4, house tours daily 10–4.*

WHERE TO STAY

¢ ⚠ **Cole's Point Plantation.** This 110-acre wooded campground on the Potomac River has a boat ramp and a 120-slip full-service marina. The facility has four log cabins that can sleep 4–13 people. Reservations are essential. **Pros:** good for boaters and fishermen. **Cons:** very limited accommodations; few amenities; open seasonally. ⊠ *Rte. 612, north of Rte. 202* ⚓ *Rte. 728, Box 77, Coles Point 22442* ☎ *804/472–3955* ⊕ *www.colespoint.com* ⇆ *74 full hookups or tent sites, 35 partial hookups or tent sites, 1 tent-only site, 4 cabins* ♿ *Pool, flush toilets, full hookups, partial hookups (electric and water), swimming (river)* ▭ *AE, MC, V* ☉ *May–Oct.*

$ ⚑ **Stratford Hall.** Of the two guesthouses on the plantation property, Cheek, the larger one, has 15 rooms, which come with either two twin beds or a king-size bed. Astor, named after Lady Astor and made from a log cabin, is directly across from the Plantation Dining Room. Both guesthouses have a fully equipped kitchen, a living room with fireplace, and decks. **Pros:** historic property; good on-site restaurant. **Cons:** limited availability. ✉485 Great House Rd. ☎804/493–8038 or 804/493–8371 ⊕www.stratfordhall.org ⬅20 rooms ⌂In-hotel: restaurant, parking (no fee) ▤MC, V ⑩CP.

WARSAW

15 mi southeast of Stratford Hall via Rte. 3.

The county seat of Richmond County, Warsaw is a pleasant town of 7,000 that's shaded by large oak trees. Near the U.S. 360 bridge over the Rappahannock, it's therefore closer to the city of Tappahannock (on the other side) than to its fellow towns on the Northern Neck.

EXPLORING

Ingleside Vineyards is one of Virginia's oldest and largest wineries, and has won the prestigious Virginia Governor's Cup more times than any other winery. It produces one of the few sparkling wines from Virginia. There are also white wines (viognier, sauvignon blanc, pinot gris, and chardonnay) and reds (sangiovese, cabernet franc, and sauvignon) as well as specially produced labels. The vineyards cover about 65 acres of gently rolling countryside whose climate and sandy loam soil is similar to that of Bordeaux, France. The winery has a tasting bar, a gift shop with grape-related gifts, a large outdoor patio with umbrella tables and a fountain, and a large indoor room for group tastings. The winery is about 40 minutes east of Fredericksburg and only a few miles from the Washington Birthplace National Monument. ✉5872 Leedstown Rd. , from Rte. 3, turn south on Rte. 638 at winery's signpost, Oak Grove ☎804/224–8687 ⊕www.ipwine.com ☉Mon.–Sat. 10–5, Sun. noon–5.

A cruise 20 mi up the river to Ingleside Vineyards leaves from Tappahannock. **Rappahannock River Cruises** enlists its ship *Capt. Thomas* to take passengers on the narrated day cruise. A buffet lunch is served at the winery ($11), snacks are served on board, or you can bring your own. To reach the dock, take Highway 17 south from Tappahannock to Hoskins Creek. The cruise departs daily at 10, returning at 4:30. They also offer a cruise from Reedville to Tangier Island. ✉Hoskins Creek ☎804/453–2628 ⊕www.tangiercruise.com ⬅$25 ☉May–Oct., daily at 10.

WHERE TO STAY

¢–$ ⚑**Heritage Park Resort & Belle Mount Vineyards.** On Menokin Bay, this campground has panoramic views overlooking the Rappahannock River and scenic wildlife settings. The rustic, wooden, two-bedroom cottages are heated and air-conditioned so they can be rented year-round. Each has a living room with navy plaid chairs and sofa, a dining room, and a fully equipped kitchen. With its banquet facilities for 300, the resort is a good place for picnics, receptions, and family reunions. There are also 78 campsites, some of which have full hookups or partial hookups. Tours and tastings at the winery on the premises are available Wednesday through Sunday from mid-March to mid-December. This is a part of the Northern Neck Wine Trail. **Pros:** free winery tours and tastings; close to Stratford Hall Plantation. **Cons:** cottage and campsite options might be too rustic for some; no Internet. ⊠ *2570 Newland Rd., Rte. 624, 2.5 mi west of U.S. 360, Warsaw* ☎ *804/333–4038* ⊕ *www.heritage park.com* ⛺ *5 cottages, 78 campsites (20 with water and electric and 25 with water, electric, and sewer)* ⚒ *In-room: kitchen. In-hotel: pool, no-smoking rooms* ⊟ *AE, D, MC, V.*

REEDVILLE

31 mi from Warsaw via U.S. 360, 46 mi from Stratford Hall via Rtes. 202 and 360.

This small town at the eastern tip of the Northern Neck was the home of wealthy fishermen and businessmen who made their fortunes from the menhaden fish abundant in the nearby Chesapeake Bay and Potomac waters.

EXPLORING

The educational and activity-oriented **Reedville Fishermen's Museum** is housed in a restored fisherman's home and a larger building. Permanent and rotating exhibits document the area's fishing industry, and there are two fishing boats here, a skipjack, the *Claud W.*, and a deck boat, the *Elva C.*, which have been named to the National Register of Historic Places. ⊠ *Main St,.* ☎ *804/453–6529* ⊕ *www.rfmuseum. org* ⛳ *$5* ⊙ *Early Mar.– Apr., weekends 10:30–4:30; May–Oct., daily 10:30–4:30; Nov–mid-Jan., Fri.–Mon. 10:30–4:30; mid-Jan.–early Mar., by appt. for groups.*

Popular cruises to quaint Smith Island in the Chesapeake Bay leave from Reedville. The 150-passenger ship *Captain Evans* and the 139-passenger air-conditioned *Spirit of Chesapeake* of **Smith Island and Chesapeake Bay Cruises** sail from the KOA Kampground at Smith Point on Route 802. The 13½-mi trip takes 1½ hours and passes a 5,000-acre waterfowl and wildlife refuge. Now a part of Maryland, Smith Island—a Methodist colony settled by British colonists from Cornwall in the early 1700s—can also be reached from Crisfield, on Maryland's Eastern Shore. Lunch is available at several restaurants on the island. Cruise reservations are required. Call ahead for the schedule and fare. *For more information on Smith Island, see Chapter 9, The Eastern Shore.* ⊠ *382 Campground Rd., behind KOA Kampground* ☎ *804/453–3430* ⊕ *www.eaglesnest.net/smithislandcruise* ⊙ *May–mid-Oct.*

Tangier is a Virginia island in the Chesapeake Bay named by Captain John Smith. This largely unspoiled fishing village with quaint, narrow streets also happens to be the soft-shell-crab capital of the nation. There's a small airport here for private planes and it also can be reached by the ship *Chesapeake Breeze* of **Tangier Island & Chesapeake Cruises** (ships also leave from Onacock, Virginia, and Crisfield, Maryland, on the Eastern Shore). The ship departs at 10 AM and returns at 3:30 PM daily, cruising 1½ hours each way. The island has several restaurants serving lunch. From the intersection of Highways 360 and 646, drive 1½ mi; then turn left on Highway 656 (Buzzard's Point Road), which leads to the dock. Reservations are required. *Also see more Tangier Island information in the Eastern Shore chapter.* ⊠*468 Buzzard's Point Rd.* ☎*804/453–2628* ⊕*www.tangiercruise.com* ⊠*$25* ⊙*May–Oct., daily.*

WHERE TO STAY

$–$$ 🏨 **Fleeton Fields.** Set amid beautifully manicured lawns and gardens, this lovely Colonial-style inn also overlooks a tidal pond on which you may be lucky enough to see ospreys, great blue herons, and eagles. Inside the inn, you're greeted by fresh flowers and soothing music before being escorted to one of the three beautifully furnished suites. Cool evenings are warmed by inviting fireplaces, and each morning's breakfast is served using china, crystal, and silver. **Pros:** on-site birding; nearby seafood restaurants. **Cons:** no restaurant on-site except for breakfast. ⊠*2783 Fleeton Rd.* ☎*804/453–5014 or 800/497–8215* ⊕*www.fleetonfields. com* ⤙*3 suites* ⚓ *In-hotel: Wi-Fi* ⊟*AE, D, DC, MC, V* ⊙*BP.*

$$–$$$ 🏨 **The Gables.** A four-story redbrick Victorian mansion built in 1909, the Gables was built by Captain Albert Fisher, one of the founders of the local fishing industry. The house has been lovingly restored and has period antiques throughout. There are two guest rooms in the main house and four more in the adjacent carriage house. The Gables has its own deepwater dock on Cockrell's Creek, with easy access to the Chesapeake Bay. **Pros:** walk to downtown Reedville; marina and boat rides next door. **Cons:** not all rooms have en suite bathroom. ⊠*859 Main St.* ☎*804/453–5209* ⊕*www.thegablesbb.com* ⤙*6 rooms* ⚓*In-hotel: public Wi-Fi, no-smoking rooms, no kids under 13* ⊟*MC, V* ⊙*BP.*

EN ROUTE After leaving Reedville on Route 360, turn left on Route 200 and drive 13 mi to Kilmarnock. Turn right on Route 3 and drive to the little town of Lancaster, home of the **Mary Ball Washington Museum and Library.** This four-building complex honors George Washington's mother, who was born in Lancaster County. Lancaster House, built about 1798, contains Washington family memorabilia and historic items related to the county and the Northern Neck. The Steuart-Blakemore Building houses a genealogical library, and the Old Jail is a lending library and archives. ⊠*8346 Mary Ball Rd., Lancaster* ☎*804/462–7280* ⊕*www.mbwm. org* ⊠*$2 museum house and grounds* ⊙*Tues.–Fri. 10–4; library Tues.– Sat. 10–4.*

IRVINGTON

5 mi south from Kilmarnock.

Although much older than the resort, the lovely town of Irvington has been associated with the Tides Inn for more than 50 years.

EXPLORING

The **Historic Christ Church** was completed in 1735, when George Washington was three years old. The Georgian-style structure, on the National Register of Historic Places, was built by Robert "King" Carter and contains a rare "triple-decker" pulpit made of native walnut. Bricks for the church were fired in a great kiln near the churchyard. A 12-minute video is screened in the museum. ⌧*420 Christ Church Rd., from Irvington drive 1.5 mi north on Rte. 200* ☎*804/438–6855* ⏚*www. christchurch1735.org* ⌦*Free* ☉*Church daily; museum weekdays 10–4; Apr.–Nov., also Sat. 10–4 and Sun. 2–5.*

WHERE TO STAY & EAT

¢–$ ✕**White Stone Wine & Cheese.** This French bistro offers sandwiches,
CAFÉ soups, and baked goods as well as a large selection of wine and cheese. There are tables available to eat your picnic, and a good selection of wines for sale. Special wine dinners are held on Saturday. ⌧*572 Rappahannock Dr. 22578* ☎*804/435–2000* ▭*MC, V* ☉ *No lunch. No dinner Sun.–Tues.*

$$ ▦**The Hope and Glory Inn.** This 1890 schoolhouse is now a pale-honey-
Fodor's Choice color Victorian B&B. The first-floor classrooms have been opened into
★ an expansive, columned lobby with a painted checkerboard floor. The upstairs bedrooms and six small cottages behind the inn are decorated romantically chic, with pastel painted floors and interesting window treatments. In the garden, surrounded by a tall wooden fence, there's a completely open-air bathroom that can be booked by adventurous couples. In 2004 the inn built new cottages, called "tents," in an allusion to turn-of-the-20th-century Methodist tent communities. On wooded bluffs overlooking the headwaters of Carter's Creek, the tents each have three bedrooms and a kitchen, and there's a pool and dock for canoes and kayaks as well as the "Detention" wine bar. **Pros:** free bikes; pet-friendly; designer aesthetic. **Cons:** limited availability. ⌧*634 King Carter Dr.* ☎*804/438–6053 or 800/497–8228* ⏚*www.hopeandglory. com* ◖*7 rooms, 4 cottages* ▭*MC, V* ⭗*BP.*

$$$–$$$$ ▦**The Tides Inn.** Surrounded by manicured grounds overlooking Cart-
☾ ers Creek, the Tides Inn, here since 1947, is sandwiched between the
★ Potomac and Rappahannock rivers. The resort offers all of the modern amenities travelers have come to expect, and features a wide variety of on-site recreational activities. Many of the rooms and suites, which are luxuriously decorated in a British Colonial style, have spectacular water views. The Golden Eagle Golf course is challenging, the par-3 course less so; the ponds are well stocked with fish; and bird-watchers should take their binoculars. There's also a sailing school that's set up for all ages and experience levels, and you can take a cruise along the Rappahannock River on a 127-foot yacht. **Pros:** full-service resort; golf, sailing lessons; kids' activities. **Cons:** expensive. ⌧*480 King Carter Dr.* ☎*804/438–5000 or 800/843–3746* ⏚*www.tidesinn.com* ◖*84 rooms, 22 suites* ☾*In-room: DVD, Ethernet. In-hotel: 4 restaurants, bar, golf courses, tennis courts, pools, gym, spa, bicycles, children's programs (ages 4–12), laundry facilities, airport shuttle, some pets allowed* ▭*AE, D, DC, MC, V.*

Williamsburg & Hampton Roads

WORD OF MOUTH

"Before you start your day in the historic area, visit the Visitors Center and see the short movie *A Story of a Patriot*. It really sets the mood and will make your visit to the historic area much more meaningful, particularly the Capitol and Raleigh Tavern."
—Gekko

Updated by
Alice Powers

PERHAPS NO OTHER REGION IN Virginia contains more variety and options for the traveler than its southeastern coastline. Colonial Williamsburg has evoked the days of America's forefathers since its restoration began during the 1920s. Jamestown and Yorktown make the area one of the most historically significant in the United States. When it's time for pure recreation, you can head to theme parks such as Busch Gardens Williamsburg and resort areas, including Virginia Beach.

At the end of the Virginia peninsula is the enormous Hampton Roads harbor, where the James, Elizabeth, and Nansemond rivers flow together into the Chesapeake Bay and then eastward into the Atlantic Ocean. Hampton Roads has also played a crucial role in the discovery and settlement of the nation, its struggle for independence, and the conflict that nearly dissolved the Union.

This entire area, known as the Tidewater, is land where water in rivers and streams is affected by tides. The cities in southeast Virginia take on different roles depending on their proximity to the Chesapeake Bay and the rivers that empty into it. Hampton contains the world's largest naval base, and enormous shipbuilding yards are in Norfolk and Newport News. The area is also committed to recreation and tourism: there are many resort hotels, a bustling beachfront, and boardwalk attractions. Virginia Beach, which in the 1950s claimed to have the world's longest public beach, has a showy boardwalk.

ORIENTATION & PLANNING

GETTING ORIENTED

The Historic Triangle. There is probably no better place in America to study this country's prerevolutionary war history than the Historic Triangle. Between Williamsburg, Jamestown, and Yorktown visitors get a full picture of life in Colonial times. The lessons are multisensory: museums, battlefields, restorations, and reenactments appeal to history buffs of every age.

Hampton Roads Area. The channel where the James, Elizabeth, and Nansemond rivers meet is surrounded by both small and larger towns that include the historic settlements of Hampton and Portsmouth, and today's cities Newport News and Norfolk. Linked to the Hampton Roads area by the unusual Chesapeake Bay Bridge-Tunnel is Virginia's "other coastline," the quiet, largely untrafficked Eastern Shore *(see Chapter 9).*

PLANNING

WHEN TO GO

During December's **Grand Illuminations** (☎*800/447–8679* ⊕*www. history.org*) in Williamsburg, Virginia, 18th-century entertainment is performed on several outdoor stages and fireworks are set off at several points through the evening. In March, **Military Through the Ages**

TOP REASONS TO GO

■ **Colonial Williamsburg:** Escape to the 18th century in the world's largest living-history museum. Virginia's capital from 1699 to 1780 and Britain's largest, wealthiest New World outpost was restored so "That the future may learn from the past."

■ **Celebrate early American history:** Jamestown was the first permanent English settlement in the Americas. Washington's momentous 1781 Revolutionary War victory at Yorktown secured the country's independence.

■ **Water, water, everywhere!** From the James River and Chesapeake Bay to the Atlantic Ocean, get in or on the waters of Tidewater Virginia.

Surf the waves, steam past the world's largest naval station, sail on a schooner, or sup on a ship.

■ **Immerse yourself in nautical and military history:** Don't miss the Mariners' Museum, the MacArthur Memorial, the Virginia Air and Space Center, and the world's largest naval base at Norfolk Naval Station.

■ **Glimpse the gracious gentry life and the hard life of slaves:** Visit America's oldest plantations and historic homes, including one chartered in 1613 and continuously occupied by 11 generations, two homes of presidents, and one claiming to have celebrated the first Thanksgiving.

5

(☎757/253–4838 ⊕*www.historyisfun.org*) in Jamestown, Virginia, uses authentic weapons in a series of reenactments of battles from the Middle Ages through the 20th century. **Yorktown Day** (☎*757/898–2410* ⊕*www.nps.gov/colo*) observances in Yorktown, Virginia, celebrate the Colonial victory in the American War of Independence (October 19, 1781) with 18th-century tactical demonstrations, patriotic exercises, and a wreath-laying ceremony.

GETTING HERE & AROUND

BY AIR The three major airports in the region are served by many national and international carriers. Ticket prices are often much less expensive to and from Norfolk and Newport News than nearby Richmond. All three airports are relatively small and easy to navigate.

BY CAR Williamsburg is west of I–64, 51 mi southeast of Richmond; the Colonial Parkway joins Williamsburg with Jamestown to the southwest and Yorktown to the east. Interstate 664 forms the eastern part of a beltway through the Hampton Roads area and connects Newport News with Portsmouth. Interstate 264 runs from I–664 to downtown Norfolk, and then extends all the way to Virginia Beach. Interstate 64 runs from Hampton to Portsmouth around the west side of Norfolk to intersect I–664.

The area is well served with expressways and interstate highways, but you have to share these routes with many local drivers. ■ TIP➜Interstate I–95 near Richmond is a perpetual bottleneck, especially from Friday to Sunday evening. If you are coming to Williamsburg from the north you may want to leave I–95 at Fredericksburg and go south on Route 17 to Yorktown.

It is a narrower road with stoplights, but may be a less frustrating drive than staying on the interstates.

Because the ragged coastline is constantly interrupted by water, driving from one town to another usually means going through a tunnel or over a bridge, either one of which may create a traffic bottleneck. The entrance to the tunnel between Hampton and Norfolk can get very congested, especially on weekends, so listen to your car radio for updated traffic reports.

In the Tidewater area, with a long list of tunnels and bridges connecting myriad waterways, it's easy to find yourself headed in the wrong direction. Highways have adequate signs, but sometimes it may be too late to merge before entering a tunnel/bridge. Traffic is highly congested during rush hour and during peak summer months, when the beach traffic can grind everything to a halt. Tune in to your car radio for traffic reports, especially during rush hours.

In congested periods, use the less-traveled I–664. The 17.5-mi Chesapeake Bay Bridge-Tunnel is the only connection between the southern part of Virginia and the Eastern Shore; U.S. 13 is the main route up the spine of the Eastern Shore peninsula into Maryland.

BY TAXI   There are a few taxi companies in Williamsburg, more in Norfolk and Virginia Beach. Unless you're at Newport News/Williamsburg International Airport or Norfolk International Airport, you must phone for a cab. Rates are metered and tipping is expected.

BY TRAIN   Amtrak trains stop in Williamsburg between Newport News and Richmond, Washington, DC, and stations to the north. There are two trains daily in each direction. At Newport News, passengers ticketed to Norfolk or Virginia Beach board a chartered bus at the station. The Williamsburg station is centrally located, sharing a building with the bus station. Service south of Richmond is slow, even for Amtrak. At Fredericksburg, Amtrak meets the Virginia Railway Express, which is cheaper, but only operates on workdays.

ESSENTIALS

Air Contacts **Hampton Roads Transit** (☎ 757/222–6100 ⊕ www.hrtransit.org). **Newport News/Williamsburg International Airport** (PHF ✉ 12525 Jefferson Ave., at I-64, Newport News ☎ 757/877–0221 ⊕ www.nnwairport.com). **Norfolk International Airport** (ORF ✉ 2200 Norview Ave., Norfolk ☎ 757/857–3351 ⊕ norfolkairport.com). **Richmond International Airport** (RIC ✉ 1 Richard E. Byrd Dr., Richmond ☎ 804/226–3000 ⊕ www.flyrichmond.com).

Train Infomation **Virginia Railway Express** (⊕ www.vre.org) .

DISCOUNTS & DEALS

The America's Historic Triangle Vacation Package includes unlimited visits to all five attractions—Colonial Williamsburg, Jamestown Settlement and Historic Jamestowne, Yorktown Victory Center and Yorktown Battlefield—in the Historic Triangle. There is also an America's Historic Triangle Ticket that does not include lodging. For information on the vacation package, visit ⊕ *www.AmericasHistoricTriangle.com* ☎ *800/495–8804* ⊕ *www.historyisfun.org/Vacation-Packages.htm*

ABOUT THE RESTAURANTS

Dining rooms within walking distance of Colonial Williamsburg's restored area are often crowded, and reservations (☎ *800/447–8679*) are necessary. Many nationally known chain eateries line both sides of U.S. 60 on the east side of the city.

ABOUT THE HOTELS

There are more than 200 hotel properties in Williamsburg. For a complete list, contact the **Williamsburg Area Convention and Visitors Bureau** (✉ *421 N. Boundary St., Box 3495, Williamsburg* ☎ *757/253–0192 or 800/368–6511*).

There are many bed-and-breakfasts in the Williamsburg area, especially near the James River Plantations off Route 10. Most are housed in historic properties with charming antiques. Rates usually include a full country breakfast.

Reservations at inns can be made through the following contacts. **Virginia is for Lovers** (☎ *800/847–4882* ⊕ *www.virginia.org*). **Virginia Beach Reservations** (☎ *800/822–3224*) can make a reservation in your choice of about 75 hotels. **Williamsburg Vacation Reservations** (☎ *800/446–9244*), representing more than 70 hostelries, provides free lodging reservation services.

Apartment and house rentals are not common in the Williamsburg area, but quite the thing to do at Virginia Beach. Rentals vary greatly in size, cost, and degree of luxury, so research possibilities thoroughly. Local agents include **Long and Foster Real Estate** (✉ *317 30th St., Virginia Beach* ☎ *757/428–4600 or 800/941–3333*) and **Siebert Realty** (✉ *601 Sandbridge Rd., Virginia Beach* ☎ *757/426–6200 or 877/422–2200* ⊕ *www.siebert-realty.com*).

WHAT IT COSTS					
	¢	$	$$	$$$	$$$$
Restaurants	under $10	$10–$16	$17–$23	$24–$30	over $30
Hotels	under $100	$100–$160	$161–$230	$231–$300	over $300

Restaurant prices are per person for a main course at dinner. Hotel prices are for a standard double room, excluding state and local taxes.

PLANNING YOUR TIME

Colonial Williamsburg recommends three or four days for their property only, but the entire Historic Triangle can be covered in that time. Try exploring chronologically, starting at the first settlement in Jamestowne, then exploring the Colonial period in Williamsburg, and finally the Revolution at Yorktown.

EXPLORING WILLIAMSBURG & HAMPTON ROADS

The beginning of both Colonial America and of the United States of America should be required visiting, and this area is home to them both. To keep the chronology straight, visit Virginia's "Historic Triangle," in the order of Jamestown, Williamsburg, and then Yorktown. Although Jamestown is somewhat overshadowed by the much-larger Williamsburg, Jamestown Island was the first permanent English settlement (1607) in North America, and celebrated its momentous quadricentennial—400th anniversary—in 2007. Just a short drive along the tree-lined Colonial Parkway is Williamsburg, which subsequently grew into the political and economic center of the Virginia Colony. The 301 acres of modern-day Colonial Williamsburg contain re-created and restored structures peopled with costumed interpreters. Everything from momentous political events to blacksmithing is portrayed. Completing the "Historic Triangle," is Yorktown, 20 mi away, the site of the battle that ended the war for independence from England. Several 18th- and 19th-century plantations lie west of Williamsburg, along the James River. South of Yorktown are Newport News, the shipbuilding capital of Virginia, and Hampton. To see the rest of this waterfront area of Virginia, you can cross the James River at Hampton and visit Norfolk, Portsmouth, and, to the east, the Virginia Beach resort area.

THE HISTORIC TRIANGLE

Virginia's number one tourist attraction has you pinching yourself to make sure you haven't entered a time machine. You'll believe you're in another century, and you really are. Colonial Williamsburg, a careful, on-the-spot restoration of the former Virginia capital, gives you the chance to walk into the 18th century and see how earlier Americans lived. The streets may be unrealistically clean for that era, and you can find hundreds of others exploring the buildings with you, but the rich detail of the re-creation and the sheer size of the city could hold your attention for days. A ticket or pass (price is based on the number of attractions and the duration of visit) admits the holder to sites in the restored area, but it costs nothing just to walk around and absorb the atmosphere. ■TIP→**Although admission is free to amble around the historic district, you will miss some of the most interesting aspects of Williamsburg by not entering the buildings or seeing the excellent programs staged by skilled reenactors. It is well worth the price of admission.**

Williamsburg anchors three elements of Colonial National Historical Park. The 23-mi Colonial Parkway links Williamsburg to Jamestown and Yorktown, two other significant historical sites on or near the peninsula bounded by the James and York rivers. Historic Jamestowne was the location of the first permanent English settlement in North America—that celebrated its 400th anniversary in 2007—and it's an excellent place to begin a visit to the area; Yorktown was the site of the final major battle in the American Revolutionary War. The sites themselves as well as the parkway are maintained by the National Park Service. Close by are Jamestown Settlement and the excellent Yorktown Victory Center, both run by the Jamestown-Yorktown Foundation. Like Colonial Williamsburg, these two sites re-create the buildings and activities of the 18th century, using interpreters in period dress.

JAMESTOWN

9 mi southwest of Colonial Williamsburg via Colonial Pkwy.

The desperate strivings of Englishmen to stay alive and establish a foothold in the New World become evident when visiting Jamestown, the beginning of English settlement in this country. Its two major sights are places to explore the early relationship between the English and Native Virginia Indians.

GETTING HERE & AROUND

From April to October, the Jamestown Area Shuttle provides loop service around the Jamestown area every 30 minutes between Historic Jamestowne, the Jamestown Settlement, and the Jamestown Glasshouse (part of Historic Jamestowne).

BY FERRY The Jamestown–Scotland Ferry began providing service across the James River in 1925. This is the best free ride in Virginia; it takes you back 400 years to when the colonists first spied the site where they founded Jamestown. The ferry leaves the Jamestown dock about every hour on the half hour, leaving the opposite port, Scotland, on the hour 24 hours a day. Wait times vary from 15 to 30 minutes (sometimes longer in summer). Cars, campers, trucks, and motorcycles are allowed on the ferry. Foot passengers may ride, but there's nowhere to park at the ferry landing.

TIMING & PRECAUTIONS

The least-visited season in the Historic Triangle is winter. During the most popular seasons—summer, fall, and spring break—there may be lines outside the Colonial Williamsburg buildings. The other attractions in the Historic Triangle are not as busy.

ESSENTIALS

Ferry Information **Jamestown–Scotland Ferry** (⊠ *2317 Jamestown Rd., Rte. 31* ☏ *757/222–6100* ⊕ *www.virginiadot.org/comtravel/ferry-jamestown.asp*).

Visitor Information **Jamestown Settlement and Yorktown Victory Center** (☏ *757/253–4838 or 888/593–4682* ⊕ *ww.historyisfun.org*).

EXPLORING

☺ **Historic Jamestowne,** an island originally separated from the mainland Fodor'sChoice by a narrow isthmus, was the site of the first permanent English settle-
★ ment in North America (1607) and the capital of Virginia until 1699. May 13, 2007, marked the 400th anniversary of its founding. The first settlers' bitter struggle for survival here, on the now uninhabited land, makes for a visit that stirs the imagination. Redbrick foundation walls roughly outline the settlement, and artists' conceptions of the original buildings can be seen at several locations. The only standing structure is the ruin of a church tower from the 1640s, now part of the Memorial Church built in 1907; the markers within indicate the original church's foundations. Other monuments around the site also date from the tercentenary celebration in 1907. Statues portray the founder of Jamestown, Captain John Smith, and his advocate, the Native Ameri-

Williamsburg & Hampton Roads

can princess Pocahontas, whom Smith credited with saving him from being beheaded.

Near the entrance to the park, you can stop at the reconstructed Glasshouse to observe a demonstration of glassblowing, an unsuccessful business venture of the early colonists. The products of today are for sale in a gift shop. Archaeological discoveries from the site are showcased at the Archaearium. You can also observe digs on-site where archaeologists from the Association for the Preservation of Virginia Antiquities continue to dig up evidence of colonists' and Native Americans' ways of life, including the remains of the original 1607 fort.

A visitor center near the main parking lot tells the history of Jamestown and the Virginia Indians, Europeans, and African peoples who lived here. Ranger-guided tours, held daily, explore many different events in Jamestown's history. Living-history programs are presented daily in summer and on weekends in spring and autumn.

A 5-mi or 8-mi nature drive that rings the island is posted with informative signs and paintings. ⊠ *Off Colonial Pkwy.* ☎ *757/898–2410* ☞ *$8; combined entry to both Jamestowne and Yorktown, $10* ☉ *Daily 9–5; gates close at 4:30.*

Adjacent to but distinct from Historic Jamestowne is a mainland living-history museum called **Jamestown Settlement.** The site marries 40,000 square feet of indoor facilities (completed in 2006) with outdoor replicas of the early James Fort, the three ships that brought the founding colonists from England, and a Powhatan Indian village. The handsome Tudor-style Great Hall borders extensive galleries arranged by decades from 1607 to 1699, when the capital was moved to Williamsburg, and leads to a 250-seat theater where the introductory film *1607: A Nation Takes Root* is shown. Within James Fort, interpreters in costume cook, forge metal, and describe what life was like living under thatch roofs and between walls of wattle and daub (stick framework covered with mud plaster). In the Powhatan Indian Village you can enter a *yehakin* (house) and see buckskin-costumed interpreters cultivate a garden and make tools. At the pier are full-scale reproductions of the ships in which the settlers arrived: *Godspeed, Discovery,* and *Susan Constant.* The new *Godspeed,* commissioned in 2006, sails to commemorative events along the East Coast; all the vessels are seaworthy. You may climb aboard the *Susan Constant* and find out more from the sailor-interpreters. Indoor exhibits examine the lives of the Powhatans and their English-born neighbors, their interaction, and world conditions that encouraged colonization. A riverfront discovery area provides information about 17th-century water travel, commerce, and cultural exchange, reflecting Powhatan Indian, European, and African traditions. Dugout-canoe making takes place in this area. Spring and fall bring lots of school groups, so it's best to arrive after 2 PM. ⊠ *Rte. 31 off Colonial Pkwy.* ☎ *757/253–4838 or 888/593–4682* ⊕ *www.history isfun.org* ⊒ *$13.50; combination ticket with Yorktown Victory Center $19.25* ⊙ *June 15–Aug. 15, daily 9–6; Aug. 16–June 14, daily 9–5.*

COLONIAL WILLIAMSBURG

51 mi southeast of Richmond via I–64.

Williamsburg was the capital of Virginia from 1699 to 1780, after Jamestown and before Richmond. Williamsburg hasn't been politically important for a long time, but now that **Colonial Williamsburg** is there to represent it in its era of glory, it's a jewel of the commonwealth. Outside the restored area is a modern city with plenty of dining and lodging options and attractions, including outlet shops and a large water park.

Colonial Williamsburg sells a number of all-inclusive tickets that cost more than a $34 one-day pass. The Freedom Pass ($59) allows you to visit for one full year. The Independence Pass ($72), also valid for a year, includes all the benefits of the Freedom Pass as well as admission to all special events and special discounts.

GETTING HERE & AROUND

BY CAR Parking near the Colonial Williamsburg historic area can be difficult during summer months and special events. It's best to park at the visitor center and ride the shuttle to the park. The parking lot behind the

Jamestown & John Smith

You can't believe everything you read in travel brochures: "Free land lush with hardwood trees! Food and water abundant! Gold for the taking! Fast side-trip to the Orient! Friendly welcoming committee!"

The real trip: 73 passengers will die. There's no gold. Fresh water and food are difficult to obtain. There is no way to sail to the Orient across North America. The land belongs to the natives, who are usually hostile, and disease-carrying mosquitoes are omnipresent.

The men and boys who settled Jamestown in 1607 had little idea of what was in store for them. Most who sailed over were intent on finding riches and hadn't given much thought to how they would survive in Virginia. Almost immediately after landing, the colonists were under attack from the Algonquian natives, and in a little over a month the settlers built a wooden fort named for King James.

One man, Captain John Smith, a soldier and adventurer who had fought in Hungary and Transylvania, was familiar with challenges and worked toward the survival of Jamestown. "America's first hero" made contact with the native chief Powhatan, from whom the colonists obtained much of their food, and became leader of the colony. After being captured by Algonquians, he may or may not have been saved by the 11-year-old princess Pocahontas, but was returned to Jamestown.

Finding the colony languishing due to lack of supplies, a drought, laziness, and conflicts, Smith instituted a policy of rigid discipline and strengthened defenses. He encouraged farming with the admonishment: "He who does not work, will not eat." Because of his strong leadership, the settlement survived and grew during the next year. Unfortunately Smith was injured and returned to England for treatment in October 1609, never to set foot in Virginia again.

Nearly 300 years later, Jamestown was acquired by the Association for the Preservation of Virginia Antiquities (APVA) and the National Park Service. Early archaeologists concluded that James Fort lay completely under the James River. In 1994, however, in preparation for the 400th Anniversary of Jamestown, APVA initiated its own excavations to search for the original 1607 fort. They uncovered evidence that James Fort had not been washed into the river, as most had believed.

Excavation has since uncovered more than 150,000 artifacts dating to the first half of the 17th century. Nearly half date to the first years of English settlement (1607–10). These objects reflect trade between Europe and the New World, patterns of warfare, day-to-day survival, and status in the early colony. You can view a sampling of these artifacts at Historic Jamestowne, whose mission is "to preserve, protect, and promote the original site of the first permanent English settlement in North America and to tell the story of the role of the three cultures—European, North American and African—that came together to lay the foundation for a uniquely American form of democratic government, language, free enterprise, and society."

Merchants Square shopping area is a good bet if you're planning a short visit or going out to eat around the area.

All vehicular traffic is prohibited within Colonial Williamsburg to preserve the illusion. Shuttle buses run continuously from 9 AM to 10 PM to and from the visitor center.

BY BIKE Biking around Colonial Williamsburg is a wonderful way to explore its 301 acres. Rental bikes are available for those staying at the Williamsburg Inn, Williamsburg Lodge, or Colonial Houses. Bikesmith, in Williamsburg, rents bikes and has especially reasonable multiday rental prices. Bikes Unlimited, close to the Williamsburg Transportation Center, also rents bikes.

TOURS Hour-long guided walking tours of the historic area depart from the Greenhow Lumber House daily from 9 to 5. Reservations should be made on the day of the tour at the Lumber House and can be made only by those with tickets to Colonial Williamsburg. "The Original Ghosts of Williamsburg" Candlelight Tour is based on the book of the same name by L. B. Taylor Jr. The tour is offered every evening at 8 (there's also an 8:45 tour June–August). The 1¼-hour, lantern-lighted guided tour through historic Williamsburg costs $8.50. Interpreters well versed in Williamsburg and Colonial history are available to lead groups on tours of the historic area. Carriage and wagon rides are available daily, weather permitting. General ticket holders may purchase tickets on the day of the ride at the Lumber House. ■TIP➔**For walking tours, be sure to park at the visitor center, as cars are not permitted on Duke of Gloucester Street.**

Lanthorn Tours take you on an evening walking tour of trade shops where jewelry and other products are made in 18th-century style. The separate ticket required for this program may be purchased at the visitor center or from the Greenhow Lumber House.

Boat tours aboard the 135-foot three-masted topsail schooner *American Rover* cruise Hampton Roads nautical historical landmarks. The *Victory Rover* and *Spirit of Norfolk* cruise the Elizabeth River to the Norfolk Naval Station. The *Spirit* has lunch, early dinner, dinner, and moonlight cruises. The *Carrie B.*, a scaled-down reproduction of a Mississippi riverboat, makes a variety of Hampton Roads cruises, including naval station, sunset, and moonlight cruises. All boats leave the Norfolk waterfront, the *Victory Rover* from beside Nauticus, and the others from beside Waterside. In addition, the *Carrie B.* stops at the Portsmouth waterfront to load passengers.

Three self-guided audio tours of Colonial Williamsburg can be rented at the Colonial Williamsburg Visitor Center: "Highlights of the Historic Area," "Reading the Restoration Architecture," and "Voices of the Revolution." Wander at your own pace; when you stop in front of a numbered location, enter the number into the player and hear all about it. Each tape is about 45 minutes and costs $6 for ticketed guests or $15 for those without tickets.

TIMING & PRECAUTIONS

Williamsburg can be very warm in summer and even in spring and fall. Be sure to carry water and replenish your bottles at the historic area's water fountains. Wear comfortable clothing and shoes since walking is the primary way to navigate Williamsburg's 301 acres. (There are horse-drawn carriages, not included in the price of admission.)

ESSENTIALS

Bike Rentals Bikesmith (⊠ *515 York St.* ☎ *757/229–9858*). **Bikes Unlimited** (⊠ *141 Monticello Ave. in the Williamsburg shopping area.* ☎ *757/229–4620*)

Boat Tours American Rover (☎ *757/627–7245*). **Carrie B.** (☎ *757/393–4735*). **Spirit of Norfolk** (☎ *757/625–3866*). **Victory Rover** (☎ *757/627–7406*).

Walking Tours Greenhow Lumber House (⊠ *Duke of Gloucester St.* ☎ *757/ 220–7645 or 800/447–8679*). **Interpreters** (☎ *800/228–8878*). **"The Original Ghosts of Williamsburg" Candlelight Tour** (☎ *757/253–1058*).

Taxi Yellow Cab (☎ *757/722–1111*).

Train Williamsburg Transportation Center (⊠ *468 N. Boundary St.* ☎ *757/ 229–8750*).

Visitor Information Colonial Williamsburg Dining and Lodging Reservations (☎ *800/447–8679*). **Colonial Williamsburg Visitor Center** (✆ *102 Visitor Center Dr. Williamsburg 23187-1776* ☎ *800/246–2099 or 757/229–1000* ⊕ *www.history. org or* ⊕ *www.colonialwilliamsburg.org*). **Greater Williamsburg Chamber and Tourism Alliance** (⊠ *421 N. Boundary St., Box 3495 23187-3495* ☎ *757/229–6511 or 800/368–6511* ⊕ *www.williamsburgcc.com*).

Numbers in the margin correspond to points of interest on the Colonial Williamsburg map.

MAIN ATTRACTIONS

⓯ The lovely brick Episcopal **Bruton Parish Church** has served continuously as a house of worship since it was built in 1715. One of its 20th-century pastors, W. A. R. Goodwin, provided the impetus for Williamsburg's restoration. The church tower, topped by a beige wooden steeple, was added in 1769; during the Revolution its bell served as the local "liberty bell," rung to summon people for announcements. The white pews, tall and boxed in, are characteristic of the starkly graceful Colonial eccle-siastical architecture of the region. When sitting in a pew, listening to the history of the church, keep in mind that you could be sitting where Thomas Jefferson, Ben Franklin, or George Washington once listened to sermons. The stone baptismal font is believed to have come from an older Jamestown church. Many local eminences, including one royal governor, are interred in the graveyard. The fully operational church is open to the public; contributions are accepted. ⊠ *Duke of Gloucester St. west of Palace St..* ■ TIP➔ Check Williamsburg's weekly program listing for free candlelight recitals in the evening at Bruton Parish Church.

❸ The **Capitol** is the building that made this town so important. It was here that the prerevolutionary House of Burgesses (dominated by the ascendant gentry) challenged the royally appointed council (an almost medieval body made up of the bigger landowners). In 1765 the House

Colonial Williamsburg Basics

The restoration project that gave birth to Colonial Williamsburg began in 1926, inspired by a local pastor, W. A. R. Goodwin, and financed by John D. Rockefeller Jr. The work of the archaeologists and historians of the not-for-profit Colonial Williamsburg Foundation continues to this day. A total of 88 original 18th-century and early-19th-century structures have been meticulously restored, and another 500 have been reconstructed on their original sites. In all, approximately 225 period rooms have been re-created with the foundation's collection of more than 60,000 pieces of furniture, ceramics, glass, silver, pewter, textiles, tools, paintings, prints, maps, firearms, and carpets. Period authenticity also governs the landscaping of the 301 acres of gardens and public greens. The restored area is surrounded by a greenbelt controlled by the foundation, which guards against development that could mar the illusion of the Colonial city.

Despite its huge scale, Colonial Williamsburg can seem almost cozy. Nearly 1 million people come here annually, and all year hundreds of costumed interpreters, wearing bonnets or three-corner hats, rove and ride through the streets (you can even rent outfits for your children). Dozens of skilled craftspeople, also in costume, demonstrate and explain their trades inside their workshops. They include the shoemaker, the cooper (he makes barrels), the gunsmith, the blacksmith, the musical instrument maker, the silversmith, and the wig maker. Their wares are for sale nearby at the Prentis Store. Four taverns serve food and drink that approximate the fare of more than 220 years ago.

Colonial Williamsburg makes an effort to represent not just the lives of a privileged few, and not to gloss over disturbing aspects of history. Slavery, religious freedom, family life, commerce and trade, land acquisition, and the Revolution are portrayed in living-history demonstrations. In the two-hour "Revolutionary City Program" you can become an active citizen in everyday life against the backdrop of momentous, world-changing events. The vignettes that are staged throughout the day take place in the streets and in public buildings. These may include dramatic afternoon court trials or fascinating estate appraisals. Depending on the days you visit, you may see the House of Burgesses dissolve, its members charging out to make revolutionary plans at the Raleigh Tavern.

Because of the size of Colonial Williamsburg and the large crowds (especially in the warmer months), it's best to begin a tour early in the day, so it's a good idea to spend the night before in the area. The foundation suggests allowing three or four days to do Colonial Williamsburg justice, but that will depend on your own interest in the period—and that interest often increases on arrival. Museums, exhibits, and stores close at 5 PM, but walks and events take place in the evening, usually ending by 10 PM. Some sites close in winter on a rotating basis.

5

Colonial Williamsburg

KEY

Pedestrian Street

0 ___ 110 yards
0 ___ 100 meters

Abby Aldrich Rockefeller
Folk Art Museum **19**
Brush-Everard House **14**
Bruton Parish Church **15**
Capitol **3**
Courthouse **10**
DeWitt Wallace
Decorative Arts Museum . **18**

George Wythe House **12**
Governor's Palace **13**
Guardhouse **8**
James Anderson's
Blacksmith Shop **6**
Magazine **7**
Palace Green **11**

Peyton Randolph
House **9**
Public Hospital **17**
Raleigh Tavern **4**
Visitor Center **2**
Wetherburn's Tavern **5**
Wren Building **16**

Waller St.

Plantation Dr.

Blair St.

Nicholson St.

Franklin St.

Botetourt St.

Duke of Gloucester St.

Colonial St.

Queen St.

MARKET SQUARE

Colonial Parkway

North England St.

South England St.

Francis St.

Buctrout Lane

Francis Ln.

Nassau St.

Scotland St.

Duke of Gloucester St.

Prince George St.

MERCHANT'S SQUARE

N. Boundary St.

S. Boundary St.

Richmond Rd.

Jamestown Rd.

Francis St.

Henry St.

Ireland St.

eventually arrived at the resolutions, known as Henry's Resolves (after Patrick Henry), that amounted to rebellion. An informative tour explains the development, stage by stage, of American democracy from its English parliamentary roots. In the courtroom a guide recites the harsh Georgian sentences that were meted out: for instance, theft of more than 12 shillings was a capital crime. Occasional reenactments, including witch trials, dramatize the evolution of American jurisprudence.

What stands on the site today is a reproduction of the 1705 structure that burned down in 1747. Dark-wood wainscoting, pewter chandeliers, and towering ceilings contribute to a handsome impression. That an official building would have so ornate an interior was characteristic of aristocratic 18th-century Virginia. This was in telling contrast to the plain town meeting halls of Puritan New England, where other citizens were governing themselves at the same time. ■TIP➡The stirring Fifes and Drums March leaves from the Capitol to the Palace Green. Don't miss the spectacle of dozens of young men dressed in period costume marching through Williamsburg's streets. Check the program guide for dates and times. ⊠*East end of Duke of Gloucester St.*

🔞 The **DeWitt Wallace Decorative Arts Museum** adds another cultural dimension that goes well beyond Colonial history. Grouped by medium are English and American furniture, textiles, prints, metals, and ceramics of the 17th to the early 19th century. If you're yawning at the thought of fancy tableware, stop: presentations here tend to be creative and surprising. Prizes among the 8,000 pieces in the collection are a full-length portrait of George Washington by Charles Willson Peale and a royally commissioned case clock surmounted by the detailed figure of a Native American. You enter the museum through the Public Hospital. ⊠*Francis St.*

⑫ The **George Wythe House** was the residence of Thomas Jefferson's law professor; Wythe was also a signer of the Declaration of Independence. General Washington used the house as a headquarters just before his victory at Yorktown. The large brick structure, built in the mid-18th century, is conspicuously symmetrical: each side has a chimney, and each floor has two rooms on either side of a center hallway. The garden in back is similarly divided. The outbuildings, including a smokehouse, kitchen, laundry, outhouses, and a chicken coop, are reconstructions. ⊠*West side of Palace Green.*

⑬ His Majesty's Governor Alexander Spotswood built the original **Governor's Palace** in 1720, and seven British viceroys, the last of them Lord Dunmore in 1775, lived in this appropriately showy mansion. The 540 weapons, including 230 muskets and pistols, arrayed on the walls of several rooms herald the power of the Crown. Some of the furnishings are original, and the rest are matched to an extraordinary inventory of 16,000 items. Lavishly appointed as it is, the palace is furnished to the time just before the Revolution. During the Revolution, it housed the commonwealth's first two governors, Patrick Henry and Thomas Jefferson. The original residence burned down in 1781, and today's reconstruction stands on the original foundation.

A costumed guide greets you at the door for a tour through the building, offering commentary and answering questions. Notable among the furnishings are several pieces made in Williamsburg and owned by Lord Dunmore. Social events are described on the walk through the great formal ballroom, where you might even hear the sounds of an 18th-century harp, clavichord, or piano. The supper room leads to the formal garden and the planted terraces beyond. ✉*Northern end of Palace Green.*

⑨ The **Peyton Randolph House** was the home of a prominent colonist and revolutionary who served as attorney general under the British, then as Speaker of the House of Burgesses, and later as president of the first and second Continental Congresses. The oak-paneled bedroom and Randolph family silver are remarkable. ✉*Nicholson and.N. England Sts.*

④ **Raleigh Tavern** was the scene of prerevolutionary revels and rallies that were often joined by Washington, Jefferson, Patrick Henry, and other major figures. The spare but elegant blue-and-white Apollo Room is said to have been the first meeting place of Phi Beta Kappa, the scholastic honorary society founded in 1776. The French general Marquis de Lafayette was feted here in 1824. In 1859 the original structure burned, and today's building is a reconstruction based on archaeological evidence and period descriptions and sketches of the building. ✉*Duke of Gloucester St., west of Capitol.*

② The **visitor center** is the logical first stop at Colonial Williamsburg. Here you can park free; buy tickets; see a 35-minute introductory movie, *Williamsburg—the Story of a Patriot*; and pick up *This Week,* which has a list of regular events and special programs and a map of the historic area. Tickets are also sold at the Lumber House in the historic area. ✉*102 Information Center Dr., off U.S. 60* ☎*757/ 229–1000 or 800/447–8679* ⊕*www.colonialwilliamsburg.com* ✍*$34–$72* ☾*Daily 9–5.*

ALSO WORTH SEEING

⑲ The **Abby Aldrich Rockefeller Folk Art Museum,** within the DeWitt Wallace Decorative Arts Museum, showcases American "decorative usefulware"—toys, furniture, weather vanes, coffeepots, and quilts—within typical 19th-century domestic interiors. There are also folk paintings, rustic sculptures, and needlepoint pictures. Since the 1920s, the 2,000-piece collection has grown from the original 400 pieces acquired by the wife of Colonial Williamsburg's first and principal benefactor. ✉*Francis St.*

⑭ The **Brush-Everard House** was built in 1717 by John Brush, a gunsmith, and later owned by Thomas Everard, who was twice mayor of Williamsburg. The wood-frame house contains remarkable, ornate carving work but is open only for special-focus tours. Temporary exhibits and vignettes on slaves' lives are held here in summer. ✉*Scotland St. at Palace Green.*

⑩ The original **Courthouse** of 1770 was used by municipal and county courts until 1932. Civil and minor criminal matters and cases involving slaves were adjudicated here; other trials were conducted at the Capitol. The stocks once used to punish misdemeanors are outside the building: they can make for a humorous photo opportunity. The courthouse's exterior has been restored to its original appearance. Visitors often participate in scheduled reenactments of court sessions. ⊠*North side of Duke of Gloucester St., west of Queen St.*

The spine of Colonial Williamsburg's restored area is the broad 1-mi-long **Duke of Gloucester Street.** On Saturday at 1 PM from March to October, the Fifes and Drums Corps marches the length of the street and performs a stirring drill. Along this artery alone, or just off it, are two-dozen attractions. Walking west on Duke of Gloucester Street from the Capitol, you can find a dozen 18th-century shops—including those of the apothecary, the wig maker, the silversmith, and the milliner.

❽ The **Guardhouse** once served in the defense of the Magazine's lethal inventory. Special interpretive programs about the military are sched-uled here. ⊠*Duke of Gloucester St. near Queen St.*

❻ At **James Anderson's Blacksmith Shop,** smiths forge the nails, tools, and other iron hardware used in construction throughout the town. The shop itself was reconstructed by carpenters using 18th-century tools and techniques. ⊠*Between Botetourt and Colonial Sts., on south side of Duke of Gloucester St.*

❼ The original **Magazine** (1715), an octagonal brick warehouse, was used for storing arms and ammunition—at one time 60,000 pounds of gun-powder and 3,000 muskets. It was used for this purpose by the British, then by the Continental army, and again by the Confederates during the Civil War. Today 18th-century firearms are on display within the arsenal. This is the largest collection of Colonial muskets in the coun-try. Every able-bodied man in Colonial times was expected to have and maintain a musket in his home. Between the ages of 16 and 55 men were expected to be a part of the militia, the civilian army that could be called to arms in defense of hearth and home. ⊠ *West of Queen St. on south side of Duke of Gloucester St.*

In **Market Square,** an open green between Queen and Palace streets along Duke of Gloucester, cattle, seafood, dairy products, fruit, and vegetables were all sold—as were slaves. Both the market and slave auctions are sometimes reenacted.

NEED A BREAK?

At the west end of Duke of Gloucester Street, for a block on both sides, Mer-chants Square has more than 40 shops and restaurants, including an ice-cream parlor, coffee shop, cheese shop, chocolatier, movie theater, peanut shop, and gourmet food store. Services also include three banks and a drug-store. The William and Mary College bookstore is operated by Barnes and Noble and has a wealth of information on Williamsburg and Virginia history. The Kimball Theatre on Merchants Square shows movies daily and has live family entertainment on weekends. For the schedule, go to ⊕ *www.kim-balltheatre.com.*

⓫ The handsome **Palace Green** runs north from Duke of Gloucester Street up the center of Palace Street, with the Governor's Palace at the far end and notable historic houses on either side.

⓱ The **Public Hospital,** a reconstruction of a 1773 insane asylum, provides an informative, shocking look at the treatment of the mentally ill in the 18th and 19th centuries. It also serves as cover for a modern edifice that houses very different exhibitions; entrance to the DeWitt Wallace Decorative Arts Museum is through the hospital lobby. ✉*Francis St.*

On the outskirts of the historic area is **Robertson's Windmill,** a Colonial mill for grinding grains. It's currently closed to the public for repairs. ✉*N. England St.*

❺ **Wetherburn's Tavern,** which offered refreshment, entertainment, and lodging beginning in 1743, may be the most accurately furnished building in Colonial Williamsburg, with contents that conform to a room-by-room inventory taken in 1760. Excavations at this site have yielded more than 200,000 artifacts. The outbuildings include the original dairy and a reconstructed kitchen. Vegetables are still grown in the small garden. ✉*Duke of Gloucester St. across from Raleigh Tavern.*

OFF THE BEATEN PATH

Williamsburg Winery. Carrying on a Virginia tradition of wine making that began with early settlers, Virginia's largest winery produces 60,000 cases yearly. The winery offers guided tours, a well-stocked wineshop, a 17th-century tasting room, and a museum of wine-making artifacts. Be sure to give the cabernets and merlots a try. The Gabriel Archer Tavern serves a casual lunch daily and dinner Tuesday to Saturday (April–October only). In 2007 a 28-room country inn, Wedmore Place, opened on the premises. The winery is off Route 199E. To get there, turn east on Brookwood Drive and left onto Lake Powell Road. ✉*5800 Wessex Hundred* ☎*757/229–0999* ⊕*www.williamsburgwinery.com* ✎*$8, includes tasting of 5–7 wines and a souvenir glass* ⊙*Apr.–Oct., Mon.–Sat. 10:30–5, Sun. 11–5; Nov.–Mar., Mon.–Sat. 10:30–4, Sun. 11–4.*

⓰ The **Wren Building** is part of the College of William and Mary, founded in 1693 and the second-oldest college in the United States after Harvard University. The campus extends to the west; the Wren Building (1695) was based on the work of the celebrated London architect Sir Christopher Wren. Its redbrick outer walls are original, but fire gutted the interiors several times, and the current quarters are largely reconstructions of the 20th century. The faculty common room, with a table covered with green felt and an antique globe, suggests Oxford and Cambridge universities, the models for this New World institution. George Wythe became America's first law professor at the college and taught law to Thomas Jefferson, Henry Clay, James Monroe, and John Marshall. Tours, led by undergraduates, include the chapel where Colonial leader Peyton Randolph is buried. Among the portraits of college presidents on the second floor of the Wren Building is an arresting painting of former Prime Minister Margaret Thatcher, who visited William and Mary during her tenure. ⊠ *West end of Duke of Gloucester St.*

WHERE TO EAT

$$
AMERICAN
✕ **Aberdeen Barn.** Saws, pitchforks, oxen yokes, and the like hang on the barn walls, but the wood tables are lacquered, and the napkins are linen. Specialties include slow-roasted prime rib; baby-back Danish pork ribs barbecued with a sauce of peach preserves and Southern Comfort; and shrimp Dijon. An ample wine list offers a wide variety of domestic and imported choices. ⊠ *1601 Richmond Rd.* ☎ *757/229–6661* ⊕ *www. aberdeen-barn.com* ⊟ *AE, D, MC, V* ⊗ *No lunch.*

$$–$$$
SEAFOOD
✕ **Berret's Restaurant and Taphouse Grill.** One of the most reliable seafood spots around, Berret's is in Merchants Square. Upscale but casual, the restaurant lights crackling fires during colder months and opens up its pleasant outdoor patio when it's warm. Entrées and appetizers employ fresh Chesapeake Bay seafood. It's usually a sure bet to try any of the nightly specials of fresh fish, which often include perfectly prepared flounder. The she-crab soup, a house favorite, blends crabmeat, cream, and crab roe with just a hint of sherry. Virginia wines and beers are featured. ⊠ *199 Boundary St.* ☎ *757/253–1847* ⊕ *www.berrets.com* ⊟ *AE, D, MC, V* ⊗ *Closed Mon. in Jan. and Feb.; no lunch in Taphouse Grill.*

¢–$
DELI
✕ **College Delly.** It's easy to forget that this is a college town, but this cheerful dive keeps up the school spirit. The white-brick eatery with forest-green canvas awnings is dark and scruffy inside. Walls are hung with fraternity and sorority pictures, graduation snapshots, and sportsteam photos. Booths and tables are in the William and Mary colors of green and gold. Deli sandwiches, subs, specialty pizzas, pasta, stromboli, and Greek dishes are all prepared with fresh ingredients and are all delicious, and there's a wide selection of beers on tap. The Delly delivers free to nearby hotels from 6 PM to 1 AM. ⊠ *336 Richmond Rd.* ☎ *757/229–6627* ⊟ *MC, V.*

$$$
FRENCH
★
✕ **Le Yaca.** A mall of small boutiques is the unlikely location for this French-country restaurant. The dining room has soft pastel colors, hardwood floors, candlelight, and a central open fireplace. The menu is arranged in the French manner, with four prix-fixe menus and 10 entrées, including whole duck breast with peach and pepper sauce, leg of lamb with rosemary garlic sauce, bouillabaisse, and fresh scallops and shrimp with champagne sauce. Le Yaca is on U.S. 60 East, near Busch Gardens. ⊠ *Village Shops at Kingsmill, 1915 Pocahontas Trail* ☎ *757/220–3616* ⊕ *www.leyacawilliamsburg.com* ⊟ *AE, D, DC, MC, V* ⊗ *Closed Sun. No lunch Sat.*

¢
SOUTHERN
☾
✕ **Old Chickahominy House.** Reminiscent of old-fashioned Virginia tearooms, this Colonial-style restaurant has delectable goodies served in an 18th-century dining room. For breakfast there's Virginia ham and eggs, made-from-scratch biscuits, country bacon, sausage, homemade

5

pancakes, and grits. Lunch brings Brunswick stew, Virginia ham biscuits, chicken and dumplings, fruit salad, and homemade pie. There's a gift shop adjacent to the restaurant. It's a great, inexpensive, and filling place for families on a budget. ⊠ *1211 Jamestown Rd.* ☎ *757/229–4689* ⊕ *www.oldchickahominy.com* ☰ *MC, V* ⊗ *No dinner.*

$$$$ ✕ **Regency Room.** This hotel restaurant is known for its elegance, atten-
CONTINENTAL tive service, and quality cuisine. Among crystal chandeliers, Asian
★ silk-screen prints, and full silver service, you can sample chateaubriand carved tableside, as well as rack of lamb, Dover sole, lobster bisque, and house-smoked and -cured salmon. It may almost seem as if you're treated like royalty. A jacket and tie are required at dinner and optional at Sunday brunch. ⊠ *Williamsburg Inn, 136 E. Francis St.* ☎ *757/229–1000* ⚒ *Reservations essential* ✆ *Jacket required for dinner* ☰ *AE, D, DC, MC, V.*

¢–$ ✕ **Sal's Restaurant by Victor.** Locals love this family Italian restaurant and
ITALIAN pizzeria. Victor Minichiello and his staff serve up pasta, fish, chicken, and veal dinners as well as subs and pizzas. It's a good choice for families who want to please the kids: parents can get quality "adult food" while their children graze on pizza and subs. An interesting side note: Chef Victor was on the International Olympics Committee. The restaurant delivers free to nearby hotels. ⊠ *1242 Richmond Rd.* ☎ *757/220–2641* ⊕ *www.salsbyvictor.com* ☰ *AE, D, MC, V.*

$$ ✕ **The Trellis.** With vaulted ceilings and hardwood floors, the Trellis is
AMERICAN an airy and pleasant place. The imaginative lunch and dinner menus change with the seasons. A good wine list complements such dishes as homemade tomato bisque, wild boar, and soft-shell crabs. The seafood entrées are particularly good, and many patrons wouldn't leave without ordering the rich Death by Chocolate, the restaurant's signature dessert. Prices on the outdoor terrace menu are lower than in the indoor dining room. ⊠ *Merchants Sq., 403 Duke of Gloucester St.* ☎ *757/229–8610* ⊕ *www.thetrellis.com* ☰ *AE, D, DC, MC, V.*

$$ ✕ **The Whaling Company.** Fresh seafood is the drawing card at this large
SEAFOOD wooden building, which wouldn't look out of place in a New England fishing village. Despite its out-of-town look, the restaurant has an authenticity sometimes hard to find in touristy towns. Locals come in for the fresh Virginia scallops, shrimp, fish, and other seafood. Steaks and lemon herb chicken are available for the non–Whalers. The restaurant is off U.S. 60 near the Route 199 interchange. ⊠ *494 McLaws Circle* ☎ *757/229–0275* ⊕ *www.thewhalingcompany.com* ☰ *AE, DC, MC, V* ⊗ *No lunch.*

COLONIAL TAVERNS

For an authentic dining experience to match the historic setting, it's nearly a requirement to dine in one of the four reconstructed "taverns" in Colonial Williamsburg—essentially casual restaurants with beer and wine available. Colonial-style and modern American fare is served at lunch, dinner, and Sunday brunch. Although the food can be uneven (excellent one night and mediocre the next), a meal at any tavern is a good way to get into the spirit of the era.

No reservations are taken for lunch (or anytime at Chowning's Tavern), but make dinner reservations up to two or three weeks in advance. Hours also change according to season, so check by calling the reservations number (☎800/447–8679). Smoking is not permitted in any of the taverns. To see tavern menus, go to: ⊕*www.history.org/visit/diningExperience*.

> ### WORD OF MOUTH
>
> "Do not miss eating dinner (or if you only have time for lunch, then lunch) in one of the restored area restaurants, for which you must make a reservation for dinner (can do that on line or by phone) well ahead of time. I like Kings Arms or Christiana Cambell, but any are fun."   —nomorecleaning

$ ✕**Chowning's Tavern.** A reconstructed
AMERICAN   18th-century alehouse, Chowning's serves casual quick fare for lunch, including traditional pit-style BBQ, beef brisket sandwiches, and Smithfield ham and Gloucester cheese on a pretzel roll. You can eat either inside the tavern or under a grape arbor behind the tavern. After 5 PM, Chownings becomes a true Colonial tavern where Gambols (18th-century entertainment), a program presented for 25 years, operates throughout the evening. Costumed balladeers lead family sing-alongs, and costumed servers play popular games of the day. From 8 PM until closing, Chowning's caters to a moremature audience. ⊠*Duke of Gloucester St.* ⊟*AE, D, DC, MC, V.*

$$$–$$$$ ✕**Christiana Campbell's Tavern.** George Washington's favorite tavern is
AMERICAN   across the street from the Capitol. Concentrating on seafood, the menu includes sherried crab stew, panfried stuffed rainbow trout, grilled sirloin of beef, and tasty oyster fritters just the way the general liked them. The Mrs. Campbell's Waterman's Supp'r assortment comes with crab-stuffed shrimp, oyster stew, grilled salmon, seared scallops, and seasonal seafood. An evening's entertainment might include storytelling or traditional music. ⊠*Waller St.* ⊟*AE, D, DC, MC, V.*

$$$ ✕**Kings Arms.** This 18th century–style chop house is where the finest
AMERICAN   gentry dined in Colonial days, and is still the best of the historic area's four Colonial taverns. The genteel surroundings imitate those experienced by Thomas Jefferson and Patrick Henry. Don't miss favorites such as peanut soup or Game Pye, made of venison, rabbit, duck, vegetables, and bacon in a wine sauce. Roast Prime Rib of Beef, tender pork, and lamb are on offer. Weather permitting, you can eat in the garden behind the tavern. ⊠*Duke of Gloucester St.* ⊟*AE, D, DC, MC, V.*

$$ ✕**Shields Tavern.** The James Shields Tavern has returned to its roots as an
AMERICAN   18th-century coffee house, with costumed interpreters engaging guests in "events of the day." The tavern's menu of light fare—gumbo soup, salads, wrap sandwiches, and pie—is served throughout the day. After 3, a part of the restaurant is given over to serving coffee, cider, and hot chocolate. ⊠*Duke of Gloucester St.* ⊟*AE, D, DC, MC, V.*

WHERE TO STAY

$ 🏠**Colonial Houses.** A stay here seems particularly moving at night, when
★   the town's historic area is quiet and you have Williamsburg pretty much to yourself. Five of the 25 homes and three lodging taverns are 18th-century structures; the others have been rebuilt on their original

foundations. Antiques and period reproductions furnish the rooms, and the costumed staff reinforces the historical air. Modern amenities include hair dryers, irons, ironing boards, coffeemakers, and a complimentary fruit basket and bottle of wine. The Colonial Houses share the facilities of the adjacent Williamsburg Inn and the Lodge. **Pros:** you can't beat the accommodations for the total Colonial experience. **Cons:** children might rather escape the summer's heat with a dip in a motel pool. ⊠ *136 E. Francis St., Box 1776* ☎ *757/229–1000 or 800/447–8679* ⊕ *www.colonialwilliamsburg.com* ➥ *77 rooms* ⟨ *In-hotel: room service, laundry service, no smoking rooms* ⊟ *AE, D, DC, MC, V.*

$$ ⟦⟧ **The Fife and Drum Inn.** On the second floor of Merchant's Square and practically across the street from the historic district stands this family-run B&B (there's no elevator). Each room is stylishly decorated by the owner in a motif that spotlights an aspect of Williamsburg town history. Modern amenities include a hair dryer and in-room phones with voice mail. Rooms have either a shower or a combination tub-shower. Included in the rates are homemade cookies, nonalcoholic beverages, and a full hot breakfast. **Pros:** in the heart of the Williamsburg commercial district and adjacent to the historic district. **Cons:** not handicapped accessible; children under eight are not accepted. ⊠ *441 Prince George St.* ☎ *757/345–1776 or 888/838–1783* ⊕ *www.fifeanddruminn.com* ➥ *7 rooms, 2 suites* ⟨ *In-room: VCR. In-hotel: parking (no fee), no elevator* ⊟ *AE, D, MC, V* ⟦⟧ *BP.*

$$ ⟦⟧ **Kingsmill Resort and Spa.** This manicured 2,900-acre resort on the
★   James River owned by Anheuser-Busch is home to the largest golf resort in Virginia: it hosts the LPGA's Michelob ULTRA Open each May. You can play year-round on three championship courses, including the River Course, renovated in 2005. The 9-hole course is free if you stay here, and so is a shuttle bus to Busch Gardens, Water Country USA, and Colonial Williamsburg. The guest rooms have fireplaces and Colonial-style furniture. The inventive menu at the expensive Bray Bistro emphasizes seafood. **Pros:** lots of space to roam around the resort and away from the hustle and bustle of Colonial Williamsburg. **Cons:** away from the hustle and bustle of Williamsburg. ⊠ *1010 Kingsmill Rd.* ☎ *757/253–1703 or 800/832–5665* ⊕ *www.kingsmill.com* ➥ *235 rooms, 175 suites* ⟨ *In-room: dial-up. In-hotel: 6 restaurants, golf courses, tennis courts, pools, gym, spa, beachfront, concierge, laundry service* ⊟ *AE, D, DC, MC, V.*

$$–$$$ ⟦⟧ **Liberty Rose.** Century-old beeches, oaks, and poplars surround this slate-roof, white-clapboard house on a hilltop acre 1 mi from Colonial Williamsburg. The inn was constructed in the early 1920s; furnishings include European antiques and plenty of silk and damask. Most remarkable is that every room has windows on three sides. The large room on the first floor has a unique bathroom with a claw-foot tub, a red-marble shower, and antique mirrors. Breakfast is served on a sun porch. This two-story bed-and-breakfast does not have an elevator. **Pros:** the whole bed-and-breakfast experience. **Cons:** may not be appropriate for children; is not handicapped accessible. ⊠ *1022 Jamestown Rd.* ☎ *757/253–1260 or 800/545–1825* ⊕ *www.libertyrose.com*

🛏4 *rooms* ☐*In-hotel: no-smoking rooms, no elevator* ☐*AE, MC, V* ☺*BP.*

¢ 🖥**Quality Inn Lord Paget.** Tall white columns front this Colonial-style motel. Four rooms are accessed via stairs off the spacious lobby, which has Oriental carpets; others have parking at the front door, and some have canopy beds. Refrigerators and microwaves are available for a fee. The property has a 2½-acre lake and lovely gardens. Newspapers and local phone calls are free, and a full, hot breakfast is included. This is a classic mid-century motel and good value for the money. Ask for a room that has been updated—not all have. **Pros:** the availability of refrigerators and microwaves make it a good value for families. **Cons:** a basic room without the frills. ✉*901 Capitol Landing Rd.* ☎*757/229–4444 or 800/537–2438* ⊕*www.qualityinn.com* 🛏*94 rooms* ☐*In-hotel: restaurant, pool, laundry service, no-smoking rooms* ☐*AE, D, DC, MC, V* ☺*BP.*

¢ 🖥**Ramada Outlet Mall Williamsburg.** Hard-core shoppers may wish to lodge directly across the street from the 200-acre Williamsburg Pottery Factory and near the numerous other outlets in the area. The contemporary building has two stories and exterior room entrances adjacent to parking. Rooms have quilted spreads, a desk, lounge chair, hair dryer, iron, ironing board, and coffeemaker. An extensive continental breakfast is included. **Pros:** very convenient to the outlets. **Cons:** basic hotel; not very convenient to the historic sites of the area. ✉*6493 Richmond Rd., I-64 to Exit 234A Lightfoot Rd., to Rte. 60* ☎*757/565–1111* ⊕*www.ramada.com* 🛏*128 rooms* ☐*In-room: refrigerator, Wi-Fi. In-hotel: restaurant, pool, parking (no fee), no-smoking rooms, no elevator* ☐*AE, DC, MC, V* ☺*CP.*

$–$$ 🖥**War Hill Inn.** This inn was designed by a Colonial Williamsburg architect to resemble a period structure: the two-story redbrick building at the center has a wood-frame wing. Appropriate antiques and reproductions decorate the interior. The War Hill is inside a 32-acre operating cattle farm, 4 mi from the Colonial Williamsburg information center. Those in search of privacy may want one of the cottages or the first-floor suite (other rooms open onto a common hallway). **Pros:** children are welcome and may enjoy the farm experience. **Cons:** breakfast, but no restaurant; no handicapped accessibility. ✉*4560 Longhill Rd.* ☎*757/565–0248 or 800/743–0248* ⊕*www.warhillinn.com* 🛏*4 rooms, 2 cottages* ☐*In-hotel: no elevator, public Wi-Fi* ☐☐*MC, V* ☺*BP.*

¢–$ 🖥**Williamsburg Hospitality House.** Across the street from the College of William and Mary and two blocks from the historic area, this hotel is a prime site for conferences and reunions, so you won't be the only one standing under the crystal chandelier in the lobby. Guest rooms are furnished in styles ranging from 18th century to art deco; all have hair dryers, irons, ironing boards, and in-room coffeemakers. The large poolside patio is very inviting after a day exploring the Historic Triangle. **Pros:** two blocks from the historic district; handicapped accessible with elevator. **Cons:** can be busy as the site of conferences and conventions. ✉*415 Richmond Rd.* ☎*757/229–4020 or 800/932–9192* ⊕*www.williamsburghosphouse.com* 🛏*296 rooms, 11 suites* ☐*In-room: Wi-Fi. In-hotel: 2 restaurants, room service, bar, pool, concierge, executive* *floor, laundry facilities, laundry service, parking (no fee), no-smoking rooms* ⊟*AE, D, DC, MC, V* �‖*CP.*

$$$$ ⊡ **Williamsburg Inn.** This grand hotel from 1937 is owned and operated
★ by Colonial Williamsburg. Rooms are beautifully and individually furnished with reproductions and antiques in the English Regency style, and genteel service and tradition reign. Rooms come with such perks as morning coffee and afternoon tea, a daily newspaper, turndown service, and bathrobes. The Providence Wings, adjacent to the inn, are less formal; rooms are in a contemporary style with Asian accents and overlook the tennis courts, a private pond, and a wooded area. **Pros:** this is the most elegant property operated by Colonial Williamsburg. **Cons:** may be pricey for families on a budget. ⊠*136 E. Francis St., Box 1776* ☎*757/229–1000* ⊕*www.colonialwilliamsburg.com* ⟳*62 rooms, 14 suites* ⊘*In-room: VCR, Wi-Fi. In-hotel: 3 restaurants, room service, bar, golf courses, tennis court, pool, gym, spa, concierge, laundry service, no-smoking rooms* ⊟*AE, D, MC, V.*

$$$ ⊡ **Williamsburg Lodge & Conference Center.** The total renovation of this classic hotel and the addition of a conference center were completed in 2006. Charmingly appointed with furnishings inspired by the collections of the Abby Aldrich Rockefeller Folk Art Museum, every room has a hair dryer, iron, ironing board, and clock radio. Rooms with fireplaces are available. **Pros:** excellent choice for families; some rooms adjoin. **Cons:** large parties (weddings, conferences) may slow check-in or check-out process. ⊠*310 S. England St.* ☎*757/229–1000 or 800/447–8679* ⊕*www.colonialwilliamsburg.com* ⟳*323 rooms* ⊘*In-room: safe, Wi-Fi. In-hotel: room service, bars, golf courses, pool, gym, concierge, laundry service, public Internet, parking (no fee), no-smoking rooms* ⊟*AE, D, MC, V.*

$ ⊡ **Williamsburg Sampler Bed & Breakfast Inn.** Charming and hospitable, this redbrick inn near the historic district is modeled after a plantation-style house from the 1700s. Rooms have 18th- and 19th-century antiques, pewter pieces, four-poster beds, and pleasant views of the city. The suites are particularly inviting: each has a separate sitting room, French doors, and a porch overlooking gardens. There are no phones in the rooms, but local calls are free from the inn's foyer. **Pros:** a trip back in time. **Cons:** not for the luxury traveler. ⊠*922 Jamestown Rd.* ☎*757/253–0398 or 800/722–1169* ⊕*www.williamsburgsampler.com* ⟳*4 rooms, 2 suites* ⊘*In-hotel: restaurant, gym, no-smoking rooms* ⊟*AE, D, DC, MC, V* �‖*BP.*

$ ⊡ **Woodlands Hotel and Suites.** An official Colonial Williamsburg property with contemporary furnishings, this 300-room hotel is adjacent to the HUZZAH! restaurant and the visitor center complex. You can enjoy the extensive free continental breakfast indoors or on the large patio—kids and adults enjoy making their own homemade waffles. There's gated free parking so you can abandon your car and walk to the free shuttle buses. **Pros:** good choice for families; suites are available; some double rooms have futons for children. **Cons:** if you want luxurious lodgings you might want to book elsewhere. ⊠*102 Visitor Center Dr.* ☎*757/229–1000 or 800/447–8679* ⊕*www.colonialwilliamsburg.com* ⟳*204 rooms, 96 suites* ⊘*In-room: refrigerator, Ethernet. In-hotel:*

restaurant, bar, pool, laundry service, public Internet, no-smoking rooms ⊟*AE, D, DC, MC, V* ⦿|*CP.*

NIGHTLIFE & THE ARTS

Busch Gardens Williamsburg (⊠*U.S. 60* ☎*757/253–3350*) hosts popular song-and-dance shows (country, gospel, opera, German folk) in several theaters; in the largest, the 5,000-seat Royal Palace, pop stars often perform. Well-known artists on tour play at the 10,000-seat **Phi Beta Kappa Hall** (⊠ *601 Jamestown Rd. entrance to campus* ☎*757/21-2674 Box office*) at the College of William and Mary.

THEME PARKING

What they don't tell you: even as expensive as they are, tickets don't include parking at either Busch Gardens or Water Country. You must pay $10 per car to enter and park ($15 for premium parking that's closer to the entrance). To avoid having to pay for parking, stay at a motel or hotel that offers free shuttle service to the parks.

SPORTS & THE OUTDOORS

AMUSEMENT PARKS

♻ **Busch Gardens Europe,** a 100-acre amusement park that has been voted the world's most beautiful theme park for 15 years, has more than 40 rides and six beautifully landscaped "countries" with re-creations of French, German, English, Scottish, Irish, and Italian areas. In addition to roller coasters, bumper cars, and water rides, the park has eight main stage shows and a magical children's area. Costumed actors add character to the theme areas while cable-car gondolas pass overhead. ⊠*U.S. 60, 3 mi east of Williamsburg* ☎*800/343–7946* ⊠*$56.95, child $49; parking $10* ⊘*Late Mar.–mid-May, weekends 10–8; mid-May–Labor Day, weekdays 10–9, weekends 10–10; early Sept.–Oct., Fri.–Sun. 10–10; call for exact hrs.*

♻ At **Water Country USA,** the more than 30 water rides and attractions, live entertainment, shops, and restaurants have a colorful 1950s and '60s surf theme. The Meltdown is a four-person toboggan with 180-degree turns and a 76-foot drop. The Nitro Racer is a superspeed slide down a 382-foot drop into a big splash. The largest attraction is a 4,500-square-foot heated pool. ⊠*Rte. 199, 3 mi off I–64, Exit 242B* ☎*757/253–3350 or 800/343–7946* ⊠*$39.95 for anyone 10 and older, child $32.90; parking $10* ⊘*Mid-May, weekends 10–6; early–mid-June, daily 10–6; mid-June–mid-Aug., daily 10–8; mid–late Aug. daily 10–7; early Sept., daily 10–6; mid-Sept., weekends 10–6.*

JOGGING & WALKING

The historic district as well as the College of William and Mary campus make for a splendid run. The best times for an amble along the sidewalks or cobblestone streets are early in the morning and at sundown. In the district is a 3-mi loop. Some of the nicest paths to run include the main thoroughfare of Duke of Gloucester Street, and the myriad side streets such as Botetourt and Blair streets. A 30-mi path starts at the college and runs all around the Colonial area.

Williamsburg Outlet Shopping

You can find many outlet malls less than 10 minutes west of Colonial Williamsburg, in the tiny town of Lightfoot. If you're driving from Richmond to Williamsburg on I-64, take Exit 234 west to Lightfoot. When you reach U.S. 60 (Richmond Road), the outlets—both freestanding and in shopping centers—are on both sides of the road. Most outlet shops are open Monday–Saturday 10–9, Sunday 10–6. In January and February some stores close weekdays at 6.

The largest of the outlets, **Prime Outlets at Williamsburg** (⌷ *U.S. 60, Lightfoot* ☎ *757/565–0702*) has more than 85 stores. Liz Claiborne, L. L. Bean, Waterford-Wedgwood, Eddie Bauer, Coach, Tommy Hilfiger, Brooks Bros., Nike, Guess, Nautica, and Cole Haan are all here.

The **Williamsburg Pottery Factory** (⌷ *U.S. 60 W, Lightfoot* ☎ *757/564–3326*) is an attraction in itself, and the parking area is usually crammed with tour buses. Covering 200 acres, the enormous store sells luggage, clothing, furniture, food and wine, china, crystal, and—its original commodity—pottery. Individual stores such as Pfaltzgraff are within the compound.

The **Williamsburg Outlet Mall** (⌷ *U.S. 60 W, Lightfoot* ☎ *757/565-3378*) has more than 60 shops, including Pendleton, Lee, Healthtex, Avon, and Lee/Wrangler.

Patriot Plaza (⌷ *3032 Richmond Rd., Lightfoot* ☎ *757/258-0767*) has Lenox, Villeroy & Boch, Orvis, Lenox, and other factory outlets.

SHOPPING

Merchants Square, on the west end of Duke of Gloucester Street, has both licensed Willliamsburg shops and non-Colonial, upscale shops that include Laura Ashley, the Porcelain Collector of Williamsburg, and the J. Fenton Gallery. There's also Quilts Unlimited and the Campus Shop, which carries William and Mary gifts and clothing.

Three Colonial Williamsburg stores have individual offerings. **Williamsburg at Home** (☎ *757/220–7749*) features the full line of Willliamsburg furniture, bedding, rugs, fixtures, and wallpapers. **Williamsburg Celebrations** (☎ *757/565–8642*) displays seasonal decorations and accessories. The **Williamsburg Craft House** (☎ *757/220–7747*) sells a full line of Willliamsburg dinnerware, flatware, glassware, pewter, giftware, and jewelry.

YORKTOWN

14 mi northeast of Colonial Williamsburg via Colonial Pkwy.

It was at Yorktown that the combined American and French forces surrounded Lord Cornwallis's British troops in 1781; this was the end to the Revolutionary War and the beginning of our nation. In Yorktown today, as at Jamestown, two major attractions complement each other. Yorktown Battlefield, the historical site, is operated by the National Park Service; and Yorktown Victory Center, which has re-creations and informative exhibits, is operated by the state's Jamestown–Yorktown

Foundation. As well, a stately Watermen's Museum educates visitors about those who earn their living from the nearby waters.

GETTING HERE & AROUND

From mid-March through the end of October, the County operates the Yorktown Trolley, providing free service between the Yorktown Battlefield Visitor Center and the Yorktown Victory Center, as well as seven stops between in the historic village. The trolley runs approximately every half hour.

ESSENTIALS

Visitor Information Colonial National Historical Park (Box 210, Yorktown 23690 757/898–3400 www.apva.org). **York County Tourism** (757-890-3300 www.yorkcounty.gov/tourism).

COLONIAL PARKWAY

For a beautiful drive along countryside that's nearly the same as land the Jamestown settlers trod, take the 23-mi scenic Colonial Parkway between Jamestown and Yorktown, a 40-minute drive one-way. The road between Yorktown and Williamsburg, which was aligned along the York River, was completed in 1937, but it wasn't until 1955, for the 350th anniversary of Jamestown, that the road was completed to America's first permanent English settlement. The limited-access highway has broad sweeping curves, is meticulously landscaped, and is devoid of commercial development.

EXPLORING

Riverwalk Landing is a group of specialty shops, an upscale restaurant, and an outdoor performance venue on the shores of the York River. Two piers for medium-size cruise ships and personal watercraft are also along the waterfront. Yet Yorktown remains a small community of year-round residents. Route 238 leads into town, where along Main Street are preserved 18th-century buildings on a bluff overlooking the York River.

Settled in 1691, Yorktown had become a thriving tobacco port and a prosperous community of several hundred houses by the time of the Revolution. Nine buildings from that time still stand, some of them open to visitors. **Moore House,** where the terms of surrender were negotiated, and the elegant **Nelson House,** the residence of a Virginia governor (and a signer of the Declaration of Independence), are open for tours in summer and are included in the Yorktown Victory Center's entrance fee.

The **Swan Tavern,** a reconstruction of a 1722 structure, houses an antiques shop. **Grace Church,** built in 1697 and damaged in the War of 1812 and the Civil War, was rebuilt and has an active Episcopal congregation; its walls are made of native marl (a mixture of clay, sand, and limestone containing fragments of seashells). On Main Street, the **Somerwell House,** built before 1707, and the **Sessions House** (before 1699) are privately owned and closed to the public: they're the oldest houses in town. The latter was used as the Union's local headquarters during General George McClellan's Peninsula Campaign of the Civil War.

The **Watermen's Museum** is sited in a Colonial Revival manor house on Yorktown's waterfront that was floated across the York River on a barge in 1987. In it you can learn more about the generations of men who have wrested a living from the Chesapeake Bay and nearby waters. The five galleries house ship models, dioramas, and artifacts themed on Chesapeake watermen, bay boats, harvesting fish, aquaculture, tools, and treasures. Outdoor exhibits include an original three-log canoe, dredges, engines, and other equipment used by working watermen past and present. ⊠*309 Water St.* ☎*757/887–2641* ⊕*www.watermens.org* ⊑*$4* ⊙*Apr.–Thanksgiving, Tues.–Sat. 10–5, Sun. 1–5; Thanksgiving–Mar., Sat. 10–5, Sun. 1–5.*

Ⓒ   **Yorktown Battlefield** preserves the land where the British surrendered to
FodorśChoice   American and French forces in 1781. The museum in the visitor cen-
★   ter has on exhibit part of General George Washington's original field tent. Dioramas, illuminated maps, and a film about the battle make the sobering point that Washington's victory was hardly inevitable. A look around from the roof's observation deck can help you visualize the events of the campaign. Guided by an audio tour purchased from the gift shop, you may explore the battlefield by car, stopping at the site of Washington's headquarters, a couple of crucial redoubts (breastworks dug into the ground), the field where surrender took place, and the Moore House, where the surrender terms were negotiated. ⊠*Rte. 238 off Colonial Pkwy.* ☎*757/898–2410* ⊑*$5; combined entry fee to both Jamestowne and Yorktown, $10* ⊙*Visitor center daily 9–5.*

Ⓒ   On the western edge of Yorktown Battlefield, the **Yorktown Victory Center**
FodorśChoice   has wonderful exhibits and demonstrations that bring to life the Ameri-
★   can Revolution. Textual and graphic displays along the open-air Road to Revolution walkway cover the principal events and personalities. A renovated *Declaration of Independence* entrance gallery and long-term exhibition, *The Legacy of Yorktown: Virginia Beckons,* debuted in 2006. Life-size tableaux show 10 "witnesses," including an African-American patriot, a loyalist, a Native American leader, two Continental Army soldiers, and the wife of a Virginia plantation owner. ■TIP➔**The "witnesses" testimony is very dramatic and makes the American Revolution real for children. This presentation brings the personal trials of the colonists to life more effectively than the artifacts of the war.**

The exhibit galleries contain more than 500 period artifacts, including many recovered during underwater excavations of "Yorktown's Sunken Fleet" (British ships lost during the siege of 1781). Outdoors, visitors may participate in a Continental Army drill at an encampment with interpreters costumed as soldiers and female auxiliaries, who reenact and discuss daily camp life. In another outdoor area, a re-created 1780s farm includes a dwelling, kitchen, tobacco barn, crop fields, and kitchen garden, which show how many Americans lived in the decade following the end of the Revolution. ⊠*Rte. 238 off Colonial Pkwy.* ☎*757/253–4838 or 888/593–4682* ⊕*www.historyisfun.org* ⊑*$9.25; combination ticket for Yorktown Victory Center and Jamestown Settlement $19.95* ⊙*June 15–Aug. 15, daily 9–6; Aug. 16–June 14, daily 9–5.*

WHERE TO STAY & EAT

$$ ✕**Nick's Riverwalk Restaurant.** Whether you dine indoors or out, enjoy
SEAFOOD the view of the York River, the Coleman Bridge, and Gloucester on the
opposite shore. Nick's Riverwalk offers casual meals of soups, salads,
and sandwiches at the Rivah Café and outdoor courtyard; the River-
walk Dining Room is more formal, with a menu featuring baked crab-
meat imperial, sautéed fillets, and local oysters. Right outside of the
café are a boardwalk and a sandy beach. Parking is available across the
street. There are many shops just outside the Riverwalk's door. ⊠*323
Water St.* ☎*757/875–1522* ▭*MC, V.*

¢ ▣**Duke of York Motel.** All rooms in this classic 1960s motel face the
water and are only a few steps from a sandy public beach on the York
River. The furnishings include quilted bedspreads and Queen Anne–
style reproduction wood furniture. The motel also has a swimming
pool and a restaurant that serves breakfast and lunch daily and dinner
Wednesday–Sunday. It is an easy walk to the riverfront and its shops
and restaurants. The free Yorktown Trolley stops right outside the hotel.
Pros: some rooms have kitchenettes; modestly priced. **Cons:** the decor
is half a century old. ⊠*508 Water St.* ☎*757/898–3232* ⊕*www.duke
ofyorkmotel.com* ↩*57 rooms* ♿*In-room: Ethernet, dial-up. In-hotel:
restaurant, pool, beachfront, no elevator* ▭*AE, D, DC, MC, V.*

CHARLES CITY COUNTY

35 mi northwest of Colonial Williamsburg via Rte. 5.

Colonists founded Charles City County in 1616. This tiny county is
unique, being the only U.S. county to have a native president (William
Harrison) and his vice president and successor (John Tyler) take office
simultaneously, in 1841. Today you can get a taste of those early days
by following Route 5 on its scenic way, parallel to the James River, past
nine plantations—some of which are now bed-and-breakfasts.

GETTING HERE & AROUND

The only effective way to get around largely rural Charles City County
is by car. The Charles City Web site has an excellent interactive map
"Find It in Charles City County," which shows attractions, restaurants,
antiques shops, and automobile services.

TIMING & PRECAUTIONS

Make sure your gas tank is full, and you may want to pack a picnic
lunch. Service stations and restaurants are few.

ESSENTIALS

Charles City County (☎*804/652–4701* ⊕*www.charlescity.org*).

EXPLORING

★ Virginians say that the first Thanksgiving was celebrated at **Berkeley** in
December 1619, not in Massachusetts in 1621. This plantation was
the birthplace of Benjamin Harrison, a signer of the Declaration of
Independence, and of William Henry Harrison, who became president
in 1841. Throughout the Civil War, the Union general George McClel-
lan used Berkeley as headquarters; during his tenure, his subordinate

general Daniel Butterfield composed the melody for "Taps" while here in 1862 with 140,000 Union troops. An architectural gem, the original 1726 brick Georgian mansion has been carefully restored and furnished with 18th-century antiques. The gardens are in excellent condition, particularly the boxwood hedges. ⊠*Rte. 5, 12602 Harrison Landing Rd., Charles City* ☎*804/829–6018 or 888/466–6018* ⊕*www.berkeley plantation.com* 🎟*$10* ⊙*Daily 9–5; last tour 4:30.*

Sherwood Forest Plantation (1720), at 300 feet said to be the longest wood-frame house in the United States, was the retirement home of John Tyler (1790–1862), 10th president of the United States. Tyler, who came into office in 1841 when William Henry Harrison died a month after inauguration, was a Whig who dissented from his party's abolitionist line in favor of the pro-slavery position of the Democrats. He died in 1862, having served briefly in the congress of the Confederate States of America. His house remains in the Tyler family and is furnished with heirloom antiques; it's surrounded by a dozen acres of grounds and the five outbuildings, including a tobacco barn. The house is only open to groups that have made a reservation in advance, but the grounds are open to the public. ⊠*Rte. 5, 14501 John Tyler Memorial Hwy., Charles City* ☎*804/829–5377* ⊕*www.sherwoodforest.org* 🎟*Grounds $5, house open to tours of 10 or more with advanced reservation, $10 per person.* ⊙*Grounds daily 9–5.*

★ **Shirley,** chartered in 1613 and the oldest plantation in Virginia, has been occupied by a single family, the Carters, for 11 generations. Their claim to the land goes back to 1638, when it was settled by a relative, Edward Hill. Robert E. Lee's mother was born here, and the Carters seem to be related to every notable Virginia family from the Colonial and antebellum periods. The approach to the elegant 1723 Georgian manor is dramatic: the house stands at the end of a drive lined by towering Lombardy poplars. Inside, the "Flying Staircase" rises for three stories with no visible support. Family silver is on display, ancestral portraits are hung throughout, and rare books line the shelves. The family lives on the upper floors, but the main floor, eight original Colonial outbuildings, and gardens of the working farm can be toured. A tour of the Shirley Plantation details stories from the 11 generations of the same family who to this day continue to own and operate it. The guided tour of the first floor of the Great House highlights family stories as well as original furnishings, portraits, silver, and woodwork. Today Shirley continues to be a working plantation, a private family home, and a National Historic Landmark. ⊠*501 Shirley Plantation Rd., Charles City* ☎*804/829–5121* ⊕*www.shirleyplantation.com* 🎟*$11* ⊙*Daily 9–5; last tour 4:45.*

Westover was built circa 1720 by Colonel William Byrd II (1674–1744), an American aristocrat and founder of the city of Richmond who spent much of his time and money in London. He was in Virginia frequently enough to serve in both the upper and lower houses of the Colonial legislature at Williamsburg and to write one of the first travel books about the region (as well as a notorious secret diary, a frank account of plantation life and Colonial politics). Byrd lived here with his beloved library of 4,000 volumes. The house, celebrated for its moldings, carvings, and classic proportions is open only during Garden Week in late April. However, it is worth the short drive off Route 5 to walk on the grounds beside the peaceful James River and smell the boxwoods. The grounds are arrayed with tulip poplars at least 100 years old, and other flowers are well tended. Three wrought-iron gates, imported from England by the colonel, are mounted on posts topped by figures of eagles with spread wings. Byrd's grave is here, inscribed with the eloquent, immodest, lengthy, and apt epitaph he composed for himself. ⊠ *Rte. 5, 7000 Westover Rd., Charles City* ☎ *804/829–2882* ⚑ *$2* ☉ *Grounds daily 9–6, house daily in late Apr.; call for hrs.*

WHERE TO STAY & EAT

$$ ✕ **Indian Fields Tavern.** Because this restaurant is the best of only a few
AMERICAN places to dine in the area, you may encounter a wait to be seated and served—especially at lunch, when visitors touring the nearby plantations descend. Dinner reservations are recommended, especially on weekends. Housed in a restored farmhouse, the tavern specializes in Southern dishes, especially regional specialties such as crab cakes and bread pudding. Other main dishes include pan-roasted oysters and tavern meat loaf. In season you can eat on the screened porch overlooking gardens. There's brunch on Sunday. ⊠ *9220 John Tyler Memorial Hwy. Charles City* ☎ *804/829–5004* ⊟ *AE, D, MC, V.*

$ 🏠 **North Bend Plantation Bed & Breakfast.** The road to this historic home winds past trailer homes and cottages before a gravel road turns to the left between farm fields. As a working farm, it stands out from similar B&Bs. The 1819 Greek Revival home was built for Sarah Harrison, sister of President William Henry Harrison, by her husband John Minge. Inside, antebellum-era antiques original to the house, as well as Civil War maps and artifacts decorate every room. Room amenities include robes and TVs. The Southern breakfast here might include buttermilk biscuits, Smithfield ham, apple butter, bacon and sausage, and strong coffee. **Pros:** set on 850 acres with nature trails, this B&B offers generously sized rooms and peaceful surroundings; golf carts are available to tour the property. **Cons:** may be too quiet for some. ⊠ *12200 Weyanoke Rd., Charles City* ☎ *804/829–5176* ⊕ *northbendplantation.com* ⊷ *4 rooms, 1 suite* ♿ *In-room: no phone, Wi-Fi, VCR. In-hotel: pool, bicycles, no elevator* ⊟ *MC, V* ⦿ *BP.*

HOPEWELL

56 mi northwest of Colonial Williamsburg via Rte. 5 and 24 mi southeast of Richmond off I–295.

City Point, the oldest part of Hopewell, was established in 1613 by Sir Thomas Dale. Across from Charles City County via the Route 106 Benjamin Harrison Bridge, Hopewell is worth a half-day exploration for its 19th-century buildings, nearby plantations, and 44 Sears Roebuck & Co. Catalog houses built from 1926 to 1937.

Stop by the Hopewell Visitor Center for maps to the Sears Catalog Homes in the Crescent Hills subdivision near downtown. The visitor center is just off I–295 at Exit 9A, and is open daily 9–5.

ESSENTIALS

Visitor Information **Hopewell Visitor Center** (⊠ *4100 Oaklawn Blvd. (Rte. 36)* ☎ *800/863–8687 or 804/541–2461*) is open 9–5 daily.

EXPLORING

The history of **City Point** includes a Revolutionary War skirmish and 10 months as General Ulysses S. Grant's Union headquarters during the Civil War, from which he directed the Siege of Petersburg. It's free to take the open-air, self-guided museum walking tour of 25 wayside exhibits and Grant's Headquarters. The City Point Early History Museum is in a former U.S. Navy church, St. Dennis Chapel. ⊠ *Appamattox St. at Cedar La.* ☎ *804/541–2461 or 800/863–8687* 🎫 *Museum $3, Weston Manor $5, combination ticket for Weston Manor and museum $7* ⊙ *Daily 9–5; closed selected federal holidays.*

Weston Manor, built in 1789 by the Gilliam family, is a classic example of Virginia Georgian architecture, a formal five-bay manor with hipped roof. The family immigrated to Virginia in the 1600s as indentured servants, eventually acquiring several area plantations. Family members were descendants of Pocahontas, and a cousin married Thomas Jefferson's daughter Maria. The distinctive interior moldings, wainscoting, and chair rails are 85% original. ⊠ *Weston La. at 21st St.* ☎ *804/458–4682* 🎫 *$8* ⊙ *Apr.–Oct., Mon.–Sat. 10–4:30, Sun. 1–4:30; Nov.–Mar., by appointment.*

WHERE TO EAT

$$　✕ **Dockside.** Broiled fresh seafood of a dozen kinds is the specialty at
SEAFOOD　this casual waterfront restaurant only a quick bridge-crossing from the James River Plantations. You could start with spiced shrimp on rice, and if you're really hungry, order the seafood platter. Other menu items include she-crab soup, Greek salads, and Italian main dishes. One of the few dining choices in the area, the Dockside is set on Big Bay Creek and overlooks salt marshes. ⊠ *700 Jordan Point Rd.* ☎ *804/541–2600* ▤ *AE, MC, V.*

HAMPTON ROADS AREA

The region known today as the Hampton Roads Area is made up of not only the large natural harbor, into which five rivers flow, but of the peninsula to the north that extends southeast from Williamsburg, and the Tidewater area between the mouth of the harbor and the Atlantic Ocean. On the peninsula are the cities of Newport News and Hampton; to the south and east are Norfolk, Portsmouth, Chesapeake, and Virginia Beach. These cities have been shaped by their proximity to the Chesapeake Bay and the rivers that empty into it, either as ports and shipbuilding centers or, in the case of Virginia Beach, as a hugely popular beach town. Hampton and Norfolk are the "old" cities of this area; recent development and revival efforts have made them worthy of a second look.

During the Civil War the Union waged its thwarted 1862 Peninsula Campaign here. General George McClellan planned to land his troops on the peninsula in March of 1862 with the help of the navy, and then press westward to the Confederate capital of Richmond. Naval forces on the York and James rivers would protect the advancing army. However, beginning with the blockade that the ironclad CSS *Virginia* (formerly the USS *Merrimack*) held on the James until May, events and Confederates conspired to lengthen and foil the campaign.

Numbers in the margin correspond to points of interest on the Hampton Roads Area map.

NEWPORT NEWS

23 mi southeast of Williamsburg.

Newport News stretches for almost 35 mi along the James River from near Williamsburg to Hampton Roads. Known mostly for its coal shipping and huge shipbuilding industry, the city is largely residential and is a suburb for both Williamsburg and the Norfolk area. Newport

News has a number of Civil War battle sites and a splendid municipal park. The fabulous Mariners' Museum may be the best museum in the state. Close by, the Virginia Living Museum is a pleasant zoo experience for kids.

Newport News first appeared in the Virginia Company's records in 1619. It was probably named after Christopher Newport, captain of the *Susan Constant,* largest of the three ships in the company of Captain John Smith that landed at Jamestown in 1607. Newport News Shipbuilding is one of the largest privately owned shipyards in the world, and with approximately 18,000 employees, probably the second-largest employer in Virginia. It's the only shipyard in the country capable of building nuclear-powered aircraft carriers.

GETTING HERE & AROUND
The city's small, but busy, airport is convenient to both Williamsburg and the beach, making it a good base from which to visit both areas.

ESSENTIALS
Train Newport News Amtrak Station (⊠ *9304 Warwick Blvd.* ☎ *757/ 245-3589).*

Visitor Information Newport News Tourism and Conference Bureau (⊠ *2400 Washington Ave.* ☎ *757/928-6843 or 888/493-7386* ⊕ *www.newport-news.org).* **Newport News Visitor Information Center** (⊠ *13560 Jefferson Ave., 1-64, Exit 250B* ☎ *757/886-7777 or 888/493-7386).*

EXPLORING
Built in 1769 by William Harwood, the Georgian-style house known as **Endview Plantation** has witnessed momentous events in American history. Situated atop a knoll near a spring, Endview's land was traversed by Native Americans of the Powhatan Chiefdom a thousand years before the coming of the English. At the outbreak of the Civil War, Endview's owner, Dr. Humphrey Harwood Curtis, formed the Warwick Beauregards, which became Company H, 32nd Virginia Volunteer Infantry. During the subsequent Peninsula Campaign of 1862, Endview served as headquarters for Confederate generals Lafayette McLaws and Robert Toombs. Maintained today as a living-history museum, Endview offers a wide variety of programs; guided tours begin every 30 minutes. ⊠ *362 Yorktown Rd., Exit 247 off I-64* ☎ *757/887-1862* ⊕ *www.endview. org* ⊠ *$6* ⊙ *Jan.–Mar., Mon. and Thurs.–Sat. 10–4, Sun. 1–5; Apr.– Dec., Mon. and Wed.–Sat. 10–4, Sun. 1–5.*

Lee Hall, an Italianate mansion constructed around 1859, was once home to one of Warwick County's leading landowners, Richard Decauter Lee, who achieved prominence using the method of scientific farming. It is the only large mid-19th-century plantation house remaining on Virginia's lower peninsula, and it served as the headquarters for Confederate generals John Bankhead Magruder and Joseph E. Johnston during the spring of 1862. Lee Hall now provides an in-depth review of the 1862 Peninsula Campaign. ⊠ *163 Yorktown Rd., Exit 247 off I-64* ☎ *757/888-3371* ⊕ *www.leehall.org* ⊠ *$6* ⊙ *Jan.–Mar., Mon. and Thurs.–Sat. 10–4, Sun. 1–5; Apr.–Dec., Mon. and Wed.–Sat. 10–4, Sun. 1–5.*

Ⓒ A world history of seagoing vessels and the people who sailed them
Fodor'sChoice occupies the outstanding **Mariners' Museum**, inside a 550-acre park. An
★ alliance between the museum and the South Street Seaport Museum in
New York City allows the two institutions to share collections, exhibitions, and educational programs. Among the more than 50 full-size
craft on display are a Native American bark canoe, a sailing yacht, a
speedboat, a gondola, a Coast Guard cutter, and a Chinese sampan.
In separate galleries you can often watch the progress of a boat under
construction; view ornate and sometimes huge figureheads; examine
the watermen's culture of the Chesapeake Bay; and learn about the history of the U.S. Navy. The museum also holds artifacts from the RMS
Titanic and remains of the ironclad USS *Monitor,* which served in the
1862 Peninsula Campaign and was recovered from the coast of North
Carolina. A 63,500-square-foot addition, the USS *Monitor* Center,
houses the ironclad ship and Civil War exhibits. ✉ *100 Museum Dr.,
I–64, Exit 258A* ☎ *757/595–0368 or 800/581–7245* ⊕ *www.mariner.
org* 🎟 *$12.50* ☉ *Daily 10–5, Sun. noon–5.*

Ⓒ The **U.S. Army Transportation Museum,** at Fort Eustis, traces the history
of army transportation by land, sea, and air, beginning with the Revolutionary War era. More than 90 vehicles, including experimental craft
and numerous locomotives and trains dating to the 1800s, are on display. The museum's Korean War and World War II–era trucks can be
toured inside and out. Be prepared to show a driver's license or other
identification at the military checkpoint at the base entrance. ✉ *Besson
Hall Bldg. 300, Washington Blvd., I–64, Exit 250A* ☎ *757/878–1115*
🎟 *Free* ☉ *Tues.–Sun. 9–4:30.*

Ⓒ At the **Virginia Living Museum,** visitors are transported to a steamy cypress
swamp and cool mountain cove, the underwater world of the Chesapeake Bay and the underground realm of a limestone cave, all with living exhibits and hands-on activities. View the sun from the observatory.
The planetarium theater was renovated in 2008. Outdoors, a 0.75–mi
boardwalk features animals native to Virginia in naturalized habitats
and wildflower gardens. ✉ *524 J. Clyde Morris Blvd.* ☎ *757/595–1900*
⊕ *www.thevlm.org* 🎟 *$15* ☉ *Memorial Day–Labor Day, daily 9–6;
Labor Day–Memorial Day, Mon.–Sat. 9–5, Sun. noon–5.*

The **Virginia War Museum** houses more than 60,000 artifacts from all
over the world. The collection includes a graffiti-covered section of the
Berlin Wall, a Civil War blockade runner's uniform, weapons, uniforms,
wartime posters, photographs, and other memorabilia. It traces military
history from 1775 to the Gulf War and includes an outdoor exhibition
of seven tanks and cannons, and the history of African-Americans and
women in the military. Several war memorials are on the grounds of
Huntington Park. ✉ *9285 Warwick Blvd., Rte. 60* ☎ *757/247–8523*
⊕ *www.warmuseum.org* 🎟 *$6* ☉ *Mon.–Sat. 9–5, Sun. 1–5.*

WHERE TO EAT

¢–$ ✕ **Bill's Seafood House.** This reasonably priced seafood restaurant is
SEAFOOD a favorite with locals. The interior is simple—café curtains, tubular
chairs, wood-grain Formica tables, and nautical paintings. The decor is

meant to mimic sea shacks that dot the area—although it's not close to water. Seafood platters (broiled or fried) and other seafood dishes arrive with hush puppies and a choice of two sides. For the landlubber, rib-eye steaks, chicken strips, and homemade pork barbecue are on the menu. No alcohol is served, but if you get iced tea it will be the "sweet tea" served in the South. ⊠ *10900 Warwick Blvd., U.S. 60* ☎ *757/595–4320* ⊟ *MC, V* ⊗ *Closed Sun.*

¢–$ ✕**El Mariachi.** This very reasonably priced cantina and restaurant has a
MEXICAN   wide variety of lunch and dinner specials and combinations. Mexican food and *cerveza* on tap are the specialties. The building resembles a former chain takeout, but the interior is festive with Mexican-print vinyl tablecloths, cut-paper doilies hanging overhead, and two overhead plasma TVs. Margaritas are another house favorite, and the restaurant also has vegetarian offerings. ⊠ *660 J. Clyde Morris Blvd.* ☎ *757/596–4933* ⊟ *D, MC, V.*

WHERE TO STAY

$ ▦**Hilton Garden Inn Newport News.** Built in 2004, this light and airy motel is within walking distance of a mall, restaurants, and movie theaters. Room amenities include free high-speed Internet access, a large work desk, irons, ironing boards, fridge, microwave, and coffeemakers. Children will enjoy the heated swimming pool and spa. **Pros:** restaurant in hotel; newer property. **Cons:** keyed to the business traveler with its business center and conference facilities. ⊠ *180 Regal Way, Exit 256B (Victory Blvd.)* ☎ *757/947–1080* ⊕ *http://hiltongardeninn. hilton.com* ⤶ *122 rooms* ⟋ *In-room: refrigerator, Wi-Fi. In-hotel: restaurant, pool, gym, spa, laundry service, no-smoking room, executive floor* ⊟ *AE, D, DC, MC, V.*

$ ▦**Omni Newport News Hotel.** The burgundy, green, and gold color scheme
★   of the lobby carries over to the guest rooms, which look out on the indoor pool below. Rooms have mahogany furnishings, granite vanities, desks, and sofas. Mitty's Ristorante and Piano Lounge serves regional Italian cuisine and local seafood, with exceptional homemade pasta and veal dishes. Specialties include ziti with broccoli and shrimp Capri (shrimp paired with spinach and fresh Italian herbs). On Friday and Saturday there is a nightclub, Tribeca, with bands and a DJ. On Thursday from 5:30 until 7 there is a manager's reception offering $1 beers and house wines. To reach the hotel, take Exit 258A off I–64 and make the first right. **Pros:** many in-house amenities; convenient to highway. **Cons:** the Omni is half a mile from the center city and there is no shuttle. ⊠ *1000 Omni Blvd.* ☎ *757/873–6664 or 800/873–6664* ⊕ *www. omnihotels.com* ⤶ *183 rooms, 4 suites* ⟋ *In-room: Ethernet, dial-up. In-hotel: restaurant, bar, pool, gym, laundry facilities, no-smoking rooms* ⊟ *AE, D, DC, MC, V.*

¢–$ ▦**Point Plaza.** This former Ramada has everything you could want in a hotel: reasonable rates and a location convenient to all the museums, plantation houses, and business centers of Newport News, plus Fort Lee, NASA Langley, Colonial Williamsburg, Yorktown, and Busch Gardens. The rooms, decorated in paisley prints and mahogany furnishings, are loaded with every necessity and convenience, like refrigerators and microwaves. They'll even loan you a wireless card for your computer.

Don't overlook the free shuttle for Newport News Williamsburg Airport, the Amtrak station, and Greyhound stop. **Pros:** barbecue pavilion and complementary use of hotel's gas grill; reliable budget option. **Cons:** basic hotel with basic decor. ⊠*950 J. Clyde Morris Blvd., Exit 258 off I–64* ☎*757/599–4460 or 800/841–1112* ⊕*www.pointplaza suites.com* ⇖*78 rooms, 71 suites* ⚿*In-room: safe, refrigerator, DVD, Wi-Fi. In-hotel: restaurant, room service, bar, pool, gym, concierge, laundry facilities, laundry service, airport shuttle, no-smoking rooms* ⊟*AE, D, DC, MC, V.*

HAMPTON

5 mi north of Newport News, 16 mi northwest of Norfolk.

Founded in 1610, Hampton is the oldest continuously existing English-speaking settlement in the United States. It also holds the country's first aviation research facility, NASA Langley Research Center. The center was headquarters for the first manned space program in the United States: astronauts for the *Mercury* and *Apollo* missions trained here.

Hampton was one of Virginia's major Colonial cities. In 1718 the pirate William Teach (better known as Blackbeard) was killed by Virginia sailors in a battle off North Carolina. As a warning to other pirates, the sailors brought his head back and mounted it on a pole at the entrance to the Hampton River (now Blackbeard Point, a residential area).

The city has been partially destroyed three times: by the British during the Revolution and again during the War of 1812, then by Confederates preempting Union invaders during the Civil War. Since the mid-1990s, Hampton has been undergoing a face-lift. It hosts many summer concerts and family festivals.

GETTING HERE & AROUND

Hampton Roads is served by the airports of both Newport News and Norfolk. Both the Virginia Railway Express and Amtrak stop there.

ESSENTIALS

Visitor Information Hampton Convention and Visitors Bureau (⊠*120 Old Hampton La.* ☎*757/727–1102 or 800/800–2202* ⊕*www.visithampton.com/*).

EXPLORING

☾ The **Cousteau Society** operates a compact gallery displaying underwater photos, models of the research vessels *Calypso* and *Alcyone,* and diving equipment from the past and present. Artifacts from famed explorer-environmentalist Jacques-Yves Cousteau's expeditions are displayed, such as a pair of minisubs, one fully equipped and one reduced to its pressure sphere; a recompression chamber from the 1950s; and a clear plastic shark cage, along with the diver's journal describing his eye-to-eye experiences. Cousteau films from various expeditions run continuously. Free parking is available at the parking garage next door. ⊠*710 Settlers Landing Rd.* ☎*757/722–9300* ⊕*www.costeau.org* 🎟*Free* ☉*Nov.–Apr. 14, Wed.–Sat. 10–4, Sun. noon–3; Apr. 15–May 29 and Sept. 5–Oct. 31, Tues.–Sat. 10–4, Sun. noon–3; May 30–Sept. 4, daily 9:30–4.*

The **Hampton History Museum** opened in 2003 with 10 galleries of permanent and changing exhibits on Native Americans and the early colonists, the city's port, the infamous Blackbeard, contraband and the Civil War, and the development of NASA Langley Research Center. ⊠*120 Old Hampton La.* ☎*757/727–1610* ⊕*www.hampton.va.us/ history_museum* ⊡*$5* ☉*Mon.–Sat. 10–5, Sun. 1–5.*

Hampton University was founded in 1868 as a freedmen's school, and ever since has had a distinguished history as an institution of higher education for African-Americans. Booker T. Washington was an early graduate. The **Hampton University Museum,** on the riverfront campus, is notable for its extensive and diverse collection, which includes more than 9,000 African, Native American, Pacific Island, and Asian art objects, as well as items related to the history of the university. Other valuable holdings include Harlem Renaissance paintings. ⊠*Museum, Huntington Bldg., off Tyler St.; I–64, Exit 267, to campus* ☎*757/727–5308* ⊕*www. hamptonu.edu* ⊡*Free* ☉*Weekdays 8–5, Sat. noon–4.*

Little of early Hampton survived the shellings and conflicts of the past, but the brick walls of **St. John's Church** (1728) have. Today a stained-glass window honors Pocahontas, the Native American princess who is said to have saved the life of Captain John Smith in 1608. The communion silver on display, made in London in 1618, is the oldest such service still used in this country. The parish, founded in the same year as the city (1610), also claims to be the oldest Protestant church in continuous service in America. You may listen to a taped interpretation or take a guided tour (by arrangement) and visit a small museum in the parish house. ⊠*100 W. Queens Way* ☎*757/722–2567* ⊕*www.stjohnshampton. org* ⊡*Free* ☉*Weekdays 9–3.*

The **Virginia Air and Space Center** traces the history of flight and space
★ exploration. The nine-story, futuristic, $30 million center is the visitor center for NASA Langley Research Center and Langley Air Force Base. Its space artifacts include a 3-billion-year-old moon rock, the *Apollo 12* command capsule, and a lunar lander. The center also holds a dozen full-size aircraft, a 3-D IMAX theater, a variety of flight simulators, and hands-on exhibits that let you see yourself as an astronaut or launch a rocket. ⊠*Downtown Waterfront, 600 Settlers Landing Rd., I–64, Exit 267* ☎*757/727–0800* ⊕*www.vasc.org* ⊡ *IMAX educational films $8, IMAX Hollywood films $10, combination ticket $15* ☉*Memorial Day– Labor Day, Mon.–Wed. 10–5, Thurs.–Sun. 10–7; Labor Day–Memorial Day, Mon.–Sat. 10–5, Sun. noon–5.*

WHERE TO EAT

$$$ ×**Captain George's.** Although you can order steaks off the à la carte
SEAFOOD   menu, the main pull here is the 70-item, all-you-can-eat buffet of fried, steamed, and broiled seafood available for $25. Highlights are steamed Alaskan crab legs, steamed shrimp with Old Bay seasoning, steamed mussels, and she-crab soup. Among the desserts are baklava and fruit cobblers. A mural of the Chesapeake Bay dominates the largest of four dining rooms, which has tables with tops embedded with seashells.

✉2710 W. Mercury Blvd., Exit 263 south off I–64 ☎757/826–1435
⊕www.captaingeorges.com ▭AE, MC, V ⊘No lunch Mon.–Sat.

¢ ✕**The Grey Goose Tearoom.** Beside the relocated Hampton History

AMERICAN Museum, you're greeted by an enticing aroma and a gift shop with tea-related items when you enter this cozy room decorated with Victorian tea-party prints in gilded frames, antique teapots, and knick-knacks. Brunswick stew, creamy Hampton blue-crab soup, and biscuits are permanent fixtures on the "everything-homemade" menu, and daily specials, such as chicken and dumplings, are posted on the wall. Desserts are especially good, but avoid the canned fruit salad on iceberg lettuce. The tearoom is open for lunch only. ✉Old Hampton La. at History Museum Way ☎757/723–7978 ⊕www.greygooserestaurant. com ▭AE, D, DC, MC, V ⊘Closed Sun. No dinner.

WHERE TO STAY

$ 🏨**Courtyard by Marriott.** The smell of homemade chocolate cookies greets you Monday through Thursday at the front desk of this modern hotel, where the chef refills a bottomless basket. As the naval items on the walls suggest, this Marriott takes in the local influence. The pool is set amid landscaped grounds. The restaurant serves breakfast only. The price of a room is reduced for long-term stays. **Pros:** the pool is unheated, but there is an indoor spa. **Cons:** Wi-Fi is available in the lobby, but Ethernet is in the rooms. ✉1917 Coliseum Dr. ☎757/838–3300 ⊕www.courtyard.com ⇆146 rooms ⌂In-room: Ethernet. In-hotel: restaurant, pool, gym, laundry service ▭AE, D, DC, MC, V.

¢ 🏨**Holiday Inn Hampton.** Halfway between Colonial Williamsburg and Virginia Beach, this complex of buildings stands on 13 beautifully landscaped acres. About half the rooms have a pink-and-green color scheme; others have a darker look, with cherrywood dressers and tables. Some rooms overlook the indoor pool in the atrium, and others have doors that open, motel-style, onto the parking lot. There's free wireless Internet, and it's free to borrow an Ethernet cord. **Pros:** very reasonable rates. **Cons:** basic hotel. ✉1815 W. Mercury Blvd. ☎757/838–0200 or 800/842–9370 ⊕www.holidayinn.com ⇆314 rooms, 6 suites ⌂In-hotel: restaurant, bar, pools, gym ▭AE, D, DC, MC, V.

FORT MONROE

Inside Phoebus, at the South end of Mellen St. and Mercury Blvd.

The channel between Chesapeake Bay and Hampton Roads is the "mouth" of Hampton Roads. On the north side of this passage is Hampton's **Fort Monroe**, built in stages between 1819 and 1834. The largest stone fort in the country, it's also the only one still in operation to be enclosed by a moat. Robert E. Lee and Edgar Allan Poe served here in the antebellum years, and it remained a Union stronghold in Confederate territory throughout the Civil War. After the war, Confederate president Jefferson Davis was imprisoned for a time in one of the fort's casemates (a chamber in the wall); his cell and adjacent casemates now house the Casemate Museum. Exhibits of weapons, uniforms, models, drawings, and extensive Civil War relics retell the fort's history, depict coastal artillery activities, and describe the military lifestyle through the Civil War years and the 20th century. ✉ *Mellen St., Phoebus* 🕾 *757/788–3391* ✇ *Free* ☉ *Daily 10:30–4:30.*

NORFOLK

16 mi southeast of Hampton.

Like many other old Southern towns, Norfolk has undergone a renaissance, one that's especially visible in the charming shops and cafés in the historic village of Ghent. There's plenty to see in this old navy town.

GETTING HERE & AROUND
Norfolk is reached from the peninsula by the Hampton Roads Bridge-Tunnel (I–64) as well as Route 460. Norfolk's free shuttle, called NET, covers the downtown area.

ESSENTIALS
Taxis Black and White Cabs (🕾 757/855–4444). **Yellow Cab** (🕾 757/857–8888).

Visitor Information Norfolk Convention and Visitors Bureau (✉ *232 E. Main St.* 🕾 *757/664–6620 or 800/368–3097* ⊕ *www.norfolkcvb.com).*

MAIN ATTRACTIONS
★ By any standard, the **Chrysler Museum of Art** downtown qualifies as one of America's major art museums. The permanent collection includes works by Rubens, Gainsborough, Renoir, Picasso, Cézanne, Matisse, Warhol, and Pollock, a list that suggests the breadth available here. Classical and pre-Columbian civilizations are also represented. The decorative-arts collection includes exquisite English porcelain and art nouveau furnishings. The Chrysler is home to one the most important glass collections in America, which includes glass objects from the 6th century BC to the present, with particularly strong holdings in Tiffany, French art glass, and English cameo, as well as artifacts from ancient Rome and the Near and Far East. ✉ *245 W. Olney Rd.* 🕾 *757/664–6200* ⊕ *www.chrysler. org* ✇ *$7; Wed. by voluntary contribution* ☉ *Wed. 10–9, Thurs.–Sat. 10–5, Sun. 1–5.*

The **MacArthur Memorial** is the burial place of one of America's most distinguished military officers. General Douglas MacArthur (1880–1964) agreed to this navy town as the site for his monument because it was his mother's birthplace. In the rotunda of the old City Hall, converted according to MacArthur's design, is the mausoleum; 11 adjoining galleries house mementos of MacArthur's career, including his signature corncob pipe and the Japanese instruments of surrender that concluded World War II. However, this is a monument not only to General MacArthur but to all those who served in wars from the Civil to the Korean War. Its Historical Center holds 2½ million documents and more than 100,000 photographs, and assists scholars, students, and researchers from around the world. The general's staff car is on display in the gift shop, where a 24-minute biography is shown. ✉ *Bank St. at*

City Hall Ave., MacArthur Square 🕾 *757/441–2965* ⊕ *www.macart-hurmemorial.org* ✉ *By donation* 🕙 *Mon.–Sat. 10–5, Sun. 11–5.*

🕭 ★ **Nauticus,** a popular attraction on Norfolk's redeveloped downtown waterfront, is a maritime science museum featuring hand-on exhibits, interactive theaters and hi-definition films that celebrate the local connection to the seaport. Visitors can touch a shark, learn about weather and underwater archaeology, and explore the mysteries of the Elizabeth River. A NOAA Environmental Resource Center is an invaluable stop for education materials. Temporary exhibits in both the Changing Gallery and Forecastle Gallery keep things fresh. The Hampton Roads Naval Museum on the second floor and the Battleship *Wisconsin* adjacent to the building are also popular attractions operated by the U.S. Navy, and are included in the Nauticus admission. ✉ *1 Waterside Dr.* 🕾 *757/664–1000* ⊕ *www.nauticus.org* ✉ *$10* 🕙 *Memorial Day–Labor Day, daily 9–5; Labor Day–Memorial Day, Tues.–Sat. 10–5, Sun. noon–5.*

> ### FREE EVENTS IN NORFOLK
>
> Town Point Park, between Nauticus and Waterside Festival Marketplace, is the site of many free outdoor festivals and concerts, the annual Fleet Week and Harborfest, and a wine festival. Fun, food, and music are here most Fridays from May through October. Check for events at ⊕ www.festeventsva.org or in the local newspapers.

🕭 Fodor'sChoice ★ The **Norfolk Naval Station,** on the northern edge of the city, is an impressive sight, home to more than 100 ships of the Atlantic Fleet. The base was built on the site of the Jamestown Exposition of 1907; many of the original buildings survive and are still in use. Several large aircraft carriers, built at nearby Newport News, call Norfolk home port and can be seen from miles away, especially at the bridge-tunnel end of the base. You may see two, each with a crew of up to 6,300, beside slightly smaller amphibious carriers that discharge marines in both helicopters and amphibious assault craft. The submarine piers, floating dry docks, supply center, and air station are all worth seeing. The *Victory Rover* and *Carrie B.* provide boat tours from downtown Norfolk to the naval station, and Hampton Roads Transit operates tour trolleys most of the year, departing from the naval-base tour office. Visitor access is by tour only, and photo ID is required to enter the base. ✉ *9079 Hampton Blvd.* 🕾 *757/444–7955* ⊕ *www.navstanorva.navy.mil/tour* ✉ *Tour $7.50 (cash only and there is no ATM on premises)* 🕙 *Tours: Jan. 1–Mar. 15, Tues. –Sun. at 1:30; Mar. 16–May 17, every ½ hr 11–2; May 18–Aug. 30, every 30 mins 10–2; Aug. 31–Nov. 1, hourly 11–2; Nov. 2–Dec. 31, Tues. –Sun. at 1:30.*

ALSO WORTH SEEING

The **Hermitage Foundation Museum,** an early-20th-century estate of the Sloane family, offers an outstanding presentation of architecture, art, and nature. The Sloanes, educated collectors with broad artistic interests, were among the founders of what is now the Chrysler Museum. Mr. Sloane was a wealthy New York businessman who moved to Virginia to operate textile mills. Docent-led tours are available on the hour. Visitors may also stroll the waterfront and 12-acre gardens and view contemporary art exhibitions. ✉7637 N. Shore Rd. ☎757/423–2052 ⊕www.thfm.org ⊠$5 ⊙Mon., Tues., and Thurs.–Sat. 10–5; Sun. 1–5.

The Federal redbrick **Moses Myers House,** built by its namesake between 1792 and 1796, is exceptional, and not just for its elegance. The furnishings, 70% of them original, include family portraits by Gilbert Stuart and Thomas Sully. A transplanted New Yorker as well as Norfolk's first Jewish resident, Myers made his fortune in Norfolk in shipping, then served as a diplomat and a customhouse officer. His grandson married James Madison's grandniece; his great-grandson served as mayor; and the family kept the house for five generations. ✉.323 E. Free Mason St. ☎757/333–1086 ⊕www.chrysler.org/houses.asp ⊠Free ⊙Wed.–Sat. 10–4, Sun. noon–4.

St. Paul's Church, constructed in 1739, was the only building in town to survive the bombardment and conflagration of New Year's Day 1776; a cannonball fired by the British fleet remains embedded in a wall. An earlier church had been built on this site in 1641, and the churchyard contains graves dating from the 17th century. Get a free visitor parking pass in the church office. ✉St. Paul's Blvd. at City Hall Ave. ☎757/627–4353 ⊠By donation ⊙Mon. 10–3, Tues.–Fri. 10–4.

WHERE TO EAT

$

MEDITERRANEAN

✕**Azars Natural Foods.** Lebanese specialties are featured at this casual restaurant in Ghent, which also has a Mediterranean food store. Indoor dining is on granite tables under the original tin ceiling and exposed air ducts. Outdoors, the terra-cotta patio has umbrellas. A sampler Mashawee Platter includes *kibbi,* seasoned beef and bulghur patties; *kefta,* spiced lamb meatballs; and lamb kebab with grilled vegetables and side dishes. Vegan and vegetarian selections are noted on the menu, which includes appetizers, wraps, pizza, and kebabs. ✉2000 Colley Ave. ☎757/664–7955 ⊕www.azarfoods.com ⊟AE, D, MC, V.

¢

BARBECUE

✕**Doumar's.** After he introduced the world to its first ice-cream cone at the 1904 World's Fair in St. Louis, Abe Doumar founded this drive-in institution in 1934. It's still operated by his family. Waitresses carry to your car the specialties of the house: barbecue, limeade, and ice cream in waffle cones made according to an original recipe. For breakfast, try the Egg-O-Doumar, a bargain at $2.70. The Food Network's "Diners, Drive-Ins, and Dives" featured Doumars twice in 2008. ✉20th St. at Monticello Ave. ☎757/627–4163 ⊕www.doumars.com ⊟MC, V ⊙Closed Sun.

$

AMERICAN

✕**Freemason Abbey Restaurant and Tavern.** This former church near the historic business district has been drawing customers for a long time, and not without reason. It has 40-foot-high cathedral ceilings and large windows, making for an airy, and dramatic, dining experience. You can sit upstairs, in the large choir loft, or in the main part of the church downstairs. Beside the bar just inside the entrance is an informal sort of "diner" area, but with the whole menu to choose from. Regular appetizers include artichoke dip and Santa Fe shrimp. There's a dinner special every weeknight, such as lobster, prime rib, and wild game (wild boar or alligator, for example). ✉209 W. Freemason St. ☎757/622–3966

⊕ *www.freemasonabbey.com*
🖃 *AE, D, DC, MC, V.*

¢ ✗**No Frill Bar and Grill.** This expan-
CAFÉ sive café is in an antique building
★ in the heart of Ghent. Beneath a
tin ceiling and exposed ductwork,
a central bar is surrounded by several dining spaces with cream-and-
mustard walls and wooden tables.

Signature items include its ribs;
the Funky Chicken Sandwich, a grilled chicken breast with bacon,
tomato, melted Swiss cheese, and Parmesan pepper dressing on rye;
and the Spotswood Salad of baby spinach, Granny Smith apples, and
blue cheese. ⊠ *806 Spotswood Ave., at Colley Ave.* ☎ *757/627–4262*
⊕ *www.nofrillsbar.com* 🖃 *AE, MC, V.*

$$ ✗**Vintage Kitchen.** In its short life, the Vintage Kitchen has racked up
AMERICAN many accolades for its focus on local foods, artisan cheeses, and micro-
brews. The chef is Paris trained, but local, and knows the specialties of
the area. It's a place where you can order "Five Spice Duck Breast" and
also a superb cheeseburger. A special seven-course tasting meal is avail-
able by appointment Monday through Wednesday. ⊠ *Dominion Tower,
999 Waterside Dr.* ☎ *757/625–3370* ⊕ *www.vintage-kitchen.com*
⌖ *Reservations essential* 🖃 *AE, D, MC, V* ⊗ *No dinner Mon.–Wed.*

WHERE TO STAY

$ 🏨**Holiday Inn Select Airport.** Surprisingly plush for a Holiday Inn prop-
erty, this airport location welcomes business travelers with an elegant
lobby bar and fireplace. Rooms are outfitted with two phone lines, high-
speed DSL Internet access, and voice mail; the lobby has free wireless.
Behind the hotel is Lake Wright, where guests may stroll or relax. Travel
forums rates this Holiday Inn one of the best in the chain. **Pros:** con-
venient to the airport. **Cons:** not convenient to the city center. ⊠ *Lake
Wright Executive Center, 1570 N. Military Hwy.* ☎ *757/213–2231*
⊕ *www.hiselect.com/norfolkva* ⤳ *147 rooms* ⌂ *In-room: refrigerator.
In-hotel: restaurant, bar, pool, gym, laundry facilities, airport shuttle*
🖃 *AE, D, DC, MC, V.*

$–$$ 🏨**Marriott Courtyard Downtown.** Built in 2005, this eight-story hotel is
near everything visitors want to see and where business travelers need
to be. It's next door to the MacArthur Memorial and near the MacArthur Center and Nauticus. A handsome, inviting lobby has a tailored
look; the modern guest rooms have a large desk, comforters, hair dryers, coffeemakers, irons, ironing boards, and a free daily newspaper.
Pros: convenient downtown location. **Cons:** the hotel has a smoke-free
policy. ⊠ *520 Plume St.* ☎ *757/963–6000 or 800/321–2211* ⊕ *www.
marriott.com* ⤳ *137 rooms, 3 suites* ⌂ *In-room: refrigerator, Wi-Fi.
In-hotel: restaurant, room service, pool, laundry facilities, laundry service, parking (fee)* 🖃 *AE, D, DC, MC, V.*

$$ 🏨**Norfolk Marriott Waterside.** This hotel in the redeveloped downtown
area is connected to the Waterside Festival Marketplace shopping area
by a ramp and is close to Town Point Park, site of many festivals. The
handsome lobby, with wood paneling, a central staircase, silk tapestries,

and Federal-style furniture, sets a high standard that continues throughout the hotel. Rooms are somewhat small, but each has most everything the business traveler could ask for—including two telephones, voice mail, and Internet access. **Pros:** great central location; two blocks from the Waterside Festival Marketplace. **Cons:** parking is pricey. ⊠*235 E. Main St.* ☎*757/627–4200 or 800/228–9290* ⊕*www.marriott.com* ⤳*396 rooms, 8 suites* ⚘*In-room: Wi-Fi. In-hotel: 2 restaurants, bar, pool* ⊟*AE, D, DC, MC, V.*

$$ 🏨**Sheraton Norfolk Waterside Hotel.** Modern is the word for this hotel's furnishings, from the bright, spacious lobby to the ample rooms and large suites. A ground-floor bar with dramatic 30-foot windows overlooks the Elizabeth—many rooms also have a beautiful view over the water. This property is convenient to the Waterside Festival Marketplace shopping area. **Pros:** the only hotel that is truly on the waterfront. **Cons:** again, parking—for Norfolk—is pricey. ⊠*777 Waterside Dr.* ☎*757/622–6664* ⊕*www.sheraton.com* ⤳*426 rooms, 20 suites* ⚘*In-hotel: restaurant, bar, pool* ⊟*AE, D, DC, MC, V.*

NIGHTLIFE & THE ARTS
MUSIC
The **Virginia Opera Company** (⊠*160 E. Virginia Beach Blvd.* ☎*757/ 623–1223*) presents some of the best operatic talent in the nation during its season (September through April) at Norfolk's elegant Harrison Opera House, which is known for its excellent acoustics. Their schedule includes the most popular operas of Europe and the United States.

SHOPPING
You can meet painters, sculptors, glassworkers, jewelers, photographers, and other artists at work in their studios at the **d'Art Center** (⊠*Selden Arcade, 208 E. Main St.* ☎*757/625–4211*); the art is for sale.

An eclectic mix of chic shops, including antiques stores, bars, and eateries, lines the streets of **Ghent,** a turn-of-the-20th-century neighborhood that runs from the Elizabeth River to York Street, to West Olney Road and Llewellyn Avenue. The intersection of Colley Avenue and 21st Street is the hub.

In Ghent the upscale clothing and shoe boutiques at the **Palace Shops** (⊠*21st St. at Llewellyn Ave.*) are a good place to search out some finery.

PORTSMOUTH

6 mi southwest of Norfolk via I-264.

Portsmouth, across the Elizabeth River from Norfolk, has a well-maintained historic area called Olde Towne, which has handsome buildings from the 18th and 19th centuries.

GETTING HERE & AROUND
A five-minute pedestrian ferry makes traveling between Portsmouth and Norfolk easy. The Elizabeth River Ferry carries passengers (but

no automobiles) between Waterside Festival Marketplace, in Norfolk, and Portsmouth's Olde Towne weekdays 7:15 AM–11:45 PM, weekends 10:15 AM–11:45 PM. Bikes and wheelchairs are allowed. Taking the ferry is more fun and normally faster than driving through the tunnel; it departs from Norfolk 15 minutes before and after every hour and leaves Portsmouth on the hour and half-hour.

ESSENTIALS

Ferry **Elizabeth River Ferry** (☎ *757/222-6100* ✉*$1*)

Visitor Information **Portsmouth Convention and Visitors Bureau** (✉*6 Crawford Pkwy.* ☎ *757/393-5111* ⊕*www.portsmouthva.gov/tourism/vstinfo.html*).

EXPLORING

The **Children's Museum of Virginia,** the largest children's museum in the state, has more than 90 hands-on exhibits for kids of all ages, including an awesome toy train collection, a planetarium, and tons more. Here kids can learn engineering and scientific principles by playing with bubbles and blocks. ✉*221 High St.* ☎*757/393-5258* ⊕*www.childrensmuseumva.com* ✉*$6* ⊗*Tues.–Sat. 9–5, Sun. 11–5.*

The **Portsmouth Naval Shipyard Museum,** one block from the waterfront and about three blocks from the paddle-wheel ferry landing, offers a history of Portsmouth, the Norfolk Naval Shipyard, and the armed forces in Hampton Roads. The museum gives visitors the opportunity to learn about this rich history through exhibited artifacts, uniforms, ship models, illustrations, and photographs. You can also explore the retired Coast Guard lightship *Portsmouth,* a floating lighthouse just outside the museum, whose quarters below deck have been authentically furnished. ✉*2 High St.* ☎*757/393-8591 shipyard museum, 757/393-8741 lightship* ⊕*www.portsnavalmuseums.com* ✉*$3, free 1st Sun. of month* ⊗*Memorial Day–Labor Day, Mon.–Sat. 10–5, Sun. 1–5; Labor Day–Memorial Day, Tues.–Sat. 10–5, Sun. 1–5.*

WHERE TO STAY

¢–$ ★ ▣**Hawthorn Hotel & Suites at the Governor Dinwiddie.** The 1940s Governor Dinwiddie hotel in the center of Portsmouth's Olde Towne business district was beautifully restored in 2005. Guest rooms are furnished in reproduction Queen Anne with satin quilted spreads, ecru walls, and moss woodwork. Museums, restaurants, and the waterfront are within a few blocks. **Pros:** a Historic Hotel of America, recognized by the National Trust for Historic Preservation. **Cons:** although it's only 3 mi from the center of Norfolk, it's a little far to compete with hotels in that city. ✉*506 Dinwiddie, at High St.* ☎*757/392-1330 or 800/527-1133* ⊕*www.hawthornhotelandsuites.com* ⇆*45 rooms, 15 suites* ⌂*In-room: refrigerator, dial-up, Wi-Fi. In-hotel: restaurant, bar, gym, laundry service* ▭*AE, MC, V.*

VIRGINIA BEACH

18 mi east of Norfolk via I–64 to Rte. 44.

The heart of Virginia Beach—a stretch of the Atlantic shore from Cape Henry south to Rudee Inlet—has been a popular summertime destination for years. With 6 mi of public beach, high-rises, amusements, and a busy 40-block boardwalk, Virginia's most populated city is now a place for communion with nature. The boardwalk and Atlantic Avenue have an oceanfront park; an old-fashioned fishing pier ($7.50) with shops, a restaurant, and a bar; and a 3-mi bike trail. The farther north you go, the more beach you find in proportion to bars, T-shirt parlors, and video arcades. Most activities and events in town are oriented to families.

GETTING HERE & AROUND

Virginia Beach has no shortage of parking lots and spaces. The cost for a day of parking is about $5 to $7 at the central beach lots and $4 or $5 for the remote beach areas. Municipal lots/decks are at 4th Street (metered only), 9th Street and Pacific Avenue, 19th Street and Pacific Avenue, 25th Street and Pacific Avenue, 31st Street and Atlantic Avenue, and Croatan and Sandbridge beaches. Metered spaces have a three-hour limit.

Bikes (two- or four-wheel) can be rented at several shops and hotels along the beach for $4 to $20 per hour. In Virginia Beach there are numerous locations along the boardwalk where you can rent bikes. Rental shops away from the boardwalk are more reasonable and have better bikes. Seashore Bikes & Fitness is near First Landing Park. Back Bay Getaways is on the other side of Virginia Beach in the Sandbridge area. They offer bikes and guided biking tours.

Hampton Roads Transit buses have bike racks, and their paddle-wheel ferries across the Elizabeth River allow bikes, so cyclists can cover a lot of territory from Newport News through Norfolk and on to Virginia Beach.

TIMING & PRECAUTIONS

Virginia Beach is one of the prime destinations for college students on spring break. Thousands of them descend on the community in April and may constitute a rowdy crowd. Avoid Virginia Beach during that time—unless you are a college student.

ESSENTIALS

Bike Rental Back Bay Getaways (✉ *3713 S. Sandpiper Rd.* ☎ *757/721–4484*). **Seashore Bikes & Fitness** (✉ *2268 Seashore Shops* ☎ *757/481–5191*).

Bus Hampton Roads Transit (☎ *757/222–6100* ⊕ *www.hrtransit.org*).

Taxis Beach Taxi (✉ *Virginia Beach* ☎ *757/486–6585*). **Yellow Cab of Virginia Beach** (☎ *757/460–0605*).

Visitor Information Virginia Beach Visitor Information Center (✉ *2100 Parks Ave.23451* ☎ *800/822–3224* ⊕ *www.vbfun.com*).

EXPLORING

Inland from the shore is the early 18th-century **Adam Thoroughgood House,** named for the prosperous plantation owner who held a land grant of 5,350 acres here in the early 1600s. This 45-by-22-foot brick house, probably constructed by a Thoroughgood grandson,

recalls the English cottage architecture of the period, with a protruding chimney and a steeply pitched roof. The four-room early plantation home has a 17th-century garden with characteristic hedges. To get there, take I–264 Exit 17 (Independence Blvd.) 4 mi, turn right on Pleasure House Road, and right on Thoroughgood Drive. ⊠ *1636 Parish Rd.* ☎ *757/460–7588* ⊕ *www.vbgov.com/dept/arts/* ☒ *$5* ⊗ *Tues.–Sat. 9–5, Sun. 11–5.*

The **Naval Air Station, Oceana,** on the northern edge of the city, is an impressive sight, home to more than 200 navy aircraft, including the F/A-18 Tomcat (the type of plane flown by the Blue Angels) and other planes assigned to the aircraft carriers of the Atlantic Fleet. From an observation park on Oceana Boulevard at the POW/MIA Flame of Hope Memorial Park, near the runways, you can watch aircraft take off and land. Non–Defense Department visitors can access the base only on the Hampton Roads Transit summer-only tours (photo ID required) or during the annual air show in September. Tours depart at 9:30 AM and 11:30 AM from the 24th Street transit kiosk on Atlantic Avenue in Virginia Beach and stop at an aviation historical park with 13 aircraft. ⊠ *Tomcat Blvd.* ☎ *757/433–3131* ⊕ *www.nasoceana.navy.mil/Visitors. htm* ☒ *Tour $7.50.*

At the northeastern tip of Virginia Beach, on the cape where the mouth of the bay meets the ocean, the historic **Old Cape Henry Lighthouse** is near the site where the English landed on their way to Jamestown in 1607. This lighthouse, however, didn't light anyone's way until 1792. Across the street to seaward is the replacement for the old lighthouse, but it isn't open to visitors. Be prepared to show a photo ID at the military checkpoint at the Fort Story base entrance. ⊠ *U.S. 60* ☎ *757/422–9421* ☒ *$4* ⊗ *Mid Mar.–Oct., daily 10–5; Nov.–mid-Mar., daily 10–4.*

Along the oceanfront, the **Old Coast Guard Station,** a 1903 Lifesaving Station, contains photographic exhibits, examples of lifesaving equipment, and a gallery that depicts German U-boat activity off the coast during World War II. ⊠ *24th St. at Atlantic Ave.* ☎ *757/422–1587* ☒ *$3* ⊗ *Tues.–Sat. 10–5, Sun. noon–5.*

The sea is the subject at the popular **Virginia Aquarium and Marine Science Center,** a massive facility with more than 200 exhibits. This is no place for passive museumgoers; many exhibits require participation. You can use computers to predict the weather and solve the pollution crisis, watch the birds in the salt marsh through telescopes on a deck, handle horseshoe crabs, take a simulated journey to the bottom of the sea in a submarine, and study fish up close in tanks that re-create underwater environments. The museum is almost 2 mi inland from Rudee Inlet at the southern end of Virginia Beach. The Virginia Aquarium and Marine Science Center has a nature trail—well worth it, but be sure to wear comfortable shoes. ⊠*717 General Booth Blvd.* ☎*757/485–3474* ⊕*www.virginiaacquarium.com* ⊠*Aquarium $11.95; combination ticket for aquarium and IMAX $16.95* ☉*Memorial Day–Labor Day, daily 9–7; Labor Day–Memorial Day, daily 9–5.*

WHERE TO EAT

$–$$
AMERICAN

✕**Five 01 City Grill.** More than a grill in name only, this restaurant has an open-grill kitchen in the dining room. It can be noisy on the bar side when live bands play in the evening. Locals get comfortable in padded chairs and some booths as they quaff the $2 beer of the month or order from the extensive wine vault. The California-inspired fusion menu offers a variety of price ranges: excellent homemade pizza from wood-burning ovens, sandwiches, pasta, chicken, steaks, and seafood followed by sinful desserts such as Homemade Bourbon Chocolate Chip Pecan Pie. ⊠*501 N. Birdneck Rd.* ☎*757/425–7195* ⊕*www.goodfood gooddrink.com* ☐*AE, MC, V.*

$–$$
IRISH

✕**Murphy's Irish Pub.** This combination Irish pub, sports bar, and restaurant has a large central dining room with an open fireplace in the middle, a bar on one side, and a smaller dining room at one end. The menu includes steaks and Irish, Italian, and seafood entrées as well as snacks and sandwiches. The Sunday brunch is reasonable, and so are the weekday dinner specials. A block from the boardwalk, Murphy's has plenty of easy parking. ⊠*2914 Pacific Ave.* ☎*757/417–7701* ☐*AE, D, DC, MC, V.*

$–$$
AMERICAN

✕**Rockafeller's.** The Down East architecture of this local favorite with double-deck porches hints at the seafood that's available. The restaurant has a bar, a raw bar, and alfresco dining in good weather (in cool weather, the large window wall still gives you a water view). Seafood, pasta, chicken, and beef share the menu with salads and sandwiches. Rockafeller's (and several others) are on Rudee Inlet. To get here, go south on Pacific Avenue and turn right on Winston-Salem immediately before the Rudee Inlet bridge. The street ends at Mediterranean Avenue. ⊠*308 Mediterranean Ave.* ☎*757/422–5654* ⊕*www.rockafellers.com* ☐*AE, D, DC, MC, V.*

$–$$
SEAFOOD
★

✕**Waterman's Beachwood Grill.** The last freestanding restaurant on the beach not inside a hotel, this aqua-painted clapboard building houses a family-owned seafood grill. Inside, the ocher walls heighten the sun rays penetrating the ceiling-to-floor windows. Awnings shade the outdoor patio where live musicians perform in season. A local menu favorite is the Crab Ripper, a crab-cake sandwich topped with mozzarella and crisp bacon. A fried seafood sampler, fish and steak platters, steamed fish, appetizers, salads, burgers, and other sandwiches fill out the menu. Banquet facilities are available, and the Beach Nut Gift Shop is also on the premises. ⊠*1423 N. Great Neck Rd.* ☎*757/496–3333* ⊕*www. watermans.com* ☐*AE, D, MC, V.*

WHERE TO STAY

$ ★ **Cavalier Hotels.** In the quieter north end of town, this 18-acre resort complex combines the original Cavalier Hotel of 1927, a seven-story redbrick building on a hill, with an oceanfront high-rise built across the street in 1973. The clientele is about evenly divided between conventioneers and families. F. Scott and Zelda Fitzgerald stayed regularly in the original hotel. If you stay in the hilltop building you can see the water—and get to it easily by shuttle van or a short walk. The newer building overlooks 600 feet of private beach. There's a fee for tennis, but the other athletic facilities are free. **Pros:** great choice of people who appreciate historic properties. **Cons:** might be too staid for spring-break students. ⊠*Atlantic Ave. at 42nd St.* ☎*757/425–8555 or 888/746–2327* ⊕*www.cavalierhotel.com* ⊅*400 rooms* ⚂*In-room: Ethernet, dial-up. In-hotel: 5 restaurants, tennis courts, pools, gym, beachfront, no-smoking rooms* ⊟*AE, D, DC, MC, V.*

$-$$ **Crowne Plaza Virginia Beach.** This sparkling white, modern hotel is well situated, midway between Norfolk and the beach, and 15 mi from Norfolk International Airport. The skylighted lobby overlooks a glassed-in indoor pool. Rooms have a sitting area with a desk; there are plush duvets and extra pillows on the beds. Every room has a hair dryer, iron, ironing board, and coffeemaker. The centerpiece of the tropical decor is a five-story atrium. **Pros:** reasonable rates in a well-maintained older property. **Cons:** hotel is 8 mi from the beach and 15 mi from Norfolk. ⊠*4453 Bonney Rd.* ☎*757/473–1700 or 800/847–5202* ⊟*757/552–0477* ⊅*149 rooms* ⚂*In-room: refrigerator, dial-up. In-hotel: restaurant, bar, pool, gym, laundry service, no-smoking rooms* ⊟*AE, D, DC, MC, V.*

$$$$ **Hilton Virginia Beach Oceanfront.** This Hilton opened in 2005 and is the only four-star hotel in Virginia Beach. Towering 21 stories over the oceanfront, it has shops, three restaurants, and a rooftop bar and infinity pool. The seafood restaurant Catch 31 has gotten good reviews, and there is great outdoor seating overlooking the boardwalk. At night the bar is a happening scene for thirtysomethings. Most rooms have balconies with panoramic views. **Pro:** a luxury hotel with all the amenities. **Con:** the priciest choice in Virginia Beach. ⊠*3001 Atlantic Ave.* ☎*757/213–3000* ⊕*www.hiltonvb.com* ⊅*290 rooms* ⚂*In-room: Wi-Fi. In-hotel: 3 restaurants, pool, gym, public Wi-Fi* ⊟*AE, D, MC, V.*

$-$$ ★ **Wyndham Virginia Beach Oceanfront.** With its 17-story tower, the former Ramada Plaza Resort Oceanfront, has been sold to private owners who promise a renovation of the 1960s-era high-rise. Rooms that do not face the ocean directly have either a partial view or overlook the swimming pool. The modern lobby has a skylighted atrium. The Surf Club Ocean Grill, serves—predictably—seafood. The hotel offers a children's program. **Pros:** the Wyndham Virginia Beach accepts pets (additional fee), but only if the reservation is made directly through the hotel. **Cons:** the hotel is north of the main action on the boardwalk. ⊠*57th St. at oceanfront* ☎*757/428–7025 or 800/365–3032* ⊕*wyndham.com* ⊅*243 rooms* ⚂*In-room: safe, refrigerator. In-hotel: restaurant, bar, pool, gym, children's programs (ages 5–13), laundry service, no-smoking rooms* ⊟*AE, D, DC, MC, V.*

NIGHTLIFE

Harpoon Larry's (✉*24th St. at Pacific Ave.* ☎*757/422–6000*) is a local watering hole with true character, not a tourist trap. Don't be surprised to see a great white shark staring back at you as you eat a juicy piece of that shark's cousin (mahimahi) stuffed with fresh Chesapeake Bay crabmeat, or enjoy raw oysters and a cold Corona. There's free nightly entertainment from April through Labor Day weekend at the 24th Street stage or 24th Street Park on the boardwalk. **Murphy's Grand Irish Pub and Restaurant** (✉*2914 Pacific Ave.* ☎*757/417–7701*) has entertainment every night in summer and Tuesday–Saturday during winter—there's typically an Irish musician or two.

SPORTS & THE OUTDOORS

GOLF

There are several public golf courses in Virginia Beach, some with moderate fees. All charge more for nonresidents and have varying fees, depending upon the day of the week and start time. **Honey Bee Golf Club** (✉*2500 S. Independence Blvd.* ☎*757/471–2768*) has greens fees of $30–$60 weekdays and $44–$69 weekends. **Kempsville Greens Municipal Golf Course** (✉*4840 Princess Anne Rd.* ☎*757/474–8441*) is a municipal course and the least expensive: weekdays $18–$23, weekends $24–$28, not including cart.

WATER SPORTS

Back Bay Getaways (✉*Sandbridge* ☎*757/721–4484*) has a variety of kayak rentals and tours, pontoon boats, surfboards, and Jet Skis in the Sandbridge area. **Lynnhaven Dive Center** (☎*757/481–7949*) leads dives and gives lessons. Their boats are at Rudee Inlet. **Wild River Outfitters** (☎*757/431–8566 or 877/431–8566*) has guided kayak tours, moonlight paddles, river tours, dolphin tours, and more.

Baltimore

WORD OF MOUTH

"There's the fabulous Oriole Park at Camden Yard, and the Babe Ruth Museum. Even people who don't like baseball enjoy going to games at Camden Yard. You can get seats standing in line before the game if you aren't picky about where you sit. The whole Inner Harbor area is lovely . . . the Aquarium is just extraordinary . . . The Baltimore Museum of Art is very fine, especially if you like furniture and glass."

—Diane

Updated by
Sam Sessa

BALTIMORE'S CHARM LIES IN ITS neighborhoods. While stellar down-town attractions such as the National Aquarium and Camden Yards draw torrents of tourists each year, much of the city's character can be found outside the Inner Harbor. Scores of Baltimore's trademark nar-row redbrick row houses with white marble steps line the city's East and West sides. Some neighborhood streets are still made of cobblestone, and grand churches and museums and towering, glassy high-rises fill out the growing skyline.

After World War II, as manufacturing jobs dried up and its populace moved to the suburbs, Baltimore declined. But in the 1970s real-estate development surged in some areas, and new arts and cultural events such as the city's ethnic festivals began to spring up. Homesteaders started moving into once-abandoned row houses, and city tourism grew dramatically when the National Aquarium opened in the early 1980s. Further development of the Inner Harbor, including Oriole Park at Camden Yards and M&T Bank Stadium, continued to fuel the city's resurgence.

Now the city's blue-collar past mixes with present urban-professional revitalization. Industrial waterfront properties are giving way to high-end condos, and corner bars formerly dominated by National Bohe-mian beer—once made in the city—are adding microbrews to their beverage lists. And with more and more retail stores replacing old, run-down buildings and parking lots, Baltimore is one of the nation's up-and-coming cities. Though Baltimore has seen a spike in develop-ment, signs of the city's pockmarked past still persist. Boarded-up row houses sit just west of downtown, and abandoned factory shells still dot the landscape—signs of the troubles the city still faces.

ORIENTATION & PLANNING

GETTING ORIENTED

Laid out in a more-or-less regular grid pattern, Baltimore is fairly easy to navigate. Pratt Street runs east along the Inner Harbor; from there the major northbound arteries are Charles Street and the Jones Falls Expressway (I–83). Cross-street addresses are marked "East" or "West" according to which side of Charles Street they are on; similarly, Balti-more Street marks the dividing line between north and south. Residents refer to areas of the city by the direction of these major arteries: thus, South Baltimore, North Baltimore, East Baltimore, West Baltimore, Northeast Baltimore, Northwest Baltimore, etc. The major down-town north–south thoroughfares are Charles and Saint Paul (north of Baltimore Street) and Light Street (south of Baltimore). Downtown, east–west traffic depends heavily on Pratt and Lombard streets. The downtown area is bounded by Martin Luther King Boulevard on the west and by the Jones Falls Expressway (President Street) on the east.

TOP REASONS TO GO

■ **Explore a revitalized addition to the Inner Harbor.** Today even more warehouses and parking lots have been converted, making this former industrial area a hot place for shops, a movie theater, and trendy restaurants. There's plenty to do in the newest addition to the decades-old Inner Harbor, called Harbor East.

■ **Tour the area on two wheels.** The Gwynns Falls Trail connects thousands of acres of wilderness in and around the city. It's a prime spot for hiking and biking.

■ **See comics and collector's items up close.** Geppi's Entertainment Museum in Camden Yards pays homage to hundreds of years of pop culture with thousands of comic books, films, toys, and more.

■ **Get wild and zany at Honfest.** Join in the fun when, for one weekend each June, thousands gussy up to celebrate Honfest in Hampden in traditional classic Hon attire: beehive hairdos and cat's-eye glasses

■ **Crack 'em and eat 'em like a Baltimorean.** Baltimore loves crabs, especially at Bo Brooks in Canton—one of the city's best crab houses—where you can crack into a piping-hot crustacean year-round.

■ **Taste the country's first tiramisu.** Piedigrotta Bakery, which has a stall in the Cross Street Market, claims to have invented tiramisu. Try it for yourself—a big wedge is only a couple of bucks.

Mount Vernon. Baltimore's arts and culture scene is focused in Mount Vernon. Some of the city's grandest architecture can be seen on Charles Street.

Charles Village. Students, professors, writers, and artists are drawn to the area's intellectual environment, centered around Johns Hopkins University.

Inner Harbor. South of the city center, the Inner Harbor is the city's biggest destination, filled with popular attractions like the National Aquarium, Harborplace shopping centers, and the Maryland Science Center.

Fells Point. To the east of Inner Harbor, Fells Point is just a water taxi away. Shops, two small museums, and the neighborhood's many pubs—most of which host live local bands daily, attract both locals and tourists.

West Baltimore. Baltimore's West Side is undergoing a transformation complete with performing arts center, high-end apartments, and two famous stadiums.

PLANNING

WHEN TO GO

Summer is definitely the best time to explore Baltimore. It's also tourist season, which means the Inner Harbor fills up with foot traffic. Though the rest of Baltimore can be humid in the summer months, there's usually a breeze blowing in from the water, which helps cool the harbor. Summer is also festival season, with a number of ethnic celebrations taking place around the city. Check ⊕ *www.bop.org* for more information, as dates and locations change from year to year.

New Year's Eve (☎*410/752–8632* ⊕*www.bop.org*) festivities in Baltimore include a concert at the Harborplace amphitheater and a 9 PM fireworks display over Inner Harbor. In February the **ACC Crafts Fair** (☎*800/836–3470*) draws more than 800 exhibitors for three days of artful displays and sales. The **Maryland Preakness Celebration** (☎*410/542–9400* ⊕*www.preakness.com*) is a weeklong festival that includes parades, street parties, fund-raisers, and hot-air-balloons. The celebration culminates in the annual running of the Preakness Stakes at Pimlico Race Course, on the third Saturday in May. **Independence Day** celebrations culminate in a major show of fireworks over the Inner Harbor. In late August the **Maryland State Fair** (☎*410/252–0200* ⊕*www. marylandstatefair.com*), in Timonium (15 mi north of Baltimore), is 10 days of horse racing, livestock judging, live entertainment, agricultural displays, farm implements, and plenty of food. **Defenders' Day** (☎*410/962–4290* ⊕*www.nps.gov/fomc*) celebrations in September at Fort McHenry commemorate—with music, drilling, mock bombardment, and fireworks—the battle that led to the writing of the national anthem.

GETTING HERE & AROUND

Baltimore is not particularly known for its public transportation. The two main transit systems, buses and the light-rail, don't reach every corner of the city and can be sluggish at times. A light-rail train runs north–south along Howard Street from Baltimore-Washington International Airport to Camden Yards and up into northern suburbs such as Hunt Valley. Cabs are your quickest option, though you will have to call for a pickup in most neighborhoods. You can also catch a water-taxi ride across the harbor.

BY AIR Traveling to Baltimore by air is fairly simple. The main airport is Baltimore-Washington International Airport (BWI), just south of town. BWI is easily reached by car, taxi, or light rail; for most agencies, rental cars are returned to lots off the airport premises.

BWI SuperShuttle provides van service between the airport and downtown hotels every half-hour 4 AM–midnight. Travel time is about 30 minutes; the fare is $20 for the first person, $5 per additional passenger. Hotel vans, which operate independently of the hotels, take 30 minutes on average.

Carey Limousines provides sedan service, which costs $80; make reservations 24 hours in advance. Private Car/RMA Worldwide Chauffeured Transportation has sedans, limos, and vans; the cost to the Inner Harbor is about $40 for a sedan.

Airport Taxis stand by to meet arriving flights. The ride into town on I–295 takes 20 minutes; a trip between the airport and downtown costs about $25. Airport Taxi service is available only *from* BWI; for transportation to the airport, consult a local cab company such as Jimmy's Cab Co. or Arrow Taxicab.

BY BUS Buses provide an inexpensive way to see much of Baltimore, though you may have to transfer several times. Route and schedule information is available by contacting the Maryland Transit Administration.

Bus and transit schedules are sometimes available inside the Charles Center metro station (Charles and Baltimore streets downtown). Fare is $1.60 (exact change is required). All-day passes are $3.50 and can be used with light-rail or metro travel. Some routes have service 24 hours daily.

BY CAR From the northeast and south, I–95 cuts across the city's east side and the harbor; Route 295, the Baltimore–Washington Parkway, follows a similar route farther to the east, and is the best route downtown from the airport. From the north, I–83, also called the Jones Falls Expressway, winds through Baltimore and ends at the Inner Harbor. Interstate 395 serves as the primary access to downtown from I–95. From the west, I–70 merges with the Baltimore Beltway, I–695. Drivers headed downtown should use I–395.

6

Parking in downtown Baltimore can be difficult; on weekdays many garages fill up early with suburban commuters. When the Orioles or Ravens play a home game, parking around the Inner Harbor can be nearly impossible to find. Best bets for parking are hotel garages, which often have spaces available. Attended parking lots are around the downtown periphery and cost less than garages.

It's hard to find a metered parking spot downtown, though in other areas it's much easier. Most meters in well-traveled areas charge 25¢ per 15-minute period and have a two-hour limit; around the Inner Harbor vicinity meters are in effect 24 hours a day.

BY METRO The Baltimore metro subway serves those coming into the city from the suburban northwest. Stops include Charles Center and Lexington Market, both within walking distance of the Inner Harbor. The single line runs from Owings Mills to Johns Hopkins Hospital, east of downtown. There's also a light rail that runs between points north and south in the city (⇨ By Train below). Fare is $1.60; day passes, which also count for bus and light-rail fares, are $3.50. Trains run weekdays 5 AM–midnight, weekends 6 AM–midnight.

BY TAXI It can be hard to catch a cab on the street in Baltimore. The best places to flag one down are at Pratt and Light streets in the Inner Harbor, Cross and South Charles streets in Federal Hill, O'Donnell Square in Canton, and at Broadway and Thames Street in Fells Point. Otherwise, your best option is to phone ahead and ask for a pickup, or ask your hotel concierge or doorman to summon one for you. Meters determine local fares, which average $7–$15, depending on how far you go.

Ed Kane's Water Taxis and the Seaport Taxi are fun and convenient ways to get around the Inner Harbor. They make stops at 12 points along the waterfront, including Fells Point, the National Aquarium, museums, restaurants, and Fort McHenry. All-day tickets for both services are $9 for adults and $4 for children 10 and under. Look for stops, marked with signs, all along the waterfront; depending on season, boats arrive every 10–15 minutes, or you can call to be picked up at a particular location.

BY TRAIN All Amtrak trains on the northeast corridor between Boston and Washington stop at Baltimore's Penn Station. Maryland Area Rail Commuter (MARC) trains travel between Baltimore's Penn Station and Washington, DC, Camden Station, and Washington, and BWI Airport and Penn Station. The trip to Washington, DC, takes about one hour and costs $7; the trip to BWI Airport from Penn Station takes about 20 minutes and costs $4. Trains run several times per hour, weekdays 4:45 AM–9:30 PM (note that MARC trains do not run on weekends).

Light rail is an easy, comfortable (if slow) way to reach downtown from the northern and southern suburbs. Stops near downtown include Oriole Park at Camden Yards, Howard Street, and Centre Street near Mount Vernon. The city's cultural center can be reached by the Cathedral Street stop. Light rail extends to Hunt Valley, BWI Airport, and Glen Burnie. The fare is $1.60 (exact change is required); day passes are $3.50.

TOURS Tours of Baltimore, on foot or four wheels, run from traditional surveys of historic buildings and sites to quirkier explorations such as the Fells Point Ghost Tour. The Baltimore Shuttle offers a 90-minute narrated trolley tour of the city; tours are $18 and depart daily at 11 and 2 from the visitor center at the Inner Harbor.

For a general overview of Baltimore, energetic, irrepressible Zippy Larson offers many different walking tours with historic, cultural, and architectural themes. Zippy's witty, well-researched tours take you outside the tourist bubble.

A particularly fascinating experience is local historian Wayne Schaumburg's guided tour to Greenmount Cemetery. Baltimore's largest and most prestigious burial ground is the final resting place of John Wilkes Booth, Johns Hopkins, and other native sons and daughters. Tours take place Saturday mornings in May and October and are $15 per person.

Baltimore Ghost Tours interweave narratives about city neighborhoods' colorful pasts with tales of its spectral inhabitants. Tours, which are suitable for children, run Friday and Saturday evenings (depending on the neighborhood) at 7 PM from March to November; the cost is $15 per adult; reservations are recommended. The Fells Point Visitors Center also offers a Fells Point Ghost Walk as well as tours focusing on such topics as maritime history and immigration.

For building buffs, the Baltimore Architectural Foundation sponsors walking tours of the historic and architecturally significant neighborhood of Mount Vernon; reservations are required and the cost is $10. The Mount Vernon Cultural District also organizes tours of Mount Vernon and other nearby neighborhoods.

A far less pedestrian way to see downtown is atop a Segway, the motorized upright two-wheel scooters. Segs in the City offers one- and two-hour historic city safaris for $45 and $70, respectively.

Most cruise and tour boats depart from docks in the Inner Harbor. Harbor Cruises, Ltd. and Pintail Yachts present lunch, dinner, and evening cruises around the harbor. Ride the Ducks of Baltimore provides a tour of the city by both land and water.

ESSENTIALS

Airport Information Baltimore-Washington International Thurgood Marshall Airport (BWI ⊠ 10 mi south of Baltimore off Rte. 295/Baltimore-Washington Pkwy. ☎ 410/859-7111 for information and paging ⊕ www.bwiairport.com).

Airport Transfers Airport Taxis (☎ 410/859-1100 ⊕ www.bwiairporttaxi.com). Arrow Taxicab (☎ 410/358-9696). BWI Airport rail station (☎ 410/672-6167 ⊕ www.mtamaryland.com). BWI SuperShuttle (☎ 800/258-3826 ⊕ www. supershuttle.com). Carey Limousines (☎ 410/880-0999 or 888/880-0999 ⊕ www.carey.com). Maryland Area Rail Commuter (MARC ☎ 800/325-7245 or 410/539-5000 ⊕ www.mtamaryland.com). Penn Station (⊠ Charles St. at Mt. Royal Ave., Mount Vernon ☎ 800/523-8720). Private Car/RMA Worldwide Chauffeured Transportation (☎ 410/519-0000 or 800/878-7743 ⊕ www.rmalimo.com).

Taxi Contacts Arrow Taxicab (☎ 410/358-9696). Ed Kane's Water Taxis (☎ 410/563-3901 ⊕ www.thewatertaxi.com). Jimmy's Cab Co (☎ 410/296-7200). Seaport Taxi (☎ 410/675-2900).

Train Contacts Amtrak Penn Station (⊠ Charles St. at Mt. Royal Ave., Mount Vernon ☎ 800/523-8720). Maryland Area Rail Commuter (MARC ☎ 800/325-7245 or 410/539-5000 ⊕ www.mtamaryland.com). Maryland Transit Administration (MTA ☎ 800/325-7245 or 410/539-5000 ⊕ www.mtamaryland.com).

Tour Information Baltimore Architectural Foundation (☎ 410539-7772 ⊕ www. baltimorearchitecture.org). Baltimore Ghost Tours (☎ 410/522-7400 ⊕ www.fells pointghost.com). The Baltimore Shuttle (☎ 410/732-5098). Fells Point Visitors Center Tours (☎ 410/675-6750 ⊕ www.preservationsociety.com). Greenmount Cemetery Tours (☎ 410/256-2180 ⊕ home.earthlink.net/~wschaumburg). Harbor Cruises, Ltd. (☎ 866/312-2469 ⊕ www.harborcruises.com). Mount Vernon Cultural District (⊠ 217 N. Charles St., Mount Vernon ☎ 410/605-0462 ⊕ www. mvcd.org). Pintail Yachts (⊠ Pier 5, Inner Harbor ☎ 410/539-3485). Ride the Ducks of Baltimore (⊠ 25 Light St., Inner Harbor ☎ 877/887-8225 ⊕ www. baltimoreducks.com). Segs in the City (☎ 410/276-7347 ⊕ www.segsinthecity. com). Zippy Larson's Shoe Leather Safaris (☎ 410/522-7334 ⊕ www.bcpl. net/~zipbooks).

Visitor Information Baltimore Convention Center (⊠ 100 W. Pratt St., Inner Harbor ☎ 410/649-7000 ⊕ www.bccenter.org). Baltimore Office of Promotion (☎ 410/752-8632 ⊕ www.bop.org). Baltimore Visitor Center (⊠ 401 Light St., Inner Harbor ☎ 877/225-8466 ⊕ www.baltimore.org). Fells Point Visitors Center (⊠ 808 S. Ann St., Fells Point ☎ 410/675-6750 ⊕ www.preservationsociety.com).

DISCOUNTS & DEALS

The Baltimore Visitor Center offers the three-day Harbor Pass, which saves you on admission to local attractions and gives you discounts on parking, hotels, and tours.

PLANNING YOUR TIME

The Inner Harbor is a must-see, and try to squeeze in a baseball or football game if you can. If you spend a long weekend in Baltimore, you can see most of the Inner Harbor attractions and get out to a few neighborhoods, too. Weekends are by far the busiest time for the Inner Harbor, but weekdays are often the best time to explore the boutiques in neighborhoods like Hampden and Federal Hill.

EXPLORING BALTIMORE

Visiting Baltimore without seeing the Inner Harbor is like touring New York City and skipping Manhattan. The harbor and surrounding area are home to a good number of the city's most popular sites: the National Aquarium in Baltimore, Camden Yards, M&T Bank Stadium, and the American Visionary Arts Museum and Science Center.

The neighborhoods themselves are fun to explore. Historic Federal Hill, just south of the Inner Harbor, is home to some of the oldest houses in the city. Fells Point and Canton, farther east, are lively waterfront communities. Mount Vernon and Charles Village have wide avenues lined with grand old row houses that were once home to Baltimore's wealthiest residents. Farther north are Roland Park (Frederick Law Olmsted Jr. contributed to its planning), Guilford, Homeland, and Mt. Washington, all leafy, residential neighborhoods with cottages, large Victorian houses, and redbrick Colonials. It's easy to tour the Inner Harbor and neighborhoods such as Mount Vernon, Federal Hill, Charles Village, and Fells Point on foot. To travel between areas or farther out, however, a car is more efficient. Most of the Inner Harbor's parking is in nearby garages, though meters can be found along Key Highway. In other neighborhoods, you can generally find meters and two-hour free parking on the street.

MOUNT VERNON

Baltimore's arts and cultural center, Mount Vernon is home to the Walters Art Museum and the Peabody Institute conservatory—one of the country's top music schools—as well as some of the city's grandest architecture.

Baltimore Beginnings

The Colonial government established Baltimore in 1729, at the end of the broad Patapsco River that empties into the Chesapeake Bay. Named for George Calvert, the first Lord Baltimore and the founder of Maryland, the town grew as a port and shipbuilding center and did booming business during the War of Independence.

A quantum leap came at the turn of the 19th century: from 6,700 in 1776, the population reached 45,000 by 1810. Because it was the home port for U.S. Navy vessels and for the swift Baltimore clipper ships that often preyed on British shipping, the city was a natural target for the enemy during the War of 1812. After capturing and torching Washington, DC, the British fleet sailed up the Patapsco River and bombarded Baltimore's Fort McHenry, but in vain. The 30- by 42-foot, 15-star, 15-stripe flag was still flying "by the dawn's early light," a spectacle that inspired "The Star-Spangled Banner."

The Walters and nearby Mount Vernon Place, a wonderfully designed park, are two of the neighborhood's must-sees. A good plan is to visit the Walters first then rest for a while in Mount Vernon Place. You'll need a breather before and after climbing the Washington Monument, which sits in the middle of the park. After, there are plenty of restaurants on or near Charles Street, the neighborhood thoroughfare. From the Inner Harbor, you can walk up Charles Street into the heart of Mount Vernon in about 25–30 minutes. You can also drive or take the No. 3 bus.

The area was named for the nation's first significant monument to George Washington, erected at the neighborhood's center in Mount Vernon Place. In the 19th century Mount Vernon was home to some of Baltimore's wealthiest residents, including Enoch Pratt, a wealthy merchant who donated funds for the first public library; Robert Garrett, of the Baltimore & Ohio Railroad; and Henry and William Walters, who founded the art gallery that bears their names. Though some of the grand houses here remain single-family residences, many have been turned into apartments or offices.

Numbers in the text correspond to numbers in the margin and on the Baltimore map.

MAIN ATTRACTIONS

❷ **Basilica of the Assumption.** Completed in 1821, the Catholic Basilica of the Assumption is the oldest cathedral in the United States. Designed by Benjamin Latrobe, architect of the U.S. Capitol, it stands as a paragon of neoclassicism, with a grand portico fronted by six Corinthian columns that suggest an ancient Greek temple. Two towers are surmounted by cupolas. The church, including 24 original skylights in the dome, which were covered over after World War II, were restored in November 2006, the bicentennial of the laying of the church's cornerstone. ⊠ *Mulberry and Cathedral Sts., Mount Vernon* ☎ *410/727–3564* ☺ *Call for hrs.*

FodorsChoice
★

⑩ Contemporary Museum. Artists come from around the world to collaborate with local communities and institutions and produce artwork that is relevant to Baltimore. The museum's minimalistic interior shifts all of your focus to the unconventional art within. Works are shown both on-site and off, using traditional mediums and innovative approaches. ⊠ *100 W. Centre St., Mount Vernon* ☎ *410/783–5720* ⊕ *www.contemporary. org* 🖼 *$5 suggested donation* ⊙ *Wed.–Sun. noon–5.*

⑨ Maryland Historical Society. More than 200,000 objects serve to celebrate Maryland's history and heritage at this museum. One major attraction is the original manuscript of "The Star-Spangled Banner." The first floor is devoted to an exhibit about Marylanders' pursuit of liberty, with a focus on religious freedom, voting rights, labor, and war. Featured on the second floor are portrait paintings by the Peale family and Joshua Johnson, America's first African-American portrait artist, as well as 18th- and 19th-century Maryland landscape paintings juxtaposed against present-day photographs of the same places. Furniture manufactured and designed in Maryland from the 18th century to the present is on the third floor. There's also a library with 7 million works that relate to the state's history. ⊠ *201 W. Monument St., Mount Vernon* ☎ *410/685–3750* ⊕ *www.mdhs.org* 🖼 *$8* ⊙ *Museum: Wed.–Sun. 10–5; library: Wed.–Sat. 10–4:30.*

۞ Maryland Zoo in Baltimore. The 150 acres of the Maryland Zoo in Baltimore—the third-oldest zoo in the country—are a natural stomping ground for little ones seeking out the spectacle of elephants, lions, giraffes, hippos, and penguins, among the more than 2,000 animals that make this their home. Don't miss the warthog exhibit, said to be the nation's only dedicated environment for the bumpy beasts. Favorite sights include a chimpanzee house and leopard lair, polar bears frolicking in an arctic pool, and a petting zoo with a re-created barnyard. If you make it all the way to the Africa exhibit and are too tired to walk back, you can hop on a tram that goes back to the entrance. Surrounding the zoo is Druid Hill Park, which was designed by Frederick Law Olmsted Jr.; the park has seen better days, but it's worth a drive through. ⊠ *Druid Hill Lake Dr., Druid Hill* ☎ *410/366–5466* ⊕ *www. marylandzoo.org* 🖼 *$15* ⊙ *Mar.–Dec., daily 10–4.*

⑥ Mount Vernon Place. One of the country's more beautifully designed pub-
★ lic spaces, Mount Vernon Place is a prime spot for relaxing. It was established when John Eager Howard donated the highest point in Baltimore as a site for a memorial to George Washington. With the monument as its center, the square is composed of four parks, each a block in length, that are arranged around Mount Vernon Place (which goes east–west) and Washington Place (north–south). Benches near the monument are great for watching water calmly trickle from the fountains. The sculptures in the parks deserve a close look; of special note is a bronze lion by Antoine-Louis Barye in the middle of West Mount Vernon Place. Northeast of the monument is Mount Vernon Methodist Church, built in the mid-1850s on the site of Francis Scott Key's home and place of death. Free concerts are held here monthly in the summertime. Take a moment to admire the brownstones along the

north side of East Mount Vernon Place. They're excellent examples of the luxurious mansions built by 19th-century residents of Baltimore's most prestigious address.

❺ **Walters Art Museum.** The Walters' prodigious collection of more than
Fodor'sChoice 30,000 artworks provides an organized overview of human history
★ over 5,500 years, from the 3rd millennium BC to the early 20th century. ■TIP➡ Thanks to a grant by the city, admission is free. The original museum (1909) houses major collections of Renaissance and baroque paintings as well as a sculpture court. Two other buildings contain Egyptian, Greek and Roman, Byzantine, and Ethiopian art collections— among the best in the nation—along with many 19th-century paintings. There are also medieval armor and artifacts; jewelry and decorative works; Egyptology exhibits; a wonderful gift shop; and a café. ⊠ *600 N. Charles St., Mount Vernon* ☎ *410/547–9000* ⊕ *www.thewalters. org* ☑ *Free* ⊙ *Wed.–Sun. 10–5.*

❼ **Washington Monument.** "If the stairs don't take your breath away, the view will." Overheard in a conversation at the top, that's Baltimore's Washington Monument in a nutshell. Completed on July 4, 1829, the monument was the first one dedicated to the nation's first president. An 18-foot statue depicting Washington caps the 160-foot white marble tower. Climb the 228 steps up the clammy spiral staircase and your reward is a stunning panoramic view of the city. The tower was designed and built by Robert Mills, the first architect born and educated in the United States; 19 years after completing Baltimore's Washington Monument, Mills designed and erected the national Washington Monument in DC. ⊠ *Mt. Vernon Pl., Mount Vernon* ☎ *410/396–1049* ☑ *$1 donation* ⊙ *Wed.–Sun. 10–4.*

ALSO WORTH SEEING

☾ **Baltimore Streetcar Museum.** This often-overlooked museum lets you travel back to an era when streetcars dominated city thoroughfares. A film traces the vehicle's evolution, and there are beautifully restored streetcars to explore. ■TIP➡ Best of all, you can take unlimited rides on a working streetcar. ⊠ *1901 Falls Rd., Midtown* ☎ *410/547–0264* ⊕ *www.baltimorestreetcar.org* ☑ *$7* ⊙ *June–Oct., weekends noon–5; Nov.–May, Sun. noon–5.*

❸ **Enoch Pratt Free Library.** Donated to the city of Baltimore in 1882 by its namesake, a wealthy merchant, the Enoch Pratt Free Library was one of the country's first free-circulation public libraries; it remains one of the country's largest. The Pratt was remarkable for allowing any citizen to borrow books at a time when only the wealthy could afford to buy them. When the collection outgrew its original fortresslike rococo structure in 1933, Pratt's democratic ideals were incorporated into the new building's grand yet accessible design. Innovations such as a sidewalk-level entrance and department store–style exhibit windows set the standard for public libraries across the country. The building is still a treat to explore. A huge skylight illuminates the Central Hall's marble floors, gilded fixtures, mural panels depicting the history of printing and publishing, and oil portraits of the Lords Baltimore. The

Children's Department, with a fishpond, puppet theater, and a large selection of books, is a real gem for little ones. An audio architecture tour of the museum is available at the circulation desk. ⊠ *400 Cathedral St., Mount Vernon* 🕾 *410/396–5500* ⊕ *www.pratt.lib.md.us* ☉ *June–Sept., Mon.–Wed. 10–8, Thurs. 10–5:30, Fri. and Sat. 10–5, Sun. 1–5; Oct.–May, Mon.–Wed. 11–7, Thurs. 10–5:30, Fri. and Sat. 10–5, Sun. 1–5.*

❹ First Unitarian Church. Designed by Maximilian Godefroy in 1819, the church that year was the site for the sermon that definitively established Unitarianism as a denomination (the sermon was given by the church's founder, Dr. William Ellery Channing). ⊠ *Charles and Franklin Sts., entrance at 1 W. Hamilton St., Mount Vernon* 🕾 *410/685–2330* ☉ *Tues.–Fri. 10–4:30.*

❽ Garrett-Jacobs Mansion. Originally built in 1893 by Stanford White for Robert Garrett, the president of the Baltimore & Ohio Railroad, this mansion was the largest and most expensive ever constructed in Baltimore (the neighbors objected to its size). After Garrett died in 1896, his widow, Mary, and her second husband, Dr. Henry Barton Jacobs, had John Russell Pope build an extension of equal size. Call ahead to book a tour. ⊠ *11 W. Mt. Vernon Pl., Mount Vernon* 🕾 *410/539–6914* ⊕ *www.garrettjacobsmansion.org* 🎟 *$5* ☉ *Tours by appointment; reservations required.*

OFF THE BEATEN PATH

Great Blacks in Wax Museum. Though not as convincing as the likenesses at a Madame Tussaud's, the more than 100 wax figures on display here do a good job of recounting the triumphs and trials of Africans and African-Americans. The wax figures are accompanied by text and audio. Baltimoreans honored include Frederick Douglass, who as a youth lived and worked in Fells Point; singer Billie Holiday; and jazz composer Eubie Blake. To get here from Mount Vernon, take Charles north and turn left at North Avenue. ⊠ *1601 E. North Ave., East Baltimore* 🕾 *410/563–3404* ⊕ *www.greatblacksinwax.org* 🎟 *$12* ☉ *Mid-Jan.–mid-Oct., Tues.–Sat. 9–6, Sun. noon–6; mid-Oct.–mid-Jan., Tues.–Sat. 9–5, Sun. noon–5. Closed Mon. except in Feb., July, Aug., and most federal holidays.*

NEED A BREAK?

Donna's (⊠ *800 N. Charles St., Mount Vernon* 🕾 *410/385–0180*) is a relaxing Mount Vernon spot for coffee; soups, salads, and sandwiches are also served. At artsy and elegant **Sascha's 527** (⊠ *527 N. Charles St., Mount Vernon* 🕾 *410/539–8880*) you can choose from a selection of salads and sandwiches.

❶ Woman's Industrial Exchange. This Baltimore institution was organized in the 1880s as a way for destitute women, many of them Civil War widows, to support themselves in a ladylike fashion through sewing and other domestic handiworks. To this day you can still purchase handmade quilts, embroidered baby clothes, sock monkeys, and many other arts and crafts. ⊠ *333 N. Charles St., Mount Vernon* 🕾 *410/685–4388* ⊕ *www.womansindustrialexchange.org* ☉ *Weekdays 10–4, Sat. 11–3.*

CHARLES VILLAGE

Though Johns Hopkins University anchors Charles Village, the Baltimore Museum of Art is the neighborhood's prime tourist draw—especially since admission is free. Students, professors, writers, and artists are drawn to the area's intellectual environment. Row houses along Charles, St. Paul, and Calvert streets—some of them quite large—were built in the late 1890s and early 1900s for merchants, bankers, and other professionals. These early developments were constructed on old family estates, one of which became the basis for the present-day Johns Hopkins campus. Some of the old mansions are now museums, including Johns Hopkins's Homewood House and the Evergreen House, which also belongs to the university. On the eastern and northern sides of the Johns Hopkins campus are the neighborhoods of Tuscany-Canterbury and Roland Park. Farther to the north and east are Homeland and Guilford, tony areas worth exploring for their beautiful homes and lovely, tree-lined streets.

MAIN ATTRACTIONS

⑪ Baltimore Museum of Art. Works by Matisse, Picasso, Cézanne, Gauguin, van Gogh, and Monet are among the 90,000 paintings, sculptures, and decorative arts on exhibit at this impressive museum near Johns Hopkins University. Particular strengths include an encyclopedic collection of postimpressionist paintings donated to the museum by the Cone sisters, Baltimore natives who were pioneer collectors of early-20th-century art. The museum also owns the world's second-largest collection of Andy Warhol works, and many pieces of 18th- and 19th-century American painting and decorative arts. The museum's neoclassical main building was designed by John Russell Pope, the architect of the National Gallery in Washington; the modern aluminum and concrete wing houses the contemporary art collection. From Gertrude's, the museum restaurant, you can look out at 20th-century sculpture displayed in two landscaped gardens. ⊠ *10 Art Museum Dr., Charles Village* ☎ *410/396-7100* ⊕ *www.artbma.org* ⊡ *Free* ⊗ *Wed.–Fri. 11–5, weekends 11–6.*

FodorśChoice ★

6

⑯ Evergreen House. Built in the 1850s, this 48-room Italianate mansion was the home of the 19th-century diplomat and collector John Work Garrett, whose father was president of the Baltimore & Ohio Railroad (the Garrett family continued to live here until the 1950s). Garrett bequeathed the house, its contents (an exquisite collection of books, paintings, and porcelain), and 26 acres of grounds to Johns Hopkins University. He required that the estate remain open to "lovers of music, art, and beautiful things." A tour of the mansion is a fascinating look at the luxury that surrounded a rich American family at the turn of the 20th century. ⊠ *4545 N. Charles St., Homeland* ☎ *410/516–0341* ⊡ *$6* ⊗ *Tues.–Fri. 11–4, weekends noon–4.*

⑬ Homewood House Museum. This elegant Federal-period mansion was once the home of Charles Carroll Jr., son of Charles Carroll of Carrollton, a signer of the Declaration of Independence. Deeded to Johns Hopkins University in 1902 along with 60 acres, the house served as faculty club and offices before being fully restored to its 1800 grandeur (it's one of the finest examples of the neoclassical architecture of the period). ⊠*3400 N. Charles St., Charles Village* ☎*410/516–5589* ≋*$6* ☉*Tues.–Fri. 11–4, weekends noon–4.*

⓬ **Johns Hopkins University.** The school was founded in 1876 with funds donated by Johns Hopkins, director of the Baltimore & Ohio Railroad. Much of the neo-Colonial architecture of the Homewood campus dates from the early 1900s, when the present-day campus was laid out. Dominating the school's main quad is Gilman Hall, which was built in 1904 and named for the university's first president, Daniel Coit Gilman. Pathways lead through campus; maps throughout can help you find your way. The medical school and hospital are in East Baltimore. ⊠*3400 N. Charles St., Charles Village* ☎*410/516–8000* ⊕*www.jhu.edu.*

ALSO WORTH SEEING

⓮ **Lacrosse Museum and National Hall of Fame.** Photos, objects, and videos tell the story of the history of lacrosse, a very popular sport in Maryland. One room is dedicated to outstanding players who have been honored by the U.S. Lacrosse Association since 1957. ⊠*113 W. University Pkwy., Tuscany-Canterbury* ☎*410/235–6882* ⊕*www.uslacrosse.org* ≋*$3* ☉*June–Jan., weekdays 10–3; Feb.–May, Tues.–Sat. 10–3.*

Lovely Lane Methodist Church. Built in 1882, Lovely Lane Methodist Church is honored with the title "The Mother Church of American Methodism." Stanford White designed the Romanesque sanctuary after the basilicas of Ravenna, Italy; the stained-glass windows are excellent examples of Italian mosaic art. The buildings to the north that resemble the church are the original campus of the Women's College of Baltimore, now called Goucher College (the school moved to Towson in the 1950s). Dr. Goucher, the college's founder, was a pastor at Lovely Lane. Today the building next to the church is occupied by the Baltimore Lab School. Tours of the church and the Methodist Historical Society are by appointment. ⊠*2200 St. Paul St., North Charles* ☎*410/889–1512* ⊕*www.lovelylane.net* ☉*Weekdays 9–3.*

NEED A BREAK? With great vegetarian food, cocktails, and doors that stay open until 2 AM every day but Sunday, it's no surprise that students love the One World Cafe (⊠**100 W. University Pkwy., North Charles** ☎**410/235-5777**). In summer, take advantage of the café's sidewalk seating.

⓯ **Sherwood Gardens.** A popular spring destination for Baltimore families, this 6-acre park contains more than 80,000 tulips that bloom in late April. Azaleas peak in late April and the first half of May. The gardens are usually at their best around Mother's Day. ⊠*Stratford Rd. at Greenway, east of St. Paul St., Guilford* ☎*410/785-0444* ≋*Free* ☉*Daily dawn–dusk.*

INNER HARBOR

The Inner Harbor has come a long way in the past 20-odd years. Before it was transformed into the city's biggest destination, the harbor consisted mostly of run-down warehouses. Now it includes the National Aquarium, Harborplace shopping centers, the Maryland Science Center, fountains, and high-rise offices. Oriole Park at Camden Yards and M&T Bank Stadium, where the NFL's Ravens play, are only a couple of blocks away. The harbor is still a working port, and visitors can get on the water with sailboat tours, water taxis, and boat rentals. Just south of the Inner Harbor and best accessed by car or water taxi, Fort McHenry was bombarded by the British during the War of 1812. Despite a long night's siege by cannon and artillery the fort never fell, and the sight of the American flag flying above the its walls inspired Francis Scott Key to pen a poem that became the national anthem.

> ## WORD OF MOUTH
>
> "Walking around the Inner Harbor is a must. It's very touristy, but that's what you will be—so you might as well join in! . . . The Aquarium is right there and a great one. I love the shark tank! Another poster mentioned the American Visionary Art Museum. I love this museum. The best way to sum it up is 'cooky'—a little out there, but I can guarantee that you have seen nothing like it. Make sure you tour all the buildings—you wouldn't want to miss the 10-foot poodle/car, would you!"   —Saytray

MAIN ATTRACTIONS

22 American Visionary Art Museum. The nation's primary museum and education center for self-taught or "outsider" art has won great acclaim by both museum experts and those who don't even consider themselves art aficionados. Seven galleries exhibit the quirky creations—paintings, sculptures, relief works, and pieces that defy easy classification—of untrained "visionary" artists working outside the mainstream art world. In addition to the visual stimulation of amazingly intricate or refreshingly inventive works, reading the short bios of artists will give you insight to their often-moving spiritual and expressive motivations. The museum's unusual, playful philosophy extends outside its walls, with large exhibits installed in a former whiskey warehouse and a 55-foot whirligig twirling in the museum's plaza. ⊠ *800 Key Hwy., Federal Hill* ☎ *410/244–1900* ⊕ *www.avam.org* ⊠ *$12* ☉ *Tues.–Sun. 10–6.*

Fodor'sChoice
★

25 Baltimore Maritime Museum. Consisting of three docked vessels and a restored lighthouse, this museum gives a good sense of Baltimore's maritime heritage as well as American naval power. On the west side of the pier, the submarine USS *Torsk*, the "Galloping Ghost of the Japanese Coast," is credited with sinking the last two Japanese warships in World War II. The lightship *Chesapeake*, built as a floating lighthouse in 1930 and now out of commission, remains fully operational. The *Taney* is a Coast Guard cutter that saw action at Pearl Harbor. Built in 1856 the Seven Foot Knoll Lighthouse marked the entrance to Baltimore Harbor from the Chesapeake Bay for 133 years before its move to the museum. ⊠ *Pier 3, Inner Harbor* ☎ *410/396–3453* ⊕ *www.*

6

baltomaritimemuseum.org ☎*$10–$16* ⏰*June–Aug., daily 10–5:30; Sept.–Nov. and Mar.–May, Sun.–Thurs. 10–5, Fri. and Sat. 10–6; Dec.– Feb., Fri.–Sun. 10–5.*

Baltimore Museum of Industry. Housed in an 1865 oyster cannery, the fascinating and kid-friendly Baltimore Museum of Industry covers the city's industrial and labor history and is well worth the 0.5-mi walk south of the Inner Harbor along Key Highway. Here you can watch and help operate the functional re-creations of a machine shop circa 1900, a print shop, a cannery, and a garment workroom. A restored steam-driven tugboat that plied the waterfront for the first half of the 20th century is docked outside. ⊠*1415 Key Hwy., Federal Hill* ☎*410/727–4808* ⊕*www.thebmi.org* ☎*$10* ⏰*Tues.–Sat. 10–4, Sun. 11–4.*

㉑ ★ Federal Hill Park. If you want to snap a photo of the Inner Harbor, Federal Hill Park is the place to do it. On the south side of the harbor, the park was named in 1788 to commemorate Maryland's ratification of the U.S. Constitution. Until the early 1900s, a signal tower atop Federal Hill displayed the "house" flags of local shipping companies, notifying them of the arrival of their vessels. Some of the oldest homes in Baltimore surround the park, and its summit provides an excellent view of the Inner Harbor and the downtown skyline. The park is also a favorite spot for watching holiday fireworks. ⊠*Battery Ave. and Key Hwy., Federal Hill.*

⑲ Fort McHenry. This star-shape brick fort is forever associated with Francis Scott Key and "The Star-Spangled Banner," which Key penned while watching the British bombardment of Baltimore during the War of 1812. Key had been detained onboard a truce ship, where he had been negotiating the release of one Dr. William Beanes, when the bombardment began; Key knew too much about the attack plan to be released. Through the next day and night, as the battle raged, Key strained to be sure, through the smoke and haze, that the flag still flew above Fort McHenry—indicating that Baltimore's defenders held firm. "By the dawn's early light" of September 14, 1814, he saw the 30-foot by 42-foot "Star-Spangled Banner" still aloft and was inspired to pen the words to a poem (set to the tune of an old English drinking song). The flag that flew above Fort McHenry that day had 15 stars and 15 stripes, and was hand-sewn for the fort. A visit to the fort includes a 15-minute history film, guided tour, and frequent living-history displays on summer weekends. To see how the formidable fortifications might have appeared to the bombarding British, catch a water taxi from the Inner Harbor to the fort instead of driving. ⊠*E. Fort Ave., from Light St., take Key Hwy. for 1½ mi and follow signs, Locust Point* ☎*410/962–4290* ⊕*www.nps.gov/fomc* ☎*$7* ⏰*Memorial Day–Labor Day, daily 8–8; Labor Day–Memorial Day, daily 8–5.*

Fodor'sChoice

㊽ Geppi's Entertainment Museum. Fans of comic books and pop culture have plenty to take in at this museum since it opened in 2006. A stone's throw from the baseball park in Camden Yards, it boasts thousands of comic books, toys, and collectibles from as far back as the 1700s. It has won awards from parents and local publications as a destination for kids (and adults with inner kids). For adults, it's a trip down memory lane. Kids will marvel at how their favorite superhero evolved over the years. ✉*301 W. Camden St., Inner Harbor* ☎*410/625–7060* ⊕*www.geppismuseum.com* ✉*$10* ⊗*Tues.–Sun. 10–6*

⑰ Harborplace and the Gallery. Inside two glass-enclosed marketplaces are a plethora of shops and eateries: the Light Street Pavilion has two stories of food courts and restaurants and the Pratt Street Pavilion is dedicated mainly to retail stores. More than a dozen restaurants, including Edo Sushi, Phillips, and Tir Na Nog, offer waterfront dining, and such local specialty shops as Best of Baltimore and Maryland Bay Company carry interesting souvenirs. In summer, performers entertain at an outdoor amphitheater between the two pavilions, and paddleboats are available for rent south of the Pratt Street building. A skywalk from the Pratt Street Pavilion leads to **The Gallery**, a four-story shopping mall with 70 more shops, including Bebe, J. Crew, Coach, and Godiva Chocolatiers. ✉*100 Pratt St. , Inner Harbor* ☎*410/332–4191* ⊕*www.harborplace.com* ⊗*Mon.–Sat. 10–9, Sun. 11–7. Harborplace and the Gallery have extended summer hrs; some restaurants open earlier for breakfast, and most close late.*

6

⑳ Maryland Science Center. Originally known as the Maryland Academy of Sciences, this 200-year-old scientific institution is one of the oldest in the United States. Now housed in a contemporary building, the three floors of exhibits on the Chesapeake Bay, Earth science, physics, the body, dinosaurs, and outer space are an invitation to engage, experiment, and explore. The center has a planetarium, a simulated archaeological dinosaur dig, an IMAX movie theater with a screen five stories high, and a playroom especially designed for young children. ✉*601 Light St., Inner Harbor* ☎*410/685–5225* ⊕*www.mdsci.org* ✉*$14.50, IMAX $8* ⊗*Memorial Day–Labor Day, Thurs.–Sat. 10–8, Sun.–Wed. 10–6; Labor Day–Memorial Day, Tues.–Fri. 10–5, Sat. 10–6, Sun. 11–5.*

㉔ National Aquarium in Baltimore. The most-visited attraction in Maryland has more than 10,000 fish, sharks, dolphins, and amphibians dwelling in 2 million gallons of water. The Animal Planet Australia: Wild Extremes exhibit mimics a river running through a gorge. It features lizards, crocodiles, turtles, bats, and a black-headed python, among other animals from Down Under. The aquarium also features reptiles, birds, plants, and mammals in its rain-forest environment, inside a glass pyramid 64 feet high. The rain-forest ecosystem harbors two-toed sloths in calabash trees, parrots in the palms, iguanas on the ground, and red-bellied piranhas in a pool (a sign next to it reads DO NOT PUT HANDS IN POOL). Each day in the Marine Mammal Pavilion, Atlantic bottlenose dolphins are part of several entertaining presentations that highlight their agility and intelligence. The aquarium's famed shark tank and Atlantic coral reef exhibits are spectacular; you can wind through an enormous glass enclosure on a spiral ramp while hammerheads and brightly hued tropical fish glide by.

Fodor'sChoice

Hands-on exhibits include such doc-
ile sea creatures as horseshoe crabs
and starfish. ■TIP➔ Arrive early to
ensure admission, which is by timed
intervals; by noon, the wait is often
two or three hours. ✉*Pier 3, Inner
Harbor* ☎*410/576–3800* ⊕*www.
aqua.org* ✑*$21.95* ⊙*Nov.–Feb.,
Sat.–Thurs. 10–5, Fri. 10–8; Mar.–
June, Sept., and Oct., Sat.–Thurs.
9–5, Fri. 9–8; July–Aug. 19, daily
9–8; Aug. 20–31, Sat.–Thurs. 9–6,
Fri. 9–8; visitors may tour for up to
1½ hrs after closing. Timed tickets
may be required on weekends and
holidays; purchase these early in the day.*

> **BEST VIEW OF THE INNER HARBOR**
>
> From the "Top of the World"—the observation level on the 27th floor of the World Trade Center—you can see for miles in any direction, or peer through binoculars for a closer look. Best free view of the Inner Harbor: Federal Hill Park, across the water from the National Aquarium, offers a good vantage point for photos and picnics.

㉗ **Port Discovery—The Baltimore Children's Museum.** At this interactive
Ⓒ museum, adults are encouraged to play every bit as much as children.
A favorite attraction is the three-story KidWorks, a futuristic jungle
gym on which the adventurous can climb, crawl, slide, and swing their
way through stairs, slides, ropes, zip-lines, and tunnels, and even cross
a narrow footbridge three stories up. In Miss Perception's Mystery
House, youngsters help solve a mystery surrounding the disappearance
of the Baffeld family by sifting through clues; some are written or visual,
and others are gleaned by touching and listening. Changing interactive exhibits allow for even more play. ✉*35 Market Pl., Inner Harbor*
☎*410/727–8120* ⊕*www.portdiscovery.com* ✑*$11.75* ⊙*Memorial
Day–Labor Day, Mon.–Sat. 10–5, Sun. noon–5; Labor Day–Memorial
Day, Tues.–Fri. 9:30–4:30, Sat. 10–5, Sun. noon–5.*

㉘ **Reginald F. Lewis Museum of Maryland African American History & Culture.**
Named for the former CEO of TLC Beatrice International, the Reginald
F. Lewis Museum is dedicated to the African-American experience in
Maryland. The contemporary, predominantly red-and-black building
holds exhibits on African-American history, art, and culture as told
through the lives of such individuals as Frederick Douglass, Billie Holiday, and civil rights leader Kweisi Mfume. Facilities include an oral history recording and listening studio and an information resource center.
✉*830 E. Pratt St., Inner Harbor* ☎*443/263–1800* ⊕*www.african
americanculture.org* ✑*$8* ⊙*Tues.–Sat. 10–5, Sun. noon–5.*

⑱ **USS *Constellation*.** Launched in 1854, the USS *Constellation* was the
Ⓒ last—and largest—all-sail ship built by the U.S. Navy. Before the Civil
War, as part of the African Squadron, she saw service on antislavery
patrol; during the war, she protected Union-sympathizing U.S. merchant
ships from Confederate raiders. The warship eventually became a training ship for the Navy before serving as the relief flagship for the Atlantic
Fleet during World War II, finally arriving in Baltimore in 1955 for restoration to her original condition. You can tour the USS *Constellation*
for a glimpse of life as a 19th-century navy sailor, and children can
muster to become Civil War–era "powder monkeys." Recruits receive

"basic training," try on replica period uniforms, participate in a gun drill, and learn a sea chantey or two before being discharged and paid off in Civil War money at the end of their "cruise." ⊠*Pratt and Light Sts., Inner Harbor* ☎*410/539–6238* ⊕*www.constellation.org* ▣*$10* ⊗*Mar.–Oct., daily 10–5:30; Nov.–Feb., daily 10–4:30.*

Visitor Center. Stop by the sweeping, all-glass center for information on the city, brochures, tickets, and hotel and restaurant reservations. ⊠*401 Light St., Inner Harbor* ☎*877/225–8466* ⊕*www.baltimore. org* ⊗*Daily 9–6.*

㉓ ★ **World Trade Center.** With 32 stories, this building, designed by I. M. Pei's firm, is the world's tallest pentagonal structure. The 27th-floor "Top of the World" observation deck allows an unobstructed view of Baltimore and beyond from a height of 423 feet. ⊠*401 E. Pratt St., Inner Harbor* ☎*410/837–8439* ⊕*www.wtci.org* ▣*$5* ⊗*Memorial Day–Labor Day, weekdays and Sun. 10–6, Sat. 10–8; Apr., May, Sept., and Oct., Wed.–Sun. 10–6.*

ALSO WORTH SEEING

㊱ **Baltimore City Hall.** Built in 1875, Baltimore City Hall consists of mansard roofs and a gilt dome over a 110-foot rotunda, all supported by ironwork. Inside you can get tours of the chambers and view exhibits on Baltimore's history. Directly across the street is **City Hall Plaza,** on what was originally the site of the Holliday Street Theatre. The theater was owned and operated by the Ford brothers; they also operated Ford's Theatre in Washington, DC, where President Lincoln was assassinated. "The Star-Spangled Banner" was first publicly sung here. ⊠*100 N. Holliday St., Downtown* ☎*410/396–3100* ▣*Free* ⊗*Weekdays 8–4:30.*

㉚ **Baltimore Civil War Museum-President Street Station.** President Street Station offers a glimpse of the violence and divided loyalties that the war caused in Maryland, a state caught in the middle. Originally the Baltimore terminus of the Philadelphia, Wilmington & Baltimore Railroad, the relocated station, built in 1849, contains exhibits that depict the events that led to mob violence. It began when troops from the Sixth Massachusetts Regiment bound for Washington, DC, walked from this station to the Camden Station (near Oriole Park). In what would be the first bloodshed of the Civil War, 4 soldiers and 12 civilians were killed; 36 soldiers and a number of civilians were wounded. The riot lasted for several hours and inspired the secessionist poem "Maryland, My Maryland," today the state song. Guided tours of the route of the Sixth Massachusetts are offered at 1 PM on weekends. ⊠*601 President St., Inner Harbor East* ☎*410/385–5188* ▣*$3, guided tour $5* ⊗*Daily 10–5.*

㉙ **Baltimore Public Works Museum.** A short walk east of the Inner Harbor, this museum is an unusual collection of artifacts displayed in an unusual location: the old Eastern Avenue Sewage Pumping Station, built in 1912. Here you can examine several generations of water pipes, including wood piping nearly 200 years old. Other exhibits tell the history of such city services as trash removal. Outdoors, a life-size model reveals what lies underneath Baltimore streets. Since the museum is still an operational sewage pumping station, it smells. ⊠*844 E. Pratt St., Inner Harbor* ☎*410/396–5565* ⊠*$3* ☽*Tues.–Sun. 10–4.*

㉜ Carroll Mansion. This was once the winter home of Charles Carroll, one of the signers of the Declaration of Independence. It's now a museum dedicated to the history of the city and the neighborhood, Historic Jonestown, as told by the various occupants of the house through the years. ⊠*800 E. Lombard St., Historic Jonestown* ☎*410/605–2964* ⊕*www.carrollmuseums.org* ⊠*$5* ☽*Wed.–Sun. noon–4 and by appointment.*

㉝ Jewish Museum of Maryland. Sandwiched between two 19th-century synagogues, the Jewish Museum of Maryland has changing exhibits of art, photography, and documents related to the Jewish experience in Maryland. The Lloyd Street Synagogue, to the left of the museum, was built in 1845 and was the first in Maryland and the third in the United States. The other, B'nai Israel, was built in 1876 in a uniquely Moorish style. Tours of both synagogues are available. ⊠*15 Lloyd St., Historic Jonestown* ☎*410/732–6400* ⊕*www.jewishmuseummd.org* ⊠*$8* ☽*Tues.–Fri. and Sun. noon–4 and by appointment.*

㉞ Nine Front Street. This cute two-story brick town house, built in 1790, was once the home of Mayor Thorowgood Smith, the second mayor of Baltimore. The Women's Civic League, which has its home here, gives tours of the house and of city hall; call for an appointment. ⊠*9 Front St., Historic Jonestown* ☎*410/837–5424* ☽*Tues.–Thurs. 9–2:30, Fri. 9–2; call ahead.*

㉟ Phoenix Shot Tower. The only remaining tower of three of this type that once existed in Baltimore, this brick structure was used to make shot pellets by pouring molten lead from the top. As the drops fell, they formed balls that turned solid in cold water at the bottom. In the summer months the tower may close due to heat. ⊠*801 E. Fayette St., Historic Jonestown* ☎*410/605–2964* ⊠*$1* ☽*May–Aug., Fri.–Sun. noon–4; Sept.–Apr., by appointment.*

㉖ The Power Plant. What actually was the city's former power plant is now a retail and dining complex that includes a Hard Rock Cafe, a Barnes & Noble, and a 35,000-square-foot ESPN Zone. Next door is the **Pier 4 Building,** which houses a Chipotle Mexican Grill and Blu Bamboo, a fast-casual Mongolian grill. The cutting-edge **Maryland Art Place** (⊠*8 Market Pl. , Suite 100, Inner Harbor* ☎*410/962–8565* ⊕*www.mdartplace.org* ⊠*Free* ☽*Tues.–Sat. 11–5*) gallery highlights works by contemporary local and regional artists. ⊠*Pier 5, 601 E. Pratt St., Inner Harbor* ☎*No phone.*

NEED A BREAK?

Espresso, cannolis, and other delicious Italian pastries can be found at **Vaccaro's** (⊠*222 Albemarle St., Little Italy* ☎*410/685–4905*). **Whole Foods** (⊠*1001 Fleet St., Inner Harbor East* ☎*410/528–1640*) has tables and chairs inside and outside for eating premade sandwiches, sushi, and salads.

WORD OF MOUTH

"Get some cannolis at Vacarro's. YUM!"   —enjoylife

31 Star-Spangled Banner House. Built in 1793, this Federal-style home was where Mary Pickersgill hand-sewed the 15-star, 15-stripe flag that survived the British bombardment of Fort McHenry in 1814 and inspired Francis Scott Key to write "The Star-Spangled Banner." The house

> **WORD OF MOUTH**
>
> ". . . the Inner Harbor is great, but I really love the Fells Point area in the evening."   —brando

contains Federal furniture and American art of the period, including pieces from the Pickersgill family. Outdoors, a map of the United States has been made of stones from the various states. A museum connected to the house tells the history of the War of 1812. ⊠ *844 E. Pratt St., Historic Jonestown* ☎ *410/837–1793* ⊕ *www.flaghouse.org* ⊠ *$7* ⊙ *Tues.–Sat. 10–4.*

FELLS POINT

Fells Point is a gathering ground for blue- and white-collar locals and tourists. Plenty of bars and small craft shops line Broadway, running north–south, and Thames (pronounced with a long "a" and thick "th"), running east–west along the water. Head here in the afternoon and tour the shops and two small museums; afterward stay for dinner and drinks at one of the neighborhood's many pubs—most of which host live local bands daily. From the Inner Harbor it takes about five minutes to reach Fells Point by car. You can also opt for the water taxi, a much more fun way to get there.

Standing in the heart of Fells Point, you get the feeling little has changed since it was founded several hundred years ago. Englishman William Fell purchased the peninsula in 1726, seeing its potential for shipbuilding and shipping. Starting in 1763 his son Edward and his wife, Ann Bond Fell, divided and sold the land; docks, shipyards, warehouses, stores, homes, churches, and schools sprang up, and the area quickly grew into a bustling seaport. Fells Point was famed for its shipyards (the notoriously speedy clipper ships built here annoyed the British so much during the War of 1812 that they tried to capture the city, a move resulting in Fort McHenry's bombardment). Frederick Douglass worked at a shipyard at the end of Thames Street in the 1830s. Around the 1840s the shipbuilding industry started to decline, in large part because of the rise of steamships, which were being constructed elsewhere.

MAIN ATTRACTIONS

39 Broadway Market. Head to the market's two pavilions to grab a drink or light snack or stock up on ethnic deli meats. You can also find pizza, sandwiches, and oysters at a raw bar. ⊠ *Broadway between Fleet and Lancaster Sts., Fells Point.*

38 Fells Point Maritime Museum. For the history of the shipbuilding industry in Fells Point and the people involved in it, go to this small museum. You can find out about the speedy Baltimore clipper schooners, which once made this area famous; the cargoes they carried; and the shipbuilders, merchants, and sailors who sought their fortunes. ⊠ *1724 Thames*

St., Fells Point ☎*410/732–0278* ⊕*www.mdhs.org* ⬚*$4* ⊙*Thurs.–Mon. 10–5.*

Fells Point Visitors Center. Be sure to take a neighborhood walking tour brochure from the gift shop. The tours depart from here on Friday evening and Saturday morning (April–October) and focus on topics such as ghosts, the War of 1812, maritime history, or slavery and Frederick Douglass's tenure in Fells Point. ✉*808 S. Ann St., Fells Point* ☎*410/675–6750 Ext. 16* ⊕*www.preservationsociety.com* ⊙*Apr.–Nov. 25, Sun.–Thurs. 10–5, Fri. and Sat. 10–8; Nov. 26–Mar., Tues.–Sun. noon–4.*

㊲ Robert Long House Museum. The city's oldest residence still standing, this small brick house was built in 1765 as both home and business office for Robert Long, a merchant and quartermaster for the Continental Navy who operated a wharf on the waterfront. Furnished with Revolutionary War–era pieces, the parlor, bedroom, and office seem as if Long himself just stepped away. A fragrant, flowering herb garden flourishes in warm months. ✉*812 S. Ann St., Fells Point* ☎*410/675–6750* ⊕*www.preservationsociety.com* ⬚*$3* ⊙*Tours daily Apr.–Nov. at 1 and 2:30.*

NEED A BREAK? The **Daily Grind** (✉*1720 Thames St., Fells Point* ☎*410/558–0399*) is the neighborhood spot for coffee and Wi-Fi.

WEST BALTIMORE

Though some sections are still dodgy, Baltimore's West Side is undergoing a much-needed transformation for the better. A multimillion dollar renovation turned the old Hippodrome movie house and its neighboring buildings into an elegant performing arts center. Up and down Eutaw and Howard streets, once-abandoned buildings are being converted into high-end loft apartments.

But the neighborhood's most popular draws are the Oriole Park at Camden Yards and M&T Bank Stadium, where the Baltimore Ravens football team plays. West Baltimore is also home to birthplaces and former residences of historic figures such as Babe Ruth, Edgar Allan Poe, and Charles Carroll, a member of the Continental Congress. The University of Maryland medical campus, including the Dr. Samuel D. Harris National Museum of Dentistry, occupies a large swath of the neighborhood. A few blocks west of the school, the B&O Railroad Museum, with more than 100 trains on display, is captivating to most small children (and the inner kid in train-loving adults).

MAIN ATTRACTIONS

㊽ Babe Ruth Birthplace and Museum. This plain brick row house, three blocks from Oriole Park at Camden Yards, was the birthplace of "the Bambino." Although Ruth was born here in 1895, his family never lived here; they lived in a nearby apartment, above a tavern run by Ruth's father. The row house and the adjoining buildings make up a museum devoted to Ruth's life and to the local Orioles baseball club. Film clips and props, rare photos of Ruth, Yankees payroll checks, a score book from Ruth's first professional game, and many other artifacts can be found here. ✉216 Emory St., West Baltimore ☎410/727–1539 ⊕www.baberuthmuseum.com 🎫$6 ⊗Apr.–Oct., daily 10–6, until 7 before Oriole home games; Nov.–Mar., daily 10–5.

🟢 **B&O Railroad Museum.** The famous Baltimore & Ohio Railroad was founded on the site that now houses this museum, which contains more than 120 full-size locomotives and a great collection of railroad memorabilia, from dining-car china and

WEST BALTIMORE TIPS

Set aside several hours for a tour of West Baltimore, and at least a half-hour for lunch at Lexington Market. Because the sights are scattered throughout the neighborhood and the streets are less safe than those in downtown Baltimore, parts of this area are best visited by car. It's safer to avoid walking through West Baltimore alone at night.

artwork to lanterns and signals. The 1884 roundhouse (240 feet in diameter and 120 feet high) adjoins one of the nation's first railroad stations. Train rides are available every day but Monday. The Iron Horse Café serves food and drinks. ✉901 W. Pratt St., West Baltimore ☎410/752–2490 ⊕www.borail.org 🎫$14 ⊗Mon.–Sat. 10–4, Sun. 11–4.

🟢 **M&T Bank Stadium.** The Baltimore Ravens football team hosts home games in this state-of-the-art stadium from August to January. ✉1101 Russell St., West Baltimore ☎410/261–7283 ⊕www.baltimoreravens.com.

🟢 **Oriole Park at Camden Yards.** Home of the Baltimore Orioles, Camden Yards and the nearby area bustle on game days. Since it opened in 1992, this nostalgically designed baseball stadium has inspired other cities to emulate its neotraditional architecture and amenities. The Eutaw Street promenade, between the warehouse and the field, has a view of the stadium; look for the brass baseballs embedded in the sidewalk that mark where home runs have cleared the fence, or visit the Orioles Hall of Fame display and the monuments to retired Orioles. Daily 90-minute tours take you to nearly every section of the ballpark, from the massive, JumboTron scoreboard to the dugout to the state-of-the-art beer-delivery system. ✉333 W. Camden St., Downtown ☎410/685–9800 general information, 410/547–6234 tour times, 888/848–2473 tickets to Orioles home games ⊕www.theorioles.com 🎫Eutaw St. promenade free; tour $7 ⊗Eutaw St. promenade daily 10–3, otherwise during games and tours; tours Mar.–Sept., Mon.–Sat. at 11, noon, 1, and 2; Oct., weekdays at 11:30 and 1:30, Sat. at 11, noon, 1, and 2, Sun. at 12:30, 1, 2, and 3; Nov., Mon.–Sat. at 11:30 and 1:30, Sun. at 12:30 and 2:30.

🟢 **Westminster Cemetery and Catacombs.** The city's oldest cemetery is the final resting place of Edgar Allan Poe and other famous Marylanders, including 15 generals from the American Revolution and the War of 1812. Dating from 1786, the cemetery was originally known as the Old Western Burying Grounds. In the early 1850s a city ordinance demanded that burial grounds be part of a church, so a building was constructed above the cemetery, creating catacombs beneath it. In the

1930s the schoolchildren of Baltimore collected pennies to raise the necessary funds for Poe's monument. Each year on Poe's birthday a mysterious stranger leaves three roses and a bottle of cognac on the writer's grave. ⊠ *W. Fayette and Greene Sts., Downtown* ☎ *410/706–2072* ⊙ *Daily 8–dusk.*

ALSO WORTH SEEING

㊷ Davidge Hall. Built in 1812 for $35,000, this green-dome structure has been used for teaching medicine for nearly two centuries. Part of the downtown campus of the University of Maryland at Baltimore, Davidge Hall is a relic of the days when dissection was illegal; the acoustically perfect anatomy theater was lighted by skylights instead of windows so that passersby would not witness students working on cadavers. ⊠ *522 W. Lombard St., West Baltimore* ☎ *410/706–7454* ⊠ *Free* ⊙ *Weekdays 8:30–4:30.*

㊸ Dr. Samuel D. Harris National Museum of Dentistry. This unusual museum, which has a set of George Washington's dentures, is on the Baltimore campus of the University of Maryland, the world's first dental school. Housed in a Renaissance Revival–style building, the museum has exhibits on the anatomy and physiology of human and animal teeth and the history of dentistry; you can also play a tune on the "Tooth Jukebox." One popular exhibit displays the dental instruments used in treating Queen Victoria in the mid-19th century. ⊠ *31 S. Greene St., West Baltimore* ☎ *410/706–0600* ⊠ *$6* ⊙ *Wed.–Sat. 10–4, Sun. 1–4.*

㊼ Mount Clare Museum House. One of the oldest houses in Baltimore, this elegant mansion was begun in 1754. It was the home of Charles Carroll, author of the Maryland Declaration of Independence, member of the Continental Congress, and one of Maryland's major landowners. The state's first historic museum house has been carefully restored to its Georgian elegance; more than 80% of the 18th-century furniture and artifacts, including rare pieces of Chippendale and Hepplewhite silver, crystal, and Chinese export porcelain, were owned and used by the Carroll family. Washington, Lafayette, and John Adams were all guests here. The greenhouses are famous in their own right: they provided rare trees and plants for Mount Vernon. ⊠ *1500 Washington Blvd., Southwest Baltimore* ☎ *410/837–3262* ⊕ *www.mountclare.org* ⊠ *$6* ⊙ *Tues.–Sat. 10–4; tours every hr until 3.*

㊶ Poe House. Though the "Master of the Macabre" lived in this tiny row house only three years, he wrote "MS Found in a Bottle" and his first horror story, "Berenice," in the tiny garret chamber that's now furnished in an early-19th-century style. Besides visiting this room, you can view changing exhibits and a video presentation about Poe's short, tempestuous life. Because of the possibility of crime, it's best to visit this neighborhood during daylight hours as part of a group. ⊠ *203 N.*

Amity St., West Baltimore ☎410/ 396-7932 ⊕*www.eapoe.org/balt/ poehse.htm* ✉$4 ⊗*Apr.–Nov. noon–3:30; call ahead.*

NEED A BREAK?

Lexington Market (✉*400 W. Lexington St., West Baltimore* ☎410/685-6169) is in a slightly sketchy area, but a trip there for Faidley's crab cakes and other famous food is definitely worth it. **Trinacria Foods** (✉*406 N. Paca. St., West Baltimore* ☎410/685-7285) is an authentic Italian grocery store a few blocks away from Lexington Market that sells meat, cheese, fresh-baked bread, pastries, and wine. There's no better sandwich in the area.

WHERE TO EAT

6

Baltimore loves crabs. Soft- or hard-shell crabs, crab cakes, crab dip—the city's passion for clawed crustaceans seems to have no end. Flag down a Baltimore native and ask them where the best crab joint is and you'll get dozens of different options. In addition to crabs and seafood, Baltimore's restaurant landscape includes Afghan, Greek, American, tapas, and other ethnic cuisines. The city's dining choices may not compare to those of New York, or even Washington, but it does have some real standouts and surprises.

Since most of the Inner Harbor only has chain and hotel restaurants, you'll want to head north up Charles Street to Mount Vernon—the city's center for fine dining. Or, you can go south down Light Street to try Federal Hill's trendy pubs, sushi bars, and bistros. A few blocks east of the Inner Harbor, Little Italy has a host of Italian restaurants, most of which serve classic southern Italian, spaghetti-with-garlic-bread fare. Yet father east, Fells Point has some renowned local restaurants. Charles Village, near Johns Hopkins University, and Hampden, just west, also have some funky casual options. Note that most places generally stop serving by 10 PM, if not earlier.

	WHAT IT COSTS				
	¢	$	$$	$$$	$$$$
AT DINNER	under $10	$10–$16	$17–$23	$24–$30	over $30

Prices are per person for a main course at dinner.

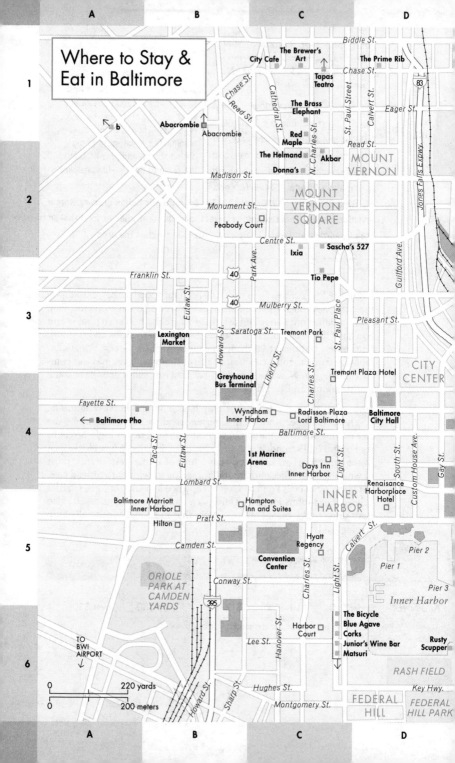

Where to Stay & Eat in Baltimore

A **B** **C** **D**

Biddle St.

City Cafe
The Brewer's Art
The Prime Rib

Chase St.
Tapas Teatro

Chase St.
The Brass Elephant

b
Abacrombie
Abacrombie

Red Maple

Read St.

The Helmand
Akbar

MOUNT VERNON

Donna's

Madison St.

MOUNT VERNON SQUARE

Monument St.

Peabody Court

Centre St.

Ixia
Sascha's 527

Franklin St.

Tio Pepe

Mulberry St.

Pleasant St.

Saratoga St.
Tremont Park

CITY CENTER

Lexington Market

Tremont Plaza Hotel

Greyhound Bus Terminal

Fayette St.

Wyndham Inner Harbor
Radisson Plaza Lord Baltimore
Baltimore City Hall

← Baltimore Pho

Baltimore St.

1st Mariner Arena

Days Inn Inner Harbor

Lombard St.

Renaisance Harborplace Hotel

Baltimore Marriott Inner Harbor

Hampton Inn and Suites

INNER HARBOR

Hilton

Pratt St.

Camden St.

Hyatt Regency

Pier 2

ORIOLE PARK AT CAMDEN YARDS

Convention Center

Pier 1

Conway St.

Pier 3

Inner Harbor

TO BWI AIRPORT

Harbor Court

The Bicycle
Blue Agave
Corks
Junior's Wine Bar
Matsuri

Rusty Scupper

Lee St.

RASH FIELD

0   220 yards

Hughes St.

Key Hwy.

0   200 meters

Montgomery St.

FEDERAL HILL

FEDERAL HILL PARK

A **B** **C** **D**

MOUNT VERNON

$$$ ✕**Abacrombie.** When new owners took over Abacrombie, local food-
AMERICAN ies wondered if it could sustain the high standards set by previous chef
Sonny Sweetman. It has. Patrons of the nearby opera house and sym-
phony hall still flock to the simple, elegant basement dining room for
seafood dishes, rich traditional entrées, and lighter fusion fare. High-
lights include the lamb served with mint chutney rather than mint jelly,
smashed chickpeas, and deep-fried potato wedges. The milk-chocolate
panna cotta is a tasty way to top off a meal. If you can, ask to sit
in the skylighted atrium section. Hosts and servers are skillful and
accommodating—even during the crush of pre-opera customers. Under
its new leadership, Abacrombie is undoubtedly still one of the city's
best restaurants. ⊠*58 W. Biddle St., Mount Vernon* ☎*410/837–3630*
⌂*Reservations essential* ⊟*AE, D, DC, MC, V* ⊘*Closed Mon. and
Tues.* ✛*1B*

$ ✕**Akbar.** A few steps below street level, this small restaurant is usu-
INDIAN ally crowded and always filled with pungent aromas and the sounds
of Indian music. Among the vegetarian dishes, *alu gobi masala,* a
potato-and-cauliflower creation, is prepared with onions, tomatoes,
and spices. Tandoori chicken is marinated in yogurt, herbs, and strong
spices, then barbecued in a charcoal-fired clay oven. Akbar also makes
a good choice for Sunday brunch. ⊠*823 N. Charles St., Mount Ver-
non* ☎*410/539–0944* ⊕*www.akbar-restaurant.com* ⊟*AE, D, DC,
MC, V.* ✛*2C*

$$ ✕**The Brass Elephant.** The rooms of this grand antebellum house on
ITALIAN Charles Street are filled with classical music and the chatter of diners
★ (the Teak Room is the quietest, the Oak Room the noisiest). The northern Italian menu includes traditional piccatas and marinaras as well as
updated versions of Italian classics, such as homemade cannelloni filled
with duck confit, woodland mushrooms, and ricotta. Upstairs, the softly
lighted Tusk Lounge is a comfortable, classy spot to meet for drinks.
⊠*924 N. Charles St., Mount Vernon* ☎*410/547–8485* ⊕*www.brass
elephant.com* ⊟*AE, DC, MC, V.* ✛*1C*

$$–$$$ ✕**The Brewer's Art.** Part brewpub, part restaurant, and part lounge, this
AMERICAN spot in a redone mansion feels young but urbane, with an ambitious
menu, a clever wine list, and the Belgian-style beers it brews itself: try
the potent, delicious Resurrection ale. The upstairs dining room serves
seasonal dishes with high-quality, locally available ingredients to create
European-style country fare that is both hearty and sophisticated. In
the dungeonlike downstairs dining room and bar the menu and decor
are more casual. Made with rosemary and garlic, the classic steak frites
are a best bet. ⊠*1106 N. Charles St., Mount Vernon* ☎*410/547–6925*
⊕*www.belgianbeer.com* ⊟*AE, D, DC, MC, V.* ✛*1C*

$–$$ ✕**City Cafe.** The lofty space and black-and-white tile floors give this
AMERICAN casual spot a feeling of classic grandeur. Come here for basic American
fare—sandwiches, salads, pasta, big brunches—and stick to that: the
more creative, ambitious attempts on the menu often fall short. But
City Cafe handles breakfast, lunch, and dinner staples with ease—a feat
of flexibility few Baltimore restaurants can match. The service could
be sharper, but the seasonal items hit the spot. In summer the frozen

cappuccino is a sweet, creamy treat. ⊠*1001 Cathedral St., Mount Vernon* ☎*410/539–4252* ⊕*www.citycafebaltimore.com* ▤*AE, D, DC, MC, V.* ✛*1C*

$–$$
AMERICAN

✕**Donna's.** Basic black and light wood are the backdrop for this casual American café and restaurant, part of a local chain (other locations are on St. Paul Street in Charles Village and in Cross Keys in Roland Park). For breakfast, bagels and muffins are served on weekdays and brunch is available Sunday; sandwiches, soups, and salads are the lunchtime offerings; dinner might include balsamic-glaze salmon, herb chicken breast with artichoke hearts, or a daily pasta dish. You can also just stop in for a cup of coffee any time of the day. ⊠*800 N. Charles St., Mount Vernon* ☎*410/385–0180* ⊕*www.donnas.com* ▤*AE, D, MC, V.* ✛*2C*

$–$$
MIDDLE
EASTERN
★

✕**The Helmand.** Owned by Hamid Kharzai's brother, Qayum Karzai, Helmand serves outstanding Afghan fare in a casual yet elegant space. Beautiful woven textiles and traditional dresses adorn the walls, adding color to the simple white table settings. Try one of the many outstanding lamb dishes such as *sabzy challow* (spinach sautéed with chunks of beef) or the vegetarian *aushak* (Afghan ravioli). For starters, *kaddo*, a sweet-and-pungent pumpkin dish, is unforgettable. ⊠*806 N. Charles St., Mount Vernon* ☎*410/752–0311* ⊕*www.helmand.com* ▤*AE, DC, MC, V* ⊗*No lunch.* ✛*2C*

$$$–$$$$
AMERICAN
Fodor'sChoice
★

✕**Ixia.** From the food to the decor, Ixia sparkles. The walls are painted blue with gold trim, and large reflective chandeliers and thin white curtains hang from the ceiling. Service is top-notch, as are dishes such as tuna tartare, which features small, tender cubes of fish in an Asian chili vinaigrette-and-cucumber soup. Entrées come in small but satisfying portion sizes. Standards such as the juicy, well-spiced filet mignon are also mouthwatering. The list of more than a dozen inventive house martinis is a must-try. ⊠*518 N. Charles St., Mount Vernon* ☎*410/727–1800* ⊕*www.ixia-online.com* ▤*AE, D, DC, MC, V* ⊗*Closed Sun. and Mon.* ✛*2C*

$$$$
AMERICAN
★

✕**The Prime Rib.** Bustling and crowded, this luxuriously dark dining room is just north of Mount Vernon Square and a five-minute drive from the Inner Harbor. Tables are set close together under a low ceiling, keeping things intimate for the bankers and lawyers who often eat here, as well as couples on expensive dates. The leopard-print carpet and live pianist lend a swanky 1960s feel to a place that seems untouched by time. The traditional menu is headed by a superb prime rib and an even better filet mignon; the jumbo lump crab cakes are also great. The wine list is predominantly California-centric. ⊠*1101 N. Calvert St., Mount Vernon* ☎*410/539–1804* ⊕*www.theprimerib.com* ⌦*Reservations essential. Jacket required* ▤*AE, D, DC, MC, V.* ✛*1D*

$–$$
ASIAN

✕**Red Maple.** Theatrical, stylish Red Maple doesn't even have a sign out front. Instead, it's only marked with a small maple-tree icon on the front door. Inside, the striking, minimalist space is warmed by a fireplace, candlelight, and sumptuous suede banquettes. The food is equally arresting: Asian-inspired tapas, artfully conceived and beautifully presented. Small plates such as wild mushroom and asparagus dumplings and shrimp and mango tapas are inexpensive, but it's easy to run up your tab because each is so compelling. ⊠*930 N. Charles*

6

St., Mount Vernon ☎410/547–0149 ⊕*www.930redmaple.com* ☰*AE, DC, MC, V* ⊗*No lunch.* ✛*1C*

$–$$ ✕**Sascha's 527.** High ceilings, warm yellow walls hung with paintings,
ECLECTIC and a giant crystal chandelier add drama to this spacious, artsy spot near
the Walters. Choose from an eclectic menu of "tastes" (appetizer-size
plates), "big plates" (chicken, lamb, or fish) served with a selection of
unusual sauces, and other American fare with a twist. At lunch there's
counter service only, with a choice of fancy sandwiches and salads on a
rotating menu. If you go for dinner, be sure to check out the lengthy wine
list. ✉*527 N. Charles St., Mount Vernon* ☎410/539–8880 ⊕*www.
saschas.com* ☰*AE, DC, MC, V* ⊗*Closed Sun. No lunch Sat.* ✛*2C*

$$–$$$ ✕**Tapas Teatro.** Connected to the Charles Theater, the place for art and
SPANISH indie films in Baltimore, the Tapas Teatro is a popular pre- and post-
movie spot. It's often a scene, especially in warm weather, when the
glass front is open and tables spill onto the street. Tapas include roasted
potatoes, spinach sautéed with crab, and lamb tenderloin. There's also
an extensive list of wines by the glass, and if you don't finish them with
dinner, you can carry drinks into the Charles. But be careful: it's so
much fun to keep sampling that it's easy to run up a hefty bill. ✉*1711
N. Charles St., Station North Arts District* ☎410/332–0110 ⊕*www.
tapasteatro.com* ☰*AE, MC, V* ⊗*Closed Mon. No lunch.* ✛*1C*

$$–$$$ ✕**Tio Pepe.** Candles light up the whitewashed walls of these cellar din-
SPANISH ing rooms, where the menu covers all regions of Spain. The staple is
paella à la Valenciana (chicken, sausage, shrimp, clams, and mussels
with saffron rice); a less-well-known Basque preparation is red snapper
with clams, mussels, asparagus, and boiled egg. Make dinner reservations well in advance; walk-in weekday lunch seating is usually available. ✉*10 E. Franklin St., Mount Vernon* ☎410/539–4675 ⊕*www.
tioperestaurant.com* ⌕*Reservations essential. Jacket and tie* ☰*AE,
D, DC, MC, V.* ✛*3C*

BOLTON HILL

$–$$ ✕**b.** In a residential neighborhood of lovely, large row houses, this casual
ECLECTIC corner bistro serves imaginative, Mediterranean-influenced fare. The seasonal menu includes such dishes as roasted vegetable ravioli in sage butter and sesame-encrusted salmon with honey horseradish crème fraîche.
Or choose from one of the chalkboard specials, such as the risotto of the
day or the "butcher's special." On Sunday b is a popular spot for brunch.
✉*1501 Bolton St., Bolton Hill* ☎410/383–8600 ⊕*www.b-bistro.com*
☰*AE, D, MC, V* ⊗*Closed Mon. No lunch.* ✛*1A*

CHARLES VILLAGE

$$–$$$ ✕**The Ambassador Dining Room.** A Tudor-style dining room in a 1930s
INDIAN apartment building is the setting for superb Indian fare. Go for the
classics such as chicken *tikka masala* (grilled chicken in a sauce of red
pepper, ginger, garlic, and yogurt) or *alu gobi* (spicy potatoes and cau-
liflower), or sample more creative options such as lamb tenderloin with
fennel-and-chive sauce. In summer the lovely garden is a favorite spot

for outdoor dining. The service does not disappoint. ⊠*3811 Canterbury Rd., Tuscany-Canterbury* ☎*410/366–1484* ⊕*www.ambassador diningroom.com* ▤*AE, MC, V.* ✛*2G*

$$–$$$ ✕**Gertrude's.** In the Baltimore Museum of Art, this casual yet classy
AMERICAN spot cooks up creative Maryland cuisine. Crab cakes, served in many forms, are one option, as are cornmeal-encrusted catfish or one of the many daily specials. In warm weather the outdoor terrace overlooking the sculpture garden makes for very pleasant dining. During the day, large windows brighten up the main dining space, which has a nautical theme. John Shields, the chef and owner, has won accolades for his homey, regional menu. ⊠*10 Art Museum Dr., Charles Village* ☎*410/889–3399* ⊕*www.gertrudesbaltimore.com* ⌦*Reservations essential* ▤*AE, MC, V* ☾*Closed Mon.* ✛*3G*

¢–$ ✕**One World Cafe.** A favorite of Johns Hopkins students, this low-key
VEGETARIAN restaurant, café, and bar is open morning until night for tasty vegetarian fare. Settle onto a couch or one of the small tables for a portobello sandwich with caramelized onions and feta cheese, tofu baked with ginger and served with steamed vegetables, or One World's version of that Baltimore specialty: a crabless crab cake. Smoothies, espresso drinks, microbrews, and mixed drinks from the full bar fill out the menu. ⊠*100 W. University Pkwy., Tuscany-Canterbury* ☎*410/235–5777* ⊕*www.one-world-café.com* ▤*AE, DC, MC, V.* ✛*2G*

¢–$ ✕**Paper Moon Diner.** Everywhere you look in this funky, colorful diner
AMERICAN are toys, and other objects glued to the ceilings and walls. People come at all hours (it's open 24/7) for the overstuffed omelets, big stacks of pancakes, burgers, and other classic fare. Stop by at 3 AM on a Friday or Saturday night to nosh on sweet potato fries with hipsters and students at nearby Johns Hopkins University. The servers have a diner attitude—they don't always seem too interested in serving, and the food might take a while—but the place is always lively and entertaining. ⊠*227 W. 29th St., Charles Village* ☎*410/889–4444* ⊕*www.papermoondiner. com* ▤*MC, V.* ✛*3F*

HAMPDEN

¢–$ ✕**Golden West Cafe.** On "The Avenue," funky Hampden's main com-
AMERICAN mercial street, Golden West is the go-to spot for breakfast, lunch, and
★ dinner. The place is colorful and eclectic, and so is the menu of diner fare with a Tex-Mex and Asian twist. Try the cold Vietnamese salad with shrimp or the hefty *huevos montuleños*—fried eggs with yellow corn cakes covered in beans, feta, salsa, and a fried banana (and served at all hours). Large tables make it a good spot for groups, and the bar makes it good for pre- or post-dinner drinks. In addition to serving food and drinks, the café occasionally hosts local folk and indie rock bands. ⊠*1105 W. 36th St., Hampden* ☎*410/889–8891* ⊕*www.goldenwest cafe.com* ▤*AE, D, MC, V* ☾*Closed Tues.* ✛*3F*

$$ ✕**Woodberry Kitchen.** This restaurant is in such high demand that it
AMERICAN books up weeks in advance. Swathed in wood and aged brick, Woodberry Kitchen has a cozy, relaxed atmosphere and the menu harks back to a simpler era. The best items are often the most basic: Eastern Shore

6

popcorn, cheddar potato gratin, and cast-iron rib-eye steak. Diners range in age from thirtysomethings to senior citizens. Ask for a table on the mezzanine, where you can peer down to the floor below and people-watch between courses. ✉ *2010 Clipper Park Rd., Hampden* ☎ *410/464–8000* ⊕ *www.woodberrykitchen.com* ⌖ *Reservations essential* ☰ *AE, MC, V* ⊙ *No lunch.* ✛ *3F*

INNER HARBOR

¢–$

ISRAELI

★

✕ **Attman's.** Open since 1915, this authentic New York–style deli near the Jewish Museum is the king of Baltimore's "Corned Beef Row." Of the three delis on the row, Attman's has the longest waits and steepest prices, but delivers the highest-quality dishes. Don't be put off by the long lines—they move fairly quickly, and the outstanding corned beef sandwiches are worth the wait, as are the pastrami, homemade chopped liver, and other oversize creations. Attman's closes at 6:30 PM daily. ✉ *1019 Lombard St., Historic Jonestown* ☎ *410/563–2666* ⊕ *www.attmansdeli.com* ☰ *AE, DC, MC, V* ⊙ *Closed Sat.* ✛ *4F*

$$–$$$

LATIN AMERICAN

✕ **Babalu Grill.** A prominent portrait of Desi Arnaz, conga-drum bar stools, live salsa music on weekends: this place is all about fun. Many of the classic Cuban dishes on the menu come from family recipes, such as savory *ropa vieja* (a stew of shredded beef) and seafood paella, brimming with shrimp, shellfish, and chorizo. The bar serves an impressive list of obscure rums and tequilas, and the wine list focuses on South American and Spanish vintages. ✉ *32 Market Pl., Inner Harbor* ☎ *410/234–9898* ⊕ *www.babalugrill.com* ☰ *AE, D, DC, MC, V.* ✛ *4E*

$$–$$$

SEAFOOD

✕ **Blue Sea Grill.** Blue is the color, cool is the mood, and the ocean is the source for the fresh seafood served here in many forms. Though the restaurant offers chicken and steak, seafood is the main focus. Start with a plate of raw oysters from the raw bar or a bowl of Maryland crab soup, then order from a selection of whole and fillet fishes—grilled, broiled, or panfried. Lobster macaroni and king-crab guacamole are two of the signature dishes. ✉ *614 Water St., Inner Harbor* ☎ *410/837–7300* ⊕ *www.blueseagrill.com* ☰ *AE, D, DC, MC, V* ⊙ *Closed Sun. No lunch.* ✛ *4E*

$$$

ITALIAN

✕ **Cinghiale.** The spotlight is on wine at Cinghiale (pronounced "ching-GYAH-lay"), Baltimore's new upscale spot for northern Italian fare opened in 2008. The restaurant is an open, inviting space with tall, wide windows. The wine list is vast—more than 400 bottles, listed on the menu by region. The service is sharp and unpretentious, but can be slightly overbearing at times. Cinghiale is split into two sections, the elegant osteria and the less-formal enoteca. Opt for the latter, where you can nibble on small plates, sample one of the city's best wine collections, and rub elbows with the professional set. ✉ *822 Lancaster St., Inner Harbor* ☎ *410/547–8282* ⊕ *www.cinghiale-osteria.com* ☰ *AE, D, MC, V* ⊙ *Closed Sun.* ✛ *6F*

$$–$$$

SEAFOOD

✕ **McCormick & Schmick's.** It may be a chain restaurant, but it's a very good one. From its expansive location at the end of Pier 5, on the east side of the waterfront, there's a terrific harbor view; ask to be seated on the patio. More than two dozen varieties of fish and seafood, available on a daily basis, are flown in from all over the world: the large menu changes daily. Choose from the more than a half-dozen varieties of oysters on the half shell, or go for the signature cedar-plank wild Oregon king salmon. ✉ *711 Eastern Ave., Inner Harbor* ☎*410/234–1300* ⊕*www.mccormickandschmicks.com* ▭*AE, D, MC, V.* ✧*6E*

$$–$$$ ✕**Rusty Scupper.** A tourist favorite, the Rusty Scupper undoubtedly has
SEAFOOD the best view along the waterfront; sunset here is magical, with the sun sinking slowly into the harbor as lights twinkle on the city's skyscrapers. The interior is decorated with light wood and windows from floor to ceiling; the house specialty is seafood, particularly the jumbo lump crab cake, but the menu also includes beef, chicken, and pasta. Reservations are essential on Friday and Saturday, and service can be spotty. ✉ *402 Key Hwy., Inner Harbor* ☎*410/727–3678* ▭*AE, D, DC, MC, V.* ✧*6D*

FEDERAL HILL

$–$$ ✕**The Bicycle.** Bright, energetic, and often noisy, Bicycle serves intel-
AMERICAN ligent, creative cuisine. Caribbean, Asian, and Southwestern flavors influence the short but engaging menu, which is supplemented by specials that make use of fresh seafood and local seasonal produce. The extensive wine list has 18 options priced at less than $20. Tables are close in this long, narrow bistro, but if you don't mind occasionally rubbing elbows with your neighbors, the proximity enhances its liveliness. ✉*1444 Light St., Federal Hill* ☎*410/234–1900* ⊕*www.bicyclebistro. com* ⬧*Reservations essential* ▭*AE, D, MC, V* ☾*Closed Mon. No lunch.* ✧*6C*

$–$$ ✕**Blue Agave.** At this authentic regional Mexican and American South-
MEXICAN western restaurant every sauce and salsa is made daily to create pure, concentrated flavors—the traditional mole sauces here are delicious. Dishes such as grilled quail served with both green and spicy yellow moles, or the more familiar chicken enchiladas with mole poblano, demonstrate the kitchen's command of this rich, complex concoction. More than 80 different kinds of tequila are available, and you would be hard-pressed to find a better margarita in the city. ✉*1032 Light St., Federal Hill* ☎*410/576–3938* ⊕*www.blueagaverestaurant.com* ▭*AE, D, MC, V* ☾*Closed Mon.* ✧*6C*

$$$ ✕**Corks.** The creative American cuisine here is as stellar as the impressive
AMERICAN wine list, and the waitstaff are adept at pairing wines with dishes. Corks
★ helped up the ante in Federal Hill fine dining. Start with a made-in-house mozzarella on top of a salad or the artisan macaroni and cheese. Other outstanding options on the seasonal menu might include monkfish osso buco or braised veal breast with woodland mushrooms. It's so cozy in the dimly lighted, wood-panel dining room that you may never want to leave. ✉*1026 S. Charles St., Federal Hill* ☎*410/752–3810* ⊕*www.corksrestaurant.com* ⬧*Reservations essential* ▭*AE, D, MC, V* ☾*No lunch.* ✧*6C*

$$ ✕ **Junior's Wine Bar.** Spacious dining areas and an affordable menu
AMERICAN make Junior's Wine Bar one of Federal Hill's better dinner destinations. Junior's sits in the building formerly occupied by the wine bar Vespa,

but most of the similarities end there. All of the entrées on Junior's menu cost less than $20, and the wine list is split into Old World and New World whites and reds. If you're in the mood for lighter fare, order one of the pizzas, which come topped with unexpected but appetizing meats like braised duck with roasted onions and Stilton cheese. The service can be sluggish at times, but the food is worth the wait. ⊠*1117 S. Charles St., Federal Hill* ☎*410/727–1212* ▤*AE, D, MC, V* ⊘*Closed Mon. No lunch Tues.–Fri., no dinner Sun.* ⊹*6C*

$–$$
JAPANESE
★
✕**Matsuri.** Sit down at the counter or make your way to one of the tables as this small sushi place, a Federal Hill favorite. And it's not just popular among Baltimoreans; the walls are covered with awards from local and national press. You can order by the roll, or opt for one of the bento boxes, udon soups, or tempura dishes like the signature crab and shrimp, wrapped in rice and seaweed and deep fried. The narrow, two-story corner row house is cozy but not cramped, and the servers are quick and accommodating. ⊠*1105 S. Charles St., Federal Hill* ☎*410/752–8561* ⊕*www.matsuri.us* ▤*AE, D, MC, V* ⊘*No lunch weekends.* ⊹*6C*

LITTLE ITALY

$$$–$$$$
ITALIAN
✕**Aldo's.** It's easy to see why Aldo's has won so many awards in the past decade. Have a meal under the skylight in the pillared two-story central dining room and you'll swoon over both the decor and food. Chef Aldo Vitale prepares unabashedly rich Italian fare, from pasta tossed in Italian black truffle butter to heavenly hunks of veal topped with melt-in-your-mouth spinach and mozzarella. The service is charming and the wine list comprehensive. A go-to for visiting celebrities and the city's upper crust, Aldo's is undeniably Little Italy's most romantic restaurant. ⊠*306 S. High St., Little Italy* ☎*410/727–0700* ⊕*www. aldositaly.com* ▤*AE, D, DC, MC, V* ⊘ *No lunch.* ⊹*5F*

$–$$
ITALIAN
☾
✕**Amicci's.** At this self-proclaimed "very casual eatery," you don't have to spend a fortune to get a satisfying taste of Little Italy. Blue jean–clad diners and walls hung with movie posters make for a fun atmosphere. Service is friendly and usually speedy, and the food comes in large portions. Try the chicken Lorenzo: breaded chicken breast covered in a marsala wine sauce, red peppers, prosciutto, and provolone. ⊠*231 S. High St., Little Italy* ☎*410/528–1096* ⊕*www.amiccis.com* ▤*AE, D, DC, MC, V.* ⊹*5F*

$$–$$$
ITALIAN
✕**Chiapparelli's.** At this neighborhood favorite, families come to celebrate milestones—baptisms, communions, graduations, and such. Pictures of the Baltimore landscape adorn the redbrick walls, and some white-cloth tables overlook one of Little Italy's main streets. The reasonably priced pasta selections rely on standards, but there's also more upscale fare such as chicken Giuseppe: breaded chicken breast with spinach, crabmeat, and provolone in a lemon wine sauce. ⊠*237 S. High St., Little Italy* ☎*410/837–0309* ⊕*www.chiapparellis.com* ▤*AE, D, DC, MC, V.* ⊹*5F*

$–$$
ITALIAN
✕**La Tavola.** Specializing in homemade, inventive pasta dishes, La Tavola is a cut above other Little Italy spaghetti houses. Don't miss the *mafalde*

alla fiorentina, wide pasta with spinach, ricotta, pine nuts, and raisins in a nutmeg-flavor cream sauce. Veal cannelloni in béchamel tomato sauce is another standout. If you're still hungry after one of La Tavola's generous plates of pasta, the fresh fish is a good bet, as is the roasted veal chop. ✉ *248 Albemarle St., Little Italy* ☎ *410/685–1859* ⊕ *www.la-tavola.com* ▤ *AE, D, DC, MC, V.* ✛ *5E*

$ **THAI** ✕ **Lemongrass.** Thriving, trendy Lemongrass is proof that Baltimore needed an upscale Thai restaurant. A two-story stone statue of a Thai princess greets diners at this stylish warehouse-turned-eatery outside Little Italy. The decor is done in deep earth tones, and the food can be fiery hot, depending on the dish. A see-and-be-seen crowd of mostly thirty- and fortysomethings flocks here for the late-night menu, served until 1 AM. Whether you come for a bar-side snack or for dinner, order a plate of crispy string beans, a hearty, addictive appetizer. ✉ *1300 Bank St., Little Italy* ☎ *410/327–7835* ▤ *AE, MC, V* ◎ *No lunch Sun.* ✛ *5F*

$$ **SPANISH** ✕ **Tapabar.** You can count the number of non-Italian restaurants in Little Italy on one hand, and now there's one more place to add. This intimate Spanish restaurant gives people good reason to branch out in this seemingly exclusive Italian neighborhood. The walls are done in deep red and yellow tones, and the south side of the building is a windowed atrium facing the sidewalk. With 25 small plates featured on the menu, diners can try a little bit of everything. The seafood soup, which is creamy but not too heavy, along with the flatiron steak stuffed with olives and smoked bacon are two standouts. ✉ *413 S. High St., Little Italy* ☎ *410/223–3020* ⊕ *www.tapabarrestaurant.com* ▤ *AE, D, MC, V* ◎ *Closed Mon. No lunch.* ✛ *5F*

FELLS POINT

$$$–$$$$ **GREEK** ★ ✕ **The Black Olive.** One of the best Greek restaurants in the country, the Black Olive specializes in impeccably fresh seafood. Let the waiter give you a guided tour of the catch of the day, which reclines on a bed of ice in the kitchen case. You can have your selection simply grilled, lightly dressed, and filleted for you table-side, accompanied by a glass from the wine list's thoughtful selection of oft-neglected Greek vintages. For an appetizer be sure to try the *kakavia,* a spicy Greek bouillabaisse served with irresistible bread warm from the brick oven. ✉ *814 S. Bond St., at Shakespeare St., Fells Point* ☎ *410/276–7141* ⊕ *www.theblackolive.com* ⌕ *Reservations essential* ▤ *AE, D, MC, V.* ✛ *6G*

¢–$ **ECLECTIC** ✕ **Blue Moon Dining House.** A cozy café with a celestial motif appropriate to its name, the Blue Moon is a favorite for breakfast, served until 3 PM daily. Start with one of the enormous house-made cinnamon rolls, but save room for excellent brunch fare such as crab Benedict and sky-high French toast with fruit compote. On Friday and Saturday the Moon reopens at 11 PM and stays open all night, attracting revelers from Fells Point's many clubs and bars. On weekend mornings there's often a line, but it's well worth the wait. ✉ *1621 Aliceanna St., Fells Point* ☎ *410/522–3940* ⌕ *Reservations not accepted* ▤ *AE, D, MC, V.* ✛ *6G*

6

$$$–$$$$ ✕**Charleston.** The kitchen here may have a South Carolina Low Country
SOUTHERN accent, but it's also skilled in the fundamentals of French cooking. Inside
★ the glowingly lighted dining room such classics as she-crab soup, crisp
cornmeal-crusted oysters, and spoon bread complement more elegant
fare, such as squab roasted with apples. Best bets are Southern-inspired
dishes such as shrimp sautéed with andouille and Cajun ham served
over creamy grits. ⊠*1000 Lancaster St., Fells Point* ☎*410/332–7373*
⊕*www.charlestonrestaurant.com* ⌂*Reservations essential* ⊟*AE, D,
MC, V* ⊘*Closed Sun. No lunch.* ✛*5F*

$$–$$$ ✕**Louisiana.** Fells Point's most elegant dining room feels like a spacious,
SOUTHERN opulent antebellum parlor. The menu mixes creole and French with a
touch of New American, and is accompanied by an expansive, thought-
ful wine list. The lobster bisque, with a dollop of sherry added at the
table by one of Louisiana's servers, is sublime, and crawfish étouffée is
a worthy follow-up course. ⊠*1708 Aliceanna St., Fells Point* ⊕*www.
louisianasrestaurant.com* ☎*410/327–2610* ⊟*AE, DC, MC, V* ⊘*No
lunch.* ✛*6H*

$$–$$$ ✕**Obrycki's Crab House.** For more than 50 years Obrycki's has served
SEAFOOD steamed crabs with its unique black pepper seasoning. Politicians and
lawyers meet at Orbrycki's after hours to talk business. It feels as though
little has changed inside the dark dining room in decades. Service can be
sluggish and prices steep, but that doesn't deter its fans. ▮**TIP➔Ask any
native of Maryland—eating crabs is an art. If you're unsure how to approach a
bushel of hardshells, go to** ⊕*www.obryckis.com* **for a demonstration.** Go for
the crabs: beyond that, the seafood menu is standard and the food just
fair. ⊠*1727 E. Pratt St., Fells Point* ☎*410/732–6399* ⊕*www.obryckis.
com* ⊟*AE, D, DC, MC, V* ⊘*Closed mid-Dec.–early Mar.* ✛*6F*

¢–$ ✕**Pazo.** An expansive 19th-century warehouse is now home to this
MEDITERRANEAN fashionable, two-level restaurant serving Mediterranean-influenced
fare. Enjoy tapas and large plates in the rich, red-hue setting lighted by
giant wrought-iron chandeliers and smaller candles on tables, or head
upstairs to the mezzanine and watch the crowd below. Service can be
pretentious at times but is always quick with orders. Tasty tapas and
warm, stylish decor make Pazo one of the city's better dinner desti-
nations. ⊠*1425 Aliceanna St., Fells Point* ☎*410/534–7296* ⊕*www.
pazorestaurant.com* ⊟*AE, DC, MC, V* ⊘*No lunch.* ✛*6G*

$–$$ ✕**Samos.** East of Fells Point is Greektown (20 minutes by car from Inner
GREEK Harbor hotels), home to Baltimore's Greek population. An informal
restaurant, done in clean, classic blue and white, Samos serves excellent Greek fare. Portions are generous, with lamb souvlaki and tender,
juicy gyros leading the menu. Be warned: the folks at Samos often take
the phone off the hook and stop offering carryout during the lunchtime
rush. Though Samos doesn't offer beer or wine, you can bring your
own. ⊠*600 Oldham St., Greektown* ☎*410/675–5292* ⊕*www.samos
restaurant.com* ⊟*AE, D, DC, MC, V* ⊘*Closed Sun.* ✛*5H*

WEST BALTIMORE

$ ✕ **Baltimore Pho.** Tucked into an up-and-coming West Baltimore neigh-
VIETNAMESE   borhood, Baltimore Pho (pronounced "fuh") is an unlikely hit. With
red and black vinyl chairs, cloth-wrapped lanterns, pressed-tin ceiling
tiles, and white linen tablecloths, the decor is sharp and funky. Meals
start with puffy white prawn chips that crackle and pop when you dip
them in a side of fish sauce. Ask for the house specialty, Baltimore Pho,
and get it "Hollins Market style"—with fewer thin noodles and more
fresh-tasting vegetables. The best way to round out a meal is with two
scoops of glorious fried ice cream. It's a sweet finish to a solid meal in
the city's newest upscale Asian spot. ⊠*1114 Hollins St., Washington
Village* ☎*410/752–4746* ▤*AE, D, MC, V* ☾*Closed Sun.* ✛*4A*

CANTON

$$–$$$ ✕**Bo Brooks.** Picking steamed crabs on Bo Brooks's waterfront deck
SEAFOOD   with a pitcher of cold beer at hand as sailboats and tugs ply the harbor
★   is a quintessential Baltimore pleasure. Locals spend hot summer days
cracking into warm, spicy crabs while a cool breeze blows in from the
harbor. Brooks serves its famous crustaceans year-round, along with
a menu of Chesapeake seafood classics. Locals know to stick to the
Maryland crab soup, crab dip, jumbo lump crab cakes, and fried oysters. ⊠*2701 Boston St., Canton* ☎*410/558–0202* ⊕*www.bobrooks.
com* ▤*AE, D, MC, V.* ✛*4H*

WHERE TO STAY

When booking a hotel or bed-and-breakfast in Baltimore, focus on the
Inner Harbor, where you're likely to spend a good deal of time. The
downside to staying in hotels near downtown is the noise level, which
can rise early in the morning and stay up late into the night—especially
if there's a baseball or football game. For quieter options, head to neighborhoods like Fells Point and Canton. All of the hotels listed are within
a half-hour drive of the harbor. If you're coming to Baltimore in summer or near Preakness (the third weekend in May), reserve your rooms
well in advance. Hunt Valley, a suburb about a 25-minute drive north
of Baltimore on I–83, has several convenient budget options.

WHAT IT COSTS					
	¢	$	$$	$$$	$$$$
FOR TWO PEOPLE	under $100	$100–$160	$161–$230	$231–$300	over $300

Prices are for a standard double room in high season, excluding 14.5% room
tax.

MOUNT VERNON

$ ⛏ **Abacrombie.** In a large, late-19th-century building, once a private
★ house, this intimate inn has rooms furnished in Victorian style and
an outstanding restaurant. It's across the street from the Meyerhoff
Symphony Hall and in walking distance of MICA, the University of
Baltimore, and Amtrak's Penn Station. Breakfast is served in the parlor room. **Pros:** within walking distance of the opera and symphony.
Cons: the four-story inn has no elevator. ⊠ *58 W. Biddle St., Mount
Vernon* ☎*410/244–7227 or 888/922–3437* ⊕*www.badger-inn.com*
⌨*12 rooms* ⛱*In-room: Wi-Fi. In-hotel: restaurant, bar, parking (no
fee), no-smoking rooms, no elevator* ⊟*AE, D, MC, V* ⫯❙*CP.* ⊕*1B*

$$$ ⛏ **Peabody Court.** Built as a luxury apartment house in 1924, this
13-story hotel faces the Washington Monument. The hotel retains its
original distinguished lobby and other period touches such as marble
bathrooms. Rooms have desks and two-line speakerphones with data
ports; a lobby business center has a fax machine, copier, and computer
station. Rooms with park views are the best choice. A courtesy shuttle
will ferry you to destinations within a 2-mi radius. The hotel bistro,
George's on Mount Vernon Square, serves American and Italian cuisine.
Pros: in the heart of Mount Vernon. **Cons:** semi-steep prices. ⊠ *612
Cathedral St., Mount Vernon* ☎*410/727–7101* ⊕*www.peabody
courthotel.com* ⌨*104 rooms* ⛱*In-room: safe, refrigerator, Ethernet,
Wi-Fi. In-hotel: restaurant, gym, parking (fee), no-smoking rooms*
⊟*AE, D, DC, MC, V* ⫯❙*CP.* ⊕*2C*

CITY CENTER

$$ ⛏ **Hampton Inn and Suites.** The free breakfast and the logo may be the
same, but this Hampton Inn tries to be more urban and chic than oth-
ers in the chain. In an early-1900s office building that lay vacant for
many years, the hotel follows the historical direction of the structure,
but keeps things contemporary. Rooms, done in warm mauve and beige
and dark wood, have a clubby, streamlined look. The biggest and most
expensive rooms, on the top floor, are studio suites in the former executive offices. **Pros:** trendier than most other Hampton Inns. **Cons:** patrons
can get loud from time to time. ⊠ *131 E. Redwood St., City Center*
☎*410/539–7888* ⊕*www.baltimorehamptoninn.com* ⌨*116 rooms,
10 studio suites* ⛱ *In room: Wi-Fi In-hotel: pool, gym, public Internet,
parking (fee), no-smoking rooms* ⊟*AE, D, DC, MC, V.* ⊕*5B*

$ ⛏ **Radisson Plaza Lord Baltimore.** Baltimore's historic landmark hotel, the
Radisson extends its Jazz Age elegance to the guest rooms, which have
been restored to their original style. Built in 1928, this 23-story hotel is
distinguished by an elegantly gilded art deco lobby. Rooms on the south
side have the best view, and from the top three floors you can see the
harbor. The hotel is quiet and comfortable, and the location is central,
three blocks from the Baltimore Convention Center or Harborplace.
Pros: centrally located. **Cons:** somewhat dated rooms and amenities.
⊠ *20 W. Baltimore St., City Center* ☎*410/539–8400* ⊕*www.radisson.
com/lordbaltimore* ⌨*440 rooms, 4 condos, 6 suites* ⛱ *In room: Wi-Fi*

In-hotel: restaurant, bar, gym, public Internet, parking (fee), no-smoking rooms ⊟*AE, D, DC, MC, V.* ⊹*4C*

$$ ⛶**Tremont Park.** Built in the 1960s as an apartment house, the 13-story
★ Tremont is now a European-style all-suites hotel that's elegant but still
comfortable. The lobby and hotel restaurant, 8 East, are intimate and
private—qualities attracting guests who might be easily recognized.
The suites come in two sizes. The Tremont is near Mount Vernon and
the Inner Harbor. The concierge will help arrange local transportation,
which in most cases is free. **Pros:** swanky but not stuffy. **Cons:** no wireless Internet in the rooms—just Ethernet cables. ⊠*8 E. Pleasant St.,
City Center* ☎*410/576–1200 or 800/873–6668* ⊕*www.tremontsuite
hotels.com* ⤶*60 suites* ⚘*In-room: kitchen, Ethernet. In-hotel: restaurant, bar, gym, concierge, parking (fee)* ⊟*AE, D, DC, MC, V.* ⊹*3C*

$ ⛶**Tremont Plaza Hotel.** This 37-story all-suites hotel, once an apartment
★ building, is in the densest part of the business district. Its plain facade
and minuscule brass-and-marble lobby belie the tasteful earth-tone
guest rooms, which are a favorite of musicians and actors performing
at local theaters. The suites come in six sizes. The best views of the city
and the small park in the center of St. Paul Place are from rooms with
numbers ending in 06. The restaurant, Tugs, has a nautical theme and a
menu rich in seafood. **Pros:** renovated rooms, kitchens in suites. **Cons:**
a somewhat long walk from the Inner Harbor. ⊠*222 St. Paul Pl., City
Center* ☎*410/727–2222 or 800/873–6668* ⊕*www.tremontsuitehotels.
com* ⤶*253 suites* ⚘*In-room: kitchen, Ethernet. In-hotel: restaurant,
bar, pool, gym, concierge, public Wi-Fi, parking (fee)* ⊟*AE, D, DC,
MC, V.* ⊹*4C*

$ ⛶**Wyndham Inner Harbor.** One of Baltimore's largest, this hotel (four
blocks from the harbor) divides its rooms between two towers and
also houses the largest ballroom in the city, which makes it especially
popular with conventioneers. Rooms, decorated in light colors, have
a contemporary flair and marble-floor bathrooms. Amenities include
in-room voice mail, Internet access, hair dryers, and ironing boards.
The hotel restaurant is Don Shula's Steak House, where the menu is
presented on an official NFL football autographed by Shula, a former coach for the Baltimore Colts. **Pros:** easy access to the convention center. **Cons:** service can be sluggish. ⊠*101 W. Fayette St., City
Center* ☎*410/752–1100* ⊕*www.wyndham.com/hotels/BWIIH/main.
wnt* ⤶*707 rooms, 21 suites* ⚘*In-room: refrigerator, Ethernet, Wi-Fi.
In-hotel: 2 restaurants, bar, pool, gym, public Internet, parking (fee),
no-smoking rooms* ⊟*AE, D, DC, MC, V.* ⊹*4C*

INNER HARBOR

$$$ ⛶**Baltimore Marriott Inner Harbor.** This 10-story hotel is a block away
from Oriole Park at Camden Yards, Harborplace, and the convention
center. The public areas are nondescript but surprisingly tranquil, as are
the rooms, decorated in teal, mauve, and gray. The best views are from
rooms facing the Inner Harbor and the ballpark. Rooms on the 10th
floor come with concierge-level privileges. Staff is generally friendly
and eager to please, and some of the views are top-notch. **Pros:** some

rooms have stunning views of historic landmarks like the Bromo Seltzer Tower; easy access to Oriole Park. **Cons:** adjacent fire department and rowdy ballpark crowds can make for a noisy night. ⊠*110 S. Eutaw St., Inner Harbor* ☎*410/962–0202 or 800/228–9290* ⊕*www.marriott. com* ➳*524 rooms, 2 suites* ♿*In-room: Ethernet. In-hotel: 2 restaurants, bar, pool, gym, concierge, public Internet, public Wi-Fi, parking (fee), no-smoking rooms* ▤*AE, D, DC, MC, V.* ✛*5B*

$–$$ 🏨 **Courtyard by Marriott Baltimore Inner Harbor.** Close to the Inner Harbor waterfront and adjacent to Little Italy, this lodging is the farthest east of the Inner Harbor hotels. With sunny rooms in soothing neutral tones, the Courtyard Inner Harbor is a comfortable and attractive alternative to more central hotels with similar amenities and higher rates. Most downtown attractions are still within walking distance, though the stadiums and convention center are more comfortably reached by car or cab. **Pros:** less expensive than most downtown hotels. **Cons:** a decent walk to many Inner Harbor attractions. ⊠*1000 Aliceanna St., Inner Harbor East* ☎*443/923–4000* ⊕*www.marriott.com/BWIDT* ➳*205 rooms* ♿ *In room: Wi-Fi In-hotel: restaurant, pool, gym, parking (fee), no-smoking rooms* ▤*AE, D, DC, MC, V.* ✛*6F*

$–$$ 🏨 **Days Inn Inner Harbor.** Less than three blocks from the Inner Harbor, this nine-story redbrick building provides reliable and relatively economical accommodations in the center of town. The utilitarian, pastel-hue guest rooms are sparsely furnished, but each has a small desk and phone with voice mail and Internet access. It's also close to the 1st Mariner Arena venue, which makes it an easy pick for concertgoers. **Pros:** inexpensive. **Cons:** this street can be sketchy at night. ⊠*100 Hopkins Pl., Inner Harbor East* ☎*410/576–1000* ⊕*www.daysinnerharbor. com* ➳*250 rooms* ♿*In-room: refrigerator. In-hotel: restaurant, bar, pool, public Wi-Fi, parking (fee), no-smoking rooms* ▤*AE, D, DC, MC, V.* ✛*4C*

$$$–$$$$ 🏨 **Harbor Court.** The entrance to the most prestigious hotel in Baltimore is set back from the street by a brick courtyard that provides ★ an immediate sense of tranquillity. A grand spiral staircase dominates the lobby, which is decorated in English country opulence. All guest rooms include such deluxe touches as twice-daily maid service, plush bathrobes, and TVs in the bathrooms; upscale suite amenities also include 6-foot marble tubs, canopied four-poster beds, and CD players. Waterside rooms have a commanding view of the harbor, but courtyard rooms are quietest. **Pros:** the city's nicest hotel. **Cons:** also city's most expensive hotel. ⊠*550 Light St., Inner Harbor* ☎*410/234–0550 or 800/824–0076* ⊕*www.harborcourt.com* ➳*195 rooms, 23 suites* ♿*In-room: refrigerator, Ethernet, Wi-Fi. In-hotel: 2 restaurants, bar, tennis court, pool, gym, concierge, public Internet, parking (fee), no-smoking rooms* ▤*AE, D, DC, MC, V.* ✛*6C*

$$$–$$$$ 🏨 **Hilton Baltimore.** Location, location, location: One of Baltimore's newest hotels has an unparalleled view of Camden Yards and a skywalk that connects to the city convention center. Opened in 2008, the towering 20-story hotel is mostly boring gray metal on the outside, in stark contrast with the brick-clad ballpark. Inside, the hotel has a nautical feel, with wave-shape fixtures hanging from the ceiling and pillars of deep

wood and blue tiles. Ask for a room on the south side, where you can peer down into the ballpark. Or you can watch the games from the fitness center on the fourth floor. Hotel staff is friendly and accommodating and the amenities are new. **Pros:** connected to the convention center; excellent ballpark view. **Cons:** pricey for its accommodations. ✉*401 W. Pratt St., Inner Harbor* 🕾*443/573–8700* ⊕*www.baltimore.hilton. com* 🛏*757 rooms,* ♿*In-room: Ethernet, Wi-Fi. In-hotel: restaurant, bar, pool, gym, public Internet, public Wi-Fi, parking (fee), no-smoking rooms* ⊟*AE, D, DC, MC, V.* ♁*5B*

$$$–$$$$ 🏨**Hyatt Regency.** This stretch of Light Street is practically a highway, but the unenclosed skyways allow ready pedestrian access to both Inner Harbor attractions and the convention center. Rooms have rich gold and black-purple prints and cherrywood furniture; most rooms have views of the harbor or the city. The lobby has glass elevators and the chain's trademark atrium. The 12th floor is the Club level, with complimentary breakfast, evening hors d'oeuvres, and a private concierge available. Atop the hotel, the Pisces restaurant and lounge provides stunning city views, especially at night. **Pros:** the Inner Harbor is just a skywalk away. **Cons:** service can be slow and unhelpful. ✉*300 Light St., Inner Harbor* 🕾*410/528–1234 or 800/233–1234* ⊕*baltimore. hyatt.com* 🛏*488 rooms, 26 suites* ♿*In room: Wi-Fi In-hotel: 2 restaurants, bars, tennis courts, pool, gym, parking (fee), no-smoking rooms* ⊟*AE, D, DC, MC, V.* ♁*5C*

$$$–$$$$ 🏨**Marriott Baltimore Waterfront.** The city's tallest hotel and the only one directly on the Inner Harbor itself, this upscale 31-story Marriott has a neoclassical interior that uses multihue marbles, rich jewel-tone walls, and photographs of Baltimore architectural landmarks. Although it's at the eastern end of the Inner Harbor, all downtown attractions are within walking distance; there's also a water-taxi stop right by the front door. Most rooms offer unobstructed views of the city and harbor; ask for one that faces west toward downtown for a splendid panorama of the waterfront and skyscrapers. **Pros:** nice amenities; great location and view. **Cons:** pricey, compared to nearby hotels. ✉*700 Aliceanna St., Inner Harbor East* 🕾*410/385–3000* ⊕*www.marriotthotels.com/ BWIWF* 🛏*751 rooms* ♿*In-room: safe, refrigerator, Ethernet. In-hotel: restaurant, bar, pool, gym, parking (fee), no-smoking rooms* ⊟*AE, D, DC, MC, V.* ♁*6F*

$$–$$$ 🏨**Renaissance Harborplace Hotel.** The most conveniently located of the Inner Harbor hotels—across the street from the shopping pavilions—the Renaissance Harborplace meets the needs of tourists, business travelers, and conventioneers. Guest rooms are light and cheerful, with amenities that include coffeemakers, terry robes, hair dryers, and ironing boards. Some rooms have a view of the harbor, the downtown landscape, or the indoor courtyard. The hotel adjoins the Gallery, a four-story shopping mall. **Pros:** snappy service. **Cons:** some rooms can be a bit threadbare. ✉*202 E. Pratt St., Inner Harbor* 🕾*410/547–1200 or 800/468–3571* ⊕*www.renaissancehotels.com/BWISH* 🛏*562 rooms, 60 suites* ♿*In-room: Ethernet. In-hotel: restaurant, bar, pool, gym, public Wi-Fi, parking (fee), no-smoking rooms* ⊟*AE, D, DC, MC, V.* ♁*5D*

6

FELLS POINT

$$ **The Admiral Fell Inn.** This inn is an upright anchor at the center of the action in funky Fells Point. By joining together buildings constructed between the late 1770s and the 1920s, the owners created a structure that resembles a small, European-style hotel, with lots of character and quirks. The rooms, which vary in shape, all have four-poster canopy beds. Three suites and eight rooms have whirlpool baths. Some hallways have a few stairs, and some rooms face a quiet, interior courtyard: if steps or street noise bother you, let the reservation agent know. **Pros:** a good sense of history; close to nightlife. **Cons:** neighborhood noise can be loud and distracting. ⊠ *888 S. Broadway, Fells Point* ☎ *410/522–7377 or 800/292–4667* ⊕ *www.admiralfell.com* ⇔ *80 rooms* ⌂ *In-room: Ethernet, Wi-Fi (some). In-hotel: restaurant, bar, public Internet, parking (no fee)* ☰ *AE, DC, MC, V* ⏀ *CP.* ✛ *6G*

$–$$ **Celie's Waterfront Bed & Breakfast.** Proprietors Nancy and Kevin Kupec oversee every detail of this small inn in the heart of Fells Point. Guest rooms, all with private bath, are furnished in Early American style; two suites accommodate large groups. Upscale amenities include down comforters, terry robes, fireplaces, and whirlpool baths. Continental breakfast is served in the cozy dining room. The rooftop deck provides a wonderful view of Baltimore's skyline and harbor. **Pros:** intimate accommodations; situated next to an entertainment district. **Cons:** prices high for what you get; it can get noisy late at night. ⊠ *1714 Thames St., Fells Point* ☎ *410/522–2323 or 800/432–0184* ⊕ *www.celieswaterfront.com* ⇔ *7 rooms, 2 suites* ⌂ *In room: Wi-Fi In-hotel: restaurant, parking (fee)* ☰ *AE, D, MC, V* ⏀ *CP.* ✛ *6H*

$$–$$$ **Inn at Henderson's Wharf.** Built in the mid-1800s as a B&O Railroad tobacco warehouse, this richly decorated, warmly inviting B&B–style inn has harbor or garden views from all of its rooms. The inn is at the water's edge, on the very peninsula that gave Fells Point its name. Adjacent to the inn is a marina with slips to 150 feet; all possible amenities are available to visiting yachters. It's a short, scenic walk from the shops, bars, and restaurants of central Fells Point. **Pros:** offers a sweeping waterfront view. **Cons:** slightly pricey for the level of accommodations. ⊠ *1000 Fell St., Fells Point* ☎ *410/522–7777 or 800/522–2088* ⊕ *www.hendersonswharf.com* ⇔ *37 rooms* ⌂ *In room: Wi-Fi In-hotel: gym, concierge, public Internet, parking (no fee), no-smoking rooms* ☰ *AE, DC, MC, V* ⏀ *CP.* ✛ *6H*

CANTON

$–$$ **Inn at 2920.** In the heart of one of the city's liveliest neighborhoods, this stylish B&B is dedicated to tranquil, luxurious living. Low-allergen surroundings (natural fiber carpeting, low-chemical cleaning products, purified air) and high-thread-count sheets are standard amenities, and each room has a Jacuzzi bathtub, satellite television with VCR, and CD player. Full-course breakfasts generally include fresh-fruit salad, omelets, and waffles or pancakes, but different dietary needs can be accommodated. **Pros:** stylish and eco-friendly. **Cons:** not within walking distance of the Inner Harbor; limited availability. ⊠ *2920 Elliott St.*

☎410/342–4450 ⊕*www.theinnat2920.com* ➷*4 rooms* ♿*In-room: no phone, VCR, . In-hotel: no kids under 13, no-smoking rooms, public Wi-Fi* ▤*AE, MC, V* ⊙*BP.* ✛*6H*

ROLAND PARK

$$–$$$ ⛺**Inn at the Colonnade.** Directly across the street from Johns Hopkins and within walking distance of the Baltimore Museum of Art, this hotel is also 15 minutes north of downtown. Rooms are welcoming, with rich, warm furnishings, and there are extras such as a glass-dome swimming pool and whirlpool baths. **Pros:** close to Johns Hopkins University. **Cons:** some rooms can feel run-down. ⊠*4 W. University Pkwy., Tuscany-Canterbury* ☎*410/235–5400* ⊕*www.doubletree.com* ➷*125 rooms, 19 suites* ♿ *In room: Wi-Fi. In-hotel: restaurant, bar, pool, gym, parking (fee), no-smoking rooms* ▤*AE, D, DC, MC, V.* ✛*2G*

$–$$ ⛺**Radisson Hotel at Cross Keys.** Ten minutes north of downtown, this secluded hotel is a respite from city bustle. Rooms come with high-speed Internet access along with cheerful French country style. The health conscious will appreciate the wooded walking trails, tennis courts, and state-of-the-art exercise equipment. The hotel is adjacent to an outdoor mall with high-end boutique shopping, though in recent years many of the boutiques have closed or moved elsewhere. There's complimentary shuttle service to the Inner Harbor. **Pros:** removed from the Inner Harbor's hustle. **Cons:** not much to do nearby. ⊠*5100 Falls Rd., Roland Park* ☎*410/532–6900 or 800/756–7285* ⊕*www.radisson.com* ➷*147 rooms, 10 suites* ♿ *In room: Wi-Fi In-hotel: restaurant, bar, pool, gym, public Internet, parking (no fee), no-smoking rooms* ▤*AE, D, DC, MC, V.* ✛*2F*

NORTHERN SUBURBS

$ ⛺**Courtyard by Marriott Hunt Valley.** About 25 minutes from downtown, in an affluent suburb that's a growing corporate center, this motel is comfortable and affordable. Guest rooms are as standardized as Courtyard's signature white-stucco exterior; coffeemakers, ironing boards, and hair dryers are added conveniences. The neighbors are office buildings, which means rooms are quiet at night but have uninteresting views. The nearby York and Shawan road corridors have many restaurants, and there's public transportation to downtown via the light-rail Hunt Valley stop. The restaurant serves breakfast only. **Pros:** inexpensive prices; comfortable accommodations. **Cons:** the drive downtown can take a while; must also drive for dinner options. ⊠*221 International Circle, Hunt Valley* ☎*410/584–7070* ⊕*www.marriotthotels.com/BWIHU* ➷*134 rooms, 12 suites* ♿*In-room: Ethernet. In-hotel: restaurant, bar, pool, gym, public Internet, parking (no fee)* ▤*AE, D, DC, MC, V.* ✛*1E*

$ ⛺**Hampton Inn Hunt Valley.** Guest rooms at this suburban hotel are brightly decorated with basic furnishings. The property is within walking distance of a light-rail station for transportation to downtown Baltimore; the city is an easy 25-minute drive directly down I-83. Although there's no restaurant in the hotel, a free breakfast bar is available every morning, and many restaurants are nearby. A note to outdoor enthusiasts: This hotel is only a short drive from Loch Raven Reservoir. **Pros:** near a light-rail station; budget-friendly. **Cons:** no hotel restaurant; long drive to downtown. ⊠*11200 York Rd., Hunt Valley* ☎*410/527–1500* ⊕*www.hamptoninn.com* ➪*125 rooms* ⚗*In-room: refrigerator. In-hotel: gym, public Internet, public Wi-Fi, parking (no fee)* ▤*AE, D, DC, MC, V* ▯◐▮*CP.* ✛*1E*

NIGHTLIFE & THE ARTS

The *City Paper* (⊕*www.citypaper.com*), a free weekly distributed in shops and yellow street-corner boxes, has the most comprehensive and complete calendar of Baltimore events; it's published every Wednesday. Other event listings appear in the Thursday edition of the *Baltimore Sun* (⊕*www.baltimoresun.com*), the monthly *Baltimore* magazine, and the daily *b* magazine.

Fells Point, just east of the Inner Harbor; Federal Hill, due south; and Canton, due east, have hosts of bars, restaurants, and clubs that draw a rowdy, largely collegiate crowd. If you're seeking quieter surroundings, head for the upscale comforts of downtown or Mount Vernon clubs and watering holes.

BARS & LOUNGES

Upstairs at **The Brewer's Art** (⊠*1106 N. Charles St., Mount Vernon* ☎*410/547–6925* ⊕*www.belgianbeer.com*) is an elegant bar and lounge with armchairs, marble pillars, and chandeliers, plus a dining room with terrific food; downstairs, the dark basement bar specializes in Belgian-style beers. With its stylized art deco surroundings, the funky **Club Charles** (⊠*1724 N. Charles St., StationNorth Arts District* ☎*410/727–8815*) is a favorite hangout for an artsy crowd, moviegoers coming from the Charles Theater across the street, and, reputation has it, John Waters. **Club Hippo** (⊠*1 W. Eager St., Mount Vernon* ☎*410/547–0069* ⊕*www. clubhippo.com*) is Baltimore's longest-reigning gay bar. The **Dog Pub** (⊠*20 E. Cross St., Federal Hill* ☎*410/727–6077*) has no TVs, so you focus more on conversation. About 10 beers are made from in-house recipes, and always served two at a time in 10-ounce glass mugs. The patio at the waterside **DuClaw Brewery** (⊠*901 S. Bond St., Fells Point* ☎*410/563–3400*) is a great spot for an early-evening pint; the restaurant serves bar fare with a twist, but stick to the standards. The well-heeled gather at the Harbor Court Hotel in the **Explorer's Lounge** (⊠*550 Light St., Inner Harbor* ☎*410/234–0550*), where there are antique elephant-tusk lamps and faux leopard-skin chairs. Enjoy a cigar and pick a single-malt Scotch from one of the largest selections in town. A pianist performs every night, and on Friday and Saturday nights there's a jazz trio. A dance club, martini bar, and pub have all helped make **Grand Central** (⊠*1003 N. Charles St., Mount Vernon* ☎*410/752–7133*) into a hip gay hot spot. The **Horse You Came In On** (⊠*1626 Thames St., Fells Point* ☎*410/327–8111*) is a dim, quiet neighborhood tavern during the day and a raucous bar with live music almost every night. The arty, funky **Idle Hour** (✉*201 E. Fort Ave., Federal Hill* ☎*410/468–0357*) is a low-key hangout with some of the city's best indie DJs. Beer lovers should visit **Max's Taphouse** (✉*737 S. Broadway, Fells Point* ☎*410/675–6297* ⊕*www.maxs.com*), which has more than 70 brews on tap and about 300 more in bottles. At **Pickles Pub** (✉*520 Washington Blvd., Inner Harbor* ☎*410/752–1784*) sports fans banter about trivia, dispute scores, and commiserate over scandals. This is a favorite postgame hangout for Orioles and Ravens fans. **Red Maple** (✉*930 N. Charles St., Mount Vernon* ☎*410/547–0149* ⊕*www.930redmaple.com*) is one of the city's most stylish spots for drinks and tapas. At the top of the Belvedere Hotel, the **13th Floor** (✉*1 E. Chase St., Mount Vernon* ☎*410/347–0888*) offers a great view, a long martini list, and live dance music. The **Tusk Lounge** (✉*924 N. Charles St., Mount Vernon* ☎*410/547–8480*), above the Brass Elephant restaurant, is a cozy, classy place for drinks.

CLASSICAL MUSIC

An die Musik (✉*409 N. Charles St., Mount Vernon* ☎*410/385–2638* ⊕*www.AndieMusikLIVE.com*) is an intimate space for classical, jazz, and world music. **Friedberg Hall** (✉*E. Mount Vernon Pl. at Charles St., Mount Vernon* ☎*410/659–8124* ⊕*www.peabody.jhu.edu*), part of the Peabody Institute, is the scene of recitals, concerts, and opera performances by students, faculty, and distinguished guests. **Meyerhoff Symphony Hall** (✉*1212 Cathedral St., Mount Vernon* ☎*410/783–8000* ⊕*www.baltimoresymphony.org*) is the city's principal concert hall and home of the Baltimore Symphony Orchestra. At the outdoor **Pier Six Concert Pavilion** (✉*731 Eastern Ave., Inner Harbor* ☎*410/783–4189* ⊕*www.piersixpavilion.com*) there's both pavilion and lawn seating for concerts showcasing top national musicians and groups. Concerts run from June to September.

COMEDY CLUBS

The Comedy Factory (✉*36 Light St., Inner Harbor* ☎*410/752–4189*) is the best local spot to see live standup.

FILM

The **Charles Theater** (✉*1711 N. Charles St., Mount Vernon* ☎*410/727–3456* ⊕*www.thecharles.com*) is Baltimore's preeminent venue for first-run, foreign, and art films. The sleek **Landmark Theatres** (✉*645 S. President St., Inner Harbor* ☎*410/624–2622* ⊕*www.landmarktheatres.com*) offer mainstream films within walking distance of the Inner Harbor. You can order a drink at the bar, take it into the auditorium, and relax in one of the black leather seats. **Rotunda Cinematheque** (✉*11 W. 40th St., Roland Park* ☎*410/235–4800*) has two small theaters showing independent films. The **Senator Theatre** (✉*5904 York Rd., Belvedere Square* ☎*410/435–8338*) is the city's grande dame, a rare surviving example of a large neighborhood theater built during Hollywood's golden age.

POP MUSIC

For some of the city's best and most authentic live blues and rock-abilly, head to the **Cat's Eye Pub** (⊠ *1730 Thames St., Fells Point* ☎ *410/276–9866* ⊕ *www.catseyepub.com*), which hosts live music every night. **The 8x10 Club** (⊠ *8–10 E. Cross St., Federal Hill* ☎ *410/625–2000* ⊕ *www.the8x10.com*) is one of the city's premier spots for live music, from rock and reggae, to jazz, blues, and soul. The spring-loaded dance floor bounces under large crowds, and there is barely a bad place to stand inside. **The Ottobar** (⊠ *2549 N. Howard St., Mount Vernon* ☎ *410/662–0069* ⊕ *www.theottobar.com*) is the city's venue for live alternative music—a hipster magnet. **Rams Head Live** (⊠ *20 Market Pl., in Power Plant Live, Inner Harbor* ☎ *410/244–8854* ⊕ *www.ramsheadlive.com*) is one of the city's newest live music venues, regularly featuring international and local bands. **Sonar** (⊠ *407 E. Saratoga St., Mount Vernon* ☎ *410/327–8333* ⊕ *www.sonarbaltimore.com*) has three separate spaces: a warehouse with a large stage, a club room, and a smaller lounge.

THEATER

The **Baltimore Theatre Project** (⊠ *45 W. Preston St., Mount Vernon* ☎ *410/752–8558* ⊕ *www.theatreproject.org*) is dedicated to showing original and experimental theater, music, and dance. **Center Stage** (⊠ *700 N. Calvert St., Mount Vernon* ☎ *410/332–0033* ⊕ *www.centerstage.org*) performs works by Shakespeare and Samuel Beckett as well as contemporary playwrights. The intimate **Fells Point Corner Theater** (⊠ *251 S. Ann St., Fells Point* ☎ *410/276–7837* ⊕ *www.fpct.org*), an 85-seat venue focused on acting and directing workshops, stages eight off-Broadway productions a year, along with readings and poetry slams. A beautifully restored 1914 movie palace is home to the **France-Merrick Performing Arts Center at the Hippodrome** (⊠ *12 N. Eutaw St., West Baltimore* ☎ *410/837–7400* ⊕ *www.france-merrickpac.com*), a stage for concerts, Broadway musicals, and other big productions. **Lyric Opera House** (⊠ *140 W. Mt. Royal Ave., Mount Vernon* ☎ *410/685–5086*) hosts plays and musicals in addition to opera productions. **Spotlighters Theater** (⊠ *817 St. Paul St., Mount Vernon* ☎ *410/752–1225* ⊕ *www.spotlighters.org*) is a true community theater, staging locally produced (and cast) works that include original productions, Shakespeare, and musicals; there's one production a month, with performances on weekends. The **Vagabond Players** (⊠ *806 S. Broadway, Fells Point* ☎ *410/563–9135* ⊕ *www.bcpl.net/~thevag*) hosts performances of recent Broadway hits and theater favorites every weekend.

SPORTS & THE OUTDOORS

PARTICIPANT SPORTS

BICYCLING

Due to the lack of street-side paths and angry motorists, exploring inner city Baltimore on two wheels is a bad idea. But the city's most defined network of bicycling paths is the Gwynns Falls Trail, which connects

2,000 acres of public land in and around Baltimore. The trail, which was completed in the past couple of years, stretches for about 15 mi. Maps are available at ⊕*www. gwynnsfallstrail.org.* Or you could head to one of the city's parks or out of town to dedicated cycling trails. Bikes can be rented from **Light Street Cycles** (⊠*1015 Light St., Federal Hill* ☎*410/685–2234*); ask for a map of local trails.

> ### DUCKPIN BOWLING
>
> Invented in Baltimore in 1900, duckpin bowling uses smaller balls and pins. For some fun and some real Baltimore character, head to the **Patterson Bowling Center** (⊠*2105 Eastern Ave., Fells Point* ☎*410/675–1011*), the oldest duckpin bowling center in the country.

Just south of the city is the **Baltimore and Annapolis Trail** (☎*410/222–6244*); to get on the trail near BWI airport, follow I–695 to I–97 south, take Exit 15 onto Dorsey Road, heading west away from the airport. Look for signs for Saw Mill Creek Park, which has 13 mi of paved trails, open space, bridges, and woodlands. North of the city, the 21-mi **Northern Central Railroad Hike and Bike Trail** (☎*410/592–2897* ⊕*www.dnr.state.md.us/publiclands/central/gunpowder.html*) extends along the old Northern Central Railroad to the Maryland–Pennsylvania line. It begins at Ashland Road, just east of York Road in Hunt Valley, and heads north 20 mi to the Pennsylvania border. Parking is available at seven points along the way.

GOLF

The *Baltimore Sun*'s **golf guide** (⊕*www.baltimoresun.com/golfguide*) gives a detailed and thorough overview of local courses.

Public **Forest Park** (⊠*2900 Hillsdale Rd., North Baltimore* ☎*410/448–4653*) has 18 challenging holes (par 71), with a tight, tree-lined front 9 and open back 9. Greens fees are $30 weekdays and $33 on weekends; reservations are accepted. Designed in 1936, **Mount Pleasant** (⊠*6001 Hillen Rd., North Baltimore* ☎*410/254–5100*) was for many years the site of the Eastern Open. It has 18 holes of par-71 golf on bent grass. Greens fees are $36 on weekdays and $42 on weekends.

HEALTH & FITNESS CLUBS

A few clubs offer temporary membership to visitors. Your hotel may provide this as a courtesy, so ask the concierge. Among hotels, the **Harbor Court** has by far the best athletic facilities.

RUNNING

Scenic places to run around the Inner Harbor include the promenade around the water; Rash Field, on the south side, adjacent to the Science Center and Federal Hill Park; and the path at the water's edge at Fort McHenry. If you're staying in Mount Vernon, head north up Charles Street toward Charles Village and Johns Hopkins University.

TENNIS

Courts can be found in the city's public parks, though if you're a serious player, you may be better off using hotel courts or tennis clubs.

Open year-round, the **Cross Keys Tennis Club** (✉ *5100 Falls Rd., Roland Park* ☎ *410/433–1800*) has courts available for $27–$37 per hour. **Druid Hill Park** (✉ *Druid Hill Lake Dr., West Baltimore* ☎ *410/396–6106*) has 24 courts. The courts at the **Orchard Indoor Tennis Club** (✉ *8720 Loch Raven Blvd., Towson* ☎ *410/821–6206*) are available to nonmembers for $25 per hour. **Patterson Park** (✉ *Eastern Ave., East Baltimore* ☎ *410/396–3774*) has 10 courts.

SPECTATOR SPORTS

BASEBALL

☺ Fodor'sChoice ★ The **Baltimore Orioles** (✉ *Oriole Park at Camden Yards, 333 W. Camden St., West Baltimore* ☎ *410/685–9800 general information, 410/481–7328 for tickets* ⊕ *www.theorioles.com*) play in their beautiful ballpark from early April until early October. Think twice about settling on a hot dog and Budweiser for your meal: the stadium also sells lump-meat crab cakes, former Orioles first baseman Boog Powell's barbecued pork loin and beef, and local microbrews, such as Clipper City's Ft. McHenry Lager.

FOOTBALL

The **Baltimore Ravens** (✉ *1101 Russell St., West Baltimore* ☎ *410/261–7283* ⊕ *www.baltimoreravens.com*) play in state-of-the-art M&T Stadium from August to January.

HORSE RACING

On the third Saturday in May the prestigious Preakness Stakes, the second race in the Triple Crown, is run at Baltimore's **Pimlico Race Course** (✉ *5204 Park Heights Ave., Northwest Baltimore* ☎ *410/542–9400* ⊕ *www.marylandracing.com*). The course has additional Thoroughbred racing. Call ahead for days and times.

LACROSSE

The **Johns Hopkins University Blue Jays** (✉ *Homewood Field, Charles St. at University Pkwy., Charles Village* ☎ *410/516–7490* ⊕ *hopkinssports. cstv.com*) are a perennial favorite.

The **Loyola Greyhounds** (✉ *Charles St. at Cold Spring La., North Baltimore* ☎ *410/617–5014*) play on their college's campus.

SHOPPING

Baltimore isn't the biggest shopping town, but it does have some malls and good stores here and there. Hampden (the "p" is silent), a neighborhood west of Johns Hopkins University, has funky shops selling everything from housewares to housedresses along its main drag, 36th Street (better known as "The Avenue"). Some interesting shops can be found along Charles Street in Mount Vernon and along Thames Street in Fells Point. Federal Hill has a few fun shops, particularly for furnishings and vintage items.

SHOPPING MALLS

About 7 mi north of downtown, at Northern Parkway and York Road, is **Belvedere Square** (⊠ *E. Belvedere Ave. at York Rd.* ☎*410/464–9773*), a small, open-air mall with shops for women's and children's clothing, furniture, and gifts, as well as a number of gourmet food shops (the soup at Atwater's is delicious). At the Inner Harbor, the Pratt Street and Light Street pavilions of **Harborplace and the Gallery** (☎*410/332–4191*) contain almost 200 specialty shops that sell everything from business attire to children's toys. The Gallery has J. Crew, Banana Republic, and the Gap, among others. **Towson Town Center** (⊠*Dulaney Valley Rd. at Fairmount Ave., 0.5 mi south of I–695 at Exit 27A, Towson* ☎*410/494–8800* ⊕*www.towsontowncenter.com*) has nearly 200 shops, including Hecht's, Nordstrom, the Gap, and Anthropologie. **Village of Cross Keys** (⊠*5100 Falls Rd., North Baltimore* ☎*410/323–1000*), about 6 mi north of downtown, is an eclectic collection of 30 stores, including Talbot's, Chico's, Williams-Sonoma, Ann Taylor, and some small, high-end boutiques for women's clothing and gifts.

DEPARTMENT STORES

For deals on designer clothes, head to **Filene's Basement** (*600 E. Pratt St., Baltimore* ☎*410/685–2637*) the city's first new department store in decades Shop for top-name designer goods accompanied by courteous, service-oriented sales staff and live music from a grand piano at **Nordstrom** (⊠*Towson Town Center, 825 Dulaney Valley Rd., Towson* ☎*410/494–9111*).

FOOD MARKETS

Baltimore's indoor food markets, all of which are at least 100 years old, are a mix of vendors selling fresh fish, meat, produce, and baked goods and a food court, with stands for street food such as crab cakes, sausages, fried chicken, and pizza. Lexington Market is the largest and most famous, and the Broadway and Cross Street markets are close behind in terms of local, taste-tempting foods. City markets are generally open year-round, every day but Sunday. Closing times depend on the market.

Broadway Market (⊠*Broadway at Fleet St., Fells Point*) has many stalls with fresh fruit, prepared foods, a raw bar, and baked goods that can be eaten at counters or taken outside for picnics along the waterfront. **Cross Street Market** (⊠*Light and Cross Sts., Federal Hill*) has stands selling produce, sandwiches, steamed crab, and baked items. Cross Street is open late on Friday and Saturday, when the market hosts one of the city's most popular happy-hour scenes, attracting crowds of youngish professionals. Be sure to stop by Piedigrotta Bakery, where you can sample what the owners claim to be the country's first-ever tiramisu. The city's oldest and largest public market, **Lexington Market** (⊠*400 W. Lexington St., between Paca and Eutaw Sts., Downtown* ☎*410/685–6169* ⊕*www.lexingtonmarket.com*) has more than 150 vendors selling meat, produce, seafood, baked goods, delicatessen items, poultry, and food products from around the world. Don't miss the world-famous crab cakes at Faidley's Seafood; other local specialties with market stalls are Rheb's chocolates, Polock Johnny's Polish sausages, and Berger's Bakery's chocolate-iced vanilla wafer cookies.

SPECIALTY STORES

ANTIQUES

Many of Baltimore's antiques shops can be found on historic Antiques Row, which runs along the 700 and 800 blocks of North Howard Street. Shops include cluttered kitsch boutiques as well as elegant, high-end galleries of furniture and fine art. Fells Point shops are concentrated on Eastern, Fleet, and Aliceanna streets. Hampden shops are found primarily on 36th Street.

Avenue Antiques (⊠ *901 W. 36th St., Hampden* ☎ *410/467–0329*) is a collection of multiple dealers, selling antiques from Victorian to mid-century modern. At **Gaines McHale Antiques and Home** (⊠ *700 S. Caroline St., Fells Point* ☎ *410/625–1900* ⊕ *www.gainesmchale.com*) the owners build new pieces with old wood, turning antique armoires, for example, into entertainment centers. There's also a large selection of unaltered, high-quality country and traditional antiques from England and France. **Second Chance** (⊠ *1645 Warner St.,Southwest Baltimore* ☎ *410/385–1101* ⊕ *www.secondchanceinc.org*) salvages unique architectural pieces from old buildings being renovated or destroyed; the five large warehouses are open Tuesday–Saturday 9–5. The **Turnover Shop** (⊠ *3855 Roland Ave., Hampden* ☎ *410/235–9585* ⊕ *www.theturnovershop.com*) is a consignment shop selling high-end antiques.

BOOKS

The **AIA/Baltimore Bookstore** (⊠ *11½ W. Chase St., Mount Vernon* ☎ *410/625–2585*) carries all kinds of architecture books. **Atomic Books** (⊠ *3620 Falls Rd., Hampden* ☎ *410/366–1004* ⊕ *www.atomicbooks.com*) specializes in obscure titles and small-press publications, including independent comics and 'zines, along with videos. There's also a formidable selection of pop-culture toys such as lunch boxes, cookie jars, and stickers. **Book Thing** (⊠ *3001 Vineyard La., Waverly* ☎ *410/662–5631* ⊕ *www.bookthing.org*) takes donations and gives away free books—as many as you like, as long as you promise not to resell them; it's open weekends 9–6. The **Children's Bookstore** (⊠ *737 Deepdene Rd., Roland Park* ☎ *410/532–2000* ⊕ *www.thecbstore.com*) is a cozy, well-stocked resource for current and classic children's literature. The **Kelmscott Bookshop** (⊠ *32 W. 25th St., Charles Village* ☎ *410/235–6810* ⊕ *www.kelmscottbookshop.com*) is known for its enormous, well-preserved stock of old and rare volumes in every major category, especially art, architecture, American and English literature, and travel. **Mystery Loves Company** (⊠ *1730 Fleet St., Fells Point* ☎ *410/276–6708* ⊕ *www.mysterylovescompany.com*) specializes in books and gifts for whodunit fans; the shop stocks an excellent selection of works by Baltimore native son (and inventor of the genre) Edgar Allan Poe.

CHILDREN'S CLOTHING

Raw Sugar (⊠ *524 E. Belvedere Ave., Belvedere Square* ☎*410/464–1240*) carries clothing for the funky, fashionable six-and-under set as well as maternity wear and toys.

GIFTS

Many of the city's museums have excellent shops, which are good sources for gifts. **Best of Baltimore** (⊠*301 S. Light St., Inner Harbor* ☎*410/ 332–4191*) carries city-related souvenirs and local specialty products. For unique, truly local mementos of Baltimore, like crab-shape twinkle lights and a kit for cleaning row-house marble steps, **Hometown Girl** (⊠*1001 W. 36th St., Hampden* ☎*410/662–4438*) is the place to go. It also stocks local history books and Baltimore guidebooks. The **Store Ltd.** (⊠ *Village of Cross Keys, Roland Park* ☎*410/323–2350*) has an eclectic mix of top-quality (and pricey) jewelry, women's sportswear, glassware, and other high-design gifts. The **Tomlinson Craft Collection** (⊠*The Rotunda, 711 W. 40th St., Roland Park* ☎*410/338–1572*) is a gallery of local artisan handiworks, from fine jewelry to ceramics and metalwork.

JEWELRY

Amaryllis (⊠*The Gallery, 200 E. Pratt St.Inner Harbor* ☎*410/576–7622*) specializes in handcrafted jewelry from more than 400 artists. Designers come from all over the world for the incredibly wide selection of beads at **Beadazzled** (⊠*501 N. Charles St., Mount Vernon* ☎*410/837–2323*); there's also a selection of already-made jewelry.

MEN'S CLOTHING

Jos. A. Bank's Clothiers (⊠*100 E. Pratt St., Inner Harbor* ☎*410/547–1700*) is a century-old Baltimore source for men's tailored clothing and casual wear. **Samuel Parker Clothier** (⊠*6080 Falls Rd., Northern Suburbs* ☎*410/372–0078* ⊕*www.samuelparker.com*) carries a fine selection of updated traditional clothing by the likes of Ralph Lauren and Samuelson.

WOMEN'S CLOTHING

Jones & Jones (⊠ *Village of Cross Keys, Roland Park* ☎*410/532–9645*) carries stylish sportswear and business attire. **Ma Petite Shoe** (⊠*832 W. 36th St., Hampden* ☎*410/235–3442*) sells chocolates as well as funky, fabulous shoes. **Oh! Said Rose** (⊠*832 W. 36th St., Hampden* ☎*410/235–5170*) carries fun, feminine clothing with a vintage look. **Ruth Shaw** (⊠ *Village of Cross Keys, Roland Park* ☎*410/532–7886*) sells the work of European designers like Gaultier and Paul Smith as well as chic evening wear. **Something Else** (⊠*1611 Sulgrave Ave., Mt. Washington* ☎*410/542–0444*) is the source for sophisticated hippie wear: Flax-brand clothes, flowing skirts, big scarves, and colorful sweaters. The **Shine Collective** (⊠*1007 W. 36th St., Hampden* ☎*410/366–6100*) carries hip accessories and clothing made by a group of local young designers.

SIDE TRIPS FROM BALTIMORE

Not far from Baltimore, Maryland's landscape is dotted with well-preserved 18th- and 19th-century towns. Harford County's Havre de Grace, at the top of the bay, and nearby Aberdeen, with a legacy of military history, make for an ideal day trip. Historic Ellicott City, southwest of Baltimore in Howard County, is a fun place to explore, have lunch, and shop.

HAVRE DE GRACE

40 mi northeast of Baltimore (via I–95).

On the site of one of Maryland's oldest settlements is the neatly laid-out town of Havre de Grace, reputedly named by the Marquis de Lafayette. This "harbor of mercy," on the Chesapeake Bay at the mouth of the Susquehanna River, was shelled and torched by the British in the War of 1812, and few structures predate that period.

TIMING & PRECAUTIONS

Depending on the season, you'll want to budget about a half day for Havre de Grace. The waterfront town has gardens and museums to tour, but none of them take too much time. It's a pleasant way to see firsthand some of the area's history. Be sure to stroll down the half-mile boardwalk and stop for a picnic in the park.

ESSENTIALS

Visitor Information **Havre de Grace Visitor Center** (✉ *450 Pennington Ave.* ☎ *410/939–2100*).

EXPLORING

The conical **Concord Point Lighthouse** is the oldest continuously operated lighthouse on the Chesapeake Bay. Built in 1827, it was restored in 1980. You can climb up 30 feet for views of the bay, river, and town. ✉ *700 Concord St.* ☎ *410/939–9040* ✉ *Free* ☉ *Apr.–Oct., weekends 1–5.*

The **Havre de Grace Decoy Museum,** housed in a converted power plant, has 1,200 facsimiles of ducks, geese, and swans made from wood, iron, cork, papier-mâché, and plastic. Three classes—decorative, decorative floater, and working decoys—are represented. A festival during the first full weekend in May includes carving contests and demonstrations by retriever dogs. ✉ *215 Giles St.* ☎ *410/939–3739* ⊕ *www.decoymuseum. com* ✉ *$6* ☉ *Mon.–Sat. 10:30–4:30, Sun. noon–4.*

★ The **Ladew Topiary Gardens** displays the life's work of Harvey Smith Ladew. The trees and shrubs are sculpted into geometric forms and life-like renditions of animals such as a fox and hounds, swans, and even a seahorse. The 15 formal gardens cover 22 acres. Besides the amazing topiary displays are rose, berry, and herb gardens, and a tranquil Japanese garden with pagoda, lily ponds, and lush flowers. In summer there are special events such as concerts and polo matches. The 18th-century manor house is filled with English antiques, paintings, photographs, and fox-hunting memorabilia. The café serves lunch and light snacks. ✉ *3535 Jarrettsville Pike, 14 mi north of I–695, Monkton* ☎ *410/557–9466* ⊕ *www.ladewgardens.com* ✉ *House and gardens $13, gardens only $10* ☉ *Mid-Apr.–Oct., weekdays 8–4, weekends 10:30–5.*

One of the few 18th-century structures in Havre de Grace, **Rodgers House** (✉ *226 N. Washington St.21078*) is a two-story redbrick Georgian town house topped by a dormered attic. The town's most historically significant building, it was the home of Admiral John Rodgers, who fired the first shot in the War of 1812. Like most of the other historic houses in Havre de Grace, it's closed to the public but still worth a drive past.

The **Steppingstone Museum** is a 10-acre complex of seven restored turn-of-the-20th-century farm buildings plus a replica of a canning house. Among the 12,000-plus artifacts in the collection are a horse-drawn tractor and an early gas-powered version, manual seeders and planters, and horse-drawn plows. A blacksmith, a weaver, a wood-carver, a cooper, a dairymaid, and a decoy artist regularly demonstrate their trades in the workshops. ✉ *Susquehanna State Park, 461 Quaker Bottom Rd.* ☎ *410/939–2299* ⊕ *www.steppingstonemuseum.org* ✉ *$3* ☉ *May–Sept., weekends 1–5.*

The **Susquehanna Museum,** at the southern terminal of the defunct Susque-hanna and Tidewater Canal, tells the history of the canal and the people who lived and worked there. From 1839 until 1890 the canal ran 45 mi north to Wrightsville, Pennsylvania. It was a thoroughfare for mule-drawn barges loaded with iron ore, coal, and crops. The museum, in a lock tender's cottage built in 1840, is partially furnished with modest mid-century antiques that recall its period of service. ⊠*Erie and Con-esto Sts.* ☎*410/939–5780* ⊕*www.lockhousemuseum.org* ⊠*Dona-tions accepted* ⊙ *Weekends 1–5.*

WHERE TO EAT

$$–$$$ ✕**Ken's Steak and Rib House.** A nautical theme prevails in this restaurant
ECLECTIC on a tree-lined avenue. Windows and mirrors on all sides keep the din-ing room well lighted whether or not the sailboat lanterns on the tables are burning. On the menu, beef, seafood, and pasta dishes are all well represented. Veal served with shrimp and lump crabmeat in a Chablis cream sauce is a specialty. ⊠*400 N. Union Ave.* ☎*410/939–5440* ⊕*www.kenssteakandribhouse.com* ⊟*AE, MC, V.*

$$–$$$ ✕**MacGregor's.** Behind the redbrick facade of a bank built in 1928,
SEAFOOD MacGregor's occupies two dining rooms on two levels, with glass walls on three sides looking onto the Chesapeake Bay. The interior is adorned with carved duck decoys, mounted guns, and antique prints of the town; there's also outdoor dining on a deck with a gazebo. Seafood is the specialty, and the kitchen claims to have the best crab cakes on the bay. ⊠*331 St. John's St.* ☎*410/939–3003* ⊕*www.macgregorsrestaurant. com.* ⊟*AE, D, DC, MC, V.*

WHERE TO STAY

$ ▦**Spencer-Silver Mansion.** This house was built in 1886 from gray granite quarried at nearby Port Deposit—the same kind of granite was used to build the Brooklyn Bridge. Characteristic Victorian details include stained-glass windows, a wraparound porch, and a turret. The carriage house is a lovely two-story stone cottage with loft bedroom, Jacuzzi, and fireplace; it sleeps up to four but is ideal for couples seeking a romantic hideaway. All rooms are furnished with period antiques sup-plemented by select reproductions. **Pro:** classic, romantic atmosphere. **Con:** few amenities; no elevator. ⊠*200 S. Union Ave.* ☎*410/939–1485 or 800/780–1485* ⊕*www.spencersilvermansion.com* ⟲*4 rooms, 1 suite* ♿ *In room: Wi-Fi In-hotel: no-smoking rooms, no elevator* ⊟*AE, MC, V* ⦿*BP.*

$ ▦**Vandiver Inn.** This three-story wood house, built in 1886 and listed on the National Register of Historic Places, is 1½ blocks from the bay. Green with dark green trim on the outside, the inn has a Victorian look, with antique beds and other period pieces. A porch extends the width of the house front, and the gazebo in the backyard is as old as the house itself. **Pro:** historic accommodations; budget-friendly. **Con:** rooms can be dusty and unkempt. ⊠*301 S. Union Ave.* ☎*410/939–5200 or 800/245–1655* ⊕*www.vandiverinn.com* ⟲*17 rooms* ♿*In-room: Ethernet. In-hotel: public Wi-Fi, no-smoking rooms, no elevator* ⊟*AE, D, MC, V* ⦿*BP.*

ABERDEEN

30 mi northeast of Baltimore.

A site for artillery testing since 1917, Aberdeen celebrates its heritage every year on Armed Forces Day (the third Saturday in May) with tank parades and firing demonstrations. The town is also the birthplace of Cal Ripken Jr., who made baseball history in 1995 by breaking Lou Gehrig's record for most consecutive games played. If you're in the area during baseball season, see a game at the intimate Cal Ripken Stadium.

ESSENTIALS

Visitor Information Harford County Tourism Council (⊠ *211 W. Belair Rd.* ☎ *410/ 272-2325 or 800/597-2649* ⊕ *www.harfordmd.com*).

EXPLORING

Cal Ripken Stadium (⊠ *873 Long Dr.* ☎ *410/297-9292* ⊕ *www.ripken baseball.com*) brings Single-A baseball to town with the IronBirds, an Orioles minor-league affiliate team. Owned by Cal Ripken, the team plays short-season ball every June to September in Ripken Stadium, a 5,500-seat venue complete with skyboxes. Future plans include opening the Ripken Museum and a hotel.

ELLICOTT CITY

12 mi southwest of Baltimore.

Ellicott City was founded in 1772 by three Quaker brothers—John, Andrew, and Joseph Ellicott. By the 1860s Ellicott City had become one of the most prominent milling and manufacturing towns in the east. Today the town retains its historical flavor and is a pleasant place to stroll and browse the many stores and antiques shops. The Howard County Office of Tourism offers walking tours of the town. It's easy to spend a day browsing shops and stopping for meals on the town's main drag. There's a large free parking lot that's well marked and within walking distance from all the stores.

ESSENTIALS

Howard County Office of Tourism (⊠ *8267 Main St.* ☎ *410/313-1900 or 800/288-8747* ⊕ *www.visithowardcounty.com*).

EXPLORING

Ellicott City was the B&O Railroad's first stop. The **Ellicott City B&O Railroad Station Museum,** built in 1831, is the oldest surviving railroad terminal in America. Exhibits focus on the history of the railroad and on its role in the Civil War. ⊠ *2711 Maryland Ave.* ☎ *410/461–1945* ⊕ *www.ecbo.org* ⊠ *$5* ☉ *Wed.–Sun. 11–4.*

Frederick & Western Maryland

7

WORD OF MOUTH

"I would encourage a trip to Antietam. For me, the area that gave me the greatest impact was at Antietam at the site of 'Bloody Lane.' To me, the air was almost palpable with the ghosts of the dead. So moving."

—jersey

"In August Deep Creek Lake in western Maryland is a great place to escape the heat and humidity. You could rent a cabin on the lake and fish, swim or canoe."

—larry

www.fodors.com/forums

Updated by
Julie Scharper

ALTHOUGH A SHORT DRIVE FROM Washington, Baltimore, and Pittsburgh, western Maryland feels a world apart, postcard-perfect, and forgotten by time. Travelers are drawn by sweeping views of the Allegheny Mountains, especially when the leaves turn rich shades of gold and russet. Others come to explore the area's Civil War past at Harper's Ferry, Monocacy, and Antietam, the scene of the bloodiest day of fighting in the nation's history. The past is inescapable—everywhere there are reminders of the boys in blue and gray who clashed here during the Civil War and the steam engines that chugged through mountainous passes into the wilderness.

Many of the area's most verdant regions were once home to mines, lumber mills, factories, and railroad stations. The crossroads of the Baltimore & Ohio Railroad, the Chesapeake & Ohio Canal, and the National Road, western Maryland buzzed with industry in the 19th century. As transportation patterns changed, businesses pulled out and the region sank into silence. Mother Nature reclaimed the land with dense stands of hickory, oak, and pine trees. The state and federal governments took advantage of the unused space and today preserve great swaths of parkland.

The dense woods of Swallow Falls State Park on the western edge of the state and Catoctin Mountain National Park in Frederick are ideal for long hikes. Swimmers and boaters explore the dark blue waters of man-made Deep Creek Lake in summer, and skiers zip down the slopes of the Wisp Resort in winter. The Potomac and Shenandoah rivers can be explored by kayak, canoe, or inner tube, and white-water rafting is popular. Cyclists bike along the C&O Canal towpath from Cumberland to Washington's Georgetown neighborhood, stopping at bed-and-breakfasts along the way. Among the region's cool forests is hidden the nation's most famous retreat—Camp David—where every president since Franklin D. Roosevelt has sought solace.

Western Maryland is changing though. In recent years, refugees from Washington have flocked to Frederick. Although housing developments and strip malls have replaced farmland on the outside of town, the new residents have also sparked an artistic revival and the opening of trendy boutiques. Staid diners have been replaced with sushi bars and restaurants featuring the cuisine of India, Ethiopia, and Thailand. Frederick's sleepier sisters—Hagerstown, Cumberland, and Oakland—have revitalized downtowns with brick walkways and restaurants and shops.

ORIENTATION & PLANNING

GETTING ORIENTED

Disagreement lingers on just where western Maryland begins. For Baltimoreans, more familiar with the Eastern Shore and Ocean City, anything west of their beltway is western Maryland. Washingtonians, on the other hand, tend to lump Frederick and points west together as a distinct region. For the people who live in the hills of Allegany and

TOP REASONS TO GO

■ **Take a hike:** Virgin forests shade stunning mountains and turn vibrant shades of orange and red in autumn. Hunt for waterfalls and camp under clear, starry skies.

■ **Explore the Civil War:** Visit Harper's Ferry, scene of John Brown's famous raid, patriot Barbara Fritchie's home in Frederick, and the hallowed Antietam National Battlefield.

■ **Splish Splash:** Swim, boat, and water-ski in frosty Deep Creek Lake, Maryland's largest man-made body

of water. Come back in winter to ski or snuggle by a fireplace at a lodge.

■ **Bike the canal:** Follow the trail past spectacular vistas along the old Chesapeake & Ohio Canal towpath. Bike from DC to Cumberland, stopping at B&Bs along the way.

■ **Fall in love:** Snuggle by the fireplace at a Victorian mansion B&B. Relax with a spa treatment, then explore the first-class restaurants and boutiques along Frederick's cobblestone streets.

Garrett counties, western Maryland begins just west of a man-made cut in a mountain called Sideling Hill. This unusual geological formation has become an attraction among motorists tooling along Interstate 68. Passing rock formations several million years old, the highway opens to sweeping views of mountain ridges, shaded blue in the fading sunset. These are the Alleghenies, Maryland's mountainside.

Frederick. Maryland's second-largest city, is surrounded by rolling farmland and rugged mountains, where outdoor activities beckon.

Side trips from Frederick. In Washington County, northwest of Frederick, Hagerstown is the county seat and a great base for excursions to the C&O Canal, various state parks, and the Appalachian Trail.

Western Maryland. Farther west, the rugged mountains of Allegany County are crossed by the Old National Highway: today the site of a scenic railroad excursion, this is the same route that westward pioneers traveled in covered wagons. Maryland's westernmost county, Garrett County, was once the vacation destination of railroad barons and Washington's high society; today it's a big destination for boaters, fishermen, and outdoor enthusiasts.

PLANNING

WHEN TO GO

At the **Antietam National Battlefield Memorial Illumination** (☎301/432-5124 ⊕*www.nps.gov/anti/planyourvisit/luminary.htm*) in early December, a sea of flickering luminaries—23,110 in all—glow in poignant tribute to Union and Confederate soldiers who were killed or wounded on September 17, 1862—the nation's bloodiest day. In early June, hundreds of artists and crafters sell their wares at the **Frederick Festival of the Arts** (☎301/694–9632 ⊕*www.frederickarts.org*), the city's numerous galleries extend their hours, and musicians and theater groups perform on three stages. A film festival and children's performances guarantee

Frederick & Western Maryland

10 miles

10 kilometers

the whole family will be entertained. As western Maryland's forests turn rich shades of russet and gold, October's **Autumn Glory Festival** (☎ *301/387–4386* ⊕ *www.visitdeepcreek.com*), in quaint Oakland, has featured an Appalachian-style fiddle and banjo competition, antiques and craft shows, and an Oktoberfest-theme dinner since 1967.

GETTING HERE & AROUND

BY AIR   Most travelers land at an international airport in the Washington-Baltimore area (Dulles, Reagan National, Baltimore-Washington International) and take a rental car to western Maryland. All three airports are about two hours away from Frederick and Hagerstown. Frederick, Hagerstown, and Cumberland each have small airports.

BY CAR   The best way to explore the verdant mountain roads of western Maryland is by car. Interstate 70 links Frederick to Hagerstown and intersects with Route 15 and I–270, the main highway to Washington, DC. West of Hagerstown, I–68—the main road through western Maryland—passes through some of the most scenic stretches of the state. Follow Route 219 off I–68 to reach Deep Creek Lake and the more remote areas of Garrett County.

BY TRAIN   The Maryland Area Rail Commuter line runs from Frederick southwest to Point of Rocks on the Potomac River and then onto Washington, DC. Amtrak service is available from Washington, DC to Cumberland.

ESSENTIALS

Train Contacts Maryland Transportation Authority (☎ *410/539–5000 or 866/743–3682* ⊕ *www.mtamaryland.com*)

ABOUT THE RESTAURANTS & HOTELS

Chain hotels are found in most larger cities and along the highways, but the best way to soak up the region's elegant tranquillity is at a B&B. Spacious rental homes are available along the shores of Deep Creek Lake.

WHAT IT COSTS					
	¢	$	$$	$$$	$$$$
Restaurants	under $10	$10–$16	$17–$23	$24–$30	over $30
Hotels	under $100	$100–$160	$161–$230	$231–$300	over $300

Restaurant prices are per person for a main course at dinner. Hotel prices are for a standard double room, excluding state tax.

PLANNING YOUR TIME

If your time is limited to a weekend, spend a few hours touring Antietam; check out the shops, museums, and restaurants in Frederick; and hike or bike one of the many mountain trails. For seekers of serious relaxation, it's easy to spend a week exploring the peaceful small towns, historic homes, and scenic forests and lakes.

FREDERICK

In recent years Frederick has become a bedroom community for Washington and, as a result, museums that chronicle the city's rich history now share the cobblestone streets with upscale boutiques and restaurants. You could spend a day or more meandering the leafy, 50-block historic district, admiring the architecture from the 18th and 19th centuries, browsing antiques and artsy stores, and eating well at the many inventive restaurants.

GETTING HERE & AROUND

Frederick is easy to navigate by car and street parking is plentiful. Frederick TransIT provides bus service within Frederick and to outlying towns, including Thurmont, Emmitsburg, Jefferson, and Walkersville.

TOURS   Guided walking tours of the city's historic district ($7) depart from the visitor center, which also offers maps for self-guided walks. At night, costumed guides leading the Candlelight Ghost Tour spin tales of the city's bloody history as you walk the city's dark streets and alleys. These tours depart from Brewer's Alley restaurant and brewery.

ESSENTIALS

Transportation Information Frederick TransIT (☎ *301/694–2065*). **Frederick Train Station** (✉ *100 S. East St.* ☎ *301/663–3311*)

Visitor Information Tourism Council of Frederick County (✉ *19 E. Church St.* ☎ *301/228–2888 or 800/999–3613* ⊕ *www.fredericktourism.org*).

MAIN ATTRACTIONS

★ **Barbara Fritchie House and Museum.** According to legend, 95-year-old Barbara Fritchie—the wife of a glove maker and friend of Francis Scott Key—hung the Union Jack from the window of her house as Confederate troops marched through Frederick in 1861. This reproduction of her home, constructed from the original bricks, is furnished with Fritchie's belongings, including the tea set from which she served George Washington. Fritchie's story caught the imagination of poet John Greenleaf Whittier. When Winston Churchill visited the home en route to a meeting at Camp David with President Franklin Roosevelt, he recited Whittier's poem, "Shoot if you must this old gray head, but spare your country's flag." ✉ *154 W. Patrick St.* ☎ *301/698–8992* ☞ *$2* ⊙ *Call for hrs.*

Frederick Visitor Center. In the heart of the historic district and a short walk from restaurants, shops, and museums, the center offers maps and brochures for attractions throughout western Maryland. Guided 90-minute walking tours leave at 1:30 PM on weekends from May through October. ✉ *19 E. Church St.* ☎ *301/228–2888 or 800/999–3613* ⊕ *www.fredericktourism.org* ☞ *Tour $7* ⊙ *Daily 9–5.*

National Museum of Civil War Medicine. Ghostly footsteps are said to echo at night through the only museum dedicated to Civil War medicine. A former funeral home that dressed the bodies of soldiers who died at Antietam, the museum is spooky by day, too. A sound track of groans and moans plays as you wander past a life-size tableau of soldiers

Frederick, Maryland

**Inset map labels:**

College Ave.
Dill Ave.
Rockwell Terr.
Bentz St.
W. 5th St.
W. 4th St.
W. 3rd St.
W. 2nd St.
E. 2nd St.
E. 3rd St.
E. 4th St.
E. 5th St.
East St.
S. Carroll St.
E. Church St.
Market St.
Court St.
40A
W. Patrick St.
E. Patrick St.
All Saints St.
E. South St.
Carroll Creek

Frederick Visitor's Center
Deloplaine Visual Arts Education Center
Community Bridge Mural
Carroll Creek Bridge
National Museum of Civil War Medicine
Barbara Fritchie House and Museum
Roger Brooke Taney House

TO HAGERSTOWN

**Main map labels:**

TO GETTYSBURG, PA
15
Military Rd.
MELBOURNE
TO MELBOURNE
13th St.
9th St.
7th St.
6th St.
Motter Ave.
7th St.
Fairview Ave.
Rosemont Ave.
2nd St.
Fleming Ave.
Carroll Parkway
W. 2nd St.
N. Market St.
SEE INSET
Gas House Pike
Rose Hill Manor Park/ The Children's and Farm Museum
Hughs Ford Rd.
Balles Lane
Shawn Lane
Monroe Ave.
Franklin St.
TO BALTIMORE
40A
70
Wisner St.
E. 2nd St.
E. Patrick St.
Carroll Creek
Clarke Pl.
Mount Olivet Cemetery
355
New Design Rd.
W. South St.
Madison St.
Center St.
Burke Ave.
Jefferson St.
W. Prospect Blvd.
15
W. Patrick St.
40A
Schifferstadt Architectural Museum
Baughman Lane
Butterfly Lane
TO HARPERS FERRY WEST VIRGINIA
180
70

1/2 mile
1/2 kilometer
0

preparing to amputate a comrade's leg. A Civil War ambulance, hospital tent, and array of surgical instruments testify to the advances in technology that the conflict fostered, and the museum invites groups of medical and military personnel for seminars on the theory of emergency medicine. A case of bones shattered by bullets and the letters written by wounded soldiers bear witness to the war. ⊠ *48 E. Patrick St.* ☎ *301/695–1864* ⊕ *www.civilwarmed.org* ⊒ *$6.50* ⊙ *Mon.–Sat. 10–5, Sun. 11–5.*

Roger Brooke Taney House. Taney, the Supreme Court Justice who wrote the 1857 Dred Scott decision which stated that blacks had no Constitutional rights, might turn over in his grave if he knew his property's slave quarters interested modern visitors as much as his brick Federal-style home. The museum highlights the life of Taney, who practiced law down the street with his brother-in-law Francis Scott Key, middle-class life in the late 1800s, and the lives of slaves. ⊠ *121 S. Bentz St.* ☎ *301/663–7880* ⊒ *$3* ⊙ *Apr.–mid-Dec., Sat. 10–4, Sun. 1–4.*

ALSO WORTH SEEING

Community Bridge Mural. An outstretched hand. A falling star. A never-ending knot. Dozens of symbols are woven into this truly remarkable trompe-l'oeil art project which makes a humble concrete bridge appear to be made of intricately carved stone. Artist William Cochrane, inspired by ideas submitted by Frederick residents, even painted life-like ivy which appears to twist over the carvings. The bridge and the waterway it spans are the centerpieces of the recently completed Carroll Creek area. Restaurants offer outside seating along the walkways that flank the creek and bands play here for summer festivals. ⊠ *Carroll Street Bridge between E. Patrick and E. All Saints Sts.* ☎ *301/228–2888* ⊕ *http://bridge.skyline.net.*

Delaplaine Visual Arts Education Center. This former mill overlooking the Community Bridge houses exhibits by local artists and a gift shop of local jewelry and crafts under its lofty ceilings. At this writing, a sculpture garden is under construction. ⊠ *40 S. Carroll St.* ☎ *301/698–0656* ⊕ *www.delaplaine.org* ⊙ *Mon.–Sat. 9–5, Sun. 1–4.*

ℭ **Rose Hill Manor Park/The Children's and Farm Museum.** The home of Maryland's first governor, Thomas Johnson, the mansion has been reinvented as a children's museum. Costumed interpreters lead children through the house and grounds, where they can don period clothing, weave on a loom, and play with reproductions of toys that would have been used when Johnson lived here from 1798 to 1819. Families can also explore a collection of carriages, herb gardens, a blacksmith shop, a smokehouse, anda log cabin, or relax in the shade of 200-year-old trees. ⊠ *1611 N. Market St.* ☎ *301/600–1646* ⊕ *www.rosehillmuseum.com* ⊒ *$5* ⊙ *Apr.–Oct., Mon.–Sat. 10–4, Sun. 1–4; Nov., Sat. 10–4, Sun. 1–4.*

Mount Olivet Cemetery. Francis Scott Key—who wrote "The Star Spangled Banner"—Barbara Fritchie, and the state's first governor, Thomas Johnson, rest in this cemetery, which dates to the 1850s. Tidy rows of graves, including some inscribed to unknown children, bear tribute to more than 800 Union and Confederate troops who were killed in the battles of Antietam and Monocacy. ✉*515 S. Market St.* ☎*301/662–1164* ⊕*www.mountolivetcemeteryinc.com* ⊙*Daily dawn–dusk.*

Schifferstadt Architectural Museum. Believed to be the oldest house in Frederick, this unusual stone structure was built in 1756 by German immigrants. Spared from the wrecking ball two decades ago by preservation-minded citizens, the house is considered one of the finest examples of German architecture in Colonial America. Ghost tours of the home are offered on Friday at 7. ✉*1110 Rosemont Ave.* ☎*301/663–3885* ▨*$3* ⊙*Apr.–mid-Dec., Wed.–Sun. noon–4.*

WHERE TO EAT

$

AMERICAN

✕**Brewer's Alley.** With more than a dozen beers brewed on the premises, a menu featuring local produce, beef, and pork, and a bright, airy dining room, Frederick's original brewpub is a guaranteed crowd-pleaser. The Germanic brews range from an award-winning golden Kölsch, to a spicy Hefeweizen and malty Maibock. The upscale twists on pub favorites include a dip with creamy chunks of Maryland crab and poblano chilies, a pulled-pork sandwich made from local pork hickory smoked for 14 hours, and grilled chicken served in a rosemary peach sauce with toasted pecans. ✉*124 N. Market St.* ☎*301/631–0089* ⊕*www. brewers-alley.com* ▤*AE, DC, MC, V.*

$$$

ITALIAN

✕**Danielle's.** From the elegant black-and-red dining room to the lush plants and trickling waterfall in the bricked courtyard, this upscale American and Italian restaurant has been a hit since opening in 2007. Try their signature decadent "exploding" shrimp appetizer, baked radiatore—lobster, scallops, and shrimp in a creamy sherry tomato sauce—and end your meal with Bananas Foster, set alight by your table. The cheerful high-ceiling bar area offers a menu of updated pub favorites like bite-size burger sliders and great happy-hour specials. Musicians play in the garden on Thursday and Friday during warm weather. ✉*6 East St.* ☎*301/663–6600* ⊕*www.danielles-restaurant.com* ▤*AE, DC, MC, V.*

$$$

AMERICAN

★

✕**Firestone's.** With its embossed tin ceiling, dark-wood bar, and cheerful service, Firestone's serves up old-fashioned elegance with an inventive menu and a telephone book of a wine list. Start with the lobster, mango, and avocado salad tossed with ginger-shallot vinaigrette and move on to the veal strip steak with tangy goat cheese gnocchi and oyster mushrooms, or the "shank of swine" braised in hard cider and served with sautéed bacon and bok choy. A lazy but sophisticated Sunday brunch can be kicked off with a bottomless mimosa. ✉*105 N. Market St.* ☎*301/663–0330* ⊕*www.firestonesrestaurant.com*▤*AE, D, MC, V* ⊙*Closed Mon.*

$$

SPANISH

★

✕**Isabella's.** A touch of Andalusia in historic Frederick, Isabella's draws lively crowds with a dazzling selection of both hot and cold tapas—small plates intended to be shared. A saffron-infused butter envelops artichokes stuffed with lumps of crab, a delicately flavored chicken mousse complements rich roasted quail, and the fritters of goat cheese and almonds pair deliciously with a glass of the house-made sangria. Savory paellas and steaks and seafood cooked with Mediterranean spices satisfy heartier appetites. ✉*44 N. Market St.* ☎*301/698–8922* ⊕*www.isabellas-tavern.com* ▤*AE, D, DC, MC, V* ⊙*Closed Mon.*

$$$ ╳**John Hagan's Tavern.** Just west of Frederick on the Old National Pike,
AMERICAN John Hagan's has been serving up hearty meals to travelers since 1785.
★ And none other than George Washington sank his wooden false teeth
into a meal here. Servers dressed in period costumes and intimate dining
rooms painted with Colonial-style murals contribute to the charm. The
"Bill of Fare," as the menu is called, is anything but antiquated. Favor-
ites include mushroom caps stuffed with escargots and goat cheese,
rack of lamb crusted with garlic and mint and drizzled with piquant
bing cherry port wine sauce, and herb-grilled chicken breasts topped
with hunks of crabmeat drenched in an Old Bay sherry cream sauce.
All of the food, from hot, crusty breads to the rich desserts, is made by
hand on the premises. ⊠ *5018 Old National Pike, Braddock Heights*
☎ *301/371–9189* ▭ *AE, D, DC, MC, V* ⊘ *Closed Mon.*

$ ╳**La Paz.** On summer evenings locals and tourists crowd onto the ele-
MEXICAN gant brick patio to sip raspberry and pomegranate-flavor margaritas and
munch on overstuffed quesadillas and blackened tilapia tacos. Inside,
the cozy dining room evokes a hacienda with rustic wooden beams and
bright paintings by Mexican artists. The marinated strip steak, creamy
chicken La Paz, and crab cakes served with jalapeño tartar sauce for
a south-of-the-border flair are a steal for the price. ⊠ *51 S. Market St.*
☎ *301/694–89802* ⊕ *www.lapazmex.com* ▭ *AE, MC, V.*

$$$$ ╳**The Red Horse.** Don't be misled by the cheerful red horse perched on
STEAK the roof—the restaurant is not a hokey tourist trap but a local institu-
tion known for sizzling, thick-cut steaks. The rustic dining room with
its centerpiece wagon-wheel chandelier looks a bit dated, but the ser-
vice is good, the wine and spirits list extensive, and the menu, though
staid, features decadent favorites such as bacon-wrapped scallops
and broiled flounder stuffed with crab imperial. ⊠ *996 W. Patrick St.*
☎ *301/663–3030* ⊕ *www.redhorseusa.com* ▭ *AE, D, DC, MC, V.*

WHERE TO STAY

$$$–$$$$ ▥ **Antrim 1844.** The graceful antebellum mansion, charming outbuild-
★ ings, and the immaculate gardens that fan out from them comprise one
of the region's premier B&Bs. Once the centerpiece of a massive planta-
tion, the mansion has been lovingly renovated into nine guest rooms.
An additional 30 suites are tucked into smaller, but equally lovely,
outbuildings, including an icehouse, carriage house, and barn. Each
suite has a unique feeling, but all include luxurious details, whether a
wood-burning fireplace, private balcony, whirlpool, steam shower, or
canopy feather bed. A swimming pool, gazebo, tennis court, croquet
field, and putting green are interspersed with the elegant topiary gar-
dens. Just 15 minutes from Gettysburg, the inn is a popular choice for
weddings and romantic getaways. **Pros:** opulent setting; restaurant on-
site. **Cons:** pricier than other area B&Bs. ⊠ *30 Trevanion Rd., Taney-
town* ☎ *410/756–6812 or 800/858–1844* ⊕ *www.antrim1844.com*
➵ *9 rooms, 30 suites* ⚭ *In-room: no phone, no TV (some). In-hotel:
restaurant, bar, tennis court, pool, no kids under 12, no-smoking rooms,
no elevator* ▭ *AE, MC, V* ⦿ *BP.*

$ ▥ **Hollerstown Hill B&B.** A century-old Victorian home embellished with
lace and chintz wallpaper, the inn is as sweet as the candy once made
at the confectionary run by the original owners. Clubfooted tubs and

pull-chain toilets add to the vintage feel, but the home features modern amenities like wireless Internet throughout the mansion. Guests can amuse themselves wandering the gardens, playing billiards or chess in the game room, or admiring the owner's collection of antique dolls. A hearty country-style breakfast with home-baked breads and casseroles is served each morning. **Pros:** quaint ambience and Wi-Fi. **Cons:** the kids can't come along. ⊠ *4 Clarke Pl.* ☎ *301/228–3630* ⊕ *www.hollerstown hill.com* ⮑ *4 rooms* ᗑ *In-room: Wi-Fi. In-hotel: public Wi-Fi, no kids under 15, no-smoking rooms, no elevator* ⊟ *AE, MC, V.*

\$–\$\$ ⬚ **Inn at Buckeystown.** A short ride south of Monocacy National Battle-field, this gracious 1897 mansion is a popular choice for weddings and weekend getaways. The rooms are lavishly decorated with period reproduction furniture, floral wallpaper, and sparkling chandeliers. The inn hosts teas, tarot card readings, and murder mystery weekends. For an additional \$75 per couple, guests enjoy sumptuous six-course dinners with choices like beef tenderloin wrapped in bacon with tangy horserad-ish mashed potatoes. Nonguests are welcome to dine, but reservations are a must. **Pros:** individual attention; tranquil setting with fun diver-sions such as tea, tarot card readings, and mystery weekends. **Cons:** a 15- to 20-minute drive to area attractions. ⊠ *3521 Buckeystown Pike, Buckeystown* ☎ *301/874–5755 or 800/272–1190* ⊕ *www.innatbuckeys town.com* ⮑ *8 rooms, 5 with bath* ᗑ *In-hotel: restaurant, no elevator* ⊟ *D, MC, V* ⊺⊙⊺ *BP.*

NIGHTLIFE & THE ARTS

Sip a latte and nibble on a sandwich in the **Frederick Coffee Com-pany** (⊠ *Shab Row–Everedy Sq., 100 East St.* ☎ *301/698–0039 or 800/822–0806*) while you watch poets and folk and jazz musicians take the stage in this intimate former 1930s gas station. The Frederick Coffee Company is open weekdays 7–9 and weekends 9–9. Feeling inspired? Tuesday is open-mike night.

A 1920s movie marquee heralds the entrance to the **Weinberg Center for the Arts,** Frederick's cultural hub for plays, musical performances, and movies in the heart of the downtown retail and dining area. Recent performers include author David Sedaris, folk singer Nancy Griffin, and South African musicians Ladysmith Black Mambazo. (⊠ *20 W. Patrick St.* ☎ *301/228–2828*).

SPORTS & THE OUTDOORS
HIKING

The famed **Appalachian Trail** crosses the spine of South Mountain just west of Frederick, from the Potomac River to the Pennsylvania line. Several well-known viewpoints along Maryland's 40-mi stretch include Annapolis Rocks and Weverton Cliffs. The best access points that have parking available are Gathland State Park, Washington Monument State Park, and Greenbrier State Park. For more information, contact the **Appalachian Trail Conference** (⊠ *799 Washington St., Harpers Ferry, WV* ☎ *304/535–6331* ⊕ *www.appalachiantrail.org*).

SHOPPING

Downtown Frederick has blossomed with a profusion of boutiques in recent years, and has emerged as one of the state's best shopping destinations. Storefronts where livestock feed and bolts of gingham were sold in the not-to-distant past are now filled with trendy clothes, eclectic home furnishings, and quirky novelties.

Old and new Frederick meet at **Cowboy Stuff: Lipstick & Spurs** (⌧9 W. Patrick St. ☎301/846–9888) where modern cowgirls can rope designer jeans, hand-tooled boots, and Annie Oakley perfume. Cross a magician's workshop with a child's daydream and you'd get something like **Dancing Bear Toys and Gifts** (⌧12 N. Market St. ☎301/631–9300), where you can find tooth-fairy boxes, a bowling set with bunny-shape pins, musical stacking boxes, and paintings with secret doors that open into mirrors. **Everedy Square & Shab Row** (⌧Corner of East and Church Sts. ☎301/662–4140) is a complex of former factories turned into arty shops and galleries. Bring home a punchy-patterned pillow or sinuously shaped salt shaker from **Home Essentials** (⌧38 E. Patrick St. ☎301/696–9070). Soaps are handmade on the premises at **Le Savon: The Soap Factory** (⌧10 E. Church St. ☎301/694–5002). Fragrances include spicy Japanese Dusk, sweet O Honey Fairest, and Frederick— a fresh woodsy scent. To deck your home like a Victorian B&B, visit **Molly's Meanderings** (⌧17 N. Market St. ☎301/668–8075) for lacy linens, sweet tea-scented soaps, and ornate silver lockets. **Social Study** (⌧203 N. Market St. ☎301/695–5671) carries the latest sneakers and skate apparel. The trendier set point their skateboards toward **Velvet Lounge** (⌧201 N. Market St. ☎301/695–4472) for jeans from Chip & Pepper, hoodies and tees from Volcom and Obey. Browsing the hundreds of thousands of books that crowd the shelves of **Wonder Book and Video** (⌧1306 W. Patrick St. ☎301/694–5955) is rather like walking through the physical equivalent of an online used-book clearinghouse, a true bibliophile's dream.

SIDE TRIPS FROM FREDERICK

Frederick is a great home base for exploring the lush mountain forests, poignant national battlefields, and quaint historic towns.

MONOCACY NATIONAL BATTLEFIELD

2 mi south of Frederick via Rte. 355.

In June 1864, Confederate General Jubal Early, who has perhaps the best name in Civil War history, marched 15,000 troops toward Frederick in the hope of capturing Washington. At Monocacy Junction, a stop on the B&O Railroad, they encountered a force of Union soldiers a third their size. Despite being outnumbered, the Union troops managed to stall the Rebels by burning a key bridge across the Monocacy River and thwarted a takeover of the capital. Roam the fields surrounding the park with an audio tour, available in the visitor center, to better under-

Side Trips from Frederick

stand this little-known battle. ✉ *5201 Urbana Pike* ☎ *301/662–3515* ⊕ *www.nps.gov/mono* 💷 *Free* ⊗ *Daily 8:30–5.*

NEW MARKET

8 mi east of Frederick via Rte. 70.

The name of the town is a little misleading, since most visitors come here seeking the old, not the new. New Market touts itself as Maryland's antiques capital. Though no longer a quiet country hamlet, the town's quaint center has managed to escape suburban sprawl. About a dozen fine antiques shops line Main Street. A day of shopping can take you through several centuries of furniture and a transatlantic tour of accessories. In early December, carolers roam the town and horse-drawn carriages take visitors past the festively decorated historic homes.

WHERE TO EAT

$$ ✕ **Mealey's.** Built in 1793, this former store and hotel is one of the few
AMERICAN   places to eat in New Market's historic district. Mealey's is much more upscale than the name might suggest. A large stone fireplace warms the spacious main dining room, especially during Sunday's all-you-can-eat brunch ($26.95) where the favorites include strawberry and cheese blintzes, applewood smoked bacon, shrimp, and prime rib. Steaks and seafood

are dinnertime specialties and the desserts are superb, especially the molten chocolate cake filled with hot rum ganache. ✉*8 Main St.* ☎*301/865–5488* ⊕*www.mealeysrestaurant.com* ▭*AE, D, DC, MC, V.*

HARPERS FERRY NATIONAL HISTORICAL PARK

24 mi southwest of Frederick via Rte. 340.

At the stunning convergence of the Potomac and Shenandoah rivers, Harper's Ferry, just over the border in West Virginia, played a key role in the events leading to the Civil War. In 2009 Harpers Ferry National Historical Park marks the 150th anniversary of the raid led by John Brown, a radical abolitionist, to take control of the town and commandeer weapons from the arsenal for the fight against slavery. Brown was later tried and hanged, but historians cite the incident as the spark that ignited the conflict between North and South. The town, at the crossroads of Maryland, Virginia, and West Virginia, has been restored to its appearance during Brown's time, and exhibits highlight early American life and Civil War history. The breathtaking rivers, shrouded by wooded cliffs, are popular spots for rafting and tubing during the warmer months.

The National Park Service will celebrate the sesquicentennial of John Brown's raid with concerts and celebrations in **Harpers Ferry** throughout 2009. New walking and driving tours will also be unveiled. Along the cobblestone streets of the town, costumed interpreters in 19th-century homes and storefronts demonstrate period activities such as candle-dipping and candy-making. Lectures and special tours are offered on weekends. Several hikes meander through the shady mountains that surround the park, passing over stone bridges and past the remains of homes and churches. Parking is virtually nonexistent at the park. Leave your car at the Cavalier Heights Visitor Center and take one of the free shuttle buses that depart every 15 minutes. ✉*Parking lot 1 mi past Shenandoah bridge on Rte. 340, Harpers Ferry, WV* ☎*304/535–6298* ⊕*www.nps.gov/hafe* ⬜*$6 per vehicle, $4 per person arriving by other means* ☉*Memorial Day–Labor Day, daily 8–6; Labor Day–Memorial Day, daily 8–5.*

SPORTS & THE OUTDOORS

The Shenandoah and Potomac rivers are idyllic spots to kayak or canoe. Drift along the refreshing waters in an inner tube or raft through the rivers' rapids. Local favorite **Butt's Tubes** (✉*10985 Harpers Ferry Rd., Purcellville, VA* ☎*877/RAFT–BTI* ⊕*www.buttstubes.com*) drops you off at the river and picks you up downstream a few hours later. They offer patriotic-theme excursions in summer and "haunted" raft tours in October. **River Riders** ✉*408 Alstadt's Hill Rd., Harpers Ferry, WV* ☎*800/325–7238* ⊕*www.riverriders.com*) offers everything from tranquil tubing for the kids to adventurous river-rafting tours. They also rent mountain bikes and lead guided fishing tours.

CATOCTIN MOUNTAIN PARK

15 mi north of Frederick via Rte. 15.

Eight square miles of thick pine and deciduous forests, rocky ledges, and magnificent views make the Catoctin a true escape from modern life. Presidents think so, too—Camp David is hidden within the park. Of course, the presidential retreat—where the famous peace accords between Egypt and Israel were resolved—is heavily guarded, so don't plan on paying a surprise visit. Across Route 77 is **Cunningham Falls State Park,** the site of an impressive 78-foot waterfall—the state's largest—and a crystal-clear man-made lake for swimming and boating. Arrive early on summer holidays and weekends: once the park fills up, additional visitors are turned away. Both parks have camping facilities. Catoctin also rents rustic cabins built by the Works Progress Administration. ✉ *Rte. 77 west of Rte. 15, Thurmont* ☎ *301/663–9388* ⊕ *www.nps. gov/cato* 🖭 *Catoctin free. Cunningham $5 per visitor June–Aug. weekends, $4 per visitor June–Aug. weekdays; $4 per vehicle Sept.–May* ☉ *Daily dawn–dusk.*

☾ **Catoctin Wildlife Preserve & Zoo,** 6 mi from the park, holds more than 350 animals on 30 acres. The zoo is easily navigable by children, and the tall trees and winding paths make for comfortable walking. Exotic animals here include tigers, macaws, monkeys, and boas. A petting zoo allows children to mingle with goats and other small animals. Throughout summer there are interactive shows, when children can touch snakes, talk to tigers, and learn about grizzlies. ✉ *13019 Catoctin Furnace Rd., Thurmont* ☎ *301/271–3180* ⊕ *www.cwpzoo.com* 🖭 *$14.95* ☉ *Mar., weekends 10–4; Apr. and Oct., daily 10–5; early to late May and early to late Sept., daily 9–5; Memorial Day–Labor Day, daily 9–6.*

WHERE TO EAT

$ ✕ **Cozy Restaurant.** After a long day of hiking, nothing is more welcome than an all-you-can eat buffet. On Wednesday and Thursday the 750-seat dining room features steak and seafood nights. On Friday and Saturday a gut-busting land-and-sea spread includes steamed oysters, clams casino, shrimp, scallops, BBQ ribs, steaks, and fried chicken. You can ratchet up the heat of your meal with one of the 200 hot sauces from the restaurant's "Wall of Fire." Family owned and operated since 1929, the Cozy drew international attention during the 1979 Camp David Accords, when swarms of reporters holed up at the adjacent inn. Newspaper clippings and photographs in the lobby recall that period. ✉ *103 Frederick Rd., Thurmont* ☎ *301/271–4301* ⊕ *www.cozyvillage. com* 🖃 *AE, MC, V.*

AMERICAN

EN ROUTE Two of Frederick County's three covered bridges span creeks near Thurmont and make a lovely detour, especially in fall. Rustic and painted red, **Loy's Station Covered Bridge** rattles when cars roll across. Snap pictures of the bridge, built in 1848 and renovated in the 1990s, then picnic at the adjacent park's tables and let the kids splash in the stream or climb on the playground. **Roddy Road Covered Bridge,** built in 1856, is north of Thurmont, just off Route 15. The smallest of the covered bridges, it's surrounded by a cooling canopy of trees on either side and a small picnic area to enjoy.

EMMITSBURG

24 mi north of Frederick via Rte. 15.

Tucked among the verdant foothills of the Catoctin Mountains, Emmitsburg is a sweet small town with a distinctly Catholic flavor. Elizabeth Ann Seton, the first American-born saint, founded the country's first order of nuns here in the early 1800s. Today the quaint streets and well-maintained historic homes are enlivened by students from Mount St. Mary's University.

Surrounded by shaded walkways and trickling brooks, the **National Shrine Grotto of Lourdes** is a meditative spot for Catholics and non-Catholics alike, in use since 1805. The grotto itself is a re-creation (from about 1875) of the spot in France where Bernadette Soubirous saw visions of the Virgin Mary. Today it attracts hundreds of thousands of visitors each year who come to pray or ask for healing. Many leave photographs, flowers, or handwritten prayers and take spring water from the grotto. The paved paths are a safe way for children, the elderly, or disabled to get a feel for Maryland's mountains. ⊠*U.S. Rte. 15* ☎*301/447–5318* ⊕*www.msmary.edu/grotto* ☜*Free* ☉*Daily dawn–dusk.*

The **National Shrine of St. Elizabeth Ann Seton** tells the story of the country's first native-born saint, whose name has been bestowed on numerous churches and schools, including Seton Hall University. Born to a wealthy New York family, Elizabeth Ann Seton (1774-1821) was a widow with five children when she converted to Catholicism. Charismatic and tireless, she started the nation's first parochial school and first order of nuns. A small white clapboard house at the shrine is a re-creation of the home where she lived with several religious sisters, her sister-in-law, and daughters surrounded by near-total wilderness. Her body is buried in a small graveyard by her former home. Mass is offered Wednesday through Sunday at the magnificent basilica dedicated to the saint. ⊠*333 S. Seton Ave.* ☎*301/447–6606* ⊕*www.setonshrine.org* ☜*Donations requested* ☉*Tues.–Sun. 10–4:30.*

WESTERN MARYLAND

Past Frederick, the highways of western Maryland twist along sweeping views and wooded mountainsides. Hikers and bikers prize the unspoiled trails along the C&O Canal towpath and the South Mountain section of the Appalachian Trail. Many of the sleepy cities have been revitalized through the state's Main Streets program, and upscale eateries now sit a stone's throw from important Civil War sites.

HAGERSTOWN

25 mi west of Frederick via I–70, 75 mi west of Baltimore via I–70.

Hagerstown has always had a bit of an identity crisis. In Colonial days it was considered the last bastion of civilization before the frontier. During the Civil War, Union and Confederate troops played a protracted game of tug-of-war with the city. The railroad brought a flurry of industry to the city, which slowly drifted away as other modes of transportation gained prominence. Now the sleepy mountain city is looking to reinvent itself with a renovated downtown area, a recently opened children's museum, and a burgeoning arts district centered around the historic Maryland Theater. The city's low profile is a boon for travelers. Bed-and-breakfasts offer a tremendous value for your money and the charming museums clustered around the leafy City Park are rarely crowded.

ESSENTIALS

Taxis Antietam Cab (☎ *301/393–8811*). **City Cab** (☎ *301/662–2250*).

Visitor Information Hagerstown/Washington County Convention & Visitor's Bureau (✉ *Elizabeth Hager Center, 16 Public Sq.* ☎ *301/791–3246* ⊕ *www. marylandmemories.org*).

EXPLORING

A full-size model of a triceratops skull welcomes you to the **Discovery Station and Hagerstown Aviation Museum,** where kids work the controls in the cockpit of a Cessna plane, squeeze through a model of an artery, and dig in sand for dinosaur fossils. Western Maryland's first hands-on science museum is set in a former bank building across from the courthouse. Other popular attractions include a National Institute of Health–sponsored exhibit on the eye and a ¼-scale model of the solar-powered NEAR spacecraft which traveled more than 200 million mi from the sun to explore asteroids. ✉ *101 W. Washington St.* ☎ *301/790–0076* ⊕ *www.discoverystation.org* ⊠ *$7 $* ⊙ *Tues.–Sat. 10-4, Sun. 2–5.*

In 1739 Jonathan Hager, an adventurous young German immigrant, built a stone home over two springs in a virgin forest. The **Hager House and Museum** still stands, a testament to Hagertown's founder and early-American life. The thick-walled home includes bedrooms, a sewing room, and a kitchen furnished with pieces from the 18th and 19th centuries, as well as a replica of the trading post that Hager operated. Guided tours include the indoor springhouse where the family preserved food and kept cool in summer. Coins, pottery, and buttons excavated from the property are on display, and Colonial-style gardens of fragrant rosemary, lavender, and thyme surround the home. ✉ *110 Key St.* ☎ *301/739–8393* ⊕ *www.hagerhouse.org* ⊠ *$3* ⊙ *Apr.–Dec., Tues.–Sat. 10–4, Sun. 2–5.*

Hagerstown Roundhouse Museum. Dubbed "Hub City" due to its importance to the Western Maryland and Baltimore & Ohio railroads, Hagerstown has a rich railway history. It's been more than a decade since the city demolished the roundhouse (a circular building used for repairing steam locomotives, adjacent to the turntable used to change their directions), but the museum preserves several cabooses, locomotives, and trolley cars as well as other railroad artifacts and memorabilia. At Christmastime the elaborate train gardens are particularly enchanting. ⊠*300 S. Burhan's Blvd. (US 11)* ☎*301/739–4665* ⊕*www.round house.org* ⌨*$3.50* ⊙*Fri.–Sun. 1–5.*

★ Shaded by trees near a placid lake at Hagerstown's **City Park**, the airy galleries of **Washington County Museum of Fine Arts** hold an eclectic mixture of American painting, from James McNeill Whistler's moody *La Mere Gerard* to Norman Rockwell's folksy *The Oculist*. Portraits by members of the Peale family and Joshua Johnson, thought to be the first African-American portrait artist, bring depth to the collection, which also includes European, Asian, and African paintings, sculptures, and prints. ⊠*91 Key St.* ☎*301/739–5727* ⊕*www.washcomuseum.org* ⌨*Free* ⊙*Tues.–Fri. 9–5, Sat. 9–4, Sun. 1–5.*

WHERE TO EAT

$ ╳**Duffy's.** An impressive classical-style frieze marks the entrance to Hag-
ECLECTIC erstown's most upscale dining spot. Inside, the converted turn-of-the-20th-century building has been renovated to show off vaulted ceilings, gleaming dark wood-floors, and a dramatic curved bar. The cuisine ranges through Asia, Mexico, Italy, and the American South. Try the spicy crab tempura, the eggplant tower with layers of the lightly fried vegetable with pistachio cream cheese, spinach, asparagus, and Asiago cheese, or the New Orleans bruschetta—blackened jumbo shrimp served on toasted crostini. Duffy's and its sister nightclub AVA's bring a cosmopolitan flair to the town. ⊠*28 S. Potomac St.* ☎*301/745–6648* ⊕*www.duffysonpotomac.com* ⊟*AE, D, MC, V.*

$ ╳**Schmankerl Stube.** If all the talk of the area's German roots gives you a
GERMAN hankering for schnitzel, knockwurst, or a refreshing Oktoberfest beer, head to Schmarkerl Stube. Waitresses dressed in traditional dirndls, looking rather like the St. Pauli beer girl, carry heaping plates of homemade sausages, veal and noodles, and sweet and sour beef with dumplings. The house favorite Knusperige Schweinshaxe—marinated pork shank with sauerkraut, apple-flavored red cabbage, and homemade Bavarian bread dumplings—must be ordered 24 hours in advance so that the pork has ample time to marinate. Intricate wood carvings and red-and-white checked tablecloths complete the style. ⊠*58 S. Potomac St.* ☎*301/797–3354* ⊕*www.schmankerlstube.com* ⊟*AE, D, MC, V* ⊙ *Closed Mon.*

WHERE TO STAY

$–$$ ▦**Inn on Potomac.** Just a few blocks away from the City Park, res-
taurants, and shopping is this restored century-old mansion. Ornately carved wooden beds and the highest quality linens are in each of the four rooms, and one suite has a Jacuzzi bathtub. Wake to a quiche seasoned with herbs from the inn's garden, then visit the attached Tranquility Salon and Spa for a comforting warm stone massage, reviving rosemary mint body wrap, facial, or hair services with Aveda products. **Pros:** spa on-site; tranquillity with a convenient location. **Cons:** no Wi-Fi; few rooms, so may book up fast. ⊠*400 N. Potomac.* ☎*301/739–5679* ⊕*www.innonpotomac.com* ⌂*4 rooms* ⌘ *In-hotel: no elevator* ⊟*AE, DC, MC, V.*

$$ ⓣ **Wingrove Manor Bed & Breakfast.**
From the white wicker furniture on the spacious veranda to the twisting stairwell that leads from the entry room to the second-floor bedrooms, this Victorian mansion on a hill invites guests to unwind in a refined, elegant setting. Each of the three ample guest rooms includes an electric fireplace, television, and

DVD player, and two feature majestic canopy beds and jetted bathtubs. The home is furnished with a mixture of antiques and period reproductions. Owners Candy and Ken Winton pride themselves on decadent breakfasts—try the French-toast baked casserole topped with pralines. **Pros:** amazing breakfasts. **Cons:** not within walking distance of most attractions. ⊠ *635 Oak Hill Ave.* ☎ *301/733–6328* ⊕ *www.wingrovemanor.com* �){3 rooms* ⚭ *In-room: Wi-Fi. In-hotel: no elevator* ⊟ *MC, V* ⓞ *BP.*

SHOPPING

Prime Outlets (⊠ *495 Prime Outlets Blvd.* ☎ *301/790–2031*), open daily, is a bargain hunter's haven featuring outlets of Banana Republic, BCBG, Puma, Coach, and Ralph Lauren.

NIGHTLIFE & THE ARTS

AVA's (⊠ *28 S. Potomac St.* ☎ *301/745–6648*) brings big-city style to Hagerstown. Sip a Glo-Tini (a fluorescent blend of Absolut Citron, peach schnapps, blue curaçao, and pineapple juice) at the sinuous brushed-metal bar, or reserve a private room with mod white leather couches. The city's only roof deck allows you to enjoy the urbane pleasure of a sophisticated cocktail under the distinctly rural pleasure of a sky crowded with stars. **The Maryland Theater** (⊠ *21 S. Potomac St.* ☎ *301/790-3500* ⊕ *www.mdtheatre.org),* in the center of the city's burgeoning arts district, brings traveling theater groups and big-name musicians and comedians to its stage.

SHARPSBURG

10 mi south of Hagerstown via Rte. 65, 20 mi west of Frederick via Alt. Rte. 40 to Rte. 34.

EXPLORING

FodorśChoice
★

Time has returned **Antietam National Battlefield,** the site of the bloodiest one-day battle of the Civil War, to its tranquil antebellum appearance, with woodlands giving way to sloping cornfields bound by rough-hewn fences. On September 17, 1862, more than 23,000 Union and Confederate troops were killed or wounded here. A self-guided auto tour follows 8.5 mi of well-preserved battlefield including Dunkard Church and Bloody Lane. An hour-long documentary is shown at the visitor center at noon each day, and there is an exhibit of Civil War artifacts. You can also hike the battlefields with an audio tour or accompanied by a ranger. A recent addition is the **Pry House Field Hospital Museum,** an extension of Frederick's National Museum of Civil War Medicine, where a re-creation of an operating room and implements used to care for the wounded are displayed. After the battle, President Abraham Lincoln visited the two-story brick house which served as Union General George B. McClellen's headquarters during the battle. ⊠*Rte. 65, Sharpsburg Pike* ☎*301/432–5124* ⊕*www.nps.gov/anti* ⊠*Battlefield $4; Pry House $2 suggested donation* ⊙*Battlefield: daily dawn–dusk. Visitor center: Labor Day–Memorial Day, daily 8:30–5; Memorial Day–Labor Day, daily 8:30–6. Pry House: Labor Day–Memorial Day, daily 11–5.*

★ Doug Bast, the founder of the **Boonsborough Museum of History**, never gave up his boyhood habit of collecting unusual curios. Among the quirky finds crammed into this small house are a wooly mammoth tusk, a still for making moonshine, a mummified bird and fish, the wrappings from a mummified dog, a piece of the White House discarded during a mid-20th-century renovation, patent medicines, a Civil War cannonball protruding from a wooden plank, and Geronimo's walking stick. ⊠*113 Main St., Boonsboro* ☎*301/432–6969* ⊠*$4* ⊙*May–Sept., Sun. 1–5 and by appointment.*

WHERE TO STAY & EAT

$$ ✕**Old South Mountain Inn.** Since 1732, this sturdy gray stone home has
CONTINENTAL welcomed travelers along a road called by turns the National Trail, the National Road, the Old National Pike, and (least romantically) Route 40. Daniel Webster and Henry Clay stopped here, and during the Civil War John Brown's men seized control of the building for a day. Just prior to the Battle of Antietam, it served as the headquarters of one of the Confederate generals. The menu is as elegant as the setting: highlights include fillet Mona Lisa, a seared filet mignon with a cabernet sauvignon demi-glace and served over crispy fried leeks, and chicken saltimbocca, a butter-sautéed boneless breast baked with prosciutto, fontina cheese, and Madeira wine. ⊠*6132 Old National Pike, Boonsboro* ☎*301/432–6155 or 301/371–5400* ⊕*www.oldsouthmountaininn. com* ⊟*AE, DC, MC, V* ⊙*Closed Mon.*

$–$$ 🏠**Inn at Antietam.** Perched on a ridge next to Antietam National Cemetery, this turn-of-the-20th-century inn makes a lovely home base for exploring Sharpsburg's history. The four suites and the penthouse all have a distinctive feel—the Rose Suite features a four-poster bed and chintz wallpaper, while the rustic Gen. Burnside Smokehouse Suite is dominated by an enormous brick fireplace. Enjoy a hearty breakfast in the dining room and meander through 8 acres of land that surrounds the inn. If you're lucky, owners Bob LeBlanc and Charles Van Metre, who met during a 1960 production of *South Pacific* will sing and play a tune for you on the parlor's baby grand. **Pros:** lovely gardens; convenient location. **Cons:** no phone in rooms; individual decor may not appeal to all. ⊠*220 E. Main St.* ☎*301/432–6601 or 877/835–6011* ⊕*www. innatantietam.com* ⊷*4 suites, 1 penthouse* &*In-room: no phone, no TV (some). In-hotel: no kids under 6, no smoking, no elevator* ⊟*AE, MC, V* ⊙*Closed Jan.*

$–$$ ⊞ **Jacob Rohrbach Inn.** Clues to the 200-year-old structure's rich past are sprinkled throughout the inn. The initials "WR" and the date 1835 are inscribed on horsehair plaster in a storeroom. A small cannonball, fired during the Battle of Antietam, flew into a wall in the summer kitchen. Some report hearing the ghostly footfalls of Rebel soldiers who shot the inn's namesake as he lay in his bed. Each of the five elegantly appointed rooms pays tribute to an aspect of the home's history. Four have private porches that look onto the inn's lush flower gardens. Breakfast includes fruit and eggs from nearby farms, pastries baked on-site, and breads from Mennonite bakeries. **Pros:** fascinating history; Federal-style inn. **Cons:** standard rooms only. ⊠ *138 W. Main St.* ☎ *301/432–5079 or 877/839–4242* ⊕ *www.jacob-rohrbach-inn.com* ⤏ *5 rooms* ♿ *In-room: no phone, no TV (some), Wi-Fi. In-hotel: no kids under 10, no-smoking rooms, no elevator* ⊟ *AE, D, MC, V.*

FORT FREDERICK STATE PARK

17 mi west of Hagerstown via I–70, 40 mi west of Frederick via I–70.

Along the Potomac River stands the only remaining stone fort from the French and Indian War, built in 1756. Named after Frederick Calvert, the sixth Lord of Baltimore, the fort's stone walls have been returned to their 1758 appearance. A visitor center displays artifacts from the French and Indian War and the Colonial era. The park offers hiking trails, skiing, boating, and canoeing. ⊠ *11100 Fort Frederick Rd., Big Pool* ☎ *301/842–2155* ⊠ *$3* ⊘ *Apr.–Oct., daily 8* AM*–dusk; Nov.– Mar., weekdays 8* AM*–dusk, weekends 10* AM*–dusk.*

EN ROUTE Interstate 68 cuts through Sideling Hill—the mountain that separates Washington and Allegany counties—thus exposing nearly 850 vertical feet of sedimentary rock formed 350 million years ago. At the top of the mountain is the **Sideling Hill Exhibit Center,** which seeks to explain one of the best rock exposures in the eastern United States. The four-story visitor center also has interpretive exhibits of animals native to western Maryland. Forty-minute tours that cover the center and the mountain's geology are given at 11, 1, and 3 daily. Picnic areas overlook the stunning valleys. ⊠ *I–68, 6 mi west of Hancock* ☎ *301/678–5442* ⊠ *Free* ⊘ *Daily 9–5.*

GREEN RIDGE STATE FOREST

23 mi west of Fort Frederick State Park via I–70 to I–68, 62 mi west of Frederick via I–70 to I–68.

At 46,000 acres, Green Ridge is the state's second-largest forest, stretching from Pennsylvania nearly to the West Virginia border. A century ago, this land was home to workers employed at an iron mine, sawmill, and apple orchard. Remains of their mossy cemeteries and the crumbling stone homes can be found among vast stands of hickory and oak trees. A victory for Maryland and Mother Nature, the second-growth forest is beautiful spot to camp, hike, and fish at a stocked lake.

✉ *28700 Headquarters Dr. NE, Flintstone* ☎ *301/478–3124* ☒ *Free* ⊙ *Park office daily 8–4.*

CUMBERLAND

17 mi west of Green Ridge State Park via I–68, 89 mi west of Frederick via I–70 to I–68, 142 mi west of Baltimore via I–70 to I–68.

Surrounded by the deep blue Allegheny Mountains, Cumberland appears plucked from a Currier-and-Ives print. Tall steeples jut into the sky and elegant 19th-century mansions line the hillsides. In the 1800s Cumberland was a major transportation hub where the Chesapeake & Ohio Canal, the Baltimore & Ohio Railroad, and the National Pike met. Railroad barons built lavish mansions, and the city bustled with tourists. But as transportation patterns shifted, Cumberland languished.

Completed in 2008, a multimillion dollar tourism project has restored the city's pulse. The stately brick Western Maryland Train Station has been renovated and a steam-powered antique train puffs through the red shale cliffs to Frostburg and back each day. At nearby Canal Place, you can follow markers from youthful George Washington's headquarters to scenic bridges, cycle over the canal towpath, and wander into shops and restaurants. A few blocks away, the cobblestone pedestrian mall feels like a small European town.

TOURS　Heritage Koaches provides horse-drawn trolley, carriage, and stagecoach tours of Cumberland. Mountain Getaway Tours offers guided bus tours of the mountains and historic sites in Allegany and Garrett counties and West Virginia and Pennsylvania. Westmar Tours conducts group bus tours of the Allegheny Mountain region and the Shenandoah Valley, led by guides in Colonial and 19th-century garb.

ESSENTIALS

Tours Heritage Koaches (✉ *13 Canal St.* ☎ *301/777–0293* ⊕ *www.wstmr.com).* **Mountain Getaway Tours** (☎ *800/459–0510).* **Westmar Tours** (✉ *13 Canal St.* ☎ *301/777–0293* ⊕ *www.wstmr.com).*

Visitor Information Allegany County Tourism Department (✉ *Western Maryland Station, 13 Canal St.* ☎ *301/777–5132 or 800/425–2067* ⊕ *www. mdmountainside.com).*

EXPLORING

In the mid- to late 19th century, Cumberland's railroad barons built homes in the **Washington Street Historic District,** which stretches along Washington Street from Wills Creek to Allegany Street and from Greene Street to Fayette Street. The six-block district, on the National Register of Historic Places, is a dream come true for architecture lovers with an eclectic mix of Federal, Greek Revival, Italianate, Queen Anne, and Georgian Revival homes. Of particular interest is the **Emmanuel Episcopal Church and Parish Hall** (✉ *16 Washington St.).* It was built in 1849–50 on the site of the former Fort Cumberland, a frontier outpost during the French and Indian War. The Gothic Revival church is built of native sandstone and contains three large Tiffany windows.

The **C&O Canal National Historical Park** is the starting point for walking and biking the towpath and tours on replica canal boats. Markers set occasionally along the towpath explain the railroad's role in the development of the town and the region's coal industry. Grab a meal or browse through the small shops or listen to a summer concert on the water at nearby Canal Place. ✉ *Western Maryland Railway Station, 13 Canal St.* ☎ *301/722–8226* ⊕ *www.canalplace.org* 🎟 *Free* ⊙ *Daily 9–5.*

In a log cabin about the size of a ice-cream stand, the father of the country mapped out strategies during the French and Indian War (1754–63). **George Washington's Headquarters**, the only remaining structure from Fort Cumberland, was used by the future president when he was an aide to General Braddock. The 250-year-old cabin contains a simple bed, desk, and fireplace, which can be viewed from outside through large windows. A walking tour that continues along the canal begins here. ✉ *Washington and Greene Sts.* ☎ *301/777–5132* 🎟 *Free* ⊙ *By appoiuntment.*

Josiah Roberts, the president of the C&O Canal, commissioned the Second Empire–style **Gordon-Roberts House** on fashionable Washington Street in 1867, a few years after he had been released from prison for being an alleged secessionist. The Allegany County Historical Society has its headquarters here today, and costumed guides lead guests through rooms of Victorian furnishings. A courting couch in the parlor has three sitting compartments—the young lady and her caller sat on opposite ends while two chaperones were perched between them. The museum hosts themed teas throughout the year. ✉ *218 Washington St.* ☎ *301/777–8678* ⊕ *www.historyhouse.alloconet.org* 🎟 *$5* ⊙ *Tues.–Sat. 10–5.*

The **Thrasher Carriage Collection Museum** has more than one hundred carriages amassed by James R. Thrasher, a local blacksmith's son who made a small fortune in business. These vehicles vary from those meant to carry royalty to ones typical of a fruit seller. ✉ *19 Depot St.,Frostburg* ☎ *301/689–3380* ⊕ *www.thrashercarriagemuseum.com* 🎟 *$4* ⊙ *May.–Dec., Wed.–Sun. 10–3; Jan.–Apr. by appointment.*

Ⓒ ★ Puffing through dark stone tunnels and along majestic cliffs, **Western Maryland Scenic Railroad** allows riders to relive the glory days of trains in Cumberland. A 1916 Baldwin locomotive carries you uphill through the Narrows and scenic mountains on a 32-mi (3½-hour) round-trip to Frostburg. A 90-minute layover in Frostburg allows time for lunch at one of the many restaurants on the city's main street, just up the hill. A diesel engine typically runs on weekdays, with the more popular steam engine saved for weekends. For a twist, try dinner and drinks on a murder-mystery train or take the kids on the North Pole Express at Christmastime. ✉ *13 Canal St.* ☎ *301/759–4400 or 800/872–4650* ⊕ *www.wmsr.com* 🎟 *$25; more for 1st-class seating or theme trains* ⊙ *Departures at 11:30 AM: May–Sept., Wed.–Sun; Oct., daily; Nov.–mid-Dec., weekends.*

WHERE TO EAT

$$–$$$
AMERICAN
✕**City Lights.** Set near a fountain on the brick pedestrian walkway, City Lights brings urbane charm to downtown Cumberland. The menu of upscale American classics features seafood with a distinctively Chesapeake touch, hand-cut steaks, freshly made pies, and espresso drinks. Lunch includes an assortment of salads and sandwiches—the portobello Reuben on rye is an unexpected twist on an old standby. ✉ *59 Baltimore St.* ☎ *301/722–9800* ⊕ *www.citylightsamericangrill.com* ☐ *AE, D, DC, MC, V* ⊘ *Closed Sun.*

$$–$$$
STEAK
✕**J. B.'s Steak Cellar.** A blazing fireplace, dark paneling, and cushioned chairs keep this basement-level restaurant cozy in winter, when skiers from the Wisp Ski Area in neighboring Garrett County stop by. Cuts of beef and fresh seafood are displayed in a glass case in one of the two small dining rooms, and steaks are grilled in front of diners. The menu, predominantly beef, chicken, and seafood, also includes pasta dishes such as seafood Alfredo and portobello mushroom linguine. Prime rib remains a favorite. ✉ *12801 Ali Ghan Rd. NE, I–68, Exit 46, 1 mi east of Cumberland* ☎ *301/722–6155* ☐ *AE, D, DC, MC, V.*

$$
ITALIAN
✕**Ristorante Ottaviani** Owned by a charismatic family from Italy by way of Baltimore, this restaurant and wine bar is a favorite of locals and tourists. Black-and-white photos of Italy hang on a textured wall painted warm shades of gold and orange, and candles flicker on tables in the covered patio. Try the slow-cooked chicken Ottaviani, the owner's Italian grandmother's signature dish, or Pasta Chivitella, penne and wild mushrooms in a rich cream sauce. There's an impressive wine list, and decadent deserts—try the tiramisu—complete the experience. ✉ *25 N. Centre St.* ☎ *301/722–0052* ☐ *MC, V.*

$
SOUTHERN
✕**When Pigs Fly.** A local favorite, this beer-and-barbecue joint is adorned with murals and statues of winged porkers. The portions are enormous, so you just might feel like a hog yourself on the way out. Ribs are slow-cooked in a sweet-and-tangy sauce, but the creamy crab dip and overloaded "pig nachos" are also favorites. The beer is said to be the coldest in town, and on rainy days draft beers sell for a buck at the bar, liquid consolation for rained-out cyclists. ✉ *18 Valley St.* ☎ *301/722–7447* ☐ *AE, MC, V.*

WHERE TO STAY

$
⟳
Inn at Walnut Bottom. Guests return again and again for the homey touches and personal attention that make this B&B unique. Enjoy peach iced tea, mulled cider, and fresh-baked cranberry-chocolate chip cookies in the back parlor in the afternoon, or borrow a bike to explore the C&O Canal towpath. The innkeepers, who live next door, chat with each guest and know everything happening in town. The inn is made of two connected 19th-century row houses, including the childhood home of Julia Dent, the wife of President Ulysses S. Grant, and is furnished with antiques and period reproductions. Three-course breakfasts cooked up by innkeeper Kirsten Hansen include dazzlers like lemon coconut bread and crème brûlée French toast. Massages using a Danish technique that unlocks stiff muscles are available. **Pros:** children are welcome; a popular spot for cyclists biking the entire canal trail. **Cons:** small rooms. ✉ *120 E. Greene St.* ☎ *301/777–0003 or 800/286–9718*

⊕*www.iwbinfo.com* ⇗*12 rooms* ♿*In–room: Wi-Fi. In-hotel: bicycles, no-smoking rooms, no elevator* ▭*AE, D, MC, V* ⦿|*BP.*

$$ ⊓*Rocky Gap Lodge and Golf Resort.* With Evitts Mountain and Lake Habeeb as a backdrop, this resort is in one of the state's most idyllic spots. The lobby, dining room, and lounge overlook a 243-acre man-made lake. In keeping with the nature outside, the colors green and brown are used throughout the six-story hotel. Rooms, larger than usual, are appointed with Shaker-style furniture, and most have views of a breathtaking ridge of mountains. If traveling with your pet, request a special "V.I.P." room, which greets your furry one with a special treat basket. Suites include a gas fireplace and sitting area. Try a spa treatment, 18 holes on the golf course, a hike along the park's trails, or boating, fishing, and swimming. At this writing, Rocky Gap was planning an expansion to include a gambling area. **Pros:** one of the region's best golf courses and a first-rate spa. **Cons:** not as intimate an experience as staying at a small B&B. ⊠*Rocky Gap State Park, 16701 Lakeview Rd., Box 1199, Flintstone* ☎*301/784–8400 or 800/724–0828* ⊕*www. rockygapresort.com* ⇗*203 rooms, 15 suites* ♿*In-hotel: 2 restaurants, bar, golf course, tennis courts, pool, gym, spa, beachfront, some pets allowed, no elevator* ▭*AE, D, DC, MC, V.*

$$ ✕⊓*Savage River Lodge.* Halfway between Grantsville and Frostburg,
★ the lodge is hidden in Maryland's largest state forest. Nestled on the wooded 45-acre plot are 18 cozy, two-level log cabins and an excellent restaurant. The handsome three-story lodge, with a towering stone fireplace that splits the room, is a short walk from the cabins. The cabins contain oversize furniture, queen-size beds draped with down quilts in a lofted nook, gas log fireplaces, oversized bathtubs, and porches with rocking chairs. Muffins and orange juice are delivered to your room every morning. **Pros:** privacy; quiet. **Cons:** no air-conditioning in rooms, although ceiling fans cool the air. ⊠*1600 Mount Aetna Rd., 5.2 mi off I–68, Exit 29, Frostburg* ☎*301/689–3200* ⊕*www.savageriverlodge. com* ⇗*18 cabins* ♿*In-room: no TV, no a/c. In-hotel: restaurant, bar, bicycles, some pets allowed (fee), no elevator* ▭*AE, D, MC, V.*

SPORTS & THE OUTDOORS

Allegany Expeditions Inc (⊠*10310 Columbus Ave. NE* ☎*301/722–5170* ⊕*www.alleganyexpeditions.com*) offers guided backpacking, caving, canoeing, fishing, and kayaking tours. The company also rents out camping equipment.

EN ROUTE Along the Old National Road out of Cumberland stands the only remaining tollhouse in Maryland. Built in 1836, the **LaVale Toll Gate House** is a four-room building that housed the gatekeepers who collected tolls until the early 1900s. ⊠*Historic National Rd., Rte. 40, LaVale* ☎*301/729–3047* ⊙*May–mid-Oct., weekends 1:30–4:30.*

GRANTSVILLE

21 mi west of Cumberland via I–68.

Two miles south of the Mason-Dixon Line, Grantsville is a village amid some of the most productive farmland in the region. It is also in the heart of the county's Amish and Mennonite communities. To the west and south is Maryland's largest forest, the 53,000-acre Savage River State Forest. Mostly undeveloped, it's used by hikers, campers, anglers, and, in winter, cross-country skiers. Also nearby is New Germany State Park, which has hiking trails, campsites, and cabins.

By the time you see the **Casselman River Bridge** (⊠ *Rte. 40*), you're almost in Grantsville. This single-span stone arch bridge 0.5 mi east of town was built in 1813; at the time it was the largest of its kind. Though the bridge is no longer in use, it serves as the backdrop for a small state park and picnic area.

In the northern end of Savage River State Forest, the much smaller **New Germany State Park** (400 acres) contains stands of hemlocks and pines planted in the late 1950s. In winter this popular hiking spot's 8 mi of trails are groomed for cross-country skiing. You can swim, fish, and boat in the 13-acre man-made lake, although low water levels and a profusion of aquatic plants have made much of the lake unusable. The park has picnic shelters, 39 campsites, and 11 rental cabins, fully equipped for year-round use. ⊠ *349 Headquarters La., 25 mi southwest of Cumberland via I-68 and Lower New Germany Rd., Exit 24* ☎ *301/895–5453* ⊕ *www.dnr.state.md.us* ☎ *$2 Memorial Day–Labor Day; $3 during ski season* ☉ *Daily dawn–dusk.*

The history and craftsmanship of Upper Appalachia are exhibited at the rustic **Spruce Forest Artisan Village and Penn Alps,** a museum village where spinners, weavers, potters, stained-glass workers, wood sculptors, and bird carvers demonstrate their skills. The Winterberg House, a log stagecoach stop, is the last remaining log tavern along the Old National Pike. It's now used as a crafts store and restaurant. ⊠ *177 Casselman Rte., at Rte. 40* ☎ *301/895–3332* ⊕ *www.spruceforest.org* ☎ *Free* ☉ *Mon.–Sat. 10–5.*

SHOPPING

Yoder Country Market (⊠ *Rte. 669* ☎ *301/895–5148*), open Monday through Saturday, began as a butcher shop on a Mennonite family farm in 1947. Today the market sells breads, cookies, pies, and pastries baked on the premises. There's also a nice selection of bulk groceries, local food products, meats, and homemade jams and jellies. A Mennonite kitchen serves a limited menu.

DEEP CREEK LAKE

21 mi southwest of Grantsville via I-68 and Rte. 219.

Garrett County's greatest asset, the 3,900-acre Deep Creek Lake was created in the 1920s as a water source for a hydroelectric plant on the Youghiogheny (pronounced "Yok-a-gainy") River—a favorite among kayakers and white-water rafters. Though much of Deep Creek Lake's 65-mi shoreline is inaccessible to the public, it's visible from Route 219 and from numerous restaurants and motels, many of which have private docks.

ESSENTIALS

Taxi **Deep Creek Lake Taxi Cab** (☎ *301/616–7407*).

Visitor Information Garrett County Chamber of Commerce (✉ *15 Visitors Center Dr., McHenry* ☎ *301/387-4386* ⊕ *www.garrettchamber.com*).

EXPLORING

The 1,818-acre **Deep Creek Lake State Park** (✉ *898 State Park Rd.* ☎ *301/387–4111* ⊕ *www.dnr.state.md.us*) hugs the eastern shore of the lake and has a public boat launch, small beach, and picnic and camping sites. The lake's indigo waters are breathtaking—literally. Even in summer the water is quite chilly, prompting frequent runs to the beach to warm in the sun. At the park's Discovery Center are hands-on educational activities for children, a freshwater aquarium, native animals on display, and a small gift shop. The center is also a staging area for organized outdoor activities, including boat tours.

The two biggest attractions in the area are the lake and Marsh Mountain, and the **Wisp Resort** takes advantage of both. Not only does the resort boast Maryland's only alpine ski slopes, but it's a virtual amusement park with water and snow tubing, mountain biking, a mountain coaster, skatepark, paintball course, climbing wall, white-water rafting, waterskiing, and even summer skiing, to name a few activities. Patient instructors teach skiing and snowboarding to all ages and ability levels. Several restaurants and bars warm up weary skiers. Called "the Wisp" by locals, the mountain has a humble history: its eastern face was once a cow pasture. Today it's one of the area's most popular destinations.

WHERE TO STAY & EAT

The area's most popular lodging choice is the ski resort, but families and groups of friends are better off renting a private house through **Railey Mtn. Lake Vacations** (☎ *800/846–7368 or 301/387–2124* ⊕ *rentals.deepcreek.com*). Year-round options include lakefront chalets as well as log cabins in the woods. Many of the rentals have amenities like outdoor hot tubs, double balconies, game rooms, stone fireplaces, whirlpool tubs, and private piers.

¢ ✕ **Canoe on the Run.** Deep Creek's best spot for sophisticated café food
AMERICAN serves breakfast burritos and homemade granola and scones in the morning. Lunch brings on an assortment of appetizers and sandwiches, including chicken breast with basil mayo, and fresh mozzarella on ciabatta bread and quesadillas with smoked Gouda, portobello mushrooms, and caramelized onions. Salads feature crisp vegetables and grilled meats. Beer and wine are available when a cappuccino just won't cut it. A short walk uphill from the lake, near the public park access, the café opens at 8 AM. ✉ *2622 Deep Creek Dr., McHenry* ☎ *301/387–5933* ▤ *AE, D, DC, MC, V.*

$ ✕ **Jearbryo's.** Above the county fairgrounds, this homey diner serves
AMERICAN affordably priced breakfasts, lunches, and dinners. Try the sweet-potato pancakes or sausage gravy and biscuits for breakfast. Homemade potato chips, cut thick and still hot from the fryer, are a surprising treat. Desserts, made in-house, are a hit, particularly the choco-fabulous Sinful Seven Cake. Free Wi-Fi is available throughout the restaurant. ✉ *145*

Bumble Bee Rd., just off Rte. 219 ☎*301/387–7667* ⊕ *www.jearbryos. com* ▤*MC, V.*

$$ ✕**Santa Fe Grille & Cantina.** The Southwest meets Appalachia at this res-
AMERICAN taurant and bar where a large wooden bear and bar stools carved from saplings greet guests. Hearty portions are welcome after a long day of skiing or swimming. Try the Painted Desert Soup with layers of pureed red peppers, corn, and beans, mesquite-grilled breast of chicken, or the huge rack of ribs slow-roasted in habanero sauce. ⊠*75 Visitors Center Dr., McHenry* ☎*301/387–2182 or 301/387–2202* ⊕*www.dclsantafe. com* ▤*AE, DC, MC, V.*

$ ⌸**Savage River Inn.** Way off the beaten path within the Savage River State Forest, this inn began as a farmhouse in 1934. Additions since have created a modern, four-story structure. The great room has a large stone fireplace and splendid views of mountain scenery. Outside, enjoy a landscaped garden, pool, and hot tub. Rooms are decorated with country furnishings, and two have sitting areas and fireplaces. **Pros:** bikes, paddleboats, and canoes to borrow. **Cons:** difficult to access in icy weather. ⊠*Rte. 495 S to Dry Run Rd., Box 147, McHenry* ☎*301/245–4440* ⊕*www.savageriverbandb.com* ⇆*4 rooms* ⌂*In-room: no TV. In-hotel: pool, bicycle, no elevator*▤*MC, V* ⧖*BP.*

$–$$ ⌸**Wisp Resort Hotel.** Western Maryland's biggest draw features activities
♻ that run the gamut from skiing, fly-fishing, and a spa to a skatepark and paintball arena. Some of the rooms are ski-in, ski-out, and they all include modern appliances, fluffy comforters, and comfortable lodge furniture to sink into after a long day on the slopes, the water, or on your derriere. Parents can take advantage of the Club Wisp Kids' Night Out program as they skip out to the spa or for a round of golf. All activities are arranged through the hotel. **Pros:** everything you want to do in one spot. **Cons:** big crowds and lots of kids make the resort feel chaotic. ⊠*290 Marsh Hill Rd., McHenry* ☎*800/462–9477 or 301/387–5581* ⊕*www.wispresort.com* ⇆*102 suites, 67 rooms* ⌂*In-room: kitchen (some), refrigerator. In-hotel: 2 restaurants, bar, pool, spa, some pets allowed (fee)* ▤*AE, D, DC, MC, V.*

SPORTS & THE OUTDOORS

BICYCLING

High Mountain Sports (⊠*21327 Garrett Hwy., McHenry* ☎*301/387–4199* ⊕ *www.highmountainsports.com*) rents mountain bikes, snow and water skis, kayaks, and snowboards, and sells outdoor gear and equipment. Kayak, mountain-bike, and other outdoor tours are available as well.

BOATING

At the docks at Deep Creek Lake State Park, **Nature Lake Tours** (⊠*898 State Park Rd.* ☎*301/746–8782*) runs sunrise, nature, dinner, and family-oriented tours of the lake daily from April through October. **Deep Creek Lake Boat Rentals** (⊠*2030 Deep Creek Dr., McHenry* ☎*301/387–9130* ⊕ *www.deepcreeklakeboatrentals.com*) rents pontoon and paddleboats and Jet Skis.

SKIING

Wisp Resort has 94 acres of trails ranging from beginner to difficult; most are open for night skiing. A "Savage Super Pipe" and two terrain parks challenge snowboarders and extreme skiers. The Bear Claw Tubing Park has nine 800-foot-long tubing lanes. Peak-season lift rates (mid-December through early March) are $39 for a full day on weekdays, $59 on weekends; prices go up about $3–$4 on holidays. Ski/snowboard rentals are $38 each. Tubing sessions run in two-hour blocks; rates are $15–$22 per person. ⊠ *290 Marsh Hill Rd., McHenry* ☎ *800/462–9477 or 301/387–4911* ⊕ *www.wispresort.com* ⊟ *AE, D, MC, V* ⊘ *Closed Apr.–mid-Dec.*

OAKLAND

11 mi southwest of Deep Creek Lake State Park via Rte. 219.

Tiny Oakland, perched on a mountain plateau at the far western end of the state, is a true escape from the big-city bustle. Its heyday was in the late 1800s, when a number of opulent hotels catered to vacationers brought by the Baltimore & Ohio Railroad. Saunter through the quaint antiques shops that line downtown's recently restored brick paths and you'll feel that you've traveled to another time.

At **Swallow Falls State Park,** paths wind along the Youghiogheny River, past shaded rocky gorges and rippling rapids, to a 63-foot waterfall. One of Maryland's hidden gems, the park is also known for its stand of 300-year-old hemlocks and for excellent camping, hiking, and fishing facilities. ⊠ *222 Herrington La., off Rte. 219* ☎ *301/334–9180* ⊕ *www.dnr.state.md.us* ⊠ *$2 Memorial Day–Labor Day, $1 Labor Day–Memorial Day* ⊘ *Daily dawn–dusk.*

WHERE TO STAY & EAT

$$ ✕ **Cornish Manor.** In its long life, this spectacular Victorian mansion, built
FRENCH just after the Civil War, has been a judge's summer home, a speakeasy, and a nursing home. Today the restaurant is a local landmark known for the elegant dishes prepared by the owner, a native of France. Try the delicately flavored rainbow trout panfried in almond butter, an immense 10-ounce crab cake, tortellini swimming in a rich Newburg sauce and topped with chunks of crab, or the zesty green peppercorn steak with brandy sauce. Work off those calories with a stroll around the manor's 7-acre grounds. ⊠ *830 Memorial Dr.* ☎ *301/334–6499* ⊕ *www.cornishmanor.net* ⊗ *Reservations not accepted* ⊟ *AE, D, MC, V* ⊘ *Closed Sun.*

$$$ ✕ **Deer Park Inn.** Within the Deer Park Inn B&B, owner Pascal Fontaine
FRENCH prepares an exceptional French menu with ingredients procured from local Amish farms. Duck confit is marinated overnight and served with savory braised red cabbage. Beef tenderloins are served with a tantalizing sun-dried cherry sauce. Desserts—such as a tart of local strawberries and rhubarb with whipped cream, or local organic blueberries with crème fraiche—are simple and elegant. During the area's off-season months, the inn and restaurant may be closed Monday–Wednesday,

so call ahead. ⊠ *65 Hotel Rd., Deer Park* ☎*301/334–2308* ⊕ *www. deerparkinn.com* ▭*AE, D, MC, V* ⊘*Closed Sun. No lunch.*

$$ **Carmel Cove Inn.** This former monastery retreat sits on a ridge above a
★   Deep Creek Lake cove. The chapel has been converted into an English-style great room, where you can play billiards or board games, watch movies, listen to music, or browse through magazines. Guests have free use of on-site sporting equipment, and a communal refrigerator is stocked with wine and beer. Breakfast can be taken in the small, bright dining room, in your room, or on the deck, weather permitting. Some rooms have private decks and fireplaces. **Pros:** sports equipment; fireplaces; complimentary wine and beer. **Cons:** few amenities compared to local resorts. ⊠*290 Marsh Hill Rd.* ☎*301/387–0067* ☐*301/387–4127* ⊕*www.carmelcoveinn.com* ⇲*10 rooms* ⌂*In-room: DVD. In-hotel: room service, tennis court, bicycles, no kids under 12, no-smoking rooms* ▭*D, MC, V* ⫶⊙⫶*BP.*

SPORTS & THE OUTDOORS

Ten minutes from Deep Creek Lake, **Precision Rafting** (⊠*715 Morris Ave., Friendsville* ☎*301/746–5290* ⊕*www.precisionrafting.com*) provides kayaking instruction and guided white-water rafting trips on the Upper Youghiogheny, Savage, Gauley, and Cheat rivers. Serious river rats can get decked out at **Upper Yough Whitewater Expeditions** (⊠*Macadam Rd., Friendsville* ☎*301/746–5808 or 800/248–1893*), which specializes in white-water rafting.

SHOPPING

A bonus of Oakland's off-the-beaten-track location is that antiques are much more reasonably priced here than in the big cities. Many shops line Second and Alder streets. **Alder Haus** (⊠*229 E. Alder St.* ☎*301/334–3233*) offers elegant iron patio furniture and decorations, stained glass, and furniture both primitive and formal. In a former pharmacy, 90 vendors within **Englander's Antiques and Collectibles** (⊠*205 E. Alder St.* ☎*301/533–0000*) sell everything from hand-stitched quilts to glassware and furniture. The best antique to be found here is in the back—the shop's original soda counter, **Dottie's Fountain and Grill**. Diners sit at pale-green stools around a wave-shape counter and drink old-fashioned thick milk shakes and eat buckwheat pancakes and sausage or hamburgers—all of which cost less than $4—just as they have for the past 40 years.

Annapolis & Southern Maryland

WORD OF MOUTH

"Do not overlook the opportunity to visit the Naval Academy. The tour is not very long and well worth it . . . There are always tidbits you pick up from a guide that you would never know if you just amble around."

—pollyvs

"We had breakfast yesterday at Chick and Ruth's on Main Street in Annapolis and somewhere around 8:30 a gong went off—everyone rose to their feet and the Pledge of Allegiance was said by everyone!! I was surprised and also delighted as everyone was quite serious."

—LN

Updated by
Alice Powers

THE PAST IS NEVER FAR away from the present among the coves, rivers, and creeks of the Chesapeake Bay's lesser-known *western* shore. In the lively port of Annapolis, Colonial Maryland continues to assert itself. Today "Crabtown," as the state capital is sometimes called, has one of the highest concentrations of 18th-century buildings in the nation, including more than 50 that predate the Revolutionary War.

The counties of Anne Arundel, Calvert, Charles, and St. Mary's, which make up the area, have all been supported since their founding in the 1600s through tobacco fields and fishing fleets. More recently, the northern parts of the counties have emerged as prime residential satellites for the Annapolis–Baltimore–DC, metro triangle—but despite the subdivisions and concomitant shopping centers, southern Maryland retains much of its rural character. With the exception of the fair-weather getaway enclave Solomons Island, and the archaeological site-in-progress Historic St. Mary's City, the region remains largely undiscovered. All the better for travelers who come to enjoy stunning water vistas, miles of scenic roads, dozens of historic sites, and a plethora of inns and bed-and-breakfasts on the water, in tiny towns, and in the fields and woodlands of its unspoiled countryside.

ORIENTATION & PLANNING

GETTING ORIENTED

The region south of Annapolis and DC is a peninsula broken in two by the Patuxent River, a 110-mi-long tributary to the Bay. Until the middle of the 20th century, the so-called Western Shore was the main vacation spot for families from Baltimore and Washington. When the Bay Bridge was completed in the 1950s and people could easily get to shore points like Rehoboth and Bethany Beach, towns like North Beach and Chesapeake Beach fell out of favor. However, in recent years the closer-in "Western Shore" has become popular again.

Annapolis. People in Annapolis live to sail on the Chesapeake Bay; its picturesque harbor with hundreds of boats is the epicenter of town. Add the Naval Academy and you have a definite nautical theme. The town is a lovely warren of historic homes and quaint shops.

Calvert County. Like the calm, nearly wave-free Bay itself, the shore resorts of Calvert County are tranquil getaways. Relatively undiscovered, it lacks the boardwalk life of the ocean resorts and its towns are often just collections of fishermen's cottages and holiday homes.

St. Mary's County. Across the Governor Thomas Johnson Bridge from Calvert County's Solomons Island, St. Mary's City was briefly the first capitol of Maryland. The historic city is gradually being restored, and is the center point of the mostly rural county.

Charles County. Charles County is slowly becoming a bedroom community to Washington, DC—especially for those who want acres and

TOP REASONS TO GO

■ **Experience much Colonial history:** The Maryland State House is both the oldest State House in continuous legislative use and also the only one in which the U.S. Congress has sat. General George Washington resigned as commander-in-chief of the Continental Army and the Treaty of Paris was ratified here, ending the Revolutionary War.

■ **Salute the Navy at Annapolis:** The U.S. Naval Academy is the most important site in town. Don't miss its centerpiece, the bright copper-clad dome of the U.S. Naval Academy Chapel, beneath which lies the crypt of the Revolutionary War naval officer John Paul Jones.

■ **Return to the golden age of the railroad:** At the Chesapeake Bay Railway Museum, housed in the railroad's 1898 track-side terminus, check out a glass-enclosed model of the town of Chesapeake Beach and a gleaming, black Ford Model T that once carried guests from the station to their hotels.

■ **Visit a 17th-century British settlement:** At Historic St. Mary's, the fourth permanent settlement in British North America and eventually the first (albeit short-lived) capital of Maryland, you can view ongoing restoration work in this much smaller, and less-refined, version of Williamsburg, Virginia.

acres of land and don't mind a long commute. But there's still plenty of relatively unspoiled parkland.

PLANNING

8

WHEN TO GO

Maryland's three-day **Historic Annapolis Antiques Show**(☎*410/267–8146* ⊕*www.annapolis.com*) in January is one of the major Mid-Atlantic events of its kind. On the last Saturday in April, rain or shine, the **Celtic Festival and Highland Gathering of Southern Maryland** (☎*443/404–7319* ⊕*www.cssm.org*) takes place south of Annapolis in St. Leonard, includes piping and fiddling competitions, dancing, games, and the foods and crafts of the United Kingdom, Ireland, and Brittany. Fifty Celtic clans are represented. In the second week of May, **Commissioning Week** (☎*410/293–0263* ⊕*www.navyonline.com*) at the U.S. Naval Academy in Annapolis, Maryland, is a time of dress parades, traditional stunts such as the Herndon Monument Climb, and a spectacular aerobatics demonstration by the navy's famous Blue Angels precision flying team.

The **United States Sailboat and Powerboat Shows** (☎*410/268–8828* ⊕*usboat.com*), the world's largest events of their kind, take place in Annapolis in October. In the second week of December more than 70 sailboats and powerboats get decked out in lights for the holidays and sail into Annapolis Harbor for the **Eastport Yacht Club Lights Parade.** Spectators watch from the center of town at City Dock. ⊠*Annapolis Harbor* ☎*410/263–0415* ⊕*www.eastportyc.org* 🎫*Free* ⊙*6* PM.

GETTING HERE & AROUND

Baltimore-Washington International Airport is convenient to Annapolis and attractions in southern Maryland. The most convenient way to get to Annapolis is by car or taxi (the fare is roughly $50). From BWI, follow airport exit signs and then take I–97 south to Route 50 East. Take Exit 24 onto Rowe Boulevard and follow signs to the Annapolis Visitor Center.

You can also reach Annapolis by bus or shuttle. The Sky Blue Bus route runs from the International Terminal Bus Stop to Annapolis. You can transfer from the Spa Road stop to other routes, several of which stop near the visitor center. BWI Ground Transportation has information on SuperShuttle and Airport Vans

ESSENTIALS

Transportation Information **Baltimore-Washington International Airport** (*BWI* ⊠ *Exit 2 off Baltimore-Washington Pkwy.* ☎ *410/859-7111* ⊕ *www.bwiairport. com*). **The Sky Blue Bus** (☎ *410/263-7964*)

ABOUT THE RESTAURANTS

In the beginning, there was crab: crab cakes, crab soup, whole crabs to crack. These days, most likely because of overfishing and habitat changes, crabs from the Bay are pretty scarce. Maryland's favorite crustacean is still found in abundance on menus, but most arrive from out of state. In addition, Annapolis has broadened its horizons to include eateries—many in the historic district—that offer many sorts of cuisines. Dinner reservations in Annapolis are recommended throughout summer and at times of Naval Academy events.

ABOUT THE HOTELS

There are many places to stay near the heart of Annapolis, as well as at area B&Bs and chain motels a few miles outside town. A unique "Crabtown" option is Boat & Breakfasts, in which you sleep, eat, and cruise on a yacht or schooner; book ahead. Hotel reservations are necessary, even a year in advance, during the sailboat and powerboat shows in spring and fall and at Naval Academy commencement in May. Like most places on the water, prices are lower in the cooler months. ■ TIP➡ You can save money on a hotel by booking a room away from the City Dock. To avoid relying on your car (and dealing with the limited parking in the historic area) ask if your hotel has a free shuttle service.

Two reservation services operate in Annapolis. **Annapolis Accommodations** (⊠ *41 Maryland Ave.* ☎ *410/280–0900 or 800/715–1000* ⊕ *www. stayannapolis.com*) specializes in long-term rentals. The office is open 9–5 weekdays. **Annapolis Bed & Breakfast Association** ⊕ *www.annapolis bandb.com*) books lodging in the old section of town, which has many restaurants and shops as well as the Maryland State House and the City Dock. The U.S. Naval Academy and St. John's College serve as the northern and western boundaries of the territory.

WHAT IT COSTS					
	¢	$	$$	$$$	$$$$
Restaurants	under $10	$10–$16	$17–$23	$24–$30	over $30
Hotels	under $100	$100–$160	$161–$230	$231–$300	over $300

Restaurant prices are per person for a main course at dinner. Hotel prices are for a standard double room, excluding state and local taxes.

PLANNING YOUR TIME

A trip through southern Maryland could be a leisurely three-day journey, including one day in quaint Annapolis, one day in bay-side towns like North Beach and Chesapeake Beach, and one day in the southern part of the region, including Solomons Island and Historic St. Mary's. Depending on your interests—sailing and water sports, hiking or birding, sightseeing in historic homes, or simply sitting dockside and digging into the region's famous crab cakes—you could spend much more time there.

EXPLORING ANNAPOLIS & SOUTHERN MARYLAND

Annapolis and southern Maryland encompass the Western Shore of the Chesapeake Bay, an area within easy driving distance of Baltimore and Washington, DC. Annapolis, on a peninsula bounded by the Severn and South rivers and the Chesapeake Bay, is a Mid-Atlantic sailing capital and the gateway to southern Maryland. Calvert County, just south of Annapolis, promises compelling bay-side scenery that includes the imposing Calvert Cliffs and several miles of Bay beaches. Beyond the Patuxent River, across the 1.3-mi Governor Thomas Johnson Bridge, lies St. Mary's County, a peninsula that protrudes farther into the Chesapeake, with the Patuxent and the Potomac rivers on either side of it.

8

ANNAPOLIS

In 1649 a group of Puritan settlers moved from Virginia to a spot at the mouth of the Severn River, where they established a community called Providence. Lord Baltimore, who held the royal charter to settle Maryland, named the area around this town Anne Arundel County, after his wife; in 1684 Anne Arundel Town was established across from Providence on the Severn's south side. Ten years later, Anne Arundel Town became the capital of Maryland and was renamed Annapolis after Princess Anne, who later became queen. It received its city charter in 1708 and became a major port, particularly for the export of tobacco. In 1774 patriots here matched their Boston counterparts (who had thrown their famous tea party the previous year) by burning the *Peggy Stewart,* a ship loaded with taxed tea. Annapolis later served as the nation's first peacetime capital (1783–84).

The city's considerable Colonial and early republican heritage is largely intact, and because it's all within walking distance, highly accessible.

Southern
Maryland

VIRGINIA

Washington D.C.

College Park

New Carrollton

Bowie

Crofton

Cape St. Clair

Parole

Annapolis
see detail map

Matapeake

Kent Island

Londontown

Beverley Beach

Romancoke

Idlewild

Forestville

Upper Marlboro

Harwood

Gunpowder Falls State Park

Sandy Point State Park

W. P. Lane, Jr. Mem. Br.

Piscataway

Clinton

Croom

Brandywine

Bristol

Lyons Creek

Friendship

North Beach

Chesapeake Beach

Patuxent River Park

Sunderland

Chesapeake Bay

Waldorf

Dr. Samuel A. Mudd House

Poplar Hill

Cedarville State Forest

Huntingtown

CALVERT COUNTY

Plum Point

Pomfret

Thomas Stone National Historic Site

Hughesville

Prince Frederick

Port Republic

Port Tobacco

Newtown

CHARLES COUNTY

Battle Creek Cypress Swamp Sanctuary

Jefferson Patterson Park and Museum

Mechanicsville

Broomes Island

Newport

ST. MARYS COUNTY

Lusby

Calvert Cliffs State Park

Newburg

Chaptico

Sotterley

Solomons

Clements

Leonardtown

Lexington Park

Tompkinsville

Gov. Nice Mem. Br.

Wicomico R.

Clements Bay

Breton Bay

Redgate

Park Hall

Cobb Island

Coltons Point

Potomac River

St. Mary's City

St. Ignatius Church

Ridge

Piney Point Lighthouse, Museum & Park

Scotland

Point Lookout

0   10 miles

0   10 kilometers

Although it has long since been overtaken by Baltimore as the major Maryland port, Annapolis is still a popular pleasure-boating destination. On warm sunny days the waters off City Dock become center stage for an amateur show of powerboaters maneuvering through the heavy traffic. Annapolis's enduring nautical reputation derives largely from the presence of the U.S. Naval Academy, whose strikingly uniformed midshipmen throng the city streets in crisp white uniforms in summer and navy blue in winter.

GETTING HERE & AROUND

Annapolis is normally 35–45 minutes by car from Washington, DC, on U.S. 50 (Rowe Boulevard exit). During rush hour (weekdays 3:30–6:30 PM), however, it takes about twice as long. From Baltimore, following Routes 3 and 97 to U.S. 50, travel time is about the same. To tour southern Maryland, follow Route 2 South from Annapolis, and Route 4, which continues through Calvert County.

■ TIP ➡ In the summertime avoid going to Annapolis from Washington on Saturday morning or returning to Washington on Sunday evening— traffic slows to a crawl, as many Washingtonian's spend their weekends on the Eastern Shore.

Parking spots on Annapolis's historic downtown streets are scarce, but you can pay $5 to park at the Navy–Marine Corps Stadium (to the right of Rowe Boulevard as you enter town from Route 50) and ride a free shuttle bus downtown. Parking garages on Main Street and Gott's Court (adjacent to the visitor center) are free for the first hour and $1 an hour thereafter with an $8 maximum but are often full on weekdays. On weekends these garages cost $4 a day. Street parking in the historic area is metered (in effect 10–7:30 daily) or limited to two hours for those without a residential parking permit.

Downtown Annapolis is accessible on foot, but to reach the malls and outlying attractions a car or taxi is necessary. To get around the Annapolis waterfront, call the Annapolis Water Taxi, which runs from mid-May to mid-September.

TOURS Discover Annapolis Tours leads one-hour narrated minibus tours ($15) that introduce you to the history and architecture of Annapolis. Tours leave from the visitor center daily April through November and most weekends December through March.

Walking tours are a great way to see Annapolis's historic district. HistoryQuest rents two self-guided (with audiotapes and maps) walking tours: "Historic Annapolis Walk with Walter Cronkite" and "Historic Annapolis African-American Heritage Audio Walking Tour." The cost for each is $5.

Guides from Three Centuries Tours wear Colonial-style dress and take you to the State House, St. John's College, and the Naval Academy. The cost is $13. Tours depart daily April through October at 10:30 from the visitor center and at 1:30 from the information booth, City Dock. From November through March one tour a week leaves on Saturday at 1:30 from the information booth.

The *Schooner Woodwind* and the *Schooner Woodwind II* are twin 74-foot boats that make two to four trips Tuesday through Sunday between April and October, with some overnight trips. Two-hour sails are $31 to $34. For more information, ⇨ *see the Sailing on the Chesapeake box, below.* When the weather's good, Watermark Journeys runs boat tours that last from 40 minutes to 7½ hours and go as far as St. Michaels on the Eastern Shore, where there's a maritime museum, yachts, dining, and boutiques. Prices range from $10 to $60. Watermark also runs land tours that depart from the information booth at the City Dock. The tours include a 90-minute "Colonial Stroll" and a two-hour "African-American Heritage Tour." Tours run from April through October, and not every tour is given every day. Check the Watermark Journey Web site for information. Prices range from $12 to $16.

Discover Annapolis runs 40- and 60-minute motorized trolley tours from April through November through Historic Annapolis Trolley Tours. Tickets are sold at HistoryQuest, at 99 Main Street. Tours leave from the Annapolis Visitor Center at Northwest and Calvert streets. There is paid parking adjacent to the center.

If you'd rather see Annapolis from a horse-drawn carriage, board "Annapolis Carriage" at the City Dock outside the Market House. The historic tours last either 25 minutes or 50 minutes and the carriages carry four adults comfortably.

TIMING & PRECAUTIONS
Swim at your own risk in the calm waters of the Chesapeake Bay. The Bay contains sea nettles that can sting like jellyfish. Some beaches are netted, but ask before you take a plunge.

ESSENTIALS
Taxis **Annapolis Cab Company** (☎ 410/268–0022). **Annapolis Water Taxi** (☎ 410/263–0033 ⊕ www.watermarkcruises.com).

Tours **Annapolis Carriage** (✉ Outside Market House, Historic District ☎ 410/349–1660 ⊕ AnnapolisCarriage.com). **Discover Annapolis Tours** (✉ 31 Decatur Ave., Historic District ☎ 410/626–6000 ⊕ www.discover-annapolis.com). **Historic Annapolis Foundation Walking Tours** (✉ 18 Pinkney St., Historic District ☎ 410/267–7619 or 800/603–4020 ⊕ www.annapolis.org). **Schooner Woodwind** (✉ Annapolis Marriott Hotel dock, City Dock ☎ 410/263–7837 ⊕ www.schooner-woodwind.com) and **Schooner Woodwind II**. **Historic Annapolis Trolley Tours.** (✉ 99 Main St. at HistoryQuest, Historic District ☎ 410/626–6000 ⊕ www.discoverannapolis.com). **Three Centuries Tours** (✉ 48 Maryland Ave., Historic District ☎ 410/263–5401 ⊕ www.annapolis-tours.com). **Watermark Journeys.** (✉ Box 3350, Annapolis, Historic District ☎ 410/268–7600 ⊕ watermarkjourney.com).

Visitor Information **Annapolis & Anne Arundel County Conference and Visitors Bureau.** (✉ 26 West St., West Side ☎ 410/280–0445 or 888/302–2852 ⊕ www.visit-annapolis.org ⊗ Daily 9–5.) **Information Booth.** (✉ Dock St. parking lot ☎ 410/280–0445.)

Annapolis,
Maryland

EXPLORING

Start your visit at Annapolis's main visitor center. Here you can pick up maps and brochures or begin a guided tour. From April to October the information booth on City Dock, adjacent to the harbormaster's office, is open and stocked with maps and brochures.

Numbers in the text correspond to numbers in the margin and on the Annapolis map.

MAIN ATTRACTIONS

3 Banneker-Douglass Museum. Named for abolitionist Frederick Douglass and scientist Benjamin Banneker, this former church and its next-door neighbor make up a museum that tells the stories of African-Americans in Maryland through programming, art, and interactive historical exhibits. The church hosts performances, lectures, and educational programs, while the four-floor addition houses changing exhibits and permanent shows. Audio and visual presentations and hands-on exhibits make the museum engaging for kids, while also bringing home the hardships of slave life. ⊠ *84 Franklin St.* ☎ *410/216–6180* ⊕ *www. bdmuseum.com* ☞ *Free* ☉ *Tues.–Sat. 10–4.*

8 Hammond-Harwood House. This is the only Colonial home in America ★ built to a design of the famous Italian architect Andrea Palladio. The

Sailing on the Chesapeake

Of course, one of the main attractions of Annapolis is the Bay itself. Short of owning your own boat, there are many ways for visitors to sample the sailing life on the Chesapeake. Many cruises—from as short as 40 minutes to as long as the entire day—leave from the City Dock. **Watermark Cruises** is Annapolis's biggest charter and tour service, with many themed tours of varying lengths (⊠ *City Dock, Historic District* ☎ *410/268–7601* ⊕ *www.watermarkcruises.com*). Children might especially enjoy Watermark's "Pirates of the Chesapeake" cruise. This "high-seas adventure" is good for short attention spans and is just one hour. Private charters are also available from Watermark. Probably the most economical way to get out on the water is on the **Water Taxi** that runs from Annapolis Harbor to Back Creek (⊠ *City Dock, Historic District* ☎ *410/263–0033*). For less than $5 per person you can get out on the water for a short trip. For a long trip, consider a Boat & Breakfast on the *Schooner Woodwind* (⊠ *80 Compromise St., at the Annapolis Marriot Waterfront Hotel* ☎ *410/263–7837* ⊕ *www.schoonerwoodwind.com*). Take a two-hour sail and then spend the night dockside in double-berth staterooms. A comprehensive listing of all of the sailing possibilities is available on the Visitors Bureau Web site (⊕ *www.visitannapolis.org*).

Anglo-Palladian residence was based on a plate of the Villa Pisani in Montagnana, Italy, by William Buckland, one of America's best-known Colonial architects. Built in 1774, on the cusp of the American Revolution, it is considered America's greatest Colonial high-style residence. This architectural "Jewel of Annapolis" was greatly admired by Thomas Jefferson when he sketched the house in 1783. The wood carvings surrounding the front door and enriching the dining room are some of the best surviving of their kind in America. Today the house museum on 4 acres of property exhibits famous Colonial art by Charles Willson Peale, Rembrandt Peale, James Peale, John Trumbull, John Hesselius, Jeremiah Theus, and John Beale Bordley. The museum also exhibits the world's largest collection of inspired Colonial cabinetwork by the Annapolis native John Shaw. The Hammond-Harwood House decorative arts collection is extensive and covers everything from Chinese export porcelain to Georgian period silver. The Colonial Revival garden is by noted landscape architect Alden Hopkins from Colonial Williamsburg. Tours leave on the hour; the last begins at 4. Children's tours are available by special appointment, call ahead to see if special children's programs are planned for the day of your visit. Regular tours may be a bit dry for children under 12. ⊠ *19 Maryland Ave.* ☎ *410/263–4683* ⊕ *www.hammondharwoodhouse.org* ⊠ *$6* ⊙ *Apr.–Oct., Tues.–Sun. noon–5; Nov–Mar., by appointment only.*

⑭ ★ **Historic London Town and Gardens.** This National Historic Landmark is on the South River, a short car ride from Annapolis. The three-story waterfront brick house, built by William Brown between 1758 and 1764, and with a dramatic view of the river, is one of two remaining original Colonial structures. The 17th-century tobacco port of London, made up of 40 dwellings, shops, and taverns, disappeared in the 18th century, its buildings abandoned and left to decay. The excavation of the town is underway, and some buildings have been restored. Docents conduct 30- to 45-minute house tours; allow more time to wander the grounds. From March 15 to December, house tours leave on the hour (the last is at 3). ⊠ *839 Londontown Rd., Edgewater* ☎ *410/222–1919* ⊕ *www.historiclondontown.com* ☜ *$8* ☽ *Mid-Mar.–Dec., Wed.–Sat. 10–4, Sun. noon–4.*

6 **Maryland State House.** Completed in 1780, the State House is the oldest state capitol in continuous legislative use; it's also the only one in which the U.S. Congress has sat (1783–84). It was here that General George Washington resigned as commander in chief of the Continental Army and where the Treaty of Paris was ratified, ending the Revolutionary War. Both events took place in the Old Senate Chamber, which is filled with intricate woodwork (attributed to Colonial architect William Buckland) featuring the ubiquitous tobacco motif. Also decorating this room is Charles Willson Peale's painting *Washington at the Battle of Yorktown,* a masterpiece by the Revolutionary War period's finest portrait artist. The Maryland Senate and House now hold their sessions in two other chambers in the building. Also on the grounds is the oldest public building in Maryland, the tiny redbrick Treasury, built in 1735. Note that you must have a photo ID to enter the State House. ⊠ *State Circle* ☎ *410/974–3400* ☜ *Free* ☽ *Welcome center weekdays 8:30–5, weekends 10–4; ½-hr tour daily at 11 and 3.*

Fodor'sChoice
★

NEED A BREAK?

Chick and Ruth's Delly (⊠ *165 Main St.* ☎ *410/269–6737*) is a longtime counter-and-table institution where the waitstaff is friendly and the deli sandwiches are named after local state politicos. Burgers, subs, milk shakes, and other ice-cream concoctions are also on offer. Built in 1901, it's been run by Baltimoreans Chick and Ruth Levitt since 1965.

7 **St. John's College.** Students at St. John's, home to the Great Books curriculum, all follow the same four-year, liberal-arts curriculum, which includes philosophy, mathematics, music, science, Greek, and French. Students are immersed in the classics, through small classes conducted as discussions rather than lectures. Start a visit here by climbing the gradual slope of the long, brick-paved path to the cupola of **McDowell Hall.** The Annapolis campus of St. John's, the third-oldest college in the country (after Harvard and William and Mary), once held the last Liberty Tree, under which the Sons of Liberty convened to hear patriots plan the Revolution. Damaged in a 1999 hurricane, the 400-year-old tree was removed; its progeny stands to the left of McDowell Hall. The **Elizabeth Myers Mitchell Art Gallery** (☎ *410/626–2556*), on the east side of Mellon Hall, presents world-class exhibits and special programs that relate to the fine arts. Down King George Street toward the water is the **Carroll-Barrister House,** now the college admissions office. Once home to Charles Carroll (not the signer of the Declaration but his cousin), the house was built in 1722 at Main and Conduit streets and moved onto campus in 1955. ⊠ *60 College Ave., at St. John's St.* ☎ *410/263–2371* ⊕ *www.sjca.edu.*

8

⑬ United States Naval Academy. Probably the most interesting and impor-
Fodor'sChoice   tant site in Annapolis, the Naval Academy runs along the Severn River
★   and abuts downtown Annapolis. Men and women enter from every part
of the United States and foreign countries to undergo rigorous study in
subjects that include literature, navigation, and nuclear engineering. The
USNA, established in 1845 on the site of a U.S. Army fort, occupies 329
waterfront acres. The centerpiece of the campus is the bright copper-
clad dome of the interdenominational **U.S. Naval Academy Chapel.**
Beneath it lies the crypt of the Revolutionary War naval officer John
Paul Jones, who, in a historic naval battle with a British ship, uttered
the inspirational words, "I have not yet begun to fight!"

☾ Adjoining Halsey Field House is the **USNA Armel-Leftwich Visitor Center**
(⊠*52 King George St.* ☎*410/263–6933*), which has exhibits on life as
a midshipman, including a mock-up of a midshipman's room, and the
Freedom 7 space capsule flown by astronaut Alan Shepard, an Academy
graduate. Don't miss the award-winning film *To Serve and to Lead.*
Walking tours of the Naval Academy led by licensed guides leave from
the center. ■TIP→ **You must have a photo ID to be admitted through the
Academy's gates,** and only cars used for official Department of Defense
business may enter the grounds. ⊕*www.navyonline.com* ⊠*Grounds
tour $7.50* ☾*USNA Armel-Leftwich Visitor Center: Mar.–Dec., daily
9–5; Jan. and Feb., daily 9–4. Guided walking tours generally leave
Mon.–Sat. 10–3 on the hr and Sun. 12:30–3 on the ½ hr; call ahead to
confirm and for Jan. and Feb. tour times.*

☾ Near the chapel in Preble Hall is the **U.S. Naval Academy Museum & Gallery of Ships** (⊠*118 Maryland Ave.* ☎*410/293–2108*), which tells the
story of the U.S. Navy through displays of model ships and memorabilia
from naval heroes and fighting vessels. The U.S. Naval Institute is also
in this building. At this writing, the museum is closed for renovation
until August 2009. Admission for the museum and institute is free;
hours are Monday through Saturday from 9 to 5 and Sunday from 11
to 5. On the grounds, midshipmen (the term used for women as well
as men) go to classes, conduct military drills, and practice or compete
in intercollegiate and intramural sports. **Bancroft Hall,** closed to the public, is one of the largest dormitories in the world—it houses the entire
4,200-member Brigade of Midshipmen. The **Statue of Tecumseh,** in front
of Bancroft Hall, is a bronze replica of the USS *Delaware*'s wooden
figurehead, "Tamanend." It's decorated by midshipmen for athletics
events; and for good luck during exams, students pitch pennies into his
quiver of arrows. ■TIP→ **If you're there at noon weekdays in fair weather,
you can see midshipmen form up outside Bancroft Hall and parade to lunch
accompanied by the Drum and Bugle Corps.**

⑨ William Paca House and Garden. A signer of the Declaration of Independence, Paca (pronounced "PAY-cuh") was a Maryland governor from
1782 to 1785. His house was built from 1763 through 1765, and its
original garden was finished by 1772. Inside, the main floor (furnished
with 18th-century antiques) retains its original Prussian blue and soft
gray color scheme. The second floor contains 18th-century pieces. The
adjacent 2-acre garden provides a longer perspective on the back of

the house, plus worthwhile sights of its own: upper terraces, a Chinese Chippendale bridge, a pond, a wilderness area, and formal arrangements. An inn, Carvel Hall, once stood in the gardens. After the inn was demolished in 1965, it took eight years to rebuild the gardens, which are planted with 18th-century perennials. You can take a self-guided tour of the garden, but to see the house you must go on the docent-led tour, which leaves every hour at half past the hour. The last tour leaves 1½ hours before closing. ⊠ *186 Prince George St.* ☎ *410/990–4543* ⊕ *www.annapolis.org* ✉ *House and garden $8, house only $6, garden only $6* ☉ *House and garden mid-Mar.–Dec., Mon.–Sat. 10–5, Sun. noon–5; Jan.–mid-Mar., Fri. and Sat. 10–4, Sun. noon–4.*

ALSO WORTH SEEING

10 **HistoryQuest.** In a redbrick building at the base of Main Street, the store occupies the site of a warehouse that held supplies for the Continental Army during the Revolutionary War. Today it's filled with maps, Maryland history books, ceramics, and nautical knickknacks. You can rent taped narrations here for 90-minute walking tours and also buy Historic Trolley Tickets. Run by the Historic Annapolis Foundation, HistoryQuest is the source for many of the historic venues, tours, and events in town. ⊠ *77 Main St.* ☎ *410/268–5576* ⊕ *www.annapolis. org* ✉ *Free* ☉ *Mon.–Thurs. 10–8, Fri. and Sat. 10–9, Sun. 10–7; fewer hrs in winter.*

11 **Kunta Kinte–Alex Haley Memorial.** A series of plaques along the waterfront recounting the story of African-Americans in Maryland lead to a sculpture group depicting the famed author reading to a group of children. On the other side of the street, a three-sided obelisk and plaque commemorates the 1767 arrival of the African slave immortalized in Alex Haley's *Roots.* This is a lovely place to reflect on African-American history and the importance of family, reading, and passing oral history from one generation to another. ⊠ *Market Sq.* ⊕ *www.kintehaley.org.*

4 **St. Anne's Church.** Residing in the center of one of the historic area's busy circles, this brick building is one of the city's most prominent places of worship. King William III donated the communion silver when the parish was founded in 1692, but the first St. Anne's Church wasn't completed until 1704. The second church burned in 1858, but parts of its walls survived and were incorporated into the present structure, built the following year. The churchyard contains the grave of the last Colonial governor, Sir Robert Eden. ⊠ *Church Circle* ☎ *410/267–9333* ✉ *Free* ☉ *Weekdays 9–5, Sat. 6–2; services on Sun.*

5 **Thurgood Marshall Memorial.** Born in Baltimore, Thurgood Marshall (1908–93) was the first African-American Supreme Court Justice and was one of the 20th century's foremost leaders in the struggle for equal rights under the law. Marshall won the decision in 1954's *Brown v. Board of Education,* in which the Supreme Court overturned the doctrine of "separate but equal." Marshall was appointed as U.S. Solicitor General in 1965 and to the Supreme Court in 1967 by President Lyndon B. Johnson. The 8-foot statue depicts Marshall as a young lawyer. ⊠ *State House Sq., bordered by Bladen St., School St., and College Ave.*

8

WHERE TO EAT

$$$–$$$$
SEAFOOD

✗**aqua terra.** This funky restaurant gives history-minded Annapolis an alternative to the Colonial flavor found at most other downtown eateries. Inside are blond-wood furniture, an open kitchen, and a handsome granite counter. The menu features ingredients from the water (aqua) and the earth (terra), with additional small plates, soups, and salads. Offerings change with the season but include seafood, beef, and pasta as regular features. ⊠*164 Main St.* ☎*410/263–1985* ⊕*www.aquaterra ofannapolis.com* ⊟*AE, MC, V.*

$$–$$$$
SEAFOOD
♻

✗**Buddy's Crabs & Ribs.** Family owned and operated, with a great location overlooking Annapolis Harbor, this fun and informal restaurant features all kinds of seafood and shellfish, including their famous "Big Buddy" crab cakes and all-you-can-eat buffets. With each full-price entrée, one child 10 and under can eat free from the kids' menu. ⊠*100 Main St.* ☎*410/626–1100* ⊕*www.buddysonline.com* ⊟*AE, D, DC, MC, V.*

$$
FRENCH

✗**Café Normandie.** Ladder-back chairs, wood beams, skylights, and a four-sided fireplace make this French restaurant homey. Out of the open kitchen comes an astonishingly good French onion soup, made daily from scratch. Bouillabaisse, puffy omelets, crepes, and seafood dishes are other specialties. The restaurant's breakfast, served only on weekends, includes poached eggs in ratatouille; eggs Benedict; seafood omelets; and crepes, waffles, and croissants. ⊠*185 Main St.* ☎*410/263–3382* ⊟*AE, D, DC, MC, V.*

$$
SEAFOOD

✗**Cantler's Riverside Inn.** Opened in 1974, this local institution was founded by Jimmy Cantler, a native Marylander who worked as a waterman on the Chesapeake Bay. The no-nonsense interior has wooden blinds and floors and nautical items laminated beneath tabletops. Food is served on disposable dinnerware; if you order steamed crabs, they'll come served atop a "tablecloth" of brown paper. Water-view outdoor dining is available seasonally. Boat owners can tie up at the dock; free parking spaces are rare during the busy summer season and carpooling is encouraged if you drive. Specialties include steamed mussels, clams, and shrimp as well as Maryland vegetable crab soup, seafood sandwiches, oysters, crab cakes, and numerous fin fish. Jimmy Buffett claims that it is one of his top 10 favorite places to have a drink waterside. This place is easiest to find by boat, so if you're coming by car, check the Web site for directions. ⊠*458 Forest Beach Rd.* ☎*410/757–1311* ⊕*www.cantlers.com* ⊟*AE, D, DC, MC, V.*

$$$
AMERICAN

✗**Carrol's Creek.** You can walk, catch a water taxi from City Dock, or drive over the Spa Creek drawbridge to this local favorite in Eastport. Whether you dine indoors or out, the view of historic Annapolis and its harbor is spectacular. The all-you-can-eat Sunday brunch ($21.95) is worth checking out, as are the seafood specialties. Any of the entrées, including the herb-encrusted rockfish or Southwestern blackened prime rib, can be turned into a four-course meal with the addition of soup, salad, and dessert for $12 more. ⊠*410 Severn Ave., Eastport* ☎*410/263–8102* ⊕*www.carrolscreek.com* ⊟*AE, D, DC, MC, V.*

¢
MEXICAN

✗**El Toro Bravo.** A local favorite, this authentic Mexican restaurant is family-owned. The wooden Colonial exterior conceals colorful, south-of-the-border scenes hand painted on the interior walls, hanging plants, and padded aqua booths. There's often a line, but takeout is available. Lunch and dinner specials include a variety of enchiladas, fish tacos, grilled shrimp, and steak. The guacamole is made on the premises. ⊠*50 West St., 1 block from visitor center* ☎*410/267–5949* ▤*AE, D, DC, MC, V.*

¢ ✕**49 West Coffeehouse and Gallery.** In what was once a hardware store, ECLECTIC this eclectic, casual eatery has one interior wall of exposed brick and another of exposed plaster; both are used to hang art for sale by local artists. Daily specials are chalked on a blackboard. Menu staples include a large cheese-and-pâté plate, deli sandwiches, and soups and salads. There's free Wi-Fi, and live music every night but Sunday. ⊠*49 West St.* ☎*410/626–9796* ⊕*49westcoffeehouse.com* ▤*AE, D, DC, MC, V.*

$$$ ✕**Harry Browne's.** In the shadow of the State House, this understated SEAFOOD establishment has a reputation for quality food and attentive service ★ that ensures bustle year-round, especially during the busy days of the legislative session (early January into early April) and special weekend events at the Naval Academy. The menu clearly reflects the city's maritime culture, but also has seasonal specialties such as rack of lamb and wild mushroom ravioli. Live Irish music is performed in the lounge once a month. The sidewalk café is open, weather permitting, April through October. ⊠*66 State Circle* ☎*410/263–4332* ⊕*www.harrybrownes. com* ▤*AE, D, DC, MC, V.*

$$ ✕**McGarvey's Saloon and Oyster Bar.** An Annapolis institution since AMERICAN 1975, this dockside eatery and watering hole is full of good cheer, great drink, and grand food. A heritage of seasonal shell- and fin-fish dishes, the finest burgers and steaks, as well as unstinting appetizers, make McGarvey's menu one of the most popular in the area. The full menu is available daily until 11 PM. Choose to eat outside in good weather, at the bar, or in the light-filled atrium. ⊠*8 Market Space* ☎*410/263–5700* ⊕*www.mcgarveys.net* ▤*AE, MC, V.*

$$$ ✕**Middleton Tavern.** Horatio Middleton began operating this "inn for AMERICAN seafaring men" in 1750; Washington, Jefferson, and Franklin were among his guests. Today two fireplaces, wood floors, paneled walls, and a nautical theme make it cozy. Seafood tops the menu; the Maryland crab soup and pan-seared rockfish are standouts. Try the tavern's own Middleton Pale Ale, perhaps during happy hour or during a weekend blues session in the upstairs piano bar. Brunch is served on weekends, and you can dine outdoors in good weather. ⊠*City Dock at Randall St.* ☎*410/263–3323* ⊕*www.middletontavern.com* ▤*AE, MC, V.*

$$ ✕**Rams Head Tavern.** A traditional English-style pub also houses BRITISH Fordham Brewing Company, which you can tour. The Rams Head ★ serves better-than-usual tavern fare, including spicy shrimp salad, crab cakes, beer-battered shrimp, and daily specials, as well as more than 100 beers—15 on tap—including six Fordham beers and others from around the world. Brunch is served on Sunday. The nightclublike Rams Head Tavern, On Stage, brings in nationally known folk, rock, jazz, country, and bluegrass artists. Dinner-show specials are available; the menu has light fare. ⊠*33 West St.* ☎*410/268–4545* ⊕*www.ramsheadtavern. com* ▤*AE, D, MC, V.*

8

WHERE TO STAY

$$$–$$$$ ⚏ **The Annapolis Inn.** An extraordinarily elegant B&B, this circa-1770 house has richly colored rooms decorated in the formal style of the home's original era. The master suite has a sitting room and two fireplaces. Each suite has a king-size bed with luxury linens and a bathroom with hand showers, bidets, and heated towel holders and marble floors. From the third-floor suite's sundeck there's a close-up view of the domes of the Naval Academy Chapel and the state capitol and the harbor. Breakfast is a sumptuous three-course event served in the stately dining room. TVs are placed in the rooms on request. **Pros:** in the heart of the historic district; you'll feel like you've truly gone back in time. **Cons:** not handicapped accessible; no elevator; children are not welcome; no parking except down the street in a public lot. ⊠ *144 Prince George St.* ☎ *410/295–5200* ⊕ *www.annapolisinn.com* 🛏 *3 suites* △ *In-room: Wi-Fi. In-hotel: restaurant, parking (no fee), no elevator, no-smoking rooms, no kids* ▭ *AE, MC, V* ⊧ *BP.*

$$$–$$$$ ⚏ **Annapolis Marriott Waterfront.** You can practically fish from your room
   ♻   at the city's only waterfront hotel. Rooms have either balconies over the water or large windows with views of the harbor or the historic district. The outdoor bar by the harbor's edge is popular in nice weather. **Pros:** a "pure room" is available for the allergy sensitive; handicapped accessible; a great place for children and offers Nintendo Wii. **Cons:** this chain is lacks the charm of some of Annapolis's bed-and-breakfasts. ⊠ *80 Compromise St.* ☎ *410/268–7555* ⊕ *www.annapolismarriott. com* 🛏 *150 rooms* △ *In-room: Wi-Fi. In-hotel: restaurant, bars, gym, concierge, laundry service, parking (fee), no-smoking rooms* ▭ *AE, D, DC, MC, V.*

¢–$ ⚏ **Country Inn & Suites.** True to its name, a cozy, country mood, as well as the gentle aroma of potpourri, permeates this suburban hotel. Rooms all have standard chain-hotel decor, but a large fireplace, wooden floors, and overstuffed sofas make the lobby an inviting place to linger. Exterior windows, trimmed with shutters and latticework, look out at a wooded area or a shopping plaza. Within walking distance of Annapolis's largest mall, the hotel also has a free shuttle that can take you to the historic district and to business parks. Four rooms have whirlpool tubs and two have fireplaces. **Pros:** continental breakfast included; reliable and inexpensive option. **Cons:** 4 mi from the dock. ⊠ *2600 Housely Rd.* ☎ *410/571–6700 or 800/456–4000* ⊕ *www.countryinns.com* 🛏 *100 rooms* △ *In-room: refrigerator, Wi-Fi. In-hotel: pool, gym, laundry facilities* ▭ *AE, D, DC, MC, V* ⊧ *CP.*

$$–$$$ ⚏ **Gibson's Lodgings.** Three detached houses from three centuries—1780, 1890, and 1980—are operated together as a single inn. One of the house's hallways is strikingly lined with mirrors. Guest rooms are furnished with pre-1900 antiques. One first-floor room, which has a private bath and porch, is designed for universal access. Free parking in the courtyards is a big advantage in the heart of this small Colonial-era city (the houses are opposite the U.S. Naval Academy). Continental breakfast is served in the formal dining room of the 18th-century Patterson House. Some rooms have free Wi-Fi. **Pros:** very conveniently located between the Naval Academy and downtown. **Cons:** children

under five are not permitted; not handicapped accessible. ⊠*110–114 Prince George St.* ☏*410/268–5555 or 877/330–0057* ⊕*www.gibson lodgings.com* ⊋*21 rooms, 17 with bath* ♿*In-hotel: parking (no fee) no kids under 5* ▤*AE, MC, V* ⦿*CP.*

\$\$–\$\$\$ 🏨**Historic Inns of Annapolis.** Three 18th-century properties in the historic ★ district are now grouped as one inn with registration for all three at the **Governor Calvert House.** Built in 1727, Calvert House is steps from the capitol building. Also on State Circle, **Robert Johnson House** was built for the Annapolis barber in 1772. At the **Maryland Inn,** on nearby Church Circle, all rooms date back to the Revolutionary era. The Treaty of Paris Restaurant and two pubs serve all three inns. Guest rooms are individually decorated with antiques and reproductions; all have hair dryers, some have sitting suites or whirlpools. **Pros:** historic properties; recent renovations include new bathrooms.**Cons:** prices vary greatly ⊠*58 State Circle* ☏*410/263–2641 or 800/847–8882* ⊕*www.historic innsofannapolis.com* ⊋*124 rooms, 14 suites* ♿*In-room: Wi-Fi. In-hotel: restaurant, bar, gym, concierge, laundry service, parking (fee), no-smoking rooms* ▤*AE, D, DC, MC, V.*

\$\$–\$\$\$ 🏨**Loews Annapolis Hotel.** Although its redbrick exterior blends with the city's 1700s architecture, this hotel's interior is airy, spacious, and modern. Guest rooms, decorated in a sailing theme, include coffeemakers and terry robes. A free hotel shuttle bus takes you anywhere you want to go in Annapolis, and a complimentary breakfast is served in the Breeze restaurant for concierge-level guests. **Pros:** many amenities; more reasonable than some of the closer-in locations. **Cons:** a mile from the dock, it's a bit removed from the action of the historic center. ⊠*126 West St.* ☏*410/263–7777* ⊕*www.loewsannapolis.com* ⊋*216 rooms, 15 suites* ♿*In-room: Wi-Fi . In-hotel: restaurant, room service, bar, gym, concierge, laundry service, executive floor, airport shuttle (fee), parking (fee), no-smoking rooms* ▤*AE, D, DC, MC, V.*

\$\$–\$\$\$ 🏨**O'Callaghan Hotel.** When this Irish-owned and -operated hotel opened in 2002, it was the city's first new downtown hotel in more than two decades. Floor-length drapes and the lush, blue carpets flecked in gold colors were custom-made in Ireland (much of the attentive staff is from the Emerald Isle as well). Meeting rooms are named after counties in Ireland, and maps and pictures of the Old Country adorn the elegant guest rooms. The first-floor restaurant and bar overlooks West Street and carries a limited but fine selection of entrées. **Pros:** Irish charm; high-speed Internet in the rooms; handicapped accessible. **Cons:** a little under a mile from the City Dock. ⊠*174 West St.* ☏*410/263–7700* ⊕*www. ocallaghanhotels.com* ⊋ *118 rooms, 2 suites* ♿*In-room: Wi-Fi. In-hotel: restaurant, bar, gym, concierge, laundry service, public Internet, parking (fee)* ▤*AE, D, DC, MC, V.*

¢–\$ 🏨**Scotlaur Inn.** On the two floors above Chick and Ruth's Delly, rooms in this family-owned B&B are papered in pastel Colonial prints. The high beds are topped with fluffy comforters and lots of pillows. Chandeliers in each room and marble floors in the private bathrooms bring this place a long way from its first days as a boardinghouse with only two bathrooms. Check-in as well as breakfast are held in the famous deli downstairs. **Pros:** a chance to stay above one of Annapolis's landmarks.

8

Cons: might not be your style if you don't like chintz. ⊠*165 Main St.* ☎*410/268–5665* ⊕*www.scotlaurinn.com* ⤙*10 rooms* ⭕*In-room: VCR, Wi-Fi. In-hotel: restaurant, no elevator* ▤*MC, V* ⎟○⎟*CP.*

$$–$$$ ⊞ **Sheraton Annapolis Hotel.** Next to Westfield Shoppingtown, and near numerous chain restaurants, this large Sheraton has a free hourly shuttle bus to and from downtown Annapolis. (Traffic and parking there can be difficult.) The lobby is outfitted with marble floors, fresh flowers and ferns, and two sitting areas among marble columns. The café is adjacent to the lobby. Rooms are furnished with blond woods, geometric carpeting, and burgundy-print bedspreads. **Pros:** reliable Sheraton experience; many in-hotel amenities. **Cons:** despite its name, the hotel is 5 mi from downtown. ⊠*173 Jennifer Rd.* ☎*410/266–3131 or 888/627–8980* ⊕*www.starwoodhotels.com/sheraton* ⤙*196 rooms* ⭕*In-room: Ethernet. In-hotel: restaurant, room service, bar, pool, gym, parking (no fee), no-smoking rooms* ▤*AE, D, DC, MC, V.*

$$$$ ⊞ **The Westin Annapolis Hotel.** The new Westin Annapolis is part of a large redevelopment complex about a mile from the City Dock. Park Place will contain not only the hotel, but offices, condominiums, and shops and the future site of the Maryland Theater of the Performing Arts. This luxury hotel offers complete spa services, a business center, and four varied restaurants, both within the hotel and outside in the larger complex. **Pros:** the complete Starwood hotel experience, including the comfortable Heavenly Bed; modern hotel with modern amenities. **Cons:** about a mile from the City Dock in a rapidly gentrifying neighborhood. ⊠*100 Westgate Circle, Park Place* ☎*410/972–4300* ⊕*www.westin. com/annapolis* ⤙*225 rooms* ⭕*In-room: Wi-Fi. In-hotel: pool, public Wi-Fi, executive floor, gym* ▤*AE, D, MC, V.*

$$–$$$ ⊞ **William Page Inn.** Built in 1908, this dark-brown, cedar-shingle, wood-frame structure was the local Democratic Party clubhouse for 50 years. Today its wraparound porch is furnished with Adirondack chairs. The third-floor suite, with dormer windows and a sloped ceiling, includes an Italian-marble bathroom with whirlpool. Breakfast is served in the common room. **Pros:** a nice alternative to large hotels; only half a block from the dock. **Cons:** no elevator; two-night minimum stay on weekends. ⊠*8 Martin St.* ☎*410/626–1506 or 800/364–4160* ⊕*www. williampageinn.com* ⤙*5 rooms, 3 with bath; 1 suite* ⭕*In-room: no TV (some). In-hotel: no elevator, parking (no fee), no-smoking rooms* ▤*MC, V* ⎟○⎟*BP.*

NIGHTLIFE & THE ARTS

BARS & CLUBS

The lounge at **Harry Browne's** (⊠*66 State Circle* ☎*410/263–4332* ⊕*harry brownes.com*) gives people something fun to do on Tuesday night: listen to live Irish music. **Middleton Tavern** (⊠*City Dock* ☎*410/263–3323* ⊕*www.middletontavern.com*) presents local and regional acoustic musicians nightly at its Oyster Bar lounge. The Oyster Shooter—raw oysters served in a shot glass with vodka and cocktail sauce and washed down with beer—supposedly originated here. The upstairs piano bar is open on Friday and Saturday nights. The **Rams Head Tavern on the**

Stage (⊠*33 West St.* ☎*410/268–4545*) hosts nationally known folk, rock, jazz, country, and bluegrass groups. Past performers include Lyle Lovett, Ralph Stanley, and Linda Thompson. Dinner combinations are available; the tavern is no-smoking.

MUSIC & THEATER

Annapolis Summer Garden Theater (⊠*143 Compromise St., at Main St.* ☎*410/268–9212*) stages a mix of musicals and plays outdoors (May–September), including occasional works by local playwrights. The **Colonial Players** (⊠*108 East St.* ☎*410/268–7373*), active since the 1940s, are the city's principal theater troupe.

Entertainment at the **Naval Academy** (☎*410/293–2439 for schedules, 800/874–6289 for tickets*) includes the Distinguished Artists Series, the Masqueraders (the Academy's theatrical club), chamber music recitals, and glee club concerts. **Naval Academy Band** (☎*410/293–0263*) concerts, many held outside during fair weather, are free.

SPORTS & THE OUTDOORS

PARTICIPANT SPORTS

BIKING

The **Baltimore and Annapolis (B&A) Trail** (⊠ *Early Height Ranger Station, 51 W. Early Height Rd., Severna Park* ☎*410/222–6244*) runs through 13 mi of farmland and forests as well as urban and suburban neighborhoods, from Annapolis to Glen Burnie. It follows the old Baltimore and Annapolis Railroad and is linked directly to the 12.5-mi trail encircling Baltimore-Washington International Airport. The trail is open sunrise to sunset to hikers, bikers, runners, and in-line skaters. Access to the northern end of the trail is via Dorsey Road off I–97 Exit 15 near Friendship Park. Parking is free but limited. **Pedal Pushers Bike Shop** (⊠*546 Baltimore, at Annapolis Blvd.,Rte. 648, Severna Park* ☎*410/544–2323*) rents bikes for the B&A Trail.

FISHING

Anglers (⊠*1456 Whitehall Rd.* ☎*410/757–3442*) sells equipment for archery and hunting as well as for fresh- and saltwater fishing. Anglers is also a full-service Orvis fly-fishing dealer.

SAILING

Annapolis Sailing School (⊠*7040 Bembe Beach Rd.* ☎ *410/267–7205 or 800/638–9192*) bills itself as America's oldest and largest sailing school. The inexperienced can take a two-hour basic lesson. In addition, live-aboard, cruising, and advanced-sailing programs are available, as are boat rentals. **Womanship** (⊠*137 Conduit St.* ☎*410/267–6661 or 800/342–9295*) is a sailing school with programs for women, for mother–daughter partners, and couples. Classes can be custom-designed for special needs or desires. Men are welcome to take classes as half of a couple or as part of a group. The Young Womanship program is for grades 7 to 12. Started in 1984 in Annapolis, Womanship now has 16 locations around the world.

8

SPECTATOR SPORTS

The teams of the **United States Naval Academy Athletic Association (NAAA)** (☎*800/874–6289 ticket office*) compete in about 20 varsity sports, most notably football. The team plays home games in fall at the Navy–Marine Corps Stadium on Rowe Boulevard in Annapolis.

BOAT RACES

Annapolis Yacht Club (☎*410/263–9279* ⊕*www.annapolisyc.org*) sponsors sailboat races at 6 PM each Wednesday from mid-May through early September in Annapolis Harbor, starting at the Eastport bridge.

CALVERT COUNTY

The long, narrow peninsula between the Patuxent River and the Chesapeake Bay is Calvert County, an area that has not yet been completely overrun by tourism. Two principal routes—Route 2 from Annapolis and Route 4 from Washington, DC—merge near Sunderland and continue on together to the county's southern tip. Exploring the bay-side and riverside communities to either side of the highway, as well as the inland sites and attractions, will immerse you quickly in the tangible history and heritage of agriculture and fishing. ■ TIP➔**Although southern Maryland is best known as a fishermen and boaters' paradise, it is also popular with cyclists. Its flat terrain and relatively uncongested roads make for perfect conditions to tour the area by bike.**

Calvert County Dept. of Economic Development & Tourism (✉*County Courthouse, Prince Frederick* ☎*410/535–4583 or 800/331–9771* ⊕*www. ecalvert.com*).

NORTH BEACH

31 mi south of Annapolis, via Rte. 2, Rte. 260, and Rte. 261.

In some ways a quieter, more-residential extension of Chesapeake Beach, North Beach has a fishing pier and a quiet boardwalk. When it was founded in 1900, it was a resort for family summer vacations, and amusement centers, bingo halls, theaters, and bathhouses defined the town until the Great Depression. Then in 1933 a hurricane ravaged the beach and destroyed many of its buildings. Post–World War II programs sponsored by the Veterans Administration facilitated a building boom, turning North Beach into a year-round community. Although sea nettles are a problem when swimming in the Chesapeake Bay, North Beach has a small, netted beach and a nearly waveless shore. Walk out on the pier where many of the benches are dedicated to the victims of September 11.

GETTING HERE & AROUND

A little over an hour from Washington and less than an hour from Annapolis, North Beach is not for those who want exciting shore resorts like Ocean City or Rehoboth. There are only a few places to eat or even get a cup of coffee, and a handful of antiques and gift shops. The main activity in North Beach is simply sitting on the shore watching the Bay or going fishing.

Access to the beach is free for North Beach residents only. In summer, out-of-county visitors must pay $7. Fishing passes are also free for North Beach residents, but out-of-county residents pay $5 or $65 for a season pass.

ESSENTIALS
North Beach Welcome Center
(☎410/286–3799 ⊕ci.north-beach.md.us).

EXPLORING

Free summer concerts are held on the second Saturday of the month from June through August on the boardwalk. Local crafts are featured at the annual Bayfest held on the fourth weekend in August. In 2008 the town inaugurated a seasonal Friday night farmers' market from 6 to 9 PM.

WHERE TO EAT

$–$$
SEAFOOD
✕**Neptune's.** Modest Neptune's claims of preparing "the world's best mussels" rings true with many, making the trip to this tiny town just north of Chesapeake Beach worthwhile. Attached to the small bar, a glass-enclosed dining room with a brick floor is a friendly, informal spot to dig in to its signature dish. Also on the menu are seafood pastas, burgers, and cuts of Angus beef. ⊠*8800 Chesapeake Ave., at 1st St.* ☎*410/257–7899* ▤*AE, D, MC, V.*

BEACH TROLLEY

In 2008 Beach Trolley Association inaugurated a regular route of motorized trolleys between North Beach and Chesapeake Beach. The trolleys run on Friday and the weekend from June through August and cost 25¢ a ride (⊕ *www.beachtrolleyassociation. org*).

CHESAPEAKE BEACH

1 mi south of North Beach via Rte. 261; 32 mi south of Annapolis via Rte. 2, Rte. 260, and Rte. 261.

This charming little town beside the Bay was founded at the close of the 19th century as a resort to rival those along the French Riviera. It was served by steamboats from Baltimore and by a railroad from Washington, DC. Steamboat service diminished over time and the railroad failed in 1935, but the town survived as private automobiles became more readily available. It boomed again in 1948 with the legalization of slot machines, although they lasted only 20 years. Today Chesapeake Beach is once again staging a tourism comeback with the addition of a water park and a new waterfront hotel.

Joined almost seamlessly to North Beach, Chesapeake Beach is the more exciting of the two relatively quiet towns. While North Beach retains the low profile of a collection of beachfront cottages, Chesapeake Beach has been built up with hotels and condominiums. Development also means that there is more to do in Chesapeake Beach—restaurants, a good museum, a hotel with a spa, a water park, and a greater number and variety of shops.

ESSENTIALS

Chesapeake Beach (☎ *410/257–2230 town hall* ⊕ *Chesapeake-Beach.md.us*).

EXPLORING

Fodor's Choice
★

The **Chesapeake Beach Railway Museum**, housed in the railroad's 1898 track-side terminus, provides memorable glimpses of the onetime resort's turn-of-the-20th-century glory days. Among its exhibits are a glass-enclosed model of the town of Chesapeake Beach and a hand-carved kangaroo from the magnificent carousel, as well as a slot machine and photos of early vacationers. One of the railroad's passenger cars rests nearby. ⊠ *4155 Mears Ave., Rte. 261* ☎ *410/257–3892* ⊕ *www.cbrm. org* ⊠ *Free* ☉ *May–Sept., daily 1–4; Apr. and Oct., weekends 1–4 and by appointment.*

Families make a day of it at **Chesapeake Beach Water Park** (⊠ *Gordon Stinnett Ave. at Rte. 261* ☎ *410/257–1404 or 301/855–3803*), which has a children's pool, beach, and many slides. The park is open from Memorial Day until the first day of school. Admission is $18.

WHERE TO STAY & EAT

$$–$$$
SEAFOOD

✕ **Rod 'n' Reel.** This family-owned restaurant opened optimistically in 1936, the year after the demise of the railroad from Washington. Since then it has remained synonymous with superb seafood. Now part of the Chesapeake Beach Resort & Spa, its bay-side location still provides stunning views. The extensive menu includes succulent southern Maryland specialties such as rockfish stuffed with crab imperial, fried oysters, and the region's ubiquitous crab cakes. ⊠ *Rte. 261 at Mears Ave.* ☎ *410/257–2735 or 877/763–6733* ⊕ *www.rodnreelinc.com* ⊟ *AE, D, MC, V.*

$$
★

🏨 **The Chesapeake Beach Resort & Spa.** Opened in 2004, this luxury hotel and spa is a key part of the revitalization of the town's tourism business. The public spaces pay homage to the beachfront community's history. A mural in the lobby depicts the old roller coaster that once thrilled vacationers, and framed photographs line the corridors, tracing the town's changes from its Victorian heyday to the present. The whitewashed oak furniture and sand-color walls give the rooms an elegant yet beachy style. The resort was built right on the water's edge, and its suites and deluxe rooms have balconies that seem to hang over the Bay. There are also three dining options, a boardwalk, and a fishing charter company at the hotel's full-service marina. **Pros:** a full-service resort with boating, an indoor pool, and spa services; a sandy beach. **Cons:** don't expect a "jumping the waves" experience at the beach—the Chesapeake is placid compared to the beach properties on the Atlantic. ⊠ *4165 Mears Ave.* ☎ *410/257–5596 or 301/855–0096* ⊕ *wwwcbresortspa.com* 🛏 *72 rooms, 6 suites* ⟨ *In-room: Ethernet. In-hotel: 3 restaurants, pool, gym, spa, parking (no fee)* ⊟ *AE, D, DC, MC, V* ❚◎❚ *BP.*

PORT REPUBLIC

17 mi south of Chesapeake Beach.

Two sites in Port Republic, Christ Church and Port Republic School No. 7, are easy to miss simply because the sign for Port Republic from Route 765 points north, but the attractions are actually south. From Route 765 turn onto Broomes Island Road. If you plan on dining near Port Republic you may have to continue to Lusby or Solomons Island.

EXPLORING

With the northernmost naturally occurring stand of bald cypress trees in the United States, the 100-acre **Battle Creek Cypress Swamp Sanctuary** provides close-up looks at the forest primeval. A 0.25-mi elevated boardwalk at the bottom of a steep but sturdy set of steps gives you a good vantage point to see the swamp, thick with 100-foot-tall trees that are 75 to 100 years old. Guides at the nature center can alert you to the seasonal permutations of the vegetation and the doings of squirrels, owls, and other wildlife. Indoor exhibits focus on the area's natural and cultural history. The swamp is about 5 mi west of Port Republic. ⊠Sixes Rd., Rte. 506, Prince Frederick ☎410/535–5327 ⊕www.calvertparks.org ☑Free ⊙Tues.–Sat. 10–4:30, Sun. 1–4:30.

Christ Church traces its origins to 1672, when a log-cabin church stood at the site. Its 1772 brick replacement, coated with plaster, is notable for its biblical garden, planted with species mentioned in the scriptures. Port Republic School No. 7 is on the church's property. Since immediately after the Civil War the grounds have been a venue for jousting (Maryland's state sport) on the last Saturday in August. ⊠3100 Broomes Island Rd., Rte. 264 ☎410/586–0565 ☑Free ⊙Daily dawn–dusk.

EN ROUTE

Behind 2.5 mi of scenic Patuxent riverfront stretch 544 acres of woods and farmland. The 70-odd archaeological sites have yielded evidence of 9,000 years of human habitation—from prehistory on through to Colonial times. At the **Jefferson Patterson Park and Museum** you can follow an archaeology trail to inspect artifacts of the successive hunter-gatherer, early agricultural, and plantation societies that once roamed and settled this land. Displays include primitive knives and axes, fragments of Native American pottery, and Colonial glassware. Stroll along the nature trails to take a look at wildlife, antique agricultural equipment, and fields of crops. The park is 2 mi south of Port Republic. ⊠10115 Mackall Rd., Rte. 265, St. Leonard ☎410/586–8501 ⊕www.jefpat.org ☑Free ⊙Mid-Apr.–mid-Oct., Wed.–Sun. 10–5.

Port Republic School No. 7, a classic one-room schoolhouse built in the 1880s, looks for all the world as if today's lesson could begin any minute. Here, you can find a restored classroom with archetypal desks, inkwells, and a school bell. Until 1932 a single teacher taught children in seven grades here. ⊠3100 Broomes Island Rd., Rte. 264 ☎410/586–0767 ☑Free ⊙Memorial Day–Labor Day, Sun. 2–4 and by appointment.

8

BROOMES ISLAND

7 mi south of Port Republic, via Rte. 264.

An area without specific boundaries, Broomes is not even an island per se, except during a very high tide or in a strong storm. It's made up of little more than a few houses and stores, a post office, and a church. This little area at the mouth of Island Creek is a portrait of a water-dependent community amid change: weather-beaten structures of its past now mingle with new, expensive waterfront homes.

WHERE TO EAT

$$$ ✕ **Stoney's Seafood House.** Popular with boaters who tie right up to the
SEAFOOD   dock, this restaurant overlooking Island Creek has one dining room
★   that actually juts out over the water and another on higher ground with great views from its floor-to-ceiling windows. There's also ample seating—and a tiki bar—outside. Stoney's hefty crab cakes are made with plenty of back-fin meat and little filler. Oyster sandwiches and Stoney's Steamer—handpicked selections of fresh seafood—are also good choices. The intense, house-made desserts, such as the strawberry shortcake and Kim's key lime pie, are not for the faint of heart. If you miss Stoney's in Broomes Island, there are two other locations in Solomons Island. ⊠ *Oyster House Rd.* ☎ *410/586–1888* ⊕ *stoneyskingfishers.com* ▭ *AE, D, MC, V* ☯ *Closed Nov.–early Mar.*

LUSBY

12 mi southeast of Broomes Island.

☯   Lusby is larger than either Port Republic or Broomes Island and has a town center as well as some of the big, convenience stores on its perimeter that are lacking in some of the smaller shore towns. And if you want to do anything after 8 PM other than watching the sunset over the dock, you might find it in Lusby.

EXPLORING

Like its better-known neighbor Calvert Cliffs State Park, **Flag Ponds Nature Park** has spectacular views of the cliffs, but with just a short stroll to the beach, this county park is the more accessible of the two. Until the 1950s the area was a busy fishery, and some of the buildings from that era still stand. Today it beckons with bathhouses, a fishing pier, 3 mi of gently graded hiking trails, observation decks at two ponds, a boardwalk through wetlands, and indoor wildlife exhibits. Soaring cliffs, flat marshland, and wildflowers (including the blue flag iris, for which the park is named) provide stunning contrasts. ■ TIP→ **A shark's tooth dating back 10–20 million years is the big prize in a fossil hunt on the beach, one of the park's most popular activities.** ⊠ *Rte. 2/4* ☎ *410/586–1477* ⊕ *www.calvertparks.org* ▭ *$6 per vehicle Apr.–Oct., $3 per vehicle Nov.–Mar.* ☯ *Memorial Day–Labor Day, weekdays 9–6, weekends 9–8; Labor Day–Memorial Day, weekends 9–5.*

NIGHTLIFE & THE ARTS

For a taste of the tropics *and* the South Pacific along St. Leonard's Creek, wet your lips with an umbrella-topped cocktail at **Vera's Beach Club** (✉ *1200 White Sands Dr., Lusby* ☎ *410/586–1182* ⊕ *verasbeachclub.com* ۵ *Closed Nov.–Apr.*). Vera's offers weekly entertainment and no cover charge. With an exotic environment and fantastic location with open-air decks overlooking a deepwater marina and delightful river views—not to mention a swimming pool—it's well worth a visit, despite its difficult-to-find location west off Route 2/4.

SOLOMONS

8 mi south of Lusby.

On the tip of the peninsula, Solomons is where the Patuxent empties into the Chesapeake. The town has become a popular getaway for sailors, boaters, and affluent professionals. But it's still a laid-back waterfront town—at least when compared with, say, Annapolis or St. Michaels. Several excellent boatyards and marinas cater to powerboaters and sailors, with nautical services from the simplest to the most sophisticated. There are several antiques, book, gift, and specialty shops and galleries side by side, parallel to the boardwalk. Wherever you go, stunning views surround you at nearly every turn.

EXPLORING

۵ A world-class sculpture and botanical venue, **Annmarie Garden** Sculpture Park and Arts Center is a 30-acre property on the St. John Creek. The sculptural art is by artists both local and from around the world. One of the more intriguing installations is a series of 13 "Talking Benches." Each tells an ecological story by depicting a plant that grows in southern Maryland, including dogwood, loblolly pines, papaw trees, and tobacco. Smooth, user-friendly pathways curve through the grounds. Don't miss the lyrical brass statue of a crabber in front of the Museum. The figure and water feature perfectly captures the dependence of the area on the seafood industry. Little here is off-limits, and picnickers are welcome to settle in virtually anywhere. Be sure to visit the mosaic-filled restrooms. ■ TIP➔ **Annemarie Garden has a special Christmas display, "The Garden in Lights," from mid-December through New Year's Eve. Children get in free and there are many specialized programs that provide a hands-on art experience.** ✉ *Dowell Rd.* ☎ *410/326–4640* ⊕ *www.annmariegarden. org* ☞ *$3* ۵ *Daily 9–5.*

8

WHERE TO STAY & EAT

$$–$$$ ✕ **DiGiovanni's Dock of the Bay.** It's rare to be able to enjoy elegant water-
ITALIAN side dining and professional service at budget prices. The chef creates succulent northern Italian dishes using fresh herbs and spices. The *cacciucco* (seafood soup) alone is worth a special trip, as is the homemade lasagna. Italian music is played during meals. There are many excellent seafood restaurants in southern Maryland, but DiGiovanni's is one of the few to give the fruit of the Bay an ethnic spin. ✉ *14556 Solomons Island Rd.* ☎ *410/394–6400* ▭ *AE, D, MC, V* ۵ *Closed Mon. Jan.–May. No lunch.*

$–$$ ⭐ 🏨 **Back Creek Inn.** Built for a waterman in 1880, this blue wood-frame house sits in a residential neighborhood on well-tended grounds at the edge of Back Creek. You can lounge on the deck next to a beautiful perennial garden. Four rooms have water views, and one opens onto the garden. Breakfast is served in the dining room or by the lily pond. The Back Creek Inn is in a residential neighborhood, but easily within walking distance to town. **Pros:** very friendly management; well-tended property. **Cons:** no elevator; only children over 12 are welcome. ✉ *Calvert and Alexander Sts.* ☎ *410/326–2022* ⊕ *www.backcreekinnbnb.com* ➘ *4 rooms, 2 suites, 1 cottage* ♿ *In-room: Wi-Fi. In-hotel: bicycles, no elevator, no kids under 12, no-smoking rooms* ▭ *MC, V* ⦿ *BP.*

> **KIM'S KEY LIME PIE**
>
> Many of the restaurants in southern Maryland serve Kim's pies, especially the key lime. The bakery is located in Solomons Island in a cottage that is a combination café, Kim's Key Lime Pie and Coffee Shop, and gift shop, Kim's Riverwalk Gifts (✉ *14618 Solomons Island Rd.* ☎ *410/326–8469).* Although the key lime is the most popular, the carrot cake is also highly recommended.

$ 🏨 **Hilton Garden Inn Solomons.** This brand new inn and convention center opened in 2008. It has all the amenities, including a heated indoor pool and a modern fitness center. It has an expansive lobby and the corporate look that signals the expectation of the convention and meeting crowd. Large rooms have desks with ergonomically designed chairs and plenty of outlets **Pros:** everything is modern and up-to-date; as a business hotel for conferences, it has many amenities. **Cons:** 2 mi from the center of town and along a highway. ✉ *13100 Dowell Rd., technically in Dowell, Maryland, rather than Solomons* ☎ *410/326–0303* ⊕ *www.solomons. stayhgl.com* ➘ *100 rooms, 8 suites* ♿ *In room: Wi-Fi. In-hotel: restaurant, executive floor, pools* ▭ *AE, D, MC, V.*

$–$$ 🏨 **Solomons Victorian Inn.** On the Back Creek side of narrow Solomons Island this three-story, yellow frame house was built in 1906 by the foremost shipbuilder on the Chesapeake Bay. Six rooms look onto Solomons Harbor and two have garden views. All are furnished with period antiques and reproductions, and every room has an ornate armoire. Afternoon refreshments and breakfast are served on an enclosed porch. **Pros:** the great room has stunning water views; all the modern amenities, but with 19th-century decor. **Cons:** only one room is handicapped accessible; no elevator. ✉ *125 Charles St.* ☎ *410/326–4811* ⊕ *www. solomonsvictorianinn.com* ➘ *8 rooms* ♿ *In-room: Wi-Fi. In-hotel: no elevator, no-smoking rooms* ▭ *AE, MC, V* ⦿ *BP.*

ST. MARY'S COUNTY

"Just at the mouth of the river, we observed the natives in arms. That night, fires blazed through the whole country and since they had never seen such a large ship, messengers were sent in all directions, who reported that a 'canoe' like an island had come with as many as there were trees in the woods."—Father Andrew White, recounting the arrival of the *Ark* and the *Dove* in 1634.

Father White arrived in the New World in 1634 as a member of Lord Baltimore's contingent of 140 colonists. The two "canoes" the Native Americans spotted were the tiny sailing vessels that had just crossed the Atlantic to reach the southernmost tip of Maryland's Western Shore, where the Potomac River meets the Chesapeake Bay. The peninsula between the Potomac and the Patuxent rivers is today St. Mary's County, easily one of the state's most beautiful regions, and gradually attracting development because of its easy access to Washington, DC, to the north.

Like so much of Maryland south of Annapolis and Washington, many scenic drives throughout St. Mary's County bring together charming inland and waterside towns and historic sites. Hearty food and homey places to stay are easy to find.

■ TIP➔ St. Mary's County also boasts another curiosity: its numerous liquor stores sell popular brands of U.S. beer in rare 8-ounce and 10-ounce cans.

St. Mary's County Tourism (✉ *23115 Leonard Hall Dr., Leonardtown* ☎ *800/327–9023* ⊕ *www.co.saint-marys.md.us*).

LEXINGTON PARK

9 mi southeast of Solomons, 68 mi south of Annapolis, via Rte. 2/4 to Rte. 235.

The Patuxent River Naval Air Station covers 25 mi of the shoreline at the mouth of the eponymous river, and it assists naval aviation operations by its research, development, and testing of aircraft and things associated with them. Its facilities are also utilized by private industry, academic institutions, and foreign governments.

EXPLORING

The St. Mary's River, which once powered **Historic Cecil's Old Mill,** is just a trickle in this area now, so the water wheel now runs on electricity. Today the building, which dates to 1900, contains an artist co-op as well as a small display of artifacts and photographs of the mill. In keeping with the setting, most of the arts and crafts on sale are quaint and rustic: rural scenes painted on circular saw blades or lighthouses on driftwood, crocheted place mats, and colorful quilts. The mill is a few miles west of the naval station and quite difficult to find—there are no signposts. ✉ *Indian Bridge Rd. off Rte. 5, Great Mills* ☎ *301/994–1510* ☉ *Mar.–Oct., Thurs.–Sat. 10–5, Sun. 11–5; Nov. and Dec., Mon.–Sat. 10–5, Sun. 11–5.*

The **Patuxent River Naval Air Museum** houses items from the research, development, testing, and evaluation of naval aircraft. Nineteen vintage aircraft are displayed outside. Inside, you can climb into a cockpit trainer and view some of the more-improbable creations that failed to pass muster, such as the Goodyear "Inflatoplane." ✉ *Patuxent River Naval Air Station, Rte. 235, 3 Notch Rd.* ☎ *301/863–7418* ⊕ *www. paxmuseum.com* ▣ *Free* ☉ *Tues.–Sun. 10–5.*

**OFF THE
BEATEN
PATH**

Sotterley. The distinguished house on the grounds of this 18th-century plantation is the earliest known (1703) post-in-ground structure in the United States: in place of a foundation, cedar timbers driven straight into the ground support it. The house is a sampler of architectural styles and interior design from the last two centuries. On the grounds of this National Historic Landmark are other buildings from the 18th through early 20th century, including a Colonial customs warehouse, a smokehouse, a "necessary" (an outhouse), and a restored slave cabin from the 1830s. The house also has Colonial Revival gardens and nature trails overlooking the Patuxent River. ⊠ *Rte. 245 near Hollywood, 12 mi north of Lexington Park via Rtes. 235 and 245* ☏ *301/373–2280* ⊕ *www.sotterley.com* ⊡ *$10.* ⊙ *May–Oct., Tues.–Sat. 10–4, Sun. noon–4. Grounds open year-round.*

POINT LOOKOUT STATE PARK

20 mi south of Lexington Park, 88 mi south of Annapolis, via Rte. 2/4 and Rte. 235 to Rte. 5.

When Father Andrew White came to Point Lookout and saw the Potomac at its side, he mused that the Thames was a mere rivulet in comparison. But instead of being overwhelmed by the wildness of the New World, he observed that "fine groves of trees appear . . . growing in intervals as if planted by the hand of man."

On the approach to Point Lookout State Park, two memorial obelisks remind travelers of the dark later history of this starkly alluring point of land. Beginning in 1863 a Union prison stood at the farthest tip of the peninsula, just across the Potomac from Confederate Virginia. During those last two years of the conflict, nearly 4,000 of the 52,000 Confederate soldiers here died because of disease and poor conditions. Point Lookout is a reminder that many men from southern Maryland fought on the side of the Confederates during the Civil War. Twenty thousand prisoners crowded the Point Lookout facilities after the Battle of Gettysburg—in space built for 10,000 people. All that remains of the prison are some earthen fortifications, partially rebuilt and known as Fort Lincoln, with markers noting the sites of hospitals and other buildings. A small museum supplies some of the details. The 1,046-acre state park has boating facilities, nature trails, and a beach for swimming. The RV campground, with hookups, is open year-round; tent camping facilities are open from April through October. Be sure to visit the lighthouse at the southern end of the park. Built in 1830 and used until 1965, the lighthouse also served as a depot. ⊠ *Rte. 5* ☏ *301/872–5688* ⊕ *www. dnr.state.md.us* ⊡ *May–Sept., weekends and holidays $5 per person, all other times $3 per vehicle* ⊙ *Year-round, daily 6 AM–sunset.*

**OFF THE
BEATEN
PATH**

St. Ignatius Church. Built in 1758, St. Ignatius is all that survives of the prerevolutionary plantation of St. Inigoes. A church dating from the 1630s had stood where this church, named for the founder of the Jesuits, stands now; the graveyard is one of the oldest in the United States. St. Ignatius is one of the most beautiful churches in Maryland, and is well worth a detour. In addition to stunning stained-glass windows, parishioners have adorned each kneeler with scenes from Maryland culture. The adjacent cemetery is a history in stone of the families of the church and the region. Several veterans of the Revolution are buried here, alongside Jesuit priests who served here. To see inside the

church, ask for the key at the sentry box of the naval installation next door. ⊠ *Villa Rd. off Rte. 5, St. Inigoes* ☎ *301/872–5590* ☐ *Free.*

SPORTS & THE OUTDOORS

Scheibel's (⊠ *Wynne Rd., Ridge* ☎ *301/872–5185*) will arrange fishing charters.

ST. MARY'S CITY

73 mi south of Annapolis, via Rte. 2/4 to Rte. 5 North.

An intrepid group of 140 English settlers sailed the *Ark* and the *Dove* up the Potomac and into one of its tributaries, the St. Mary's River. About halfway up, on an east bank, they founded St. Mary's City, the fourth permanent settlement in British North America and eventually the first (albeit short-lived) capital of Maryland.

Long before a Constitution or a Bill of Rights, the first law of religious tolerance in the New World was enacted in St. Mary's City, guaranteeing the freedom to practice whatever religion one chose. Here, too, almost three centuries before American women achieved suffrage, Mistress Margaret Brent challenged the status quo and requested the right to vote (she didn't get it). The settlement served as Maryland's capital city until 1695, when the legislature moved to Annapolis and the county seat moved to Leonardtown. St. Mary's City virtually vanished, its existence acknowledged only in historical novels and textbooks. Today the city is home to a living-history park and a small liberal-arts college that shares its name. St. Mary's College of Maryland, which dates to 1840, functions as the cultural center for the surrounding community.

EXPLORING

In 1934 a first step in the rebirth of St. Mary's was taken. In commemoration of the 300th anniversary of Maryland, the Colony's imposing State House, originally built in 1676, was reconstructed. In the early 1970s a vast archaeological-reconstruction program began in earnest, a project that has revealed nearly 200 individual sites. The entire 800-plus acres have become a living-history museum and archaeological park called **Historic St. Mary's City.** In 2009 St. Mary's marked its 375th anniversary of the founding of Maryland. Historic St. Mary's is an ongoing archaeological dig and a work in progress. Don't expect Colonial Williamsburg.

The historic complex includes several notable reconstructions and reproductions of buildings. The **State House of 1676,** like its larger and grander counterpart in Williamsburg, has an upper and a lower chamber for the Council and General Assembly. This 1934 reproduction is based on court documents from the period; the original was dismantled in 1829, with many of the bricks used for Trinity Church nearby. The square-rigged ship *Maryland Dove,* docked behind the State House, represents the smaller of the two vessels that conveyed the original settlers from England.

OFF THE BEATEN PATH

Piney Point Lighthouse, Museum & Historic Park. The first permanent lighthouse constructed on the Potomac River is now the center of a small, 6-acre park. The grounds, which are free, have a boardwalk, pier, and picnic tables. The 1990 lighthouse is a replica of the 1861 original. ⊠*Lighthouse Rd., Piney Point* 🕿*301/494-1471* ⊕*www.stmarysmd. com/recreate/museums* ⊠*$3* ☉*Mid-May–Oct., daily*

Godiah Spray Tobacco Plantation depicts life on a 17th-century tobacco farm in the Maryland wilderness. Interpreters portray the Spray family—the real family lived about 20 mi away—and its indentured servants, enlisting visitors in such household chores as cooking and gardening or in working the tobacco field. The buildings, including the main dwelling house and outbuildings, were built with period tools and techniques.

Throughout Historic St. Mary's City, you're encouraged to explore other sites and exhibits-in-progress, including the town center, the location of the first Catholic church in the English Colonies, a "victualing" and lodging house, and the Woodland Indian Hamlet. Historic interpreters in costume—some in character—add realism to the experience. ⊠*Rte. 5* 🕿*240/895–4990 or 800/762–1634* ⊕*www.stmaryscity.org* ⊠*$10* ☉ *Wed.–Sun. 10–5.*

WHERE TO STAY

$$ ★ **Brome-Howard Inn.** Set on 30 acres of farmland, this 19th-century farmhouse provides a trip through time to life on a tobacco plantation. Rooms are decorated with original family furnishings. Relax on one of the big outdoor porches or patios and watch the lazy St. Mary's River nearby. In the evening there are two candlelit dining rooms—the foyer or the formal parlor. Five miles of hiking trails lead to St. Mary's City, and the inn has bikes for the use of guests. The in-house restaurant specializes in seafood and occasionally serves such exotic items as bison, ostrich, or shark. **Pros:** breathtaking setting overlooking the St. Mary's River—the reason that many couples pick it as a wedding site. **Cons:** the inn is remote and is a destination itself, so unless you get in your car, you will not be strolling to other sites. ⊠*18281 Rosecroft Rd.* 🕿*301/866–0656* ⊕*www.bromehowardinn.com* ➾*3 rooms, 1 suite* ⌂*In-hotel: restaurant, bicycles, no elevator* ☐*AE, MC, V* ⦿*BP.*

CHARLES COUNTY

To the north of St. Mary's County and about 35 mi southwest of Annapolis, relatively rural Charles County is flanked on its west by the Potomac River's big bend as it flows south from Washington, DC. In what used to be tobacco country, less-traveled county and state roads crisscross the pristine countryside dotted with depot towns, riverfront ports-of-call, wildlife preservation centers, and unsung historic sites.

ESSENTIALS

Visitor Information **Charles County Office of Tourism** (⊠ *103 Centennial St., Suite C, La Plata* ☎ *800/766–3386*). **Crain Memorial Welcome Center** (⊠ *U.S. Rte. 301, 12480 Crain Hwy., near Newburg, 1 mi north of Governor Nice bridge over the Potomac River* ☎ *301/259–2500*).

WALDORF

40 mi south of Annapolis on Rte. 301.

The lovely rural fields of other parts of eastern Maryland give way to developments and higher-density traffic when you reach Waldorf.

EXPLORING

The **Dr. Samuel A. Mudd House** is where John Wilkes Booth ended up at 4 AM on Good Friday, 1865, his leg broken after having leaped from the presidential box at Ford's Theater. Most likely, the 32-year-old Dr. Mudd had no idea his patient was wanted for the assassination of Abraham Lincoln. Nonetheless, Mudd was convicted of aiding a fugitive and sentenced to life in prison. (President Andrew Jackson pardoned him in 1869.) Today the two-story house, set on 10 rolling acres, looks as if the doctor is still in. The dark purple couch where Mudd examined Booth remains in the downstairs parlor, 18th-century family pieces fill the rooms, and the doctor's crude instruments are displayed. There's a 30-minute guided tour of the house, an exhibit building, and Mudd's original tombstone. ⊠ *14940 Hoffman Rd.* ☎ *301/645–6870* ☞ *$4* ⊙ *Late Mar.–late Nov., Wed. and weekends 11–4.*

8

PORT TOBACCO

11 mi southwest of Waldorf via Rte. 301 and Rte. 6.

One of the oldest communities in the East, Port Tobacco first existed as the Native American settlement of "Potopaco." (The similarity between this Native American name—meaning "the jutting of water inland"— and the name for the plant that was to become a cornerstone of the region's economy is purely coincidental.) Potopaco was colonized by the English in 1634, and later in the century emerged as the major seaport of Port Tobacco. The historic district includes the reconstructed early-19th-century courthouse; Catslide House, one of the area's four surviving 18th-century homes; and a restored one-room schoolhouse, dating to 1876 and used as such until 1953.

EXPLORING

★ **Thomas Stone National Historic Site,** built in the 1770s, was the Charles County home of Thomas Stone, one of four Maryland signers of the Declaration of Independence. It has been painstakingly rebuilt after a devastating fire left it a shell in the late 1970s. The restoration re-created the distinctive five-part Georgian house inside and out. The two-story main plantation house is linked to the two wings and adjoining hallways in an arc rather than a straight line. All the rooms have exquisite details, such as built-in cabinets, elaborate moldings, a table set in fine china, gilded mirrors, and a harpsichord. The house and family grave site are just a short stroll from the parking lot and visitor center, where you can examine a model of the house or watch a video about Stone. This is one of the least-visited National Park Service sites, but is in a lovely rural setting. ✉ *6655 Rose Hill Rd., between Rtes. 6 and 225, 4 mi west of La Plata* 🕾 *301/392–1776* 🌐 *www.nps.gov/thst* 🎫 *Free* 🕙 *Mid-June–Aug. daily 9–5; Sept.–mid-June, Wed.–Sun. 9–5.*

The Eastern Shore

WORD OF MOUTH

"If you are looking for a quiet, peaceful place, then Virginia's Eastern Shore is the place for you . . . It's a great balance of fields, forests, and quaint little villages."

—hansman

"Assateague Island has wild (sort of) ponies living on it. Lots of birds. Nice paths to walk in search of ponies and scenery. The kayaking is very nice. You can sometimes see ponies from the kayaks as well. There's a couple of places there to rent boats. April would be a nice time to visit. You would be there before the mosquitos."

—AlJ

Updated by
Pete Nelson

SAILING THE CHESAPEAKE BAY NEARLY four centuries ago in search of new territory for his English king, Captain John Smith wrote that "heaven and earth never agreed better to frame a place for man's habitation." Today the counties of Maryland and Virginia on the eastern side of the Bay retain an enchanting culture and landscape of calm despite their proximity to Baltimore and Washington, DC.

The Eastern Shore's first permanent English settlement—indeed, the first in Maryland and one of the earliest along the Atlantic—took root on Kent Island, now Queen Anne's County, in 1631. The region's long heritage is recorded in architecture and on paper and canvas, and many Eastern Shore families have been here for many generations; residents of Smith Island still retain a peculiar Elizabethan lilt in their speech.

A visit to the Shore might consist of exploring hospitable communities and historic sites, strolling through wildlife parks and refuges, pausing at a few of the myriad shops, dining at third-generation-owned waterfront restaurants, and overnighting at inns and bed-and-breakfasts. One of the region's most popular summertime destinations is Ocean City, which clings to a narrow barrier island off the southeastern edge of Maryland's Eastern Shore. Its ocean-side culture differs dramatically from that of the Chesapeake, lacking as it does the early-American aura that pervades the rest of the peninsula.

ORIENTATION & PLANNING

GETTING ORIENTED

To understand the Eastern Shore, look to the Bay. The Chesapeake is 195 mi long and the nation's largest estuary (a semi-enclosed body of water with free connection to the open sea). Freshwater tributaries large and small flow south and west into the Bay, ensuring the agricultural wealth of the peninsula as well as the bounty of the Bay ("Chesapeake" is an Algonquian word meaning "great shellfish"). At day's end look west across the Chesapeake Bay and you can see the sun set over water—a rare sight for any East Coast resident.

Cecil County. The northern gateway to Maryland's Eastern Shore caps the headwaters of the Chesapeake Bay, including some 12,000 acres of park- and forestland as well as a National Resource Area of more than 5,600 acres. It is known best, however, for its world-renowned horse farms

Kent County. Immediately to the south of Cecil County lies a delightful blend of agriculture and maritime culture, its principal towns successful combinations of Colonial-era history and 21st-century modernity.

Queen Anne's County. Best known as the eastern gateway to Maryland's Eastern Shore, Queen Anne's Kent Island is the site of the eastern end of the double-span William Preston Lane Jr. Bridge—known colloquially as the "Bay Bridge." On the island's eastern shore, Kent Narrows, with its variety of lodging, restaurant, and water-related recreation opportunities has emerged as an attractive travel destination.

Talbot County. Much of this county is threaded with waterways of various sizes that yield myriad untrammeled peninsulas and almost-islands that welcome explorers. Its county seat, Easton, is a vibrant small town.

Dorchester County. Dorchester exudes an aura of gentility reminiscent of the Southern states. Home of one of the region's largest wildlife refuges, it, too, has a wildly ragged western shoreline, undeveloped and unsung, and a mix of agriculture and maritime heritage.

Lower Eastern Shore. Maryland's southernmost shore is comprised of three counties: Wicomico, whose county seat, Salisbury, is the area's second-largest port city (after Baltimore); Worcester, which includes the ever-popular year-round Atlantic resort destination Ocean City; and quiet Somerset, with the state's southernmost locales (opposite the mouth of the Potomac River).

Virginia's Eastern Shore. State highway 13 crosses into Virginia out of Maryland's Worcester County and meanders for some 70 mi southward to the extraordinarily engineered Chesapeake Bay Bridge-Tunnel complex, bisecting its narrow rural peninsula like an extension of Delmarva. Funky, mostly waterside hamlets are tucked away against the Chesapeake and Atlantic shorelines to either side of the highway. The most celebrated of these is Chincoteague, dominating an island of the same name and known for its famous ponies.

PLANNING

WHEN TO GO

Traditional summertime months, i.e. school vacation time, are the busiest throughout the region. Ocean City attracts not only visitors for weeks-long stays but also day-trippers, particularly on weekends, and that means heavy traffic. July and August are the hottest and humidity can be high, but literally thousands of miles of water's edge produces cooling breezes.

Shallower edges of the Chesapeake Bay can freeze over in January and February. However, the relatively temperate climate of this region—winters without any snow at all are not uncommon—means year-round appeal. Many large and small towns celebrate winter months as heartily as the warmer ones with regional festivals and local tours.

In May a weekend-long festival called the **Chestertown Tea Party** (☎410/778–0416 ⊕www.chestertownteaparty.com) commemorates a little-known Colonial rebellion in 1774 that includes an authentic reenactment of their hurling British tea into the Chester River, in support of a similar event in Boston a year earlier. Late July's **Pony Swim and Auction** (☎757/336–6161 ⊕www.chincoteaguechamber.com) is the renowned annual roundup of wild ponies from Assateague Island, Virginia, which are then herded to Chincoteague where select foals are auctioned off to support the volunteer fire department. This tradition

9

is the basis of the 1947 classic children's book, *Misty of Chincoteague* by Marguerite Henry. In September, Crisfield's **National Hard Crab Derby** (☎*410/968–2500* ⊕*www.crisfieldchamber.com/crabderby.htm*) celebrates the Eastern Shore's crabs with a crab race, steamed crabs, and all things crabby, including the crowning of a Miss Crustacean.

Ocean City, Maryland, celebrates the quest for endless summer in mid-September with **Sunfest Kite Festival** (☎*410/289–7855* ⊕*www. kiteloft.com*), a four-day blowout with all sorts of entertainment, kite contests, and a crafts show. In October, **Chincoteague Oyster Festival** (☎*757/336–6161* ⊕*www.chincoteaguechamber.com*), on Virginia's Eastern Shore, recognizes the significance, current and historic, of the Bay's famed oysters. This giant all-you-can-eat oyster feast typically sells out long in advance. On or close to the first weekend in November, a small fleet of vessels—from historic working boats and traditional sailing ships to majestic "tall ships"—gathers in the Chester River's broad waters in front of Chestertown for **Downrigging Weekend** (☎*410/778–5954* ⊕*www.sultanaprojects.org/thefleet.htm*), hosted by the town's resident schooner *Sultana*. During **Waterfowl Week** (☎*757/336–6122* ⊕*www.chinco.fws.gov*), around Thanksgiving every year, the Chincoteague National Wildlife Refuge opens a portion not accessible to motor vehicles during the rest of the year to allow close-up observation of Canada and snow geese on their southward migration.

GETTING HERE & AROUND

In general, this is a driving and walking region—you arrive by car and either walk or bike around your destination. Taxis are few and far between. One of the most thorough transportation resources is the non-profit Chesapeake Bay Gateways Network.

BY AIR   The most convenient major airport for travel throughout eastern Maryland is Baltimore-Washington Thurgood Marshall Airport (BWI), approximately 30 minutes' drive from the Chesapeake Bay Bridge.

BY CAR   A car is indispensable for touring the region. To reach the Eastern Shore from Baltimore or Washington, DC, travel east on U.S. 50/301 and cross the 4.5-mi Chesapeake Bay Bridge northeast of Annapolis (toll, $2.50, eastbound only). The extraordinary 17.5-mi Chesapeake Bay Bridge-Tunnel is the only access between Virginia's Eastern Shore and Norfolk, Virginia Beach, and other Tidewater-area towns. The bridge-and-tunnel complex comprises 12 mi of trestled roadway, two tunnels, two bridges, almost 2 mi of causeway, among four man-made islands (toll, $12, in either direction).

Weekend traffic going to the beach can be exceptionally heavy during summertime months. Times to avoid if possible are Friday afternoon and evening and Saturday morning, eastbound, and Sunday afternoon and evening, westbound.

ESSENTIALS

Transportation Information Chesapeake Bay Gateways Network (⊕*www.bay gateways.net*). **Chesapeake Bay Bridge-Tunnel** (☎*757/331–2960 in Maryland,*

TOP REASONS TO GO

■ **Sail on a historic skipjack:** Though they once dominated the Chesapeake Bay waterways, these traditional fishing vessels under sail—several of which have been designated National Historic Landmarks—today are nearly extinct. Fortunately, you can still experience a bit of unique history by sailing aboard one of the few that remain.

■ **Tuck into Maryland's trademark crustacean:** Don't leave the Eastern Shore without sampling the slightly sweet taste of the Chesapeake renowned blue crab at a down-home eatery, cracking shells with your own wooden mallet. Or join in the perpetual arguments over who prepares the best crab cake and who serves the most succulent soft-shell crabs.

■ **Get back to nature:** Bike the Blackwater National Wildlife Refuge or paddle the tidal marsh pathways of the unique Fishing Bay Water Trail and view the American bald eagles that call this place home. Or stroll the pristine Atlantic beaches of Assateague Island's National Seashore and National Wildlife Refuge.

■ **Amble along Ocean City's boardwalk:** With year-round leisure-time opportunities—mid-summer for 24/7 activity and unparalleled people-watching, mid-winter for bracing coastal solitude, or during the idyllic months in between—Maryland's Atlantic barrier island Ocean City is a versatile coastal destination.

410/974–0341 in Virginia ⊕ www.cbbt.com). **William Preston Lane Jr. Bridge– Chesapeake Bay Bridge** (*P877/229–7726 ⊕ www.baybridge.com*)

ABOUT THE RESTAURANTS

Clearly "seafood"—finned fish and shellfish from the Chesapeake and its tributaries—reigns. Many menus include local dishes and seasonal highlights, such as corn and cantaloupe ("'lopes") in the summertime.

ABOUT THE HOTELS

Outside of Cambridge's singular Hyatt Regency and Ocean City's approximately 10,000 hotel rooms—the great majority of accommodations throughout this region are B&Bs, inns, and budget chain hotels. The scope of choice is broad, yet as might be expected, the quality and level of service of these smaller enterprises varies dramatically. Many B&Bs and inns have teamed up with other tourism enterprises to create packages that include boating, golf, and tennis, visits to art galleries and museums, and more.

Of note: B&Bs and inns throughout Maryland's and Virginia's Eastern Shore commonly require two-night minimum stays on weekends during periods of high demand, most often throughout the summer months, sometimes in late spring and early fall, and during special events such as town-wide festivals.

9

WHAT IT COSTS					
	¢	$	$$	$$$	$$$$
Restaurants	under $10	$10–$16	$17–$23	$24–$30	over $30
Hotels	under $100	$101–$160	$161–$230	$231–$300	over $300

Restaurant prices are per person for a main course at dinner. Hotel prices are for a standard double room, excluding state tax.

PLANNING YOUR TIME

Among the nine counties of Maryland's Eastern Shore and the two on Virginia's Eastern Shore, planning a circuitous, nonrepetitive route can be difficult. Most travelers follow the Eastern Shore's county roads from small town to town along the Chesapeake Bay. The north–south orientation of the region, bridges and ferries, narrow roads, and small towns require getting off the highway and slowing down. In Virginia, the narrowness of the land makes it easy to go between the Atlantic and the Bay. The Bay's enigmatic islands are easy day trips, but an overnight on one of them means planning within the limited schedules of the ferries that serve them.

EXPLORING THE EASTERN SHORE

Maryland's Eastern Shore is readily accessible from the north via any number of routes out of eastern Pennsylvania and northern Delaware and from the east out of Delaware. However, only two bridges cross the Chesapeake Bay, one connecting the region to the Maryland mainland to the west, the other to the Virginia mainland to the south. The William Preston Lane Jr. Bridge,"the Bay Bridge," crosses northeast of Annapolis; its dual spans stretch 4.5 mi across. From the south, the impressive 17.5-mi Chesapeake Bay Bridge-Tunnel connects Norfolk, Virginia Beach, and other Tidewater-area towns to the south with lower Delmarva, Virginia's Eastern Shore.

QUEEN ANNE'S COUNTY

The eastern landfall of the Bay Bridge, which carries U.S. 50/301, is Kent Island, home to historic Stevensville and a thriving cluster of waterside restaurants, bars, lodging, and marinas surrounding the slim Kent Narrows channel. This island gateway is 5.5 mi wide where U.S. 50/301 crosses it, and 14 mi long. William Claiborne established Maryland's first permanent settlement here in 1631 as part of Virginia.

ESSENTIALS

Queen Anne's County Office of Tourism & Exploration Hall (⊠ *425 Piney Narrows Rd., Chester* ☎ *410/604–2100 or 888/400–7787* ⊕ *www.discover queenannes.com*).

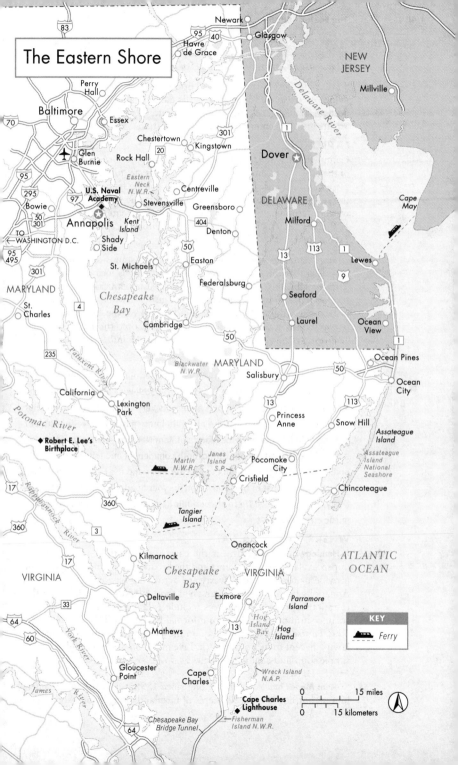

STEVENSVILLE

10 mi east of Annapolis via U.S. 50/301.

Stevensville, just north of the Bay Bridge's eastern landfall, is a growing village of artists and craftspeople. Its galleries and studios sell original pottery, stained glass, and painted furniture as well as antiques and fine art. Its historic center has been on the National Register since 1986.

EXPLORING

Completed in 1809, the **Cray House** is a glimpse into middle-class life of the early 19th century. The two-story cottage, furnished with period pieces, sits in a little yard surrounded by a picket fence. Also on the site, the restored **Stevensville Train Depot,** from the early 1900s, was the western terminus of the old Queen Anne's Railroad Company system. ⊠*Cockey La.* ☎*410/643–5969* 🖃*Donations accepted* 🕑*May–Oct., 1st Sat. of month and by appointment.*

Guitar aficionados will understand what PRS stands for, but might be surprised that the **Paul Reed Smith Guitars factory** is located not in New York or Chicago, but in Stevensville. Visitors can take tours of this revered name in music and admire the intricate woodworking of each instrument. Tours Monday–Wednesday at 4 PM the first three weeks of the month require a minimum of four people (no children under 12); reserve four to eight weeks in advance. ⊠*380 Log Canoe Circle* ⊠*410/643–9970* 🖃*Free.*

NEED A BREAK? With its glow-in-the-dark green and yellow exterior colors, the **Jetty** (⊠ *201 Wells Cove Rd., Grasonville* ⊠ *410/827–4959* w*www.jettydockbar.com*) strives for an aura of the tropics among its very laid-back crowd. Popular with area residents and visitors alike, its large, partially covered outdoor seating area juts out over the waters of Kent Narrows—hence its name. It's a prime spot to watch boat traffic, both commercial and leisure, traversing under a drawbridge between the Chester River and the Eastern Bay. Drinks are strong and most of the food is bad for your health, but it's fun and (relatively) family-friendly. There are periodic karaoke nights and occasional live music on weekends.

WHERE TO STAY & EAT

$$–$$$ ✕**Hemingway's.** Perched near the eastern end of the Bay Bridge, the
SEAFOOD upper-level indoor dining area and the broad veranda of this restaurant provide panoramic views westward across the Bay and of the city of Annapolis beyond. Sunsets can rival those off Key West, home of the restaurant's namesake. Entrées include Atlantic salmon and coconut sesame shrimp. In summer an informal bar and grill, Lola's, opens at 5 PM Thursday through Sunday on the lower level, with tables on the lawn adjacent to its private dock. Live music on weekends enhances its simple soup-and-sandwich menu. ⊠ *357 Pier 1 Rd.* ☎*410/643–2722* 🖃*AE, D, MC, V.*

$$ 🏨**Kent Manor Inn.** A summer hotel since 1898, this imposing antebellum manor house is on 226 acres of farmland along Thompson Creek

near the Chesapeake Bay. Many guest rooms have cozy window seats, others Italian marble fireplaces. All rooms on the upper floors open onto semiprivate verandas. The in-house restaurant serves continental meals in two elegant Victorian dining rooms or in an enclosed porch. **Pros:** pleasant, relaxed environment; waterside setting is perfect for wandering around; unique alternative to many chains in the area. **Cons:** as a popular wedding venue, it is often busy weekends; book well in advance. ⊠ *500 Kent Manor Dr.* ☎ *410/643–7716 or 800/820–4511* ⊕ *www.kentmanor.com* 🛏 *20 rooms, 4 suites* ♿ *In-hotel: restaurant, bar, tennis court, pool, no-smoking rooms, no elevator* ⊟ *AE, D, MC, V* ⫣ *BP.*

SPORTS & THE OUTDOORS

You can stroll or roll along the 6-mi **Cross Island Trail** between Kent Narrows on the western edge of Kent Island and Bay beachfront on its eastern side. Here the flat, smoothly paved or hard-packed trail joins the **Terrapin Nature Area,** 279 lush acres comprised of five identifiable habitats: wetlands, woodlands, wildflower meadows, tidal ponds, and sandy beaches. There is ample parking at both ends of the trail.

Bicycles are available for rent at Chester's **Happy Trails Bicyle Shop** (⊠ *Castle Marina Rd., behind McDonald's, Chester* 21619 ☎ *410/643–0670*), which also hosts escorted group rides of 15 to 30 mi Sunday at 9 AM, weather permitting.

SHOPPING

Old Stevensville's popular art gallery, the **Kent Island Federation of Art** (⊠ *405 Main St.* 21666 ☎ *410/643–7424*), showcases local artists. **Ye Olde Church House** (⊠ *426 Love Point Rd.* 21666 ☎ *410/643–6227*) in old Stevensville is just that, a de-sanctified church, but now it's a shop filled with crafts and hand-spun yarn, hand-dipped candles, old-fashioned soap and candy, and the occasional antique. With sheep grazing in the pasture next door, it's hard to miss and worth seeking out.

9

GRASONVILLE

7 mi east of Stevensville, 21 mi east of Annapolis via U.S. 50/301.

Follow the scenic byway, old two-lane Route 18, across Kent Island and over an aging drawbridge across Kent Narrows to reach quiet Grasonville. The modest homes and shops of the town are a pleasant alternative to the east–west U.S. 50 highway route. Most restaurants and lodging are clustered around scenic Kent Narrows, the waterway between Kent Island's eastern side and the mainland.

SPORTS & THE OUTDOORS

Operated by the Wildfowl Trust of North America, the 500 acres of the **Chesapeake Bay Environmental Center** will open your eyes, ears, and mind to the wildfowl and waterscapes that characterize Maryland's Eastern Shore. The aviary and waterfowl ponds are full of ducks, geese, swans, and birds of prey. Pause a moment in a secluded blind and explore native woodlands, marshes, and meadows along 4 mi of trails. A visitor center and picnic facilities are on the grounds. ⊠ *600 Discovery*

BOATING IN QUEEN ANNE'S COUNTY

Experienced and hospitable, **C&C Charters** (⊠ *Mears Point Marina, 506 Kent Narrows Way N* ☎ *410/827–7888 or 800/733–7245* ⊕ *www.cccharters.com*) has a fleet of power- and sailboats over 30 feet for bare-boat or captained charter. **Tuna the Tide Charter Service** (⊠ *404 Greenwood Creek La.* ☎ *410/827–5635 or 410/827–6188*) has two boats for light tackle and fly-fishing expeditions as well as for crabbing or a sightseeing cruise.

Queen Anne's County has 18 public landings for boats of all sizes. Of these, nine have trailer-launching ramps, but the others are "unimproved" and can be used only for canoes, kayaks, and other small boats that can be carried to the water. A seasonal or daily permit is required to launch a boat from public landing ramps and for parking at these sites. For locations where permits may be purchased, contact **Parks and Recreation** (☎ *410/758–0835*).

La., Grasonville ☎ *410/827–6694* w*www.bayrestoration.org* ⊠ *$5* ☉ *Daily 9–5, except major holidays.*

WHERE TO EAT

$$–$$$ ✕ **Harris Crab House & Seafood Restaurant.** On the mainland side of Kent
SEAFOOD Narrows, this family-friendly institution serves fresh catch directly from
☺ local watermen, some of whom are Harris family members. Nautical
★ decor prevails in the large dining room, including an intriguing collection of oyster cans from an adjacent abandoned oyster house. Views over the shallow, twisting northern end of the Narrows toward the Eastern Neck National Wildlife Refuge can be stunning. Cream-of-crab soup and back-fin crab cakes are among the best around—the cakes are spicy enough to promote plenty of beer drinking. ⊠ *433 Kent Narrows Way N, Grasonville* ☎ *410/827–9500* ⊕ *www.harriscrabhouse. com* ⊟ *MC, V.*

$$–$$$ ✕ **The Narrows.** The spacious contemporary dining room, its porchlike
SEAFOOD extension, and an adjacent bar all face southward to the Eastern Bay
Fodor'sChoice and across this restaurant's slim namesake waterway separating Kent
★ Island from the Eastern Shore mainland. One of the region's largest commercial fishing fleets is harbored next door. Specialties include a Caesar salad with fried oysters and grilled peppered tuna, served over sautéed spinach; and Crab Imperial, lump crabmeat, and select oysters baked with imperial sauce, topped with bacon. The Narrows's dinner menus include "Light Suppers," that encourage a second look at the to-die-for—or –from—desserts listing. ⊠ *3023 Kent Narrows Way S, Grasonville* ☎ *410/827–8113* ⊕ *www.thenarrowsrestaurant. com* ⌂ *Reservations essential* ⊟ *AE, D, DC, MC, V.*

QUEENSTOWN

11 mi east of Stevensville

The cove of Queenstown's harbor is protected by a bend of the mouth of the Chester River. Established in 1707 as "Queen Anne's Town," it became an important-enough port to be attacked by the British during the War of 1812. An erstwhile fishermen's community, it's worth a quick drive through and along its north-side water's edge

SPORTS & THE OUTDOORS

Queenstown is home to a pair of the finest golf courses in the region, both of which are part of **Queenstown Harbor Golf Links** (✉ *32 Links La., off Rte. 301, just beyond Rte. 50/301 split* ☎ *410/827–6611 or 800/827–5257* ⊕ *www.mdgolf.com*). The River Course and the adjacent Lakes Course, par 71 and par 72 respectively, have 36 holes beside the place where the Chester River flows into the Bay. Fees range from $49 for 9 holes on weekdays on "The Lakes," to $69 for 18 holes on weekends on "The Lakes," and $119 for 18 holes on weekends along "The River."

SHOPPING

A major lure to discount seekers year-round—and a traditional stopover between the urban centers to the west of the Chesapeake Bay and the beaches in the summertime—**Prime Outlets Queenstown** (✉ *441 Outlet Center Dr., at the U.S. 50/301 split* ☎ *410/827–8699 wwww.prime outlets.com* ☉ *Apr.–Dec, daily 9–9; Jan.–Mar., daily 10–9*), just 10 mi east of the Bay Bridge at the Routes 50/301 split, is a factory outlet complex comprised of 60 upscale factory outlet stores.

KENT COUNTY

Not unlike most of Maryland's Eastern Shore, Kent County is steeped in history and determined to preserve it. Its idyllic location between the Chester and Sassafras rivers is enhanced by a long, ragged Chesapeake Bay shoreline, many of its hidden hamlets untouched by time and savoring their quiet anonymity, while others struggle to balance their discovery by immigration from northern states with their heritage of 300 years.

ESSENTIALS

Kent County Tourism Development Office (✉ *400 High St., Chestertown* ☎ *410/778–0416* ⊕ *www.kentcounty.com*).

CHESTERTOWN

47 mi northeast of Annapolis via U.S. 50/301 to Rte. 213, 24 mi north of Queenstown via U.S. 301 to Rte. 213.

Second only to Annapolis in its concentration of 18th-century houses, Chestertown was a major international port in Colonial days: a tall, brick customhouse continues to dominate the High Street waterfront. Still the home of families whose local roots go back many generations, the town has its share of newer residents, many of them retirees. Today inns and good restaurants, fine-art galleries, and antiques shops line the brick pavements of High Street, Chestertown's broad, tree-lined main street. To walk along its narrow streets, some of them cobbled, is to commune quietly with some of the country's oldest history. At the northern edge of Chestertown is **Washington College,** one of the nation's oldest liberal-arts institutions. George Washington helped found the college in 1782 through a gift of 50 guineas.

TOURS   **Historic Chestertown and Kent County Tours** (☎*410/778–2829*) schedules guided, narrated walking tours (by appointment only) that focus on history and architecture.

EXPLORING

Geddes-Piper House, home of the Historical Society of Kent County, is a splendid Federal-style home containing 18th-century furniture and an impressive teapot collection, a historical library, and a shop. It's a good place to begin a visit to Chestertown. ☒*Church Alley* ☎*410/778–3499* ☒*Donation suggested* ☉*Hrs. vary seasonally.*

The **Sultana**, a reproduction of a 1768 Colonial schooner by the same name, was launched in 2001. With a length of 97 feet, the original *Sultana* was the smallest schooner ever registered on the Royal Navy Lists. The modern mission of this "Schoolship of the Chesapeake" is to provide unique, hands-on educational experiences in Colonial history and environmental science. Several two-hour public sails are available each month from April through November. Daylong public sails are scheduled on occasion. The *Sultana* can be seen close-up when she is anchored in the Chester River, at the end of Cannon Street *(see also When to Go).* Additionally, half-day guided paddle tours operated by Sultana management are also available a few times a year in various Kent Count rivers. ☒*105 S. Cross St.* ☎*410/778–5954* ⊕*www.sultana projects.org* ☒ *$30* ⚓*Reservations essential.*

OFF THE
BEATEN
PATH   ★

About 10 minutes drive east of Chestertown is **Dixon's Furniture Auction** (☒*2017 Dudley Corner Rd., at intersection of Rtes. 290 and 544, Crumpton* ☎*410/928–3006* ⊕*www.crumptonauctions.com*), a Maryland Eastern Shore institution—with much more than just furniture (although there are literally a couple of acres of that). Hundreds of pieces, "other people's junk" and real treasures, are sold out in the open, regardless of the weather. A huge shed houses smaller items defying easy description, from atlases to zithers. The auction is held every Wednesday of the year (Christmas week excepted) beginning at 8 AM.

WHERE TO EAT

$$–$$$ ✕**Blue Heron Café.** This relaxed, contemporary dining room has high,
SEAFOOD   sloped ceilings and skylights. Among its crab offerings and pasta, as well as chops and steaks, the café's most sought-after entrée is baked rockfish, but don't overlook the oyster fritters, a signature dish. Weekend nights are busy, and the service here is genuine and attentive. ☒*236 Cannon St.* ☎*410/778–0188* ⊕*www.blueheroncafe.com* ☐*AE, MC, V* ☉*Closed Sun.*

$$ ✕**Brooks Tavern.** A pair of seasoned professionals have converted Colo-
ECLECTIC   nial-era Radcliffe Mill—"the old mill"—into one of the finest restau-
Fodor'sChoice   rants in the area. In an atmosphere rustic and casual, yet chic, diners
★   sit between solid wooden floors and exposed supporting beams. The superbly talented chef co-owner describes his cuisine as evolutionary and ever-changing, his ingredients as local, seasonal, and fresh. Favorite

entrées include roast and stir-fried duck with rice noodles and vegetables in a coconut curry sauce and a trademarked crab steak in lemon-butter sauce. There is also a "kitchen table," where you can watch the preparations, and a small separate bar. ⊠ *870 High St.* ☎*410/810–0012* ⊕*www.brookstavern.com* ⌃*Reservations not accepted* ▤*AE, MC, V* ⊘*Closed Sun. and Mon.*

¢ ✕**Feast of Reason.** Head to this popular boutiquelike lunch spot for the
CAFÉ daily quiche special or innovative sandwiches with uncommon ingredients, including roast beef with pesto mayonnaise on French bread; or tomatoes, spinach, zucchini, and sprouts in a garlic herb wrap. "The Feast" will wrap your lunch to go for a picnic on the dock of the river. For dessert, try a cookie, a brownie, a granola bar, or a "fuslbous." A "fuslbous"? Try one, then ask the proprietor how this item got its name. ⊠*203 High St.* ☎*410/778–3828* ▤*MC, V* ⊘*Closed Sun. No dinner.*

¢ ✕**Play It Again, Sam.** This is the place to mingle with C'town residents
AMERICAN as well as with Washington College students and local pols, for good conversation—indoors or alfresco—over fresh coffee (including excellent espresso) or fine wine, by the glass or bottle, to accompany hearty, healthy soups, salads, and sandwiches. Friday night is "wine night" with complimentary hors d'oeuvres, often accompanied by live music. Wi-Fi's in the air here. ⊠*108 S. Cross St.* ☎*410/778–2688* ▤*AE, D, MC, V.*

WHERE TO STAY

$$ 🏨**Brampton Bed & Breakfast Inn.** On 20 wooded acres between the Chester River and the Chesapeake Bay, about 1 mi south of downtown Chestertown, this mid-19th-century inn, known for its gracious hospitality, still resembles the plantation house it once was. The brick building's entrance has a 3½-story walnut-and-ash staircase, pine floors, and plaster ceiling medallions. All of the spacious, well-appointed guest rooms have working fireplaces, and five have hot tubs. Classic movies, available from the innkeepers' private collection, can be viewed in the library, which also has an extensive supply of books. Rates include a full country breakfast and afternoon tea with homemade pastries. **Pros:** exceptional waterside locale; hospitable B&B experience. **Cons:** not in the center of Chestertown. ⊠*25227 Chestertown Rd., Rte. 20 W* ☎*410/778–1860* ⊕*www.bramptoninn.com* ⇗*10 rooms* ⌂*In-room: no phone, no TV (some). In-hotel: no kids under 12, no-smoking rooms, some pets allowed, no elevator* ▤*AE, D, MC, V* �🍴*BP.*

$$ 🏨**Great Oak Manor.** On 12 acres sloping gently to a gazebo on the edge of its private Chesapeake beach, this stately 18th-century Georgian brick manor house provides a taste of Eastern Shore gentility. Its antique furnishings and Oriental rugs, along with an airy sunporch, re-create a bygone era. Of its 11 impeccably decorated guest rooms, 5 have working fireplaces. The manor's formal library is well stocked with both books and films. If needed, guests are provided transportation to the restaurant of their choice for dinner. Golf and tennis are available at neighboring Great Oak Landing. **Pros:** stunning waterside location. **Cons:** formal period decor may be stuffy. ⊠*10568 Cliff Rd.* ☎*410/778–5943 or 800/504–3098* ⊕*www.greatoak.com* ⇗*11 rooms*

9

&In-room: VCR. In-hotel: beachfront, bicycles, no-smoking rooms, no elevator, no kids ⊟AE, D, MC, V ○|BP.

$–$$ 🏨 **Imperial Hotel.** This three-story brick structure on Chestertown's main street was built in 1903 for traveling salesmen. Today it is a gathering center for residents and visitors alike. Guest rooms and suites with authentic period furnishings, as well as custom-designed and hand-crafted pieces, some of which hide TVs and telephones, strive for a blend of 20th-century eras. The heated towel rack in every room gently breaks the mold. The hotel's four dining areas, including one outside in the summertime, all serve regional dishes such as rack of lamb with toasted pecans and peanuts, as well as Asian-Mediterranean creations, described as "eclectic contemporary cuisine." **Pros:** a pleasant alternative to pervasive Colonial historical sites; good on-site dining. **Cons:** historic property's amenities may not be up to modern travelers' expectations. ⊠*208 High St.* ☎*410/778–5000* ⊕*www.imperialchestertown. com* ⇨*11 rooms, 2 suites* &*In-room: Wi-Fi. In-hotel: restaurant, no-smoking rooms, no elevator* ⊟*AE, MC, V.*

$$ 🏨 **White Swan Tavern.** Step back in time at this inn restored to its appear-
★   ance circa 1790. Built as a home in 1733, it was a tavern, then a general store; it may be the town's oldest building. Brick fireplaces and deep window seats, an old writing desk, and pewter candleholders are all in keeping with its Colonial past. The original kitchen, shaded by a giant elm, is the inn's most requested guest room. Its rough ceiling beams, brick floor, and large fireplace attest to its antiquity. Afternoon tea is served in the dining room, on the rear stone patio, or in guest rooms. **Pros:** historic inn; in the heart of the historic district. **Cons:** small rooms; few amenities. ⊠*231 High St.* ☎*410/778–2300* ⊕*www.whiteswan tavern.com* ⇨*4 rooms, 2 suites, 2 apartments* &*In-room: no phone, no TV. In-hotel: public Wi-Fi, no-smoking rooms, no elevator* ⊟*MC, V* ○|*CP.*

NIGHTLIFE & THE ARTS

Younger and older C'town residents alike head to **Andy's** (⊠*337½ High St.* ☎*410/778–6779* ⊕*www.andys-ctown.com*) when they're looking for an unpretentious nightspot with the aura of an "everybody-knows-your-name" neighborhood pub.

ROCK HALL

13 mi southwest of Chestertown via Rte. 291 to Rte. 20.

No longer just a side trip, Rock Hall, its hardy maritime character intact, has emerged as a viable destination in its own right, to be reached either by road or by boat. It reveres its heritage, despite the pleasure boats anchored in its waters and moored at its docks—which far out-number actual working fishing boats.

EXPLORING

Fodor'sChoice   At the tip of the Eastern Neck peninsula, at the mouth of the Chester
★   River, is the superb **Eastern Neck National Wildlife Refuge.** This 2,285-acre park, 8 mi south of Rock Hall, is a prime place to spot migratory water-fowl, wild turkeys, Delmarva fox squirrels, and southern bald eagles,

undeterred by the experimental power-generating solar panels and wind turbines installed nearby. Nearly 6 mi of roads and trails and an observation tower provide excellent vantage points. ✉*1730 Eastern Neck Rd.* ☎*410/639–7056* ⊕*www.fws.gov/northeast/eastern neck* ☉*Daily dawn–dusk.*

The **Waterman's Museum** profiles the hard life on the Bay in absorbing detail, celebrating a Chesapeake way of life that is dying out. On display are exhibits on oystering and crabbing that include historical photos and local carvings, as well as preserved examples of the watermen's all-important boats and a reproduction of a waterborne shanty. ✉*20880 Rock Hall Ave.* ☎*410/778–6697* ✉*Free* ☉*May–Sept. daily 8–5; Oct.–Apr., weekdays 8–5, Sat. 9–5, Sun. 10–4.*

WHERE TO STAY & EAT

$–$$
SEAFOOD
✕**Waterman's Crabhouse.** This casual dockside restaurant looking southward toward the Chesapeake Bay Bridge in the distance has lots of local color. The menu includes ribs, steaks, and fried oysters, but its crab dishes are legendary, as are its homemade cheesecake and key lime pie. Warm summer weekends mean live entertainment and seating on the 40-foot deck. There's a deep-draft dock for diners arriving by boat. ✉*21055 Sharp St.* ☎*410/639–2261* ⊕*www.watermanscrabhouse. com* ▤*AE, D, MC, V* ☉*Closed Jan. and Feb.*

$–$$
AMERICAN
▥**The Inn at Osprey Point.** On 30 lush acres along Swan Creek, this stately Colonial-era building welcomes guests with brick fireplaces and exposed beams; four-poster, canopied beds; and a spacious two-room Escapade suite with French doors and a marble bath with a whirlpool hot tub. But it's worth staying here for the views alone. At the inn's restaurant regional fare is served. The cream-of-crab soup with sherry is a favorite among regulars, as are entrées such as Maryland jumbo lump crab cakes and pan-seared duck breast. Osprey Point Marina, with 160 slips, welcomes transient boaters year-round. **Pros:** great views; quintessential Chesapeake Bay elegance. **Cons:** some visitors may find modern marina clashes with historical ambience. ✉*20786 Rock Hall Ave.* ☎*410/639–2194* ⊕*www.ospreypoint.com* ⇆*15 rooms, 1 suite* ⌂*In-room: no phone. In-hotel: restaurant, pool, no-smoking rooms, bicycles, no elevator* ▤*D, MC, V* ☉*CP.*

SPORTS & THE OUTDOORS

Canoeing and kayaking on quiet creeks and rivers throughout the Eastern Shore's ragged western shorelines are popular pastimes here. Two firms in Kent County provide rentals, tours, and lessons for the area: there are also good sources for waterside camping advice.

The folks at **Chester River Kayak Adventures** (✉*5758 Main St., Rock Hall* ☎*410/639–2001* ⊕*www.crkayakadventures.com*) also operate two B&Bs. Gear up at **KayakCanoe** (✉ *7280 Swan Creek Rd., 4 mi north of Rock Hall* ☎*410/639–9000*).

CECIL COUNTY

Cecil County includes the northern extremities of Chesapeake Bay. Its western boundary with Harford County, the Susquehanna River, is the Bay's principal northern tributary. Its southern boundary with Kent County is another tributary, the Sassafras River. The all-important Chesapeake and Delaware (C&D) Canal is cut between Cecil's third major river, the Elk, and the Delaware River, a major shipping route that connects Chesapeake Bay with Delaware Bay and the Atlantic Ocean. Its many acres of public parks and forests and well-known horse farms help preserve connections to the land.

ESSENTIALS

Cecil County Tourism (⊠ *1 Seahawk Dr., Suite 114, North East* ☎ *410/996–6290 or 800/232–4595* ⊕ *www.seececil.org*).

CHESAPEAKE CITY

31 mi north of Chestertown via Rte. 213.

As it's a town split dramatically in two by the Chesapeake and Delaware (C&D) Canal, Chesapeake City homes and businesses face each other across the busy waterway. Those sitting at the restaurants and taverns next to the canal often marvel at the giant oceangoing vessels that slide by—seemingly within arm's reach.

TOURS   On half- or full-day itineraries, **Chesapeake Horse Country Tours** (☎ *410/885–2797 or 800/466–1402*), operated by Uniglobe Hill Travel in Chesapeake City, guides visitors through Cecil's stunning emerald acres to historic area churches as well as horse farms that have produced such notable racing legends as Northern Dancer and Kelso.

WHERE TO STAY & EAT

$-$$ ✕ **The Bayard House.** One of the few restaurants in Chesapeake City, the
SEAFOOD Bayard House boasts cuisine and service that would stand out anywhere.
★   Patrons in the know travel to this canal-shop eatery for dishes such as tournedos Baltimore, twin fillets of beef topped with crab and lobster; stuffed Anaheim pepper, chilies stuffed with lobster, crabmeat, and shrimp; and de rigueur Maryland crab cakes. The Maryland crab soup is even more widely renowned. ⊠ *11 Bohemia Ave.* ☎ *410/885–5040* ⊕ *www.bayardhouse.com* ☐ *AE, D, MC, V.*

$-$$ ⌂ **Ship Watch Inn.** Three levels of broad decks mean that every room has a place from which to relax and watch all manner of watercraft, including international shipping vessels, sail in and out of the Chesapeake & Delaware Canal just yards away. (A canal-side hot tub offers an even closer view.) Built as a residence in 1920, this elegant, waterfront B&B blends eclectic furnishings with modern amenities. The decades-old black-and-white photos hanging in the public areas reveal much about the roles the owner-innkeepers' families played in the history of Chesapeake City. The Ship Watch is one of several B&Bs in Chesapeake City. **Pros:** extraordinary location literally on the edge of the C&D Canal; two-night stay not required. **Cons:** few amenities. ⊠ *401 1st*

*St. 📞410/885–5300 ⊕www.shipwatchinn.com ⇥8 rooms, 2 suites
♿In-hotel: no-smoking rooms, no elevator ▤AE, MC, V ⦿BP.*

NORTH EAST

12 mi northwest of Chesapeake City via Rte. 213 and Rte. 40.

Uncommon neighborliness along a main street of antiques and collectibles shops and homey eateries gives Cecil's riverside county seat its welcoming charm.

EXPLORING

The **Day Basket Factory** has been crafting oak baskets by hand since 1876. Skilled craftspeople and weavers use techniques passed down through the generations; you can often watch them as they work. ⊠*714 S. Main St. 📞410/287–6100 wwww.daybasketfactory.com ⊘ Wed.–Fri. 10:30–5, Sat. 10–5, Sun. 1–5; until 6 PM on Sat. in summer.*

About 6 mi south of the town of North East, **Elk Neck State Park** juts into the headwaters of the Chesapeake Bay to its west, with the Elk River flowing along its eastern flank. You can drive almost the length of the peninsula and then walk about a mile through pleasant woodlands to the cliffs on its tip. There you can find the sparkling-white Turkey Point Lighthouse, albeit no longer in use. The 270-plus-degree view from Turkey Point is stunning. Campsites are available here, as are some charming 1950s-era wooden cabins that are admirably well maintained. Elk Neck is a prime location for picnicking as well as for fishing and swimming off sandy beaches. ⊠*Rte. 272 south of North East 📞410/287–5333 or 888/432–2267 ⊕www.dnr.state.md.us/public lands/central/elkneck.html.*

You could spend a weekend in the **5&10 Antique Market.** Originally the Hotel Cecil, it became Cramer's 5&10, an old-fashioned variety store operated by a pair of proprietors who themselves became historic treasures. The building's enterprising current owner created an antiques mart, but fully restored the building's exterior and retained its well-worn wood flooring, candy jars, and display counters. ⊠*111 S. Main St. 📞410/287–8318.*

The two spacious buildings of the **Upper Bay Museum** at the head of the North East River preserve the rich heritage of both the commercial and recreational hunter. This unusual museum houses an extensive collection of boating, fishing, and hunting artifacts native to the Upper Chesapeake Bay: sleek sculling oars, rare working decoys, and the outlawed "punt" gun and "gunning" rigs. ⊠*Walnut St. at Rte. 272 📞410/287–2675 ⊘Sat. 10–3, Sun. 10–4.*

WHERE TO STAY & EAT

$–$$
SEAFOOD
🐛

✕**Woody's Crab House.** You can buy crabs here, of course, and have them served any number of imaginative ways. But slurp one of the thick homemade soups, or down the famous Carolina shrimp burger, to understand why this funky little eatery is so popular. The children's menu is a thoughtful extra. But go easy on the real food: Woody's ice-cream parlor, next door, includes seasonal favorite flavors such as apple, pumpkin, and Fourth of July (a celebration of red, white, and blue ice creams). ⊠*29 S. Main St.* ☎*410/287–3541* ⊕*www.woodyscrabhouse. com* ⌂*Reservations not accepted* ▭*D, MC, V.*

¢–$ ☲ **Elk Forge B&B Inn and Retreat.** An easy 20-minute drive from North
★ East, Elk Forge is nestled among 5 acres of woods and gardens along Big Elk Creek. Each of the 12 guest units is beautifully furnished and uniquely decorated, inspired by area locales and cultures, and creature comforts are plentiful. A daily afternoon tea includes the innkeepers' own herbal blends; services at the Spa in the Garden include Swedish massage and aromatherapy facials. With easy access to sites of interest in Delaware and Pennsylvania as well as Maryland, Elk Forge is indeed a miniresort. **Pros:** attractively priced considering available spa amenities. **Cons:** might seem somewhat remote to some. ⊠*807 Elk Mills Rd., Elk Mills* ☎*410/392–9007 or 877/355–3674* ⊕*www.elkforge. com* ➥*7 rooms, 5 suites* ⌂*In-room: VCR, Wi-Fi. In-hotel: spa, gym, no-smoking rooms* ▭*AE, MC, V* ⦶*BP.*

TALBOT COUNTY

Water defines the landscape of Talbot County, which has some of the region's most vibrant little towns, including Easton and St. Michaels. The Chesapeake Bay forms its western border, and the meandering Choptank River slices through the Delmarva Peninsula to form its southern and eastern borders. Waterfront hamlets that started as fishing villages now include comfortable inns and downtown B&Bs. Fine waterside restaurants and folksy main-street taverns are also part of this comfortably refined region.

ESSENTIALS
Talbot County Office of Tourism (⊠*11 S. Harrison St., Easton* ☎*410/770–8000* ⊕*www.tourtalbot.org*).

EASTON

★ *79 mi south of North East and 36 mi south of Chestertown via Rte. 213 and U.S. 50, 36 mi southeast of Annapolis via U.S. 50/301 to U.S. 50.*

Well-preserved buildings dating from Colonial through Victorian times still grace this affluent, genteel town. Fine art galleries, high-quality antiques shops, and gift boutiques sit side by side along North Harrison Street as well as the small midtown mall called Talbottown. Downtown Easton's tree-lined streets present an eclectic collection of boutique-style shops. Strolling Harrison Street—between the Talbottown shopping complex and the Academy Art Museum—and parts of parallel Washington Street, as well as their cross streets, can be at once eminently rewarding and soberingly expensive.

EXPLORING

★ In its 1820s-era schoolhouse, the **Academy Art Museum** houses a permanent collection of fine art by such American artists as James McNeil Whistler, Grant Wood, Lichtenstein, and Rauschenberg, as well as Chagall and Dürer. Special exhibitions often cover local artists, and the juried art show the museum holds in early October is one of the finest in the region. ⊠ *106 South St.* ☎ *410/822–2787 or 410/822–0455* ⊕ *www.art-academy.org* ⊡ *$3* ⊙ *Mon., Fri. and Sat. 10–4; Tues.–Thurs. 10–8.*

A three-story Federal brick house restored by a Quaker cabinetmaker in 1810 houses the **Historical Society of Talbot County,** which maintains a small museum of local history and manages Tharpe Antiques. The society also operates Three Centuries Tours, a one-hour overview of authentically furnished homes of the 17th through 19th centuries. ⊠ *25 S. Washington St.21601* ☎ *410/822–0773* ⊕ *www.hstc.org* ⊡ *$5* ⊙ *Mon.–Sat. 10–4. Guided house tours Tues.–Sat. 11:30 and 1:30.*

Rebellious citizens gathered at the **Talbot County Courthouse** to protest the Stamp Act in 1765 and to adopt the Talbot Resolves, a forerunner of the Declaration of Independence. Today the courthouse, built in 1712 and expanded in 1794, along with two wings added in the late 1950s, is still in use. ⊠ *11 N. Washington St.* ☎ *410/770–8001* ⊙ *Weekdays 8–5.*

WHERE TO EAT

$$ ╳ **General Tanuki's.** A most unusual and exciting blend of Pacific Rim,
ECLECTIC California surf, and grandma's kitchen await adventurous taste buds in this intimate venue. A *tanuki* is akin to a Japanese leprechaun, and the creative flavors here play tricks on traditional dishes. Imagine a restaurant serving buttery sushi and sashimi, lamb lettuce wraps, thai mussels simmered in Woodpecker cider, and a classic Hawaiian pizza under one roof. Run, don't walk, to this place, and make sure to check out happy hour (4–6 PM) at the U-shape bar. ⊠ *25 Goldsborough St.* ☎ *410/819–0707* ⊕ *www.generaltanukis.com* ⊟ *MC, V.*

$$$$ ╳ **Inn at Easton Restaurant.** The inn's owner-operator chef Andrew Evans
ECLECTIC uses his international training and only the finest ingredients to create global fare. Opened in 2000 within an upscale B&B in a Federal mansion, the inn combines antiques with modern art. The focus is on a three- and four-course prix-fixe menu that is updated regularly. Among the more-unusual items from each course are puree of celeriac soup (whipped crème fraîche and American sturgeon caviar), panfried kasseri cheese with balsamic and oven-roasted vine-ripened tomatoes), and *barramundi en papillote* (red thai curry, jasmine rice, and chili jam). Creative seasonal desserts make up the fourth course, and wine pairings are available starting at an additional $50. ⊠ *28 S. Harrison St.* ☎ *410/822–4910 or 888/800–8091* ⊕ *www.theinneaston.com* ⊟ *AE, D, MC, V* ⊙ *Closed Mon. and Tues. No lunch.*

$$$–$$$$ ╳ **Mason's.** A family-run landmark for more than 30 years, Mason's
AMERICAN uses fresh ingredients from its own garden. The chef brings bold flavors
★ like pan-seared crab cakes topped with a corn and soybean succotash, crispy-skin red snapper surrounded by braised artichokes, and gentle rockfish stuffed with lump crab meat, a local delicacy. Sip a classic

9

martini in the swanky lounge while waiting for a table—make sure to ask for one on the porch in warm weather. Next door is a coffee bar and a food store that sells hard-to-find cheeses and meats, wonderful handcrafted chocolates, and all manner of esoteric edibles. ⊠*42 E. Dover St.* ☎*410/822–3204* ⊕*www.masonsgourmet.com* ⊟*AE, D, MC, V* ⊙*Closed Sun.*

$$$–$$$$
ITALIAN
Fodor'sChoice
★

✕**Scossa.** Surrounded by shops, lodging, and other eateries so very American, sophisticated Scossa almost seems out of place. From Scossa Café, its sidewalk patio with wall-mounted fountains, to its superb menus, it is unmistakably northern Italian. The well-trained co-owners create lunch and dinner dishes with an Italian influence that does not overwhelm the fine ingredients. Samples of daily specials include braised lamp shank with artichokes, short ribs with Borolo wine sauce, roast rabbit *campagnola,* and soft-shell crabs *alla provinciale.* Brunch is available on weekends. Jackets are not required, but the cosmopolitan style of Scossa definitely attracts a well-dressed clientele who reserve ahead. ⊠ *8 N. Washington St.* ☎*410/822-2202* ⚜*Reservations essential* ⊕*www.scossarestaurant.com* ⊟*AE, MC, V* ⊙*Closed Mon.*

WHERE TO STAY

$$–$$$
★

⊞**Inn at Easton.** This B&B is a bit like a boutique hotel, with just seven rooms and suites. While the original molding, doors, plaster walls, and hardwood floors have been preserved in every room of this Federal mansion, built in stages between 1790 and 1894, the guest rooms are stunningly furnished with uncommon contemporary elements complemented by gracious decorative touches and carefully selected color. Australian aboriginal artwork adorns the walls here while original paintings by the Russian impressionist Nikolai Timkov hang in the common areas. Trivia note: The 2006 movie *Wedding Crashers* filmed a reception scene here. **Pros:** exceptional on-site restaurant; old-time charm with modern amenities and style. **Cons:** expensive; not a traditional inn. ⊠*28 S. Harrison St.* ☎*410/822–4910 or 888/800–8091* ⊕*www.theinnateaston.com* ⮡*3 rooms, 4 suites* ⚷*In-room: no TV. In-hotel: restaurant, no kids under 9, no-smoking rooms, no elevator* ⊟*AE, D, MC, V* ⊙*No lunch* ⧀*BP.*

$–$$

⊞**The Tidewater Inn & Conference Center.** This stately four-story brick hotel was built in 1949. Beyond its entry archways, an early-20th-century aura pervades its spacious common areas enhanced by huge fireplaces and paintings of old Easton. Mahogany reproduction furniture fills the guest rooms, most in greens and golds. In the hotel's full-service dining room a "hunting breakfast" is available early every morning in season. To one side of the porte cochere, broad awnings shade an alfresco lobby and sometime dining area. A small on-site spa offers manicures and massages. The Tidewater is a member of the Historic Hotels of America. **Pros:** welcome contrast to ubiquitous Colonial-era lodging; large property has more amenities than local B&Bs. **Cons:** if inn is hosting a conference, individual guests may feel marginalized. ⊠*101 E. Dover St.* ☎*410/822–1300 or 800/237–8775* ⊕*www.tidewaterinn.com* ⮡*114 rooms, 7 suites* ⚷*In-hotel: restaurant, bar, pool, spa, no-smoking rooms, some pets allowed* ⊟*AE, D, MC, V.*

NIGHTLIFE & THE ARTS

With a name like **Chez Lafitte** (⊠*13 S. Washington St.* 21601 ☏*410/770–8868*), you might think that this bar is going to ooze pretentiousness. But no. The owners, a New York actress and her husband, named this intimate yet welcoming piano jazz bar after their Great Dane. The rich furnishings, including giant gilded mirrors and crushed velvet drapes, evoke Parisian bistros. The **Washington Street Pub** (⊠*20 N. Washington St.* 21601 ☏*410/822–9011*) has a raw bar, 19 beers on tap, hardwood floors, a brick wall behind a bar that stretches on and on, and serves the town's legendary "pub chips."

SPORTS & THE OUTDOORS

Most of the fishing and boating tours depart a few miles away in the towns of St. Michaels and Tilghman Island.

Easton Cycle & Sports (⊠*723 Goldsborough St.* ☏*410/822–7433*) specializes in bike rentals as well as kayaks and canoes. **Eastern Shore Adventure Company** (⊠*28290 St. Michaels Rd.* ☏*410/827–0552*) offers kayak rentals and tours of the scenic Wye Island and Tuckahoe rivers.

Hog Neck Golf Course (⊠*10142 Cordova Rd.* ☏*410/822–6079 or 800/280–1790*), one of the best public courses in the state, has an 18-hole, par 72 championship course and a 9-hole, par 32 "Executive" course ($25 walk/$35 ride). Nonresident greens fees are $60–$70.

ST. MICHAELS

9 mi west of Easton via Rte. 33, 49 mi southeast of Annapolis.

St. Michaels, once a shipbuilding center, is today one of the region's premier leisure-time destinations. Its ever-growing popularity has resulted in more and more shops, cafés, waterfront restaurants, and inns. In warmer months, tourists and boaters crowd its narrow streets and snug harbor. Talbot Street is lined with restaurants, galleries, and all manner of shops, including a hardware store that doubles as a retro gift shop.

EXPLORING

Besides any number of tours by boat from several of the waterside towns on Maryland's and Virginia's Eastern Shore, there are day-trip tours into the region from Annapolis and Baltimore. Larger towns, including Annapolis as well as St. Michaels, are home port for diesel- or gasoline-powered tour boats and yachts. **The Patriot** (⊠*Docked near Crab Claw Restaurant and Chesapeake Bay Maritime Museum, End of Mill St., at Harbor* ☏*410/745–3100* ⊕*www.patriotcruises.com*), a 65-foot steel-hull yacht, departs four times daily, from March through September, for one-hour cruises on the Miles River. The tour covers the ecology and history of the area as it passes along the tranquil riverfront landscape.

☾
★ The **Chesapeake Bay Maritime Museum,** one of the region's finest, chronicles the Bay's rich history of boatbuilding, commercial fishing, navigating, and hunting in compelling detail. Exhibits among nine buildings on the 18-acre waterfront site include two of the Bay's unique skipjacks

among the museum's more than 80 historic regional boats. There's also the restored 1879 Hooper Strait Lighthouse, a working boatyard, and a "waterman's wharf" with shanties and oystering and crabbing tools. In the Bay Building you can see a crabbing skiff as well as a dugout canoe hewn by Native Americans. The Waterfowl Building contains carved decoys and stuffed birds, including wood ducks, mallards, and swans. ☒*End of Mill St. at Navy Point, near harbor* ☎*410/745–2916* ⊕*www.cbmm.org* ☜*$13.* ⊙ *Open daily year-round—except Tues.– Thurs. Nov. 14–Jan. 14, but hrs vary seasonally.*

WHERE TO EAT

$–$$ ╳**Crab Claw Restaurant.** Owned and operated by the same family since
SEAFOOD 1965, this St. Michaels landmark started as a clam- and oyster-shucking house for watermen long before that. Diners at both indoor and outdoor tables have panoramic views over the harbor to the river beyond, but dockside tables are the best. As the name suggests, this is *the* down-home place for fresh steamed and seasoned blue crabs. But the extensive menu also includes sandwiches and other light fare as well as other seafood and meat dishes. Children's platters are available, too. ☒*End of Mill St., at harbor* ☎*410/745–2900 or 410/745–9366* ⊕*www.the crabclaw.com* ▤*No credit cards* ⊙ *Closed Dec.–early Mar.*

$$–$$$ ╳**Town Dock Restaurant.** Every seat in this vast restaurant overlooks St.
SEAFOOD Michaels Harbor and the Miles River, every window framing its own scene; the deck is also open. Fresh seafood dishes such as sesame-seared tuna and grilled Atlantic salmon, as well as roast duck with dried cherry glaze—their preparation carefully supervised by award-wining restaurateur Michael Rork—are favorites. Or if you just can't decide, tackle the Land and Sea Buffet, and for a finale sample some strawberries hand-dipped in chocolate. ☒*125 Mulberry St.* ☎*410/745–5577* ⊕*www.town-dock.com* ▤*AE, D, DC, MC, V* ⊙ *Closed Mon.–Thurs. Nov.–Mar.*

$$$–$$$$ ╳**208 Talbot Restaurant & Wine Bar.** Unobtrusively situated on St.
SEAFOOD Michaels's busy main street, 208 Talbot, long a favorite among dis-
★ criminating diners, has several intimate dining rooms with exposed brick walls and brick floors. Specialties include such original first-course dishes as house-cured gravlax served with fresh mango, avocado, jalapeño pesto, and grilled flat bread; and more-traditional second-course entrées such as whole grilled rockfish accompanied by braised greens, grape tomato relish, and hush puppies; as well as a welcome variety of meat dishes. Small plates ($8–$14) are available for more conservative appetites, and on Saturday there's a four-course prix-fixe menu available ($55). ☒*208 N. Talbot St.* ☎*410/745–3838* ⊕*www.208talbot. com* ▤*D, MC, V* ⊙ *Closed Mon.*

WHERE TO STAY

$$–$$$ ▦**Five Gables Inn & Spa.** Three circa-1860 houses have been turned into
★ an elegant and comfortable getaway. All rooms have a private porch or balcony, and all are decorated with antique furnishings, fine linens and towels, and down comforters. The hot stone massage and invigorating rosemary mint body wrap are treatments in the spa. Refreshments are served daily at 3. This St. Michaels bed-and-breakfast also features a

fine needlepoint shop B's Stitches, and an upscale pet boutique Flying Fred's. **Pros:** easy walking throughout St. Michaels thanks to main-street location; shopping and spa options in-house. **Cons:** true resort feel challenged by main-street location. ☒*209 N. Talbot St.* ☎*410/745–0100 or 877/466–0100* ⊕*www.fivegables.com* ⟳*12 rooms, 8 suites* &*In-room: no phone (some), DVD. In-hotel: restaurant, pool, spa, bicycles, no-smoking rooms, some pets allowed (fee), no elevator* ▤*AE, MC, V* ◉*CP.*

$$$$ ⊞**Inn at Perry Cabin.** On 25 acres beside the Miles River, this luxury
★   inn—operated by the world-renowned Orient Express Hotels group—employs a nautical theme throughout to elegant effect. Each unique guest room has elegant appointments; standard amenities include heated towel racks, fresh flowers in all rooms, and afternoon tea. Above all, staying here means impeccable service. Dining at the inn's restaurant with its flawless cuisine and stellar wine selection is an event. The signature crab spring roll with pink grapefruit, avocado, and toasted almonds, and the lamb shank glazed with honey and tarragon are both exquisite. **Pros:** great customer service; riverside location; spa and pool. **Cons:** expensive for the area. ☒*308 Watkins La.* ☎*410/745–2200 or 800/722–2949* ⊕*www.perrycabin.com* ⟳*54 rooms, 27 suites* &*In-room: Wi-Fi. In-hotel: restaurant, spa, bar, pool, concierge, no-smoking rooms* ▤*AE, DC, MC, V.*

$$–$$$ ⊞**The Oaks, a Country Inn.** Antebellum grace defines this 1748 mansion on 17 acres along the banks of Oak Creek, 3 mi from St. Michaels. The antiques-filled inn has a stunning black-and-white tile foyer; its best rooms have fireplaces, private porches, and hot tubs. The day starts with a full country breakfast served in the sunny yellow-and-red dining room. After that, you might want to go fishing off the pier, or head no farther than one of the rockers in the screened porch overlooking the water. **Pros:** affordable; waterside location. **Cons:** some decor clashes with inn's heritage; a short drive from downtown. ☒*Rte. 329 at 329 Acorn La., Royal Oak* ☎*410/745–5053* ⊕*www.the-oaks.com* ⟳*22 rooms, 1 cottage* &*In-hotel: restaurant, pool, bicycles, no-smoking rooms, no elevator* ▤*MC, V* ◉*BP.*

$$–$$$ ⊞**Victoriana Inn.** Adirondack chairs line a sloping expanse of lawn leading to the formal gardens of what was once a Civil War army officer's home. Set on the town's harbor and across a footbridge from the Maritime Museum, this inn is a relaxing haven. All rooms include queen-size beds; two have fireplaces, and three overlook the water. The suite has a private water-view deck and a fireplace as well as a TV. There's a nightly happy hour that includes wine, beer, and light hors d'oeuvres. No children under 13 are allowed on weekends. **Pros:** a revered St. Michaels institution among many favored town sites. **Cons:** location near the harbor can be heavily trafficked. ☒*205 Cherry St.* ☎*410/745–3368* ⊕*www.victorianainn.com* ⟳*6 rooms, 1 suite* &*In-room: no phone, no TV (some). In-hotel: bicycles, no-smoking rooms, no elevator* ▤*MC, V* ◉*BP.*

SPORTS & THE OUTDOORS

Town Dock Marina (✉ *305 Mulberry St.* ☎ *410/745–2400 or 800/678–8980*) rents bicycles as well as surrey-top electric boats and small powerboats.

★ The 1955 32-passenger skipjack HM **Krentz,** (✉ *Docked at the Chesapeake Bay Maritime Museum* ☎ *410/745–6080* ⊕ *www.oystercatcher. com*), captained by owner Edward Farley, is available to the public for sails between early April and late November.

TILGHMAN ISLAND

13 mi southwest of St. Michaels via Rte. 33.

A visit to Tilghman Island provides intriguing insight into the Eastern Shore's remarkable character. Leave your car and explore by bike or kayak. A handful of B&Bs and inns provide excellent accommodations here. A small fleet of working fishing boats, including a few of the region's remaining skipjacks, call Dogwood Harbor their home port.

WHERE TO STAY

$$$ 🏨 **Tilghman Island Inn.** Warm, welcoming conviviality and casual elegance define this compact, modern resort overlooking the Chesapeake Bay and a waterfowl marsh. Decor and furnishings throughout are bright and modern, with lots of white enhanced by splashes of color. Five deluxe waterside suites have hot tubs, fireplaces, and spacious decks. The 5-acre complex includes a 20-slip transient marina and a small fleet of tandem and single kayaks available for rent. Dishes served at the Gallery Restaurant are at once innovative and traditional, enhanced by a well-selected wine list. **Pros:** truly panoramic Bay views; aura of a miniresort. **Cons:** not historic setting; lacking small B&B feel of island's other options. ✉ *Coopertown Rd. (2nd right after Knapps Narrows Bridge)* ☎ *410/886–2141 or 800/866–2141* ⊕ *www.tilghmanislandinn. com* 🛏 *15 rooms, 5 suites* ⚙ *In-room: Wi-Fi. In-hotel: restaurant, bars, tennis court, pool, no-smoking rooms, some pets allowed, no elevator* ▭ *AE, D, DC, MC, V* ⎮◎⎮*CP.*

SPORTS & THE OUTDOORS

★ Built in 1886, the 49-passenger **Rebecca T. Ruark,** (✉ *21308 Phillips Rd., at Dogwood Harbor* ☎ *410/829–3976 or 410/886–2176* ⊕ *www. skipjack.org*), captained by owner Wade Murphy Jr., offers hands-on learning charters from early April into late October. She is the oldest working skipjack on the Bay, and is one of several skipjacks designated as National Historic Landmarks.

OXFORD

7 mi southeast of St. Michaels via Rte. 33 and Rte. 333.

Tracing its roots to 1683, tiny Oxford remains secluded and untrammeled. Robert Morris, a merchant from Liverpool, lived here with his son, Robert Morris Jr., a signer of the Declaration of Independence. The younger Morris helped finance the Revolution but ended up in

The Venerable Skipjacks of the Chesapeake Bay

Settlement along the fertile shores of the Chesapeake Bay was an obvious choice for 17th-century English immigrants, who soon farmed the cash crop of tobacco and plucked plentiful blue crabs and plump oysters from its bottom. Among the reminders of the Bay's fishing culture, which endures, is its dwindling fleet of native skipjacks: broad, flat-bottom wooden sailing vessels for dredging oysters. Economical to build, skipjacks had the shallowest draft—the distance from the waterline to the lowest point of the keel—of any boat in the bay. This made them excellent for cruising above the grassy shoals favored by oysters.

At first, oyster harvesters would stand in small boats and use simple, long-handle tongs, to grasp clumps of oysters from the bottom and bring them aboard. It was tiresome, difficult work. In the early 1800s, sturdy Yankee schooners, having left the depleted waters of New England, entered the Chesapeake Bay with dredges, iron contraptions that dragged up oysters along the bottom. With their first large harvest, Chesapeake's fishing industry changed forever.

Dredging was initially banned as being exploitative and intrusive, first by Virginia and later by Maryland. However, after the Civil War drained the region's economy, Maryland legalized the practice, allowing it under certain conditions for boats powered only by sails. By 1875 more than 690 dredging licenses were issued. Soon more-sophisticated dredgers emerged; all were loosely called *bateaux,* French for "boats."

The oyster bounty was not to last. After peaking in 1884 with 15 million bushels, less than a third of that amount was caught in 1891. Despite the growing use of steam and gasoline power on land and water, "only under sail" dredging laws prevailed in the Bay. As the 19th century drew to a close, boatbuilders were forced to experiment with boat designs that were cheap to build yet had sails that would provide enough power for dredging and transporting the harvests. In 1901 one of these new bateaux appeared in Baltimore's harbor. She caught the eye of a *Baltimore Sun* newspaper reporter, who wrote that their "quickness to go about may have earned for them the name of skipjack." The name stuck. On occasion, skipjacks have been compared to bonito tuna because, like the great Atlantic fish, they seem to skip over the surface of the water.

Oysters—and the Chesapeake's renowned blue crab—are still harvested by a diminishing number of watermen, their fleets of small, flat-bottom boats—sometimes powered by modified automobile engines—concentrated in locales such as Crisfield and Kent Narrows as well as Smith and Tangier islands, but less than a dozen sail-powered skipjacks are still working. Sailing on one of them (generally from early April through October, when they're not dredging) is an exhilarating way to fully experience the culture and history of the Chesapeake. The *Herman M. Krentz,* built in 1955, sails from St. Michaels, and the 80-foot *Rebecca T. Ruark,* originally built in 1886, from Tilghman Island. An authentic replica skipjack, the *Nathan of Dorchester,* also available for sails by the public, is berthed in Cambridge.

9

debtor's prison after losing at land speculation.

Reserve time for Oxford, via the Oxford-Bellevue Ferry, its Bellevue terminus near St. Michaels, if early U.S. history is paramount and time permits. (See also ⊕ *www.portof oxford.com.*)

EN ROUTE The **Oxford-Bellevue Ferry,** begun in 1683, may be the oldest privately owned ferry in continuous operation in the United States. It crosses the Tred Avon River between Bellevue, 7 mi south of St. Michaels (via Routes 33 and 329), and Oxford in 7 to 10 minutes. ⊠ *N. Morris St. at Strand, Oxford* ☎ *410/745–9023* ⊕ *www.oxfordbellevueferry.com* ⊡ *Ferry: $7 car and driver one-way, $4 motorcycle, $3 bicycle, $2 pedestrian* ⊙ *Mar.–Memorial Day and Labor Day–Nov., weekdays 7 AM–sunset, weekends 9 AM–sunset; Memorial Day–Labor Day, weekdays 7 AM–9 PM, weekends 9–9.*

EXPLORING

The **Oxford Museum** displays models and pictures of sailboats. Some boats were built in Oxford, site of one of the first Chesapeake regattas (1860). Check out the full-scale racing boat by the door. Other artifacts include the lamp from a lighthouse on nearby Benoni Point, a sailmaker's bench, and an oyster-shucking stall. Docents elaborate on the exhibits, which set the context for a walking tour of nearby blocks. ⊠ *Morris and Market Sts.* ☎ *410/226–5122* ⊡ *Free* ⊙ *Apr.– Oct., Fri.–Sun. 2–5.*

WHERE TO STAY & EAT

$$–$$$ ✕ **Latitude 38.** A whimsical red, white, and green color scheme; painted
AMERICAN   vines climbing the walls; and polished wooden floors distinguish this bistro. Weather permitting, you can eat outdoors at wrought-iron tables in a brick courtyard. The creative and diverse menu changes twice a month, offering such dishes as veal fettuccine Montrachet topped with goat cheese and a tomato cream sauce, and sauté of seafood including lobster, shrimp, and scallops. ⊠ *26342 Oxford Rd.* ☎ *410/226–5303* ⊕ *www.latitude38.org* ⊟ *AE, D, MC, V* C Closed Mon.

$$$–$$$$ ▥ **Combsberry.** This 1730 brick manor house, together with the carriage
★   house and the Oxford cottage, is set amid magnolias and willows on the banks of Island Creek, a few minutes' drive from Oxford. Inside are five arched fireplaces, floral chintz fabrics, and polished wood floors. All the rooms and suites of this luxurious B&B have water views and are furnished with English manor–style antiques, including four-poster and canopy beds. Some also have hot tubs and working fireplaces; the two-bedroom carriage house has a kitchen. **Pros:** elegantly appointed inn; impeccable service. **Cons:** expensive option. ⊠ *4837 Evergreen Rd.* ☎ *410/226–5353* ⊕ *www.combsberry.net* ⊷ *2 rooms, 2 suites, 1-bedroom cottage, 2-bedroom carriage house* ⚭ *In-room: no phone, no TV. In-hotel: restaurant, no kids under 12, some pets allowed, no elevator* ⊟ *AE, MC, V* ⊚*BP.*

$$–$$$ 🏠**Robert Morris Inn.** In the early 1700s this building on the banks of the Tred Avon River was crafted as a home by ships' carpenters using ship nails, hand-hewn beams, and pegged paneling. In 1738 it was bought by an English trading company as a house for its Oxford representative, Robert Morris. Four guest rooms have handmade wall paneling and fireplaces built of English bricks used as boat ballast. Other buildings in the complex include a newer manor house on a private beach. Breakfast is included. **Pros:** whiffs of history exude from every corner; riverfront setting. **Cons:** three-centuries-old accommodations are difficult to maintain. ⊠*314 N. Morris St.* ☎*410/226–5111* ⊕*www.robertmorrisinn. com* ⇨*35 rooms* ⌂*In-room: no phone, no TV (some), Wi-Fi. In-hotel: beachfront, no-smoking rooms, no elevator* ⊟*AE, MC, V* ⦿*BP.*

DORCHESTER COUNTY

One of the larger, yet more sparsely populated, counties on Maryland's Eastern Shore, Dorchester retains bits of early America in its picture-postcard towns and waterfront fishing villages. The expansive Choptank River, its northern boundary, and the rambling 28,000-acre Blackwater National Wildlife Refuge are idyllic locales for biking and boating, hiking and camping, and hunting, fishing, and crabbing.

ESSENTIALS

Dorchester County Tourism Department (⊠ *2 Rose Hill Pl., Cambridge* ☎*410/ 228–1000 or 800/522–8687* ⊕*www.tourdorchester.org*).

CAMBRIDGE

15 mi southeast of Oxford via U.S. 50, 55 mi southeast of Annapolis via U.S. 50/301 to U.S. 50.

Once upon a time renowned resident Annie Oakley would shoot waterfowl from the ledge of her waterfront home here. Today graceful Georgian, Queen Anne, and Colonial Revival buildings abound, and with an art gallery here and a museum there, a night or two in this county seat can be very refreshing.

EXPLORING

The small **Harriet Tubman Museum & Learning Center** is dedicated to the former slave, born and raised in and around Cambridge, who helped lead more than 300 other slaves to freedom along the Underground Railroad. At the museum, artifacts and documents about her life are on display. ⊠*424 Race St.* ☎*410/228–0401* ✉*Donations accepted* ⊗*Fri. 10–3, Sat. noon–4.*

The **La Grange Plantation** is headquarters to the Dorchester County Historical Society, and houses two historic homes on its property. The three-story, 18th-century Georgian **Meredith House** is rich with Chippendale, Hepplewhite, and Sheraton period antiques, and the Children's Room holds an impressive doll collection, cradles, miniature china, and baby carriages. Portraits and effects of seven former Maryland governors from Dorchester County adorn the Governor's Room.

In the **Neild Museum** are agricultural, maritime, and Native American artifacts. There's also a restored smokehouse, blacksmith's shop, and medicinal herb garden on the grounds. Fall is ablaze with vibrant leaves and many family activities. ⊠ *902 La Grange Ave.* ☎ *410/228–7953* ▦ *Free* ☉ *Weekdays 10–3, and by appointment.*

OFF THE BEATEN PATH

Old Trinity Church. Seven miles southwest of Cambridge stands tiny Old Trinity Church. Built around 1675 and extensively altered in the 1800s, the church has been restored to its 17th-century appearance. In the churchyard are the graves of four governors of Maryland and several members of the distinguished political and clerical Carroll family. Services are still held here every Sunday at 11. ⊠ *Rte. 16 near Church Creek* ☎ *410/228–2940* ☉ *Tours by appointment.*

Spocott Windmill. Maryland's only English post windmill—which, unlike stationary Dutch windmills, can rotate 360 degrees—stands 6 mi west of Cambridge on Route 343. It's a replica of one destroyed in an 1888 blizzard. Also open to the public are the miller's tenant house, a one-room schoolhouse dating to 1868, a country store from the 1930s, a blacksmith's shop, and a period doctor's office. The windmill operates only sporadically for celebrations, but a good gust of wind will give you a great snapshot to take home. ⊠ *Rte. 343* ☎ *410/476–5058* ▦ *Free; donations accepted* ☉ *Mon.–Sat. 10–5.*

WHERE TO STAY & EAT

$$–$$$
AMERICAN

✕ **Snappers Waterfront Cafe.** Join regulars at this casual waterside restaurant and bar on the edge of town that has a wide-ranging menu with a Southwestern flavor. Mexican quesadillas are a Snappers specialty, but there is also an array of burritos, enchiladas, and fajitas. Jamaican jerk spices enhance burgers and crab cakes. From waters close to home, there's shrimp, stuffed or simply fried. Sandwiches, wraps, and pasta also satisfy the local lunch crowd. ⊠ *112 Commerce St.* ☎ *410/228–0112* ⊕ *www.snapperswaterfrontcafe.com* ▤ *AE, D, MC, V.*

$$$$

▦ **Hyatt Regency Chesapeake Bay Golf Resort, Spa and Marina.** This 370-acre complex is the Eastern Shore's first full-service, year-round resort, and one that takes full advantage of the soothing natural light and spectacular views of the Choptank River. The resort includes an 18-acre Blue Heron rookery, an 18,000-square-foot spa, and a golf course designed by Keith Foster. All rooms and suites have a private balcony; those on the upper level have raised ceilings. The resort's restaurants include the self-service Bay Country Market and the Blue Point Provision Company for seafood. Two outdoor sandstone fireplaces make perfect s'more hubs, and a 30-foot-high wall of windows welcomes you to Michener's Library. **Pros:** features and amenities worthy of any world-class resort; expensive. **Cons:** strangely isolated in a region devoid of comparable lodging; can be overwhelmingly large. ⊠ *100 Heron Blvd.* ☎ *410/901–1234* ⊕ *www.chesapeakebay.hyatt. com* ⊅ *384 rooms, 16 suites* ⚿ *In-room: safe, refrigerator, Wi-Fi. In-hotel: 5 restaurants, room service, bar, golf course, tennis courts, pool, gym, spa, beachfront, concierge* ▤ *AE, D, MC, V.*

$$

▦ **Lodgecliffe on the Choptank.** Located on a rise overlooking the river, this elegant turn-of-the-20th-century country home was the first bed-

and-breakfast in the county (1986) and remains one of the most charming. Accommodations include Sarah's Loft, named for the original innkeeper, a delightfully contemporary second-floor room. Don't sleep through breakfast or you might miss cranberry French Toast made with sourdough bread, Chesapeake puff pancakes, or phyllo dough egg blossoms, freshly made and hot from the oven and often served out on the screened-in porch. Guests feel as personal guests of the innkeepers and their two young sons. **Pros:** traditional B&B in the truest sense; less expensive option. **Cons:** almost too personalized an enterprise for some. ✉*103 Choptank Terr.* ☎*866/273–3830* ⊕*www.lodgecliffeonthechoptankbandb.com* ⇆*4 rooms* ♿*In-room: Wi-Fi. In-hotel: restaurant, no-smoking rooms, no elevator* ▤*AE, D, MC, V.*

SPORTS & THE OUTDOORS

All of the land of the **Fishing Bay Wildlife Management Area,** bordering Blackwater National Wildlife Refuge, is along **Fishing Bay** at the southern end of Dorchester County. Here you can take a pair of "water trails" through some scenic rivers and streams—it's reminiscent of Florida's Everglades. A short canoeing or kayaking trek down one of these water trails—recommended only for experienced paddlers—is an exceptional way to experience a salt marsh and the wildlife that lives in one. Contact the Dorchester County Department of Tourism (☎*410/228–1000*) for more information, as well as for a waterproof map.

Rent kayaks and bikes at **Blackwater Paddle & Pedal Adventures** (✉*4303 Bucktown Rd.* ☎*410/901–9255* ⊕*www.blackwaterpaddleandpedal. com*), which also provides guided instruction.

★ The *Nathan of Dorchester,* a skipjack replica commissioned in 1994, cruises the Choptank River from the foot of High Street in Cambridge. In summer the 28-passenger *Nathan* sets sail on most Saturday evenings and Sunday afternoons for two-hour cruises. ✉*Long Wharf, 526 Poplar St.* ☎*410/228–7141* ⊕*www.skipjack-nathan.org.*

BLACKWATER NATIONAL WILDLIFE REFUGE

8 mi south of Cambridge via Rte. 16 to Rte. 335, 63 mi southeast of Annapolis.

The largest nesting bald eagle population north of Florida makes Blackwater its home. You can often see the birds perching on the lifeless tree trunks that poke from the wetlands here, part of nearly 28,000 acres of woods, open water, marsh, and farmland. In fall and spring some 35,000 Canada and snow geese pass through in their familiar V formations to and from their winter home, joining more than 15,000 ducks. The rest of the year, residents include endangered species such as peregrine falcons and silver-hair Delmarva fox squirrels. Great blue heron stand like sentinels while ospreys dive for meals and tundra swans preen endlessly. By car or bike you can follow a 5-mi road through several habitats or follow a network of trails on foot. Exhibits and films in the visitor center provide background and insight. ✉*2145 Key Wallace Dr., at Rte. 335* ☎*410/228–2677* ⊕*www.fws.gov/blackwater* ▤*$3*

9

car, $1 pedestrian or cyclist ⊗ *Wildlife drive daily dawn–dusk. Visitor center weekdays 8–4, weekends 9–5.*

**OFF THE
BEATEN
PATH**
Believed to have been first settled on a Choptank Native American trail in the 1660s, **East New Market** contains some 75 buildings of historic significance—churches, schools, businesses, and residences—representing three centuries. In this living museum of architecture, every exhibit is in its original location. An illustrated walking-tour map is available from the Dorchester County Tourism office (☎ *410/228–1000*).

THE LOWER EASTERN SHORE

The three counties of Maryland's Lower Eastern Shore—Wicomico, Worcester, and Somerset—contain the contrasting cultures of the Chesapeake Bay and the Atlantic coast but still share a common history.

The Nanticoke River flows out of southern Delaware across fertile farmland between Dorchester and Wicomico counties into the Chesapeake Bay's Tangier Sound near the Blackwater National Wildlife Refuge. To the east the Atlantic alternately caresses and pounds Worcester County's sturdy shorelines and fragile barrier islands stretching from the Delaware Bay to easternmost Virginia. Somerset County, comprising the Eastern Shore's southeastern corner, includes a few communities clinging to the shoreline of Tangier Sound among sprawling Wildlife Management Areas and an island State Park.

The Main Street shops, early-American inns, and unsung restaurants of the small towns in this region seem a century removed from the boutiques and galleries, high-rise hotels and condos, myriad eateries, and nightlife of nearby Ocean City.

SALISBURY

32 mi southeast of Cambridge via U.S. 50, 87 mi southeast of Annapolis via U.S. 50/301 to U.S. 50.

Barges still ply the slow-moving Wicomico River between the Bay and Salisbury, the Eastern Shore's second-largest port after Baltimore. This urban center is a hub of commercial activity in the region and the home of Salisbury University, but its leisure options pale compared to the excitement of nearby Ocean City. The tree-shaded waterfront draws bikers and shoppers. Antiques shops and galleries, along with some exemplary Victorian architecture, fill its downtown six blocks.

EXPLORING

★ Operated in partnership with Salisbury University, the **Ward Museum of Wildfowl Art** presents realistic marshland and wildfowl displays. Two brothers from Crisfield, Lem and Steve Ward, helped transform decoy making from just a utilitarian pursuit to an art form; their re-created studio is a must-see exhibit. Besides the premier collection of wildfowl art, the 30,000-square-foot museum has some 2,000 other artifacts as well as a gift shop and library. ✉*909 S. Schumaker Dr.* ☎*410/742–4988* ⊕*www.wardmuseum.org* 🎟*$7* ⊗*Mon.–Sat. 10–5, Sun. noon–5.*

WHERE TO EAT

$$
AMERICAN

✕**The Red Roost.** Inside a former chicken barn, inverted bushel baskets now serve as light fixtures at this down-home crab house, where hammering mallets rival the beat of piano and banjo sing-alongs. The Red Roost gets rave reviews for its seafood specialties and ribs, as well as its meaty steamed crabs. ✉*Rtes. 352 and 362, Whitehaven* ☎*410/546–5443 or 800/953–5443* ⊕ *www.theredroost.com* ▭*AE, MC, V* ⊗*Closed Nov.–Mar. and Mon. and Tues. Labor Day–Memorial Day. No lunch.*

EN ROUTE

At this writing, the **Delmarva Discovery Center** is scheduled to be fully operational by spring 2009. This modern structure on the banks of the Pocomoke River promises to deliver hands-on experiences of the region's history. Exhibits will focus on the work- and lifestyles of indigenous communities and early settlers, on local wildlife, and on the river as a fishing and shipbuilding industry hub and a major port for Chesapeake Bay steamers during the 19th century. ✉*2 Market St. (BR 13 at Riverside Dr.), Pocomoke* ☎*410/957–9933* ⊕*www.delmarvadiscovery center.org.* 🎟*$10* ⊗*Wed.–Sat. 10–4, Sun. 12–4.*

SNOW HILL

19 mi southeast of Salisbury via Rte. 12, 106 mi southeast of Annapolis.

The streets of Snow Hill, the Worcester County seat, are lined with huge sycamores and stately homes that reflect its days as a shipping center in the 18th and 19th centuries. Today's visitors are often drawn to kayak on the Pocomoke River.

9

WHERE TO STAY

$$$

🏨**River House.** With its welcoming icon the prancing carousel horse on the front porch, this Victorian home and its adjacent cottages are on 2 lovely acres on the banks of the Pocomoke River. This small inn, on the National Register, is impeccably appointed and maintained, including the lovely gardens. Decor is traditional Early American. A free day of canoeing is offered with any stay of two nights or more, courtesy of the Pocomoke River Canoe Company (see below). **Pros:** relaxing riverside setting; attractive for paddlers; complimentary breakfast. **Cons:** pricey; may be too quiet for some. ✉*201 E. Market St.* ☎*410/632–2722* ⊕*www.riverhouseinn.com* 🛏*2 private cottages, 2 rooms* ⊛*In-room: no phone, refrigerator, VCR. In-hotel: pool, no-smoking rooms, some pets allowed, no elevator* ▭*AE, D, MC, V* ⊗*Closed Dec.–Feb.*

SPORTS & THE OUTDOORS
CANOEING

Pocomoke River Canoe Company (✉*312 N. Washington St., Snow Hill* ☎*410/632–3971* ⊕ *www.atbeach.com/amuse/md/canoe*) rents canoes, offers lessons, and leads tours along the Pocomoke River, a habitat for bald eagles, blue herons, and egrets.

BERLIN

15 mi northeast of Snow Hill via Rte. 113, 22 mi east of Salisbury via U.S. 50; 7 mi west of Ocean City via U.S. 50.

Berlin—named not for the German city, but evolving from Burleigh Inn, a Colonial-era way station— is a short drive from Ocean City yet could not be more different. Magnolias, sycamores, and ginkgo trees line streets filled with predominantly Federal- and Victorian-style buildings, of which 47 are on the National Register of Historic Places. Berlin still clings to its now decade-long claim to fame as the principal location for the filming of *Runaway Bride,* in which several of the town's shops were featured along with the bride's home and half the residents "starred" as extras. A delightful short-visit destination onto itself, Berlin is also a great break from the hoopla of Ocean City, particularly when inclement weather precludes beach time.

> ## PADDLING INN-TO-INN
>
> You can canoe miles of pristine woodland in the Bald Cypress tidal river on an **inn-to-inn tour** (☎ 410/632-2722 ⊕ *www.inntours.com*) arranged by the River House B&B. After a full breakfast at a participating inn, you spend the day drifting past waterside homes, hidden landings, and abundant wildlife. Have a picnic lunch on a quiet bank or in a riverside park. Dinner awaits at your next overnight inn; then continue on for a second day (luggage transfers are included).

WHERE TO STAY & EAT

$$$
ECLECTIC
✕ **The Globe.** Housed inside a brilliantly converted theater, its stage area retained and periodically used for a variety of presentations, this eclectic eatery is well worth a meal, from spicy black bean soup and the vegetarian Globe sandwich—to appetizers such as cashew-encrusted crab cakes with strawberry horseradish sauce and entrées like jerked tilapia. Allow some extra time to wander the upper-level art gallery, its works all for sale. And you might luck into one of the periodic screenings of *Runaway Bride.* Sunday brunch and weekend dinners are popular with locals. ⊠ *12 Broad St., Historic District* ☎410/641-0784 ⊕*www.globetheater.com* ▤*AE, MC, V.*

$–$$
★
▥ **Atlantic Hotel.** This fully restored 1895 inn blends the taste of grand living with modern conveniences. Spacious, hardwood-floor guest rooms all offer four-poster beds. The second-floor parlor, done in bold red-and-green hues with ornate furnishings, is a perfect place to escape with a fat book or a stack of magazines. The curved entry drive has been closed to vehicles and landscaped into a delightful people-watching alfresco lobby and optional dining area. Beneath sparkling chandeliers, the hotel's formal dining room serves scrumptious entrées that may include a pistachio duck dish or rockfish topped with oysters, ham, and crabmeat. **Pros:** excellent in-house restaurant; historic inn with modern updates. **Cons:** style may be too formal for some. ⊠*2 N. Main St. Historic District* ☎410/641–3589 or 800/814–7672 ⊕*www.atlantichotel.com* ➲*17 rooms* ⌂*In-hotel: restaurant, no-smoking rooms* ▤*AE, MC, V.*

OCEAN CITY

7 mi east of Berlin and 29 mi east of Salisbury via U.S. 50.

Stretching some 10 mi along a narrow barrier island off Maryland's Atlantic coast, Worcester County's Ocean City draws millions annually to its broad beaches and the innumerable activities and amenities that cling to them, as well as to the quiet bay side between the island and the mainland. "O.C." is a premier mid-Atlantic leisure travel destination, at once big and small, sprawling and congested, old and new, historic and hip, noisy and quiet, sophisticated and tacky, expensive and not, and everything in between.

The town grew into a city south to north. On the older, southern end of the island a restored 19th-century carousel and other traditional amusement park rides churn above a long fishing pier along the inlet connecting the Atlantic and Assawoman Bay. On the opposite side of the inlet is the northern tip of the pristine 37-mi-long Assateague Island, federally and state-protected lands devoid of man-made elements beyond the most rudimentary.

From this southern end, O.C.'s renowned and brilliantly maintained 3-mi-long boardwalk reaches northward as far as 27th Street, nothing but sand to one side, everything else—hotels and eateries and shops—crowding every available square inch lining the other. Beyond 27th Street , the cross streets climb to 145th at the Delaware state line. High-rise condominium complexes prevail farther to the north, interspersed with more hotels and shopping complexes. While it seems a little less hectic toward O.C.'s northern end, beaches are not necessarily less crowded, depending on the season and on the presence of condominium residents. The western side, along the Bay, tends to be comprised of smaller enterprises, including cruise and fishing-boat firms.

GETTING HERE & AROUND

You can avoid the aggravation of driving in often heavy traffic by taking **The Bus,** which travels the 10-mi-long Coastal Highway 24 hours a day in its own lane. Service is about every 10 minutes from bus stops every other block. A $2 ticket is good for 24 hours. A park-and-ride facility on the mainland—on Route 50 just west of Ocean City—has free parking for some 700 vehicles. It's on the Bus's route. A walking map of Ocean City's historic sites is available at its Visitor Information Center.

TIMING & PRECAUTIONS

A year-round destination, Ocean City is particularly appealing in fall and spring, when the weather is mild. Most hotels and better restaurants remain open year-round, although the latter may operate on fewer days and/or shorter schedules. Furthermore, many festivals and other special events are scheduled for the off-season. Weekend traffic to and from Ocean City on U.S. 50 and MD 404 can be exceptionally heavy, not only during summertime months but often from late spring into early fall as well.

ESSENTIALS

Bus Contacts **The Bus** (☎ *410/723–1607*).

Taxi Contacts **Light Up Your Night** (☎ *410/289–9700*). **Sunshine Cab** (☎ *410/208–2828*).

Visitor Information **Ocean City Department of Tourism** (✉ *4001 Coastal Hwy., at 41st St., Ocean City* ☎ *410/289–2800 or 800/626–2326* ⊕ *www.ococean.com*).

EXPLORING

Jacob Fussell began a wholesale ice-cream business in Baltimore in 1851, the first in the United States. Today privately owned and operated ice-cream parlors abound along Maryland's Eastern Shore, but **Dumser's Dairyland,** established in 1939, takes ice cream to new heights at its vast "factory" and parlor (601 South Atlantic Avenue), open in the summertime from noon to midnight. They also operate branch locations at 49th Street and Coastal and 124th Street and Coastal, as well as three smaller outlets on the boardwalk.

★ On the southernmost tip of the island, the **Ocean City Life Saving Station Museum** traces the resort to its days as a tiny fishing village in the late 1800s. Housed in an 1891 building that once held the U.S. Lifesaving Service and the Coast Guard, the museum's exhibits include models of the grand old hotels, artifacts from shipwrecks, boat models, five saltwater aquariums, an exhibit of sands from around the world, and even itchy wool swimsuits and an old mechanical laughing lady from the boardwalk. Press the button, and you can be laughing with her. ✉ *Boardwalk at inlet* ☎ *410/289–4991* 🎟 *$3* ☉ *June–Sept., daily 11–10; May and Oct., daily 11–4; Nov.–Apr., weekends 10–4.*

Trimper's Amusement Park, at the south end of the boardwalk, has a "boomerang" roller coaster; the rickety and terrifying "Zipper"; and the Hirschell Spellman Carousel, from 1902. The park has been owned by the Trimper family since it opened in 1890. ✉ *Boardwalk at S. 1st St.* ☎ *410/289–8617* 🎟 *Pay per ride or attraction* ☉ *Memorial Day–Labor Day, weekdays 1 PM–midnight, weekends noon–midnight. Labor Day–Memorial Day indoor portion only, weekends noon–midnight.*

WHERE TO EAT

"Fresh catch" is the magic phrase, but note that this is the one area of Maryland's and Virginia's Eastern Shore region in which crab is not king. Many diners like to time their meals with the view: don't forget that the sun rises over the Atlantic and sets behind Assawoman Bay.

$$$–$$$$ ✗**Fager's Island.** This fine-dining restaurant adjacent to and operated
AMERICAN by the same owners as the Lighthouse Club and the Edge hotels, gives
★ you white-linen treatment and views of soothing wetlands and the Bay, and stunning sunsets through its large windows. In addition to ubiquitous fresh-catch seafood, Fager's is renowned for its prime rib. There's an outside deck for more informal dining and a raw bar with lighter fare. ✉ *60th St. at Bay* ☎ *410/524–5500* ⊕ *www.fagers.com/restaurant* 🍴 *Reservations essential* ▤ *AE, D, DC, MC, V.*

$$–$$$ ✗**Fish Tales Bar and Grill.** When the children need a break from the stan-
SEAFOOD dard boardwalk fare, take 'em to this incredibly family-friendly restau-
  rant where children are part of the action. They can play on an awesome pirate ship or on the soft beach with the Frisbee that comes with their meals. The food is as easygoing as the atmosphere, from a fried chicken

and barbecued ribs combo to skewered surf and turf. There's also a slew of economical offerings "From the Dock" and "From the Farm" as well as an extensive menu for "L'il Skippers." At night, a bit of a rowdy (yet civilized), older bar crowd likes to congregate on the waterfront benches. ⊠ *Bay side between 21st and 22nd Sts.* ☎ *410/289–7438* ⊕ *www.ocfishtales.com* ▤ *AE, D, DC, MC, V.*

$$$–$$$$
AMERICAN
✕ **Galaxy 66 Bar & Grill.** This unusual watering hole is a welcome breeze of creative cuisine. Appetizers are light and delicate, like seared foie gras and asparagus shrimp risotto. Equally innovative mains include homemade manchego cheese gnocchi, seared duck with sun-dried cherries, and a pistachio-encrusted rockfish. The second and third floors open up to outdoor seating and views of the Bay. The cosmic Star Bar is a hot spot for local celebs and those looking for creative cocktails in a dark hideaway—and it serves tapas until midnight. ⊠ *66th St. at Bay* ☎ *410/723–6272* ⊕ *www.galaxy66barandgrille.com* ▤ *AE, D, DC, MC, V.*

$$–$$$
SEAFOOD
✕ **Phillips Crab House & Seafood Buffet.** Feast on crab cakes, crab imperial, or stuffed and fried shrimp at the original 1956 home of an O.C. institution that is the original of three Phillips locations here and has since grown into a regional chain. Considered the city's most popular dining site, the dark-panel dining area has decorative stone floors, Tiffany-style hanging lamps, stained-glass windows, and funky wall art. Its seafood buffet is served in an upstairs dining room. Phillips By the Sea is at 1301 Atlantic Avenue, and Phillips Seafood House is at 14101 Coastal Highway . ⊠ *21st St. at Philadelphia Ave.* ☎ *410/289–6821 or 800/549–2722* ⊕ *www.phillipsseafood.com* ▤ *AE, D, MC, V.*

$$–$$$
SEAFOOD
✕ **The Shark.** A restaurant you shouldn't be afraid of at the beach, this upscale place takes advantage of every Bay view, including from the sweeping rooftop bar. The namesake dish can be prepared any way you like. Other dishes experiment with unusual flavors like the tuna with wasabi cream sauce and pineapple meringue, and the plank-grilled salmon with raspberry-chipotle BBQ sauce. Go for the Eggplant Tower stuffed with layers of shrimp, lump crab, and wild mushrooms with fresh-shaved Parmesan. Entrées are $5 from 3 to 5 PM, and a live jazz band plays on Thursday nights. ⊠ *46th St. at Bay, behind Sunsations* ☎ *410/723–1221* ⊕ *www.ocshark.com* ▤ *AE, D, DC, MC, V.*

WHERE TO STAY

Ocean City's narrow barrier island means that no lodging is far from either the ocean or the Bay. Rates vary dramatically through the year, the lowest typically between mid-November and mid-March, and the highest during July and August. Ocean-view rooms are always considered premium.

$
⊞ **Atlantic Hotel.** Family-owned and -operated since 1923, the three-story, H-shape frame hotel—Ocean City's oldest—is a replacement of the original Victorian hotel, opened on July 4, 1875, that was destroyed as part of the Great Ocean City fire of 1925. The present structure was quickly rebuilt by 1926, its rooms today plainly furnished and decorated just as they were originally, but now with modern comforts, such as private baths and air-conditioning throughout. A rooftop deck

affords truly panoramic views over the ocean and the Bay. **Pros:** ocean side; classic vacationing spot. **Cons:** in a noisy area. ⊠*Boardwalk at Wicomico St.* ☎*800/328–5268 or 410/289–9111* ⊕*www.atlantichotel ocmd.com* ⤳*90 rooms* ⅋*In-hotel: pool, parking (no fee)* ▭*MC, V* ⊙*Closed Oct.–Apr..*

$–$$ ☷ **Castle in the Sand Hotel.** This compound of castles is a popular family
ↄ   destination for its sheer amount of kid-friendly amenities. "Castle Kid" activities include tales of pirates and ghosts of Assateague Island told by Captain J. one night a week in summer, and Lady Sunshine is on hand to pamper young princesses. All rooms are basic, with pastel walls and random, motel-esque furniture. But all are oceanfront, looking onto a wide swath of beach, with some overlooking the largest pool in Ocean City. Two off-site cottages a block away provide a cozy home-away-from-home atmosphere. **Pros:** ideal for families with younger children; oceanfront location. **Cons:** simple rooms; "kid-friendly" focus not for everyone. ⊠*3701 Atlantic Ave.* ☎*410/289–6846 or 800/552–7263* ⊕*www.castleinthesand.com* ⤳*179 rooms* ⅋*In-room: kitchen (some), refrigerator, VCR. In-hotel: restaurant, bar, pool, parking (no fee)* ▭*AE, D, DC, MC, V.*

¢–$ ☷ **The Lankford Hotel & Apartments.** Opened in 1924, the Lankford is
still owned by the family of the original owners. Many combinations of rooms in the hotel and the adjacent lodge are available for small groups of friends and families. Bicycle storage and Ocean City Golf Course privileges are included in the rate. Lazing in a rickety rocking chair on the front porch off the small (un-air-conditioned) lobby, cooled by overhead fans, is a true throwback to quieter times. (All guest rooms are air-conditioned.) **Pros:** good for groups; a genuine aura of classic seashore vacations. **Cons:** small in size; little privacy from boardwalk and beachfront activity. ⊠*8th St. at boardwalk* ☎*410/289–4041, 800/282–9709 late May–Sept., 410/289–4667 Oct.–late May* ⊕*www. lankfordhotel.com* ⤳*23 rooms, 28 suites* ⅋*In-hotel: laundry facilities, parking (no fee)* ▭*No credit cards* ⊙*Closed Columbus Day–Apr.*

$$$–$$$$ ☷ **Lighthouse Club Hotel.** This elegant boutique hotel is a Chesapeake Bay
★   lighthouse lookalike of quiet luxury, just blocks from the busy Coastal Highway. Its airy, contemporary suites have high ceilings and views of sand dunes that slope to Assawoman Bay. Suites have white-cushion rattan furniture and marble bathrooms, some with two-person hot tubs, and the allure of wet bars and fireplaces. Sliding glass doors lead to private decks with steamer chairs. **Pros:** comfortably luxurious; quiet bay-side location. **Cons:** pricey in high season; not beachfront. ⊠*56th St. at Bay* ☎*410/524–5400 or 888/371–5400* ⊕*www.fagers.com* ⤳*23 suites* ⅋*In-room: refrigerator, Wi-Fi* ▭*AE, D, DC, MC, V.*

$–$$ ☷ **Park Place.** Filling a need for more affordable, family- and child-
ↄ   friendly accommodations, this small, multistory hotel on the boardwalk is owned and operated by a family with over a century of experience. All rooms are efficiencies with fully equipped kitchenettes and sofa beds. Some have extra-long beds and hot tubs. Conner's Beach Café, a full-service restaurant, and Conner's Sail Loft Deck Bar, a beachside bar and restaurant, are part of the complex. **Pros:** prime location for lower O.C. activities; on the boardwalk. **Cons:** "family-friendly" features not

for everyone. ⊠*2nd and 3rd Sts. at boardwalk* ☎*410/289–6440 or
888/212–7275* ⊕*www.ocparkplacehotel.com* ⇌*89 rooms* ⌂*In-room:
kitchen, refrigerator, Wi-Fi. In-hotel: restaurant, bar, pool, parking (no
fee)* ▭*AE, D, MC, V.*

NIGHTLIFE & THE ARTS

In summer Ocean City provides enough entertainment for everyone,
ranging from refined to rowdy. Some bars and clubs close in midwinter,
but most of those with live music remain open.

BARS

Open since 1976, the large sports saloon known as the **Greene Turtle**
(⊠*Coastal Hwy. at 116th St.* ☎*410/723–2120*) is a beach landmark
and a must for casual drinks to soothe the afterburn. The waterside
Seacrets Bar and Grill (⊠*49th St. at Bay* ☎*410/524–4900*) often presents four live bands at four different entertainment venues. The crowds
run in age from those in their early twenties on through baby boom-
ers, proving that you're never too old to sip a piña colada while on an
inner tube.

DANCE CLUBS

The huge **Bonfire Restaurant & Nightclub** (⊠*71st St. at Ocean Hwy.*
☎*410/524–7171*) serves an all-you-can-eat buffet and an à la carte
menu. It caters to thirties-and-over diners enjoying the live Top 40 music
played by local groups. It's closed Monday–Thursday mid-October–mid-
March. One of the most versatile complexes for twenty-one-plus-some-
things, the **Party Block** (⊠*Coastal Hwy. at 17th St.* ☎*410/289–6331*)
encompasses a handful of somewhat raunchy, yet crazy popular nightclub venues. **Big Kahuna** is a DJ-driven "party place"; others include
the **Paddock,** pumping out heart-thumping recorded and live music
with a bit more volume and flash; and **Rush,** a Miami-style dance club
for a well-dressed clientele.

SPORTS & THE OUTDOORS

Although Ocean City is primarily a beach resort, there are ample outdoor activities once you feel like getting off your beach towel, many
of them offering classes for first-timers. In addition to fishing, powerboating, and sailing opportunities, there's kite-boarding, parasailing,
and jet-skiing. For the less adventurous or perhaps just more quiet,
kayak or canoe through the gentle Bay wetlands. Back on land there's
biking, tennis, volleyball, and (especially) golf.

BICYCLING

A portion of Coastal Highway has been designated for bus and bicycle
traffic. Bicycle riding is allowed on the Ocean City boardwalk from 5
AM to 10 AM in summer and 5 AM to 4 PM the rest of the year. The bike
route from Ocean City to Assateague Island (U.S. 50 to Route 611) is
a 9-mi trek, and Assateague itself is crisscrossed by a number of clearly
marked, paved trails.

Bike rentals are available throughout Ocean City. **Mike's Bikes** is one of
the oldest bike rental, sales, and service enterprises and highly respected
(⊠*N. Division St. at Baltimore Ave.* ☎*410/289–5404* ⊠*N. 1st St. at*

boardwalk ☎410/289–4637). Rates are $5 for the first hour, $3 for every hour thereafter for regular adult bikes up to $20 an hour for a six-passenger-and-two-toddler surrey.

BOATING

Assawoman Bay, between the Ocean City barrier island and the mainland, is lined with enterprises for all manner of waterborne activities. To name just one, **Sailing, Etc** (✉*5305 Coastal Hwy.* ☎*410/723–1144*) rents sailboats and windsurf boards—and teaches both—as well as other small watercraft.

FISHING

No fishing licenses are required in Ocean City. Public fishing piers on the Assawoman Bay and Isle of Wight Bay are at (south to north) 3rd, 9th, 40th, and 125th streets and at the inlet in Ocean City. Other fishing and crabbing areas include the U.S. 50 bridge, Oceanic Pier, and Ocean City Pier, at Wicomico Street and the boardwalk. Crabbing is especially good at Northside Park.

Bahia Marina (✉*21st St. at Bay* ☎*410/289–7438 or 888/575–3625*) is a great venue for sportfishing enthusiasts. It has spotless charter boats, live bait and tackle, and opportunities for bottom fishing. **Ocean City Fishing Center** (✉*U.S. 50 at Shantytown Rd., West Ocean City* ☎*410/213–1121*) is Ocean City's largest deep-sea charter-boat marina with some 30 vessels and Coast Guard–licensed professional captains. In addition to catering to preformed groups, the Fishing Center will form fishing groups of individuals who are on their own.

GOLF

Now rivaling premier golfing destinations around the United States, Ocean City is within easy driving distance of more than 21 golf courses. The Web site **Ocean City Golf Getaway** (⊕*www.oceancitygolf.com*) provides thorough information about courses.

SHOPPING

Ocean City's 3-mi-long boardwalk is lined with retail outlets for food, souvenirs, more food, and more souvenirs, with a smattering of surprising specialty stores. Side streets are filled with still more shops, as are the avenues parallel to the beachfront in the older, southern end of the island. Farther north, the atmosphere changes; the beaches a block away become almost incidental. Shopping plazas—several comprised of factory outlets—vie for attention behind acres of parking.

The Kite Loft (✉*5th St. at boardwalk* ☎*410/289–6852* ✉*45th Street Village* ☎*410/524–0800* ✉*Coastal Hwy. at 131st St.* ☎*410/250–4970*), with its dazzling line of kites as well as banners, flags, wind socks, hammocks, sky chairs, whirligigs, and wind chimes, is more than just a store. It's symbolic of Ocean City. Their kites, thriving on the oceanside winds, flying high over the boardwalk all day long, and visible for long distances, are an iconic welcome to the beachfront.

ASSATEAGUE ISLAND

11 mi south of Ocean City.

Fodor's Choice
★

The Assateague Island National Seashore, established in 1962, occupies the northern two-thirds of a 37-mi-long barrier island, encompassing a small portion operated as Assateague State Park. ("Assateague" means "a marshy place across.") Although most famous for the small, shaggy, wild horses (adamantly called "ponies" by the public) that roam freely along the beaches and roads, this stunning island is also worth getting to know for its wildland, wildlife (including the beautiful Sika deer), and for simply enjoying a pristine ocean-side environment. In summer the seashore's mild surf is where you can find shorebirds tracing the lapping waves back down the beach. There are three self-guided nature trails behind the dunes that encourage exploration of the island's forests and bay-side marshes.

Driving is permitted the length of—and several miles south of—the state park. Appropriate off-road vehicles with special permits may drive the length of the National Seashore as far as the Maryland-Virginia line. Remember that the animals here are wild, and follow the signs about not feeding or trying to pet the horses (or ponies).

Swimming, biking, hiking, surf fishing, picnicking, and camping are all available on the island. The visitor center at the entrance to the park has aquariums and hands-on exhibits about the seashore's birds and ocean creatures as well as the famous ponies. ⊠*7206 National Seashore La.), Rte. 611, south of Ocean City, southeastern extremity of Rte. 611* ☏*410/641–1441* ⊕*www.assateagueisland.com, www.nps.gov/ asis and www.dnr.state.md.us/publiclands/eastern/assateague* ☞*7-day pass MD/VA section $3–$10 per vehicle; $2 per person for bicycles and pedestrians* ☉ *Visitor center daily 9–5, park daily 24 hrs.*

CRISFIELD

33 mi southwest of Salisbury via U.S. 13 to Rte. 413.

In William W. Warner's study of the Chesapeake Bay, *Beautiful Swimmers,* Crisfield was described as a "town built upon oyster shells, millions of tons of it. A town created by and for the blue crab, Cradle of the Chesapeake seafood industries, where everything was tried first." Unfortunately, visitors can see the creeping hand of development changing the face of this charming, end-of-the-road town with the sprawling condominium complex at the end of Main Street. The many bustling seafood processing plants here—where workers still pick crabs and shuck oysters by hand, as they have for more than a century—have dwindled to just 3 from more than 150, but you can still marvel at the craft and listen to workers singing hymns as they work.

9

Crisfield's Visitor Center, operated by the Crisfield Heritage Foundation, is known as the J. Millard Tawes Museum & Visitor's Center. Guided tours of Crisfield are run from here; from May through October the tours include a visit to a crab processing plant. (⊠*3 9th St.* ⊗Weekdays 9 AM–3 PM; Sat. 9 AM–4 PM ☎*410/968–2501* ⊕*www.crisfieldheritagefoundation.org*)

SHOPPING
The **Ice Cream Gallery** (⊠*5 Goodsell Alley* ☎*410/968–0809*) is a sweets emporium that doubles as a crafts outlet for local artisans. From here there's a pleasant view out over the Bay. **Tropical Chesapeake** (⊠*712 Broadway* ☎*410/968–3622*) prepares oven-baked deli sandwiches and sells gifts and clothing.

SMITH ISLAND

12 mi west of Crisfield by boat.

For more than three centuries, Smith Islanders have made their living coaxing creatures from the Chesapeake Bay. Today, the tiny island's three villages (Tylerton, Ewell, and Rhodes Point), made up of simple homes, churches, and a few stores, remain reachable only by boat, fiercely independent, and fairly remote (cable TV didn't arrive here until 1994). A midday visit by passenger ferry allows ample time for a stroll around the island and a leisurely meal overlooking watermen's shanties and workboats. Stop by **Ruke's,** a venerable general store that serves excellent fresh seafood. And don't skip the island's nationally known cakes—stacked 8 to 10 layers high and frosted—and recently designated Maryland's state cake by lawmakers.

GETTING HERE & AROUND
The air-conditioned Smith Island Cruises leave Crisfield's Somers Cove Marina for the 60-minute trip to Smith Island at 12:30 PM daily, returning at 4 PM, from Memorial Day to mid-October. Another way to get to Smith Island is via the mail boat, *Island Belle*. There are two departures daily (12:30 and 5 PM). Two freight boats, *Captain Jason I* and *Captain Jason II*, also take passengers to Smith Island. All three boats (including the above-mentioned *Island Belle*) depart daily at 12:30 PM and return to Crisfield at 5:15 PM, year-round, weather permitting. You can ride back to Smith Island later in the evening; both captains live on the island. See also w*www.visitsmithisland.com*.

ESSENTIALS
Ferry Services Captain Jason I & II (☎410/425–4471 ⊠$22 round-trip). **IslandBelle** (☎410/968–1118 ⊠$22 round trip). **Smith Island Cruises** (⊠*Somers Cove Marina, Crisfield* ☎410/425–2771 ⊕www.smithislandcruises.com ⊠$25 round-trip.)

EXPLORING

Weather permitting—and, mid-winter excepted, it usually does—exploring the creeks and inlets of Smith Island (actually a mini-archipelago) by canoe or kayak is truly memorable. See ⊕*www.paddlesmithisland.com* for photos and detailed information—including a pdf map—on exploring by water. Waterproof copies of *Smith Island Water Trails Paddlers Guide* are available from dlitedirector@comcast.net.

Started in 1996 by 12 gutsy Smith Island women, **Smith Island Crabmeat Co-op** produces the finest, shell-less quality crabmeat, with all proceeds going straight back to the women and their families. Visitors can drop by and see the lightning-fast pickers at work. Don't forget to pick up a pound before you leave, and ask Janice (the founder and president) about her secret crab-cake ingredient. ⊠*3019 Union Church Rd., Tylerton* ☎*410/968–1344.*

WHERE TO STAY

An overnight on Smith Island—at one of the few inns—gives new meaning to the term "getaway." Your neighbors include more egrets, heron, osprey, and pelicans than people.

¢ 🏠**Ewell Tide Inn and B&B.** On the northern tip of Smith Island, down-home hospitality is heartily extended by a licensed ferry- and charter-boat captain and his wife. Dinner is available, but must be ordered in advance. Open year-round, the inn—one of three lodging options in Ewell—welcomes children, as well as pets, on weekdays, and complimentary drinks and snacks are served throughout the day. This couple also operates Ewell's Driftwood General Store as well as the adjacent marina. **Pros:** innkeepers of true Smith Island stock offer insight into local culture. **Cons:** may be simply too secluded; too quiet for some. ⊠*Ewell21824* ☎*410/425–2141 or 888/699–2141* ⊕*www.smithisland.net* ⇱*4 rooms, 2 with bath* ♿*In-room: no phone, dial-up. In-hotel: restaurant, bar, bicycles, no-smoking rooms, some pets allowed* ☐*MC, V* ⏐⊘⏐*BP.*

$ 🏠**Inn of Silent Music.** Part of a town that's separated by water from the other two villages on Smith Island, this remote English cottage–style inn takes its soothing name from a phrase in a poem by the mystic St. John of the Cross, a Carmelite monk. The rooms are small with antique linens and big windows. Tylerton has no restaurants, but the eclectic innkeepers will cook a fresh seafood dinner for guests for an extra charge. **Pros:** on the quietest end of a very quiet island. **Cons:** location can be vulnerable to the whims of Chesapeake weather patterns. ⊠*Tylerton* ☎*410/425–3541* ⊕*www.innofsilentmusic.com* ⇱*3 rooms* ♿*In-room: no phone, no TV. In-hotel: restaurant, bicycles, no kids under 12, no-smoking rooms* ☐*No credit cards* ☉*Closed mid-Nov.–early Mar.* ⏐⊘⏐*BP.*

TANGIER ISLAND, VIRGINIA

Crab traps stacked 10 feet high, watermen's shanties on the water, and a landscape virtually devoid of modern commercialization characterize this Virginia island fishing community. Ferry service to Tangier operates from Crisfield, Maryland (and Reedville, Virginia) only (see Crisfield, above). Note that Tangier Island is "dry"; you may bring your own alcohol for personal use, but you must use discretion.

Stop by the **Waterfront Sandwich Shop** (⊠ *16125 Main Ridge Rd.* ☎ *757/891–2248*), where you can also rent golf carts to roam the few narrow roads. You can join a guided tour near the boat dock or simply soak in the timelessness on foot.

WHERE TO STAY

⊄ 🖭 **Bay View Inn.** An overnight on Tangier Island is an experience. A fanciful complex of gingerbread-style cottages, this inn is an enchanting and relaxing place to experience the Bay. Breakfast is served on 100-year-old china, and dinner consists of—what else—crab served up in cakes, soup, or imperial-style. In addition to the Bay View Inn, there are two B&B's on Tangier Island. **Pros:** unique experience on quiet island. **Cons:** island can feel too remote for some. ⊠ *16408 W. Ridge Rd.* ☎ *757/891–2396* ⊕ *www.tangierisland.net* ⏎ *2 rooms, 9 cottages* ⚄ *In-room: no phone, refrigerator. In-hotel: beachfront, no-smoking rooms, public Internet, some pets allowed* ⊟ *No credit cards.*

SMITH & TANGIER ISLANDS

Two Chesapeake Bay island groups with intriguing heritages have begun to attract increasing numbers of travelers: Smith Island (Maryland) and Tangier Island (Virginia). Both are the realms of Bay fishermen, direct descendents of late-17th-century English settlers, among the earliest Europeans to have ventured across the Atlantic. The residents of both Smith and Tangier speak with a charmingly distinct accent, echoing the speech patterns of their forebears. These islands are readily accessible by ferry from Crisfield and from Onancock on Virginia's Eastern Shore as well as from Reedville on mainland Virginia to the west.

VIRGINIA'S EASTERN SHORE

This is the "-va" in Delmarva, a narrow 70-mi-long tail tacked onto the southern tip of the "Delmar-" Peninsula. It has one main artery bisecting its full length, U.S. 13, its occasional gentle curves interrupting an otherwise straight, flat route through unremarkable landscape. The appeal of Virginia's Eastern Shore is out of sight from the highway, among its barrier islands in the Atlantic to the east, along its wetlands and Chesapeake Bay shoreline to the west. It's the wild ponies, a small slice of NASA, gloriously uncrowded beaches, and waterfront views in every direction that draw thousands of snowbirds here every summer. Tiny hamlets are scattered among farms and protected wildlife habitats, or cling to the edges of the ocean or the Bay where watermen still struggle for their living. Part of the appeal here is its more recent 19th- and early-20th-century history, a welcome change from the Colonial eras that predominate elsewhere.

At its southernmost tip, the extraordinary Chesapeake Bay Bridge-Tunnel sweeps 17.5 mi across the Chesapeake Bay, salted by the close-by

Atlantic, to connect with the Virginia Tidewater towns of Hampton Roads, Norfolk, and Virginia Beach.

GETTING HERE & AROUND

The key to exploring the 70-mi-long peninsula known as Virginia's Eastern Shore is getting off Route 13 onto the byways leading eastward toward the Atlantic and westward toward the Chesapeake Bay.

ESSENTIALS

Eastern Shore of Virginia Southern Gateway Welcome Center (☎ *410/787–8268* ⊕ *www.esvatourism.org)* **New Church Welcome Center** (✉ *3420 Lankford Hwy. (Rte. 13), New Church* ☎ *757/824–5000* ⊕ *www.esvatourism.org).*

CHINCOTEAGUE

27 mi southeast of Snow Hill, MD via U.S. 13 to Rte. 175, 43 mi southeast of Salisbury, MD via U.S. 13 to Rte. 175.

Just south of the Maryland-Virginia line, a few miles east of U.S. 13, the Virginia Eastern Shore's island resort town of Chincoteague (pronounced *shin'*-coh-teeg), which means "large stream or inlet,"—also known as Chinoteague Island—exudes a pleasant aura of seclusion. Small, but bustling, with affordable eateries and myriad shops, it is eminently walkable. Within a few minutes' drive or an easy bike ride, relatively uncrowded beaches stretch northward for miles. Small inns and B&Bs abound.

GETTING HERE & AROUND

Chincoteague is less than 10 mi east of U.S. 13, just south of the Maryland-Virginia line. Driving is permitted through two picturesque sectors of the Chincoteague National Wildlife Refuge, occupying the southern third of Assateague (Barrier) Island. Appropriate off-road vehicles with special permits may drive to the southernmost tip, known as Tom's Cove Hook. Some 10 mi of pristine beaches to the north are readily accessible on foot.

TIMING & PRECAUTIONS

Late July's renowned Pony Swim and Auction draws thousands and can create maddening traffic congestion and parking challenges. Follow the signs in regard to the wild horses and do not feed or try to touch them.

ESSENTIALS

Visitor Information Chincoteague Chamber of Commerce (✉ *6733 Maddox Blvd.* ☎ *757/336–6161* ⊕ *www.chincoteaguechamber.com).*

EXPLORING

Virginia's **Chincoteague National Wildlife Refuge** occupies the southern third of Assateague Island, directly off Chincoteague Island. (The northern two-thirds, part of Maryland, comprise the Assateague Island National Seashore.) Created in 1943 as a resting and breeding area for the imperiled greater snow goose as well as other birds, this refuge's location makes it a prime "fly-over" habitat. It also protects native and migratory nonavian wildlife, including the small Sika deer, that

Virginia's Eastern Shore

MARYLAND

Assateague Island

Chincoteague Island ◆

Chincoteague

New Church

175

Temperanceville

Tom's Cove Hook

Wallops Island ◆

Crisfield

Bloxom

Nelsonia

Smith Island

Cedar Island Great Fox

Watts Island

Tangier Island ■

Onancock

Tasley

Cedar Island

NORTHAMPTON

Potomac River

Chesapeake Bay

Pungoteague

Wachapreague

Parramore Island

Quinby

Exmore

Nassawadox

13

Hog Island Bay

Hog Island

Rappahannock River

Cobb Island Bay

Cobb Island

Eastville

Wreck Island

VIRGINIA

17

MATHEWS

Cheriton

Cape Charles

South Bay

Mobjack Bay

Townsend

York River

Yorktown Battlefield ✕

Eastern Shore of VA & Fisherman Island N. W. R.

Colonial Williamsburg

Yorktown

238

Poquoson

Jamestown Island

64

Langley Air Force Base

Buckroe Beach

Chesapeake Bay Bridge Tunnel

Hampton

Hampton Roads Bridge Tunnel

60

Newport News

17

James River

Hampton Roads

Elizabeth River

Norfolk

58

44

Virginia Beach

664

Pungo

13

Portsmouth

17

Nansemond River

264

Chesapeake

64

VIRGINIA BEACH

KEY

✕ Battlefield

0   10 miles
0   10 kilometers

inhabit its interior pine forests. A 3.2-mi self-guided wildlife loop is a great introduction to the refuge. Bike or walk it; it's open to vehicles only between 3 PM and dusk.

The famed Chincoteague ponies occupy a section of the refuge isolated from the public, but they may still be seen in the distance from a number of spots. Swimming, surf fishing, picnicking, and camping are all available on the island. ⊠*Herbert H. Bateman Educational and Administrative Center and entrance: 8231 Beach Rd.* ☎*757/336–6122* ⊠*$10 per car, valid for 7 days* ☉*Refuge hrs: May–Sept., daily 5 AM–10 PM; Oct. and Apr., daily 6 AM–8 PM; Nov.–Mar., daily 6–6. Visitor center hrs vary seasonally; call for information.*

NEED A BREAK?

From the street, **sea star café gourmet carryout** (⊠*4121 Main St.* ☎*757/336–5442*) doesn't look very gourmet, but the shacklike exterior of this take-out place belies the delectable salads, sandwiches, and roll-ups, much of it vegetarian, inside. Most items are less than $5.

Each of the three ice-cream parlors on the island has its own personality: The **Island Creamery** (⊠*6243 Maddox Blvd.* ☎*757/336–6236*), more than a quarter century in business, sells ice cream as well as sorbets, sherbets, and frozen yogurt. On a warm summer night, visit **Muller's Old Fashioned Ice Cream Parlour** (⊠*4034 Main St.* ☎*757/336–5894*) for soda-fountain treats, like malted milk shakes, root beer, and warm Belgian waffles served with ice cream, fresh fruit, and homemade whipped cream. Soft-serve shop **Mr. Whippy's** (⊠*6201 Maddox Blvd.* ☎*757/336–5122*) is another local favorite.

The **Oyster and Maritime Museum** chronicles the local oyster trade with displays of mostly homemade tools; elaborate, hand-carved decoys; marine specimens; a diorama; and audio recordings based on museum records. ⊠*7125 Maddox Blvd.* ☎*757/336–6117* ⊠*$3* ☉*July–Sept., daily 10–5; Mar.–May, Sat. 10–5, Sun. noon–4.*

WHERE TO EAT

$–$$
SEAFOOD
☺

✕**Etta's Channel Side Restaurant.** On the eastern side of the island, happily ensconced along the Assateague Channel away from the more heavily trafficked main streets of town, this meticulously maintained family-friendly restaurant has a vista as soothing as its food. Its dishes include pastas and popular meat dishes as well as typical fish and shellfish creations. Its signature dish is flounder stuffed with crab imperial. A trip to Chincoteague is incomplete without a meal at Etta's. ⊠*7452 East Side Dr.* ☎*757/336–5644* ▭*D, MC, V* ☉*Closed Jan.–Mar. No lunch Mon.–Thurs.*

$
SEAFOOD
★

✕**Shucking House Café.** This relaxed eatery is just the place to unwind after a day on the water. A covered deck houses a bar overlooking the Chincoteague Channel, a favorite feeding site for myriad wildfowl. Featuring oyster, crab, and fish sandwiches along with fish-and-chips, this café is a pleasant change from fancy restaurants or fast-food franchises. Be sure to try the rich New England or Manhattan clam chowder, both prepared with local mollusks. A sister property adjacent to the Shucking House Café, **Landmark Crabhouse** (☎757/336–3745) is a bit more upscale, with the same fresh, locally harvested seafood dishes and peaceful waterfront views. ⊠6162 *Landmark Pl.* ☎757/336–5145 ▤*MC, V.*

WHERE TO STAY

$–$$ ▦**Channel Bass Inn.** This three-story, beige clapboard house just off
★   Chincoteague Bay was built in the 1870s, then expanded and converted to an inn 50 years later. Its luxurious rooms all have comfortable sitting areas, and outside is a lovely Japanese garden with delicate waterfalls. In addition to its full breakfast, the inn serves afternoon tea daily in the public tearoom. Delicacies such as *Apfelkuchen* (German apple cake), butterscotch pecan tarts, and firm ginger scones, all homemade, are served on Wedgwood china. The innkeeper herself is charming, personable, and a wealth of information. **Pros:** welcoming hosts; delectable food. **Cons:** not directly on the Bay. ⊠6228 *Church St.* ☎757/336–6148 *or* 800/249–0818 ⊕*www.channelbass-inn.com* ☛8 *rooms, 1 suite* ☐*In-room: no phone, no TV. In-hotel: no kids under 6, no-smoking rooms, some pets allowed* ▤*AE, D, MC, V* ⦿*BP.*

$ ▦**The 1848 Island Manor House.** The unusual design of the Island Manor
★   House was a result of splitting the home in two, providing adequate privacy for the original owners, who were brothers, and their wives, who were sisters. Most rooms have water views of the channel and an intimate brick patio, with a multitier fountain, that makes a nice summer gathering place. Decor is delightfully eclectic, highlighting the regional landscape and history. Full spa and massage services are readily available for hotel guests. **Pros:** Chincoteague's largest B&B. **Cons:** streets on three sides; not all rooms have views. ⊠4160 *Main St.* ☎757/336–5436 *or* 800/852–1505 ⊕*www.islandmanor.com* ☛7 *rooms, 5 with bath* ☐*In-room: no phone, no TV. In-hotel: spa, no kids under 10, no-smoking rooms* ▤*MC, V* ⦿*Closed Jan.* ⦿*BP.*

$–$$ ▦**Miss Molly's.** This unassuming 1886 Victorian inn claims fame as the temporary home of author Marguerite Henry, who wrote *Misty of Chincoteague.* Here, in 1946, she spent two of her six weeks in Chincoteague preparing the background for her renowned children's novel. Miss Molly, the daughter of the home's builder, spent most of her life here. Guests have their pick of five bay-front porches loaded with comfy rocking chairs, and traditional English high tea is served every afternoon (for an additional fee). **Pros:** literary history; inviting bay-front porches; Victorian-style home. **Cons:** smaller rooms; afternoon tea costs extra. ⊠4141 *Main St.* ☎757/336–6686 *or* 800/221–5620 ⊕*www.missmollys-inn.com* ☛7 *rooms* ☐*In-room: no phone, no TV. In-hotel: bicycles, no kids under 6, no-smoking rooms* ▤*AE, D, MC, V.*

OFF THE BEATEN PATH

Wallops Island. NASA's Wallops Flight Facility Visitors Center fires the imagination with full-scale rockets, films on space and aeronautics, and displays on NASA projects. Although this was the site of early rocket launchings and NASA occasionally sends up satellites here, the facility now focuses primarily on atmospheric research. ⊠*Rte. 175, 20 mi southwest of Chincoteague* ☎757/824–2298 *or* 757/824–1344 *wwww.wff.nasa.gov* ⌧*Free* ☉*July and Aug., daily 10–4; Sept.–Nov. and Feb.–June, Thurs.–Mon. 10–4.*

ONANCOCK

30 mi southwest of Chincoteague via Rte. 175 to U.S. 13.

Four miles from the Chesapeake Bay at the mouth of Onancock Creek, Onancock (pronounced oh-*nan*'-cock), which means "foggy place," was once the home of a handful of Algonquian families. It was established by early English settlers as a port in 1690 and later emerged as an important ferry link with the burgeoning waterside cities of Maryland and Virginia. Today, this quiet community of 1,600, the second-largest town on Virginia's Eastern Shore, is worth a short visit for a flavor of its past as a transfer point between water and land.

WHERE TO STAY & EAT

$–$$ ✕**Hopkins & Bros. General Store.** Beside the wharf, inside a general store
SEAFOOD (circa 1842) on the National Register of Historic Places, you can imagine yourself waiting for a steamer to Baltimore. At the charming eatery adjacent to the store there's fresh baked grouper with locally picked crabmeat stuffing as well as prime meats that are hand cut to order. Hopkins & Bros. is a great opportunity to meet the locals, folks whose roots here are deep, capturing the aura of a post–Civil War Chesapeake. ⌧*2 Market St.* ☏*757/787–3100* ▤*MC, V* ☉*Closed Sun.*

$–$$ 🏨**Charlotte Hotel.** Creative funk meets island culture at Onancock's boutique hotel, four blocks from the harbor on Onancock Creek. Built as the White Hotel a century ago, the Charlotte went through a number of permutations before returning full circle to its original role. Rooms and public space are delightfully, imaginatively appointed. (Many of the floors were hand-painted by a co-owner.) In addition to the adjacent Next Door Art Gallery, there is a full-service bar and an intimate dining room. The restaurant's menu features local and regional produce and seafood. **Pros:** unique character and personality; bar and art gallery on-site. **Cons:** main street location away from the water. ⌧*7 North St.* ☏*757/787–7400* ⊕*www.thecharlottehotel.com* ⤴*8 rooms* ⚷*In-room: DVD, Wi-Fi. In-hotel: restaurant, no kids under 10* ▤*AE, MC, V.*

SPORTS & THE OUTDOORS

Broadwater Bay Ecotours (⌧*6035 Killmon Point Rd., Exmore* ⊕*www. broadwaterbayecotour.com* ☏*757/442–4363 or 757/710–0568*) custom schedules tours on the flat, quiet waters among the myriad barrier islands stretching the eastern length of Virginia's Eastern Shore aboard one of two comfortable shallow draft boats.

CAPE CHARLES

30 mi south of Onancock via U.S. 13.

Cape Charles, established in the early 1880s as a railroad-ferry junction, quieted down considerably after its heyday, but in the past few years its very isolation has begun to attract people from farther and farther away. The town holds one of the largest concentrations of late-Victorian and turn-of-the-20th-century buildings in the region. Clean, uncrowded public beaches beckon, as do a marina, a renowned golf course, and two National Wildlife Refuges a dozen miles farther south.

TOURS **Bay Creek Railway** (☎757/331–8770 ⊕*www.baycreek.net/railway.asp*) is a single-car train that meanders through the peninsula flatlands north from Cape Charles for dinner excursions lasting about two hours and "fun run" trips lasting about one hour.

WHERE TO STAY

$ ⛺ **Pickett's Harbor.** Clinging to the southernmost tip of the peninsula, this land parcel is part of a 17th-century grant to the owner's family. The current clapboard B&B was built in 1976 according to a Colonial-era design, with floors, doors, and cupboards from several 200-year-old James River farms reinstalled here. All guest rooms overlook small sand dunes and the Chesapeake; the backyard is actually 27 acres of private beach. Runners and bikers will find the area's long country lanes and untrafficked paved roads a delight. **Pros:** exudes an inescapable aura of the 18th century; reproduction well suited for modern comforts. **Cons:** truly the back of beyond. ✉*28288 Nottingham Ridge La., Cape Charles* ☎*757/331–2212* ⊕*www.pickettsharbor.com* 🛏*6 rooms, 4 with bath* ⚒*In-room: no phone, no TV. In-hotel: beachfront, bicycles, no-smoking rooms, some pets allowed* ⊟*No credit cards* ⏍*BP.*

SPORTS & THE OUTDOORS

Remote **Bay Creek Golf Club** (✉*1 Clubhouse Way* ☎*757/331–9000*) has been a popular public course since it opened in 2002. The "front 9" of the 18-hole Arnold Palmer course play right along the edge of the Chesapeake Bay. It's a view rivaled by few other courses.

SouthEast Expeditions offers kayak rentals and instruction, as well as tours among the wetlands of the still-pristine shoreline of the Chesapeake Bay. (✉*611 Mason Ave.* ☎*757/331–2680 or 877/225–2925*).

NATIONAL WILDLIFE REFUGES

13 mi south of Cape Charles.

At the southernmost tip of the Delmarva Peninsula, the unique Eastern Shore of Virginia and the Fisherman Island National Wildlife Refuges—including nearby Skidmore Island—established in 1984, are among the most untrammeled havens for winged wildlife, resident and migrating alike, in the region.

Each fall, between late August and early November, millions of song-birds and monarch butterflies and thousands of stunning raptors converge on these forests and wetlands in myrtle and bayberry thickets, grasslands and croplands, on their voyage south. ✉*Southern extremity of Rte. 13* ☎*757/331–2760* ⊕*easternshore.fws.gov* 🎫*Free.*

Travel Smart Virginia & Maryland

WORD OF MOUTH

"Colonial Williamsburg, Jamestown and Monticello (in Charlottesville) are must-sees. I would add Yorktown, which is co-located, roughly, with Colonial Williamsburg and Jamestown: the mapped battlefield walk, and accompanying recorded narrative, are very interesting."

—NewbE

"I love May and June in Baltimore when the azaleas and rhododendrons bloom in the elegant residential neighborhoods . . . near Johns Hopkins University."

—ncounty

GETTING HERE & AROUND

▌BY AIR

Flying time to Baltimore-Washington International (BWI) Airport is just over one hour from New York; approximately two hours from Chicago; and five hours from Los Angeles. Flying time to Richmond International Airport is approximately 1½ hours from New York, 2 hours from Chicago, and 7 to 9 hours from Los Angeles (because there are no nonstop flights). A flight to DC is a little more than an hour from New York, about two hours from Chicago, and five hours from San Francisco. Those flying from London can expect a trip of about six hours. A trip from Sydney takes about 20 hours.

Flying into BWI Airport could save money; airlines, including Southwest, often have good deals to this airport. Good sales can sometimes be found to Dulles and occasionally to Reagan National. Fares into Richmond International are sometimes more expensive.

Airlines & Airports Airline and Airport Links.com (⊕ www.airlineandairportlinks.com) has links to many of the world's airlines and airports.

Airline Security Issues Transportation Security Administration (⊕ www.tsa.gov) has answers for almost every question that might come up.

AIRPORTS

Virginia has Richmond International Airport (RIC), 10 mi east of Richmond; the busy Ronald Reagan Washington National Airport (DCA), 3 mi south of downtown Washington; and Washington Dulles International Airport (IAD), 26 mi northwest of Washington. There is considerable service nationwide into and out of Norfolk (ORF) and even Newport News (aka Patrick Henry, PHF). Maryland's Baltimore-Washington Thurgood Marshall International Airport (BWI) is about 25 mi northeast of Washington and

10 mi south of Baltimore. Amtrak and commuter trains stop at BWI.

Most travelers fly to the nearest major airport and rent a car to get to areas covered by smaller regional airports. Many smaller airports have flights or connections to Washington, Baltimore, Richmond, Norfolk, and Philadelphia. Hagerstown Regional Airport has flights to Pittsburgh and other Pennsylvania airports (but not to Washington or Baltimore). Salisbury-Ocean City-Wicomico Regional Airport serves the lower Eastern Shore with service to Philadelphia. Airports at Staunton, Charlottesville, Lynchburg, and Roanoke have scheduled service.

Airport Information Newport News/ Williamsburg International Airport (PHF ☎ 757/877–0221 ⊕ www.nnwairport.com). **Norfolk International Airport** (ORF ✉ 2200 Norview Ave., Norfolk ☎ 757/857–3351) ⊕ norfolkairport.com. **Richmond International Airport** (RIC ☎ 804/226–3000 ⊕ www.fly richmond.com). **Ronald Reagan Washington National Airport** (DCA ☎ 703/417–8000 ⊕ www.metwashairports.com/National). **Thurgood Marshall Baltimore-Washington International Airport** (BWI ☎ 410/859–7111 or 800/435–9294 ⊕ www.bwiairport.com). **Washington Dulles International Airport** (IAD ☎ 703/572–2700 ⊕ www.metwashair ports.com/dulles).

Secondary Airports Charlottesville Albemarle County (CHO ☎ 434/973–8342). **Hagerstown Regional** (HGR ☎ 240/313–2777). **Lynchburg Regional** (LYH ☎ 434/455–6090). **Roanoke Regional Airport** (ROA ☎ 540/362–1999). **Salisbury-Ocean City-Wicomico Regional** (SBY ☎ 540/548–4827).

GROUND TRANSPORTATION

Reagan National, Dulles, and BWI airports are served by SuperShuttle, which takes passengers to or from a hotel or residence. Buy tickets and request service at the SuperShuttle counter, or book online for returns to the airports.

The most reasonable way to BWI is by Maryland Transit Administration (MTA) train, MTA light rail, Washington Metropolitan Transit Authority (WMATA) bus, or a combination thereof. All northbound Amtrak and MTA Penn Line trains from Washington's Union Station or southbound from Baltimore Penn Station make a BWI stop, where there's a free shuttle bus to the terminal. MTA costs about a third of the Amtrak fare, but only operates on workdays. MTA light trains run from BWI to downtown Baltimore and the suburbs daily. WMATA has an express bus (B30) to BWI every 40 minutes from its Greenbelt, MD, Metrorail station.

Taxi fare to Baltimore's Inner Harbor is about $25.

Dulles is served by Washington Flyer bus and WMATA's Metrobus. Washington Flyer operates between Dulles and the West Falls Church Metrorail station every half hour from 5:45 AM (7:45 on weekends) until 10:15 PM for $9. WMATA Metrobuses and trains operate from the Metrorail station. ■ TIP→ **The little-known express Metrobus, route 5A, runs hourly between Dulles and L'Enfant Plaza Metrorail station in downtown Washington. It costs only $3, but exact change is required.**

Taxi fares from Dulles to downtown Washington range from $51 to $58; drivers accept major credit cards.

Reagan National has its own Metrorail station just outside the main terminal. There is virtually no bus service to the airport. Taxi drivers must accept credit card payment, and they charge a $1.75 airport-access fee. Fare to the U.S. Capitol is about $10, though a small gas surcharge may also apply.

TRANSFERS BETWEEN AIRPORTS

Taxi service is by far the most expensive option between airports; sample fares are $70 between BWI and National, $100 between BWI and Dulles, and $55 between Dulles and National.

Travel between BWI and National for $6.85: Take WMATA's express bus from BWI to the Greenbelt Metrorail station, then switch to the Metrorail and transfer at Gallery Place. Between BWI and Dulles, take WMATA's express bus, then the Metrorail to L'Enfant Plaza, then switch to the 5A express bus; total fare is $8.30.

For a little more comfort on weekdays, take the MTA train to or from BWI and transfer to the Metrorail at New Carrolton or Union Station. It adds about $2.50 to the fare.

Contacts **Maryland Transportation Administration** (☎ 410/539–5000 ⊕ www.mtamaryland.com). **SuperShuttle** (☎ 800/258–3826 ⊕ www.supershuttle.com). **Washington Flyer** (☎ 888/927–4359 ⊕ www.washfly.com). **WMATA** (☎ 202/637–7000 ⊕ www.wmata.com).

■ BY BOAT

Water sports and activities are popular recreational pursuits in Virginia and Maryland, which share the expansive Chesapeake Bay and the Potomac River. Harbor and river cruises are offered in Baltimore, St. Michaels, Annapolis, Washington, DC (along the Potomac), Hampton, and Norfolk, to name a few starting points. Sailboats and other pleasure craft can be chartered for trips on the Chesapeake Bay or inland rivers. Popular ports include Rock Hall, Havre de Grace, and Solomons in Maryland, and Newport News and Chincoteague in Virginia.

For a complete list of ferries operating in Virginia, including commercial ferries and those operating to the Maryland shore, see ⊕ www.vdot.virginia.gov/comtravel/ferry.asp.

■ TIP→ **If you're over 60, chances are you qualify for greatly discounted transit fares in Virginia and Maryland. If you're over 60 in the Norfolk area, they almost pay you to ride their excellent system of buses and** ferries. And if you're over 65 Maryland and WMATA let you ride their trains, buses, and subways at half price. All state-operated ferries in Virginia are free. The Elizabeth River ferry between Portsmouth and Norfolk costs $1. Ferries to Tangier and Smith islands cost about $25 round-trip, but be sure to confirm the price in advance.

Information Hampton Roads Transit (☎ 757/222–6100 ⊕ www.hrtransit.org/ ferryservice.html). **Smith Island Cruises** (☎ 410/425–2771 ⊕ www.smithisland cruises.com). **Tangier Island Cruises** (☎ 410/968–2338 or 800/863–2338 ⊕ tangieris landcruises.com). **Virginia Department of Transportation** (☎ 804/786–2801 ⊕ www. vdot.virginia.gov/comtravel/ferry.asp).

▌ BY BUS

A bus is a very practical way to get to a one-stop resort destination such as Ocean City or Virginia Beach, but many of Maryland's and Virginia's more scenic attractions lie outside the cities served by bus routes. Municipal buses do provide point-to-point transportation in Baltimore, Richmond, the Hampton Roads area, and metropolitan Washington, DC.

Greyhound Lines has extensive service to Virginia and Maryland, supplemented by Peter Pan from Washington to points north to Massachusetts. Unfortunately, there is no system for reserving or assigning seats, so even ticket holders may not get a seat or may lose their seat during stops to change buses. Buses in Virginia and Maryland tend to be quite crowded, so competition is fierce for seats.

A low-cost alternative is the system of "Chinatown" buses, which operate primarily between little travel agencies in northeastern cities. Reservations can be made in person or online, and the price is about half the equivalent Greyhound ticket or less. Chinatown Bus Lines has information for some (but by no means all) "Chinatown" bus companies on the East Coast.

New arrivals BOLTBUS and Megabus run discounted trips several times a day between Washington and New York. Fares are cheapest when you reserve well in advance.

Bus Information Chinatown Bus Lines (⊕ www.staticleap.com/chinatownbus). **Greyhound Lines** (☎ 800/231–2222 ⊕ www. greyhound.com). **Peter Pan Trailways** (☎ 800/343–9999 ⊕ www.peterpanbus.com). **BOLTBUS** (⊕ www.boltbus.com). **Megabus** (⊕ www.megabus.com).

▌ BY CAR

A car is by far the most convenient means of travel throughout Maryland and Virginia, and in many areas it's the only practical way to get around. (Where it exists, public transportation is clean, reasonable, and comfortable, but too often it bypasses or falls short of travel high points.)

HIGHWAYS

Interstate 95 runs north–south through Maryland and Virginia, carrying traffic to and from New England and Florida and intermediate points. U.S. 50 links I–95 with Annapolis and Maryland's Eastern Shore. U.S. 97 links Baltimore with Annapolis. Interstate 695 forms a beltway around Baltimore, and I–495 and I–95 form a beltway around Washington. The Baltimore-Washington Parkway is an old four-lane road that parallels I–95 between the two beltways. Interstate 895 parallels I–95 near Baltimore, offering an alternative route around the city (a $2 toll applies to tunnels on both roads). Interstate 64 intersects I–95 at Richmond and runs east–west. At Staunton, I–64 intersects I–81, which runs north–south. Interstate 70 runs west from Baltimore's Beltway, I–695, to Hancock in western Maryland. Interstate 270 stretches north from the Washington beltway to I–70 at Frederick, Maryland. Interstate 68 connects Hancock to Cumberland and Garrett County. U.S. 40—the National Pike—travels east and west, the entire length of Maryland. Interstate 83 journeys south from Pennsylvania to the top of I–695, the Baltimore Beltway.

ROAD MAPS

The state tourist offices of Maryland and Virginia *(⇨ Visitor Information)* publish official state road maps (and special-interest maps like bike maps and scenic highway maps), free for the asking, that contain directories and other useful information. For the excellent, free *Maryland Scenic Byways* guide, call ☎ 877/632–9929 or look for one at a state welcome center.

RULES OF THE ROAD

The maximum speed limit is 65 mph on stretches of major highways in both states. Radar detectors are legal in Maryland, but are not permitted in DC or Virginia. Front-seat passengers in all jurisdictions must wear seat belts.

In Virginia, DC, and Maryland, you may usually turn right at a red light after stopping if there's no oncoming traffic and no pedestrians present. Watch the signs.

In both states, HOV (high-occupancy vehicle) lanes are restricted to a minimum of two (three in some places) people during rush hour. Look for the diamond on the highway and on signs telling you when the restrictions are in effect.

Talking on cell phones while driving is not allowed in DC.

Children must be in approved child restraints if they are under six in Maryland and Virginia (or under 40 pounds at any age in Maryland). In DC they must be in an infant, toddler, or booster seat up to age eight.

▌ BY TRAIN

Amtrak trains run out of Baltimore, Maryland, north toward Boston and south toward Washington, DC, along the busy "northeast corridor." A rail station at Baltimore-Washington International

Airport serves both Baltimore (about 15 mi to the north) and Washington, DC (about 30 mi to the south). Some trains running between New York and Chicago stop at Charlottesville, Virginia, and at two locations in western Virginia. Trains run between Newport News, Virginia, and New York City, stopping in northern Virginia, Richmond, and Williamsburg in between. Stops in Richmond and northern Virginia are also made on runs between New York City and Florida.

The Maryland Transit Administration operates commuter trains (on weekdays only) between Baltimore's Penn Station and DC's Union Station. It also operates trains from Baltimore's downtown Camden Station and from Union Station in Washington, DC. There's free bus transportation between the Baltimore-Washington International Airport Rail Station and the airport passenger terminal.

Virginia Railway Express, or VRE, provides workday commuter service between Union Station in Washington and Fredericksburg and Manassas, with additional stops near hotels in Crystal City, Alexandria, and elsewhere.

Information Amtrak (☎ *800/872–7245* ⊕ *www.amtrak.com*). **Maryland Transit Administration** (*MTA* ☎ *800/325–7245* ⊕ *www.mta maryland.com*). **Virginia Railway Express** (*VRE* ☎ *800/743–3873* ⊕ *www.vre.org*).

▌ ACCOMMODATIONS

The lodgings we list are the cream of the crop in each price category. We always list the facilities that are available, but we don't specify whether they cost extra; when pricing accommodations, always ask what's included and what costs extra.

■ TIP➔ Assume that hotels operate on the European Plan (EP, no meals) unless we specify that they use the Breakfast Plan (BP, with full breakfast), Continental Plan (CP, continental breakfast), Full American Plan (FAP, all meals), Modified American Plan

FOR INTERNATIONAL TRAVELERS

CURRENCY

The dollar is the basic unit of U.S. currency. It has 100 cents. Coins are the penny (1¢); the nickel (5¢), dime (10¢), quarter (25¢), half-dollar (50¢), and the very rare golden $1 coin and even rarer silver $1. Bills are denominated $1, $5, $10, $20, $50, and $100, all mostly green and identical in size; designs and background tints vary. You may come across a $2 bill, but the chances are slim.

CUSTOMS

U.S. Customs and Border Protection (⊕ *www.cbp.gov*).

DRIVING

Driving in the United States is on the right. Speed limits are posted in miles per hour (usually between 55 mph and 70 mph). Watch for lower limits in small towns and on back roads (usually 25 mph to 40 mph). Most states require front-seat passengers to wear seat belts; many states require children to sit in the back seat and to wear seat belts. In major cities rush hour is between 7 and 10 AM; afternoon rush hour is between 4 and 7 PM. To encourage carpooling, some freeways have special lanes, ordinarily marked with a diamond, for high-occupancy vehicles (HOV)—cars carrying two people or more.

Highways are well paved. Interstates—limited-access, multilane highways designated with an "I–" before the number—are fastest. Interstates with three-digit numbers circle urban areas, which may also have other limited-access expressways, freeways, and parkways. Tolls may be levied on limited-access highways. U.S. and state highways aren't necessarily limited-access, but may have several lanes.

Gas stations are plentiful. Most stay open late (24 hours along major highways and in big cities) except in rural areas, where Sunday hours are limited and where you may drive for long stretches without a refueling opportunity. Along larger highways, roadside stops with restrooms, fast-food restaurants, and sundries stores are well spaced. State police and tow trucks patrol major highways. If your car breaks down on an interstate, pull onto the shoulder and wait for help, or have your passengers wait while you walk to an emergency phone (available in most states). If you carry a cell phone, dial *55, noting your location on the small green roadside mileage marker.

ELECTRICITY

The U.S. standard is AC, 110 volts/60 cycles. Plugs have two flat pins set parallel to each other.

EMBASSIES

Australia (☎ *202/797–3000* ⊕ *www. austemb.org*). **Canada** (☎ *202/682–1740* ⊕ *www.canadianembassy.org*). **United Kingdom** (☎ *202/588–7800* ⊕ *www.britainusa. com*).

EMERGENCIES

For police, fire, or ambulance, dial 911 (0 in rural areas).

HOLIDAYS

New Year's Day (Jan. 1); Martin Luther King Jr. Day (3rd Mon. in Jan.); Presidents' Day (3rd Mon. in Feb.); Memorial Day (last Mon. in May); Independence Day (July 4); Labor Day (1st Mon. in Sept.); Columbus Day (2nd Mon. in Oct.); Thanksgiving Day (4th Thurs. in Nov.); Christmas Eve and Christmas Day (Dec. 24 and 25); and New Year's Eve (Dec. 31).

MAIL

You can buy stamps and send letters and parcels in post offices. The United States no longer makes aerograms. Stamp-dispensing machines can occasionally be found in airports, bus and train stations, office buildings, drugstores, and convenience stores. U.S. mailboxes are stout, dark-blue steel bins; pickup schedules are posted inside the bin (pull down the handle to see them). Parcels weighing more than a pound must be mailed at a post office or at a private mailing center.

Within the United States a first-class letter weighing 1 ounce or less costs 42¢.

To receive mail on the road, have it sent c/o General Delivery at your destination's main post office (use the correct five-digit ZIP code). You must pick up mail in person within 30 days, with a driver's license or passport for identification.

DHL (☎ *800/225-5345* ⊕ *www.dhl.com*). **Federal Express** (☎ *800/463-3339* ⊕ *www. fedex.com*).**Mail Boxes, Etc./The UPS Store** (☎ *800/789-4623* ⊕ *www.mbe.com*).**United States Postal Service** (⊕ *www.usps.com*).

PASSPORTS & VISAS
Visitor visas aren't necessary for citizens of Australia, Canada, the United Kingdom, or most citizens of European Union countries coming for tourism and staying for fewer than 90 days. If you require a visa, the cost is $100, and waiting time can be substantial, depending on where you live. Apply for a visa at the U.S. consulate in your place of residence; check the U.S. State Department's special Visa Web site for further information.

Destination USA (⊕ *www.unitedstatesvisas. gov*).

PHONES
Numbers consist of a three-digit area code and a seven-digit local number. Within many local calling areas you dial only the seven digits; in others you dial "1" first and all 10 digits—just as you would for calls between area-code regions. The same is true for calls to numbers prefixed by "800," "888," "866," and "877"—all toll free. For calls to numbers prefixed by "900" you must pay—usually dearly.

For international calls, dial "011" followed by the country code and the local number. For help, dial "0" and ask for an overseas operator. Most phone books list country codes and U.S. area codes. The country code for Australia is 61, for New Zealand 64, for the United Kingdom 44. Calling Canada is the same as

calling within the United States, whose country code, by the way, is 1.

For operator assistance, dial "0." For directory assistance, call 555–1212 or occasionally 411 (free at many public phones). You can reverse long-distance charges by calling "collect"; dial "0" instead of "1" before the 10-digit number.

Instructions are generally posted on pay phones. Usually you insert coins in a slot (usually 25¢–50¢ for local calls) and wait for a steady tone before dialing. For long-distance calls the operator tells you how much to insert; prepaid phone cards, widely available in various denominations, can be used from any phone. Follow the directions to activate the card (there's usually an access number, then an activation code), then dial your number.

CELL PHONES
The United States has several GSM (Global System for Mobile Communications) networks, so multiband mobiles from most countries (except for Japan) work here. Unfortunately, it's almost impossible to buy a pay-as-you-go mobile SIM card in the United States—which allows you to avoid roaming charges—without also buying a phone. That said, cell phones with pay-as-you-go plans are available for well under $100. The cheapest ones with decent national coverage are the GoPhone from Cingular and Virgin Mobile, which only offers pay-as-you-go service.

Cingular (☎ *888/333-6651* ⊕ *www. cingular.com*). **Virgin Mobile** (☎ *No phone* ⊕ *www.virginmobileusa.com*).

(MAP, breakfast and dinner), or are all-inclusive (AI, all meals and most activities).

APARTMENT & HOUSE RENTALS

At shoreline resorts, as well as Deep Creek Lake in western Maryland, real estate agents generally handle apartment, condo, and town-house rentals. For rentals in Deep Creek Lake, contact Railey Mountain Lake Vacations or Coldwell Banker. Call Atkinson Realty for Virginia Beach and Bud Church Coldwell Banker for Ocean City. Seashore homes usually rent by the week.

Online Booking Resources Atkinson Realty (☎ 757/428–4441 ⊕ www.atkinsonrealty.com).**Bud Church Coldwell Banker** (☎ 800/851–7326 ⊕ www.coldwellbankerbudchurch.com).**Coldwell Banker** (☎ 301/387–6187 ⊕ www.deepcreekrealty.com). **Hideaways International** (☎ 603/430–4433 or 800/843–4433). **Interhome** (☎ 954/791–8282 or 800/882–6864 ⊕ www.interhome.us). **Property Rentals International** (☎ 804/378–6054).**Railey Mountain Lake Vacations** (☎ 800/846–7368 ⊕ http://realty.railey.com/). **Vacation Home Rentals Worldwide** (☎ 201/767–9393 or 800/633–3284 ⊕ www.vhrww.com). **Villas International** (☎ 415/499–9490 or 800/221–2260 ⊕ www.villasintl.com).

BED & BREAKFASTS

Houses in this region make it a natural area for bed-and-breakfast accommodations. The majority of B&Bs in Virginia and Maryland are Victorian structures with fewer than 10 rental units; a full or a continental breakfast is typically included in the lodging rate, and rooms rarely have their own TV. Most rooms, however, have private bathrooms.

Reservation Services Bed & Breakfast.com (☎ 512/322–2710 or 800/462–2632 ⊕ www.bedandbreakfast.com) also sends out an online newsletter. **Bed & Breakfast Accommodations Ltd. of Washington, DC** (☎ 202/328–3510). **Bed & Breakfast Association of Maryland** (☎ 301/432–5079). **Bed & Breakfast Inns Online** (☎ 615/868–1946

or 800/215–7365 ⊕ www.bbonline.com). **BnB Finder.com** (☎ 212/432–7693 or 888/547–8226 ⊕ www.bnbfinder.com). **Maryland Office of Tourism** (☎ 410/767–3400 or 800/634–7386 ⊕ www.mdisfun.org). **Virginia Tourism Corporation** (☎ 804/786–2051 or 800/847–4882 ⊕ www.virginia.org).

CAMPING

Camping is popular in the Shenandoah and Blue Ridge mountains—particularly on the Appalachian Trail, which crosses Virginia and Maryland—and at state forests and parks in western Maryland. The Maryland Department of Natural Resources sells trail guides online. You can reserve sites at Virginia state parks online or by phone.

Assateague Island State Park in Maryland, the Assateague Island National Seashore (in Maryland and Virginia), and the state park at Cape Henry in Virginia are popular campgrounds. State-maintained sites include primitive and full-service sites (with showers, bathrooms, and hookups). Private campgrounds offer more amenities.

There are 30 free National Park Service campsites along the C&O Canal towpath in Maryland with water, chemical toilets, and grills. Bike camping is a very practical way to travel the towpath, and five drive-in campsites rent for $10. For large groups, two additional drive-in campsites are available for $20 a night.

Information C&O National Historical Park (⊕ www.nps.gov/choh/Recreation/Camping.html). **Go Camping America** (⊕ www.gocampingamerica.com). **Maryland Department of Natural Resources** (☎ 410/260–8100 ⊕ www.dnr.state.md.us). **Virginia Department of Conservation and Recreation** (☎ 804/786–1712 ⊕ www.dcr.state.va.us).

HOSTELS

With few exceptions, hostels in Virginia and Maryland are near popular outdoor spots or resort communities. In Maryland, the HI-Harpers Ferry is near the

Appalachian Trail in Knoxville, across the Potomac River from Harpers Ferry. Virginia's Bears Den Lodge is near the Appalachian Trail in Bluemont, HI-Galax is near the Blue Ridge Parkway, and HI-Angie's Guest Cottage is in Virginia Beach.

Information **Bears Den Lodge** (☎540/554-8708 ⊕ www.bearsdencenter. org). **HI-Angie's Guest Cottage Hostel** (☎757/428-4690 ⊕www.angiescottage.com). **HI-Galax** (☎276/236-4962). **HI-Harpers Ferry** (☎310/834-7652 ⊕www.harpersferry hostel.org). **Hostelling International–USA** (☎301/495-1240 ⊕www.hiusa.org).

HOTELS

The large hotels of Baltimore, Richmond, Norfolk, DC, and the Virginia suburbs of Washington, DC, are in competitive markets for business travelers: standards and prices are high. The beach and mountain resorts in the region are among the oldest and largest in the country, and on the expensive side. Accommodations at beach resorts in Maryland and Virginia can be difficult to find during summer holiday weekends—be sure to make reservations. Off-season, rates often go down in both metropolitan areas and resorts.

All hotels listed have a private bath unless otherwise noted.

■ COMMUNICATIONS

INTERNET

Local Internet cafés are listed in the Contacts of each chapter. Larger hotels often have Wi-Fi available but some smaller B&Bs may not.

Contacts **Cybercafes** (⊕www.cybercafes. com) lists more than 4,000 Internet cafés worldwide.

■ EATING OUT

The restaurants listed are the cream of the crop in each price category.

CON OR CONCIERGE?

Good hotel concierges are invaluable—for arranging transportation, getting reservations at the hottest restaurant, and scoring tickets for a sold-out show or entrée to an exclusive nightclub. They're in the know and well connected. That said, sometimes you have to take their advice with a grain of salt.

It's not uncommon for restaurants to ply concierges with free food and drink in exchange for steering diners their way. Indeed, European concierges often receive referral *fees*. Hotel chains usually have guidelines about what their concierges can accept. The best concierges, however, are above reproach. This is particularly true of those who belong to the prestigious international society of Les Clefs d'Or.

What can you expect of a concierge? At a typical tourist-class hotel you can expect him or her to give you the basics: to show you something on a map, make a standard restaurant reservation (particularly if you don't speak the language), or help you book a tour or airport transportation. In Asia, concierges perform the vital service of writing out the name or address of your destination for you to give to a cab driver.

Savvy concierges at the finest hotels and resorts can arrange for just about any good or service imaginable—and do so quickly. You should compensate them appropriately. A $10 tip is enough to show appreciation for a table at a hot restaurant. But the reward should really be much greater for tickets to that U2 concert that's been sold out for months or for those last-minute sixth-row-center seats for *The Lion King*.

The treasure of the Chesapeake Bay is the blue crab. In Maryland and Virginia, and DC, the locals like crabs steamed in the shells, seasoned by the bushel, and dumped on brown-paper-covered tables in spartan crab houses. Diners use wooden mallets to crack the shells, and nimble fingers to reach the meat. Crab cakes, soft-shell crab, crab imperial (enriched crabmeat stuffed back into shells), crab soup, and a host of other such dishes can be found throughout the region. Pollution in the Bay, however, has largely depleted the crop of local crabs in recent years, raising prices. Rockfish (striped bass) is another seafood delicacy, harvested in summer and fall.

In Virginia, country ham, biscuits, collard greens, and fried chicken—Southern staples—are popular Sunday meals. Grits (often served for breakfast) and pecan and sweet-potato pies are other popular Southern foods.

MEALS & MEALTIMES

Unless otherwise noted, the restaurants listed in this guide are open daily for lunch and dinner.

RESERVATIONS & DRESS

Regardless of where you are, it's a good idea to make a reservation if you can. In some places (Washington, DC, for example), it's expected. We only mention them specifically when reservations are essential (there's no other way you'll ever get a table) or when they are not accepted. For popular restaurants, book as far ahead as you can (often 30 days), and reconfirm as soon as you arrive. (Large parties should always call ahead to check the reservations policy.) We mention dress only when men are required to wear a jacket or a jacket and tie.

Online reservation services make it easy to book a table before you even leave home. OpenTable covers most states, including 20 major cities, and has limited listings in Canada, Mexico, the United Kingdom, and elsewhere. DinnerBroker has

restaurants throughout the United States as well as a few in Canada.

Contacts OpenTable (⊕ *www.opentable.com*). **DinnerBroker** (⊕ *www.dinnerbroker.com*).

WINES, BEER & SPIRITS

In Maryland and Virginia, restaurants and bars can serve wine, beer, and spirits seven days a week.

■ **TIP→** **In Virginia the state-run ABC liquor stores are open daily. In Maryland, some counties prohibit liquor sales on Sunday, but some restaurants and bars package alcohol to go, even on Sunday.** Beer and wine are sold throughout the region in convenience stores, markets, drugstores, and even gas stations every day. Sunday liquor sales in DC are limited to wine and beer.

■ HOURS OF OPERATION

The business week runs from 9 to 5 weekdays, and in some instances, on Saturday in the metropolitan regions of Virginia and Maryland, and in Washington DC. Stores, restaurants, and other services maintain longer hours. Hours vary in small towns and resort areas, especially those dependent on seasonal visitors. In rural areas many retail establishments close on Sunday.

Most businesses in the area close for many religious holidays and all holidays that are celebrated on a Monday. However, shopping malls and plazas, as well as restaurants, remain open.

Most art and historical museums in the region are open Monday through Saturday from 10 or 11 to 5 or 6, and Sunday noon to 5. Some museums are closed Monday and/or Tuesday. Many parks and historic homes tend to have later closing hours in summer, and some close during the winter months. In this book's sight reviews, open hours are denoted by a clock icon.

In the metropolitan areas, retail stores and shopping malls are open Monday through Saturday 10–9 and Sunday 11–6. In suburban Baltimore, Washington, and Richmond, grocery stores and superstores often are open 24 hours. Retailers in small towns and in the downtown office districts close earlier and are often not open on Sunday.

∎ MONEY

Generally, lodging, restaurants, and attractions are most expensive in Washington, DC, Baltimore, Richmond, suburban Washington, and resort areas, especially Ocean City and Virginia Beach. Gas prices tend to be higher in the mountainous regions. Lodging and restaurant costs are considerably lower in the western Maryland mountains and rural Virginia.

Coupons for hotel discounts and services in Maryland and Virginia can be printed at ⊕ *www.travelcoupons.com.*

Prices throughout this guide are given for adults. Substantially reduced fees are almost always available for children, students, and senior citizens.

CREDIT CARDS

Throughout this guide, the following abbreviations are used: **AE**, American Express; **D**, Discover; **DC**, Diners Club; **MC**, MasterCard; and **V**, Visa.

It's a good idea to inform your credit-card company before you travel. Otherwise, the credit-card company might put a hold on your card owing to unusual activity—not

---

WORST-CASE SCENARIO

All your money and credit cards have just been stolen. In these days of real-time transactions, this isn't a predicament that should destroy your vacation. First, report the theft of the credit cards. Then get any traveler's checks you were carrying replaced. This can usually be done almost immediately, provided that you kept a record of the serial numbers separate from the checks themselves. If you bank at a large international bank like Citibank or HSBC, go to the closest branch; if you know your account number, chances are you can get a new ATM card and withdraw money right away. **Western Union** (☎ *800/325–6000* ⊕ *www. westernunion.com*) sends money almost anywhere. Have someone back home order a transfer online, over the phone, or at one of the company's offices, which is the cheapest option.

---

a good thing halfway through your trip. Record all your credit-card numbers—as well as the phone numbers to call if your cards are lost or stolen—in a safe place, so you're prepared should something go wrong. Both MasterCard and Visa have general numbers you can call if your card is lost, but you're better off calling the number of your issuing bank, since MasterCard and Visa usually just transfer you to your bank; your bank's number is usually printed on your card.

Reporting Lost Cards American Express (☎ *800/992–3404 in U.S.* ⊕ *www.american express.com*). **Diners Club** (☎ *800/234–6377 in U.S.* ⊕ *www.dinersclub.com*). **Discover** (☎ *800/347–2683 in U.S.* ⊕ *www.discover card.com*). **MasterCard** (☎ *800/622–7747 in U.S.* ⊕ *www.mastercard.com*). **Visa** (☎ *800/ 847–2911 in U.S.* ⊕ *www.visa.com*).

∎ PACKING

If you're visiting the mountains and the caverns of Virginia, prepare for colder-than-average temperatures. Hiking along the Appalachian Trail, even in spring and fall, frequently requires a coat.

Where dress is concerned, Washington, Baltimore, and Richmond are relatively conservative. In the more expensive restaurants men are expected to wear a jacket and tie.

At the Bay and ocean resorts, "formal" means long trousers and a collared shirt for men, and shoes for everybody. A tie might never get tied during a stay in these areas.

▌ TAXES

Sales tax is 5.75% in DC; 6% in Maryland; and 4% in Virginia, though a 1% local tax is often added, bringing Virginia's total sales tax to 5% for most purchases. The hotel tax varies because a local tax is added to the state tax. The result in Maryland varies from 6% to 13.5% and in Virginia from 6.5% to 12.5%; in DC it's 13%.

▌ TIME

Maryland, Virginia, and Washinton DC are in the eastern time zone. In 2009, daylight saving time goes into effect on March 8 and ends November 1. Starting in 2010, daylight saving time goes into effect on the second Sunday in March and ends on the first Sunday in November. Eastern standard time occupies the rest of the year. The area is 3 hours ahead of Los Angeles, 1 hour ahead of Chicago, 5 hours behind London, and 14 hours behind Sydney.

▌ TIPPING

Tipping is expected in restaurants and bars. Waiters receive 15%–20% of the total bill, depending on the level of service; for groups of six or more, a 15%–20% gratuity may be tacked onto the bill (if gratuity is covered, additional tips aren't necessary). Bartenders get $1–$2 or more, depending on the number of drinks and

the number of people in the party. Taxi drivers are generally tipped 15% of the total price of the ride; more if they have been particularly helpful. Doormen carrying bags to the registration desk and porters carrying bags between the lobby and the room are usually tipped $1 per bag, as are Red Caps at the airport or the train station. Chambermaids are generally tipped $1 to $3 a night for inexpensive-to-average hotels and up to $5 a night per guest for high-end properties. Barbers, hairdressers, and masseuses are usually tipped 10%–20% of the total cost of the service, depending on the place and the amount of time spent.

TIPPING GUIDELINES FOR VIRGINIA AND MARYLAND	
Bartender	$1–$5 per round of drinks, depending on the number of drinks
Bellhop	$1–$5 per bag, depending on the level of the hotel
Hotel Concierge	$5 or more, if he or she performs a service for you
Hotel Doorman	$1–$5 for help with bags or hailing a cab
Hotel Maid	$1–$3 a day (either daily or at the end of your stay, in cash)
Hotel Room-Service Waiter	$1–$2 per delivery, even if a service charge has been added
Porter at Airport or Train Station	$1 per bag
Skycap at Airport	$1–$3 per bag checked
Taxi Driver	15% but round up the fare to the next dollar amount
Tour Guide	10% of the cost of the tour
Valet Parking Attendant	$1–$2, but only when you get your car
Waiter	15%–20%, with 20% being the norm at high-end restaurants; nothing additional if a service charge is added to the bill

TIPPING GUIDELINES FOR VIRGINIA AND MARYLAND	
Spa Personnel	10-20% of the cost of your service
Restroom Attendents	$1 or small change
Coat Check	$1-$2 per item checked unless there is a fee, then nothing

▌VISITOR INFORMATION

State Tourism Offices Maryland Office of Tourism Development (☎ *410/767–3400 or 800/634–7386* ⊕ *www.mdisfun.org*). **Virginia Tourism Corporation** (☎ *804/786–2051 or 800/847–4882* ⊕ *www.virginia.org*). **Washington, DC Convention and Tourism Corporation** (☎ *202/789–7000 or 800/422–8644* ⊕ *www.washington.org*).

National Park Service The **National Park Service** (☎ *202/619–7222* ⊕ *www.nps.gov/parks.html*).

Weather Accuweather.com (⊕ *www.accuweather.com*) is an independent weather-forecasting service with especially good coverage of hurricanes. **Weather.com** (⊕ *www.weather.com*) is the Web site for the Weather Channel.

For Civil War buffs, ⊕*www.civilwartraveler.com* has information on battlefields and war-related sites and events. Wine enthusiasts can learn the basics of Maryland and Virginia wines (including winery locations) at ⊕*www.marylandwine.com* and ⊕*www.virginiawines.org*, respectively.

Find arts and entertainment listings online for Baltimore at the *Baltimore Sun,* for Richmond at the *Richmond Times-Dispatch,* and for DC at the *Washington Post.* For DC gay bars and clubs, click on the Web site for the gay newspaper *Washington Blade* or the bar guide *Metro Weekly.*

All About Virginia & Maryland Baltimore Sun (⊕ *www.baltimoresun.com*). **Metro Weekly** (⊕ *www.metroweekly.com*). **Richmond Times-Dispatch** (⊕ *www.timesdispatch.com*). **Washington Blade** (⊕ *www.washblade.com*). **Washington Post** (⊕ *www.washingtonpost.com*).

INDEX

NOTES

NOTES

NOTES

NOTES